HISTORY OF THE SECOND WORLD WAR

The authors of this, as of other official histories of the Second World War have been given free access to official documents. They alone are responsible for the statements made and the views expressed.

BRITISH FOREIGN POLICY IN THE SECOND WORLD WAR

BY

SIR LLEWELLYN WOODWARD

Professor at the Institute for Advanced Study
Princeton, N.J.,
formerly
Professor of Modern History
at the University of Oxford.
in collaboration with

M. E. LAMBERT, M.A.

Volume V

LONDON
HER MAJESTY'S STATIONERY OFFICE

First Published 1976

HER MAJESTY'S STATIONERY OFFICE

Government Bookshops

49 High Holborn, London WC1V 6HB
13a Castle Street, Edinburgh EH2 3AR
41 The Hayes, Cardiff CF1 1JW
Brazennose Street, Manchester M60 8AS
Southey House, Wine Street, Bristol BS1 2BQ
258 Broad Street, Birmingham B1 2HE
80 Chichester Street, Belfast BT1 4JY

Government publications are also available through booksellers

ISBN 0 11 630191 0*

Printed in England for Her Majesty's Stationery Office by
Butler & Tanner Ltd., Frome and London
Dd. 288561 K.32 12/75

History of the Second World War
British Foreign Policy in the
Second World War Volume V

CORRECTION

Page 13 line 3.
Insert 'earlier' before memorandum.
Page 91 footnote 1, last line.
Amend pp.313–91 to read 313–19.
Page 117 3rd para. line 2.
After Court, insert 'and' 3rd para. line 3.
After Japan insert comma 3rd para. line 4.
Amend 'satellities' to read 'satellites'.
Page 253 footnote 1. 1st line.
Amend p.266 to read p.226.
Page 431 source reference (a) in margin.
Move down one line.
Page 469 source reference (a) at foot of page.
Amend to read F(Terminal) 1st meeting.
Page 470 source reference (a) in margin.
Move down two lines.
Page 471 source reference (a) in margin.
Move down one line.
Source reference (b) in margin.
Move down two lines.
Page 539 foot of second column.
Amend 476 to read 407.

AUGUST 1976
CABINET OFFICE
LONDON: HER MAJESTY'S STATIONERY OFFICE

Chapter LXIII summarises the discussions at the Dumbarton Oaks Conference on the World Security Organisation and describes the deadlock arising out of the failure to agree on the voting procedure and, particularly, whether the rule of unanimity among the Great Powers in the case of decisions of the Security Council should apply to disputes in which one of these Powers was a party, i.e. whether the vote would also be a veto. The question was left for discussion at the forthcoming conference of the Great Powers.

Meanwhile the problems of the post-war treatment of Germany were becoming urgent as the end of the war seemed to be approaching. Chapter LXIV deals with the discussion of these problems, and particularly with the question whether, in the interest of future security, the German Reich should be dismembered and what economic measures should be applied to prevent German rearmament. No agreement (except to discard the so-called Morgenthau plan for the complete destruction of German industry and the 'pastoralisation' of the country) was reached before the Yalta Conference[1]. Chapter LXV recounts the discussions at Yalta on the World Security Organisation and the treatment of Germany. President Roosevelt came to the Conference in the belief—or at all events strong hope—that the United States was more likely than Great Britain to make a satisfactory agreement with the Russians. His Majesty's Government, though no less anxious to secure Russian co-operation, without which there could be no hope of lasting peace, was more inclined to fear that the Russians did not think such co-operation in their interests, and that they were intending to establish their own exclusive control of all central and south-eastern Europe which their armies could reach. In order to commit the Russians at least on paper to a common policy with the Western Powers the Americans brought before the Conference a Declaration on Liberated Europe, reaffirming the principle laid down in the Atlantic Charter that peoples had a right to choose their own government and offering the help of the three Powers to this end.

Between the Yalta and Potsdam Conferences (Chapter LXVI) the three Powers gave up plans for the dismemberment of Germany. The Russians, who had been the strongest supporters of such a policy, seem to have realised that they could not combine it with an attempt at getting a large amount of reparations. His Majesty's Government also took this view, and realised the great difficulty of preventing in a dismembered Germany a movement for reunification. Meanwhile no agreement was reached about reparation, and long before the

[1] *Note by Collaborator.* Chapters LXII and LXIV also include an account of the views of Mr. Churchill and of Mr. Eden and the Foreign Office on a regional grouping of Western Europe.

meeting of the Potsdam Conference the Russians had shown their disregard of the Declaration on Liberated Europe and other engagements, e.g. with regard to Poland, made at Yalta, and their clear intention of excluding their Allies from any share in the control of that part of Europe over which their armies had advanced. Mr. Churchill's repeated advocacy with the Americans of a tripartite conference while the Anglo-American forces were at full strength shows the measure of his anxiety. The briefs drawn up for the British Delegation to the Potsdam Conference were concerned, in Mr. Eden's words, with 'calculating what cards we hold for a general negotiation with the Russians, in the shape of things which the Russians want from us and which it is in our power to give or to withhold'.

The German unconditional surrender had come before this bargaining took place. Chapter LXVII describes the final capitulation in which the shadows of Russian suspicion of their western Allies fell across even the celebrations of victory. The chapter also deals with German 'peace-feelers' received during the later years of the war. Some of those approaches were intended merely to divide the Allies: other more genuine approaches were of little practical value. The German civil and military opposition to the régime included men of high integrity and personal courage: but they never devised a successful plan for getting rid of Hitler, and the terms which they regarded as essential if they were to gain popular support in Germany were unacceptable to the Allies. His Majesty's Government had endorsed President Roosevelt's demand for 'unconditional surrender'; they had also made it clear that this term did not foreshadow utter ruin for the German people, but only that the Allies were unwilling to commit themselves in advance to any set of terms and that they intended to avoid a repetition of the controversy (which every German Government had used for propaganda purposes) about the conditions of German surrender in 1918. When, in 1944, the Foreign Office considered whether a modification of the words 'unconditional surrender' might be to our military advantage, the Prime Minister doubted whether a full knowledge of the actual terms in preparation for this would be any more reassuring than the vague 'unconditional surrender'.

Chapters LXVIII and LXIX give an account of the Potsdam Conference. The Conference had failed to bring agreement on the main issues between Russia and the Western Powers before Mr. Churchill and Mr. Eden resigned office after electoral defeat in Great Britain. The deadlock at Potsdam was then broken on the initiative of Mr. Byrnes, United States Secretary of State, who suggested a compromise on the disputed question of reparation in return for recognition of the western Neisse frontier for Poland, and for promises on the part of the Russian-controlled Polish Government to hold free elections. Even at the time these promises were given there was obviously little likelihood that they would be fulfilled. In spite, therefore, of verbal agreements, the position at the end of the Conference, from the point of view of Russian co-operation, was bleak. Mr. Attlee sent a mildly hopeful account of the proceedings to the Commonwealth Prime Ministers. In the House of Commons Mr. Bevin stated frankly that in Hungary, Roumania and Bulgaria our impression was that 'one kind of totalitarianism is being replaced by another'; Mr. Churchill, also in the House of Commons, described what was happening in the areas of Europe under Russian control and gave a warning against the delusion that the most serious questions at the Conference 'were brought to good conclusions'.

Against this sombre background the fighting ended in the Far East with a surrender of Japan as complete as the German surrender in Europe. Chapter LXX describes the circumstances before and after the use of the atomic bomb. His Majesty's Government acquiesced in the American use of the bomb, but the decisions on the matter were taken by the United States Government. The Western Powers during the Potsdam Conference gave Japan a warning of a destructive attack on her if she did not surrender. The warning was intended at the same time to let the Japanese know that the Allied demand for unconditional surrender did not necessarily mean a demand for the deposition of the Emperor. The Japanese Government, however, failed to understand the Allied statement in this sense, and in any case the military leaders of a 'no surrender' party were still confident that the resistance of the Japanese army to an invasion of their country would still be strong enough to compel the Western Powers to offer tolerable terms. Hence the rejection of the Allied warning and the employment of the atomic bomb.

LLEWELLYN WOODWARD

COLLABORATOR'S NOTE

SIR LLEWELLYN WOODWARD had not completed the revision of the text of this volume before his death, but he left detailed notes of his intentions. I have, to the best of my ability, carried out these intentions. Such relatively minor changes as I have considered it necessary to make are in harmony with what I believe would have been his wishes, and largely comprise corrections of small errors of fact and minor clarifications of the text. Additional material from published sources not available for the original official history has, as explained in the Foreword to Volume I, been added in footnotes. The present volume is thus substantially as Sir Llewellyn Woodward left it.

I should like to thank all those who have helped Sir Llewellyn Woodward and myself in the preparation for publication of the five volumes. The staff of the Record Branches of the Cabinet Office and of the Foreign and Commonwealth Office, latterly under Mr. C. J. Child O.B.E., and Mr. B. Cheeseman O.B.E., respectively, have provided invaluable assistance in tracing documents, and the authors have benefited from the great care and knowledge devoted to the checking and polishing of the text by Miss Jean Dawson B.LITT., and Mr. W. Todhunter, B.A. I am also grateful to Mr. Todhunter for preparing the Index.

M. E. LAMBERT

CONTENTS

Page

KEY TO REFERENCES

Foreign Office Records

The great majority of the references quoted in this book are to Foreign Office files. These references are always preceded by a letter, indicating the department responsible for the file in question. Thus, A indicates the American department, N the Northern, U the Reconstruction, etc.

Cabinet Office Records

CA	Confidential Annex (or Secretary's Standard File) to Cabinet Conclusions
JSM	Joint Staff Mission, Washington
PMM . . .	Cabinet Office printed series of Prime Minister's minutes
WM	War Cabinet Conclusions
WP	War Cabinet Papers

Public Record Office Group

PREMIER 3	State papers, formerly known as the Churchill Papers, covering Sir Winston Churchill's period of office as Premier and Minister of Defence.

Printed Sources

F.R.U.S. . . .	*Foreign Relations of the United States*

Note

Throughout these volumes, footnotes are indicated in the text by numerals, 1, 2, 3, etc. The marginal notes in brackets, (a), (b), (c), etc., indicate references to sources which are printed at the foot of each page.

CHAPTER LXI

Foreign Office views on a world security organisation and on the post-war settlement of Europe, with special relation to the future of Germany and Austria, September 1942–July 1943

(i)

Consideration of post-war problems: Mr. Jebb's memorandum of October 5, 1942, on a 'Four-Power' plan: Mr. Eden's note of November 8, 1942: Mr. Eden's memorandum of January 16, 1943, on 'The United Nations Plan'.

UNTIL the autumn of 1942, although there had been much informal discussion in the Foreign Office on British policy with regard to the organisation of security and the resettlement of Europe after the war, no definite conclusions had been reached or brought before the War Cabinet. The Prime Minister was disinclined, and indeed unable, to give time to large questions of post-war policy while the military situation remained critical on every front. In any case it was clear from the attitude of the Russians towards the two large declarations already published—the Atlantic Charter and the Declaration of the United Nations—that a closer definition of policy would cause difficulties. The terms of the Charter were for the most part vague, but there was a reference in it to 'the establishment of a wider and more permanent system of general security'. The Charter also gave an assurance—without any specific mention of Europe—that territorial changes would be recognised only if they were in accordance with the 'freely expressed will' of the peoples concerned, and that independent sovereignty and self-government would be restored to peoples deprived of them.

The Russians had put their own interpretation on these terms—and had insisted, even at the time of their worst military disasters, upon territorial claims which in the British view were incompatible with the spirit, if not the letter, of the Charter. It was clear, therefore, that if British policy were to be based both on the Anglo-Soviet alliance and upon close collaboration with the United States, a great deal of negotiation—and hard bargaining—would be necessary. It was also desirable that the British Government should take the initiative in proposing plans both for a future world organisation and for a political settlement of Europe, and that they should agree on these plans with the United States Government.

In fact the Foreign Office had no definite information about American views, and assumed that the United States Government had also not gone beyond the stage of tentative suggestions. As far as the (a) Foreign Office knew,[1] the President and the State Department, in spite of their emphasis on the 'United Nations', were inclined to favour a world organisation which would be directed and controlled by the four Great Powers—the President insisted on treating China as a Great Power. They envisaged a 'Supreme Council' of these four Powers, with an 'Assembly of the United Nations' on which certain neutrals would be represented. The plan did not exclude regional organisations in western and eastern Europe and in the Far and Middle East, but such organisations would be presided over by one of the four Great Powers. There might also be some scheme for the internationalisation of colonial resources, and even of certain colonial areas, and a number of technical commissions dealing, if possible on a world-wide range, with matters such as communications and transport. The system would rest on an immense American sea and air power and (in a slightly secondary degree) on the British Navy and Air Force and the Russian army. Agreements might be made for sharing bases, and thus, in fact, establishing American power in the four non-American Continents. There was considerable reason for thinking that the United States Government had in mind that only the four Great Powers should be allowed any major armaments.

(b) The Americans were also known to have tentative views on the post-war settlement of Europe. These views implied a drastic treatment of Germany, probably to the extent of breaking up the Reich into a confederation of five or six sovereign States (of which Bavaria, with Austria, might be one). The arrangement would not be federal; it would merely be a loose confederation with such functions as the control of communications and public utilities. Even in these matters the confederation would be subject to international supervision in the exercise of its powers. The Germans would be deprived of all arms, and of the machine tools and machine tool plant required for the armament industry. The supervision and control of order in Europe would be enforced with the aid of an air police provided by the three major Powers and stationed in central key positions, possibly with outlying posts as far away as Bizerta. Such land forces as were necessary for the occupation of European countries and the maintenance of international order would be provided at first by the

---

[1] Mr. Law, the Parliamentary Under-Secretary, and Mr. Ronald, an Assistant Under-Secretary, visited the United States in August 1942.

(a) U742/742/70. (b) U216/71/70 (1943).

three major Powers and later by an international police force. The Americans also appeared to favour the absorption of 'Walloon' Belgium by France, and the creation of a new national unit by the amalgamation of Flanders,[1] Luxembourg, Alsace-Lorraine, the Eiffel and Palatinate areas, and possibly the Ruhr.

The plans for a World Security Organisation which involved, by definition, the unity of the Great Powers, had a logical and practical priority over schemes for the future of Germany. If the Great Powers remained united, and if they set up a general security organisation dominated by themselves, they could determine without much difficulty the future of a defeated Germany. They had already announced in the Declaration of the United Nations that they would continue the war until the defeat of Germany was complete. The Atlantic Charter had implied earlier that this defeat would be complete, since it referred to the disarmament of aggressor Powers.

The first definite attempt in the Foreign Office to formulate a British plan for a world organisation was made in a long memorandum submitted by Mr. Jebb[2] to Mr. Eden. Mr. Eden gave a summary of (a)
the memorandum on October 5, 1942, to the Prime Minister. This memorandum (which subsequently underwent many changes of (b)
phrasing) was headed 'The Four-Power Plan'. Mr. Jebb. began by outlining the American views, as far as they were known. He then asked whether this conception of 'four-power' control was practicable, and how far it would accord with British interests. The practicability of the scheme depended upon certain assumptions. Clearly the first assumption must be that the three Great Powers—China would not in reality be on a level with the United States, the United Kingdom, and the U.S.S.R.—would realise their world-wide interests and responsibilities and be both able and willing to enter into world-wide commitments to prevent any other nation from again troubling the peace.

Before examining the validity of this assumption as far as concerned the United Kingdom, the memorandum defined the main objectives of British post-war policy as (i) development or restoration of our export trade, overseas investments, and other 'invisible exports' in order to maintain the imports without which we could not maintain our standard of living, (ii) the establishment of an international system designed to restrict the power of Germany and Japan, (iii) the maintenance of armed forces strong enough to inspire

[1] In the document summarising American views, no clearer indication is given of what was meant by 'Flanders'. See also below p. 32.

[2] Mr. Jebb was in charge of the Economic and Reconstruction Department of the Foreign Office. He was assisted by Professor Sir Charles Webster in the formulation of plans for a World Security Organisation.

(a) U742/742/70. (b) See Lord Gladwyn, Private Papers.

confidence in our Allies and respect in our enemies, and to enable us to make an adequate contribution to any international system of collective security, (iv) the consequent maintenance of our power and influence—political and economic—in those parts of the world where we had hitherto exercised such influence and where it represented a civilising and educational force, and (v) more generally the promotion of world peace and world trade by means of international co-operation, provided that we were not placed thereby at the mercy of any Foreign Power or combination of Powers.

Towards the achievement of these objectives we had already entered into major commitments in the Atlantic Charter, the Mutual Aid Agreement which indeed bound us to pursue economic policies favoured by the Americans, and the Anglo-Soviet Treaty, which engaged the two parties to mutual assistance if either were attacked by a member of the Axis. These documents all connoted, in varying degrees, the willingness of the United Kingdom to play a leading part in world affairs after the war in collaboration with the United States and the U.S.S.R. It seemed likely therefore, that we should have to pursue these objectives whatever Government was in power and whatever theories were held about world organisation. There might indeed be those who would question whether we were physically able to act as a world Power on a level with our two great Allies. Our population was only 45 millions and thus we could hardly hope to have an industrial capacity equal to that of the United States, Germany, Japan or the U.S.S.R. Even if the whole Empire were reckoned as a unit, its undustrial capacity was far less than that of the United States and potentially less than that of the U.S.S.R. The Dominions might not support us in applying a world policy, and India might break away altogether. It would be pointed out that we should end the war with no financial resources; we should be a debtor nation with the problem of huge sterling balances held against us. Finance would in future be a weapon not for, but against us and, in addition, if there were any serious measure of inflation, the consequent impoverishment of the nation might have far-reaching political effects on the United Kingdom's future status in the world.

On the other hand there were more hopeful factors. Even if our Navy would no longer exercise a preponderating influence in the world, we had a powerful air force and the factories for maintaining it. Although the Dominions might become increasingly independent-minded, they would possibly realise that active collaboration with us in the maintenance of general, and not merely local, peace was in their interests, and distrust of American control often reinforced loyalty to the British Crown. Against our financial weakness we could set off the possibility that the war might finally break the dictatorship which finance had wielded hitherto. Our productivity had increased during the war, Germany and Japan were unlikely to challenge us for a number of years and our internal market was of great importance.

If we had the ability to maintain our position as a Great Power, should we also have the will to do so? There were important sections of British public opinion in favour of abdicating our position in the world in order to concentrate on the improvement of standards of living at home. This tendency went with a kind of defeatism based on the theory that 'we had had our day!' Unless therefore we could find a rallying cry which would inspire such doubters with a belief in the necessity of our fulfilling our world-wide mission, it was possible that we should sink to the level of a second class Power. This process might be painless, and possibly even profitable in the short run, but if it took place, sooner or later we should probably experience an agonising collapse from which we should emerge as an American, Soviet or German satellite. Such might be the unimagined outcome of the adoption of a theory based on our abdication as a Great Power, and could not be seriously advocated by many people. We must, therefore, hope that our great experience and good judgment as a nation would continue to generate the will to power which alone would save us from such disasters, and that we should continue to be blessed with leaders who would give expression to that will. Even so we should not blind ourselves to the fact that, whereas the United States and the U.S.S.R. could relapse into isolation, we should have no choice. We must have some powerful ally or allies, or cease to be a World Power; we could not expect to have powerful allies unless we were powerful ourselves.

The memorandum then considered the first 'assumption' from the point of view of the United States, the U.S.S.R. and China. (i) The United States would certainly emerge from the war in a position to play a world role. The internal problems of the nation were serious but would not invalidate its capacity as a World Power. On the other hand, American traditional distrust of Europe would persist, and, even if the United States Government accepted at the outset commitments in Europe, experience might lead to disappointment and withdrawal. At present, however, the tendency of American thought was in the other direction, and towards the use of American power co-operatively and the acceptance of binding commitments.

(ii) The capacity of the U.S.S.R. to act as a World Power was also obvious. The Russians, however, were much more interested in their own future than in the good of the world. They suspected that the British and Americans regarded the U.S.S.R. as a useful instrument in winning an Anglo-Saxon war leading to a post-war world dominated by the two western democracies. Their own primary aim was immunity from attack; they hoped to secure it by building a defensive barrier against the rest of Europe and preventing a hostile Continent from uniting against them. They could achieve their object by establishing communist governments in Germany and elsewhere or by standing on the defensive against the Anglo-Saxon democracies, playing off the small States against them, and impeding plans for the settlement of Europe. For the time, however, Stalin seemed to be thinking rather in terms of collaboration with us and with the United States as the best method of securing Russian aims in Europe and as bringing them advantages also in the Far and Middle East. Stalin might therefore accept a 'four-Power' plan if he were satisfied that we and the Americans were determined to keep Germany down and to admit the U.S.S.R. into full collaboration in running the world. Nevertheless the Russians were unlikely to commit themselves finally until after the war had been won; meanwhile they would judge the sincerity and value of our co-operation solely by results.

(iii) The interests of China were limited to the Far East. She could not for a long time to come assume anything like the role of a World Power or even take the main burden of keeping Japan under restraint. She would be included among the Great Powers solely owing to American wishes, and American views in the matter were due not only to admiration for Chinese resistance to Japan and sympathy for a 'fellow democracy' but also to a fear of ultimate Chinese territorial ambitions and a realisation that close association with the United States would provide the best means of restraining any such tendencies.

A second assumption therefore followed that—China apart—a four-Power plan was a practical conception provided that its real, if not its declared object was to hold down Germany and Japan for as long as possible, and that it was not based on the alternative theory that these Powers should be readmitted to the ranks of Great Powers. Mr. Jebb regarded this provision as essential to the success of the plan. The Russians would not accept anything on the lines of the League of Nations. President Roosevelt had also made statements implying that he was unfavourable to an attempt at a World Concert including Germany and Japan. Clause 8 of the Atlantic Charter provided for the unilateral disarmament of the aggressor States pending the establishment of a wider and permanent system of general security. Under the four-Power plan this system would consist in the conservation of as much physical force as possible in the hands of the four Great Powers. Germany and Japan as the two great potential threats to the system would never be admitted to it on terms of equality. There must be no talk of *Gleichberechtigung*; the four-Power plan would differ in essence from the conception underlying the League of Nations.

If these two assumptions were accepted—i.e. if it were agreed that the United Kingdom, the United States and the U.S.S.R. had both the power and the will to act with China on a 'four-Power basis', and if the object of their plan was to prevent a recurrence of German and Japanese aggression, how could the plan be applied in practice? The first and most obvious question concerned the position of France. If France took an important part in our ultimate victory, and recovered her independence, her unity and a measure of her greatness, she would have a claim to be included among the Great Powers and could make a valuable contribution to any world system. We should therefore try to secure American and Russian agreement that a place should be kept open for her. A second question concerned the place of regional arrangements in a world system. Obviously we did not want a 'limited liability' arrangement whereby one Great Power was responsible for keeping the peace in a given area. The four Powers (or rather the three Powers, since China would have less concern in the matter) would be equally interested in principle with the maintenance of peace everywhere, and should speak and act together whenever peace was threatened.

Nevertheless in many areas one particular Power would be expected at the outset to provide the chief physical means of keeping the peace. In the Far East, for example, there might be a Regional Council—on which the United States would predominate—to co-ordinate defence and economic arrangements. In Europe primary responsibility would fall on Great Britain and the U.S.S.R., each of whom would arrange to control, as far as possible, the policies of the smaller Powers in the best use of military and economic power. Western Europe was still of the greatest historic and cultural importance, and contained a population almost equal in numbers and surpassing in intelligence the population either of the United States or the U.S.S.R. Furthermore the developed physical resources of the area were not much inferior to those of the two Great Powers—the United States and the U.S.S.R. The greatest responsibility for the restoration of this western European area would rest with us.

In eastern Europe two confederations might emerge, one grouped round Czechoslovakia and Poland, and the other around Greece and Yugoslavia.[1] If these confederations could achieve a common military, economic and political system, and act in collaboration with the U.S.S.R., they might form a real buttress against German penetration. In north-west Europe Great Britain might expect to exercise an effective regional control and to have the use of regional naval and air bases on the Continent. All the Great Powers should take some part in each of the regional organisations, and each of these latter

[1] See note at end of this section.

should be related directly to the four-Power plan, and regular meetings of the four Powers held to discuss problems of world-wide interest.

After rejecting as impracticable President Roosevelt's idea that only the Great Powers should possess major armaments, and after making suggestions for technical and economic collaboration, the memorandum considered the question of colonies. One of the principal implications of the four-Power plan would be our own acceptance —conditional on a similar acceptance by other Powers—of some measure of international supervision over our possessions in the Far East. We should maintain our right to administer these possessions on the grounds both of our long-standing obligations to the territories in question and of our special local knowledge and experience. American opinion was much less interested in our African colonies; we should make it clear that the régime for Far Eastern colonies did not necessarily apply elsewhere.

In spite of these arguments we could not be sure that a four-Power plan would work. The uncertainties of American policy, the suspicions of the U.S.S.R., dislike of 'Great-Power' tyranny among the smaller Powers and in the Dominions would be difficult obstacles. Nonetheless from our point of view there was no satisfactory alternative. If the United States refused to enter into any commitment, we should be compelled to base our policy on an alliance with the U.S.S.R., but we should then have to accept measures, especially in the economic field, which would tend to estrange us from the United States and the Dominions. It the Russians rejected co-operation, and followed a policy of their own in Europe and the Middle East, we should be compelled to oppose them and, in so doing, we should eventually have to accept the collaboration of Germany. If both the United States and the U.S.S.R. rejected the four-Power idea and took no effective steps to hold Germany down, we should have to choose between the impossible task of attempting the subjection of Germany with such European support as we could obtain or of collaborating with the Germans and Italians in the feeble hope that these aggressive countries would undergo a change of heart.

We ought therefore to support a four-Power plan and, above all, to try to secure a treaty under which the United States would enter into certain definite commitments. We had the bargaining advantage that neither the United States nor the U.S.S.R. wanted us to make an alliance with the one in opposition to the other, but we should not succeed in persuading either to support our plan unless we knew clearly what we wanted, and unless we were ourselves convinced of the important part which we had to play in world politics.

In sending the summary of this memorandum to the Prime

Minister, Mr. Eden said that the arguments in favour of our agreeing now on the broad lines of our foreign policy were obvious, and that the absence of any clear directive hampered our negotiations with the Americans, our day-to-day relations with our European Allies and our attempts by propaganda to sustain the morale of the occupied countries. Mr. Eden proposed—if the Prime Minsiter agreed—to circulate the summary and the original memorandum to the War Cabinet.

The question of post-war security was also raised in a positive (a) form by Mr. Lie and Dr. van Kleffens, respectively Norwegian and Dutch Ministers for Foreign Affairs. Mr. Lie regarded it as essential to the security of Norway and the peace of Europe that permanent measures should be taken for the defence of the Atlantic, and that bases for this purpose should be put at the disposal of Anglo-American forces in Norway, Iceland and the Faroes, and possibly in Denmark, Greenland, Ireland and France. Dr. van Kleffens had said that the Governments of Belgium, Norway and the Netherlands were considering the submission of joint proposals to the British and American Governments. Dr. van Kleffens had also discussed the matter with the American Secretary of State Mr. Hull and the Under-Secretary of State Mr. Sumner Welles and had suggested that other areas than the Atlantic—e.g. the Pacific and Indian Oceans, and even the Mediterranean and the Baltic, should be treated in a similar way for purposes of regional defence. The United States Government had been favourably disposed to the idea and had promised to consider it.

On November 3, 1942, Mr. Eden brought before the War Cabinet (b) the draft of a despatch to H.M. Ambassador at Washington who (c) had reported that, in a conversation on October 28, 1942, Mr. Roosevelt had indicated that he wanted to begin talks on the post-war settlement. The President had suggested that the discussion should begin on the statement in the Atlantic Charter about the disarming of aggressors. He also put forward the principle of trusteeship as the best method of dealing with the administration of Colonial territories Mr. Eden suggested that Lord Halifax should put to the State Department the British view of the proposals. This view was that on political grounds the scheme was desirable, since it presupposed the abandonment of the conception of neutrality, and might be developed into a general international policing arrangement. Our aim was to achieve by joint action the security and political and economic stability of Europe as a whole, and the proposals for bases was a step towards these objectives. We could not hope for permanent stability

---

(a) WP(42)480, N5554/463/30.
(b) WM(42)149; U1238/155/70. (c) U1211/155/70.

in Europe unless the United States shared to some degree in the responsibility for maintaining it. We should therefore specially welcome the proposals if they were acceptable to American opinion. Furthermore, Stalin's statements to Mr. Eden in December 1941[1] showed that at that time the Soviet Government were unlikely to raise any objections.

On military grounds we were less certain of the advantages of the plan. A commitment to maintain bases in foreign countries involved a commitment to defend the territories of those countries, and experience had shown that bases in hostile or undefended territory were not of much value in themselves. Nevertheless the existence of bases would go far to provide the element of confidence which had been lacking since 1918.

The War Cabinet considered that these proposals went too far, and that before instructing Lord Halifax to engage in detailed discussions they should come to a decision on the general lines upon which international security should be established after the war. Mr. Eden was therefore asked to prepare a further memorandum on the wider issue.

(a) This memorandum, which Mr. Eden submitted on November 8, pointed out that, although any decisions could be no more than provisional, we ought to try to lay down certain guiding principles for our post-war policy, since our relations with all our Allies were affected by the absence of any sign of our intentions. The Russians suspected that we and the Americans wanted them to be weakened permanently by the war; the Americans doubted whether we should have sufficient determination to undertake wide responsibilities in or outside Europe. The smaller Allies were disturbed because we seemed unable to give a lead or to provide for them the framework under which they could hope to survive in a post-war Europe which would continue to be overshadowed even by a defeated Germany.

The memorandum was based on the two assumptions:

That Great Britain would continue to exercise the functions and to bear the responsibilities of a World Power, and that we should aim not only at liberating but at preserving Europe. We could not afford a Europe unfriendly to us or dominated by Germany. If we refused the leadership of Europe, the smaller Powers would inevitably drift into the German orbit.

We could not attain our objectives in Europe or elsewhere unless we ourselves were acting with other Powers as part of a wider organisation. Since we did not know whether the League of Nations could, or should, be revived in anything like its old form, we ought

---

[1] See Volume II, p. 222.

(a) WP(42)516; U742/742/70.

to take the United Nations as our starting point. At the same time we should remember that, in addition to the fundamental defect—the absence of the United States—one reason for the breakdown of the League was the failure of the Great Powers to accept the responsibilities of leadership within its framework. The smaller Powers at Geneva had been unwilling to move without such leadership. It was therefore clear that the United Nations would not provide the necessary cohesion and stability unless the Great Powers were willing to work together in the exercise of these responsibilities of leadership. Without their co-operation and collaboration there would be only a precarious balance; the Great Powers, each with its circle of client States, would drift into mutual rivalry and hostility.

The simplest and, perhaps, the most desirable solution would be for the British Commonwealth and the United States to take the leadership of the United Nations, but neither the Russians nor the other European States would accept an Anglo-Saxon hegemony. The Americans themselves would be less likely to assume commitments towards the world at large if they were asked to do so solely in co-operation with us. We needed, therefore, a combination at least of three of the Great Powers. In fact we should have to agree to four because—however unreal the conception might seem to us—the Americans insisted on regarding China as a Great Power and on including her as such in any world organisation.

We should therefore aim at a four-Power plan. China or even, on a pessimistic view, the United States might withdraw; France might come in. For the time, however, we must work on the basis of collaboration with the United States, the U.S.S.R. and China. Mr. Eden asked for the general approval of the Cabinet that in his speeches and his dealings with the Allies he should assume that the world organisation of the future would rest upon this four-Power collaboration. The Americans were putting forward the idea in public speeches. The smaller Allies would welcome it, and the Russians, while they resented too close an association between Great Britain and the United States, might co-operate if we offered them a workable plan which gave them, from their point of view, a satisfactory position in relation to ourselves and the Americans.

Sir S. Cripps, after reading Mr. Eden's memorandum, submitted (a) on November 19 to the War Cabinet an important note on the 'four-Power' Plan. He thought it necessary to take the consideration of policy a stage further and to develop a programme of common action by the four Powers. He regarded Europe as the most important area of such action. The major danger in Europe was the strong central position of Germany with her large population and highly

(a) WP(42)532; U1505/742/70.

developed industries. Hence the safety of Europe depended on reducing the economic power of Germany and increasing that of her neighbours, and bringing the small States into larger federal units.

For some time after the war the four Powers (or the three Powers most intersted in Europe) would have to establish a 'policing system' which might gradually develop into an international world police force. It would also be necessary to set up a Council of Europe to deal with political, economic and social issues (including minority issues) likely to disturb the peace. Great Britain, the United States, and the U.S.S.R. would all be members of this Council. Africa (outside the area of sovereign States, e.g. Egypt and the Union of South Africa) would have to be dealt with in association with Europe. The American continent was primarily the concern of the American countries. All the Great Powers were interested in the Far East hence a Council of Asia should be set up with China as the leading member. The British Commonwealth had an Imperial Conference which would be in close touch with the other three Councils. The U.S.S.R., owing to its great size and its multiplicity of Republics, would be recognised as one of the five 'World Councils'—i.e.; European, American, Far Eastern, British Commonwealth, and Soviet Union—each of which would be represented on a Supreme World Council.

(a) The War Cabinet considered Mr. Eden's memorandum and Sir S. Cripps's note on November 27, 1942. Four days earlier Mr. Eden had mentioned a speech by Mr. Sumner Welles which seemed to show that the United States administration was becoming more inclined to conversations on post-war political problems. The War Cabinet had agreed that we should take advantage of this situation. They now accepted in general terms the idea of four-Power cooperation (including China as the fourth Power). They discussed the possibility of setting up a World Council, with four subsidiary councils covering Europe, America, the Far East, and the British Commonwealth. Each of the subsidiary Councils would be represented on the World Council; the United States, Great Britain, and the U.S.S.R. would be members of the European Council.

The War Cabinet decided to give further consideration to Mr. Eden's plan and to the proposal for a system of Councils, but to avoid for the time any commitments on the matter. Mr. Eden also suggested that he might combine in a single memorandum the ideas suggested in his own and in Sir S. Cripps's paper. No further discussion of the four-Power plan took place in the War Cabinet before Mr. Eden's visit to Washington early in March 1943. Mr. Eden, however, submitted on January 16, 1943, a revised version of his paper of

---

(a) WM(42)157, 161; U1713/27/70.

November 8. The paper was drawn up after consultation with Sir S. Cripps, and was now headed 'The United Nations Plan' and summed up both the paper of November 8 and Mr. Jebb's memorandum on a four-Power plan.

The reason for re-submitting the paper at this time was that the Foreign Office were beginning to be concerned that the major Allies might not have reached agreement on a common policy at the end of the war. The end of the war seemed much nearer in January 1943 than in October 1942, and, apart from the question of a World Security Organisation, there were urgent reasons for getting an agreed plan for the treatment of Germany. Other matters required decision, e.g. the 'transitional' problem of the establishment or (a) maintenance of a legal authority in the countries occupied by Germany and in the lesser enemy States. This problem was unlikely to be troublesome in France, Norway, Belgium and the Netherlands. Elsewhere the exiled Governments might not be able to reassert their authority on their return. In any case they would have at first no armies at their disposal, since it would take a considerable time to bring back from Great Britain or the Middle East the small Allied armies built up in exile during the war. On the other hand the smaller enemy States—Roumania, Hungary and Bulgaria—would try to keep their armies in being, and to hold on to territories belonging to Allied States which they had occupied or annexed during the war.

In this situation there might be fighting and chaos unless the major Allied Powers were able to intervene effectively. The position would be even more difficult if the Soviet armies advanced beyond their 1941 frontiers without some agreement with ourselves, the Americans, and the lesser Allies. The case of Poland was particularly difficult. It was probable that the Soviet Government alone would have the armed forces available to impose a provisional régime in the eastern and south-eastern regions of Europe, and that we might be unable to hold them to any agreements made before the actual circumstances of the situation after the German collapse were known. This possibility, however, was no argument against doing our best to secure an agreement now for post-war collaboration; indeed there was every reason for trying to reach agreement and for removing causes of suspicion which might lead to separate and non-cooperative action by the Soviet Government.

These problems—immediate, transitional, and 'ultimate'—could not easily be separated, and indeed the first steps taken at the time of the surrender of the enemy might well be decisive for any future world

(a) U321/67/70.

organisation. The Foreign Office wished therefore to begin consultations with the United States and Soviet Governments, but before doing so they needed to be sure of the agreement of the War Cabinet upon the general lines of post-war policy. Mr. Eden explained that his memorandum merely attempted 'to plot a course'. He asked only for an approval in principle of this course; criticism of details would come at a later stage.

(a) The memorandum was in the following terms:

'The aim of British foreign policy must be, first, that we should continue to exercise the functions and to bear the responsibilities of a World Power; and, secondly, that we should seek not only to prevent Europe from being dominated by any one Power, but to preserve the freedom of Europe as essential to our own.

2. We cannot realise these objectives through our own unaided efforts. We can only hope to play our part either as a European Power or as a World Power if we ourselves form part of a wider organisation.

3. Towards the achievement of these objectives we have already entered into certain major commitments, namely the Atlantic Charter, the Mutual Aid Agreement with the United States, and the Anglo-Soviet Treaty.

4. It is impossible to say whether the League of Nations can ever be revived in its old form, or even whether we would wish to see it revived as it was. Certainly we should make every effort to preserve those technical and humanitarian services of the League which have been so conspicuously successful in the past and for which there will be scope in the future. It is perhaps needless to add that the I.L.O. would continue in existence, its functions indeed being extended if necessary. In the meantime, we have the conception of the United Nations, a conception at once less ambitious and more practical than the conception of the League. Upon this idea of the United Nations we must build up the machinery of international co-operation.

5. International co-operation between the United Nations will not provide the necessary cohesion and stability unless the Great Powers are prepared to accept the responsibilities of leadership *within* the United Nations. For this purpose the Great Powers must agree between themselves on a common world policy and be prepared, as leaders of the United Nations, to take joint action to enforce it. Failing this, we shall be confronted by the prospect of a world in precarious balance, with the Great Powers, each with its circle of client States, facing each other in a rivalry which will merge imperceptibly into hostility.

6. The leadership of the United Nations will have to come from three, at least, of the Great Powers—the British Commonwealth, the United States, and Russia. In view of the attitude of the United

(a) WP(43)31.

States, China, too, must be included as one of the Great Powers; though it is to be expected that for a long time to come she will not be a Great Power in anything but the name. We should, therefore, regard the conception of the Four Powers, working within the framework of the United Nations, as the immediate basis of our present and post-war foreign policy. Later on this conception may be widened to include other States in the category of Great Powers.

7. The successful application of the United Nations conception will, however, depend on the validity of two assumptions:

(i) that the United Kingdom, the U.S.S.R. and the U.S.A. will all, after the war, recognise their world-wide interests and responsibilities and be willing to enter into world-wide commitments in order to guard against other nations again troubling the peace; and

(ii) that, politically speaking, the real, if not the declared object of the Concert of the Four Powers will be to restrict the power of Germany and Japan for as long a period as possible, and will not be based on the alternative theory that both these Powers should be readmitted to the ranks of Great Powers. (Italy had never been a Great Power except by courtesy, and it would probably not be necessary to treat her and the smaller Axis Allies in the same way as Germany and Japan.)

8. It follows that the most desirable *political* set-up at the end of the war would be a Council consisting of representatives of the British Commonwealth, the United States, the U.S.S.R., and (*pro forma*) China, to act, as it were, as a provisional Executive Committee of the United Nations.

9. The future of France is obscure, but from our point of view it would be desirable that, provided she recovers her independence and a measure of her greatness, she should be associated with the other Four Powers in the government of the world, if only because without the assistance of a rejuvenated France the problem of preventing a renewed German effort to dominate the Continent will be much more difficult.

10. For a period after the war and until some more comprehensive international system is established, the Four Powers will thus have to undertake the military responsibility for maintaining order and preventing the building up of aggressive forces in Europe and the Far East. This will entail the maintenance by them of a considerable measure of armaments throughout Europe and in Asia; the complete disarmament of the defeated Powers; and the establishment of an Air Force and Naval policing system towards the financing of which the defeated Powers, relieved of the burden of armaments, should, if practicable, contribute heavily.

11. The most suitable agency for these purposes would seem to be an Inter-Allied Armistice Commission, which might be charged with the duty of supervising a certain number of Reconstruction activities.

12. International friction and aggression frequently have their

roots in economic and social disharmonies. If standards of living are too unequal, for instance, frictions will be created leading to dangerous crises and even to war itself. Consequently it will be of the highest importance for the Four Powers to concern themselves with world economic and social problems, subject, however, to the considerations advanced in paragraph 15 below.

13. It will, for instance, be highly desirable, if not essential, to obtain general consent to schemes on the lines of the Clearing Union and the "Commodity Control" schemes, so that an "expansionist spiral" of world trade can be initiated. Unless such an expansion of world trade takes place the economic conditions of many countries, including our own, may become completely intolerable, and desperate solutions may be urged by desperate people.

14. It will also be desirable to retain some organisation, such as the I.L.O., to smooth out discrepancies in social standards by the encouragement of progressive policies in less advanced countries.

15. It is at this point that a reconciliation is possible between the power-doctrines underlying our conception of the role of the Four Great Powers and the economic interest of smaller States. If the Four Powers accept the responsibilities of effective and overwhelming leadership for reasons of security, they should be very careful to allow economic affairs, so long as they do not endanger security, to be handled by wider assemblies, whether on a world basis or on regional lines.

16. The most important and also the most dangerous area which will have to be dealt with is Europe. Here, in Europe, is the cradle, and until recently the home, of the civilisation which has now spread to almost every corner of the globe. Here, too, is to be discovered the source of most of the worst conflicts in modern history.

17. The major danger in Europe is the strong central position of Germany, with her large population and highly developed industries, which are the bases of her military power. The ultimate safety of Europe will depend on the economic as well as the military disarmament of Germany, and an increase in the relative economic status and power of Germany's neighbours.

18. In addition, however, the joint occupation of Germany by the three major Allies should be accompanied by a very close control over its economic life. If this control were successful it would represent an important large-scale experiment in European international administration.

19. The Armistice and Reconstruction Commission (on which the smaller European Allies should also be represented) would have wide powers, and might well co-ordinate certain essential European services, such as transport, outside as well as inside Germany.

20. It is to be hoped that the European neutrals (if any in fact remain at the end of the war) will agree to work in with this Commission, but it should not be the intention of the Allies to force them to do so against their will.

21. Further, the Allied Forces under the control of the Com-

mission would, in fact, if not in name, constitute an international Police Force, which might at a later stage have a more formal international constitution, and which might also be given a wider field of usefulness in appropriate circumstances.

22. In some cases, particularly in Eastern Europe, we may hope to amalgamate the smaller Powers into Confederations. Two such Confederations are already under discussion (one centring round Czechoslovakia and Poland, and the other round Greece and Yugoslavia) and others might be formed elsewhere.

23. Generally speaking, regional groupings should be encouraged, subject always to the principle that there must not be a kind of "limited liability" system, whereby one Power is solely responsible for keeping the peace in any given area. For the conception, if so applied, would give rise to rivalries as between one group and another, and hence sow the seeds of future war. In discussing "regionalism" therefore, we must assume that all the Four Powers (with the exception of China) are in principle equally interested in maintaining the peace everywhere in the world, and that they will speak with one voice and act together whenever and wherever it may be threatened.

24. Thus the measures taken by the United Nations to pacify Europe and to restore its economic life, will, if they are well conceived and executed, go far towards creating the conditions under which European unity may eventually become a reality. To provide a unifying political framework for the various military and economic measures which are envisaged, it is to be hoped that the Armistice and Reconstruction Commission (see paragraph 19) may at some stage become a "Council of Europe" on which all European States should be represented, including the United Kingdom, the Soviet Union, and, if possible the United States. But the admission of neutrals and *a fortiori* of ex-enemies to full membership of the Council would be a gradual, in some cases a very gradual, process.

25. The military security and economic welfare of backward areas with the status of colonial dependencies would most appropriately be dealt with by Regional Commissions, composed of representatives of parent States, and of other nations with a major defence or economic interest in the regions concerned. Such regions might be, first, South-East Asia; secondly, Africa; and thirdly, the Western Atlantic. Responsibility for the internal administration of particular territories would rest with the individual parent State concerned.

26. In various other parts of the world the political and economic affairs of particular areas should be dealt with by regional meetings of all the States concerned. Thus, many of the problems of the American Continent would be handled, as at present, by the Pan-American Union. The British Commonwealth already has its Imperial Conference. The Soviet Union is clearly an entity on a comparable scale. Europe has already been dealt with. A Council of the Far East might conceivably be formed with China as a leading figure. In the Middle East we ourselves might attempt, together with the Soviet

Union and the United States, and in co-operation with Turkey, to set up an organisation dealing with Middle Eastern questions as a whole. "Backward Areas" have been considered in paragraph 25. But all these Regional Councils would ultimately be subordinate, so far as political issues are concerned, to some Council of the World which, in the early stages after the war at any rate, can for all practical purposes only consist of the representatives of the Four Powers and possibly also of France, who would represent in their turn all the United Nations. (See diagram on opposite page.)

27. What we want to suggest to the world as a whole, here and now, is that there shall, in the World Council, be some ultimate Court of Appeal, but that in the period after the war it will be necessary for the Great Powers to undertake obligations on behalf of the World Council until the latter can be fully organised.

28. In any case unless something like the United Nations Plan can after this war be established on a firm and durable basis, it is only too likely that the course of history will repeat itself and that in the fullness of time Germany will once again resume the struggle for world hegemony, and that she will employ for the purpose the same subtle and gradual methods as were employed so successfully by Hitler between 1933 and 1939. If, therefore, we believe that the United Nations Plan offers the best hope for the future, we should make every possible effort to get it generally agreed without delay.'

Note to Section (i). Foreign Office views on the formation of Confederations in Europe.

A good summary of the Foreign Office views up to June 1942, about a possible confederation of the central European and south European States is to be found in a memorandum by Sir O. Sargent a Deputy
(a) Under Secretary of State. This memorandum was headed: 'Suggested Confederation of the States lying between Germany and Italy, on one side, and Russia and Turkey, on the other.' Sir. O Sargent began by pointing out the unsatisfactory position, from their own point of view and from that of European security, of the small States of Europe, whose existence was justified only on ethnological grounds and without reference to strategic and economic factors. The value of a collection of small States desirous individually of defending themselves against an aggressor had been shown to be almost nil. If, however, the small States were to be fused into some form of confederation in which the idea of individual nationalism founded on an ethnographical basis were subordinated to the idea of collective nationalism based on a common economic and strategic interest, such a group might constitute a really effective deterrent to future German aggression.

(a) R3793/43/67.

POLITICAL

WORLD COUNCIL

(British Commonwealth, U.S.A., U.S.S.R., China, ?France.)

- British Imperial Conference.
- Pan-American Union.
- European Council (Armistice and Reconstruction Commission) U.K., U.S.A., U.S.S.R., European Allies: eventually neutrals and ex-enemies.
- Far Eastern Council (China, Korea, U.K., U.S.A., U.S.S.R., Canada, ?India, ?Australia: eventually Japan).
- S.E. Asia Council (U.K., Australia, Canada, New Zealand, U.S.A., China, France, Holland, Thailand, ?India).
- Middle East Council (U.K., ?U.S.A., U.S.S.R., Turkey, Iran, Iraq, Syria, Saudi Arabia, Egypt, ?Palestine).
- Africa Council (U.K., ?U.S.A., Union of S.A., France, Portugal, Spain, Ethiopia, Belgium).
- Caribbean Commission (U.K., U.S.A., Canada, Holland, France, ?Mexico, Cuba, Puerto Rico, San Domingo, Venezuela).

ECONOMIC

WORLD ECONOMIC COUNCIL

(If established.)

- Board of Clearing (? and Commercial) Union (4 Powers, plus 8 others).
- International Investment Board.
- Commodity Control.
- I.L.O. (Governing Body).
- League of Nations Humanitarian and Economic Services (Directors responsible to Four/Five Powers).
- Relief Organisation (Seven-Power Executive Committee).

N.B.—1. Political issues arising in the economic councils would be referred either to one of the political regional councils or to the World Council.
2. The 'Africa Council' would only apply to Africa south of the Sahara. Alternatively there might be more than one Council for Africa.

For some time past the Governments of Poland, Czechoslovakia, Yugoslavia, and Greece had been working, with British encouragement, at schemes for two separate confederations. This work had resulted in agreements between Poland and Czechoslovakia,[1] and between Yugoslavia and Greece.[2] Such agreements did not solve the questions which would arise if the arrangements were to be extended to a large number of States. In this event the first problem would be the form of the confederation. In order to secure adequate provisions for defence, the constituent units would have to set up a system of collective national sovereignty with executive machinery for enforcing the will of the confederation on its members. The machinery would require a common foreign policy and a customs union and common currency.

Neither of the proposed confederations would be capable of resisting both Russia and Germany; our aim should be to see that they were strong enough to resist Germany, though they might also be considered a barrier against the spread of Russian influence. Sir O. Sargent pointed out that the Yugoslav Government, which had suggested the Greco-Yugoslav agreement for a Balkan Union, undoubtedly regarded it as directed as much against Russian as against German imperialism. The Russians, after the defeat of Germany, could easily secure the adherence of Bulgaria—where popular opinion was largely pro-Russian—and could also get support in Macedonia and Serbia for the constitution of a Serbo-Bulgarian Union under Soviet protection. A union of this kind would isolate Greece and Roumania.

The Russian attitude towards the idea of confederation was indeed uncertain. The Soviet Government argued that the confederations would be directed against their interests. Special treaty arrangements would therefore be necessary between the two confederations and the U.S.S.R., possibly allowing the latter to occupy certain strategic bases on the Roumanian and Bulgarian coast.

The proposed Central European confederation would include Poland (with any part of the Baltic States not absorbed by Russia, and possibly East Prussia), Czechoslovakia, Hungary and possibly Austria. The case of Austria was particularly difficult; it was doubtful, for example, whether the other countries would be willing to be associated with so large a German population. The other main difficulty was the relationship between the Hungarians and the Czechoslovaks. The friendship between Poland and Hungary might be of help to get over this difficulty, but, if necessary, the great Powers might have to compel Hungary to enter and remain in the confederation.

---

[1] December 3, 1941. [2] January 15, 1942.

The South-Eastern European confederation would include all the Balkan States. It might be better for the Serbs, Croats, and Slovenes to form separate units in the confederation, since the experiment of uniting them in a single kingdom had failed. The Soviet Government would probably demand the return of Bessarabia and the northern Bukovina. Some surrender of territory to Greece and Yugoslavia might be necessary in the case of Bulgaria, and Bulgaria, like Hungary, might have to be brought into, and kept in the confederation by force. Albania could hope to maintain its national identity only as a member of a Balkan confederation; otherwise Yugoslavia and Greece might well partition the country between them. The frontiers of the confederations could not as yet be defined; there would certainly be difficulties both over the external frontiers and over territories—such as Teschen—already in dispute between members of the same confederation. Transylvania would be a particularly troublesome case, since its allocation as a whole or in large part either to Roumania or to Hungary would cause friction between the two countries.

During the twelve months after this summary was written, the Foreign Office, though still regarding in principle the confederation plan as desirable, came increasingly to doubt whether it could be put into effect. The internal problems of the States concerned, and the hostility of the Soviet Government to the idea were seen to be almost insuperable obstacles. On the other hand, and especially as the menace of Russian predominance over the whole of the area concerned grew more serious, the Foreign Office were reluctant to give up a plan to which there seemed no satisfactory alternative.[1]

(ii)

The Casablanca declaration on unconditional surrender; Foreign Office memorandum of March 8, 1943, on the future of Germany; Mr. Eden's discussions in Washington in March 1943.

In submitting his memorandum of January 16, 1943, to the War Cabinet as the first step in the long process of obtaining Allied agreement on the general lines of a post-war settlement, Mr. Eden had in mind that he would go to Washington for preliminary discussions with the President and his advisers. Before any such visit was arranged the President had publicly stated at a press conference held on January 24 after the conclusion of the Casablanca Conference that the Allies would insist on the 'unconditional surrender' of

[1] See also below, pp. 42–3.

Germany, Italy and Japan. This term, which was used by the Americans[1] on the analogy of General Grant's action in the American Civil War, and accepted by Mr. Churchill (and the British Cabinet), referred only to the character of the actual surrender, and was put forward by the President without any discussion of the kind of terms which would be imposed after the surrender had been made. Neither the President nor Mr. Churchill was concerned with the ambiguity of the term (e.g. surrender of what and by whom, and on whose behalf). At the press conference on January 24 the President said that 'unconditional surrender' would alone provide a reasonable assurance of future world peace—it meant not the destruction of the population of Germany, Italy or Japan, but the destruction of the philosophies in those countries which were based on conquest and the subjugation of other peoples.[2]

The Casablanca announcement at a time when the Allies still did not know what terms they would enforce after they had received the unconditional surrender of their enemies made Anglo-American discussions seem more necessary. There was no chance of holding the discussions in London. Mr. Roosevelt had said—informally— at the end of the Casablanca meeting that he very much wished to come to England but that he had to consider the internal situation in the United States and to keep all elements of the people united behind him; if he paid a visit to England, the Irish and German elements would have an opportunity of making trouble over it. Mr. Roosevelt added that he looked forward to seeing Mr. Eden in the near future. The Prime Minister seems to have agreed to raise with the President the question of a visit by Mr. Eden to Washington, but it is not (a) certain that he did so. At all events Mr. Churchill telegraphed to Mr.

---

[1] The term seems to have been used in American official discussions as early as May 1942. Mr. Roosevelt said before leaving Washington for Casablanca that he proposed to mention it to Mr. Churchill (*F.R.U.S. 1943, Casablanca and Washington Conferences*, 506, and 833–8). Mr. Churchill's first reaction was to suggest the exclusion of Italy on the ground that this omission might encourage the Italians to make a separate peace. Mr. Churchill consulted the War Cabinet on January 20 about the President's proposal and his own suggestion. Mr. Attlee and Mr. Eden replied on January 21 that, in the opinion of the War Cabinet, the balance of advantage lay against excluding Italy, not only because the exclusion might cause misgivings in Turkey, the Balkans and elsewhere, but also because Italian morale was more likely to be affected by a knowledge of 'the rough stuff coming to them'. The term 'unconditional surrender' was not used in the official communiqué of the Casablanca Conference. Mr. Churchill did not mention to the War Cabinet any reason for its omission, though the reason seems to have been his own feeling against applying it to Italy. The War Cabinet received the draft of the communiqué but made no comment on the omission of a reference to unconditional surrender.

[2] It is probable that the American use of the term 'unconditional surrender' was intended to remove any recurrence of the controversies following the German surrender in November 1918 on the basis of President Wilson's ambiguous Fourteen Points. For American documents bearing on the statement of 'unconditional surrender', see note 1 above. For later discussions on 'unconditional surrender' see Volume III, Chapter XXXVIII, sect. (v) (Germany) and below, Chapter LXVIII, section (vi) (the German satellites).

(a) T142/3, No. 266, Premier 3/476/9.

Roosevelt on February 11 suggesting a visit.[1] Mr. Roosevelt replied (a) on the following day that he would be glad to see Mr. Eden as soon as possible.

Mr. Roosevelt thought that the purpose of Mr. Eden's visit should (b) be announced in a communiqué as a 'general exchange' with the United States Government on all aspects of the war situation, and a discussion on the most effective method of preparing for the Conference of all the United Nations on questions arising out of the war. The Foreign Office were uncertain whether Mr. Roosevelt had in mind a conference to be held before the armistice, possibly within the next few months, or whether he was thinking of a peace conference. In the latter case we should be unwilling to be committed in a public communiqué to the convocation of a conference of all the United Nations to deal with so comprehensive an agenda. The Foreign (c) Office suggested that the communiqué should read: 'The purpose of Mr. Eden's visit is to discuss political aspects of the war situation and to exchange preliminary views with the United States Government on questions arising out of the war which will have to be considered by the United Nations.'

Mr. Eden also telegraphed to Lord Halifax on February 20 that he did not want formal conversations and thought it better not to propose a list of subjects for discussion. Lord Halifax replied on February (d) 22 that the President's draft should have read 'conferences.' Mr. Roosevelt had in mind a conference in the United States on post-war food supplies, possibly a monetary conference in London, and a conference somewhere else about metals, 'and so on'. He disliked the phrase in the Foreign Office draft about discussing 'the political aspects of the war situation', since he thought that these words would cause difficulties in the United States and also with the Russians and other Allied Nations. He therefore proposed to keep his sentence about a general exchange of views, and to substitute the words 'meetings between the Governments of all the United Nations' for the word 'conference'. Mr. Eden accepted the President's wish in the matter.

Owing to the Prime Minister's illness, Mr. Eden had to postpone his visit to Washington until the end of the second week of March. Meanwhile on February 16—the day on which the Prime Minister

---

[1] After the Casablanca Conference Mr. Churchill went to Cairo and to a meeting with Turkish Ministers at Adana. For the memorandum that he gave to the Turkish Ministers of his own ideas of post-war international organisation and his hopes of British, American, and Russian co-operation, see Volume IV, Chapter I, section (v), and W. S. Churchill, *The Second World War*, (London, 1951) *Vol. IV*, Ch. XXXIX.

(a) T148/3, No. 260, Premier 3/476/9. (b) Washington tel. 821, PRISEC.
(c) Tels. 1180–1, to Washington, FO 800/404/20/18–19. (d) Washington Tel. 885, FO 800/404/20/21.

fell ill—Mr. Eden considered with members of the Foreign Office the line which he should take in his discussions with the Americans. It was agreed that the best way of approaching the 'four-Power plan' would be to concentrate on the practical problem presented by Europe. Mr. Eden could point out that, unless the Americans, the Russians, and ourselves worked on some agreed plan, there was scarcely any hope of putting an end to the chaotic conditions which would follow the collapse of the Nazi régime. A continuance of these chaotic conditions would prevent us from diverting our maximum effort to the war in the Pacific. Hence in the period immediately after the fighting was over in Europe a three-Power system was almost inevitable, though we should hope to bring our European Allies into it, and especially, in the first instance, to secure the co-operation of France.

A discussion of the problem of Europe would be likely to involve some reference to the German problem, including the question of frontiers. Mr. Eden could then introduce the general problem of world security. Mr. Eden would not put too much emphasis on the 'regional idea' (except to the extent to which it was implicit in the initial treatment of Europe, and in the proposed Colonial Declaration).[1] He would try to get a general discussion on the form which a World Council ought to take, and, if possible, on the place or places where it should be established. He might also attempt to get agreement on the principle that the composition of a World Council should be on a functional basis, i.e. representation on a Political Council should be limited to those nations which could contribute materially to an international policing system. This provision would limit membership immediately after the war to four

---

[1] On December 9, 1942, the War Cabinet had approved (subject to the agreement of (a) the Dominion Governments), a draft declaration on future colonial policy. The question had been raised actively in the United States, and the President had large, though somewhat vague, ideas about substituting a system of trusteeship under the United Nations for all colonial régimes throughout the world. The War Cabinet therefore considered some statement necessary in order to satisfy American opinion. They had in mind a unilateral declaration, but Lord Halifax reported that Mr. Hull favoured a joint Anglo-American statement, possibly supported by other colonial Powers, e.g. the Dutch. After discussion with the Dominions, and some amendments, the draft text was sent to Lord Halifax on February 1, 1943, and communicated by him on February 4 to Mr. Hull. The Americans did not reply to this communication until Mr. Eden was in Washington. Mr. Hull then produced a redraft on March 29—just as Mr. Eden was leaving for Ottawa. The redraft was unacceptable from the British point of view; e.g. it called for the fixing of dates for the grant of full independence to all colonies, and made no distinction between dependent territories and countries which had lost their independence. Mr. Eden gave the American Ambassador an *aide-mémoire* on the subject on May 26. Mr. Winant promised a draft of his own, but did not submit one or send Mr. Eden's *aide-mémoire* to Washington. Since the United States Government seemed for the time to have lost interest in the matter, the British Government took no further steps, though the Colonial Secretary, Mr. Oliver Stanley, made a statement on British policy in the House of Commons on July 13, 1943. See also below, p. 73, note 3, and p. 91, note 1.

(a) WM(42)166.

Powers, but the World Economic Council, on the same functional principle, might well have a larger membership.

It would hardly be possible to prevent the Americans from raising the issue of bases, especially since Mr. Lie, the Norwegian Foreign Minister, would be in the United States at the same time as Mr. Eden. In spite of the feeling in the War Cabinet that the grant of bases would involve us in commitments without adding greatly to our security, we should show a sympathetic interest in any proposals, if only for the reason that the establishment of American forces, e.g. at Bergen, would be likely to involve the United States in a war against a European aggressor far earlier than would otherwise be the case. Moreover, if an attempt were made to set up an international police force, the common use of certain bases would be necessary at all events for the major Allied Powers. The War Cabinet also agreed that Mr. Eden should try to secure Anglo-American, and, if possible, Anglo-Soviet-American planning to deal with the technical problems involved in the termination of hostilities.

On March 8, 1943, a few days before he left England for Washing- (a) ton, Mr. Eden circulated to the War Cabinet a paper on the future of Germany. He described this paper as a 'preliminary study'. He did not attempt to suggest what should ultimately be the relationship of Germany to her neighbours or how Germany could fit into the proposed European and world organisation. He pointed out that after the first World War German opinion was divided on the question whether the future of the country lay in association with the West or with the East. In 1925, Stresemann, through the Locarno Pact, took the first step towards the West. The attraction of the East—especially in view of the German 'worship of strength'—might now be very great. We ought, therefore, not to lose sight of the possibility that, in order to forestall any orientation of German policy towards the U.S.S.R. and the conclusion of a Russo-German alliance directed against the West, we might have to convince the German people that their best long-term interest lay in an association with Western Europe.

Mr. Eden said that we hoped for the establishment at some time of a democratically-minded central government in Germany. At this stage or, preferably, after a further trial period, the main forces of occupation would be withdrawn from the country. We should have to impose discriminatory measures after the war, but it would be easier later on to bring Germany back into the 'family of nations' if such measures could be merged into a wider system of international controls, and thereby become 'non-discriminatory'.

The paper began by asking what would be the most likely internal

(a) WP(43)96.

developments in Germany immediately before the Germans asked for an armistice. There were several possibilities, of which the least probable was a request for an armistice from Hitler. We should reply with an absolute refusal to treat with Hitler, or with Air Minister Göring—the only other Nazi leader who, for this purpose, could take Hitler's place. On the other hand there might be complete disintegration of order in Germany. This disintegration might result from revolutionary outbreaks coincident with or arising out of a clash between the army and the Party, leading to civil war; it might also be the last stage in a 'fight to the end' in which the army was not strong enough to eliminate the Party, and therefore remained with it. The army, however, would probably try to avoid a situation of this kind, and would insist on asking for an armistice when further resistance was hopeless and would mean huge and senseless losses among the soldiers and, possibly, the civilian population.

We should refuse any request from the army commanders until they had got rid of the Nazi leaders. They might then ask for terms without having substituted any other civilian government or they might support the establishment of a civilian government consisting of certain conservative political, industrial, and possibly, religious groups, and headed by someone like the former President of the Reichsbank, Schacht, or von Papen, the German Ambassador to Turkey. This government might seek terms, in the name of the army and the people, either by direct appeal to the Head of one or more of the major Allied Powers or through neutral intermediaries. The army chiefs, under the articles (which had not been abrogated) of the Weimar Constitution, might stage an election in Germany, and present the United Nations with a democratically elected, representative central government behind which they (the army) would try to shelter.

In view of the course of events at the end of the first World War, and afterwards, it was essential for us to secure the agreement of the United States and Soviet Governments (i) to the negotiation of the armistice between soldiers; otherwise the German army and even the German people might later repudiate the action of the civilian Government as the German negotiators at Versailles were afterwards repudiated; (ii) to a refusal, at least at the outset, to recognise or transact business with a German civilian central Government, as distinct from the central administrative machine with which at first we could not dispense. We should thus undertake the total military occupation of Germany, and announce that no recognised central Government existed and that the Allied occupying forces would deal with the regional or provincial authorities. In order to avoid a complete breakdown of essential services, the Allies might also make a joint announcement inviting the regional authorities to carry on. We should, however, have to act with caution. Party influence was very deep in Germany; we could not remove all Nazis at once without dislocating the administrative machinery, but we should have to be on our guard against allowing ourselves to be exploited by nationalist groups interested in the suppression of Liberal movements which we should wish to support.

The paper then dealt with future Allied policy towards Germany. The basis of our policy should be the disarmament of Germany and the prevention of German rearmament. We knew from past experience that in the course of time the will to enforce measures against rearmament might weaken, and, although we might now have learned our lesson, we should consider what additional measures, in the nature of reinsurance, might be applied to Germany. In this connexion five different types of policy had been suggested:

(i) We should deprive Germany not only of all territory which she had occupied during the war, but also of territory acquired by acts or threats of violence before the war, i.e. Austria, Memel, the Sudeten areas, and the 'Protectorate of Bohemia and Moravia.' On this policy there would be general agreement. The Allies, however, would almost certainly want more than a 'restitution' which would leave pre-*Anschluss* Germany intact.

(ii) The Allies might therefore dismember Germany, either by their own act or by encouraging separatist tendencies. A policy of dismemberment would mean that there would no longer be a State called Germany, but only a number of independent German States. Thus south Germany and old Prussia might be lopped off. This action would leave an amorphous region in the centre and north-west for which it would be difficult to devise a reasonable political structure owing to the interlocking of the old German Länder. A subdivision of the area into independent States would mean creating new political units which would have little chance of becoming stabilised. If, on the other hand, old Prussia were allowed to remain united with this residual territory to the west of it, we should have a largely Prussian North German State of considerable size and industrial resources.

There would thus be three independent, or quasi-independent German States: North Germany (the 'new' Prussia with Saxony), Western Germany (the Rhine-Ruhr area) and South Germany (Baden, Württemberg, Bavaria). We should require a strong political control to prevent their reunion as well as an economic control to prevent their rearmament. It might be possible, by encouraging separatist tendencies, to split Germany into more than these three States, but the more radical our measures of dismemberment, the harder it would be to prevent the units from coming together as their desire for reunion developed and the Allies' determination to oppose it weakened.

(iii) A third type of policy—'truncation'—would consist of depriving Germany of large frontier areas in order to ensure that the remaining 'Rump State' would be too weak to endanger the peace of Europe. This policy would aim at security, and would not be based on the specific territorial claims of Germany's neighbours. Thus in 1918 the Danish Government had claimed only those parts of Slesvig whose inhabitants wished for incorporation in Denmark; a policy of 'truncation' might demand the cession, for strategic reasons, of Slesvig and Holstein, with or without their German populations, in order to deprive Germany of the Kiel Canal. Similarly, the principal industrial areas on the right bank of the Rhine, including the Ruhr, might be taken from Germany in order to deprive her of her most important source of war potential. Or again, the whole of East Prussia, with its German population, might be detached.

This policy would probably mean the transfer of considerable German populations to non-German States, since the 'Rump State' could not absorb all the Germans who might otherwise be transferred to it. It would also mean—unlike the policy of dismemberment—that a 'Rump State'—a 'Germany'—would remain in which strong irredentist feelings would arise. The 'Rump State' would exert a pull on the Germans in the severed parts, but they could not respond to it without defying the political authorities under whom they had been placed. These authorities in turn would have to maintain a strong armed force.

(iv) A fourth type of policy would consist only of 'frontier rectification' on the basis of historical, ethnic, economic or strategical claims put forward by Germany's neighbours. Unlike 'truncation', this policy would allow the removal to the Reich of at least a considerable proportion of the German inhabitants of the transferred territories. The cession of Upper Silesia to Poland (though hardly that of East Prussia) would fall into this category.

(v) The fifth policy was that of 'decentralisation', i.e. 'federalisation', with or without removing the control of military and foreign affairs from the central Government. A federal solution would reduce the danger of German aggression; it was not out of harmony with German ideas and political evolution and might give the best chance of establishing a stable democratic régime. There was, however, an important difference between compulsory and voluntary federation. The former assumed that federation would be imposed and maintained by force on an unwilling people. It might, however, be possible, particularly during the period of occupation, to foster the natural development of particularist sentiment and to encourage the establishment of a federal constitution such as could be maintained without the direct application of outside force.

In deciding which of these four possible policies should be adopted in addition to the first one of restoring the 1937 frontiers we should attempt an estimate of the strength of the centripetal forces in Germany. Modern German nationalism had developed in the early years of the nineteenth century but owed a good deal to a tradition dating back to the Middle Ages. The concept of German unity was based on the idea of the people rather than on the idea of the State, and, since it had not depended on the continuance of any particular structure, would survive the destruction of the political entity—the third Reich—to which it was at present attached. It might adapt itself to new ideas about national sovereignty, but it could not be reconciled with a system, such as dismemberment, which refused it all recognition. During the last hundred years the component parts of Germany had been brought closer together, and all the main political parties had supported German unity. Even the opponents of a particular form of unity had accepted it—once it had become established—because their desire for unity was stronger than their dislike of the actual form it had taken. Regional sentiment was particularist rather than separatist, and the supporters of particularism did not press their claims to a point which would endanger the existence of a united Germany.

The centrifugal tendencies which emerged after the first World War were likely to do so again even more strongly. National Socialism had gone much further than the Weimar Constitution in a centralising direction. There might be a reaction in favour of regional self-government combined with economic unity. Furthermore, if, in the internal chaos after the war, no stable central government emerged for some time and the regions were thrown on their own resources, the result might be favourable to greater permanent decentralisation. Different political trends might appear in different parts of the Reich—Communism in the Rhineland, or Catholicism associated with the Centre Party in South Germany.

On the other hand particularist feelings which might be strong in the hour of defeat would lose much of their force when internal conditions—and the policy of the United Nations—had made possible the establishment of a central government. The ultimate aim, at any rate, of the Communists, would be not regional autonomy, but the seizure of power in a united Germany. Separatism, as distinct from particularism, would have little support after the war. There was little separatism in 1918 even when Prussia and the Prussian military caste might have been held responsible for the war. The power of the National Socialists, however, was not based on Prussia. National

Socialism was ideological not local, and at one stage was strongest in Bavaria and Thuringia and weakest in Prussia.

On the economic side a dismemberment of Germany sufficient to prevent a concerted plan for rearmament would have a serious effect on the general economic prosperity of the country. The German economy had been built up as a unity; the economic differences between regions were manifestations of that unity; regional specialisation was also evidence of regional interdependence. If economic or political barriers prevented full co-operation between the dismembered parts of Germany, some of them would be greatly impoverished while the destruction of the unity of the social services would cause a lowering of the standard of welfare in certain areas. The several parts of Germany would also seek to escape from political isolation along the paths indicated by their economic interests, i.e. by federation.

This federal movement would be supported in Germany, not only by aggressive nationalists, but by the Liberals and Social Democrats. They would argue that forcible resistance to it would be contrary to world interests and to the Atlantic Charter, since it would be denying to the Germans the right to choose their own form of government when there was no evidence of any intention to abuse that right in such a way as to endanger world security. In these circumstances, we should begin to make concessions, and should find ourselves drawn on from economic agreements to economic collaboration and from political understandings to political federation and finally to unification. The stability of the peace settlement would be endangered and there might well be disagreement among the Allies.

These arguments applied equally to the policy of 'truncation'. The neighbouring States would probably not be sufficiently willing or sufficiently strong to ensure the permanent separation of their German minorities from the German homeland. The Rhineland was a case in point. The cession to France of the territory on the left bank might be strategically desirable, but the French people were unlikely to accept the responsibilities involved in it. The compulsory federation of Germany, against the wishes of the people, was hardly more practicable. A federal constitution demanded positive collaboration, and could not be maintained merely by forbidding Germans to take certain action. In any case the balance of power in such a constitution was so delicate a matter that we could not easily specify in advance what internal political changes would be a breach of the peace treaty.

There were less objections to the policy of frontier rectification. In certain cases the cession of territory, and the transfer of population, would be necessary. We could assume that any such measures applied to the pre-1937 territory of the Reich would arouse irredentist feeling and therefore that the transfer of territory, however great its strategical value, would be only an aid to other security measures and not a substitute for them. Hence we must be sure that the States receiving German territory would have the will and the ability to hold and assimilate it. We could expect the Poles to do so in East Prussia and in the Oppeln district of Silesia. The cession of these areas was desirable on political, strategic and economic grounds. France or the Low Countries would probably not be able or willing to hold and assimilate the Rhineland or the Ruhr.

There remained voluntary federation. This would be the best solution, but its practicability must depend on the strength of the particularist movements and on the skill with which the Allies could foster them.

As a conclusion the paper suggested the following measures, designed to limit German powers of making war, as strategically necessary, politically expedient, and economically desirable, and also as reasonably likely to survive as part of a permanent peace settlement, if the victorious Powers maintained a preponderance of armed force and were willing to use it in case of need: (i) Restoration of a free and independent Austria, possibly connected with some Central European Confederation. (ii) Restoration of Czechoslovakia, possibly with minor agreed frontier rectifications, e.g. in the Eger triangle. (iii) Restoration to France of Alsace-Lorraine. (iv) Cession to Poland of East Prussia, Danzig and the Oppeln district of Silesia. (v) Transfer (if desired) of the control of the Kiel Canal to the United Nations. (vi) Restoration of the pre-war territorial *status quo* in the Low Countries and Luxembourg. (vii) Imposition of some form of international control of German industry generally, and particularly in the Rhineland. (viii) Encouragement of any spontaneous particularist or even separatist movements with a view to the development of a federal Germany.

Mr. Eden arrived in Washington on the night of March 12–13, 1943.[1] On March 13 he dined with the President, Mr. Winant and the President's Special Assistant, Mr. Hopkins. He telegraphed to (a) the Prime Minister on March 14 that the President clearly wanted to lead American opinion to understand that American assistance on Lend-Lease lines must be continued after the war. The President also agreed with Mr. Churchill's view of the desirability of a meeting with Stalin, and appeared to be thinking of a date in July. On March 16 Mr. Eden saw Mr. Hull and again dined with the President—Mr. Hopkins was the only other person present. Mr. Eden reported

[1] The Permanent Under-Secretary, Sir A. Cadogan was unable, owing to illness, to accompany Mr. Eden. Mr. Strang, an Assistant Under-Secretary, and Mr. Jebb went with him.

(a) U1273/320/70.

(a) to the Prime Minister the President's general views on the European situation. These views remained much as they had been at Casablanca. The President thought that, after the war, armaments should be concentrated in the hands of the 'policing Powers in Europe—Great Britain, the U.S.S.R. and the United States of America. The smaller Powers might have rifles, but nothing more dangerous.' Mr. Eden explained the obvious difficulties in the way of this plan. The President's main preoccupation was about American relations with the U.S.S.R. Mr. Eden told the President about the demands put to him by M. Maisky the Soviet Ambassador on 10 March.[1] To Mr. Eden's surprise Mr. Roosevelt did not seem to find any difficulty in the Polish question. He thought that, if Poland received East Prussia, and some concessions in Silesia, she would gain rather than lose by agreeing to the Curzon line.[2] The main question, however, was whether it was possible to work with Russia 'now and after the war'.

Mr. Roosevelt said that Mr. Bullitt[3] held the view that Russia wished to see Communist States everywhere in Europe and to overrun the Continent. Mr. Eden thought that, even if this view were correct, our attempts to work with Russia would not make the position worse, and that we should continue to assume that Stalin meant what he had said in the treaty which he had signed with us. Mr. Roosevelt agreed with Mr. Eden, and did not take exception to the Russian claim to the Baltic States. He hoped for some arrangement for a plebiscite in these States, but considered that, if Russia decided to take them, no one could turn her out. He was also willing to accept the Russian demands on Finland.

Mr. Roosevelt seemed to favour dismemberment as the only wholly satisfactory solution of the German problem. He thought that the three Great Powers would have to police Germany for a long period of years and that they should obtain authority from the other States to carry out this work. He was doubtful about the position in Belgium after the war, and thought that the King of the Belgians had gravely undermined his authority. The President put forward tentative ideas about the creation of a new state, to be named Wallonia, on the western borders of Germany and including parts of Belgium, the Rhineland, Luxembourg and the Ruhr. Mr. Eden pointed out the difficulties of such a project, and the President did not return to it. The President also suggested the establishment of a separate kingdom of Serbia. Mr. Eden said that we did not like the idea of adding to the

---

[1] See Volume II, pp. 621–2.

[2] See Volume II, pp. 650–1.

[3] Mr. Bullitt, Special Assistant to the U.S. Secretary of the Navy, was a former Ambassador to Moscow.

(a) U1274/320/70.

number of small States, and hoped rather that the tendency to do so would be reversed, and that some of the existing States would be grouped together. Finally the President spoke of the need to associate China with the other World Powers. Mr. Eden showed no enthusiasm for this proposal, but the President maintained that China was at least a potential World Power, and that anarchy in the country would be so grave a misfortune that we ought to give General Chiang Kai-shek our fullest support.

On March 24 Mr. Welles explained to Mr. Eden his views on a (a)
future World Organisation to prevent war. His plan was that the four major Powers should be responsible for keeping the peace and should form something like an executive committee of the United Nations. In order to avoid giving to the smaller nations the impression that they would be faced with a dictatorship of the Great Powers, we should authorise regional groups—Europe, the American Continent, the Pacific[1]—to elect one or more members to sit on a World Council. If this Council failed to settle a dispute, the four Great Powers, with or without the approval of the Council as a whole, would take action to enforce their decision. Mr. Welles also wanted a general body like the Assembly of the League, upon which every nation would have an opportunity to state its views.

Mr. Welles and Mr. Eden discussed methods of fitting this scheme into the Prime Minister's plan for a Council of Europe.[2] Mr. Eden said that the Prime Minister wanted the United States to take part in the Council of Europe. Mr. Welles thought that American public opinion would not accept such a responsibility if the matter were stated in these terms. There was a great difference between asking the United States Government to become involved in European affairs and asking them to share in the general policing of the world. Mr. Welles thought that a Council of Europe might deal with matters of common European interest such as economics, transport or health, but that political matters should go directly or through the proposed Assembly, to a World Council.

On March 27, Mr. Eden, Lord Halifax and Mr. Strang had a long (b)
conversation with the President, Mr. Hull, Mr. Welles, Mr. Hopkins, and Mr. Winant. The President first raised the question of the post-war organisation of the United Nations. He thought that there should be (i) a General Assembly, meeting about once a year, at which all the members would be represented; this meeting would give the

---

[1] In reporting the conversation, Lord Halifax did not state more closely what was meant by the term.

[2] In a broadcast of March 21, 1943, the Prime Minister had spoken of the necessity of a Council of Europe and a Council of Asia as distinct from, but subsidiary to a World Organisation of the United Nations.

(a) U1679/320/70. (b) WP(43)130; U1430/320/70.

representatives of the smaller Powers an opportunity to 'blow off steam'. (ii) an executive committee of representatives of the four Great Powers (United States, Great Britain, U.S.S.R. and China). This committee would take all the more important decisions and control the police powers of the United Nations. (iii) an Advisory Council composed of representatives of the four Great Powers, and about six or eight other representatives elected on a regional basis for areas roughly equal in population, e.g. there might be one representative from Scandinavia and Finland, and one or two from groups of the Latin American States. This Council would meet as required to settle questions which might be brought before it. The chief official of the organisation would be a Moderator (the President preferred this title to that of Secretary-General).

The President again insisted on the inclusion of China as one of the Four Powers,[1] and upon giving the organisation a world-wide rather than a regional basis. He made it clear that American opinion would agree to undertake international responsibilities only on this world-wide basis, and would suspect organisations of a merely regional kind. The President then raised the question of international trusteeship for certain areas in the world. He did not say much about the case of disputed territories in Europe. On the question of colonial territory the State Department was already considering amendments to a draft submitted from the British side.[2] The discussion therefore was mainly over certain Far Eastern and Pacific territories, and certain parts of the French Empire. The President's view was that Manchuria and Formosa should be returned to China and southern Sakhalin to Russia. The Japanese-mandated islands in the Pacific should pass under the trusteeship of the Allied Nations and all other Pacific Islands (except the French Marquesas and Tuamotu islands) should remain under their existing sovereignty, but should have a common economic policy on lines similar to those proposed for the West Indies. The two French groups of islands would pass to the United Nations for use respectively as stages on the northern and southern air routes across the Pacific from the Caribbean area to Australia and New Zealand. An international trusteeship would be set up for Korea and French Indo-China; for the former the trustees might be the United States, the Soviet Union and China. Timor would have to be dealt with on similar lines owing to its importance for Australia.

Mr. Eden thought that experience in the New Hebrides had shown the practical difficulties of international administration even under trusteeship, and that it would be desirable to entrust the administra-

---

[1] Mr. Eden thought that the President was using the American interest in China as a means of leading the people of the United States to accept international responsibilities.

[2] See above, p. 24, note 1.

tion to a single trustee. Mr. Roosevelt considered that a good deal depended upon the personalities of the local agents exercising a joint trusteeship. He also mentioned Dakar and Bizerta as examples of places likely to be of great strategic importance; he thought that the United States should act as 'policemen' at Dakar and Great Britain at Bizerta.

Mr. Eden said that the President was being very hard to the French, and that they would strongly oppose his suggestions.[1] Mr. Roosevelt agreed, but said that France would need assistance after the war, and might be willing in return to place certain parts of her territory at the disposal of the United Nations. Mr. Welles reminded the President that the United States Government had promised the restoration of French possessions. Mr. Roosevelt thought that this promise referred only to North Africa, but Mr. Welles said that there was no such limitation. The President thought that matters of this kind could be settled in the general 'ironing out' after the war.

In discussing Germany the President again returned to the idea of dismemberment as necessary for the security of Europe. Mr. Eden said that Mr. Churchill had often spoken in favour of the idea, and that he (Mr. Eden) was inclined to agree with it. The President thought that German unity did not go back far in history and that there might well be a tendency—which we should encourage—for the country to split up into a number of separate entities.

In conclusion[2] Mr. Hopkins pointed out that an attempt to set up a Council of Europe would give the Isolationists an opportunity to ask for a similar regional Council for the American continent; on the other hand we should take care that our discussions did not look like an Anglo-American attempt to settle the future of the world. Mr. Eden added that he wanted the Soviet Government to be informed of the conversations by the United States Government as well as by ourselves.

Mr. Eden's report to the Cabinet on his visit added little to his tele- (a)
grams. He explained that Mr. Hull and Mr. Welles had emphasised the need of some machinery for considering the political aspect of military operations. If such machinery had existed, the difficulties which had arisen in North Africa might have been avoided. Mr. Eden had found that there was still a difference of view over the

[1] The Prime Minister, in a later message to Mr. Eden, agreed that proposals to rank France lower than China even in matters affecting Europe and to subjugate all Europe (b)
after disarmament to the four Powers would certainly meet with opposition. The Foreign Office also regarded the conversation as unsatisfactory, since it was difficult to know how far the President was giving a considered opinion and not merely putting forward ideas for discussion. In any case we could not accept a proposal to reduce France to the rank of a second-rate Power. See also Volume II, Chapter XXXI.

[2] Mr. Eden also reported a discussion of shipping problems and of the post-war organisation of civil aviation.

(a) WM(43)53, 2, C.A. (b) Tel. 2077 to Washington, FO 800/404/20/71.

future handling of French affairs. Mr. Hull wished to continue dealing with the various French overseas territories separately rather than through a provisional central administrative body. Mr. Welles was also afraid that, however much we might emphasise the provisional character of such a central authority, we should find it establishing a claim to be regarded as a possible future administration for Metropolitan France. The American view remained in favour of keeping the field free in France in order that a new administrative authority might emerge in accordance with the will of the French people expressed, possibly, through the Conseils Généraux.

Mr. Eden mentioned to the War Cabinet the President's view that the United States could not be a member of the Council of Europe and that China ought to have a place among the four Great Powers, and that she would have no imperialistic ambitions and would be unlikely to become aggressive. Mr. Roosevelt indeed thought that China would be a useful counterpoise to the U.S.S.R. Mr. Eden had suggested to Mr. Roosevelt that much would depend on the kind of situation existing in China after the war.[1]

Note to section (ii). Views of the State Department on post-war organisation.

(a) On March 24, 1943, Mr. Strang and Mr. Jebb had an informal conversation at the State Department with Mr. Dunn, Adviser on political relations, and Mr. Atherton, Head of the European Division. The British officials explained their organisation in London for the consideration of armistice problems. The American officials agreed (i) that at some stage we should bring the Russians into the discussion of these problems and of the kind of machinery which we ought to set up to deal with the situation in Europe after the end of the fighting, (ii) that the only hope of establishing order lay in three-Power collaboration, subject to the provision that, if France recovered her strength, she might be associated with the three Powers on a basis of equality.

Mr. Strang and Mr. Jebb then mentioned the British suggestion for a United Nations Commission for Europe[2] which might in the first instance co-ordinate the activities of the various armistice commissions. We thought that three-Power action in the war would lead necessarily to three-Power concern with the terms of capitulation, and thence to three-Power collaboration in the re-establishment of order in Europe. Mr. Dunn and Mr. Atherton were much interested in the proposal, and especially with the consideration that, for example, European transport problems could be handled as a whole only if

---

[1] See also *F.R.U.S.* 1943, III, 9–43. [2] See below pp. 46–8.

(a) WP(43)217.

some such organisation were set up. Mr. Dunn thought it essential to establish something on the lines of the British plan since, if there were no machinery for getting order in Europe, the Americans might think that the position was hopeless. Finally Mr. Strang said we should like an exchange of ideas now with the Americans on the military aspects of armistice problems.

On the following day Mr. Strang and Mr. Jebb saw Mr. Norman Davis of the American Advisory Committee on post-war foreign policy. Mr. Davis made it clear that the Americans had been considering armistice problems but had not yet made up their minds about them. Mr. Davis doubted whether the President's idea of denying any arms to the minor Allies was practicable, but he regarded some scheme for the regulation of armaments as necessary. He said that the Americans had been thinking about a plan whereby all Powers should have arms sufficient for police purposes, and should also contribute on an agreed scale to some international system. He agreed with the British view that we needed a strong France, and that Germany must be completely and finally disarmed. The President favoured the dismemberment of Germany. Mr. Hull had not come to any decision on the question, and the American Chiefs of Staff (and Mr. Davis himself) were not sure whether enforced dismemberment would not merely increase the strength of centripetal forces.

Mr. Davis said that until recently he had been in favour of the plan that each of the three major Allies should occupy a separate area in Germany, but that the United States military authorities had brought forward powerful arguments in favour of 'mixing up' the Allied forces, though with the proviso that no two Powers would be stationed in the same town. The American view was that the allotment of large areas to any one Power would result in the creation of zones of influence and thus cause difficulties. Moreover the Russians were likely to treat the Germans far more brutally than the British or the Americans would, and a more unified policy towards the population might be possible in the 'mixing-up' plan.

Mr. Davis's reaction to the suggestion of a United Nations Commission for Europe was favourable, though the idea seemed new to him. He said that he knew that there was a general assumption that British and American relations with the U.S.S.R. would continue to be friendly. He had some doubts about the point, but he entirely agreed that we should make the greatest possible effort to bring Russia into the peace and to work out arrangements with her in advance. He agreed with the view that the Soviet Government had not decided upon their post-war policy, and that, if we showed confidence in them now, they might wish to co-operate with us. On the other hand, if they refused co-operation, they could do great harm with their Communist propaganda. Mr. Davis thought that the best course was to talk 'very straight' with Stalin, who 'appreciated the direct method'. In any case the United States would not go to war with Russia for the Baltic States or for any frontiers in Eastern Europe.

Mr. Davis said that he was speaking personally and informally, and that Mr. Eden might shortly have another interview with the President. The President, however, was inclined to go slowly, and to avoid the risk of appearing to dictate to the smaller Powers.

(iii)

The Prime Minister's conversation in Washington on May 22, 1943, about a post-war World Organisation: Foreign Office views on the conversation.

After Mr. Eden's return from Washington the Foreign Office considered that there was for the time sufficient agreement on the general lines of a post-war world security organisation, and that it
(a) was unnecessary, and indeed, inexpedient to try to settle details. Mr. Jebb wrote a paper analysing the differences between the ideas put forward by the President and those of the Prime Minister. Sir A. Cadogan, however, in a minute of April 13, 1943, wrote that, if, owing to continued agreement between the Great Powers and a readiness on their part to use force when necessary, we retained the means for checking German and Japanese aggression, we should not find it difficult to construct 'ancillary organs which might have their uses'. If we did not retain the means for checking aggression, all these ancillary constructions were nothing but card castles, as in the case of the League. Hence, at the present stage, we need not discuss in detail the various possible forms of organisation. We might, however, try to reach an agreement with the United States and the U.S.S.R. on our respective functions and aims after the end of the European war, i.e. the broad lines of an armistice, the nature and extent of the occupation of enemy countries, precautions for maintaining disarmament, the economic control which we should exercise, etc. If we could reach agreement on these lines, we might be able to organise an effective 'policing' of Europe with which other countries might be associated. The 'grim' feature in the outlook was that everything depended upon agreement between the three Powers and upon their determination to use force, if necessary, to restrain a breach of the peace. At all events, we should concentrate upon trying to get such agreement before we began to design 'all the outbuildings of the future Palace of Peace'.

A further exchange of Anglo-American views, or at all events of

(a) U1535/320/70.

the views held respectively by the Prime Minister and President Roosevelt, took place at Washington during the latter part of May 1943. The Prime Minister's visit to Washington was concerned, like the Casablanca Conference, primarily with military matters. He asked Lord Halifax, however, to invite to luncheon at the British (a) Embassy on May 22 a number of Americans specially interested in the question of post-war arrangements.

The American guests were Mr. Wallace, who was at this time Vice-President, Mr. Stimson, Secretary of War, Mr. Ickes, Secretary of the Interior, Mr. Sumner Welles and Senator Connally, Chairman of the Foreign Relations Committee of the Senate. Mr. Churchill said that he hoped for an association of the United States, Great Britain and Russia to prevent future aggression by Germany or Japan. If the United States wished to include China, he would agree, although China was not comparable in importance with the other three Powers. These three, or four, Powers should form a Supreme World Council, with three Regional Councils (Europe, the American Hemisphere, and the Pacific) subordinate to them.

The European Council might be formed from some twelve States or Confederations. It was important to recreate a strong France, since otherwise there would be no strong country between Great Britain and the U.S.S.R.; in any case neither the United States nor Great Britain would be able to keep large numbers of men indefinitely on guard in Europe, though the four Powers would doubtless be associated in the policing of Europe. There would also be Spain and Italy, and, if possible, a Danubian and a Balkan Confederation. The Prime Minister wanted Prussia to be separated from the rest of Germany; he reserved judgment on the question whether Prussia should remain as a unit or be subdivided. He hoped that Bavaria might join the Danubian Confederation. Poland and Czechoslovakia should stand together in friendly relation with Russia. There remained the Scandinavian countries and Turkey; Turkey might be willing to take some part with Greece in a Balkan Confederation. Switzerland would continue to be a 'special case'.

Mr. Wallace suggested that Belgium and the Netherlands might join with France. Mr. Churchill thought that an arrangement of this kind was possible, or that the two countries might form with Denmark a Low Countries Confederation.[1] Each of the European countries should send a representative to the European Regional Council, and thus create a form of United States of Europe. The Prime Minister thought that Count Coudenhove-Kalergi's ideas on this subject

---

[1] Mr. Churchill's words about Switzerland were in answer to a question from Mr. Wallace about the possibility of Switzerland joining France. The Prime Minister said that Switzerland was a 'special case'.

(a) WP(43)233; U3060/1814/70.

had much to recommend them.[1] He suggested a Regional Council for the Americas on which Canada would represent the British Commonwealth, and a similar Council for the Pacific on which Russia would probably be represented. The Prime Minister hoped that the United States would be represented on all three Regional Councils.

Mr. Wallace said that the other countries would not agree to a World Council consisting solely of the four major Powers. Mr. Churchill agreed that other Powers should be added by election in rotation from the Regional Councils. The central idea was that of a three-legged stool—the World Council resting on three Regional Councils. Mr. Churchill repeated that 'the last word would remain with the World Council', but that he attached great importance to the regional principle, since only the countries whose interests were directly affected by a dispute could be expected to apply themselves with sufficient vigour to secure a settlement. He also wanted an agreement between the United Nations on the minimum and maximum armed force which each member would maintain. The forces of each country might be divided into two contingents, of which one would form the national forces of the country, and the other a contingent to an international police force at the disposal of the Regional Councils under the direction of the Supreme War Council. The personnel of this international contingent provided by each country would be bound to undertake operations against any country other than their own.

Mr. Churchill said that these proposals did not exclude 'special friendships' devoid of sinister purpose against others. He saw little hope for the world unless the United States and the British Commonwealth worked together in 'fraternal association'. He would like the citizens of each country, without losing their present nationality, to be able to settle and trade with freedom and equal rights in the territories of the other. There might be a common passport or a special form of passport or visa, or even some common form of citizenship under which citizens of the United States or of the British Commonwealth might enjoy voting privileges after residential qualification and be eligible for public office in the territories of the other. Mr. Churchill, in answer to a question from Mr. Wallace, also said that he would support 'the common use of bases for the common defence of common interests'. The Americans present at the conversation said that they agreed generally with the Prime Minister's views and thought that American opinion might accept them, or

---

[1] Count Coudenhove-Kalergi was an active supporter of European Union. He had written a number of books on the subject and had founded a Pan-European Union for the advocacy of his plans.

something like them, especially if such plans were presented during the war and as a continuation of existing co-operation.

At the end of the conversation Mr. Welles repeated to Lord Halifax how important it was from the point of view of American opinion to secure the adoption of at least the essentials of a post-war security organisation before the end of the war. He also thought it desirable to take advantage of good relations with the Soviet Government. Mr. Welles suggested the conclusion during the war of two protocols. The first protocol would consist of an agreement between the four major Powers on their joint responsibility for the maintenance of peace. The four Powers would undertake to maintain minimum and maximum forces for the purpose. The second protocol would be an agreement among all the United Nations to co-operate in the preservation of peace.[1]

Mr. Welles was unwilling to put his suggestions on paper since he had not submitted them to the President or the Secretary of State. On June 10, 1943, he told Lord Halifax and Mr. Richard Law, who was (a) visiting the United States, that he hoped to get the President's approval for his plans. He explained in greater detail his ideas of the 'World Council'. He proposed that the Council should consist of eleven members, i.e. representatives of the four major Powers, two members elected by the European and two by the American Regional Councils from a panel of accepted names, and three members elected respectively by the Pacific Regional Council, the independent countries of the Middle East and North Africa and the British Commonwealth of Nations. Mr. Welles thought that the World Council should act only on a unanimous decision of the four Great Powers. This condition would not only recognise political 'realities', but would also be valuable from the point of opinion in the United States. Mr. Welles was sure that we need not be afraid of a revisal of American policy once a commitment had been assumed.[2]

On his return to England early in June the Prime Minister circulated to the Cabinet an account of his conversation. The Foreign Office regarded it as generally satisfactory that a number of leading Americans, including Mr. Welles, should have agreed upon the

[1] See also *F.R.U.S., 1943 Conferences at Washington and Quebec*, 166–72.

[2] On June 29 Lord Halifax asked Mr. Welles how matters stood with regard to his suggestion for an early negotiation of protocols. Mr. Welles said that he had had a long talk with the President on the matter. The President's general attitude was favourable. Mr. Welles said that he would speak to the President again before July 1; he was then (b) going on leave for three weeks. Lord Halifax made another enquiry on August 7. Mr. Welles said again that he had discussed the question with the President and also with Mr. Hull. The President was more disposed than Mr. Hull to favour immediate action; Mr. Hull was inclined to think it necessary to talk first to the party leaders in Congress and the Senate. Mr. Welles, however, thought that some action would be taken, though not at once; he also hoped that the President would discuss the matter with the Prime Minister at their forthcoming meeting.

(a) U2695/1816/70. (b) U2902, 3520/1816/70.

desirability of the United States, together with the three major Allies, adopting the principle of joint responsibility for keeping the peace. If the United States Senate accepted the two protocols suggested by Mr. Welles, the consequences would be of the greatest value. The Foreign Office welcomed American assent to the idea of a Supreme World Council consisting of the four Powers and other members chosen on a regional basis. On the other hand a number of points in the Prime Minister's proposals seemed impracticable or
(a) undesirable. Mr. Eden, therefore, circulated a memorandum to the War Cabinet on July 1, 1943, discussing the proposals in some detail. On the question of membership of the World Council, he thought that France would want a permanent seat (he agreed with the Prime Minister's desire for the complete restoration of France as a Great Power). He also saw difficulties in the proposal for a 'panel' of candidates for election, and doubted whether Canada would wish to join a Pan-American Union.

Mr. Eden's main criticisms concerned the European proposals. He did not agree with the implication of the Prime Minister's plan for the separation of Prussia, as a unit, from the rest of Germany. He pointed out that the 'Nazi virus' was not confined to north Germany or to 'Prussia'; that Prussia extended from Aachen to the Polish frontier, and included a large number of Catholics and other West Germans who were not 'ethnic' Prussians and did not share the conventional Prussian outlook. In any case there was the difficulty that the greater part of German industry was in north Germany, and that, as soon as the Allied occupation ceased, the two parts of Germany would seek reunion. If this reunion took place, and if Austria—as the Prime Minister had suggested—were included in south Germany, we should be faced again with the 'grossdeutsche Reich' of 1937, and the position of Czechoslovakia would again be dangerous. The situation would be even more serious if Hungary and even Roumania were associated with a south German federation. We should then ensure German economic predominance in south-eastern Europe. We could not therefore expect either our European Allies or the Soviet Union to accept proposals of this kind as the basis of a settlement.

Mr Eden therefore suggested that we should try to secure the association of Austria with Czechoslovakia, and possibly with Hungary and Yugoslavia in a Danubian Federation. Mr. Eden considered that the other proposed federations would be valuable but that there was little chance of bringing them about. We were encouraging proposals for a Greco-Yugoslav confederation[1] but it was difficult to

[1] Mr. Eden did not distinguish in any detail between the terms 'federation' and 'confederation'.

(a) WP(43)292; U3061/1816/70.

make much progress while the Governments of the two countries were in exile. We could not forecast what would happen after an Axis collapse: a good deal would depend on whether at the time of collapse we were in occupation of the countries. The prospects of a Polish–Czechoslovak confederation were slight, and indeed nothing could be done until there was an improvement in Polish–Soviet relations. A Scandinavian confederation was not impossible, but the Soviet Government would probably not allow Finland to join it, and relations between Norway and Sweden were not good. Belgium and the Netherlands were unlikely to unite; both countries looked towards us, and neither wished, at all events for the present, to be more closely associated with France. Denmark was even less likely to agree to association with the Low Countries. Spain and Italy were most unlikely to come together, and in any case there was Portugal to be considered. Finally, a Balkan *bloc* which included Turkey might arouse Russian suspicions.

Mr. Eden thought, however, that, in spite of the difficulties, we should continue to work for confederations in Europe. Such confederations were unlikely to come about except through fear of aggression. We could assume that, even after unconditional surrender, there would be fear of renewed German aggression in Europe during the next twenty or thirty years. It might indeed be that fear of Russian aggression would be greater, but we could not make our plans on this assumption. Mr. Eden thought that Mr. Churchill's proposals did not put sufficient emphasis on the absolute need for co-operation between the United Kingdom, the United States, and the U.S.S.R. He would have liked a suggestion that one of the main functions of the World Council would be to settle differences between the Great Powers and to reach agreement on their respective rights, obligations and aims during the period after the war when they would have the duty of policing and reconstructing Europe. Mr. Eden agreed in principle with the idea of an International Police Force, but doubted whether we could get agreement immediately after the war on minimum and maximum forces. He also thought that other States, especially the Soviet Union, would refuse to accept the principle of two contingents. In general, and taking into account the great difficulties of securing inter-Allied agreement on the various urgent and important questions connected with an armistice, Mr. Eden considered that we should avoid raising contentious European issues in a scheme for a world organisation. We should rather work towards the plan for a United Nations Commission for Europe which the Cabinet had agreed to put forward to the American and Soviet Governments.[1]

---

[1] See also below, pp. 49–50. The Foreign Office also had doubts on other points in the Prime Minister's paper which were not mentioned in Mr. Eden's memorandum. Thus

(*continued on page 44*)

Meanwhile, although Mr. Eden's memorandum of March 8, 1943, on the future of Germany had not required any action by the War Cabinet, the proposals were being considered by other Ministers.
(a) Lord Selborne, Minister of Economic Warfare, circulated a memorandum to the War Cabinet on April 8, containing important comments on the Foreign Office paper. He pointed out that the Ministry of Economic Warfare had reached discouraging conclusions about the possibility of controlling Germany's war potential. The great difficulty was that a lasting peace required a prosperous Germany. Economic distress and unemployment would reproduce the conditions in which Hitler rose to power. On the other hand practically all the great industries of peace played their part in total war, and a country's power of making war could not be reduced by economic measures without impairing its capacity for peacetime prosperity.

There had been suggestions for getting round this dilemma: (i) the destruction of 'Ersatz' war industries such as synthetic oil and rubber. Germany might accept this prohibition since it would be cheaper for her to buy natural oil and rubber. On the other hand, owing to technical advances, 'Ersatz' substances might be manufactured at a cheaper price than that of the natural articles. In any case an economic control not forming part of an international system applicable to all nations perpetuated on the country subjected to it the status of a conquered but potentially dangerous and hostile Power. (ii) The destruction of key war industries such as the machine-tool making industry. We might destroy all existing tool-making factories, but how could we prevent the Germans from recreating the industry? It was hard to define a machine tool, and we could maintain our veto only by policing German industry in permanence. (iii) The transfer of whole sections of German industrial equipment to other European countries. This policy might well result, after a few years, in the industries of Germany having a more modern equipment than those of her rivals. (iv) Limitation of German stocks of raw materials. This proposal involved policing the key raw materials of the world, such as nickel, copper and chrome, control of the German customs and some system of checking stocks at works.

Lord Selborne asked whether, from our previous experience, we were justified in thinking that German opinion would willingly accept any of these economic measures or the territorial changes regarded by

---

(*continued*)
they considered that the proposals for joint 'American-British Commonwealth' citizenship would give the impression of an Anglo-Saxon dictatorship, and would lead to requests from many other nations for similar facilities, and that generally the Prime Minister had given insufficient attention in his proposals to the question of the Commonwealth, the problem of Middle Eastern organisation, and the desirability of world economic organisation.

(a) WP(43)144.

the Foreign Office as strategically necessary. If these measures were not so accepted, what chance had a peace built upon them of surviving longer than the Treaty of Versailles? *A fortiori* these considerations also applied to a proposal to abolish the German aircraft industry, or to the decision in the Atlantic Charter to deny Germany an air force and a navy. A peace treaty placing Germany in a position of permanent inferiority in any respect to the Great Powers would be a grievance which the Germans would rapidly come to regard as intolerable. They would then repeat the tactics which they had followed from 1919. There would be continuous propaganda to Great Britain and the United States, and demands, at first for minor concessions, but increasing in magnitude as Germany grew stronger. On the other side the will of the victorious Powers would be in inverse ratio to the strength of Germany, and these Powers would finally persuade themselves that the only way to live peaceably with the Germans was to give them what they wanted.

It was impossible for us to re-educate the Germans from outside, and useless to hope that their own Liberals could do the work for us. We had no reason to suppose that the establishment of democracy in Germany would result in a pacific régime unless the German people themselves were pacifically inclined. Lord Selborne's view therefore was that we should insist upon the political dismemberment of Germany, and try to make British and American opinion realise that such a policy—accompanied by measures to secure German economic prosperity—was morally justifiable and the only means of securing a lasting peace.

A second memorandum came, on July 19, 1943, from Mr. Attlee; (a) his main argument was that the real aggressive element in Germany was the Prussian Junker class, with its strong roots in the Reichswehr and the Civil Service. This class, which had allied itself to the masters of heavy industry in Westphalia and elsewhere with their special industry in armaments, might now liquidate the Nazis and come forward as the only body which could save central Europe from anarchy. Some general would no doubt provide a convenient figurehead. After the first war we had allowed these aggressive elements to remain owing to our fear of Bolshevism. We must not do so again and, unless we secured their liquidation, it was useless to talk about encouraging particularist tendencies. The 'Prussian virus' had spread very widely throughout the Reich, and only strong action could eradicate it. Mr. Attlee also thought that we should not give back to the German capitalists the sections of German industry which Göring had now taken under his control, and that we should break

(a) WP(43)322.

up the big German capitalist combines and control German industry in the interests of central and south-east Europe. Mr. Attlee's memorandum was short, and did not attempt to enter into detail or to explain how his proposals should be carried out.

(iv)

Foreign Office memorandum of May 25, 1943, on 'Armistices and Related Problems': Sir S. Cripps's comments (June 15) on the memorandum: discussion of the memoranda in the War Cabinet, June 16, 1943.

(a) On May 25, 1943—while the Prime Minister was in Washington—Mr. Eden circulated another Foreign Office memorandum to the War Cabinet on 'Armistices and Related Problems'. He wrote that he had not yet asked for any cabinet decisions on his earlier memorandum about 'The United Nations Plan'.[1] Since his conversations at Washington[2] the paper would have to be revised. The first step must be an approach to the Dominions; the Foreign Office were therefore discussing with the Dominions Office the best way of making this approach. Meanwhile we should define our own views and convey them to the Russians and Americans, and, after obtaining their agreement, to the minor Allies. We had to settle the form of an armistice with Germany and the means of putting it into effect. We also had to decide what system, from our own point of view, would be best for co-ordinating the activities of the United Nations authorities, military and civil, and for maintaining order in Europe after the fighting was over. Mr. Eden then referred to the conversations between Mr. Strang and Mr. Jebb and officials of the State Department on March 24–5.[3]

Mr. Eden thought that we should go slow with inter-Allied discussions of a theoretical kind on a substitute for the old League of Nations, and that we should begin with practical problems the solution of which could not be delayed. He suggested certain principles as governing our approach to the United States and Soviet Governments:

(i) The terms to be imposed on any European member of the Axis should be presented as one comprehensive document covering all the United Nations at war with that member, and embodying the principle of unconditional surrender.

(ii) If there existed a central enemy Government with which we were

---

[1] See above, p. 12 ff.
[2] See above, pp. 31–8, and *F.R.U.S. 1943.* III, 9–41.
[3] See above, note to Section (ii).

(a) WP(43)217; U2256/25/70.

prepared to treat, a fully accredited representative of that Government should be associated with its Commander-in-Chief for purposes of signature; or alternatively the Armistice should not come into force until confirmed by that Government.

(iii) If there were no such Government the Armistice should be signed by the enemy Commander-in-Chief only. In that case provisions which the enemy Commander-in-Chief lacked authority to execute would have to be omitted from the Armistice, which would thus be primarily a military document. Non-military provisions should so far as necessary be embodied in a Declaration or Proclamation issued by the United Nations.

(iv) If there were neither an enemy Government nor Commander-in-Chief with whom we could or were prepared to treat, military resistance would presumably be brought to an end by a series of local capitulations. It would, however, probably be desirable that the United Nations should issue a Declaration stating their intentions in respect of the defeated Power. This would be followed by a series of proclamations issued by the Allied Commander-in-Chief containing instructions to the local authorities and population.

(v) The administration of any Armistice should be placed in the hands of an Inter-Allied Armistice Commission, the President to be alternately representative of the United States, U.S.S.R. and the United Kingdom. The Commission would establish its headquarters in the Axis country concerned, and would be responsible for controlling the execution of the Armistice terms; these terms would involve in the first place, the disarmament and demobilisation of enemy armed forces, the collection and disposal of surrendered war material and other mobile property and the handing over of fortifications and other fixed property. Representatives of the Armistice Commission would be despatched to liberated Allied territory to perform a similar task in respect of the enemy troops there located and to regulate their evacuation or internment.

(vi) In the absence of an Armistice (see paragraph (iv)), a Control Commission should administer the appropriate portions of the Declaration.

(vii) Any Armistice or Declaration would presumably provide for the occupation, whether total or partial, of the country concerned. Germany, in any case, should be totally occupied, and might be divided into three main zones, convenient for administration by ourselves, United States and U.S.S.R. In these zones the occupying forces would be predominantly British, United States and Russian respectively, but would in each case include forces of the other Allies and be under Inter-Allied Command. The principle of a joint United Nations occupation would then be maintained, but problems of supply and administration would be simplified.

(viii) The United Nations Commander-in-Chief in any occupied country should have complete responsibility for the maintenance of law and order.

(ix) There should be established a supervisory body entitled 'United Nations Commission for Europe', composed of high-ranking political representatives of the three major Allies, of France and the minor European Allies, and possibly of any Dominion prepared to contribute to the policing of Europe. The Commission should be situated at some convenient point on the Continent.

The Commission would act as the supreme United Nations authority in Europe to direct and co-ordinate the activities of the several Armistice Commissions, the Allied Commanders-in-Chief and any United Nations civilian authorities that might be established; and to deal with current problems, military, political, and economic, connected with the maintenance of order. A 'Steering Committee', consisting of the representatives of the three major Allies and of France, if she recovered her status,[1] should be established as the directing body of the Commission. In the 'Steering Committee' the unanimity rule should apply.

(x) A number of civilian authorities would probably be set up by agreement between the United Nations, some on a world and others on a European basis. Apart from the United Nations Relief and Rehabilitation Administration and the Intergovernmental Committee which might emerge from the Bermuda Conference on refugees, the establishment of a United Nations Shipping Authority and a United Nations Inland Transport Authority for Europe had been suggested. Analogous bodies might well be required to control telecommunications and propaganda, and to handle reparation, restitution and other economic problems. These authorities might, in respect of their European activities, establish their headquarters in the same city as the United Nations Commission for Europe, to whom they would be responsible and provide the necessary technical advice.

Mr. Eden regarded the acceptance of these 'principles' as necessary if we were to avoid the signature by the Soviet Union of a separate armistice and the creation of a situation in which the Russians would organise an independent system of their own in Eastern Europe. Mr. Eden did not despair of an agreement with the Russians. He thought it wiser not to raise for the present questions such as the future of Germany, but to concentrate upon the establishment of the machinery necessary for the collaboration of the Great Powers. The Soviet Government might refuse to discuss even this matter, and might eventually go their own way in Europe without regard to the wishes of the Americans and ourselves, but we had nothing to lose by suggesting

[1] The memorandum actually used the vague term 'greatness'.

to them a contrary course. Unless we could harmonise British, American and Soviet policy and, probably, unless we could get machinery established to ensure such harmony, no settlement would be possible, and 'we should have very shortly, after the conclusion of the war, to set about preparing for the next'.

On June 15, 1943, Sir S. Cripps circulated a paper to the War Cabinet commenting on Mr. Eden's proposals of May 25. He agreed that we should not initiate inter-Allied discussions of a theoretical kind on the constitutional framework of post-war co-operation until we had reached some measure of agreement with our major Allies on more immediate questions. He did not think, however, that we should postpone for too long the consideration of the larger questions, since we might be confronted at any time with American or Russian proposals relating to post-war international organisation. On the immediate issue of 'armistices and related problems', Sir. S. Cripps also agreed with Mr. Eden subject to one important qualification. Sir S. Cripps did not like the suggestion that occupied territory should be divided into three main zones to suit the convenience of British, American and Russian administration. He recognised that there was much to be said for the plan from the military side. On the other hand he thought that there were sound reasons for a 'mixed' form of United Nations administration throughout the occupied territory. He agreed with the American argument[1] that the allotment of large areas to any one Power would mean the creation of zones of influence which would not conduce to harmony between the three major Allies and might become a serious embarrassment at a later stage when a definite settlement had to be reached. It would also be very difficult to enforce a unified policy with regard to the population if separate parts of Germany were under the control of men with such different administrative traditions as the Russians, the Americans and ourselves. The comparatively slight differences between ourselves, the French and the Belgians had most unfortunate consequences in the zoned administration of the Rhineland in 1919 and after. Sir S. Cripps also thought that the success of the 'United Nations idea' would depend on the development of habits of co-operation in practical matters serving mutually agreed purposes. Hence officials from the major (and minor) Allies should learn to work side by side; only on the basis of such intimate collaboration would it be possible to create a tradition of disinterested international co-operation. (a)

The War Cabinet considered Mr. Eden's and Sir S. Cripps's memoranda on June 16, 1943. They agreed that, although it was (b)

---

[1] See above, pp. 36–7.

(a) WP(43)243; U2720/25/70. (b) WM(43)86.

difficult to forecast the situation at the end of the war, we could not wait to discuss at the last minute problems of great complexity. Moreover the Americans had already begun the consideration of these questions and the Russians were showing interest in them. In general the War Cabinet approved of Mr. Eden's proposals, and agreed that he should discuss them informally with the United States and Soviet Ambassadors in London, but that he should not yet raise the question of the extent or method of the occupation of Germany. The War Cabinet thought that we should not yet commit ourselves to a total occupation of Germany by the Allies. We did not wish to incur the burden of maintaining and administering a large part of the country though we might well have to occupy the main centres of German industry. There was some agreement with Sir S. Cripps's argument against creating three zones of occupation, but it was recognised that there would be great administrative difficulties in mixing up contingents of each of the three Allies in each zone.

(a) Mr. Eden saw M. Maisky on July 2, and Mr. Winant on July 14. He gave each of them an *aide-mémoire* (dated July 1) summarising the British proposals, but omitting any reference to the discussion about the occupation of Germany. Mr. Eden told M. Maisky that we had been considering the possibility of an Italian collapse and had even drawn up draft armistice terms for such an event, but that this problem was only one among the many problems concerned with the end of the war in Europe. It was therefore essential to begin thinking about the organisation of a supreme United Nations authority in Europe and unless the three Great Powers reached some agreement, there would be chaos when the war ended. M. Maisky, who was about to go to Moscow on leave, said that he would take the paper with him.

(v)

Foreign Office memorandum of July 7, 1943, on 'The United Nations Plan for Organising Peace'.

(b) On March 6, 1943, before leaving with Mr. Eden for the United States, Mr. Jebb drew up another memorandum[1] entitled 'Suggestions for a Peace Settlement'. He wrote the paper, after discussions in the Foreign Office, in order to sum up the conclusions reached over the past few months. During the next three months this paper

[1] This memorandum—especially the section 'General Considerations'—was in part a revised and enlarged version of the memorandum of January 16 on the United Nations Plan. The paper also took account, in its final form, of the memorandum of May 25 on 'Armistice and Related Problems' and of the Prime Minister's conversations in Washington.

(a) U3009, 3140/25/70. (b) U2066/402/70.

underwent considerable alteration; a revised version was drawn up on June 21, and a second revise was entitled 'United Nations Plan for Organising Peace and Welfare'.[1] The paper was circulated on July 7 to the War Cabinet. It is worth quoting in full as a general indication of the views put forward at this time in the Foreign Office about post-war organisation. (a)

A. GENERAL CONSIDERATIONS

1. The Atlantic Charter

The principles embodied in the Charter will be the basis of any international world order after the war. But they will need to be applied and interpreted so as to provide definitely both for a world security system and for world economic arrangements.

2. Necessity for an International System and International Machinery

(i) It is improbable that the League of Nations can be revived in its old form, but it is highly desirable that some international machinery, embodying many of the good features of the League, should be established on the conclusion of hostilities.

(ii) In any case, every effort should be made to preserve those technical and humanitarian services of the League which have been so conspicuously successful in the past, and for which there will be scope in the future.

(iii) The International Labour Office should also continue in existence as such, its functions being expanded as necessary.

(iv) But, quite apart from these existing machines, world opinion will undoubtedly demand with increasing insistence that some system should be devised for ensuring political co-operation, the sphere in which the League was least successful. The foundations upon which such a system must be built already exist in the idea of the United Nations.

3. Position and Duties of the World Powers

International co-operation between the United Nations will not provide the necessary cohesion and stability unless the World Powers are prepared to accept the responsibilities of leadership *within* the United Nations. For this purpose these Powers, before the war in Europe comes to an end, should agree between themselves on a common world policy and be prepared, as leaders of the United Nations, to take joint action to enforce it. Failing this, we shall be confronted

[1] The last two words were omitted in the title of the paper circulated to the Cabinet.

(a) WP(43)300; U2889/402/70.

by the prospect of a world in precarious balance, with the World Powers, each with its circle of client States, facing each other in a rivalry which may merge imperceptibly into hostility.

4. What States should rank as World Powers

(i) The Four Powers

The leadership of the United Nations will have in some way to be shared between the British Commonwealth (and more especially the United Kingdom), the United States and the Soviet Union, if only for the reason that the refusal of any one of these Powers to enter into a world system would render any world system impracticable. In view of her vast area and population and her potential development it would be desirable for China, too, to be included in the ranks of the World Powers, who between them would thus comprise about two-thirds of the population of the globe. We should therefore regard the conception of these Four Powers, working within the framework of the United Nations, as the basis of any scheme for world organisation.

(ii) France

The future of France is obscure, but it would seem essential that, when she has recovered a measure of her greatness, she should be given the same position as the Four Powers, if only because without the willing assistance of a rejuvenated France the problem of recreating a sound and free Europe would be much more difficult.

(iii) Germany, Japan and Italy not to be re-admitted as World Powers

It must be assumed that the policy of the United Nations towards the Axis Powers will be to restrict the power for evil of Germany and Japan for as long a period as is necessary, and will not be based on the alternative theory that both these Powers should be readmitted in the foreseeable future to international society on the same footing as the Four (or Five) Powers mentioned above. Italy, on the other hand, has never been a world Power in any real sense, and, in addition, she probably went to war against the real wishes of a considerable proportion of her population. It is therefore possible to contemplate a non-Fascist Italy adhering to the United Nations after the war (although not in any leading capacity) perhaps after some period of probation, and the same applies in varying degrees to the minor Axis allies.

5. The World Council

(i) Composition

It follows that there should be a World Council, consisting in the first place of the U.S.S.R., the United States of America, China and the United Kingdom and possibly also of France. To these might be added the representatives of smaller Powers chosen on a regional basis (see paragraph 24), and with certain defined functions (see sub-paragraph (ii) below). Should it prove difficult to obtain the general agreement of the United Nations to this or any other method of selection or to these functions, the Four (or Five) Powers should, nevertheless, constitute themselves a Provisional World Council until such time as general agreement can be obtained.

(ii) Functions

The functions of any World Council would be two-fold, as follows:

(*a*) Since all the World Powers would always be present, its primary and most important task would be to smooth out any frictions existing between them so as to achieve that unity of purpose without which no ordered progress will be possible and the peace of the world is bound to be threatened. Where necessary, discussions on these subjects could be limited to the World Powers themselves.

(*b*) But, in addition, it would have to take such dispositions for the restraint of aggression and for ensuring the peaceful settlement of disputes as the needs of a general security system may dictate. It may be hoped that the other nations (whether numbered during this war among the United Nations or among the neutrals) will, as a result of their recent experience, consent to the assumption by the World Powers of leadership for that purpose. Naturally the decisions of the World Powers on all such subjects must be unanimous. The smaller Powers should, however, be given adequate representation on the Council and allowed to influence its decisions. In addition, smaller Powers should always be summoned to sit on the Council when their special interests are under discussion. If the smaller Powers accept this method there is no reason why they should not play an important role in the discussions of the Council. But no opposition on their part should be allowed to prevent the World Powers from taking the necessary action for the restraint of aggression and for ensuring the peaceful settlement of disputes. In other words, the final decision on such questions should rest with the World Powers acting unanimously.

6. Judicial and Arbitral Machinery

The experience of the League and other bodies has shown the advantage of establishing arbitral and fact-finding machines for the settlement of the various kinds of disputes that arise between nations. It will be the duty of the Council to see that such machinery is used, and it may be hoped that only rarely will the Council itself be called upon to make the actual decisions.

7. Armaments

An essential part of any future world order will be some agreement between the World Powers as to the forces to be maintained by each of them for internal and external purposes, and also the adoption of some principle regulating the armament of smaller Powers. The armaments which the latter can claim to maintain will in turn depend on (1) how far the policy and undertakings of the World Powers, together with the machinery instituted, guarantee the security of the smaller Powers, and (2) on how far the latter are themselves prepared to play their part, whether active or passive, in a general security system. National independence should no longer be considered as a natural right, but as a privilege entailing for the independent State such corresponding obligations and contributions as may be necessary to ensure the maintenance of international well-being, security and peace. If a satisfactory solution of these points is achieved, the principle to be adopted might be that the armament of each country should be proportionate to the part it would be called upon to play in that system.

8. Immediate Post-war Period

(i) For a period after the war, during which they will have a virtual monopoly of armed strength, the World Powers will, however, have to undertake by themselves the military responsibility for maintaining order and preventing the building up of aggressive forces in Europe and the Far East. This will entail the maintenance by them of a considerable measure of armaments throughout Europe and in Asia; the complete disarmament of the defeated Powers; and the establishment of a policing system towards the financing of which the defeated Powers relieved of the burden of armaments, should, if practicable, contribute heavily.

(ii) For these immediate purposes the most suitable agencies would seem to be some such bodies as United Nations Commissions which would have the task, one in Europe, and one in the Far East, of co-ordinating the activities of the various Armistice Commissions, and those of other United Nations bodies (see paragraphs 14 and 18). In such Commissions the smaller Allied Powers would co-operate.

B. ECONOMIC AND SOCIAL CONSIDERATIONS

9. Economic Aspects of World Order

International friction and aggression frequently have their roots in economic and social disharmonies. Thus, if standards of living are too unequal, stresses will be created leading to dangerous crises and even to war itself. Consequently, it will be of the highest importance for the United Nations, and in particular for the World Powers, to concern themselves with world economic and social problems.

10. Relief and Reconstruction

It will, for instance, be highly desirable, if not essential, to obtain general consent before the end of the war to schemes which will be proof that the combined United Nations can bring and intend to bring early relief to the peoples of disorganised countries. These should include schemes covering monetary control, primary products (especially food-stuffs), etc., so that an "expansionist spiral" of world trade can be initiated. Unless such an expansion of world trade takes place, the economic conditions of many countries may become completely intolerable, and desperate solutions may be urged by desperate people.

11. Development of Backward Countries

It will also be necessary to inaugurate steps to smooth out discrepancies in social standards by the encouragement of progressive policies in the less advanced countries. This will require internationally concerted measures to assist the development of the more backward countries. It will also be necessary to utilise the International Labour Office to bring about progressive improvement in labour conditions in the industries of the less advanced countries.

12. Role of Smaller States in World Economic Organisations

It is at this point that a reconciliation is possible between the military and political realities underlying the conception of the role of the World Powers as defined above and the economic interest of smaller States. If the World Powers accept the responsibilities of leadership as the only practicable means of maintaining the peace, they should be careful to see that schemes which deal with economic issues, so long as they do not endanger security, are handled by wider assemblies, whether on a world basis or on regional lines. In other words, the construction of any world authority should be guided by considerations of function. Politically the World Powers, as alone possessing any considerable force, should not hesitate to take the lead. Economically, on the other hand, many Powers other than the World Powers would have much to contribute, and, in so far as they can contribute, they should have a real voice in the direction of affairs.

C. APPLICATION OF THE PLAN TO EUROPE

13. Action in regard to Germany

(i) It is likely that any United Nations plan will have to be applied in the first instance to Europe. Moreover, the European situation is potentially more dangerous than the Far Eastern as a cause of future wars. The major danger in Europe is the strong central position of Germany, with her large population, natural resources, and highly developed industries, which are the bases of her military power. The maintenance of peace in Europe will consequently depend on the economic as well as the military disarmament of Germany, and on an increase in the relative economic status and power of Germany's neighbours.

(ii) In order to secure this result, the joint occupation of Germany by the three major Allies should be accompanied in the early stages by a very close control over the German economic machine. If this control were successful it would represent an important large-scale experiment in European international administration.

(iii) To prevent the re-emergence of anything like an aggressive German "Unitary State" it would probably in addition be desirable:

(*a*) to encourage "particularist" or federal tendencies in any local governments which may set themselves up in Germany when the collapse takes place, subject always to not allowing such Governments to escape the consequences of the war, and

(*b*) so to organise the occupation of Germany as to foster any particularist, and even eventually separatist tendencies that may reveal themselves.

(iv) If these political and economic precautions were taken, and Germany was occupied for a considerable number of years, it might not be desirable at once and radically to alter the 1937 (i.e. pre-*Anschluss*) boundaries of the Reich, with the exception of the transfer of East Prussia, Danzig, and certain districts of eastern Germany to Poland. If such transfers took place however, they should in principle be accompanied by transfers of population. Finally, the Kiel Canal should be internationalised and an international régime applied to the principal German waterways.

14. The United Nations Commission for Europe

(i) But the best safeguard of all against renewed German attempts to dominate the Continent would lie in the creation of a United Nations Commission for Europe (see paragraph 8(ii)), consisting of representatives of the United Kingdom, the Soviet Union and the United States, with whom a French representative should, if practicable, be associated on an equal footing. Also associated with them, as might be required, would be representatives of the smaller European Allies, and also of Canada and South Africa, if these Dominions so desired and were prepared to make a military contribution to the European policing system. The Commission might be established at some central point in Europe (e.g. Copenhagen or Vienna), and would have wide powers. It might well, for instance, in addition to the functions described in paragraph 8 (ii) above, co-ordinate certain essential services—such as transport—outside as well as inside the Axis territories. Apart from that it would be the organ for exercising all the powers of the United Nations necessary to cope with civil disturbances and any minor hostilities that may flare up after major hostilities have been abandoned.

(ii) It is to be hoped that the European *neutrals* (if any, in fact, remain at the end of the war) would agree to work in with this Commission. If they did not do [*sic*] so agree, however, the United Nations should not shrink from exercising pressure on them.

(iii) Further, the Allied Forces which would be under the higher control of the Commission would, in fact, if not in name, constitute an *International Police Power*, which might at a later stage have a more formal international constitution.

15. European Confederations

(i) In some cases, particularly in eastern Europe, we may hope to see the amalgamation of the smaller Powers into Confederations. The bases for two such Confederations already exist and others might be formed elsewhere. But it is evident that any durable grouping in eastern Europe can only come about as a result of complete co-operation between the Soviet Government and other leading members of the United Nations.

(ii) It is also assumed that it will not be the intention of the World Powers to attempt to force European nations into unions against their will. Subject to this, it might be possible for the United Nations Commission for Europe, for instance, to encourage "regional" tendencies by centralising certain services in certain specified areas.

16. The Future of Europe

The measures taken by the United Nations to pacify the peoples of Europe and to restore their means of livelihood and of production will, if they are well conceived and executed, go far towards creating the conditions under which European co-operation may eventually become a reality. To provide a political framework for the various military and economic measures contemplated, it is to be hoped that the United Nations Commission for Europe (see paragraph 14) may at some stage become a "Council of Europe", on which all European States should be represented, including the United Kingdom and the Soviet Union, with the addition, it is to be hoped, of the United States. Neutrals (and Austria) should be admitted to the Council as soon as practicable, and at a fairly early stage Italy and the lesser enemy States; but the admission of Germany must be delayed until at any rate after the occupation has ended and could only then take place as a result of some unanimous decision of the World Council. A Council of Europe in which the United Kingdom, the United States of America, and the U.S.S.R. did not play an active part might become in course of time an instrument through which Germany could recover peacefully that hegemony over Europe which she has momentarily established by force of arms during the present war.

D. APPLICATION TO THE FAR EAST

17. Security Measures in respect of Japan

(i) Disarmament

The Far Eastern situation will differ from the European in several important respects. It will be necessary to disarm Japan and for that purpose an Armistice Commission on the lines of that proposed for Germany should be set up. In order to achieve its purpose it must insist on the abolition of fortified zones in Japan and other internal arrangements designed to preserve secrecy as to her intentions. But once these measures have been carried out a prolonged military occupation of Japan may be neither necessary nor desirable, for, in contra-distinction to Germany, it should be possible to control Japan's armaments by economic means provided adequate naval and air forces are available in the background.

(ii) Control of Japan's armaments by indirect means

It is assumed that Japan will be deprived of her Empire, including Korea and Formosa. This would mean in effect the confinement of the Japanese people to the islands of Japan proper. In such circumstances they will scarcely be able to feed themselves, let alone carry on their industries, without a considerable international trade. Moreover, Japan has only one primary product with an export surplus, silk, and after the war this will lose much of its economic importance owing to the development of nylon. Unless, therefore, it is proposed to allow a large number of Japanese to starve, it will be necessary to permit the Japanese to develop their imports and exports. But this can be done in such a manner as to allow them to exist but at the same time prevent them from becoming a danger to other countries. The Japanese, it is true, are a united and highly disciplined people who are likely to seek to evade the controls imposed on them. But in order to build up aggressive armaments Japan would have to import the necessary raw materials. If these materials are rationed by an international authority commanding wide control she will be helpless. Such machinery must, therefore, be set up in the first place under the Armistice Commission, but perhaps later developing into a more permanent economic body.

(iii) Permanent Defence System for the Far East

It will also be necessary to construct a permanent defence system, as a further precaution against Japanese aggression and to make possible the economic control of Japan suggested in sub-paragraph (ii) above. For this purpose all suitable bases in the western Pacific and in eastern Asia might be put at the disposal of a United Nations Pacific Council of Defence, composed of the United States of America, United Kingdom, U.S.S.R., China, Canada, (possibly France), Australia, New Zealand, (possibly Portugal) and the Netherlands, which would command the necessary air and naval forces.

18. Economic and Political Measures

There will have to be a Relief and Rehabilitation Commission to assist China and other countries, including Japan. Both this body and the Armistice Commission might be co-ordinated by a United Nations Far Eastern Commission, and this might some day develop into a "Council of the Far East", which could deal in the first instance with the economic and political problems of that area. Representation of the smaller Far Eastern countries on the World Council (China being in any case a member *ex officio*) might also be arranged by means of this body.

19. India

The immediate future of India is too uncertain for her place in the world system to be very exactly defined. It is to be hoped that she will find it as a Dominion. She might immediately be associated in some way with the Permanent Defence System of the Far East (see paragraph 17 (iii)) and/or the South-Eastern Asiatic regional system (see paragraph 24). Communal difficulties might possibly stand in the way of her association with the Middle East regional system (paragraph 23) in spite of her interest in the defence of that area.

E. EVENTUAL WORLD ORGANISATION

20. Principles governing "Regionalism"

Generally speaking, tendencies towards regional groupings should be encouraged, subject always to the principle that no one World Power by itself should be given the task of maintaining order in any particular region. For the contrary principle, if admitted, would give rise to rivalries as between one group and another and hence sow the seeds of future war. In discussing "regionalism", therefore, we must assume that all the World Powers are in principle equally interested in maintaining the peace, and that they will speak with one voice and act together whenever and wherever it may be threatened.

21. Regional Institutions

To enable the Great Powers to exercise effective control and to associate the smaller Powers to the greatest possible extent in a world system it may be found convenient to set up regional institutions. Such institutions would have several different objects. They might be used for security, for political and economic collaboration, or for the development and control of dependencies. It has already been mentioned (paragraphs 16 and 18) that a "Council of Europe" and a "Council of the Far East" may eventually result from the immediate measures which must be taken in these two areas. But such developments will take time, and meanwhile regions of smaller extent may be used to obtain the objects mentioned above.

22. Regional Defence Systems (Atlantic and Pacific)

Thus there might come into existence two regional systems whose main object was to maintain security against Germany and Japan. (i) There might be an Atlantic System which associated the United

Kingdom, the U.S.S.R., and the United States with the countries of the western sea-board of Europe (including Denmark) and Canada for purposes of common defence, including the provision of air and sea bases in, e.g., Bergen or the Atlantic Islands. It might well be necessary to sub-divide this system into a Northern and Southern Atlantic system. The latter, if formed, would of course include certain South American States, and notably Brazil and the Argentine. (ii) A similar system could, as contemplated in paragraph 17(iii) be set up in the Pacific. Here again it might be found desirable to associate with this system some South American State with a Pacific seaboard, such as Mexico, Chile, or Peru.

23. Mixed System (Eastern Europe and Middle East)

A Confederation or Confederations in Eastern Europe might form the nucleus, with the assistance of the World Powers (other than China) of a regional system not only for military, but also for political and economic defence against Germany. The Middle East is in a special position, since it contains neither enemy States nor (except to a very limited extent) colonial areas; but here also there might be a system which should enable the World Powers concerned to some extent to share the responsibility for its defence and provide the leadership necessary to overcome obstacles in the way of political and economic collaboration. Such arrangements, however, should not conflict with the treaty position of Great Britain, under which the independent sovereignty of many of the nations comprised in the area at present rests.

24. Colonial Systems

Three regional systems might be set up for colonial dependencies consisting in the first instance of the "Parent States" concerned, together with other States having a major economic or strategic interest in the area. Thus, dependencies in South-East Asia might be associated together not only for economic collaboration but also in order to establish the responsibility of the Powers administering them and to encourage the gradual development of self-government. The tropical dependencies in Africa might also be combined in one or more regional groups for similar purposes, while the Caribbean Colonies (and the Guineas [*sic*? Guianas]) might fall into another group.

25. Regional Representation in the World Council

In addition to the functions mentioned above, regions might be used as the means of selecting representatives to sit on the World Council with those of the World Powers. The Pan-American System would naturally be one region and might elect two representatives. Europe might also choose two representatives, possibly one from

Western and one from Eastern Europe if the systems suggested in paragraphs 22 and 23 came into existence. The Far Eastern region, the Middle East and the British Commonwealth of Nations (other than the United Kingdom) might each select one representative.

26. Functions of the Council and Assembly

Such a Council of 11 or 12 members, meeting at regular intervals, would not be too large for effective business under the leadership of the World Powers, while it would link all parts of the world together and serve as a final Court of Appeal for all political or economic issues capable of threatening the peace. But an Assembly of all the United Nations might in addition be summoned at fairly long intervals (say every two years) to receive and discuss reports from the Council and the economic bodies described in paragraph 10.

27. Alternative Methods of Representation

On the other hand (as already stated in paragraph 5(i), it must be recognised that it may be difficult or impossible to establish such a system of regional representation. If this should prove to be the case it might be possible to fall back on election of seven representatives by an annual Assembly. Failing this, the only alternative would be the Four (Five)-Power Council referred to in paragraph 5(i).

28. Where should all this International Machinery be?

How far the Council (and consequently the Assembly) should have a regular meeting place is primarily a matter for consideration by the World Powers. But the Council, like the League Council in its earlier stages, could, if desired, meet at different places according to convenience. The international economic and social bodies would, however, certainly need a permanent centre, which it is suggested might be in the Western Hemisphere, as well as a permanent secretariat in which the existing staffs of the League and the I.L.O. should be incorporated. It might well be that the Council would often in practice find it convenient to meet at that centre.

29. Secretariat

It might be better not to form any elaborate international political secretariat until it is seen how the Council and Assembly are going to work and where the headquarters of the new organisation is likely to be. But it would obviously be necessary to have some "Secretary-General" or "Moderator" with a small staff to produce the agenda, conduct correspondence with the economic and regional organisations and generally make arrangements for the meetings of the Council and Assembly.'

(a) On July 29, 1943, the Prime Minister suggested that his own and other memoranda[1] on the structure of a post-war settlement should be considered in the first instance by a small Cabinet Committee. This committee held only four meetings. A fifth meeting was arranged for September 1, 1943, but did not take place. The Committee did not report to the War Cabinet, and no further reference was made to it in the War Cabinet minutes. The Committee seems to have been allowed to lapse in view of the proposals at the Quebec Conference for a three-Power meeting to discuss main issues of policy in connexion with the post-war settlement.

(b) A second committee, however, suggested by the Foreign Office and approved by the Prime Minister, was of more importance. The Prime Minister circulated a memorandum to the War Cabinet on August 4, 1943, to the effect that the growing volume and complexity of the political and civil problems connected with liberated or occupied enemy territories made it necessary to establish a ministerial committee to settle questions of lesser importance and to make recommendations to the War Cabinet on major issues. The Prime Minister had therefore set up a Ministerial Committee on Armistice Terms and Civil Administration, under the chairmanship of Mr. Attlee.[2]

---

[1] The Prime Minister's memorandum was the record of his conversation in Washington on post-war organisations. See above pp. 39–41.

[2] The Committee was, in fact, a continuation of an *ad hoc* committee which had been formed to consider armistice terms for Italy. On April 19, 1944, the Prime Minister agreed that the Committee of the War Cabinet on Armistice Terms and Civil Adminis-
(c) tration should be given wider terms of reference. The Committee was instructed 'to consider and, where necessary, advise the War Cabinet on questions affecting armistice terms and their execution, and the administration of territories, liberated or conquered, and general political and military questions in the post-war period'. The Committee was to be known henceforward as the Armistice and Post-War Committee. The Deputy Prime Minister continued to be Chairman. For the discussion of political and military post-war problems the Foreign Secretary (or Minister of State), the Ministers of Labour and Production, and the Secretaries of State for Dominion Affairs and for Air were always to be invited to attend. The First Lord of the Admiralty, and the Secretaries of State for War, India, and the Colonies would receive all papers and notices of meetings, and would be invited to attend, or be represented at meetings when matters affecting them were under discussion. The Committee was expected to work in a series of panels. Thus, when it was dealing with questions of procedure affecting the meeting of the Dominions Prime Ministers, the Secretary of State for Dominion Affairs would preside. When questions of military administration of liberated or conquered territories were under discussion the panel of Ministers would always include the Secretary for War. Mr. Jebb represented the Foreign Office on the Secretariat for matters connected with major post-war political questions.

(d) A Post-Hostilities Planning Sub-Committee of the Chiefs of Staff was established on August 9, 1943, under the chairmanship of Mr. Jebb. Its purpose was to consider, primarily, post-hostilities strategic questions, to prepare instruments for the formal suspension of hostilities with enemy Powers and to submit plans for the enforcement of such instruments. It would maintain close touch with the three Service Departments and the Foreign Office. The Committee was instructed to report normally to the Chiefs of Staff Committee or to the Committee on Armistice Terms and Civil Administration. The Sub-Committee continued to function after the latter Committee had changed its title to Armistice and Post-War Committee.

(a) WM(43)107.
(b) WP(43)350; U3368/324/70; U3369/3497/25/70; U3657/3657/74.
(c) APW(44)1. (d) PHP(43)1.

(vi)

British statements on changes effected in Austria and Czechoslovakia during, or since, 1938: Foreign Office memorandum on the future of Austria, May 25, 1943, and subsequent communication of the proposals to the United States and Soviet Governments.

The future of Austria was as complicated and intractable a problem, from the point of view of the resettlement of Europe, as the larger problem of the future of Germany. The two problems were linked together historically and politically. It could indeed be said that the misfortunes which Germany had brought upon herself and Europe had been due largely to the failure in the nineteenth century of German and Austrian statesmanship to find a satisfactory solution of the special difficulties of the multinational Habsburg Empire. The Habsburgs themselves, and the ruling classes of the Empire, had been clumsy, unimaginative, and feckless in their own attempts—such as they were—to stave off internal collapse. The Empire had broken up in the last stages of military defeat during the first World War. The treaty settlement had merely registered this collapse. The successor States from 1918–19 onwards had repeated, in a different form, many of the blunders of the imperial bureaucracy which they had displaced. Hitler's 'solution', the annexation, first of Austria, and then of Czechoslovakia, had been the worst and most impolitic of all the solutions of the problem.

The British Government, on August 2, 1938, had recognised, for all practical purposes, the German annexation of Austria by withdrawing the Legation from Vienna and replacing it by a Consulate-General. They were obviously not bound by this decision; Mr. Eden had stated in the House of Commons on September 9, 1942, that the British Government did not regard themselves as committed to the recognition of any change effected in Austria during or since the year 1938.

At this time, also, the British Government informed the Czechoslovak Government officially of its attitude to the consequences of the Munich Agreement. Already on the second anniversary of the agreement, September 30, 1940, Mr. Churchill had told the Czechoslovak people in a special broadcast message that: 'Our hopes had been frustrated—the solemn promises of the Germans had been broken within six months, and the Agreement had been destroyed with a ruthlessness which unmasked the true nature of the Germans' reckless ambition . . . We have refused to recognise any of the brutal conquests of Germany in central Europe and elsewhere and we (a)

(a) *The Times*, October 1, 1940.

have welcomed a Czechoslovakian Provisional Government in this country, and I have made the restoration of Czechoslovakian liberties one of our principal war aims. That aim will be achieved.'

In the following year, on July 18, 1941, the British Government gave full recognition to the Czechoslovak Government, and to Dr. Benes as President of the Czechoslovak Republic. This step was taken after the Soviet Government had given full recognition. The letter conveying recognition, however, contained reservations concerning the future frontiers of the State, the juridical continuity of the Government and the authority of the Government over the Sudeten Germans in British territory.

Dr. Benes felt that these reservations implied a difference in status between the Czechoslovaks and other Allies of Great Britain. He asked for some further declaration and, in particular, for an expansion of the Prime Minister's broadcast statement that the Germans had destroyed the Munich Agreement. He also wanted the withdrawal of the three reservations.

The Czechoslovak position was in fact different from that of the other Allied Governments in that in the case of the latter it had not been necessary to make a formal act of recognition, and therefore to refer in a formal way to their frontiers. The Sudeten problem was also in a special category, since the cession of the Sudeten territories resulted from an international agreement to which the British Government was a party, and Sudeten German refugees had been received in Great Britain.

No step was taken to meet Dr. Benes's wishes until the summer of (a) 1942 when, on July 2, Mr. Eden submitted a memorandum to the War Cabinet suggesting a declaration to the Czechoslovak Government repeating the view of the British Government that, owing to German action, they were free from the engagements contracted in the Munich Agreement and that at the settlement of the Czechoslovak frontiers after the war they would not be influenced by any changes in these frontiers effected in or since 1938.

Mr. Eden considered that in view of the hard trials suffered by the Czechoslovak people since the death of Heydrich[1] it was desirable to do everything possible to meet their wishes. He did not propose to express an opinion on the question of legal continuity—or to commit the British Government to any details about future frontiers. There was, however, one important question affecting not only the position of the Sudeten Germans in Great Britain, but the whole subject of a post-war settlement in Europe. Dr. Benes was known at that time to

---

[1] German reprisals for a bomb attack in May 1942 on the German Acting Protector Reinhard Heydrich, who died of his injuries, included the destruction of the village of Lidice and the massacre of its population.

(a) WP(42)280; C6671/326/12.

be in favour of allowing Germany to retain the Eger triangle and two other districts containing in all some 6–700,000 Sudeten Germans. He wanted to expel about 3–400,000 Sudetens as war criminals and transfer another million to Germany. In this way the Sudeten minority of $3\frac{3}{4}$ million—which Dr. Benes regarded as too large for successful absorption—would be reduced to something over a million.

A transfer—not an exchange—of population on such a scale was a difficult undertaking. There were no precedents other than those set by Hitler. On the other hand, unless some measure of this kind were carried out in an orderly and peaceful way, the Czechoslovaks and Poles were likely to expel their German minorities by force. Mr. Eden thought that we should therefore accept the general principle of transfer without discussing its application.

The War Cabinet approved these proposals on July 6 subject to (a)
the Dominions being consulted. After further discussion with the Czechoslovak Government, Mr. Eden informed the Czechoslovak (b)
Minister for Foreign Affairs, on August 5, 1942, that 'as Germany has deliberately destroyed the arrangements concerning Czechoslovakia reached in 1938, in which His Majesty's Government in the United Kingdom participated, His Majesty's Government regard themselves as free from any engagements in this respect. At the final settlement of Czechoslovak frontiers to be reached at the end of the war they will not be influenced by any changes made in and since 1938.' No mention was made in the British note of the continuity of the Czechoslovak State or of the position of the Sudeten Germans, though Mr. Eden informed Dr. Benes verbally that the British Government were, in principle, in favour of transfers of population. The Czechoslovak Government accepted this note as 'a practical solution of the questions and difficulties of vital importance for Czechoslovakia which emerged between our two countries as the consequence of the Munich agreement', and maintained their own political and juridical position regarding agreement. The Czechoslovak reply concluded: 'Between our two countries the Munich Agreement can now be considered as dead.' These notes were published in Cmd. 6379 (1942).

Later in the year, on December 16, Mr. Eden referred in the House of Commons to a speech which he had made at Leamington on September 26, 1942. In this speech he had mentioned the Polish-Czechoslovak and Greco-Yugoslav agreements and had said that we should encourage the smaller European States to form larger, though not exclusive groupings. Mr. Eden now said:

> 'Whether it will be possible or desirable to include Austria or Hungary within a federation based upon Poland and Czechoslovakia must

(a) WM(42)86; C6788/326/12. (b) C6834, 6867, 7210, 7307, 7361, 7517, 7666/326/12.

clearly depend, amongst other things, upon the views of the Polish and Czechoslovak Governments and peoples, and upon the future attitude of the Austrians and Hungarians who are now fighting in the ranks of our enemies.'

During the first half of 1943 the Foreign Office gave much consideration to the problem, without coming to a definite decision. On May 25, 1943, Mr. Eden submitted a memorandum to the War (a) Cabinet on the future of Austria. The memorandum considered four possible solutions. (i) The association of Austria with Germany as an integral part of the Reich or on a federal basis. The political and strategic arguments against this solution were very strong. Austria under German control was a permanent threat to Italy and the Successor States, and also added several million German-speaking people to the war potential of the Reich. Although a democratic Germany might have some attraction for Austrians, and especially for Austrian Socialists, the condition of Germany after the war was unlikely to make an *Anschluss* attractive. The Austrians would hope to escape their share of responsibility and retribution by repudiating the Nazis, and in our own interest we should encourage a policy of separation by differentiating between the treatment of Germany and that of Austria.

(ii) The inclusion of Austria, in a South German Confederation, with Bavaria and possibly Württemberg and Baden. There was, however, little reason to suppose that this solution would be desired either by Bavarians or by Austrians, since their mutual relations had never been particularly friendly. Furthermore a German state extending from Stuttgart or Freiburg or even from Munich to Vienna, could not be a member of a south-east European Confederation without making such a confederation preponderantly German. We should therefore be cutting Austria off from a claim to be treated as a Danubian State and we should be driving her into a closer association with Germany.

(iii) The restoration of Austria as an independent State. Here one difficulty was that there was no Austrian Government in exile representing Austrian opinion, and ready to return to the country and take control. There was also no chance of building up an Austrian Council or Committee from the Austrians in Great Britain or the United States. The amount of support in Austria for a restoration of the Habsburgs was difficult to estimate, but was certainly not great. In any case Austria under a Habsburg could not be in close relations with Poland, Czechoslovakia or Yugoslavia or be included in any confederation.

On the other hand the link between Austria and the Reich was of

(a) WP(43)218.

Nazi creation and could easily be broken, and the United Nations would be free to decide, when they occupied Germany, whether they would administer Austria as a part of Germany. The chances of re-establishing an independent Austrian Government would depend largely on economic conditions. Austria had failed to settle her economic problems between the wars partly owing to the lack of initiative of her successive Governments in carrying out an active policy of employment for the labour and capital of the country, and partly owing to the various forms of trade barriers affecting her relations with her neighbours. Unless the Great Powers could give in the future to an independent Austrian State a degree of political and economic security not substantially lower than the inhabitants might expect from association with Germany, the chances of the maintenance of an Austrian 'will' for political independence were slight.

(iv) The inclusion of Austria in a Central or East European Confederation. Membership of a confederation might give Austria more economic and political security, especially if it led to the re-establishment of her trading, financial and other connexions with the former Habsburg territories. Austria might render other important services to such a confederation. The Austrians were less nationalistic than most of the peoples of Europe, and might exercise a moderating influence on their Danubian neighbours. Furthermore, although an independent Austria would never be strong enough to defend herself alone, the strategic protection which her territories provided for her neighbours could be used to the full only if she were included in a confederation with them. On the other hand, some of these neighbours might well feel nervous of the possible development, within the confederation, of something like the old Austro-Magyar alliance. They had also built up their own banking systems and industries, and might be afraid of Austrian economic predominance. Above all, they might fear that Austria would serve as a stepping-stone for German penetration and as a camouflage for activities pursued in German interests. Thus they might well feel, with their experience of German minorities, that a confederation would be safer without a number of Germans in it. Hence, although, from our point of view, the federal solution was probably the best, we could not regard it as an easy or an immediate solution. We could not even be sure that any central or south-east European confederation would be formed, at all events immediately after the war, and the first step must be the restoration of a free and independent Austrian State. Whatever international guarantee such a State might receive, it would be weak, and a potential danger point. All that we could do for the present would be to bring Austria into any plans for relief and reconstruction in central and south-east Europe in such a way that her subsequent inclusion in a confederation would be the fulfilment and not the reversal of a policy already in process of execution.

In a covering note to this memorandum Mr. Eden pointed out that, as the military situation turned in our favour, we should have more chance of embarrassing the Germans by the encouragement of resistance and sabotage in Austria. At present, however, we were hampered because we had no declared policy for Austria. Mr. Eden asked that, as a first step, the War Cabinet should give general approval to the conclusions in the memorandum. He would then communicate it to the Dominions, and enter into discussion with the United States and Soviet Governments with a view to getting their agreement to the policy which we were proposing and later, perhaps, to the issue of a declaration promising a free and independent Austria.

(a) The War Cabinet considered the memorandum on June 16, 1943. They thought that, especially from the economic point of view, we should aim at a Central European or Danubian group[1] centred on Vienna. Such a group should combine the economic stability of a larger unit with the maximum degree of freedom in local affairs for the successor states of the Austro-Hungarian Empire. The presentation of this idea would need great care, but we might get the larger group set up before opinion had time to harden in another sense. It was pointed out in the discussion that the Austrian experience from 1918 to 1938 did not give the concept of independence much of an appeal, and that we should put our emphasis rather on freeing Austria from Prussian domination. Subject to these considerations, the War Cabinet approved of the policy laid down in the memorandum. The memorandum was then sent to the Dominions.

(b) The Foreign Office considered that, although the War Cabinet might be in favour of a Danubian Confederation, the Russians would certainly oppose it. Nevertheless Lord Halifax and H.M. Ambassador at Moscow, Sir A. Clark Kerr, were instructed on August 14 to communicate the memorandum respectively to the United States and Soviet Governments, and to give them also the draft of a declaration regarding the re-establishment of a free and independent Austria which we thought it desirable to issue without long delay. The United States Government replied on October 11 agreeing generally with the proposals and putting forward a re-draft of the declaration. The Foreign Office were willing to accept this re-draft. Sir A. Clark Kerr thought it a mistake to give the memorandum, as it stood, to the Russians in view of their known opposition to federa-

---

[1] This term appears to be used to mean 'confederation'.

(a) WM(43)86. (b) C6162/321/18; C7012, 9546, 9915, 11201, 11609, 11820/321/18.

tions. He communicated it, however, on September 29, though at this date we had already told the Soviet Government of our wish to include the question of Austria on the agenda of the Moscow Conference.

CHAPTER LXII

Discussions on post-war questions at the Quebec, Moscow and Teheran Conferences, 1943: Exchanges of view between the British, United States and Soviet Governments with regard to a World Security Organisation, January–August 1944: British memoranda on a World Security Organisation: the Prime Minister's views

(i)

President Roosevelt's proposals at the Quebec Conference: statement of British policy before the Moscow Conference: the Four-Power declaration and the establishment of the European Advisory Commission: discussion on the future of Germany at the Teheran Conference (August 21–December 1, 1943).

THE Prime Minister, in suggesting the establishment of a committee of Ministers to survey the whole field of post-war arrangements, and a second committee to consider problems connected with liberated or occupied territories, was not merely finding a way to deal with a growing accumulation of proposals. He realised the importance of coming to a decision on the many important issues of policy raised in the memoranda submitted to the War Cabinet by the Foreign Office on the post-war organisation of security and the future re-settlement of Europe. The Prime Minister was, however, primarily concerned with the question of an Italian surrender. The fall of Mussolini on July 25—fifteen days after the invasion of Sicily—made it likely that this surrender would come very soon. The Prime Minister also knew that at his forthcoming meeting with President Roosevelt at Quebec, he would be asked to subscribe to another of the Declarations in which the President was inclined to set out his policy.

The Prime Minister left London for Quebec on August 4. Here, on
(a) August 21, Mr. Hull gave Mr. Eden (who had then joined the Prime Minister in Quebec) a draft four-Power declaration to be made by

(a) U3876/402/70.

the Governments of the United States, the United Kingdom, the U.S.S.R. and China. This text was as follows:

'The Governments of the United States, Great Britain and the Soviet Union and China, united in their determination, in accordance with the declaration by the United Nations of January 1, 1942, and subsequent declarations, to continue hostilities against those Axis powers with which they respectively are at war until such powers have laid down their arms on the basis of unconditional surrender; conscious of their responsibility to secure the liberation of themselves and the people allied with them from the menace of aggression; recognising the necessity of ensuring a rapid and orderly transition from war to peace and of establishing and maintaining international peace and security with the least diversion of the world's human and economic resources for armaments, jointly declare:

1. That their united action, pledged for the prosecution of the war, will be continued for the organisation and maintenance of peace and security.
2. That those of them at war with a common enemy will act together in all matters relating to the surrender and disarmament of that enemy, and to any occupation of enemy territory and of territory of other States held by that enemy.
3. That they will take all measures deemed by them to be necessary to provide against any violation of the requirements imposed upon their present enemies.
4. That they recognise the necessity of establishing at the earliest practicable date a general international organisation, based on the principle of the sovereign equality of all nations, and open to membership by all nations, large and small, for the maintenance of international peace and security.
5. That for the purpose of maintaining international peace and security pending the re-establishment of law and order and the inauguration of a general system of security, they will consult and act jointly on behalf of the community of nations.
6. That, in connexion with the foregoing purpose, they will establish a technical commission to advise them on the military problems involved, including the composition and strength of the forces available in an emergency arising from a threat to the peace.
7. That they will not employ their military forces within the territories of other States except for the purposes envisaged in this declaration and after joint consultation and agreement.
8. That they will confer and co-operate to bring about a practicable general agreement with respect to the regulation of armaments in the post-war period.'

The Foreign Office already knew the general tenor of the draft (a) since the text had been read to Mr. Jebb by an official at the State

(a) U3624, 3625, 3626/1816/70.

Department. Mr. Jebb. had also been told that a proposal had been made to link the Declaration with a protocol for signature by all the United Nations, and pledging them to set up a world organisation after the war. The President, however, thought that this protocol was too detailed and complicated, and that it would require the approval of the Senate, whereas the Declaration could be made on the basis of the President's war-time authority.

(a) The Foreign Office regarded the Declaration as less valuable than a document which the Senate could have ratified at once; nonetheless it was obviously of great importance to obtain American support in principle for the establishment of a post-war organisation, and the terms of the Declaration were generally acceptable. On the other hand there seemed little chance that the Declaration would satisfy the Soviet Government unless the proposed tripartite conference[1] dealt with matters directly concerning Russian interests. The Foreign Office therefore suggested that the four-Power Declaration should follow, and not precede the conference with the Russians.

(b) The Prime Minister told the President on August 23, 1943, that he would have to submit the Declaration to the Cabinet on his return, and that no decision could be taken about it at Quebec. He said that there would be no serious Anglo-American difference of view about the text. The President accepted the Prime Minister's proposals about procedure, and agreed that in any case the text should not be put to the Soviet Government as already agreed between the British and United States Governments but as a matter for tripartite discussion.

(c) Mr. Eden circulated the American draft text of the four-Power declaration to the War Cabinet on September 4. In a discussion of the draft on September 6 the War Cabinet were doubtful about the reference to the 'sovereign equality of all nations'; the phrase might be taken to mean that every nation should be given an equal weight in the World Organisation. The War Cabinet, after submitting the draft to the Dominion Governments, finally approved it with the following alterations: (i) Article 2. The second half to read 'to any occupation of enemy territory and the liberation of the territory of other States held by that enemy'. (ii) Article 3. The concluding words to read: 'Any violation of the terms imposed upon the enemy'. (iii) Article 4. After the words following 'sovereign equality of all nations' to add 'for the maintenance of international peace and security in which all peace-loving nations, great and small, may play their part'. (iv) Article 5. The final clause to read: 'They will consult

[1] See Volume II, Chapter XXXIV, Section (iv).

(a) U3875/402/70. (b) U3876/402/70.
(c) WP(43)389, 412; WM(43) 124, 131; U4153, 4425, 4658/402/70; N6921/3666/38.

with one another, and as occasion requires with other Members of the United Nations, with a view to joint action on behalf of the community of nations.' (v) Article 8, after the words 'confer and co-operate', to add 'with one another and with other Members of the United Nations to bring about, etc'. This revised text was sent to Washington on September 27, and to Moscow and Chungking on October 2 for communication to the three Governments.[1]

On September 14, 1943, the Prime Minister[2] telegraphed that the President thought that we should raise with Stalin, in the first instance at the tripartite conference, the question of post-war world organisation, and that our proposals should assume an interim or emergency period of unspecified duration in which a permanent organisation could be shaped and built. During this period there would be three forms of United Nations collaboration: (i) the Four Powers, who would guarantee the maintenance of peace and order, and the enforcement of armistice conditions; (ii) an executive council, reaching, step by step, a number of 11 members; (iii) a general assembly of all the United Nations, including 'respectable' neutrals. The assembly would pass resolutions, but would not have executive powers. (a)

The Foreign Office agreed that the subject might suitably be discussed at Moscow. They suggested that the United States Government should put it on their proposed agenda. The Foreign Office did not expect that any conclusions would be reached; they regarded an exchange of views as useful and as likely to clear the way for decisions at a later date. On September 28 the State Department said that they doubted whether they would put the subject on their agenda, but that Mr. Hull might raise it orally.[3]

The Prime Minister drew up, and circulated to the War Cabinet, a (b)

---

[1] The British text at the Moscow Conference was therefore a separate document from the American text which was itself slightly different from the original draft.

[2] The Prime Minister was on this day at Halifax on his way home from Washington.

[3] The President had also given Mr. Churchill at Quebec a draft declaration on National Independence. This document (*F.R.U.S. 1943, Washington & Quebec Conferences*, 717–720) was the American redraft of the declaration regarding colonial territory which the British Government had sent to the United States Government in February 1943 (see above, p. 24, note 1). The Prime Minister expressed no opinion on the draft to the President. Mr. Hull also mentioned the declaration to Mr. Eden. who said he did not very much like the American draft (*F.R.U.S.* ibid., p. 726). Mr. Hull had not seen the *aide-mémoire* which Mr. Eden had given to Mr. Winant in May stating the British objections to the American redraft. This *aide-mémoire* was now brought to Mr. Hull's notice. Mr. Eden did not think it necessary to submit any further comment on the American text. Mr. Hull tried to raise the subject again at the Moscow Conference. He circulated his draft text (though it was not printed as one of the Conference memoranda). Mr. Eden said that he was not prepared to discuss the text. He told Mr. Hull that, from what he had said earlier to Mr. Winant, it would be clear that the British Government could not accept the document in its present form. M. Molotov said that he would study it. See also below, p. 91, note 1. (c)

(a) Welfare 736, U4349/1816/70; N5412/3666/38.
(b) WP(43)447 Revise; WM(43)137.4, C.A.; C12155/696/62. (c) U4486/402/70.

note on British policy for the use of Mr. Eden at the Conference of Foreign Ministers in Moscow. This note was drafted with reference to the four-Power declaration discussed at Quebec. The note was itself in the form of a declaration; it was also framed to take special account of Russian demands and susceptibilities. The Prime Minister began by the assurance given so often to the Russians that Great Britain sought no territory or special advantage for herself as the outcome of the war 'which she entered in pursuance of her obligations and in defence of public law. We hold strongly to a system of a League of Nations, which will include a Council of Europe, with an International Court and an armed power capable of enforcing its decisions. During the Armistice period, which may be prolonged, we hold that the three Great Powers . . . with the addition of China, should remain united, well-armed, and capable of enforcing the Armistice terms and of building up the permanent structure of peace . . . . We consider that states and nations that have been subjugated by Nazi or Fascist violence during the war should emerge at the Peace Conference with their full sovereign rights, and that all questions of final territorial transference must be settled at the peace table, due regard being paid to the interests of the populations affected. We reaffirm the principles of the Atlantic Charter, noting that Russia's accession thereto is based upon the frontiers of June 22, 1941. We also take note of the historic frontiers of Russia before the two wars of aggression waged by Germany in 1914 and 1939.' The draft then mentioned—in similarly guarded terms—'the British hope of a Russo-Polish agreement which would allow a strong and independent Poland and also give to Russia 'the security necessary for her western frontier'.

Mr. Churchill then referred to the extirpation of Nazism and Fascism and the establishment of

> 'democratic Governments based upon the free expression of the people's will, obtained under conditions of reasonable tranquility. . . . This should not exclude measures of military diplomacy or relations with interim Governments which may come into being, so that our main objects may be achieved with the minimum of slaughter, especially to the forces of the Allies.'

After these references, which envisaged—obviously—the situation in Italy, the Prime Minister stated the British view that all German acquisition of territory under the Nazi régime should be repudiated, and that

> 'the future structure of Germany and the position of Prussia as a unit of the German State should be subject to an agreed policy among the three Great Powers.'

Finally the Prime Minister mentioned the need for 'prolonged control' to maintain the disarmament of the aggressor Powers and the British desire not

> 'to keep any branch of the European family of nations in a condition of subjection or restriction except as may be required by the general needs and safety of the world',

and the general British resolve that the authority of the three Great Powers should be used for the general good.[1]

Before the meeting of the Foreign Secretaries, however, it was clear that the main Russian interest in the conference was military; the Russians wanted to be sure that the Western Powers intended to carry out the invasion of northern France in the spring of 1944, and to suggest other measures, such as bringing Turkey and Sweden into the war, which they regarded as likely to bring about a more rapid defeat of Germany. The conference, however, at Mr. Hull's suggestion, accepted the proposal for a Four-Power Declaration,[2] and, at Mr. Eden's suggestion, a plan for setting up a European Advisory Commission to consider the problems which would arise in Germany and elsewhere when the Nazi régime was nearing collapse.[3] The Four-Power Declaration was published on October 30.[4]

On October 26, after the text of the Four-Power Declaration had been agreed, M. Molotov suggested setting up a Commission to work out jointly, and on a preliminary basis, the questions relating to the establishment of the World Organisation envisaged in the Declaration. Mr. Hull said, however, on October 29, that he was not in favour of a formally constituted Commission since it would get publicity, and politicians and interested organisations in the United States would therefore ask for representation on it. Mr. Hull proposed that informal discussions should be held in Moscow, London or Washington, and that the three Governments should exchange

---

[1] The first version produced by the Prime Minister brought considerable criticism from the Foreign Office on the grounds of its vagueness. Thus the Prime Minister had suggested the 'isolation of Prussia from the rest of Germany'. Mr. Eden, in a minute of (a)
October 6 referring to some of the points made by the Foreign Office, asked the Prime Minister if he were thinking of a partition of Germany into a North and a South German State. Prussia stretched across the whole of north Germany; hence this plan would leave a large and powerful Prussian State which might again extend its influence over Germany. Mr. Eden suggested that the Prime Minister might have in mind the restriction of Prussia to 'Old Prussia' and the subdivision of the rest of Germany into two or more areas. Mr. Eden agreed that we should work towards this objective.

[2] After M. Molotov had raised objections to the inclusion of China as a signatory of the declaration, Mr. Hull explained to him in private conversation that 'it was the attitude of the United States Government that China had been in the world picture as one of the Big Four for the prosecution of the war and for her now to be dumped out on her face by Russia, Great Britain and the United States' in connection with the four-Power agreement would have the most serious repercussions in the Pacific area and on American opinion. *F.R.U.S. 1943*, I, 602–3.

[3] For the discussion of these questions at the Conference see Volume II, Chapter XXXIII, section (v).

[4] *British and Foreign State Papers*, Volume 154, 362–3.

(a) PM/43/291, C12155/696/62.

papers on the subject. Mr. Eden and M. Molotov accepted Mr. Hull's proposal.

(a) The question of the future of Germany was raised, though not fully discussed at the Conference, since a detailed examination was expressly left to the European Advisory Commission. Mr. Hull submitted a memorandum dealing mainly with the immediate steps to be taken after the German unconditional surrender, but covering also a number of long-term proposals.[1] The memorandum suggested the appointment of a Reparation Commission consisting at first of American, British and Russian representatives, with provision for the representation of other directly interested Governments, and proposed the complete disarmament of Germany, the dismantling of all German facilities for the manufacture of arms, and the maintenance of a permanent system of inspection under the supervision of the United Nations. Mr. Hull's memorandum stated that we did not as yet know whether the effect of defeat would be to strengthen the trend towards political unity in Germany or whether the reaction against the defeated Nazi régime would produce a movement for the creation of several separate States out of the Reich. The American view was that in the long run the most desirable form of Government for Germany would be a broadly based democracy operating under a bill of rights to safeguard the civil and political liberties of the individual. Among the conditions required for the success of a new democratic experiment would be a tolerable standard of living, the restriction of measures of control to the requirements of general security, and harmony of policy and purpose among the British, Soviet and American Governments. Early steps should be taken to restore political freedom in Germany and, as soon as possible, preparations should be made for the holding of free elections for the establishment of a central German Government to which the Occupying Authorities would gradually transfer responsibility for the internal administration of the country. The potential threat of German aggression might be lessened if the political structure of Germany were decentralised by giving wide administrative control to the federal units and encouraging any movement in favour of the diminution of Prussian domination over the Reich. All questions of frontiers should be left to the general settlement at the end of the war.

Mr. Hull's memorandum was considered at a meeting of the conference on October 25. Mr. Eden said that he agreed generally with the proposals dealing with immediate action; he suggested that they should be sent to the European Advisory Commission for examination. Mr. Hull and M. Molotov accepted this suggestion. They also

---

[1] See also Volume II, pp. 592–3.

(a) N6921/3666/38.

agreed that the Commission should consider the question of reparation. M. Molotov said that he did not want to go into detail, but that the special interest of the Soviet Government in obtaining reparation was evident. The Foreign Sectaries were also in general agreement about the total disarmament of Germany. They decided that it would be inadvisable, for obvious reasons, to publish any statement about weakening Germany from a political, economic or military point of view.

The meeting then discussed the question of the permanent status of Germany. Mr. Eden said that the British Government would like to see Germany after the war divided into a number of separate States. They would particularly like Prussia to be separated from the rest of the country, and thought that separatist movements should be encouraged. They were, however, unable as yet to assess the prospects of imposing separation by force. Mr. Eden asked M. Molotov what were the views of the Soviet Government. M. Molotov was inclined at first not to commit himself, but it became clear that he regarded Mr. Hull's proposals as insufficient, and believed that the British Government were not inclined to go even as far as the United States Government. Mr. Eden repeated that we wanted to encourage separatism in Germany, and that we had an open mind about enforced dismemberment and would be glad to know the Soviet view.

Mr. Hull explained that the United States Government had started with a definite inclination towards dismemberment and that the trend of opinion was still in this direction, though less strongly so. M. Molotov said that the Soviet Government were somewhat backward in their study of the question probably owing to the military preoccupation of their leaders.[1] He was certain, however, that they would give weight to any opinion in favour of dismemberment by force. M. Molotov also commented that not much was said in Mr. Hull's memorandum about frontiers. He asked whether Mr. Hull proposed the return of territory captured by Germany. Mr. Hull replied that the United States Government had not yet considered territorial questions. Mr. Eden said that it could surely be agreed that Germany should revert at least to her pre-*Anschluss* frontiers. M. Molotov strongly assented. Mr. Eden also brought up at the meeting the British draft declaration on Austria[2] incorporating certain American amendments. This declaration, which was published at the end of the Conference, stated that the three Governments regarded the union imposed on Austria by Germany as null and void,

---

[1] Mr. Eden commented on this remark that the Soviet position seemed to be about the same as our own, and that therefore no reply was needed and no remarks called for about the activities of their respective leaders in connexion with military operations.

[2] See above, pp. 68–9.

and that they wished to see the establishment of a free and independent Austria, and thereby to open the way for the Austrian people as well as neighbouring States faced with similar problems to find that political and economic security which was the only basis for lasting peace. They added that the Austrian people, however, must remember that they had a responsibility which they could not evade, and that in the final settlement account would be taken of their own contribution to the liberation of their country.

Mr. Hull put forward a memorandum on reparation at the meeting on October 29. This memorandum stated that Allied policy on reparation should be formulated with a view to speeding economic recovery and achieving the peace aims of the United Nations. Germany should be required to contribute goods and services—not money—to the recovery of the Allied countries, without, however, injuring third countries or affecting German standards of living and productive plant in such a way as to create serious economic and political problems. The countries claiming reparation from Germany should be given shares of the total amount exacted in proportion to their losses of non-military property resulting from military operations or the action of German forces of occupation. The period of Germany's obligation should be limited as far as possible to the time required for the first stage of European reconstruction. If reparation were regarded as a measure of economic reconstruction, it should not be relied upon as a major instrument of control over German military power.

Mr. Eden said that he was in general agreement with Mr. Hull's principles. M. Molotov, on the other hand, was not satisfied with the memorandum. He did not understand why it was limited to Germany. He thought that if German living standards deserved attention, even greater attention should be paid to living standards in countries which had suffered at German hands during the war. The Conference took no further action on the matter.

(a) At a conversation with Stalin on November 28, 1943, before the formal opening of the Teheran Conference, the Prime Minister discussed shortly the question of the future of Germany. Stalin said that Germany had every possibility of recovering from the war within fifteen or twenty years, and might start a new war within a comparatively short time. The Prime Minister replied that the world must be made safe for at least fifty years. He would forbid the Germans to have a General Staff or to engage in civil or military aviation. We should also supervise German factories and enforce far-reaching territorial changes. Prussia should be isolated and reduced, and Bavaria, Austria and Hungary might form a 'broad, peaceful, cow-

(a) WP(44)8; U88/88/70 (1944).

like confederation'. Stalin inclined to regard these proposals as insufficient. The Prime Minister, on the other hand, thought there was no reason why the Germans should not be controlled if the three Great Powers were able to 'keep a close personal friendship and supervise Germany in their mutual interest'.

The German question was discussed at the Conference indirectly, in relation to the proposed western frontier of Poland,[1] and directly at a meeting on December 1. At this discussion the President and Stalin favoured the break-up of Germany. Mr. Roosevelt suggested a division into five parts: (i) Prussia, (ii) Hanover and the north-western area, (iii) Saxony and the Leipzig area, (iv) Hesse-Darmstadt, Hesse-Cassel, and the area south of the Rhine, (v) Bavaria, Baden and Württemberg. These five parts would be self-governing; Kiel and the Canal and Hamburg, and the Ruhr and Saar areas would be under the control of the United Nations as trustees.

The Prime Minister said that this plan was a new one.[2] He thought that, if Germany were divided into a number of small units, these units would have no means of independent existence and would re-unite. Hence it was necessary to give some kind of life to them by attaching them to other combinations. It would be desirable to detach Prussia from the rest of Germany. The Prime Minister regarded the south Germans as less belligerent, and therefore less likely to start another war. We should treat them less harshly than we should treat the Prussians, and give them sufficient inducement to prevent their reunion with Prussia. They might 'work in' with a Danubian Confederation.[3] Stalin and the President regarded the south Germans as equally dangerous. Stalin favoured partition on something like the President's plan, and did not believe in the viability of a Danubian Confederation. He realised that the Germans would try to unite, but we should have to prevent them, if necessary by force, from so doing. The Prime Minister agreed with the idea of some kind of partition, but said that they were making only a preliminary survey of a vast historical problem. President Roosevelt—with Stalin's approval—suggested that a special committee of the three Powers should be set up, under the European Advisory Commission to study the question.[4]

---

[1] See Volume II, Chapter XXXV, section (v).

[2] The Prime Minister used the American term that the President had 'said a mouthful'.

[3] The Prime Minister intended this southern group to include Bavaria, Württemberg, the Palatinate, Saxony, and Baden. He did not mind whether they formed one group or two groups.

[4] There is no record of a discussion of the future World Security Organisation at the plenary meetings of the Teheran Conference. President Roosevelt, however, put forward his proposals for a four-Power policing of the world in private conversations with Stalin, remarking that he felt it was premature to consider them at Teheran with Mr. Churchill. Stalin suggested the the President's plan might require the sending of American troops to Europe. He was doubtful about Chinese participation and thought that the small

(*continued on page* 80)

(ii)

Preliminary discussions between the British, United States, and Soviet Governments with regard to a World Security Organisation: arrangements for tripartite conversations in Washington (January–August 1944).

(a) On November 5, 1943, the United States Senate passed (by eighty-five votes to five) a resolution recognising the necessity of establishing 'at the earliest practicable date a general international organisation based on the principle of the sovereign equality of all peace-loving States, and open to membership of all such States, large and small, for the maintenance of international peace and security'. A fortnight
(b) later the United States Chargé d'Affaires in London presented a note to the Foreign Office suggesting that the Four Powers should announce that they would welcome the adherence of all peace-loving States to article 4 of the Moscow Declaration. A similar note was presented to the Soviet Government. The Foreign Office replied that they considered this step to be premature because the Moscow Conference had agreed that the three Powers should hold preliminary discussions. It would therefore be better to make some progress with these discussions before inviting enquiries from other Governments. The Dominion Governments were informed of the proposal, and the Canadian Government, in particular, thought that a longer document should be prepared before other signatures were invited. The
(c) State Department then changed their plan and, early in January 1944, told Lord Halifax that they intended to ask British, Russian and possibly Chinese representatives to come to Washington for preliminary discussions. They wanted first, however, to formulate their own views on a United Nations Organisation. They had not yet brought the matter before the President, but they were working on lines of Regional Councils under a World Council. The crucial point was whether the consent of each of the major Powers should be required for a decision to use force against an aggressor or whether a majority vote would suffice. Mr. Dunn, of the State Department, thought that American opinion would more easily accept the principle of unanimous decision.

(d) The Foreign Office replied to Lord Halifax on January 15, 1944, that they were doubtful about Chinese participation in the discussions, and thought that we should not come to any decision on the

---

(*continued*)
European nations would not favour the plan and would resent China's being one of the enforcing authorities. *F.R.U.S.*, *The Conferences at Cairo and Teheran*, 1943, 530–2, 595–6: see also Churchill, *Second World War*, Volume V, pp. 320–1.

(a) A10131/144/45. (b) U6136/402/70; U3128/180/70 (1944).
(c) U180/180/70. (d) U180/180/70.

point until we knew whether the Russians would agree. The British Government thought it sufficient to inform the Chinese of the discussions, but would not oppose bringing them in if the Americans strongly wished to do so. We had not yet made up our minds on the kind of security organisation we should want, and we doubted whether the Russians had given much thought to the question. We should like a few weeks' delay before the discussions. Lord Halifax replied on (a)
January 22 that the Americans themselves would not be ready until the end of January. On January 26 the State Department mentioned (b)
a date not earlier than February 22. Eight days later they said that they would need a longer time for preparation. On February 8 they (c)
suggested an exchange of papers with ourselves and the Russians before the proposed meeting took place.

The Foreign Office replied on February 15 with a 'summary of topics'. They described the summary as, in a sense, the chapter headings of the detailed papers which we should submit and also as a draft agenda for the discussions. The headings were as follows:

A. *Nature and membership of any World Organisation*

1. Membership, functions and powers of a General Assembly.
2. Membership of a smaller body (Council).
3. Functions and powers of such a Council.

(*a*) Maintenance of international peace and security.
(*b*) Settlement of international disputes.
(*c*) Nature of relation of Council to world economic bodies—see C below.
(*d*) Question of unanimity.

4. The role of an international court for the settlement of juridical disputes.
5. The nature of the instrument establishing world organisation and method of amendment.
6. Secretariat.

B. *System of General Security*

1. Methods of co-operation and co-ordination between members e.g. question of concerted military advice to Council.
2. Relation of mutual defence arrangements and any regional systems which may be established to the general security system.
3. Provision of bases for common use.

C. *International economic and functional organisations*

1. Their relation to Council and Assembly; their relation to one another; should there be attached to the Council some body for the purpose of co-ordinating them?
2. Should such a body dispose of an economic general staff?

(a) U529/180/70. (b) U637/180/70; U879/80/70. (c) U1033/84/70.

3. Management and secretariat.

4. Future role of the International Labour Organisation and any functional bodies of the League of Nations which may be continued.

D. *Future procedure*

1. Method of discussion with other United Nations.
2. Method of registering agreement reached.
3. Time-table.

(a) The State Department replied on February 19 with a similar outline as follows:

(*a*) *General character of an International Organisation*

What should be the general structure, functions and powers of an international organisation for the maintenance of peace and security established in accordance with the provision of the Moscow Four-Nation declaration?

(*b*) *A General Assembly*

1. What should be the functions and powers of a representative General Assembly with regard to:

a. General policy of the organisation?
b. Promotion of international co-operation?
c. Settlement of disputes and security action in relation to a Council?

(*c*) *An Executive Council*

1. What should be the composition of an Executive Council?
2. What should be its functions and powers with regard to:

a. Settlement of disputes?
b. Restraint or suppression of threats to or breaches of the peace?
c. A system of regulation of armaments?
d. Economic and social co-operation.

3. By what vote should decisions be reached?

(*d*) *A Court of Justice*

1. How should an International Court of Justice be constituted and what should be its position and its functional relation to other organs of the International Organisation?

2. What should be the jurisdiction of the Court in the settlement of disputes?

3. Should the Court be empowered to render advisory opinions?

(*e*) *Arrangements for Security*

What arrangements and procedures should be provided:

1. For pacific adjustment of [disputes][1] or settlements of disputes likely to lead to a breach of the peace.

---

[1] The text of the telegram containing the American proposals was at this point uncertain. The text printed in *F.R.U.S., 1944*, 626, reads: 'conditions'.

(a) U1364/84/70.

2. For the establishment of a system of regulation of armaments and for its enforcement.
3. For the determination of threats to or breaches of the peace.
4. For the application of non-military measures.
5. For the availability and use of armed forces and facilities in the prevention or suppression of threats to or breaches of the peace.

(*f*) *Economic and Social Co-operation*

What functions and powers should the organisation have with regard to the development of international co-operation in economic and social activities and co-ordination of international agencies and action in these fields?

(*g*) *Territorial Trusteeships*

What provision should be made for the performance of such territorial trusteeship responsibilities as may devolve upon the international organisation?

(*h*) *Administration and Secretariat*

What should be the nature and functions of the Administration and Secretariat Services that may be necessary for central and related organs and agencies of the Organisation?

(*i*) *Establishment*

When and by what procedures should the Organisation be established?

On March 14, 1944, the Foreign Office sent a memorandum to the (a)
United States Government and the Soviet Government (whom they and the Americans had kept informed of their proposals). They suggested that the three Governments might now start work on papers which they would communicate to one another, and that these papers should cover the points raised in their own and the American summaries. This procedure would keep the discussions on broad lines before more detailed controversial topics were considered. The Foreign Office expected that their papers would be ready in one or two months and wished to know the American time-table.

The State Department replied on March 27 that they were making (b)
considerable progress, but could not yet suggest a time-table. At the end of the month Senator Connally, the Chairman of the Senate (c)
Foriegn Relations Committee, announced to the press that Mr. Hull thought that the work of the State Department on an International Peace Organisation had reached a point at which special consultative committees of Congress should be formed to discuss the subject. Mr. Dunn told a member of the British Embassy on April 1 that the (d)
discussions between the three Powers might take place at the end of May. Mr. Dunn said that the Americans were thinking in terms of

(a) U2101/180/70. (b) U2546/180/70. (c) U2671/180/70. (d) U2851/180/70.

a small World Council, an Assembly of all peace-loving nations, a World Court, and national contingents rather than an International Police Force. Regional Councils might deal with disputes in their area, but a major dispute anywhere would soon become a matter for the World Council. In any case it was necessary, from the point of view of American public opinion, that emphasis should be laid on the world character of the organisation.

During his visit to London in April 1944 for political and economic (a) discussions, Mr. Stettinius met Mr. Eden (who was away on leave).[1] Among other matters concerning post-war organisation, they discussed the level at which the proposed talks at Washington should be held. Mr. Eden thought that the talks should be on a high official level—he mentioned Sir A. Cadogan as a possible British representative—but that the final stage of the discussions should be at a high ministerial level. Mr. Stettinius remarked that it was a mistake to hold all the conferences in Washington. Mr. Eden replied that there was no objection on the British side in the case of these particular talks if the Americans thought Washington the best place in an election year, but that it would be a good thing to offer the Russians a conference in Moscow on some other subject if opportunity arose. Mr. Stettinius also had a conversation in very general terms with Mr. Law and Sir A. Cadogan. Here again he suggested tentatively the proposed talks might be held in London, but he told Sir A. Cadogan later that the suggestion was not practicable.

(b) During Mr. Stettinius's visit a number of talks took place at the Foreign Office with Dr. Bowman, an adviser to the State Department. Dr. Bowman explained the views of the State Department on various points: (i) The organisation should be as simple and flexible as possible, and should include some definite means to ensure action for the maintenance of peace and security. The Foreign Office thought that the Americans seemed prepared to be 'tougher' than we were towards the small States. (ii) The Assembly should occupy itself mainly with economic and social matters, but any State should be able to raise in it questions of peace and security. The Council, however, and not the Assembly, would take action. (iii) The Council should be small. The Americans had not yet come to any conclusion about the method of electing small States to it. They had given up the idea of a four-Power executive committee, but wished the four Powers to have a predominant authority; they were prepared for this purpose to consider a voting rule in which all four Powers would have to be included in any majority decision. (iv) The Political Secretariat of

---

[1] Mr. Stettinius had recently been appointed Under-Secretary of State. For his visit to London, see also Volume III, p. 36; Volume IV, Chapter LVI, p. 387.

(a) U3337/180/70. (b) U3316, 3409, 3574, 4024, 4025, 6555/180/70.

the Organisation would be established at a fixed centre (which would not be Geneva) but the Council and Assembly might be peripatetic. (v) The International Court should deal with justiciable disputes. Dr. Bowman was unable to say how far the State Department could go towards making the jurisdiction of the Court compulsory (the Foreign Office thought that as yet the Americans had not given much consideration to the Court). The Council would deal with all other disputes; the State Department were still considering whether the decisions of the Council should be binding. There would be no guarantees of territorial integrity on the lines of Article X of the Covenant. A refusal to obey the directions of the Council for the maintenance of peace in a dispute which threatened to lead to a rupture would bring sanctions into operation. (vi) The State Department no longer favoured the establishment of an international police force, but had not gone far in considering the problems of security and armaments. They thought that there should be only a few United Nations bases. Dr. Bowman could say little about their views on the nature of these bases. (vii) Dr. Bowman was also vague on the subject of regionalisation, though he agreed that 'security regions' might usefully come into existence if the World Organisation were firmly established.[1]

Up to the end of March 1944, the Soviet Government had made no positive contribution to the exchange of documents. On March 31 (a)
the Foreign Office instructed Sir A. Clark Kerr to ask for their views. M. Molotov gave a written reply on April 5 that the British and American documents would assist the discussions in Washington but that the acceptance of a list of questions for discussion did not mean the settlement of all of them in a favourable sense, or even the adoption of the same order of subjects on the agenda. M. Molotov thought that we should first discuss fundamental questions, e.g. the relationship between the general organisation and the directing body, the methods of reaching decisions, the relations of mutual defence arrangements and any regional systems to the general security system. M. Molotov did not object in principle to an exchange of documents, but regarded it as necessary to settle first the order of questions, and to exchange the documents on those questions which, as a result of negotiations in Washington, were recognised to have 'first priority'.

The Foreign Office replied that we also thought that we should begin with the discussion of fundamental questions, and that M. Molotov's first example was in fact the first on our list of papers.

---

[1] For Dr. Bowman's statements on a Colonial Declaration, see below, p. 91, note 1.

(a) U2546, 2954/180/70.

Sir A. Clark Kerr was asked to see M. Molotov again and to encourage him to produce papers in his own chosen order of priority. The Foreign Office considered that we should hint to the Russians that, if they were too slow, we should have to begin discussions with the Americans.

The rate of progress on the American side, however, was not rapid. (a) On May 29 Mr. Hull announced that the first phase of the informal conversations with eight Senators had been completed, and that the State Department, with the approval of the President, were ready to begin informal discussions on the subject of an International Security (b) Organisation with Great Britain, the U.S.S.R. and China. Mr. Hull told Lord Halifax on May 30 that the United States Government wanted to know when the British and Soviet Governments would be (c) ready to start discussions. Nearly three weeks later the President made a general statement about the American proposals, but the British Embassy in Washington was not given a copy of the American proposals until July 18.[1]

(d) Meanwhile on June 12 Mr. Hull repeated his earlier question to Lord Halifax, whether, if the Russians were unwilling to join in conversations with the Chinese, we would agree to Anglo-American-Chinese talks. Mr. Hull explained the difficulties which he would meet if there were an appearance of treating the Chinese on any basis other than that of equality. He said that he had no illusions about Chinese strength, and that the question was 'entirely psychological', but he was uncertain whether he could put forward the general proposal for conversations unless the Chinese were brought into them.

Lord Halifax was instructed that we regarded the holding of two parallel conferences as likely to involve a waste of time and energy, but that we would agree to his proposal provided that it was made clear to the Russians that the procedure was being adopted merely to put China in a position of technical equality. We should have to (e) concentrate on the talks with the Americans and Russians, and not on those with the Chinese.

The Russians were delaying a formal and definite reply, although they had made it clear that they agreed in principle to the proposed talks.[2] On July 12 Mr. Hull told Sir R. I. Campbell, Minister in H.M. Embassy at Washington, that the formal Russian acceptance had been received. Mr. Hull then asked whether we would wish to

---

[1] For these proposals see below, pp. 133–4.

[2] On June 21 Lord Halifax reported that the Soviet Embassy in Washington had told (f) the State Department that the Soviet Government would send a definite reply in a few days' time.

(a) U4874/180/70. (b) U4887/180/70. (c) U4887, 5639/180/70.
(d) U5466, 5877/180/70. (e) U6366/180/70. (f) U5877/180/70.

hold the talks with the Chinese simultaneously with the main conversations or whether these talks should follow the conversations with the Russians. Sir R. I. Campbell was instructed to say that we thought 'parallel' conversations the more convenient method. We also wanted time—at least a fortnight—to consider the American written memoranda (which we had not then received). The Russians themselves, however, asked for a postponement until 'approximately August 12'. They also hoped that the talks with the Chinese would follow the Anglo-American-Russian conversations. Mr. Hull therefore asked whether we would agree to this proposal on condition that the Chinese were kept fully informed of the tripartitie conversations. (a)

In the third week of July 1944 Mr. Winant wrote to Mr. Eden that the United States Government contemplated that Mr. Hull would be the senior representative of the American group taking part in the discussions and, particularly, in dealing with considerations of basic policy.[1] Mr. Eden asked Sir R. Campbell to explain that, if Mr. Hull took part in the discussions, he (Mr. Eden) would be asked why he was not attending them. Mr. Eden could not arrange participation at such short notice, and did not think that a meeting of Foreign Secretaries was desirable at the present stage of the discussions. Mr. Eden also communicated his views on the matter to M. Molotov. (b) (c)

M. Molotov let Mr. Eden know on July 24 through the Soviet Ambassador in London that he agreed with the British view and that the conversations were to be entirely preliminary; the Russians would be represented by the Soviet Ambassador in Washington. Mr. Eden said that we should be represented by Sir A. Cadogan, and that Lord Halifax (who was at this time in England) would take part if he were back in time. (d)

Mr. Eden's view was that, if the conversations were successful, they should be followed later by a meeting of Foreign Secretaries. The Americans had also proposed a meeting to launch the world organisation; on July 31 Mr. Stettinius,[2] in the absence of Mr. Hull, asked Sir R. I. Campbell our views about a possible meeting in September. Mr. Hull suggested Casablanca as a meeting place. After the British

---

[1] On June 7 President Roosevelt, in conversation with Lord Halifax, had seemed surprised at the British view that the proposed discussions should be held entirely on an official level. He said that Mr. Hull would want 'to be in on them from day to day'; he thought therefore that Mr. Eden might have wanted Lord Halifax to take part in them. Lord Halifax said that Mr. Eden had discussed the matter with Mr. Stettinius, and that they had agreed that the purpose of the discussions was to fit together various drafts rather than to take decisions on policy. (e)

[2] See above, p. 84, n. 1.

(a) U6518, 6526/180/70. (b) U6478/180/70. (c) U6552, 6652/180/70.
(d) U6552/180/70. (e) U5241/180/70.

(a) Delegation had left for Washington Mr. Stettinius repeated the suggestion of a meeting in North Africa. Mr. Eden telegraphed on August 12 to Sir. A. Cadogan that he would go anywhere: if the meeting was held in North Africa, we should have to include French representatives. Mr. Eden was in favour of doing so but doubted whether Mr. Hull would agree. He suggested London as a possible place. As for a date, he doubted whether any date before the beginning of October was practicable if, as he expected, the Washington talks did not end until the middle of September. He also thought that it would be a mistake to exclude the Chinese from the ministerial talks after they had been brought into the preliminary discussions, since we should be giving the impression that we regarded Chinese membership of the Big Four as merely camouflage. If the Russians objected to inviting the Chinese, the onus should rest on them.[1]

The opening of these discussions was postponed once again owing (b) to a request from the Russians. On the evening of August 5 the Foreign Office heard from Washington that Mr. Stettinius had telephoned to the British Embassy to repeat a message from Mr. Harriman in Moscow. This message was to the effect that M. Vyshinsky wished to postpone the opening of the discussions in Washington from August 14 to August 21 in order to give the Soviet Government more time for study of the proposals. Mr. Stettinius thought it desirable to accept this proposal.

Sir A. Cadogan and the staff of the British Delegation were leaving on August 6. The Foreign Office regarded the delay as tiresome, and considered that M. Vyshinsky or Mr. Harriman should have told Sir A. Clark Kerr that a postponement was being suggested. It was, however, impolitic not to agree to it. The Foreign Office

(c) [1] The Prime Minister commented on August 23 on this telegram to Washington. He agreed that the proposed meeting should be held in London, 'as it is our turn'. He hoped that the French would not be admitted to the discussion until they had broadened their Government. The rapid liberation of France should make it possible to obtain some national authority which we could recognise. The Prime Minister thought it 'an absolute farce' to include China as one of the four Great Powers of the World. He had told the President that he would be 'reasonably polite about this American obsession'; he could not agree that we should 'take a positive attitude in the matter. The latest information from China points to the rise already of a rival Government to supplant Chiang Kai-shek, and there is always a Communist civil war impending there'. The Prime Minister would not oppose the President's wish, but would 'object very much if we adopted other than a perfectly negative line, leaving him [the President] to do the needful with the Russians'. Mr. Eden noted on the Prime Minister's minute: 'It is no doubt true that Chiang's authority is weakening, but it is not in our interest that China should relapse into chaos, which will, I fear, occur, if he cannot win through.'

Mr. Eden did not reply to the Prime Minister's minute. The Foreign Office pointed out, in regard to the Prime Minister's view, (i) that we had implied in our proposals that France would be a permanent member of the Council, and that the Americans explicitly, and the Russians implicitly, agreed that the Organisation would be constituted, and hold a first meeting before the admission of France as a permanent member; (ii) that we had recognised China as one of the 'Big Four' and would run into many difficulties if we did not treat her as such in practice.

(a) U6681/180/70. (b) U6756/180/70. (c) U7314/180/70.

considered letting M. Vyshinsky know that he had caused unnecessary inconvenience, but the Soviet Ambassador apologised to (a) Mr. Eden for the delay, and no telegram was sent to Moscow.

(iii)

British memoranda on a World Organisation (April–May 1944).

During these months of prolonged negotiations with the United States and Soviet Governments, a special interdepartmental committee in London had been considering in detail the proposals which the British Government would desire to put forward with regard to a World Security Organisation. The committee, under the chairman- (b) ship of Mr. Law, Minister of State, reported on April 19, 1944, to the Armistice and Post-War Committee.[1] They had prepared[2] five memoranda, and a covering explanatory note. They suggested that—subject to the approval of the War Cabinet—these memoranda, and the note, should be submitted to the meeting of Dominion Prime Ministers which was to take place in London in May. The documents could then be used as a basis for the discussions with United States and Soviet representatives in Washington. The memoranda and covering note, after a few changes made by the Armistice and Post-War Committee, were circulated to the War Cabinet on April 22.

The five memoranda were on the following subjects: (*a*) the scope and nature of a permanent international organisation; (*b*) the pacific settlement of disputes, the question of guarantees, and the conditions in which action should be taken for the maintenance of peace and security. (*c*) The military aspect of any post-war security organisation. (*d*) The co-ordination of political and economic international machinery. (*e*) The method and procedure for establishing a world organisation.

In his covering note of April 16 to the War Cabinet Mr. Law summarised the course of events since the Moscow Declaration of

---

[1] See above, p. 62, note 2.

[2] There is a very large amount of material in the Foreign Office archives on the preparation of these memoranda. Mr. Jebb, in particular, took a leading part in the work on the official side. For reasons of space the preparation of the memoranda has not been dealt with in detail; a good deal of the material indeed is outside the scope of this history. Nevertheless, owing to the importance and interest of the memoranda, they have been inserted in full into the text of this section, apart from a lengthy technical discussion omitted from the end of memorandum C. The text of memorandum D submitted by Mr. Law's committee was criticised by the Armistice and Post-War Committee as not indicating sufficiently clearly the relation of the specialised international economic institutions to the general political organisation. The revised text prepared for the Cabinet in accordance with the instructions of the latter Committee is therefore included in place of the original version.

(a) U6829/180/70.
(b) WP(44)220; APW(44) 1st meeting; APW(44)4; U3128/180/70.

November 1943, which had led to the preparation of the memoranda. He then described the general principles upon which they were based:

> 'The Organisation suggested has much in common with the Covenant of the League of Nations, and, in accordance with the expressed intention of the Prime Minister, it tries to retain all the best features of its predecessor. But it is meant to be more flexible, less bound by rigid definitions which hamper or prevent necessary action, and above all endowed with the machinery to make action effective. In short, our plan is based on the acceptance of certain essential principles and we leave the means by which these principles shall be carried out to be adapted to the varying circumstances of human intercourse which cannot be foreseen.
>
> It is thus that the institutions of Britain and the Commonwealth have grown, and it is this method that their peoples will best understand. Our method of approach may possibly make less appeal to the more legally-minded people of the United States, who attach so much importance to the details of a written constitution, or to the Russians, whose way of thinking is very different from our own, or to the peoples of the Continent of Europe, who have a different system of law and have always desired explicit undertakings no matter how often they have been broken, But, though changes may have to be made to meet these points of view, we believe that something like what we suggest represents the maximum of effective international co-operation that can be secured at the present time.
>
> Naturally we must not agree to anything which might impair the harmony of the Commonwealth or the integrity of the British Empire. But subject to this it will be essential to obtain an organisation embracing the United Kingdom and the Dominions, the United States and the U.S.S.R., and, it might perhaps be added, France. This, therefore, should be our primary object and no minor considerations should be allowed to stand in its way.
>
> The establishment of a centre where the policies of the principal States of the world can be harmonised is in the great tradition of British policy, and we believe that the present proposals carry on a development which was supported by Castlereagh, Palmerston, Salisbury and Grey before the last war and by Lord Balfour, Sir Austen Chamberlain and Mr. Arthur Henderson in the period between the wars.
>
> We attach great importance to the establishment of some permanent machinery by which rapid and effective action may be taken against any threat to world peace. The world has seen so many promises broken that faith in the new institution can only be obtained if the means of action are visible, and will, perhaps, only be confirmed after such action has taken place.
>
> It is essential to the interests of the British Commonwealth that the Organisation should be world-wide. We have, therefore, subordinated the creation of regional organisations to this end. But we believe that in due course regional organisations (which will probably

develop naturally) may play an important part in the world and that if they are suitably guided within the World Organisation their advantages will outweigh their disadvantages.

In Memorandum A we have assumed that the World Council will consist of the Four Powers and a number of other States. We have left open the method by which these States are chosen because we think that it would be premature to put forward a cut-and-dried scheme at this stage. We have not even laid down the principle that one of the members of the Commonwealth other than the United Kingdom should always have a place on the World Council. Such a demand may very likely provoke a counter demand from the Soviet Government that one of the constituent republics of the U.S.S.R. should always have a seat on the World Council. Whether it can be ensured that one of the Dominions shall always have a place on the Conucil must obviously depend on the number of Council members. But we recognise that it should be our object to obtain this result.

We have also left open the questions of the Secretariat and the seat of the Organisation, problems closely interrelated. They raise issues on which it is likely to be difficult to come to an agreement and we think that it would be better to postpone them to a later stage of the discussions.

Under our proposals, great power would rest in the hands of the World Council. It would, for instance, take the initiative in action to maintain peace, and other members would be bound to follow its decisions. We have, however, left open the question of placing permanently a special responsibility on the Great Powers for the maintenance of international peace and security. By doing so the association of the United States in the burden would be more explicitly obtained, but it may well be possible to secure that advantage without such definition as might seem to imply too great a recognition of the position of the Great Powers in the Organisation.

We have not mentioned the Colonial question. It may have to appear on the Agenda of the tripartite discussions in deference to the wishes of the United States. They have, however, preferred to raise it privately with the United Kingdom in the first instance, and informal discussions have been taking place with members of Mr. Stettinius's mission.[1]

---

[1] Dr. Bowman had made a number of references while in London to the proposed Colonial Declaration (see above, p. 24, note 1, and p. 73, note 3). He said that the (a) State Department still wanted such a declaration. Their idea now was to emphasise the promotion of material well-being and self-government rather than political independence, but they envisaged international machinery of a supervisory and not merely a consultative character. Dr. Bowman insisted that American opinion would want something to be said on the subject in connexion with the World Organisation. He thought that the colonial Powers might report periodically to the Organisation. Dr. Bowman saw the Secretary of State for the Colonies on April 18, and was disappointed that he would not go beyond his statement of July 13, 1943, in the House of Commons. The Foreign Office suggested that the American insistence on a declaration might in part be attributed to their desire to justify their own plans to annex certain Japanese islands in the Pacific, and in part to the risk that, unless some statement were made the President might be accused in his election campaign of being a champion of imperialism. See also below, pp. 313–91.

(a) U3409, 4025/180/70.

In Memorandum B the machinery for the pacific settlement of disputes and the maintenance of peace and security has been made as flexible as possible. The members of the British Commonwealth have always been opposed to such guarantees of territorial integrity and political independence as those contained in Article X of the Covenant. Our proposals contain three main propositions:

(i) That the members of the Organisation shall promise to settle all disputes in such a manner as not to endanger the maintenance of international peace and security without, however, guaranteeing the territorial integrity and political independence of member States. (We have attempted in this manner, so far as can be done at the present stage of international relations, to throw the balance rather more in the direction of change.)
(ii) That the World Council shall be given the initiative to take action for the maintenance of peace and security. (It is only in this way that machinery can be set up to make the promises of the members effective.)
(iii) That action by the Organisation shall be based on principles rather than on elaborate definition (which we believe defeats its own purpose).'

The memorandum C on military questions was based on two earlier papers already approved by the Chiefs of Staff. The memorandum said little about the regulation of armaments which the United States had included as one of the subjects for discussion, but our proposals would enable us to deal with the question positively, as a part of the process of sharing the burden of armaments necessary to maintain international peace and security rather than negatively by the process of limiting armaments.

The fourth Memorandum D on economic questions was an attempt to co-ordinate new and untried economic and technical organisations without depriving them of the necessary control over their own actions. The interdepartmental committee regarded such coordination as essential for the maintenance of full employment and proper use of resources after the war.

The committee realised that the United States Government would decide for itself the best way of securing the assent of Congress to American participation in setting up an international organisation. They put forward their proposals in memorandum E as a possible assistance to the discussion of the subject.

The memoranda were as follows:[1]

[1] Certain paragraphs in these memoranda were re-drafted before their final Approval by the Cabinet. For the re-drafts, see below, pp. 122–6.

Memorandum A

SCOPE AND NATURE OF THE PERMANENT ORGANISATION

I. *The Principles and Objects of the Organisation*

1. The World Organisation will consist of independent States freely associated and working together for the better realisation of the common good of mankind.

2. The principles and objects of the Organisation should be stated in the preamble of the document which brings it into existence. The Organisation should be as simple and flexible as possible. Thus the statement of its principles and objects becomes specially important, since they lay down the conditions in which action is taken by the members of the Organisation.

3. Article 4 of the Moscow Declaration lays down that the Organisation shall be based on the 'sovereign equality' of States. Two principles follow from these words. In the first place members must agree to respect each other's political independence, and secondly all members enjoy equality of status, though not necessarily equality of function.

4. Members should not be entitled to receive the benefits of the Organisation unless they are prepared to accept the obligations that go with them. Moreover, it is the assumption of such obligations by all members that ensures to all the benefits of the Organisation. This should be recognised, therefore, as one of the principles of the Organisation.

5. The object of the Organisation is stated in Article 4 to be the 'maintenance of international peace and security', and this must be regarded as its primary purpose.

6. But if recourse to violence is ruled out, means must be provided by which Members of the Organisation can settle their disputes by other than violent methods; and the establishment of machinery for achieving this must be one of the objects of the Organisation.

7. Moreover, in order that international peace and security shall be maintained there must be in the world some means by which States meet together to review and harmonise their political action. One of the objects of the Organisation, therefore, must be to create a meeting-place where statesmen can come together for that purpose.

8. But international peace and security must be made positively, and not only kept by the negative means of suppressing violence. They will be confirmed and strengthened by guarding the right of man to seek his freedom, and by increase in the well-being of human society. Statesmen of the United Nations have declared this to be

both the purpose and the condition of development in international order.

9. It will be necessary, therefore, for the Organisation to create institutions to promote the betterment of world-wide economic conditions and the removal of social wrongs, and to support and extend institutions which now exist for these purposes.

10. Thus the principles and objects of the Organisation, and consequently the conditions in which its members receive its benefits and accept its obligations and on which actions taken under its authority are based, may be described as follows:

11. *Principles*

(i) That all Members of the Organisation undertake to respect each other's political independence.
(ii) That all members are equal in status though not necessarily in function.
(iii) That all members undertake to fulfil towards each other the obligations which are the conditions of receiving the benefits of the Organisation.

12. *Objects*

(i) To ensure that peace and security shall be maintained so that men shall not live in fear of war.
(ii) To provide means by which all disputes arising between States may be so dealt with that peace and security are not endangered.
(iii) To provide a centre in which the political action of States can be reviewed and harmonised, and directed towards a common end.
(iv) To promote the betterment of world-wide economic conditions and the well-being of all men by international agreement so that the fear of want may be removed from the world.
(v) To guard and enlarge the freedom of man by institutions for the removal of social wrongs.

II. *The Nature of the Organisation*

13. In Article 4 of the Moscow Declaration it is laid down that the Organisation is to be founded on the sovereign equality of its Members. Its Members will, therefore, retain control of their own actions except so far as they are limited by the obligations into which they freely enter and by international law.

14. Nothing has been more clearly proved during the present war than the interconnexion of peace and security in all parts of the world. The future organisation must recognise this fact and be a World Organisation in which all peaceful States in every part of the world can co-operate together for their mutual benefit.

15. Though the status of all Members is equal and all will enjoy

the same rights and undertake the corresponding obligations, their differences in power make necessary some recognition of differences in function. The initiative for the formation of the Organisation has come from the Four Powers, the United States, the U.S.S.R., the United Kingdom and China, and it is generally recognised that its success will depend more upon their continued co-operation than on any single factor. The machinery of the Organisation should make it possible for them to carry out the responsibilities which they will have agreed to undertake. The same principle applies to all other States. The more power and responsibility can be made to correspond, the more likely it is that the machinery will be able to fulfil its functions.

16. We look forward to the liberation of France and her restoration to the ranks of the Great Powers. It is assumed that she will then have the same position in the Organisation as the Four Powers.

17. It is presumed that there will come into existence a number of specialised technical organisations through which States will combine together for various purposes. There are already such organisations in existence as part of the system of the League of Nations. The relations of these bodies to one another and to the main organisation are considered in paper D. Here it need only be said that such bodies are unlikely to survive as effective instruments in a world from which reasonable security is absent.

18. Just as there are special functional organisations, so there may be regional associations for various purposes when there is obvious advantage to be obtained by limitation of the sphere of action. Such regional associations might come into existence for security, for economic co-operation, for the promotion of welfare in colonial territories or for other purposes. It is, however, essential that they should not conflict with the world-wide organisation but rather assist it to carry out its purposes.

III. *Constitution of the Organisation*

19. It is generally recognised that it will be necessary to set up two main bodies, one as a centre of discussion on which all States are represented and the other, a smaller body, as a centre of action. It is suggested that these bodies be termed the World Assembly and the World Council respectively.

20. *Membership.* It is assumed that at the outset all the United Nations will be invited to be members of the Organisation. What States now neutral shall be admitted and at what period is a matter for consideration. The enemy States cannot be admitted until they have shown by their conduct that they accept the objects of the Organisation and intend to pursue them.

21. All the Members of the Organisation should share in some

manner in the admission of new members. It will have to be considered how far it is necessary to lay down conditions under which a State shall cease to be a member of the Organisation.

22. *World Assembly.* The Sovereign equality of all Members should be recognised by their representatives meeting together on a footing of equality in a World Assembly at least once a year. The right of information and criticism should belong to all Members of the Organisation.

23. It is not suggested that this body should have all the powers that were possessed by the Assembly of the League. The specialised and technical bodies should undertake some of the duties which that body performed and the initiative in preventing breaches of the peace should lie with the World Council.

24. It is a matter for consideration whether the World Assembly should have the control over finance and the admission of new members which the Assembly of the League possessed; but it is suggested that the States cannot be expected to contribute to the finances of an organisation without some share in their determination, nor to belong to a society to which other States may be admitted without consultation with them.

25. *World Council.* This body should be sufficiently small and compact to ensure action and of such a character as to possess the confidence of all Members of the Organisation.

26. The *constitution* of this body raises many difficult problems. The relation between the Great Powers and other States has been matter of dispute for over a century. The principle has been generally accepted that where the interests of any State are specially affected it should have the right of representation on the Council. It is also clearly necessary that the Four Powers, which between them are directly responsible for the peace and security of nearly two-thirds of the world's inhabitants, should always be represented on it.

27. The number and method of representation of other States is a matter for grave consideration and the manner in which the decisions of the Council shall be made may depend on the method adopted. The object should be to ensure that the other States on the World Council command general confidence. Some form of election is probably essential and the World Assembly can obviously be used for this purpose.

28. Some means must be found to ensure that the various regions of the world are adequately represented. The size and area of States vary so greatly and are so unevenly distributed over the Continents that some agreement on this subject is essential. Thus, the Caribbean area has more independent States than all the rest of Latin America, which includes Brazil, Argentina and Chile. Both Europe and South

America have many more States than North America or Asia. Hitherto States as different in power and status as Canada and Panama have had equal rights of representation. The principle of rotation has deprived the Council of experienced statesmen, while the creation of 'semi-permanent' seats was much resented by some of the States that did not enjoy the privilege.

29. If the principle which governs the election of the Governing Body of the I.L.O.[1] could be accepted, a more satisfactory result might be obtained, but it is difficult to find the principle to apply to a political body.

30. Should Regional Associations of sufficient importance be formed they might furnish a basis for representation on the Council. But for the most part States do not recognise other States as 'representing' them on institutions in which they have a major interest.

31. It is clear that this subject will need careful examination—not only amongst the Four Powers themselves but with the other States whose wishes must be taken into account.

32. The main *function* of the World Council will be to ensure such intercourse between the statesmen of the countries represented on it as to enable them to secure solutions of international problems by discussion and co-operative action. For this purpose regular meetings with an appropriate procedure and secretariat are indispensable. No other single factor is likely to be so influential in producing harmony between the policies of States. The experience of the last thirty years shows that there is no adequate substitute for it.

33. The functions suggested for the World Council as the body responsible for the peace of the world are described in Memorandum B.

34. It will also be necessary for the World Council to give some common direction to the functional bodies. This question is considered in paper D.

35. In general it is hoped that the Council may become a centre where Governments reconcile their attitudes towards major international problems so as to be able to act decisively towards a common end.

36. *Permanent Court of International Justice.* It is assumed that there will be general agreement that a Permanent Court of International Justice will be set up. The proposals of the Informal Inter-Allied Committee which recently reported on this question seem to indicate the general lines that should be followed.[2]

---

[1] The Governing Body of the International Labour Organisation consisted of thirty-two members elected triennially. Eight were appointed by the States of chief industrial importance and eight selected from the representatives of other governments. The representatives of the employers and workers each elected eight members. Six governmental representatives and two representatives of employers and workers respectively were from non-European States.

[2] See Cmd. Paper Misc. No. 2 of February 10, 1944.

37. *Secretariat.* A permanent secretariat will be indispensable. The experience of the League of Nations and the I.L.O. should be utilised. It is assumed, however, that a number of new specialised technical bodies will come into existence. Further consideration of this question might, therefore, await more definite information concerning them.

38. The suggestion that the head of the Secretariat should be given the right of bringing before the World Council any matter which in his opinion threatens the peace of the world might well be incorporated in the rules of the Organisation.

39. *Specialised and Technical Organisations.* This question is considered in Memorandum D. The position of the International Labour Organisation will need special consideration.

40. *Seat of the Organisation.* This problem should be left open until further information is available on the number and character of the functional organisations.

41. *Name of the Organisation.* The term 'United Nations' is now in general use and there does not seem to be any strong reason to substitute any other for it.

Memorandum B

THE PACIFIC SETTLEMENT OF DISPUTES, THE QUESTION OF GUARANTEES AND THE CONDITIONS IN WHICH ACTION SHOULD BE TAKEN FOR THE MAINTENANCE OF PEACE AND SECURITY

I. *Introduction*

If war is to be prevented there must be in existence a means to make those decisions which in the past have been made by violence. If an organisation is set up to achieve this end there must be some guarantee that its members will be protected should States, inside or outside it, threaten to subject them to violence. For the purpose of providing protection, action may have to be taken against an offending State, and this necessitates some statement of how and when such action shall be taken.

2. The maintenance of peace and security is not merely an end in itself but a means by which an ordered and progressive community of States may come into existence. The principles and objects of such a society have been indicated in Part I of Memorandum A, and it is on them that all action by the Organisation should be based. A state of peace should be regarded as not simply the acceptance of the *status quo* but active co-operation between States for the objects and principles of the Organisation.

3. Such ends cannot be obtained by any system of procedure how-

ever skilfully designed. Everything depends on the unity of purpose of those States which possess the greatest means of carrying out their purposes. It is impossible to ensure that these States will always be in agreement, and no set of rules will do so. But an agreement to act under certain specific principles in a World Organisation will make their co-operation easier and will enable other states to be associated with them for their common purpose.

4. If all the Great Powers are members of the Organisation and show their intention of acting in accordance with it, all States will be more ready to accept the responsibilities commensurate with their power. The absence of the United States and, for a long period, of the U.S.S.R. from the League of Nations caused the United Kingdom to review its responsibilites. For the same reason smaller States were often reluctant to accept full responsibility.

5. For the same reason also there was great anxiety on the part of many States to define very closely the occasion for action by the organs and members of the League of Nations. As is explained below, this attempt failed in its purpose. Moreover, public opinion did not understand the elaborate safeguards against arbitrary action that existed. It is suggested that the methods embodied in the constitution of the Organisation should be simple and flexible. They should be extended and elaborated only as the result of experience.

6. It is believed also that, whatever procedure be adopted, it is only by setting up some definite security system such as is suggested in Memorandum C that reality will be given to the promises made and that the States of the world will come to believe that by accepting the rights and responsibilities given to them by the Organisation they will be spared such sufferings as they are now enduring.

II. *The Pacific Settlement of Disputes*

7. Disputes between States are divided into two main categories, those, often termed 'justiciable', that can be settled by a legal tribunal, and those in which other considerations are predominant.

8. It is the second class which produces the most intractable and dangerous disputes, including those in which the legal position is entirely clear. In the past, States have promised not to attempt settlement of their disputes by violent means, but they have not promised to settle their disputes. It is suggested that it might be well if they now promised to 'settle' their disputes in the sense that they will not allow them to endanger peace and security.

9. *Justiciable Disputes*. It would seem that there is likely to be general agreement that justiciable disputes should be generally settled by a Permanent Court of International Justice. The Informal Inter-Allied Committee suggested in its recent report that the Court

be open to all States, whether they accept compulsory jurisdiction or not. It would be possible for the International Organisation to make the acceptance of such an obligation a condition of membership, but in such a case it would be necessary to allow States to make certain reservations.

10. The difference between accepting compulsory jurisdiction with reservations and retaining full freedom of action is likely to have more psychological than practical effect, especially if the World Council can obtain advisory opinions from the Court on some point in a dispute which has been submitted to it.

11. *Other Disputes.* Reference to the World Council is the obvious method of dealing with other disputes. Though other elaborate methods of conciliation have been set up they have hardly ever been used and they have the disadvantage of placing the case in the hands of persons who are not responsible for the consequences of failure to preserve peace. It is only in the World Council itself that a body of rules and a technique of procedure can be gradually established as the result of accumulated experience.

12. It should be for the World Council to decide what method should be used for dealing with the dispute. Any decision of this nature should be regarded as a decision of procedure and consequently be adopted by a majority vote.

13. There have been suggestions that even on questions of principle (as opposed to questions of procedure) decisions should be taken by (say) a two-thirds majority of the Council rather than by unanimity. We leave this important question open, but it seems desirable that in all such cases all the Four Powers should be included in the majority. In any event, the votes of the parties to the dispute should not, of course, be taken into account.

14. States are not likely to bind themselves to accept the decision of the Council in all cases. Nor would it be likely that they would undertake the obligation to enforce it on other States in all cases. But it would still be the function of the World Council to see that disputes did not threaten peace and security and for the other States to co-operate with it to the utmost of their power for that purpose, so that there would still be large opportunities for action to deal with even the most difficult disputes.

15. For, as has been indicated, if peace and security are to be maintained, some method must be devised for the settlement of all disputes between States. 'Settlement' in this sense may, as is often the case in domestic disputes, show that no remedy exists for a legitimate grievance. But if States promise to 'settle' their disputes in the sense defined in paragraph 8 above, the balance is thrown more in the direction of change. The *status quo* is sufficiently safeguarded by the mere existence of a universal system for the maintenance of peace and

security. Should the dispute be such as to threaten peace and security, it will be for the World Council (and in such cases action will depend largely on the Great Powers) to decide what action should be taken to deal with it.

16. If the dispute involves the Great Powers themselves the machinery for decision may prove inadequate; but there is hope that the habit of co-operative leadership in the settlement of other disputes and the restraints imposed by their own promises to one another and to other States may suffice to achieve a settlement, even where the machinery seems to be inadequate to do so. Much will depend on whether a sufficient number of States, great and small, come to attach so much importance to the preservation of the system that they are prepared to run risks and make sacrifices to support and preserve it.

17. There was considerable agreement in the period between the two wars that the vague words of Article XIX of the Covenant of the League of Nations were hardly a sufficient recognition of the fact that there must be a change in the world. When, in the thirties, it was perceived that there was no great desire in some countries to go to war to defend some of the frontiers erected by the Peace Treaties, there was much discussion of a process which became known as 'Peaceful Change'. Examination of this concept shows that it cannot be obtained by a clause in a Covenant, but can only be a continual process achieved through discussion and compromise between the Great Powers and, in their due place, the smaller States concerned. But it is essential that such a process be guided by principle and subject to an ordered procedure, and it is necessary, therefore, that it should take place within an international organisation.

18. It may be hoped that the international functional organisations which are being brought into existence will contribute to furthering the process of peaceful change in an orderly manner.

III. *The Question of Guarantees*

19. In considering this question the history of the guarantees given in the Covenant of the League of Nations must be taken into account, since it throws great light on the nature of the problem. For by Article X the Members of the League 'undertook to respect and preserve as against external aggression the territorial integrity and existing political independence of all Members'. The formula had first been devised by President Wilson for the Western Hemisphere and it was at his instance that it was applied universally. No method was laid down as to how the obligation should be carried out except that the Council should 'advise' upon that question.

20. *Territorial Integrity*. There was much opposition to the proposed Article, attention being concentrated on the question of

'territorial integrity'. Lord Cecil[1] suggested that the guarantee should be withdrawn if the State concerned refused to accept a modification of frontier desired by a large majority of the Members of the League of Nations. The vague phraseology of Article XIX of the Covenant was all that resulted from this proposal. Mr. Lansing and Dr. Miller[2] were also opposed to inserting Article X, though the latter came to believe that it made little difference. Sir Robert Borden[3] tried to abolish it before the Covenant was signed, and the Canadian Delegation renewed the attempt at the First Assembly. In 1923 an interpretative resolution was adopted by the Assembly (though as Persia dissented it had no legal force) which laid down that it was for each State to decide how it should carry out its obligations under this head, while the Council was to take into account, in any advice that it might give, the geographical situation and special conditions of each State.

21. In fact, Article X was hardly ever used in the disputes which came before the League of Nations. But it was constantly referred to when some State wished to remind others that its existing frontiers were guaranteed by them. It was also constantly used by critics of the League of Nations to show that its members had guaranteed for all time frontiers which they possessed no legal means of changing without the consent of the State concerned.

22. Much smaller attention has been paid to this subject in recent discussions, though there may, of course, be a shift of interest when the treaties that register any changes of frontier which may be made come into existence. There is, however, reason to think that many States will be more interested in the establishment of some concrete security system ready for immediate action than in guarantees of frontiers which in themselves do little to prevent the invasion and occupation of territory by the armed forces of another State.

23. Many other States would be likely to refuse to accept an Organisation which committed them to a guarantee of the territorial integrity of all States.

24. It is suggested, therefore, that no such guarantee be included in the obligations undertaken by members of the Organisation.

25. *Political Independence*. The question of 'political independence' raises issues of a rather different character. The Moscow Declaration has already based the Organisation on the 'sovereign equality' of all States, which implies that the Members of the Organisation will retain legal control over their own actions except in so far as they agree

[1] Viscount Cecil of Chelwood (Lord Robert Cecil), Assistant Secretary of State for Foreign Affairs, 1918–19 and a member of the British Delegation to the Paris Peace Conference, had been closely concerned in the drafting of the Covenant.

[2] Mr. Lansing, U.S. Secretary of State 1915–20, was a member, and Dr. D. Hunter Miller a technical adviser to the U.S. Commision at the Paris Peace Conference in 1919.

[3] Prime Minister of Canada, and a member of the Canadian Delegation to the Paris Peace Conference.

by treaty to limit it. All States naturally attach the highest value to their political independence, and the principal statesmen have made repeated declarations that they intend to respect the independence of other States.

26. But an undertaking to respect the political independence of other States does not necessarily involve a commitment to guarantee it. It is, moreover, not easy to define exactly what political independence is. One State may control the actions of another State by indirect means. It is impossible to distinguish the line which divides such actions from what is generally regarded as the legitimate influence which one State may exercise on the actions of another. Any guarantee of 'political independence', therefore, can only extend to external and legal forms. If cannot take into account more indirect methods.

27. For this reason the inclusion of a guarantee of political independence in the obligations of the Organisation seems undesirable. But it should be recognised that mutual respect for the political independence of its members is one of the essential principles of the Organisation as already pointed out in Part I of Memorandum A.

28. *The Maintenance of International Peace and Security.* By the Covenant of the League, States undertook to inflict sanctions on another State which broke its promises to submit a dispute to pacific settlement *and* resorted to war. It was for each State to determine its own actions after the Council (or Assembly) had declared that the occasion for action had arisen. Doubt was constantly expressed as to the sufficiency of this promise, though, so far as words can guarantee action, a definite promise was made. But the duty of enforcing action to be taken was laid on the members.

29. Also by Article XI of the Covenant the duty of safeguarding the 'peace of nations' was laid on the League, but no specific obligations as regards the action to be taken were laid on the Members.

30. The Four Powers have already, by Article 4 of the Moscow Declaration, laid down that the main purpose of the international organisation is the 'maintenance of international peace and security', and have asserted by Article 5 that 'they will consult with one another and, as occasion requires, with other Members of the United Nations, with a view to joint action on behalf of the community of nations' for this purpose until a system of general security is inaugurated. It would seem that it is along these lines that any guarantee should be given.

31. The duty of co-operating to the utmost of their power in the maintenance of international peace and security should be undertaken by all Members of the Organisation. The degree of such co-operation

must obviously depend on the geographical situation of States, the amount of their resources, their own internal situation and possibly other factors which cannot be accurately weighed in advance. But the duty of co-operating to the utmost of their power in an Organisation which is essential to the peace and security of all should be laid upon all members.

32. The duty of maintaining international peace and security should be laid in the first instance on the World Council acting on behalf of the other Members of the Organisation. It will be for the World Council to take the initiative to give effect to the undertaking to maintain international peace and security.

33. It is for consideration whether any special obligations for the maintenance of international peace and security should be explicitly assumed within the permanent Organisation by the Four Powers who have undertaken such a responsibility pending the establishment of a general system.

34. If regional organisations are set up for security purposes, part of the responsibility in the first instance might fall on them, but, as is suggested in Memorandum A, paragraph 18, not in such a manner as to conflict with the final responsibility of the World Council or the maintenance of peace and security.

IV. *The Conditions in which Action should be taken for the Maintenance of Peace and Security*

35. It is generally recognised that there must be some statement in the constitution of the Organisation as to the conditions in which action is taken to maintain international peace and security. In the Covenant of the League of Nations and in the attempts to elaborate the Covenant great attention was given to this question.

36. In the Covenant the sanctions of Article XVI came into force only if there was resort to war after a Member had broken the promises made in Articles XII–XIV. Even then each State necessarily determined for itself whether the *casus foederis* had arisen.

37. In Article X the guarantees were against 'external aggression' only. It was by this article that the unfortunate word 'aggression' was introduced into the Covenant and became the subject of so many debates at Geneva. But the more the word was discussed the more difficult it became to define exactly what it meant. The definition of aggression was considered important because it was thought that it might affect the right of the Council to advise that sanctions be employed. The most notable contribution to the debate was the suggestion that aggression should be determined by the acceptance or refusal of arbitration or some other peaceful method of settling disputes. But this did not cover the preparations for aggression, nor did it take the time element sufficiently into account. Moreover, the

discussion and analysis of aggression enabled States to use a procedure calculated to defeat the objects of the Covenant. Illustration of this fact was given by the Japanese attack on China in Manchuria.

38. In Article XI sanctions were not mentioned, and the obligations of the Council were stated in the most general terms. These obligations could be interpreted as giving the right to take drastic action, but in the light of other articles it was difficult to find in them any right to use force against a State. In actual practice a number of dangerous situations that arose between small States were dealt with successfully under Article XI, and a technique which involved such matters as the setting up of commissions of enquiry and the establishment of neutral zones was gradually developed.

39. In the Protocol of 1924 an attempt was made to make the sanctions 'automatic' by setting up an elaborate set of rules. But the discussions showed that such a course was impossible. Sanctions depend upon the will of Governments and peoples and cannot be automatically brought into existence.

40. As has been noted above, one test of aggression is the acceptance or refusal of some method of settling the dispute. But the acceptance may by merely a method of delay while preparations for aggression are being made (as in the case of Italy's attack on Abyssinia) or actual force is used (as in Japan's attack on China). It can be argued that in both these cases the lack of effective action was due not to any defect in the Articles of the Covenant but to the lack of will on the part of the other States, and notably of the Great Powers involved, to go to war with the recalcitrant State. But it was also true that Japan was able to use her right of veto under Article XI to place obstacles in the way of the necessary enquiry, and that preventive action against Italy before she attacked was difficult to take legally under the Covenant. Under the Locarno Treaties the signatory States could act without League authority in the case of 'flagrant aggression', but not preventively. If the question of Germany's rearmament had been brought before the Council it is not easy to see what sanctions could have been taken against her under the Covenant.

41. In actual fact there was never any doubt, in the cases in which the League of Nations was concerned, as to the identity of the aggressor, though sometimes as to the character of the provocation to aggression. States, it is true, adapted their actions and procedure to the language and resolutions adopted at Geneva and later to the Pact of Paris. But in no case were the real intentions and motives of the aggressive States concealed from the Governments of the other members of the League or from public opinion. The discussions at the Council and the Assembly made them sufficiently clear.

42. This experience suggests that too rigid a definition of the occasion for action is as likely to hinder as to facilitate the maintenance of peace and security. If the World Council is given power to act for this purpose it will be able to work out for itself the necessary procedure in the light of experience. It will be easier also in such circumstances to refer matters to regional associations if any such come into existence which can be used for that purpose.

43. At the same time the principles and objects governing the actions of Members will have been laid down in the Preamble to the document bringing the Organisation into existence. These, as suggested in Part I of Memorandum A, should include not only the maintenance of peace and security but also respect for the 'sovereign equality' and 'political independence' of its Members. If, therefore, it is laid down that the World Council shall only take action in accordance with these principles and objects, action for other purposes will be excluded. It is suggested that States will be protected from arbitrary action by the World Council as much by this safeguard as by elaborate definition, while the World Council will be more free to act to protect States from violence.

V. *Conclusions*

44. *As to the Pacific Settlements of Disputes*—

(i) That all States should promise to settle their disputes by peaceful means in such a manner that international peace and security are not endangered.

(ii) That justiciable disputes should generally be decided by a Permanent Court of International Justice.

(iii) That other disputes should be subjected to a process of discussion and conciliation in the World Council, which should have power to determine the procedure to be followed without the consent of the parties to the dispute.

45. *As to Guarantees*—

(i) That all Members should undertake to co-operate to the utmost of their power in the maintenance of international peace and security, and that the World Council should be required to take the initiative for this purpose.

(ii) That no guarantee should be given of the territorial integrity of Members.

(iii) That no guarantee should be given of the political independence of Members, but that respect for it should be recognised as one of the principles of the organisation.

46. *As to the conditions in which action should be taken for the maintenance of peace and security*—

That there should be no attempt to lay down in advance any rigid definition of the occasions on which such action should be taken, but that the Members of the Organisation and the World Council should only be empowered to take action in accordance with the principles and objects of the Organisation.

Memorandum C

1. THE MILITARY ASPECT OF ANY POST-WAR SECURITY ORGANISATION (a)

1. *Introduction*

1. The Moscow Declaration on General Security contemplates the creation, at the earliest possible date, of an international organisation charged with the maintenance of world peace and security. This organisation is to be founded on the principle of the sovereign equality of all peace-loving States, and all such States are to be eligible for membership.

2. An attempt is made in the present paper to sketch out the general lines on which the organisation of International Security might be attempted after the conclusion of the present war. The proposals deal, however, with the form which the Permanent Security Organisation might eventually take and do not relate to the intervening period. During this last period it is evident that some temporary arrangements will have to be made, but these will be obviously affected if there is some previous general agreement as to the form which the permanent organisation might assume.

2. *General Considerations*

A. *Nature of the Organisation*

3. The proposed world organisation, whatever its form, is bound to fail unless:

(*a*) The U.K., U.S.A., U.S.S.R. and China continue to co-operate wholeheartedly in its support.

(*b*) The governments and peoples of those Powers at least retain the will to enforce peace.

(*c*) The organisation is simple, its objects are clear-cut, and the machinery is of a kind to which member States are already accustomed.

B. *The Objects*

4. The objects should be:

(*a*) to disarm Germany and Japan;

(*b*) to keep them disarmed, and

(a) U3319/180/70.

(*c*) to prevent them or any other aggressor from again upsetting the peace of the world.

C. *The Means*

5. The proposed organisation will have to rely, in the main, on the combined military forces of the United Nations and, in particular, of the Four Powers, working together to a common end. Most of the States concerned are already accustomed to such a system.

6. Economic measures, also, may operate to deter potential aggressors, but unless backed by force or the effective threat of it are unlikely to prove an adequate check on a State which is, itself, ready to resort to force.

D. *The Idea of an 'International Police Force'*

7. In some quarters it is contended that the co-ordination of military forces could best be expressed in a completely international 'Police Force'. Whatever its theoretical merits, this postulates a greater advance in international co-operation than States are yet prepared to make, as it implies the existence of a world State. Practical questions of size, composition, maintenance, location and command would give rise to controversies on which international agreement would almost certainly be unobtainable.

8. We conclude that the time has not yet come for the creation of such an international force.

3. *Proposals*

A. *Higher Military Organisation*

9. The proposed world organisation implies the existence of some sort of World Council. This Council will need military advice and this advice will have to be given by States, not individually but in concert. Apart from the 'strategic' side of the work, e.g., the preparation of plans to resist potential aggression, there are a number of general questions such as the regulation of armaments on which combined military advice will be required.

10. If the Higher Military Organisation is to advise the World Council and provide machinery whereby plans can be made in advance and the efforts of the forces of member States co-ordinated, it follows that it must form part of, and receive directions from, the World Council.

11. It thus becomes clear that there will have to be a Military Staff Committee serving the World Council.

B. *Composition of the Military Staff Committee*

12. Since for many years to come the Four Powers will have to play the predominant part in safeguarding world peace, the perma-

nent members of this Committee should be the military representatives of those Powers. The co-operation of States other than the Four Powers will, however, be essential in providing forces and making available bases, shipping and other facilities, and these States will expect to be given a voice corresponding to their obligations. These States should, therefore, be associated in some form or other with the work of the Military Staff Committee. The form which this association should take raises difficult problems, and must depend to a considerable extent on the form which the World Council itself takes. As a beginning, the Committee might be strengthened, when dealing with particular security problems, by the addition of military representatives of States having special concern with the question under discussion.

13. It is important that the members of the World Council should not receive military advice from more than one source. It is, therefore, essential that the members of the Military Staff Committee should be the supreme military authorities in their own countries, or their representatives.

C. *Functions of the Military Staff Committee*

14. The primary duty of the Committee would be to prepare and keep up to date plans for the prevention of any renewed aggression by Germany or Japan, or by any other State which might at any time give signs of becoming an aggressor. The Committee would also be responsible for any necessary co-ordination of the national forces of the member States.

D. *Force at the Disposal of the World Council*

15. The World Council would dispose of the aggregate of the national forces which member States were prepared to place at its disposal for the purpose of resisting aggression. On an emergency arising, it would be for the World Council, on the advice of the Military Staff Committee, to decide what proportion of the forces at its disposal would be needed to deal with the situation.

16. The mere existence of national forces and their availability in emergency would not, however, by itself, suffice to ensure the maintenance of security, even if plans for their employment were made in advance by the Military Staff Committee. It would be essential that these forces should have worked together in time of peace if their co-operation were to be smooth and efficient in time of emergency. In this connection it is difficult to exaggerate the psychological effect of constant co-operation.

E. *Co-operation between Forces of different States*

17. In time of peace co-operation could best be fostered:

(*a*) By the joint garrisoning or occupation of certain areas; and (*b*) By means of joint cruises and flights, and other joint exercises.

There are a number of areas which a more detailed study may show to be suitable for joint occupation. The Kiel Canal area is a case in point. As regards joint exercises, it is desirable that displays of force should periodically be made with the object of impressing would-be aggressors.

18. The rights and facilities necessary for joint garrisoning or occupation, joint exercises and joint access to ports and airfields would have to be secured by agreement between member States and, where necessary, by express provisions in the peace treaties with ex-enemy States. The question of bases is very complicated and is dealt with in Part II of this paper.

4. *Regions*

19. There is considerable support for the suggestion that, for purposes of an international security system, the world should be divided into fixed regions, each containing forces which, under the supreme control of a World Council, would be responsible for preventing aggression in that region. It has been argued that such an arrangement would limit the military commitments of the smaller States and increase efficiency and rapidity of action.

20. From a military point of view, there are certain objections to a world organisation constructed on a basis of separate regions. These objections may be stated as follows:

(*a*) It is impossible to draw the boundary of a region so as to confine within it all military operations which the member States in that region might have to undertake.

(*b*) If an attempt were made to fix the operational boundary of a region, States on the perimeter would necessarily form part of the neighbouring geographical region. Thus neighbouring regions would overlap extensively.

(*c*) The defence arrangements of some Powers are based primarily on sea and air power, which do not lend themselves to regionalisation.

The advantages of regional organisation may be summarised as follows:

(*a*) The main attraction of a regional political organisation is that it would give the smaller nations a more direct concern in security problems, and so encourage their co-operation in security measures, thus reducing the burden on the Four Powers.

(*b*) Regional organisation might increase the efficiency and rapidity of both political and military action by member States of the region.

(*c*) A regional organisation, through its attached military staff, would facilitate military co-operation between the States concerned.

21. An argument in favour of the proposals contained in this paper is that the suggested military organisation is not dependent on the existence of regional political councils, yet could be adapted to a regional system if the latter proved desirable on political grounds. In such a case the Military Staff Committee would serve to co-ordinate the activities of the military staffs attached to the regional organisations.

5. *Conclusions*

22. Our conclusions, therefore, are as follows:

(*a*) Any complete international 'Police Force' is impracticable in present circumstances.

(*b*) The success of any world security organisation depends on the whole-hearted co-operation of the principal member States and on their resolution to use force to prevent aggression.

(*c*) The object, in the first instance, of any world security organisation should be the prevention of renewed aggression by Germany and Japan.

(*d*) Forces for this purpose would have to be placed by Member States at the disposal of the organisation as requisite.

(*e*) Military advice and direction would be afforded to such World Council as may be set up by a military staff composed of the supreme military authorities of appropriate Member States or their representatives.

(*f*) National forces associated for the above purpose should train and work together in peace to the greatest possible extent.

(*g*) There would be some military difficulty in the division of the world for security purposes into fixed geographical regions, but, if Regional *Political* Councils were set up as part of some world organisation, it would follow that they should have Military Advisory Staffs, and this might facilitate local co-operation.

NOTE—It will be noticed that the system proposed above differs from the system which existed prior to the war in the following three main points:

(*a*) The establishment of an effective Military Staff Committee of the World Council with power to formulate plans and to co-ordinate the action of national forces prior to any emergency which may necessitate their action.

(*b*) The joint garrisoning of certain areas by combined detachments of national forces.

(*c*) The training and exercising together of national forces in peace time, making use of certain specified seaports and airfields.

Memorandum D

(a) CO-ORDINATION OF POLITICAL AND ECONOMIC INTERNATIONAL MACHINERY

There will inevitably be set up, as part of the permanent international system, a number of specialised bodies dealing with economic and social questions. Some of these bodies have already been considered in considerable detail, e.g., the Permanent Organisation for Food and Agriculture. Others are in earlier stages of development. There are already in existence the technical organisations attached to the League of Nations, such as those which deal with Health, the abolition of the Drug Traffic, Transport, etc.

2. It will be necessary to make provision—

(*a*) To co-ordinate the activities of these bodies on their technical side.

(*b*) To bring them into relation with the World Organisation.

3. The obvious methods by which these objects can be achieved are by means of discussions both between the specialised organisations themselves and in the world organisation, and by means of an economic and social secretariat attached to the World Council.

4. No doubt some form of consultation will be arranged between the specialised bodies themselves so that their activities may be directed towards a common end. This co-ordination will be assisted by the existence of an economic and social secretariat attached to the World Council. The specialised international bodies should also have the obligation of sending reports to the World Organisation as well as to their constituent members. These reports can be considered and discussed in the World Organisation, so far as it is desirable to do so, in order to facilitate co-operation between the specialised bodies and the maintenance of international peace and security.

5. These discussions will be assisted by the existence of an economic and social secretariat attached to the World Council, and there may thus come into being for economic and social questions an equivalent to the machinery which (see Memorandum A, paragraph 38 [37]?), will, it is hoped, be in existence for political questions.

Memorandum E

METHOD AND PROCEDURE FOR ESTABLISHING A WORLD ORGANISATION

It may be hoped that the exchange of memoranda and preliminary discussions between the three Powers will result in a considerable

(a) Copy from U4072/180/70.

measure of agreement. The question thus arises how such agreement shall be recorded, in what form it shall be submitted to the three Governments for their approval, and how and when the views of the other United Nations shall be obtained.

2. In Article 4 of the Moscow Declaration the Four Powers recognised the necessity of establishing an international organisation 'at the earliest practicable date', and an obligation lies on them to make every effort to fulfil this promise.

3. Moreover, if agreement can be obtained between the United Nations on a definite scheme to maintain international peace and security a new hope will arise in the world which may do much to render less difficult the painful process of reconstruction. The reception of the Moscow Declaration by public opinion shows how anxious the world is to receive some assurance that such a scheme is ready for adoption.

4. There appear to be considerable advantages in obtaining at the earliest possible moment agreement on the essentials of the permanent International Organisation, leaving the more detailed working out of its several parts to a later stage.

5. If it is decided to set up any regional associations in any part of the world it will be much easier to fashion them in accordance with a general plan after the outline of the World Organisation has been determined.

6. Moreover, the existence of such an agreement will facilitate negotiation for the establishment of specialised and technical bodies. It will also make possible the adaptation of such parts of the temporary machinery set up immediately after the war as it is desired to incorporate in the permanent Organisation.

7. In the Moscow Declaration the Four Powers have assumed a responsibility for the maintenance of peace and security pending the establishment of a general system of security. This duty is likely to be less onerous if the other United Nations, and possibly States now neutral, are associated with the Four Powers for that purpose at the earliest possible date. In this way the new permanent Organisation will more quickly become a reality and take its proper position in the new world community.

8. Moreover, the Treaties of Peace will be more easily made if the form and character of the new permanent organisation are already known. Solutions of difficult problems will be more easily found and there is less likelihood of decisions being made which are incompatible with the terms of the permanent organisation.

9. It is suggested, therefore, that the aim of the preliminary talks at Washington should be to reach such agreement as can be referred to the three Governments in the form of a Draft Declaration, similar to that signed at Moscow but containing in its several clauses a more

extended survey of the objects and principles of the permanent International Organisation and an outline of the machinery which it is proposed to set up to obtain them.

10. It may be necessary to omit from the draft Declaration many important particulars, e.g., the exact methods by which the members of the World Council are chosen and their number. Some of these points may perhaps be left to the new organisation itself to determine. But it may be hoped that agreement may be obtained on what political bodies shall be set up, e.g., a World Assembly, a World Council and a World Court; on the principles on which action will be taken for the pacific settlement of disputes and the maintenance of international peace and security; on the necessity for agreeing some permanent method by which the military forces necessary to maintain international peace and security can be co-ordinated; and on the principles which shall govern the relations of the specialised organisations with one another and with the World Council and World Assembly.

11. It will then be for the Governments of the three Powers to determine how far they can approve the draft Declaration and it may be necessary to have a more formal exchange of views between them for this purpose.

12. If agreement is thus obtained it will be necessary to communicate it to the other United Nations for consideration, and immediately thereafter to publish it. After a suitable interval the United Nations would be invited to attend a Conference at which the Declaration, with such amendments as had been found desirable, would be definitely adopted.

13. It should then be possible to set up a body to work out a more detailed instrument in the form of a Convention or Treaty on the lines of the Declaration. It would be the coming into force of this instrument, after the ordinary procedure required for ratification, which would bring the Permanent Organisation into existence. The exact date on which it was put into force might well be left to be determined by the Four Powers who are specially responsible for the maintenance of international peace and security in the interim period.

14. This method would have the advantage that, while the Permanent Organisation can, of course, only be brought into existence with the full consent of the Governments concerned after they have consulted the peoples which they represent, its form and character will have been to a large extent decided in consequence of the adoption of the Declaration. Many of the Governments of the United Nations might find it impossible to sign a treaty at that stage. Some of them may not survive the transition from war to peace. But many of them could record their agreement to a Declaration of the kind

described and so prepare the way for themselves or their successors to take part in the preparation and signature of the final instrument.

The Armistice and Post-War Committee, after considering the five memoranda and the covering note submitted to them by Mr. Law's Committee, circulated a report on them to the War Cabinet on April 22, 1944. The first question which they raised was whether His Majesty's Government in the United Kingdom should come into the proposed new scheme as the United Kingdom or as the British Empire. Under the scheme great weight was rightly thrown on the Great Powers. We could not, however, be certain whether individual Dominions would wish to be considered as component parts of a British Empire *bloc*, operating as a single Great Power, or as individual small nations. The Dominions and the smaller Powers might also be alarmed at the absence of specific guarantees of territorial integrity and political independence, and by the authority given to the World Council, composed of the Great Powers, to determine the method of settling disputes. On the other hand an undertaking of members to respect the political independence of one another appeared in the principles of the World Organisation (Memorandum A, paragraph 11). (a)

The Committee recognised that some difficulty might be experienced over the question of Dominion representation on the World Council. We should try to secure such representation but if we pressed for it we might get a demand from Russia for the representation of her constituent republics.

In their discussion of the memoranda the Committee proposed a number of minor changes. The only question which led to considerable discussion was that of earmarking certain specific forces as at the immediate disposal of the Great Powers. The majority of the Committee regarded such earmarking as essential, but the Vice-Chiefs of Staff felt that it would be impracticable to go beyond an acceptance in principle of the plan. This question was discussed on May 3 with the Vice-Chiefs of Staff, and, on their suggestion, a new wording was proposed for Memorandum C, paragraph 15:[1] 'For the purpose of dealing with major aggression it is contemplated that when necessary the full resources of all Member States would be made available. To deal with minor emergencies, part of the obligation to be assumed by Member States would be the earmarking of a quota of their national forces or other resources to be at the disposal of the Council. It would be for the (b)

[1] This wording was not included in the memorandum as circulated to the War Cabinet, but was incorporated in it before the memoranda were given to the Dominion Prime Ministers.

(a) APW(44) 1st meeting; WP(44)220.
(b) APW(44) 2nd, 3rd and 4th meetings; APW(44)10, 15.

World Council to decide on the advice of the Military Staff Committee:

(i) What the size and composition of the quotas of individual States should be
(ii) in the event of an emergency arising what particular forces should be called on to deal with it.'

(a) The War Cabinet did not discuss at this time the memoranda in detail or the points raised by the Armistice and Post-War Committee. There was, however, an informal exchange of views on post-war organisation at a Cabinet meeting on April 27. No definite conclusions were reached, but the general view expressed was that the real authority and force in shaping the future of the world lay with the three or four Great Powers. The Prime Minister mentioned favourably the proposal for setting up Regional Councils for Europe, America, and Asia, and—less probably—for Africa.

(b) On May 4, 1944, Mr. Eden sent a summary of the five memoranda to the Prime Minister and asked for his consent to their circulation to the Dominion Prime Ministers. With the Prime Minister's agreement the drafts of the five papers were given to the Dominion Prime Ministers on May 8 and discussed at their meeting in London on May 11, 1944. The Foreign Office drew up a covering note explaining the circumstances in which the papers had been written and the general policy outlined in them. The note was largely on the lines of the note submitted by Mr. Law to the War Cabinet. It stated that the memoranda were put forward merely to serve as a basis of study, and that the British Government were not committed to the proposals in them.

(iv)

The Prime Minister's proposals for a World Peace Council, and for three Regional Councils and a 'United States of Europe': withdrawal of the Prime Minister's proposals: Foreign Office suggestions for meeting the Prime Minister's requirements: redraft of certain paragraphs in the British memoranda (May 8–June 2, 1944).

During this period in which the Foreign Office were formulating and co-ordinating British proposals for a world organisation, they had some difficulty in convincing the Prime Minister. Mr. Churchill at this time was occupied, among other things, with the complex and momentous military problems of the cross-Channel invasion.

(a) U4098/180/70. (b) PMM(44)4; U3872, 4072/180/70.

It was not therefore possible for him to find to time to study in detail the large number of Foreign Office and other departmental papers on matters of post-war organisation. He therefore tended to keep to certain general ideas which he had already expressed to President Roosevelt and Stalin on the nature of post-war security arrangements.

On May 8, 1944, the Prime Minister put forward his views in a (a) memorandum in connexion with the meeting of Dominion Prime Ministers in London. He wrote that he was in general agreement with the Foreign Office memorandum[1] and that his differences from it were largely in 'emphasis and degree'. He thought that a World Peace Council should come into existence at the time of the armistice with Germany, or, if possible, earlier. This Council would consist at first of the British Empire and Commonwealth, the United States, the U.S.S.R. and, for the reasons put forward by Mr. Eden,[2] China. These four Powers would probably be actively engaged in the defeat of Japan and would thus be in the closest military contact. Hence after the war they would naturally take the lead in regulating the immediate transition from war to peace, and in setting up a world organisation to preserve peace.

This organisation might consist of the World Peace Council, the World Court, a consultative Assembly upon which all recognised States, except Germany and Japan would have a place. The position of the 'satellities' who had become 'co-belligerents' would have to be examined. The World Peace Council would also set up as soon as possible three Regional Councils: a Council of Asia, which in the first instance would be, practically, the War Council of those States which had been fighting Japan, a Council of Europe, and a Council of the Americas or, alternatively, of the Western Hemisphere. Each Regional Council would consist of twelve to twenty representatives, and would send one member to the World Council. The method of choosing such representatives would be open to discussion, but, in order to avoid the undue predominance of any one Power, the representative of a Regional Council should not be of the same nationality as any of the four Powers already on the Council. We should, however, encourage the representation on the Regional Councils of the original four members of the World Council, e.g. we should hope that

---

[1] It is not wholly clear whether the Prime Minister was referring to the covering note or to the memoranda as a whole. He used the reference number PMM(44)4 under which the memoranda were circulated to the Dominion Prime Ministers.

[2] In the summary of the memoranda sent on May 4 to the Prime Minister, Mr. Eden (b) wrote: 'China must also be a Member, and though she is obviously not at present a Great Power, her population, resources, and relations with the United States make it necessary to treat her as such.'

(a) PMM(44)5; U4194/180/70. (b) U3872/180/70.

the United States, the Soviet Union, and the United Kingdom would be represented on the European Regional Council, and that we should be represented on the Council of the Americas, either by ourselves or through Canada, and that we and all Powers, including the Dominions, with Pacific or Indian interests, should be represented on the Asiastic Regional Council.

The Regional Councils would have the duty of doing all they could do to improve the prosperity and harmony of their respective regions; their first obligation would be to prevent the rearmament of the vanquished Powers and to try to allay at any early stage potential causes of war. Neither the Regional Councils nor their members would be entitled to make war on any other Power, but they would enjoy all rights of self-defence. In the event of a threat of war they must lay their case before the World Council which would take the measures necessary to prevent violent outbreaks. They must also be ready to co-operate by armed force, or by any other way required of them, in carrying out decisions of the World Council or procuring compliance with decisions of the World Court approved by the World Council. There would also be a number of functional Committees, covering part or all of the world, and dealing with particular economic or financial questions or questions connected with aviation, the welfare of backward races, illicit drug traffic, etc. The Prime Minister pointed out that the plan contemplated derogations from national sovereignty only in connection with the prevention of war. The World Council would attempt to reduce armaments only by persuasion, except in the case of the guilty Powers disarmed by the Peace Treaty. The members of the World Council would, however, be under an obligation to maintain sufficient armaments in aggregate to overawe any Power or group of Powers seeking to pursue policy by war.

Finally the Prime Minister hoped that the British Empire would find itself unitedly able to pursue (i) 'The Union of our World-Wide Brotherhood by every lawful and innocuous means'; (ii) 'a Fraternal Association with the United States', possibly in the form of maintaining the machinery of the Combined Chiefs of Staff and the reciprocal use of bases, at any rate until a period in the world had been reached when 'words and wishes of peace have been translated into facts, thoughts and customs deeply rooted in the hearts of men'. (iii) Within this framework, and, the Prime Minister hoped, with the agreement of the Dominions, the United Kingdom should help and favour the formation of a 'United States of Europe'. This organism would arise naturally out of the European Regional Council and might well take as its model the British Empire and Dominions, with all the additional intimacy which would come from geographical proximity. 'In this way only'—so Mr. Churchill concluded—'can the glory of Europe rise again and its ancient nations dwell together in peace and mutual goodwill instead of tearing themselves and the world to pieces in their frightful and recurring quarrels.'

The Foreign Office thought that Mr. Churchill's plan for a Council of Europe was not practicable since—if it included United States representatives—it would be hardly distinguishable from the World Council, at all events in matters concerned with the settlement of disputes. From the point of view of British interests, the most questionable suggestion in the memorandum was the proposal for a 'United States of Europe'; the Foreign Office, however, did not think that there was any chance of the Russians agreeing to it, since they would regard it as restoring the power of Germany.[1] (a)

The Prime Minister withdrew his paper after the discussions with the Dominion Prime Ministers because he found that they objected to his proposed Councils of the Americas and of Asia and to his plan that the Dominions should be represented on the World Council by the United Kingdom. He wanted the Foreign Office to make a further study of the plan for a Council of Europe, and to keep in mind the ultimate possibility of a 'United States of Europe'. (b)

There was at first some doubt in the Foreign Office about the Prime Minister's instructions. It seemed, however, that the Prime Minister had not changed his own views; he merely wanted the Foreign Office to re-examine their papers from the point of view of emphasis, and to recast them in order to show 'in more non-committal terms' the 'alternative solutions to particular problems'.

Mr. Eden therefore sent to the Prime Minister on May 15 a minute with two documents, of which the first was an insertion proposed for the 'covering note' to the Dominion Prime Ministers. The second document consisted of revised versions of certain passages in Memoranda A and B. Mr. Eden thought that the effect of these additions and revisions would be to draw attention to the Prime Minister's suggestions and to set out the arguments for and against these suggestions. Mr Eden also proposed that the revised documents should be circulated to the Dominion Prime Ministers in order to get their opinions as quickly as possible. (c)

The insertion in the covering note was to be made in the following terms:[2]

'4. The Moscow Declaration in Article 4 laid down the principle of a general organisation, though it reserved in Article 5 the special

---

[1] For a further criticism in the Foreign Office of the Prime Minister's proposals for Europe, and for alternative suggestions, see also Chapter LXIV, section (i).

[2] These new paragraphs were to follow the summary of events since the Moscow Declaration. See above, p. 89.

(a) U4194/180/70. (b) U4367/180/70. (c) U4367/180/70.

position of the Four Powers in maintaining peace and security on behalf of the community of nations during the interim period.

5. The problem of a world organisation can, however, be considered in a very concrete way if it is envisaged as a combination of the three Great Powers, the British Commonwealth, the United States and the Union of Soviet Socialist Republics, and China linking up the continental organisations in which the other States find their due place. The world might then be organised in the three continental *blocs* of Europe, Asia and the Western Hemisphere each with its own special machinery adapted to its own special needs. (Africa must remain under the final control of the British Commonwealth and France, while the Middle East will be in the charge of the United Kingdom with such assistance as the United States and the U.S.S.R. may, perhaps, find it necessary to give there.) The advantages of such a system are fourfold.

6. In the first place it will foster that European unity which should emerge out of European civilisation and enable the problems of Europeans to be decided by Europeans themselves in a "United States of Europe", without the participation of other States which can only be partially aware of the vital factors involved. The same is true of the problems of the Western Hemisphere and of Asia in each of which the relative scales of power and values are quite different to those of Europe.

7. Secondly, if the Continents were each represented on the World Council in addition to the Four Powers, it would enable that body to be constructed so as to be representative of the whole world yet sufficiently small in numbers to be capable of rapid and efficient action.

8. Thirdly it would enable the smaller States to combine together with their neighbours to form compact *blocs* of power inside the continental organisation and thus prevent their weakness from offering a temptation to the rapacity of stronger states.

9. Fourthly it would help towards the solution of many economic and technical problems, and in particular those of transport and power which must play so great a part in the modern world.

10. It is of course impossible to bring into existence immediately a fully developed regional system. In the meantime however some United Nations Commission for Europe, such as was suggested in the Foreign Secretary's memorandum of July 1, 1943,[1] could be set up in which the smaller States of Europe could be associated with the three Powers in the responsibility of controlling the occupation of Germany, the disarmament of her satellites, and gradually the establishment of European or regional functional bodies, such as transport, within the framework of the World Organisation.

11. It is more difficult to foresee what will happen in Asia and the Pacific, but at any rate in South-East Asia and the South-West Pacific

---

[1] See above, p. 51.

regional organisations should come into existence which may ultimately share with China in the establishment of some common institutions for the whole area in which the British Commonwealth would be strongly represented. In the Western Hemisphere the framework of a continental organisation already exists, and it will be for the United States to take the lead in making it more compact and united than it has hitherto been.

12. Meanwhile the maintenance of world peace would remain as the special charge of the British Commonwealth, the United States and the U.S.S.R. with China contributing in her own special sphere. It might be necessary for the three Powers to intervene in either Europe or Asia with commanding authority and power if any threat to world peace seemed to be emerging out of the play of forces. But they would so far as possible encourage the other States to co-operate together in the settlement of their own problems in such a manner as finally to reach the objectives of a "United States of Europe" and its equivalent in the other continents.

13. But though this objective should be constantly in the mind of our delegation at Washington it is not possible to state it there explicitly or include it in the papers which we have undertaken to exchange before the meeting with the United States and the U.S.S.R. Mr. Hull has committed himself publicly to a world organisation of a quite different kind, and we have been repeatedly warned by Mr. Hull and others that any attempt to organise the world on continental lines before the world organisation itself is set up would probably cause the United States to refuse any permanent responsibility outside its own hemisphere. To suggest, therefore, that the discussions in Washington should run on these lines might mean abandoning the whole project and with it the best chance that we possess of associating the United States permanently with the British Commonwealth in the maintenance of world peace and security. We must, therefore, seek to secure these objectives by indirect means so far as possible inside a world organisation based on a drastic reorganisation of the League of Nations in the light of the experience of these last fateful 25 years. By enhancing the role of the Council in which the Four Powers combine, by limiting its membership and ensuring so far as possible that the other members represent as far as practicable the different continents, an organisation will be obtained in which there will be opportunity for the regional and ultimately continental organisations to grow up. The same objective can be kept in view in any regional security organisations which may come into existence. But the offers of co-operation which we make to the United States and the U.S.S.R. must be based on a world organisation and not on the separation of the world into continents and regions.

14. Our five papers therefore are on the five topics enumerated above and are designed, subject to any observations on the part of the Dominion Prime Ministers, to be handed . . .' (a)

(a) U4367/180/70.

The redrafts of certain paragraphs in Memoranda A and B were as follows:

Memorandum A

'15.[1] Though the status of all Members is equal and all will enjoy the same rights and undertake the corresponding obligations, their differences in power make necessary some recognition of differences in function. The initiative for the formation of the Organisation has come from the Four Powers, the United States, the U.S.S.R., the United Kingdom and China, and it is generally recognised that its success will depend more upon their continued co-operation than on any other single factor. The machinery of the organisation should make it possible for them to carry out the responsibilities which they will have agreed to undertake. They must be given, therefore, a special position in the organisation in order effectively to maintain peace and security. In general, the more power and responsibility can be made to correspond, the more likely is it that the machinery will be able to fulfil its functions.'

'18.[2] Just as there are special functional organisations, so there should be regional association when there is obvious advantage to be obtained by limitation of the sphere of action. For instance, it is possible that out of some "United Nations Commission for Europe" as proposed in Mr. Eden's memorandum of July 1, 1943, there might grow a European organism which, under the guidance of the three major allies, might foster peaceful tendencies, heal the wounds of Europe, and at the same time prevent Germany from again dominating the Continent. Such Regional associations might also come into existence for electing representatives to a World Council, for economic co-operation, for the promotion of welfare in colonial territories, etc. It is, however, essential that they should not conflict with the world-wide organisation but rather assist it to carry out its purposes.'

'26.[3] The *constitution* of this body [the World Council] raises many difficult problems. The relation between the Great Powers and other States has been a matter of dispute for over a century. It is clearly necessary that the Four Powers, which between them are directly responsible for the peace and security of nearly two-thirds of the world's inhabitants, should always be represented on it. The principle has been generally accepted that where the interests of any State are specially affected it should have the right to lay its case before the Council.

27. While it is desirable that the World Council should be strictly limited in size, and while it would be desirable, from many points of view, that its membership should be restricted to the three or four

---

[1] See above, p. 94. [2] See above p. 95. [3] See above, p. 96.

Powers upon whom the responsibility for maintaining peace principally depends, it is open to question whether the other States would agree to the establishment of a Council so limited in number. In this case the number and method of their representation is a matter for grave consideration and the manner in which the decisions of the Council shall be made may depend on the method adopted. The object would be to ensure that the other States on the World Council command general confidence. Some form of election is probably essential and the World Assembly might be used for this purpose.'

'30.[1] Should Regional Associations of sufficient importance be formed (e.g. the Regional Council for Europe) they might furnish a basis for representation on the Council. But for the most part States do not recognise other States as "representing" them on institutions in which they have a major interest.'

Memorandum B

'13[2] Even on questions of principle (as opposed to questions of procedure) decisions might be taken by (say) a two-thirds majority of the Council rather than by unanimity. In all such cases all the Four Powers should of course be included in the majority. In any event, the votes of the parties to the dispute should not be taken into account.

14. States are not likely to bind themselves to accept the decision of the Council in all cases. Nor would it be likely that they would undertake the obligation to enforce it on other States in all cases. But it would still be the function of the World Council, and particularly of the Great Powers on it, to see that disputes did not threaten peace and security and for the other States to co-operate with it to the utmost of their power for that purpose, so that there would still be large opportunities for action to deal with even the most difficult disputes.'

The revised drafts were shown informally to the Dominion (a)
representatives on May 17, 1944, and discussed unofficially, since Mr. Churchill had not yet given his opinion on them. Mr. Fraser, Prime Minister of New Zealand, took strong exception to them, especially if they were to be taken as guidance for the United Kingdom representatives in the discussions on the World Organisation with the Americans and the Russians. Mr. Fraser wrote to Mr. Eden on May 18 that the New Zealand Government were fundamentally opposed to the idea of organising the world in three continental *blocs*, and that he had assumed that, with the withdrawal of the Prime Minister's paper, no further plan of this kind would be put forward. Mr. Eden sent Mr. Fraser's letter to the Prime Minister, with the comment that he believed these views to be held by other Dominion Ministers.

---

[1] See above, p. 97. [2] See above, p. 100.

(a) U4406/180/70; U4562/180/70.

(a) The Prime Minister replied on May 21 that he had withdrawn his paper on the assumption that the original Foreign Office paper[1] was to be amended 'in the sense of weighing the alternatives of regional organisations under the supreme body versus general mob. We were not to declare ourselves against regional organisations nor in favour of them; but to leave the arguments in a balanced way on each side.'

The Prime Minister asked for the 'revise' of the Foreign Office paper. He added: 'the only thing I am pressing for is a United States of Europe in some form or other, with a Council of its own of which I trust Russia, Great Britain and the United States will be members.' Mr. Eden considered an answer drafted for him on May 22 that the amendments to the Foreign Office paper had been sent to the Prime Minister with his (Mr. Eden's) minute of May 15. The paper had not been reprinted as a whole because Mr. Eden wanted first to get the Prime Minister's agreement to the changes. On May 23 Mr. Eden also considered sending another minute to the Prime Minister to the effect that there was now no real difference of view between them on the establishment of some regional organisation provided that it were linked up with the World Organisation. Mr. Eden also thought of giving the Prime Minister a copy of Mr. Jebb's paper on 'British policy in Europe'.[2]

Mr. Eden decided not to send to the Prime Minister either of the proposed minutes or, at this time, the text of Mr. Jebb's paper. Instead he sent a minute on June 2 explaining that the Dominions
(b) representatives had objected to the inclusion of some of the 'revised' passages in the covering note and the memoranda. Mr. Eden therefor proposed to substitute a new revision which would certainly satisfy the Dominions and also meet the point raised by the Prime Minister. This new revision tacitly omitted any reference to the proposed changes in the 'covering note'. It was pointed out in the Foreign Office that this covering note had not been written as an instruction to the British Delegation; it had been drawn up firstly, for use by the Armistice and Post-War Committee, and secondly for the information of the Dominion Prime Ministers. On Mr. Churchill's instructions it had been altered to include a kind of résumé of his views as an alternative to the plans contained in the five memoranda. We had undertaken to let the Americans and Russians have a considered statement of our views, and should merely confuse them if we sent them alternative, and mutally contradictory plans.

---

[1] This term is not clear, but the reference seems to be to the 'covering note' (PMM(44)4) as well as the memoranda.

[2] See below, pp. 183–5.

(a) U4635/180/70. (b) U5050/180/70.

The proposed redraft of certain paragraphs in memoranda A and B was as follows:

Memorandum A

Paragraph 15 as in redraft of May 15.[1]

'18.[2] Just as there are special functional organisations, so there may be regional associations for various purposes when there is obvious advantage to be obtained by limitation of the sphere of action. In particular there should be some regional organisation for the Continent of Europe if only to prevent a repetition of the circumstances which have caused two World Wars to originate in that area. The condition of Europe at the close of this war will demand the special care and assistance of the three Great Powers and means must be found to prevent its becoming the centre of a third world tragedy. It is possible that out of some "United Nations Commission for Europe", as proposed in Mr. Eden's memorandum of July 1943, there might grow a European organisation which under the guidance of the three major allies, might foster peaceful tendencies, heal the wounds of Europe, and at the same time prevent Germany from again dominating the Continent. Such regional associations might also come into existence for economic co-operation, for the promotion of welfare in colonial territories, etc. It is, however, essential that they should not conflict with the world-wide organisation but rather assist it to carry out its purposes.'

Paragraph 26 as in redraft of May 15.[3]

'27. It is desirable that the World Council should be strictly limited in size, and it has been suggested in some quarters that its membership should be restricted to the three or four powers upon whom the responsibility for maintaining peace principally depends. It is, however, open to question whether the other States would agree to the establishment of a Council so limited in number. In any case the number and method of their representation is a matter for grave consideration and the manner in which the decisions of the Council shall be made may depend on the method adopted. The object would be to ensure that the other States on the World Council command general confidence. Some form of election is probably essential and the World Assembly might be used for this purpose.'

Paragraph 30 as in redraft of May 15.[4]

Memorandum B. Paragraphs 13–14 as in redraft of May 15.[5]

Mr. Eden pointed out in his minute that the new paragraphs met the only point to which the Prime Minister attached capital importance—i.e. the establishment of some regional European machine

[1] See above, p. 122. [2] See above, pp. 95, 122.
[3] See above, pp. 96, 122. [4] See above, p. 123. [5] See above, p. 123.

on which the United Kingdom, the Soviet Union, and the United States would be represented. Mr. Eden mentioned that he had made very similar suggestions to the United States and Soviet Ambassadors on July 1, 1943, in accordance with a previous Cabinet decision. He enclosed a copy of his *aide mémoire*.[1] He suggested that if the Prime Minister approved of the draft revise, we should telegraph it to the Dominions. With their approval we could then send the five memoranda to the American and Soviet Governments. We should act as quickly as possible since the Americans were proposing to hold a conference in the 'fairly near future'.

(v)

Consideration by the War Cabinet and the Armistice and Post-War Committee of the instructions to the British Delegation to the Dumbarton Oaks Conference; American proposals for a World Organisation (June 26–August 4, 1944).

On June 26 Mr. Eden asked the Prime Minister whether he would (a) be able to give an early decision on the papers sent to him on June 2. Mr. Eden said that on May 30 Mr. Hull had told Lord Halifax that the United States Government wanted to make as early progress as possible.[2] Mr. Hull had asked when we could begin the talks. The Russians on June 21 had promised a reply in a day or two,[3] and Mr. Hull had informed the press that he was waiting to hear from the British Government and from the Russians and Chinese. We had suggested earlier that time would be saved by an exchange of written 'studies' before the official talks. We therefore ought to decide upon the final texts of our memoranda.

The Prime Minister answered on June 29 that Mr. Eden should (b) bring the question before the War Cabinet. Mr. Eden therefore circulated to the War Cabinet on July 3 the revised copies of the five memoranda and the covering note. He explained that these memoranda had been considered at the meeting with the Prime Ministers of the Commonwealth; certain alterations had then been made in Memoranda A and B, but that C, D and E remained unchanged.[4] The alterations had since been discussed with the Dominions representatives at the official level; we had reason to suppose that they would be accepted by the Dominions Governments.

Mr. Eden said that the two suggestions in regard to which these Governments had, in varying degrees, expressed strong opposition were the idea of any unitary representation of the British Common-

[1] See above, p. 50. [2] See above, p. 85. [3] See above, p. 87.
[4] See, however, above, p. 115, note 1.

(a) U6210/180/70. (b) WP(44)370.

wealth and the constitution of regional *political* bodies. The Prime Ministers, however, recognised that Europe was to some extent a special case; they would probably not dissent from the creation of some machinery for dealing with the affairs of Europe on condition that the overriding authority of a World Organisation in regard to the settlement of political disputes was explicitly recognised.

The new paragraph 18[1] of Memorandum A accordingly brought forward the scheme which Mr. Eden had put forward to the Soviet and United States Ambassadors in July 1943, for a 'United Nations Commission for Europe'. The Dominion Governments had approved generally of this scheme. Mr. Eden felt strongly that at present we ought not to go further in the direction of encouraging specifically European organisations, since, apart from other dangers, we might give the Russians the impression that we were trying to organise Europe against them and we might also tend to encourage isolationism in the United States.

We had promised to send the five memoranda (or something like them) to the United States and Soviet Governments. Mr. Hull now seemed to think that we might exchange papers about three weeks before the opening of the discussions in which, at his urgent request, the Chinese Government had also been invited to take part. It was not certain when the discussions would be held, since the Russians had not yet replied to Mr. Hull's request to fix a date, but we expected the conference to meet towards the end of July.

Mr. Eden therefore asked for the approval of Memoranda A–E in order that they might be communicated to the Governments concerned after they had been finally accepted by the Dominion Governments. He called attention to the fact that on a number of points these memoranda set out alternative solutions. We had to instruct our Delegation in each of the alternatives which we preferred. Mr. Eden suggested that the Cabinet should ask the Armistice and Post-War Committee to consider all these points. Finally he pointed out that the discussions at Washington would be purely exploratory and would not commit Governments.

The War Cabinet agreed on July 7 to Mr. Eden's suggestions for (a) procedure, and accepted generally the policy laid down in the five memoranda. Mr. Eden sent the memoranda to the Armistice and Post-War Committee on July 17 with a covering note on the questions (b) to which he wished them to give special consideration. These questions were as follows:

(i) *The size of the Council.* This question had been left open in

[1] See above, p. 125.

(a) WM(44)88. (b) APW(44)45.

Memorandum A but would certainly be discussed, and might affect decisions on other points. The Russians might ask for a Council consisting solely of representatives of the Great Powers; the United States might wish to limit to four the number of small States. Mr. Eden's own view was that a Council of four Great Powers would not be a practicable solution, and that the limitation of the smaller Powers to four representatives would probably be insufficient. If, as we hoped, France were given a permanent seat among the Great Powers, the smaller Powers might have six or seven representatives, and the Council would then consist of eleven or twelve members. This number was not too large for convenience, and there were great advantages in associating a sufficient number of States to ensure the representation of different interests and continents. We should also try to secure a seat for the Dominions. On the other hand we did not want the Council to be as large as it became in 1934–5, i.e. sixteen members, and it might therefore be better to start with a smaller number than twelve. Mr. Eden suggested that we should aim at a number not smaller than nine and not larger than twelve.

(ii) *The method by which the Council should reach decisions and the question of the special status of the Great Powers in this respect.* We had suggested in Memorandum A that on questions of procedure a majority vote should suffice; there was no strong reason why the votes of the Great Powers should enjoy any special status in this regard. The more important decisions of principle taken by the Council might be of two kinds: (*a*) for the settlement of non-justiciable disputes and (*b*) for the application of force to maintain or restore peace and security. With regard to (*a*) neither we nor any other State would agree that States should be obliged to accept and carry out such decisions against their will. Any rule of this kind would imply something like the immediate creation of a super-State. Nonetheless, decisions of the Council for the settlement of disputes would carry a very great weight, and should enable a State which accepted them to count on the full support of the Council if attacked. Mr. Eden's view was that these decisions should be made only by the unanimous vote of all the members of the Council not parties to the dispute. A unanimous decision would carry more moral weight than a two-thirds majority, even though all the Great Powers not parties to the dispute were included in it. We had not found that there were in the League any inconveniences in the unanimity rule outweighing the advantages of the moral weight attached to it.

(*b*) The situation was somewhat different in the case of decisions of the Council for the application of force to maintain or restore peace and security. In such cases the responsibility for carrying out the decisions would fall mainly on the Great Powers; the decision (except as provided below) should therefore always include their votes. There was, however, much to be said for the principle that in decisions involving the application of force individual smaller States should not have the power to prevent coercive action against disturbers of the peace to whom they might be united by special ties. It was therefore desirable that a two thirds majority of the Council, including all the Great Powers, should suffice for such decisions.

The exception was that, if coercive action were directed against one of the Great Powers, the vote of this Power would not count among the votes necessary for the requisite majority. In such a case the World Organisation would become, in practice, an alliance against the dissident Great Power, and the stage would be set for a major war. It would obviously be one of the main purposes of the Organisation to prevent the occurrence of a situation of this kind. If it occurred, we should have failed, and there was little use in asking what would happen.

There was one general difficulty in these proposals. Owing to American pressure, we had to admit China as one of the Great Powers. In fact, however, China for a long time would depend so much on the other Great Powers that she would be unlikely to pursue any very independent policy in matters affecting international peace and security.

(iii) *Abstention by a Great Power.* The United States Government might suggest that in certain cases a Great Power should have the right to abstain from voting on the Council, and thus free itself from responsibility while allowing other States more immediately interested to take such action as they desired. Mr. Eden thought that such an escape clause was against the spirit and letter of our proposals that each State should assist in the maintenance of peace and security, due regard being paid to its resources, geographical position, etc. Our Delegation should therefore be instructed to oppose the insertion of any such clause.

(iv) *The question of withdrawal.* There was much to be said for making the Organisation permanent; the whole peace settlement would indeed assume the existence of a security Organisation. On the other hand, States would probably not wish to forgo in advance the right of withdrawal, and an unwilling member of the Organisation might do more harm than good. We might also wish at some time to amend the constitution of the Organisation and could hardly insist that States must be bound to remain members of an Organisation whose constitution was changed in a manner of which they did not approve. Nevertheless, if the other Powers at Washington were willing to accept a permanent organisation with no right of withdrawal, there would be advantages in agreeing to it. Obviously, if one of the three Great Powers should break its obligations and leave the

Organisation, all other States would have the right to reconsider their position.

(v) *Relation of the Council to the Military Staff Committee.* This question was of the greatest importance in building up a workable system for the maintenance of peace and security and especially for keeping Germany and Japan from again challenging the world. The Military Staff Committee would give technical advice, but decisions for translating such advice into action would have to be taken by the representatives of the Governments on the Council. Should these decisions be made directly by the whole Council, or should the Great Powers form a Defence Committee of the Council, whose normal function would be to recommend measures to the main body, but which would possess the right to act immediately if such action were necessary to maintain peace and security? Should all the States on the Council have the right to be represented on the Military Staff Committee? Mr. Eden thought that in this latter case a number of the representatives would be constantly changing, and that only the Great Powers should have representation as a right, and that other States, whether members of the Council or not, should be represented only when they had a special interest in the subjects to be discussed. If this procedure were adopted, the question of a Defence Committee of the Great Powers might be of less importance, since the control of the Great Powers would be assured primarily by their special position on the Military Staff Committee. On the other hand, the demand for machinery ensuring rapid and effective action in the event of a sudden challenge to the Organisation was so great that the smaller States might be willing to accept a Defence Committee. Mr. Eden suggested that the Delegation should discuss the whole question with the American and Russian representatives, and refer back for instructions in the light of these views.

(vi) *Regional Associations.* Mr. Eden agreed with the general view of the Dominion Prime Ministers that regional political bodies should be entirely subordinate to the World Organisation, and that they were unsuitable for the settlement of important disputes. The Prime Ministers, however, in Mr. Eden's opinion, had conceded that regional defence associations might perform a very useful role within the framework of a general world organisation. Mr. Eden said that he had been considering for some time whether there should be a regional association for the Western European or Atlantic area. The Chiefs of Staff had been asked to review a paper on the subject, and after receiving their comments Mr. Eden proposed to make some suggestions on the matter to the Armistice and Post-War Committee. He did not think it necessary to press for any reference to this subject in any draft declaration if it were likely to add to the difficulty of reaching agreement.

Mr. Eden said that paragraph 18 of Memorandum A introduced the possibility of a 'United Nations Commission for Europe'. Mr. Eden had no doubt that such a Commission would be most useful; it would be 'a projection into the peace of the European Advisory Commission', and might reinforce the Anglo-Soviet Treaty as a kind of bridge between Eastern and Western Europe. It would be designed, however, primarily as part of the machinery for 'clearing up the war' and would not necessarily form part of the eventual world machinery for maintaining peace. In particular, major political disputes in Europe would be referred to the World Council and not to a 'United Nations Commission for Europe'. Mr. Eden proposed that the Delegation should put forward an explantion on these lines to their Soviet and American colleagues.

(vii) *A fixed place for the Organisation.* This question had been left open in our memoranda, but we had assumed some fixed location, and Mr. Stettinius and his advisers seemed to agree with us. On the other hand there was reason for thinking that President Roosevelt would favour a peripatetic Council and Assembly. We should therefore instruct our Delegation that we wished the Organisation to be established in some definite place—i.e. the Secretariat at least should have a permanent home. The Council should also have a permanent seat for its normal meetings, though provision might be made, if necessary, for meetings elsewhere. The suggestion of a peripatetic Assembly offered even more difficulty. We should, however, try to avoid discussion on the actual location of the Organisation until a later stage when there was a measure of agreement on questions of principle.

(viii) *Time.* From reports of Mr. Hull's discussions with the special non-party sub-committee of the Senate, it appeared that a fairly considerable body of opinion in the United States thought that the attainment of a satisfactory peace settlement should be a previous condition of American participation in a World Organisation. On the other hand it was argued that such a settlement was among the most vital tasks of a World Organisation, and that, for this reason, and in order to secure the continuance of American co-operation, we should press very strongly for the establishment of the Organisation *before* the peace settlement. Mr. Eden suggested that the Delegation should be instructed to this effect.

The Armistice and Post-War Committee sent their report to the War Cabinet on July 24, 1944. The report, which was signed by Mr. Attlee as Chairman of the Committee, dealt in order with Mr. Eden's questions. (i) They accepted his recommendation for the size of the Council. (ii) They agreed that a two-thirds majority should be (a)

(a) WP(44)406.

adopted for decisions under category (*b*),[1] but did not think that there was sufficient justification for a distinction between cases under category (*a*) and category (*b*). Hence they recommended that the British Delegation should advocate the principle of a two-thirds majority, including the Great Powers, for cases in both categories. The Committee noted that China was to be included as a Great Power. On questions (iii), (iv) and (v) the Committee agreed with Mr. Eden's recommendations. In view of Mr. Eden's wish to postpone the framing of definite proposals for a regional association for Western Europe or the Atlantic area, the Committee made no recommendations on the matter. Otherwise they agreed with his proposals under heading (vi). They accepted the proposals under headings (vii) and (viii).

(a) The War Cabinet considered the report of the Armistice and Post-War Committee on August 4. They agreed that the recommendations of the Committee should be taken as the instructions to the British Delegation. Mr. Eden explained that, since the Committee had reported, we had received the text of the draft scheme which the United States Government proposed to bring forward at the meeting. This scheme was very satisfactory from our point of view. The only point left in doubt was a reference to arrangements for territorial trusteeships, the details of which had not been filled in. The United States Government might have omitted the details because they
(b) preferred to observe the turn taken in the discussions. Our own position was quite clear. We should hold to the policy already approved by the Cabinet that Commissions might be established for certain regions. These Commissions would provide machinery for international consultation and co-operation, but each State would remain responsible for the administration of its own territory. Our delegates should therefore be instructed to refer to London if any proposals conflicting with our views were put forward.

The Prime Minister referred to the importance of bringing the French, and also the Dutch, into the next stage of the discussions with the Americans. Our Delegation should be instructed that the meetings were for preliminary exploration and discussion on an official level. The issues involved were of great importance and the Prime Minister regretted that the pressure on the War Cabinet had been so great that they had not been able to give closer attention to such matters.

(c) The American proposals for a World Organisation, which were received on July 18, did not differ in essentials from those of the

---

[1] See above. p. 128.

(a) WM(44)101; U6806/180/70.
(b) WP(44)211; WM(44)58. (c) U6519/180/70; U6572/180/70.

United Kingdom. They defined the purpose of the proposed international organisation as (i) to maintain international peace and security and (ii) to foster conditions of stability and well-being essential to the maintenance of security and peace. The organisation would comprise, in the first instance, the United and Associated Nations and such others as they might invite, but it would be open to membership by all 'sovereign and peace-loving States'. It would have power to make effective the principle that no nation be permitted to maintain or use armed force in a manner inconsistent with the purposes of the basic instrument or give assistance to any State contrary to the preventive or enforcement action undertaken by the organisation. It would be constituted in such a manner as to allow the existence of regional organisations or arrangements or policies which might function on their own initiative or by instructions from the general organisation. It would also include arrangements for co-operation in the fields of economic and other specialised activities.

The principal organs and agencies would be a General Assembly, an Executive Council, an International Court of Justice, and a General Secretariat. There would also be additional bodies for co-operation in international economic and social activities and for territorial trusteeship.

The Assembly would consist of representatives of all Member States. Each Member would have one vote. The Executive Council would consist of four Permanent Members—the United States, the United Kingdom, the U.S.S.R. and China—and seven Members elected annually. France would be added to the Permanent Members 'whenever the Executive Council finds that a Government freely chosen by the French people has been established and is in effective control over the territory of the French Republic'.

The Executive Council would have primary responsibility for the peaceful settlement of international disputes, for the prevention of threats to peace or breaches of the peace and for such other activities as might be necessary for the maintenance of international security and peace. Each Member of the Council would have one vote, and decisions would be taken by a majority vote, including the votes of the Permanent Members, on the following matters: (*a*) the assumption of jurisdiction over a dispute (*b*) the terms of settlement of disputes (*c*) the negotiations for a general agreement on the regulation of armaments and armed forces, (*d*) the determination of a threat to peace or a breach of the peace or acts obstructing measures for the maintenance of security and peace, and (*e*) the institution and application of measures of enforcement. All other decisions would be taken by a simple majority. In every case a Member would have the right to abstain from voting but would be bound by the decision taken by the voting Members.

The draft did not make any recommendation with regard to voting in the event of a dispute in which one or more of the Permanent Members of the Council might be directly involved. It considered in some detail the machinery by which the Assembly and the Council would deal with disputes and enforce the decisions of the organisation. It also enumerated the powers and composition of an Economic and Social Council, but left blank a chapter on 'arrangements for territorial trusteeships' with a note that documents on the subject would be available later.

The draft envisaged the establishment of the organisation at the earliest practicable date, and, if possible, before the termination of hostilities. The 'four Moscow Powers' were to take immediate steps to agree in principle on the fundamental features of the plan. They would then send to the Governments of the other United and Associated Nations an agreed statement of those fundamental features and invite comments and suggestions. The next step would be a general conference of the United and Associated Nations for the formulation and signature of the Agreement which would constitute the basic instrument of the organisation.

(a) The Foreign Office were most satisfied to find that these American plans coincided largely with our own. The Americans had given rather more prominence than we had done to regional associations, and had agreed with us in admitting that the Organisation as such could not settle disputes involving the Great Powers, though it could do much to facilitate a settlement.

On the other hand the American plan was more legalistic than ours, and seemed to derive more from a 'written constitution'. The Foreign Office recommended that we should advocate generally the adoption of principles rather than rules. The American suggestions for security did not differ much from our own proposals for a military staff committee. There was, indeed, only one large contentious point—the question of territorial trusteeship. The Americans, however, were unlikely to go beyond ensuring 'accountability' and to ask that the Governments of all non-selfgoverning dependencies should furnish an annual report to a central body dependent on the World Organisation. They were unlikely to demand any measure of supervision for an international authority.

(a) U6772/180/70.

CHAPTER LXIII

The Dumbarton Oaks Conference and subsequent discussions (to January, 1945) on post-war security arrangements[1]

(i)

The opening of the Conference: Anglo-American discussions: Soviet insistence on a full Great Power veto and refusal to agree to the British and American proposals with regard to voting on the Security Council (August 15–September 6, 1944).

THE much-postponed conversations on proposals for a World Security Organisation opened at Dumbarton Oaks near Washington on August 22, 1944. Sir A. Cadogan telegraphed to the Foreign Office on the night of August 15–16 that, if the conversations resulted in agreement, Mr. Hull wanted the four Powers to give their approval to it. At the same time he did not want to appear to be presenting the smaller Powers with a *fait accompli*. He therefore thought that the Great Powers should consult or at least inform them before making an announcement or summoning a conference of the United Nations. If, therefore, an agreement were reached at Dumbarton Oaks and confirmed by the four Powers, it might be communicated to the other United Nations who would then have time to consider it before the full conference. On the other hand, if any important points were left unsettled at Dumbarton Oaks the Foreign Ministers of the United States, Great Britain and the U.S.S.R. would have to meet in order to try to reach agreement. (a)

Sir A. Cadogan suggested to Mr. Eden that, if he and the Prime Minister were at Quebec about the time of the conclusion of the Dumbarton Oaks conversations—probably on September 10 or 12—the British Delegation could report to them there. Mr. Eden and the Prime Minister could pass on their views to the Cabinet. Sir A. Cadogan hoped to keep the Dominion representatives informed from

[1] Without adding unduly to the length of this chapter it has been impossible to deal with anything more than the main issues at the Dumbarton Oaks and San Francisco Conferences on the establishment of a World Organisation.

(a) U7020/180/70.

day to day so that it might not take very long to get the approval of the Dominion Governments.

Mr. Eden replied on August 19 that he did not yet know whether he would go to Quebec with the Prime Minister, but that he agreed in general with the proposals in Sir A. Cadogan's telegram. Mr. Eden asked whether London would be a suitable meeting place for the proposed Conference. He also thought that if no agreement were reached at Dumbarton Oaks, and there did not seem to be much chance of settling the differences at an immediate meeting of Foreign Ministers, or if the Dominions were not in agreement with us, no meeting should be held at Quebec, and we should fall back on the procedure which he (Mr. Eden) had suggested in a telegram of August 12.[1]

(a) Sir A. Cadogan reported to the Foreign Office on August 17 that he and his colleagues on the British Delegation had been holding informal talks with the Americans before the opening of the Conference. The Americans, at Sir A. Cadogan's suggestion, had agreed to take their plan as a basis for the discussions, and hoped that the Russians would accept this procedure. The two Delegations had gone carefully through their respective instructions; the points of divergence—with one exception—were so few that they had reached something like provisional agreement. Thus, the Americans were disposed to accept our statement of 'principles and objects' and to embody it in their own plan. Our Delegation had objected to the American proposal that the non-permanent Members of the Council should be elected annually, and the Americans had said that there was much force in our objections. The Americans seemed ready to agree that France should be co-opted to membership by the four Permanent Members and that it might be undesirable to wait until the establishment of 'a Government freely chosen by the French people'. On the other hand both Delegations thought that it would be difficult for France to become a Permanent Member until her Government had been recognised by the Great Powers. On military matters the American view was that discussion between experts would be necessary before making any more definite proposals, but they did not disagree with anything in our Memorandum C on the subject. They wanted some scheme for the earmarking of forces to be put forward as early as possible.

The Americans seemed to be willing to leave the question of territorial trusteeship out of the discussions, at any rate for the time, though they might want to have private talks about it with our Delegation. The outstanding point was the question of a veto. The

[1] See above, p. 88.

(a) U6916/180/70.

Americans appeared to have come provisionally to the conclusion that the Permanent Members of the Council should have a right of veto on a decision in which their own interests were involved, and that parties to a dispute should therefore be allowed—as in the League—to vote on it.

Sir A. Cadogan understood that the Americans were divided on the question. He had pointed out that there would be strong opposition within the Commonwealth to a system in which the United Kingdom could veto any action against itself, whereas Canada, for example, could not do so. There would be similar opposition among the other smaller Powers, and especially, perhaps, in Latin America. The American reply was that without a provision of this kind it would be difficult or impossible to get the scheme through the Senate. The press, however, had now published on August 16 a statement by the Republican Presidential candidate, Governor Dewey of New York, criticising a dictatorship of the four Powers, and suggesting that something of the kind was implied in the American plan. It was therefore possible that the American Delegation would bring forward other proposals. On the night of August 22–3 Sir A. Cadogan tele- (a)
graphed that there was likely to be a controversy over this question of a 'Great Power veto.' Within a few days the matter became critical not only for the conference but for the whole future of the World Organisation.

The instructions to the British Delegation had been that if a Member—permanent or otherwise—of the Security Council were a party to a dispute (i.e. not involved indirectly, but directly engaged in a dispute which threatened the maintenance of international peace and security, or directly involved in a threat of a breach of the peace) such Member should not be entitled to vote at any stage of the consideration of the dispute by the Security Council. The British attitude was determined by the consideration that, if the unanimity rule were to apply in the case of disputes to which a Great Power were a party, the Great Power could veto not only all decisions by the Security Council against it, but also all discussion of the dispute in the Council. A small Power would have no such right of veto and would therefore be in a position of inequality before the Council. Small Powers would thus have no assurance that in disputes between themselves and a Great Power the Security Council would even consider their case. The general question of relations between major and secondary Powers was a matter on which the Dominions felt strongly; all the smaller Powers were likely to share their view.

In the proposals put forward by the Soviet Government and trans- (b)
mitted to the Foreign Office by the Soviet Ambassador on August 12,

(a) U7016/180/70. (b) U6845/180/70; APW(44)75.

1944, the suggestion was made that all questions concerned with countering aggression should be decided by a majority vote provided that the Permanent Members of the Council were in agreement. The Americans had also put forward a proposal for the unanimity of the Permanent Members; the British proposal had been for a two-thirds majority including the votes of the Permanent Members. The Soviet memorandum did not state clearly whether members of the Council who were parties to a dispute should vote on it. This point was of greater importance than the question of a two-thirds or a simple majority. The Russian Delegation at the Conference stated that the rule concerning the unanimity of the Permanent Members should apply in all cases including those in which one or more of the Members was involved in a dispute.

(a) On August 29 Sir A. Cadogan reported that the Americans, at a meeting of the Steering Committee, had come down in favour of the proposal that parties to a dispute, whether they were Great Powers or not, should not vote. They argued that the Great Powers ought to set a good example to other nations, and that they could do so only if they accepted the same obligations as every other Power. If a Great Power ever reached the point of refusing to listen to the rest of the world, a war-like situation would clearly be developing, and in such case the Organisation would be likely to break down. We did not want to consider the possibility of anything of this kind; we also wished the smaller Powers to come into the Organisation. Hence we ought to have a 'system of law' applicable to all countries. We should, however, have to work out a formula dealing with the exclusion of disputes coming within the domestic jurisdiction of a State and the unanimity of the Great Powers would be required in respect of all disputes in which no Permanent Member of the council was involved.

The American Delegation pointed out that the matter was one of fundamental importance, and that a decision to accept the same obligations as other Powers would enhance, and not diminish the status of the Great Powers. Sir A. Cadogan, on behalf of the British Delegation, agreed that the question was the most difficult of those which the Conference had to settle. We hoped that the Soviet Government would accept the view which we had already put forward, and to which the Americans now agreed, since otherwise we should have the greatest difficulty in persuading other States to join the Organisation.

Sir A. Cadogan reported that the American statement was clearly something of a shock to the Soviet Delegation. M. Gromyko[1] said that

[1] M. Gromyko, Soviet Ambassador to the United States, was the leader of the Soviet Delegation.

(a) U7098/180/70.

the American proposals violated the basic principle of unanimity on the part of the Great Powers. They would report the British and American views to the Soviet Government, but they did not suggest that the latter would agree.

On September 1 Sir A. Cadogan telegraphed that Mr. Stettinius had told him that Mr. Hull had sent for M. Gromyko on August 31 and impressed upon him the importance of the provision that parties to a dispute should not vote on it. Mr. Hull thought that his talk had had some effect, but M. Gromyko had not shown as yet any evidence of a change of mind. On the night of September 3–4 Sir A. Cadogan telegraphed that there was no sign that the Soviet representatives were willing to give way on this question whether parties to a dispute should vote on it. The Americans, however, seemed to be increasingly aware of the importance of the point, and public opinion in the United States was generally favourable to the idea that the Great Powers should not regard themselves as above the law. (a) (b)

Mr. Eden replied to Sir A. Cadogan on September 6 that we regarded it as a matter of fundamental principle that the Great Powers should not claim the right to vote on disputes in which they were themselves involved. If we gave way on this point and thus allowed a Great Power veto, we should undermine the moral authority of the new Organisation from the start, and should have great difficulties from the smaller States, including the Dominions, who would feel strongly on the subject. Mr. Eden was unable to consult his Ministerial colleagues before sending this telegram to Sir A. Cadogan. On September 7, however, he brought the matter before the Armistice and Post-War Committee. The Committee agreed with his view.[1] (c) (d)

(ii)

Further unsuccessful British and American attempts to persuade the Soviet Government to accept their voting proposals: Sir A. Cadogan's compromise proposal: Field-Marshal Smuts's message of September 20 to the Prime Minister: Soviet objections to the proposed explanatory communiqué accompanying the publication of the agreed recommendations (September 7–October 9, 1944).

On the night of September 7–8 Sir A. Cadogan reported that he had explained in a private talk with M. Gromyko, that it would be (e)

[1] Sir A. Cadogan also reported that the Delegations at the Conference had left unsettled the question whether the normal vote (i.e. leaving out of account the question of (*continued on page* 140)

(a) U7160/180/70. (b) U7204/180/70. (c) U7223/180/70. (d) APW(44) 16th meeting. (e) U7274, 7323/180/70.

useless for the British and United States Governments to accept the Soviet proposal on voting, since no other Government would do so, and there would thus be no Organisation. M. Gromyko 'remained immovable'. Sir A. Cadogan doubted whether he really understood the British and American arguments; he suggested that Sir A. Clark Kerr might raise the question with M. Molotov. Meanwhile President
(a) Roosevelt had also spoken to M. Gromyko and had sent a message on the subject to Stalin. The Foreign Office therefore thought that the best plan would be for Mr. Harriman to put the case to M. Molotov in Moscow, and for Sir A. Clark Kerr to support him. Mr. Stettinius,
(b) however, asked on September 11 that Sir A. Clark Kerr should take the initiative with M. Molotov and tell him that the British Government held strongly the views which Sir A. Cadogan had put to M. Gromyko. Mr. Harriman would then support Sir A. Clark Kerr's
(c) representations. Sir A. Cadogan thought this the better plan. Sir A. Clark Kerr was instructed accordingly on September 14.

(d) On September 13, however, the Soviet Ambassador told the Steering Committee of the Conference that the Soviet Government had 'finally and unalterably' decided that they could not agree to anything short of the principle of complete unanimity among the Great Powers. The Soviet Government thought that the smaller Powers would accept this principle, since their one concern was security. Mr. Stettinius and Sir A. Cadogan said that the American and British Governments could not accept a system which would place a Great Power 'above the law', and that the smaller Powers would not join an Organisation based on the Russian plan. Mr. Stettinius pointed out that the United States Government, if they accepted the Russian view, would find themselves in a most difficult position with regard to the South American States; Sir A. Cadogan spoke in similar terms about our own position with regard to the Dominions.

The Committee then considered what could be done. They did not wish to leave a blank in the Charter on the question of voting or to put in an explanatory footnote stating that on this crucial matter they had failed to agree. If they tried to work out an alternative plan for something like a consultative council, they would have to recast much of the document to which they had already agreed. Sir A.

(*continued*)
whether interested parties should vote) of the Council should be by a two-thirds or a simple majority (including all the Permanent Members). The Armistice and Post-War Committee on September 7 had agreed with Mr. Eden's view that a two-thirds majority was the better solution, especially since it would give the representatives of the smaller States a considerably greater part in the shaping of policy.

In the draft scheme telegraphed by Sir. A. Cadogan on September 10 the section on voting in the Council was left without recommendations other than that each Member of the Council should have one vote.

(a) U7281/180/70. (b) U7323/180/70. (c) U7274/180/70. (d) U7374/180/70.

Cadogan suggested in his telegram reporting the proceedings that there were now four possible courses of action: (i) The Charter could be 'watered down' and published with a statement to the effect that in the present position of the world it was impossible to visualise how the Council would organise itself and take decisions. Sir A. Cadogan thought that a statement of this kind would cause deep public disappointment. In any case the United States Delegation were strongly opposed to it.

(ii) We might ask the Russians to agree to the ommission from the document of all references to unanimity on the part of the Great Powers. The Russians were most unlikely to accept this solution.

(iii) We could ask the Russians to agree to a formula whereby the Council would 'call upon' a Great Power to forgo its right to vote in a dispute to which it was a party. We should normally obey this 'behest', but the Soviet Government would be most unlikely to do so. Hence this plan also was unsuitable.

(iv) We might try to get the Russians to agree to a Great Power forgoing the right of veto on the first two stages in the settlement of a dispute, in other words, on the proposals in section VIII(*a*).[1] A Great Power would thus be left free to block action by the Council. In the case of a dispute between a great and a small Power the Council, acting by a majority, would investigate the dispute, urge suitable solutions, and formulate recommendations. The Great Power would not be able to block these processes by a negative vote. On the other hand the Great Power could use its veto to block the determination by the Council that a threat to security existed, and any enforcement of the Council's recommendations. The advantage of this plan was that the Great Powers would not place themselves altogether 'above the law' and that it would be possible at least to find out the attitude of world opinion towards a dispute. The smaller Powers would not like the plan, but they might be brought to agree to it.

Sir A. Cadogan thought that this plan (iv) was the only practicable alternative to a breakdown. It recognised the hard fact that, if sanctions were to be applied against a Great Power, a major war was likely to ensue, and that the preparation for such a war, or conduct of it, could not be the concern of the proposed World Organisation. Sir A. Cadogan said that, as time was pressing, he had asked Mr. Jebb to put plan (iv) hypothetically to the Russians and to see how they reacted to it.

Mr. Attlee telegraphed to the Prime Minister and Mr. Eden at (a)
Quebec on September 15 that he and Lord Cranborne, Secretary

[1] See below, pp. 157–8.

(a) Cordite 278, U7374/180/70.

of State for Dominions Affairs, disliked all the possibilities put forward by Sir A. Cadogan. They thought that very many members of their respective parties would regard it as wrong for us to accept a position which would place us and the other Great Powers in a position to veto, if not discussion, at all events action in a case in which we or they were involved. The Dominions were likely to take a similar view; it would therefore be better to have a 'show-down' with the Russians than to try to gloss over a real difference. The Prime
(a) Minister and Mr. Eden took a similar view.

President Roosevelt sent a message[1] on September 13, 1944, to
(b) Stalin explaining the attitude of the United States. He said that

> 'traditionally, since the founding of the United States, parties to a dispute have never voted on their own case. . . . Public opinion in the United States would never understand or support a plan of international organisation which violated this principle. . . . Furthermore . . . many nations of the world hold this same view and . . . would find it difficult to accept an international organisation in which the Great Powers insisted upon the right to vote in the Council in a dispute involving themselves. They would be most certain to see in this an attempt on the part of the Great Powers to set themselves up above the law.'

The President added that he would himself have 'real trouble' with the United States Senate if he accepted the Russian view.

(c) The President showed the Prime Minister on September 15 a reply from Stalin. Stalin said that the order of voting on the Council would be of great significance for the success of the World Organisation

> 'having in mind the importance that the Council work on the basis of the principle of co-ordination and unanimity of the four leading Powers on all questions, including those which directly relate to one of these nations.'

The initial American proposal for a special procedure of voting in the case of a dispute in which one or several Permanent Members of the Council were involved seemed to Stalin to be correct. Otherwise the agreement reached at the Teheran Conference would be 'brought to naught'. This agreement meant that the unanimity of the four Powers was necessary for the struggle against aggression in the future. Such unanimity presupposed that there were no mutual suspicions among the leading Powers. The Soviet Union could not ignore 'the presence of certain absurd prejudices' which often

---

[1] Owing to an oversight the text of this message was not transmitted to the Foreign Office until December 3, 1944.

(a) Gunfire 188, U7374/180/70. (b) U8496/180/70. (c) U7469/180/70.

hindered an 'objective attitude towards the U.S.S.R.' The other nations should also weigh the consequences which the lack of unanimity among the leading Powers would bring about. Stalin concluded by hoping that the President would understand the seriousness of the considerations which he had expressed.

Meanwhile Sir A. Clark Kerr had given M. Molotov on the night (a) of September 14–15 a memorandum stating the British view. In reply M. Molotov had made a long statement on the lines of Stalin's message. He said that the Soviet Government did not want to undertake anything without agreement with the other three Powers and also did not want any of them to do anything without Soviet agreement. The four Powers were in a special position just because they were bound to act unanimously. The worst would happen if this principle were broken, and departure from it could be due only to the sustained existence of mutual suspicion. Unless this suspicion disappeared, there could be no solid world organisation for peace. The Soviet Government could not ignore the 'wild prejudices' in certain quarters against the U.S.S.R. A departure from the principle of unanimity would merely strengthen these prejudices and provide material to inflame them.

Sir A. Clark Kerr explained the objection that under the Soviet plan a Power committing a breach of the peace could veto action against itself. M. Molotov's answer was that if the breach were a minor one, there were scores of ways of settling it, but if it were a major breach, nothing would be left of the peace organisation but an empty form, whatever provision had been laid down. If now, before the end of the war, we were suspicious of one another and admitted the possibility of an act of aggression by any one of the four Great Powers, our peace organisation was being built on a foundation of sand.

During the night of September 16–17 Sir A. Cadogan telegraphed (b) to Mr. Eden (who was leaving Quebec) that Mr. Stettinius proposed to go to see the President and Prime Minister at Hyde Park to discuss the situation. Mr. Stettinius was inclining to think that rather than invite the United Nations to a Conference after the Dumbarton Oaks talks, it would be better to put out a short statement indicating in broad outline both the field on which the officials of the three Governments had reached agreement and the points left open for consideration at a meeting of representatives of the Powers. Mr Stettinius thought that, since a meeting at a high level would soon have to take place, there could be no question of calling a larger Conference. Sir A. Cadogan considered that the Soviet Government might agree to this plan, but that they would probably

(a) U7393/180/70. (b) U7406/180/70; U7410/180/70.

refuse to come to a conference at which they would be in a minority of one.

(a) On September 17 M. Gromyko told Mr. Stettinius that the Soviet Government could not accept the tentative British proposal which Sir A. Cadogan had asked Mr. Jebb to put to the Russians. After a telephone conversation with the President, Mr. Stettinius summoned a meeting of the Steering Committee in the afternoon of September 18. He said that the United States Government wished to close down the discussions with the Russians as soon as possible, with the issue of a short communiqué, and to publish a four-Power statement at some date soon after the discussions with the Chinese. This statement would mention the points on which agreement had been reached, and would in fact be the text of the proposals. The section relating to voting on the Council would be left blank, with a note that proposals referring to this and other matters not yet settled would have to be worked out by the four Powers with a view to the submission of final proposals to a United Nations Conference. Mr. Stettinius suggested November 15 as a date upon which the proposals should be ready.

(b) The Prime Minister also telegraphed to Mr. Eden on September 18 that, in view of the Russian attitude, the President had decided to postpone the United Nations Conference until November 15.[1] The President was sending a message to Stalin to this effect. The Prime Minister mentioned to Mr. Eden that he had heard that the American military authorities considered the Russian plan to be the right one, and in the interest of the United States. He also said that enough had leaked out 'to give rise to some newspaper discussion'. It was soon evident that the United Nations Conference could not be held as early as November 15, and that a meeting of the three Great Powers (without China) would have to be held in order to try to reach agreement. Moreover, from the Prime Minister's reference to American military opinion, there was now some doubt whether the United States Government might not change their views, and, in such case, whether the British Government could maintain their objections to a compromise on the lines of Sir A. Cadogan's proposal.

The Prime Minister was also changing his mind. He was much (c) influenced by a message to him on September 20, 1944, from the South African Prime Minister. Field-Marshal Smuts described his message as a 'warning note' against undue haste, especially with

[1] The Prime Minister appears to have thought that Mr. Stettinius's date for the conclusion of the further discussions was the date proposed for a conference. The Foreign Office told Sir A. Cadogan that they considered it better not to specify a date for the conclusion of the discussions. No date was mentioned in the communiqué.

(a) U7416/180/70. (b) Gunfire 264, U7416/180/70. (c) U7593/180/70.

regard to the *impasse* on the question of voting. He said that his first view had been that the Russian attitude was absurd. On second thoughts, however, he was changing his opinion. The Russians regarded the matter as involving the honour and standing of their country among the Allies. They asked whether they were to be trusted and treated as equals, or were they still outlaws and pariahs? A misunderstanding on this point was more than a mere difference and might poison European relationships; Russia, conscious of her power, might become ever more grasping. If she were not included in a World Organisation, she would become the power centre of another group, and we should be heading for World War III. If the United Nations did not form any World Organisation, they would be stultified before history.

In view of these dangers Field-Marshal Smuts thought that the smaller Powers should be prepared to make a concession to Russian amour-propre and that they should not insist in the matter on theoretical quality of status. Such insistence might have devastating results for the smaller Powers themselves. Where questions of power and security were concerned it would be most unwise to raise the theoretical issues of sovereign equality, and the United Kingdom and United States should use their influence in favour of common-sense and safety rather than of status for the smaller nations. On the merits there was much to be said for unanimity among the Great Powers, at least for the years immediately after the war. If the principle proved unworkable, the situation could be reviewed later when mutual confidence had been established. If the unanimity rule were adopted, the United Kingdom and the United States would have to exert all their influence on Russia to be moderate and sensible and not to flout world opinion. They were likely to be largely successful. If Russia proved impossible, the world organisation might have to act, but the blame would be Russian.

> 'At worst the principle of unanimity will have only the effect of a veto, of preventing action where it may be wise or even necessary. It will be negative and slow down action. It will also make it impossible for Russia to embark on crises (*sic* courses?) disapproved of by the United Kingdom and the United States. Where people are drunk with new-won power, it may not be so bad a thing to have a brake like unanimity. I do not defend it, I dislike it, but I do not think it is at present so bad that the future of world peace and security should be sacrificed on this issue.'

The Prime Minister told Mr. Eden that he agreed with Field-Marshal Smuts, and was convinced that no further progress could be made on 'this dangerous path' until a meeting between the three (a)

(a) M(O) 13/4, U7593/180/70.

(a) Heads of Government. Mr. Churchill said that he was forwarding Field-Marshal Smuts's telegram to President Roosevelt and to the (b) Prime Minister of Canada. The President replied on September 28 that he agreed upon

> 'the necessity of having the U.S.S.R. as a fully accepted and equal member of any association of the Great Powers formed for the purpose of preventing international war. It should be possible to accomplish this by adjusting our differences through compromise by all the parties concerned, and this ought to tide things over for a few years until the child learns how to toddle.'

(c) Mr. Mackenzie King replied on September 28 that he too thought that the question needed the most careful consideration. He also had doubts about other points in the proposed Charter, and suggested (d) that the official publication of the plan should be deferred. Mr. Churchill answered on October 7 that we also would have wished to postpone publication but that the Americans had been pressing us hard to publish the plan on October 9. The United States Administration felt that the best way of securing acceptance for it was by putting it before public opinion at once. In any case much of the document had already leaked into the American press and 'the rest is sure to leak too'. If this happened it would embarrass us if we could not give the authorised version to Parliament and our own press.

(e) The Foreign Office had been uneasy for some time about the publicity given to the proceedings of the Conference. The President and Mr. Hull had encouraged this publicity because they wanted to get popular support for American participation in the World Organisation. For this reason Mr. Hull, before and during the Conference, took care to let members of both parties in Congress know in considerable detail the plans of the Administration and the progress made towards their realisation. The Foreign Office, however, were afraid that the document containing the recommendations agreed by the Delegates at the Conference might appear to public opinion to be a kind of treaty binding the three Governments. Sir A. Cadogan had repeatedly emphasised that the discussions were non-committal. The Foreign Office suggested to him on September 15 that he might put on record at the end of the Conference a statement that the agreed document represented only a set of recommendations for consideration by the participating Governments.

On September 25 the Foreign Office agreed that, in view of the

(a) T1813/4, No. 785, Premier 3/472; U7593/180/70.
(b) T1835/4, No. 624, Premier 3/472. (c) U7593/180/70. (d) U7593/180/70.
(e) U7426/180/70.

leakages, the statement of recommendations should be published as soon as possible, but they asked for time to study them before fixing a definite date. Sir A. Cadogan reported on September 27 that Mr. Stettinius had suggested publication on October 9. A short communiqué closing the Russian talks was issued on September 29. There was, however, some trouble with the Soviet Government over the proposed longer statement. The British and United States Governments suggested including an explanatory communiqué with the list of agreed recommendations. The Soviet Government objected to the inclusion in this communiqué of a paragraph reading:

> 'Meanwhile [i.e. while the principal Powers were preparing complete proposals for the full Conference] the three (or four) Governments are resolved to work together, and with all other Governments jointly engaged in the suppression of the forces that have disturbed the peace of the world, for the future enforcement of the terms of surrender to be imposed on the common enemy.'

Sir A. Cadogan had proposed the insertion of this paragraph for the purpose of accustoming the American public to the idea of accepting obligations in Europe whether or not a World Organisation were established, and also to make it clear that the failure to reach complete agreement at Dumbarton Oaks did not affect the solidarity of the Powers in carrying on the war and imposing terms on Germany. (a) The original draft of the paragraph referred only to the Great Powers. The additional reference to 'working with' all other Governments was included to meet the criticism that the principal Allied Powers were assuming a sort of dictatorship and excluding the other Allies, who had taken part in the fighting, from the preparation and enforcement of the terms of surrender. The Dominion Governments had particularly strong feelings on the point.

The Soviet Government objected to the inclusion of this reference to the 'other Governments'. The Foreign Office were afraid that the Soviet Government would not give way. Throughout the meetings of the European Advisory Commission they had caused delay and embarrassment by insisting rigidly upon the principle of three-Power responsibility in connexion with the terms of surrender for Germany and the plans for occupation and control. Nonetheless the Foreign Office instructed Sir A. Clark Kerr on October 3 to try to persuade the Soviet Government to treat the communiqué as a separate issue and not to link it with the objections which they had made on the European Advisory Commission. Sir A. Clark Kerr was told to remind M. Molotov that Article 5 of the Four-Power Declaration at the Moscow Conference of October 1943 provided that the Four Powers 'will consult with one another and *as the occasion*

(a) U7582/180/70.

requires with other Members of the United Nations' in maintaining peace and security pending the inauguration of a system of general security.

If the Soviet Government still refused to accept the draft of paragraph 4 in the communiqué, Sir A. Clark Kerr was instructed to ask whether M. Molotov could suggest an alternative wording, e.g. a shorter formula by which the three (or four) Governments would merely reaffirm their determination to give effect to Article 5 of the Moscow Declaration.

(a) The War Cabinet consented on October 6 to the publication of the 'agreed recommendations' subject to agreement also on the accompanying communiqué, and on the understanding that it was made clear that the British Government were not committed in any way to the acceptance of the recommendations.

(b) M. Molotov, however, would not give way, and, in view of his refusal, the Foreign Office thought it best to leave out the whole paragraph, since there was no point in retaining it without a reference to the smaller States. The State Department, independently, took the same view. Hence the communiqué issued with the statement of agreed recommendations on October 9, 1944, merely announced the fact that each of the Governments had received from the Conference a 'statement of tentative proposals indicating in detail the wide range of subjects on which agreement has been reached at the conversations', and that they (the Governments represented at the Conference) had agreed that, after further study of these proposals, they would 'as soon as possible take the necessary steps with a view to the preparation of complete proposals which could then serve as a basis of discussion at a full United Nations Conference'.

Note (i) to section (ii). Other points concerning the Dumbarton Oaks proposals.

In addition to the questions of voting and of the inclusion of the sixteen constituent Republics of the Soviet Union as founder Members,[1] certain other matters were left without any recommendation from the Delegations at Dumbarton Oaks.

(i) The site of the World Organisation was not considered.

(c) (ii) The United States Delegation proposed that the original Members of the Organisation and those to be invited to the 'full Conference' of the United Nations should be the United and

---

[1] See below, section (iv) of this Chapter.

(a) WM(44)133; U7720/180/70. (b) U7699/180/70.
(c) U7665/180/70.

Associated Nations.[1] The Soviet Delegation opposed this proposal on the ground that if membership were restricted to the United Nations, States now neutral or 'Associated' might be encouraged to join the Allies in the prosecution of the war. The point was left open in the recommendations.

(iii) The United States Delegation had originally tabled for discussion the question of 'territorial trusteeship'; at the beginning of the discussions they announced that they had decided not to raise the matter. No discussion on the subject took place.

(iv) The United Kingdom Delegation had tried to secure in Chapter VI (A)[2] the insertion of a provision whereby, in electing non-permanent members of the Security Council, the Assembly should pay due regard to the contribution of the States concerned 'towards the maintenance of peace and security and towards the other purposes of the Organisation'. This insertion was proposed in the interests of the Dominions, but the two other Delegations would not agree to it.

(v) Military questions. On September 2, 1944, the Joint Staff (a) Mission in Washington telegraphed to the Chiefs of Staff in London that three main questions were being considered in the discussions at Dumbarton Oaks on military matters. These questions were the provision of forces for use by the Council, the composition of the Military Staff Committee and the provision of bases and facilities.

On the first question there was agreement that the Member States should undertake to provide quotas of forces for use by the Council when required. The Russians, however, were pressing for the provision, in addition, of an Air Force which would be composed of contingents of national Air Forces and would be permanently under the orders of the Council. The Russians argued that such a force would deter potential aggressors and that, in case of aggression, it could take action at once which would suffice to hold off the aggressor until the national quotas could come into operation.

The British military representatives were arguing that the provision of an additional 'international force' was unnecessary and undesirable, and that it would be possible to devise machinery for making the national quota forces available as rapidly as an 'international force.' The Americans agreed with the British view. The

---

[1] i.e. (in the American view) States which had broken off relations with the Axis and had been invited to recent international conferences, namely Egypt, Venezuela, Chile, Peru, Ecuador, Paraguay and Uruguay. Turkey (but not Argentina) would also be included. The Americans were much alarmed at the possible consequences if this proposal became publicly known. In their own memoranda they spoke of it as 'proposal X'. They also asked—without effect—that M. Gromyko should agree to allow his mention of the proposal to be omitted from the minutes of the Steering Committee. *F.R.U.S. 1944*, I. 753.

[2] See below p. 155.

(a) U7184/180/70.

British military representatives thought that the Russians would not insist on their view if it were made clear that the 'international force' could be brought into existence at any time when the Council regarded it as necessary. The British representatives pointed out to the Chiefs of Staff that we had nothing to fear from the Russian proposals since on the Council the Great Powers had to be unanimous in such matters, and would be advised by the Military Staff Committee which would be composed of their military representatives.

Mr. Eden considered that the British military representatives should not have argued so strongly against an 'international force'. The Foreign Office suggested to the Chiefs of Staff that it would be a mistake for us merely to reject the Russian proposal, as the Chiefs of Staff proposed, without mentioning the possibility of an 'international force'. The British representatives were therefore informed that, although we did not regard the provision of such a force as necessary, we could not allow it to be said that we had completely rejected the proposal. The proposal, however, had such wide military and political implications that we needed time to examine it. The British military representatives were instructed to suggest the following form of words to meet the Russian suggestion:

> 'In order to increase the speed with which urgent military measures could be taken, member States should undertake to examine the practicability of organising contingents from national air forces into an International Air Force, the composition of which would be determined by the Council with the assistance of the Military Staff Committee.'

On the question of the composition of the Committee, the British military representatives reported general agreement that the Committee must be small, and that it should be composed only of the military representatives of the Great Powers; other Powers would be associated with it when their interests were affected.

In the discussion of the third question—bases and facilities—the Russians explained that they had in mind that States unable to provide substantial forces but possessing territory suitable for strategic bases should agree to hand over such territory to the World Organisation for the construction of international bases. The British and American representatives did not like this plan. The British representatives thought that it might lead, for example, to a demand for the construction of an international base on Australian territory. They secured, however, provisional assent to a form of words to the effect that Member States should undertake to provide, for use by the Council, forces, facilities, and assistance in accordance with an agreement or agreements to be entered into between Member

States and subject to ratification in accordance with the constitutional procedure in force in each State.

(vi) Another proposal caused considerable disquiet to the Chiefs of Staff. Sir A. Cadogan reported on September 9 that the Americans wished to insert in the agreed proposals a statement of principle to the effect that (a)

> 'the International Organisation should refrain from intervention in the internal affairs of any State, it being the responsibility of each state to see that conditions prevailing within its jurisdiction do not endanger international peace and security, and to this end to respect human rights, and fundamental freedoms of all its people and to govern in accordance with principles of humanity and justice.'

The Chiefs of Staff thought that this 'principle' which the Americans had suddenly brought forward was 'objectionable *in toto*' since it could be interpreted as precluding intervention in Germany to stop a revival of Nazism, or justifying a State such as Egypt or Panama in obstructing the strategic needs of the World Organisation, or preventing us from protecting our own rights, e.g. in Egypt. On the other hand the Chiefs of Staff realised that the 'principle' might also prevent the World Organisation from interfering in the affairs of a State with which we had a special relationship. The British Delegation was instructed on September 15 to try to persuade Mr. Stettinius to withdraw the 'principle' or at all events to word it less vaguely. Sir A. Cadogan replied that the British Delegation had not wanted this American insertion, but thought that they would have to make some concession in the matter to satisfy American left-wing opinion. Sir A. Cadogan's own objection was not that, as the Chiefs of Staff thought, it would limit the right of intervention but that it would encourage too much interference with internal matters, e.g. in India or Burma, especially if the term 'responsibility' were retained. In fact the Americans withdrew their proposal, largely owing to Russian objections.

Note (ii) to Section (ii). The 'Agreed Recommendations' of the Dumbarton Oaks Conference.[1]

The conversations on World Organisation at Dumbarton Oaks, between representatives on the official level of the United Kingdom of Great Britain and Northern Ireland, the United States of America and the Union of Soviet Socialist Republics came to an end on September 28, 1944. The agreed recommendations are set out in the document reproduced below, which was signed by the Heads of Delegations. (b)

[1] The recommendations were published as a White Paper, Cmd. 6560 of 1944.

(a) U7426, 7427/180/70. (b) U7585/180/70.

PROPOSALS FOR THE ESTABLISHMENT OF A GENERAL INTERNATIONAL ORGANISATION

There should be established an international organisation under the title of The United Nations, the Charter of which should contain provisions necessary to give effect to the proposals which follow.

Chapter I.—Purposes

The purposes of the Organisation should be:

(1) To maintain international peace and security; and to that end to take effective collective measures for the prevention and removal of threats to the peace and the suppression of acts of aggression or other breaches of the peace, and to bring about by peaceful means the adjustment or settlement of international disputes which may lead to a breach of the peace;

(2) To develop friendly relations among nations and to take other appropriate measures to strengthen universal peace;

(3) To achieve international co-operation in the solution of international economic, social and other humanitarian problems; and

(4) To afford a centre for harmonising the actions of nations in the achievement of these common ends.

Chapter II.—Principles

In pursuit of the purposes mentioned in Chapter I the Organisation and its members should act in accordance with the following principles:

(1) The Organisation is based on the principle of the sovereign equality of all peace-loving States.

(2) All members of the Organisation undertake, in order to ensure to all of them the rights and benefits resulting from membership in the Organisation, to fulfil the obligations assumed by them in accordance with the Charter.

(3) All members of the Organisation shall settle their disputes by peaceful means in such a manner that international peace and security are not endangered.

(4) All members of the Organisation shall refrain in their international relations from the threat or use of force in any manner inconsistent with the purposes of the Organisation.

(5) All members of the Organisation shall give every assistance to the Organisation in any action undertaken by it in accordance with the provisions of the Charter.

(6) All members of the Organisation shall refrain from giving assistance to any State against which preventive or enforcement action is being undertaken by the Organisation.

The Organisation should ensure that States not members of the Organisation act in accordance with these principles so far as may be necessary for the maintenance of international peace and security.

Chapter III.—Membership

Membership of the Organisation should be open to all peace-loving States.

Chapter IV.—Principal Organs

(1) The Organisation should have as its principal organs:

(*a*) A General Assembly;
(*b*) A Security Council;
(*c*) An International Court of Justice; and
(*d*) A Secretariat.

(2) The Organisation should have such subsidiary agencies as may be found necessary.

Chapter V.—The General Assembly

(A) composition

All members of the Organisation should be members of the General Assembly and should have a number of representatives to be specified in the Charter.

(B) functions and powers

(1) The General Assembly should have the right to consider the general principles of co-operation in the maintenance of international peace and security including the principles governing disarmament and the regulation of armaments; to discuss any questions relating to the maintenance of international peace and security brought before it by any member or members of the Organisation or by the Security Council; and to make recommendations with regard to any such principles or questions. Any such questions on which action is necessary should be referred to the Security Council by the General Assembly either before or after discussion. The General Assembly should not on its own initiative make recommendations on any matter relating to the maintenance of international peace and security which is being dealt with by the Security Council.

(2) The General Assembly should be empowered to admit new

members to the Organisation upon the recommendation of the Security Council.

(3) The General Assembly should, upon the recommendation of the Security Council, be empowered to suspend from the exercise of any rights or privileges of membership any member of the Organisation against which preventive or enforcement action shall have been taken by the Security Council. The exercise of the rights and privileges thus suspended may be restored by the decision of the Security Council. The General Assembly should be empowered upon the recommendation of the Security Council to expel from the Organisation any member of the Organisation which persistently violates the principles contained in the Charter.

(4) The General Assembly should elect the non-permanent members of the Security Council and the members of the Economic and Social Council provided for in Chapter IX. It should be empowered to elect upon the recommendation of the Security Council, the Secretary-General of the Organisation. It should perform such functions in relation to the election of the Judges of the International Court of Justice as may be conferred upon it by the Statute of the Court.

(5) The General Assembly should apportion the expenses among the members of the Organisation and should be empowered to approve the budgets of the Organisation.

(6) The General Assembly should initiate studies and make recommendations for the purpose of promoting international co-operation in political, economic and social fields and of adjusting situations likely to impair the general welfare.

(7) The General Assembly should make recommendations for the co-ordination of the policies of international economic, social and other specialised agencies brought into relation with the Organisation in accordance with agreements between such agencies and the Organisation.

(8) The General Assembly should receive and consider annual and special reports from the Security Council and reports from other bodies of the Organisation.

(C) VOTING

(1) Each member of the Organisation should have one vote in the General Assembly.

(2) Important decisions of the General Assembly, including recommendations with respect to the maintenance of international peace and security; the election of members of the Security Council; the election of members of the Economic and Social Council; the admission of members, suspension of exercise of the rights and privileges of members, and the expulsion of members; and budgetary

questions, should be made by a two-thirds majority of those present and voting. On other questions, including the determination of additional categories of questions to be decided by a two-thirds majority, the decisions of the General Assembly should be made by a simple majority vote.

(D) PROCEDURE

(1) The General Assembly should meet in regular annual sessions and in such special sessions as occasion may require.

(2) The General Assembly should adopt its own rules of procedure and elect its president for each session.

(3) The General Assembly should be empowered to set up such bodies and agencies as it may deem necessary for the performance of its functions.

CHAPTER VI.—THE SECURITY COUNCIL

(A) COMPOSITION

The Security Council should consist of one representative of each of eleven members of the Organisation. Representatives of the United States, the United Kingdom of Great Britain and Northern Ireland, the Union of Soviet Socialist Republics, the Republic of China, and in due course France, should have permanent seats. The General Assembly should elect six States to fill the non-permanent seats. These six States should be elected for a term of two years, three retiring each year. They should not be immediately eligible for re-election. In the first election of the non-permanent members three should be chosen by the General Assembly for one-year terms and three for two-year terms.

(B) PRINCIPAL FUNCTIONS AND POWERS

(1) In order to ensure prompt and effective action by the Organisation, members of the Organisation should by the Charter confer on the Security Council primary responsibility for the maintenance of international peace and security and should agree that in carrying out these duties under this responsibility it should act on their behalf.

(2) In discharging these duties the Security Council should act in accordance with the purposes and principles of the Organisation.

(3) The specific powers conferred on the Security Council in order to carry out these duties are laid down in Chapter VIII.

(4) All members of the Organisation should obligate themselves to accept the decisions of the Security Council and to carry them out in accordance with the provisions of the Charter.

(5) In order to promote the establishment and maintenance of

international peace and security with the least diversion of the world's human and economic resources for armaments, the Security Council with the assistance of the Military Staff Committee referred to in Chapter VIII, Section (B), paragraph 9, should have the responsibility for formulating plans for the establishment of a system of regulation of armaments for submission to the members of the Organisation.

(C) VOTING

[NOTE.—The question of voting procedure in the Security Council is still under consideration.]

(D) PROCEDURE

(1) The Security Council should be so organised as to be able to function continuously and each State member of the Security Council should be permanently represented at the headquarters of the Organisation. It may hold meetings at such other places as in its judgment may best facilitate its work. There should be periodic meetings at which each State member of the Security Council could, if it so desired, be represented by a member of the Government or some other special representative.

(2) The Security Council should be empowered to set up such bodies or agencies as it may deem necessary for the performance of its functions including regional sub-committees of the Military Staff Committee.

(3) The Security Council should adopt its own rules of procedure, including the method of selecting its President.

(4) Any member of the Organisation should participate in the discussion of any question brought before the Security Council whenever the Security Council considers that the interests of that member of the Organisation are especially affected.

(5) Any member of the Organisation not having a seat on the Security Council and any State not a member of the Organisation if it is a party to a dispute under consideration by the Security Council should be invited to participate in the discussion relating to the dispute.

CHAPTER VII.—AN INTERNATIONAL COURT OF JUSTICE

(1) There should be an International Court of Justice which should constitute the principal judicial organ of the Organisation.

(2) The Court should be constituted and should function in accordance with a Statute which should be annexed to and be a part of the Charter of the Organisation.

(3) The Statute of the Court of International Justice should be either (*a*) the Statute of the Permanent Court of International

Justice, continued in force with such modifications as may be desirable, or (*b*) a new Statute in the preparation of which the Statute of the Permanent Court of International Justice should be used as a basis.

(4) All members of the Organisation should, *ipso facto*, be parties to the Statute of the International Court of Justice.

(5) Conditions under which States not members of the Organisation may become parties to the Statute of the International Court of Justice should be determined in each case by the General Assembly upon the recommendation of the Security Council.

Chapter VIII.—Arrangements for the Maintenance of International Peace and Security, including the Prevention and Suppression of Aggression

(A) The Pacific Settlement of Disputes

(1) The Security Council should be empowered to investigate any dispute, or any situation which may lead to international friction or give rise to a dispute, in order to determine whether its continuance is likely to endanger the maintenance of international peace and security.

(2) Any State, whether a member of the Organisation or not, may bring any such dispute or situation to the attention of the General Assembly or of the Security Council.

(3) The parties to any dispute the continuance of which is likely to endanger the maintenance of international peace and security should obligate themselves, first of all, to seek a solution by negotiation, mediation, conciliation, arbitration or judicial settlement, or other peaceful means of their own choice. The Security Council should call upon the parties to settle their dispute by such means.

(4) If, nevertheless, parties to a dispute of the nature referred to in paragraph 3 above fail to settle it by the means indicated in that paragraph, they should obligate themselves to refer it to the Security Council. The Security Council should in each case decide whether or not the continuance of the particular dispute is in fact likely to endanger the maintenance of international peace and security and, accordingly, whether the Security Council should deal with the dispute, and, if so, whether it should take action under paragraph 5.

(5) The Security Council should be empowered at any stage of a dispute of the nature referred to in paragraph 3 above to recommend appropriate procedures or methods of adjustment.

(6) Justiciable disputes should normally be referred to the International Court of Justice. The Security Council should be empowered

to refer to the Court for advice legal questions connected with other disputes.

(7) The provisions of paragraphs 1–6 of Section VIII (A) should not apply to situations or disputes arising out of matters which by international law are solely within the domestic jurisdiction of the State concerned.

(B) DETERMINATION OF THREATS TO THE PEACE OR ACTS OF AGGRESSION, AND ACTION WITH RESPECT THERETO

(1) Should the Security Council deem that a failure to settle a dispute in accordance with the procedures indicated in paragraph 3 of Section A, or in accordance with its recommendations made under paragraph (5) of Section (A), constitutes a threat to the maintenance of international peace and security, it should take any measures necessary for the maintenance of international peace and security in accordance with the purposes and principles of the Organisation.

(2) In general the Security Council should determine the existence of any threat to the peace, breach of the peace or act of aggression and should make recommendations or decide upon measures to be taken to maintain or restore peace and security.

(3) The Security Council should be empowered to determine what diplomatic, economic or other measures not involving the use of armed force should be employed to give effect to its decisions, and to call upon members of the Organisation to apply such measures. Such measures may include complete or partial interruption of rail, sea, air, postal, telegraphic, radio and other means of communication and the severance of diplomatic and economic relations.

(4) Should the Security Council consider such measures to be inadequate, it should be empowered to take such action by air, naval or land forces as may be necessary to maintain or restore international peace and security. Such action may include demonstrations, blockade and other operations by air, sea or land forces of members of the Organisation.

(5) In order that all members of the Organisation should contribute to the maintenance of international peace and security, they should undertake to make available to the Security Council, on its call and in accordance with a special agreement or agreements concluded among themselves, armed forces, facilities and assistance necessary for the purpose of maintaining international peace and security. Such agreement or agreements should govern the numbers and types of forces and the nature of the facilities and assistance to be provided. The special agreement or agreements should be negotiated as soon as possible, and should in each case be subject to approval

by the Security Council and to ratification by the Signatory States in accordance with their constitutional processes.

(6) In order to enable urgent military measures to be taken by the Organisation, there should be held immediately available by the members of the Organisation national Air Force contingents for combined international enforcement action. The strength and degree of readiness of these contingents and plans for their combined action should be determined by the Security Council, with the assistance of the Military Staff Committee, within the limits laid down in the special agreement or agreements referred to in paragraph (5) above.

(7) The action required to carry out the decisions of the Security Council for the maintenance of international peace and security should be taken by all the members of the Organisation in co-operation or by some of them as the Security Council may determine. This undertaking should be carried out by the members of the Organisation by their own action and through action of the appropriate specialised Organisations and agencies of which they are members.

(8) Plans for the application of armed force should be made by the Security Council with the assistance of the Military Staff Committee referred to in paragraph (9) below.

(9) There should be established a Military Staff Committee, the functions of which should be to advise and assist the Security Council on all questions relating to the Security Council's military requirements for the maintenance of international peace and security, to the employment and command of forces placed at its disposal, to the regulation of armaments and to possible disarmament. It should be responsible under the Security Council for the strategic direction of any armed forces placed at the disposal of the Security Council. The Committee should be composed of the Chiefs of Staff of the permanent members of the Security Council or their representatives. Any member of the Organisation not permanently represented on the Committee should be invited by the Committee to be associated with it when the efficient discharge of the Committee's responsibilities requires that such a State should participate in its work. Questions of command of forces should be worked out subsequently.

(10) The members of the Organisation should join in affording mutual assistance in carrying out the measures decided upon by the Security Council.

(11) Any State, whether a member of the Organisation or not, which finds itself confronted with special economic problems arising from the carrying out of measures which have been decided upon by the Security Council should have the right to consult the Security Council in regard to a solution of those problems.

(c) REGIONAL ARRANGEMENTS

(1) Nothing in the Charter should preclude the existence of regional arrangements or agencies for dealing with such matters relating to the maintenance of international peace and security as are appropriate for regional action provided such arrangements or agencies and their activities are consistent with the purposes and principles of the Organisation. The Security Council should encourage settlement of local disputes through such regional arrangements or by such regional agencies either on the initiative of the States concerned or by reference from the Security Council.

(2) The Security Council should, where appropriate, utilise such arrangements or agencies for enforcement action under its authority but no enforcement action should be taken under regional arrangements or by regional agencies without the authorisation of the Security Council.

(3) The Security Council should at all times be kept fully informed of activities undertaken or in contemplation under regional arrangements or by regional agencies for the maintenance of international peace and security.

CHAPTER IX.—ARRANGEMENTS FOR INTERNATIONAL ECONOMIC AND SOCIAL CO-OPERATION

(A) PURPOSE AND RELATIONSHIPS

(1) With a view to the creation of conditions of stability and well-being which are necessary for peaceful and friendly relations among nations, the Organisation should facilitate solutions of international economic, social and other humanitarian problems and promote respect for human rights and fundamental freedoms. Responsibility for the discharge of this function should be vested in the General Assembly and under the authority of the General Assembly in an Economic and Social Council.

(2) The various specialised economic, social and other Organisations and agencies would have responsibilities in their respective fields as defined in their statutes. Each such Organisation or agency should be brought into relationship with the Organisation on terms to be determined by agreement between the Economic and Social Council and the appropriate authorities of the specialised Organisation or agency, subject to approval by the General Assembly.

(B) COMPOSITION AND VOTING

The Economic and Social Council should consist of representatives of 18 members of the Organisation. The States to be represented for this purpose should be elected by the General Assembly for terms of three years. Each such State should have one representative, who should have one vote. Decisions of the Economic and Social Council should be taken by simple majority vote of those present and voting.

(C) FUNCTIONS AND POWERS OF THE ECONOMIC AND SOCIAL COUNCIL

(1) The Economic and Social Council should be empowered:

(*a*) To carry out, within the scope of its functions, recommendations of the General Assembly;

(*b*) To make recommendations on its own initiative with respect to international economic, social and other humanitarian matters;

(*c*) To receive and consider reports from the economic, social and other organisations or agencies brought into relationship with the Organisation, and to co-ordinate their activities through consultations with, and recommendations to, such organisations or agencies;

(*d*) To examine the administrative budgets of such specialised organisations or agencies with a view to making recommendations to the organisations or agencies concerned;

(*e*) To enable the Secretary-General to provide information to the Security Council;

(*f*) To assist the Security Council upon its request; and

(*g*) To perform such other functions within the general scope of its competence as may be assigned to it by the General Assembly.

(D) ORGANISATION AND PROCEDURE

(1) The Economic and Social Council should set up an Economic Commission, a Social Commission, and such other Commissions as may be required. These Commissions should consist of experts. There should be a permanent staff which should constitute a part of the Secretariat of the Organisation.

(2) The Economic and Social Council should make suitable arrangements for representatives of the specialised organisations or agencies to participate without vote in its deliberations and in those of the commissions established by it.

(3) The Economic and Social Council should adopt its own rules of procedure and the method of selecting its president.

CHAPTER X.—THE SECRETARIAT

(1) There should be a secretariat comprising a Secretary-General and such staff as may be required. The Secretary-General should be the chief administrative officer of the Organisation. He should be elected by the General Assembly on recommendation of the Security

Council, for such term and under such conditions as are specified in the Charter.

(2) The Secretary-General should act in that capacity in all meetings of the General Assembly, of the Security Council, and of the Economic and Social Council, and should make an annual report to the General Assembly on the work of the Organisation.

(3) The Secretary-General should have the right to bring to the attention of the Security Council any matter which in his opinion may threaten international peace and security.

Chapter XI.—Amendments

Amendments should come into force for all members of the Organisation when they have been adopted by a vote of two-thirds of the members of the General Assembly and ratified in accordance with their respective constitutional processes by the members of the Organisation having permanent membership on the Security Council and of a majority of the other members of the Organisation.

Chapter XII.—Transitional Arrangements

(1) Pending the coming into force of the special agreement or agreements referred to in Chapter VIII, section (B), paragraph (5), and in accordance with the provisions of paragraph 5 of the Four-Nations Declaration, signed at Moscow, the 30th October, 1943, the States parties to that declaration should consult with one another and as occasion arises with other members of the Organisation with a view to such joint action on behalf of the Organisation as may be necessary for the purpose of maintaining international peace and security.

(2) No provision of the Charter should preclude action taken or authorised in relation to enemy States as a result of the present war by the Governments having responsibility for such action.

Note

In addition to the question of voting procedure in the Security Council, referred to in Chapter VI, several other questions are still under consideration.

For the United States of America: Ed. D. Stettinius, Jr.
For the United Kingdom of Great Britain and Northern Ireland: Alexander Cadogan.
For the Union of Soviet Socialist Republics: A. Gromyko.

Washington, D.C.
September 28, 1944.

(iii)

Consideration of British policy with regard to the deadlock on the question of voting on the Security Council: memoranda by Sir S. Cripps and Sir A. Cadogan: President Roosevelt's compromise proposal; decision of the War Cabinet to accept the proposal: the Prime Minister's unwillingness to resist a Russian refusal to accept the compromise.

At the end of September 1944, the Foreign Office drew up a draft (a) memorandum on the voting question for submission to the Armistice and Post-War Committee. The memorandum pointed out that one common feature of the three sets of proposals which formed the basis of the the Dumbarton Oaks recommendations was a desire to avoid the mistake made by the League of Nations in ignoring the fact that the responsibility for the maintenance of peace and security must rest with the Great Powers. The British, American and Russian proposals thus agreed in providing for a small Council of eleven Members of whom five would have permanent tenure; decisions of the Council required a unanimous vote of the permanent Members. The difference between the Powers was that the Russians held there should be no exceptions to this rule of unanimity. We and the Americans thought that permanent members should not be allowed to vote on disputes in which they themselves were involved. The memorandum then stated the arguments for and against each view, and concluded that if we had to choose between giving way to the Russians and abandoning the chances of a World Security Organisation, we should choose the former course in our interests and those of the world in general. We ought to be able to convince the smaller States and the majority of public opinion that the balance of advantage lay in getting the U.S.S.R. into the Organisation. We might also be able to reassure them to some extent by promoting a declaration on the part of the Great Powers that they would not make improper use of their privileged position under the unanimity rule to prevent the consideration by the Council of disputes in which they were concerned.

Hitherto we had looked at the question of a Great Power veto from the point of view of its broad effect upon the establishment and operation of the new World Organisation. The Soviet Government were considering it from the narrow viewpoint of their own national interests, and there were signs that the United States might take a similar line. We might therefore reasonably ask how the matter affected us as an Imperial Power. The Russian thesis might well prove

(a) U7664/180/70.

a safeguard to us with regard to our scattered and sometimes disputed possessions throughout the world. We could not ignore the possibility that a majority of the World Council might vote against us over disputes affecting territories such as Hong Kong, the Falkland Islands or British Honduras. The fact that we had not persuaded the United States and Soviet Governments to adopt the rule of a two-thirds majority for decisions by the Council was also relevant.

Mr. Eden decided that for the time being he would not submit this memorandum to the Armistice and Post-War Committee. Sir A. Cadogan, in a minute on the proposals, had pointed out that the Russians would probably not give way, and that the Americans were unlikely to agree—in spite of the views of their military authorities—to put to their own people and to the world a scheme on the Russian basis. Sir A. Cadogan thought that we had to choose between a Four or Five-Power Alliance dominating a World Organisation, and a 'democratic' universalised Organisation to deal with all eventualities. We were aiming at the latter type, but we might be mistaken. There was something wrong with a 'Charter' implying that, in certain circumstances, we and the Americans and French would go to war with the Russians over the Polish question when in fact we should not, and could not do so. We were indeed falling into the errors of the League Covenant. A Four or Five-Power Alliance might be repugnant to many people, but it might take various forms, e.g. it might be an instrument, at the centre of the World Organisation, for continuing to impose terms of surrender on Germany and Japan, while other arrangements could be made for the rest of the world. At all events the whole question needed careful thought. The Prime Minister also considered that we could make no progress until after a meeting of the three Heads of Governments.

In conversation with Mr. Jebb on November 24 M. Sobolev[1] said
(a) that the Soviet Government were likely to insist only that all decisions on the Security Council should be unanimous, i.e. that the Council should not be obliged to take action against one of the Permanent Members. The Soviet Government did not wish to prevent the discussion of disputes to which a Great Power was a party. Mr. Jebb said that in this case the outlook was more hopeful since most people would admit that, at all events in the present state of the world, the organisation of sanctions against a permanent Member of the Security Council would be absurd. Mr. Jebb then mentioned the compromise proposed at Dumbarton Oaks.[2] M. Sobolev did not make a direct

[1] Minister in the Soviet Embassy in London, and a member of the Soviet Delegation to the Dumbarton Oaks Conference.

[2] See above, p. 141.

(a) U8512/180/70; APW(44)122.

response to the suggestion; at the same time he did not appear to regard a compromise as out of the question.

Meanwhile on October 7, 1944, Sir S. Cripps had put the case for (a) the Soviet proposal from a somewhat different angle. His views impressed the Prime Minister, and, at the latter's request, were circulated (with Sir A. Cadogan's reply to Sir S. Cripps) on November 21 to the War Cabinet. Sir S. Cripps considered that it was impracticable to try to apply majority rule internationally. The consent of all the five[1] major Powers would be essential to the acceptance of a decision by the Security Council. All five Powers need not agree that a decision was right, but they must give their consent to the action arising out of the decision when it had been taken. A parliamentary minority in Great Britain would not consent to a decision unless it had been able to express an opinion and to vote on the matter at issue. The Security Council was a political, not a judicial body, and therefore the only chance of obtaining consent to its decisions was that all its members should have a right to vote even when their own conduct was being called in question.

In addition to these general considerations, Sir S. Cripps gave some illustrations of the practical difficulties which might arise if interested parties were not allowed to vote. Thus there might be a dispute whether Hong Kong should become an international base in the Pacific. The United States might put forward a request in this sense; we might resist it, and China might come in as a claimant for the return of Hong Kong to Chinese sovereignty. The United States, China and the United Kingdom would be excluded from voting, and the only major Power with a vote would be the U.S.S.R. The United States, the U.S.S.R. and the United Kingdom might claim rights to land aircraft in Greenland. The decision by vote would then remain largely in the hands of China.[2] Similarly, if the U.S.S.R., China and the United Kingdom claimed the right to land aircraft in Honolulu, the decision would rest entirely with France and the smaller Powers.

Sir A. Cadogan replied to Sir S. Cripps on October 30 that the controversy with the Russians was not, in fact, whether a great Power who was a party to the dispute should have a vote in deciding the dispute, but whether this vote should also be a veto. Since unanimity of the Great Powers was required for all important decisions, a vote by a Great Power against a decision was equivalent to a veto, whereas a smaller Power party to a dispute had no such

---

[1] Sir S. Cripps was including France as well as China.

[2] It will be noticed that in these two examples Sir S. Cripps had omitted to include France whom he had previously counted as one of the five permanent Members of the Council.

(a) U7737/180/70; WP(44)667.

right of veto. The Soviet plan, therefore, would set up two entirely different systems—one for the Great Powers who would be subject to no control whatever except to the extent that they might be influenced by the other Powers, and another for the smaller States who would be subject to the most drastic penalties if they refused to accept a decision of the Council. Sir A. Cadogan pointed out that this position could hardly be reconciled with the 'sovereign equality' promised in Article 4 of the Four-Power Declaration in Moscow.

Sir A. Cadogan himself drew up a memorandum which was
(a) circulated to the Armistice and Post-War Committee on November 22, 1944. Mr. Eden told the Prime Minister that the paper was sent out under Sir A. Cadogan's name because he (Mr. Eden) had not yet
(b) made up his mind on the question. Sir A. Cadogan explained that it was intended to settle the question at the forthcoming meeting of Heads of Governments, and that, whatever advantages there might be in going slowly, the Americans would insist upon bringing up the subject and attempting to decide it at the meeting. The view of the United States Administration seemed to be that, if it were apparent that the major problem concerning the Council remained unsolved, enthusiasm for a World Organisation might wane in the United States. Since from our point of view the greatest advantage of a World Organisation would be that the United States could accept under it commitments impossible for them to agree to under any kind of alliance, we ought to make the greatest effort to secure agreement on this major question of voting.

Sir A. Cadogan then stated the reasons for the Russian attitude and for our own and the American refusal to accept it. He said that obviously there was much force in the Russian argument that unanimity was necessary if the World Organisation were to work, and that it was impracticable to introduce any qualifications of such unanimity. On the other hand the Soviet Government did not seem to realise the importance of getting the full co-operation of the secondary States. We might not carry them with us if they thought that a single Great Power could frustrate the purpose of the organisation by exercising a privileged vote. If a distinction were made between Great and Secondary Powers with regard to voting in disputes to which they were parties, the whole Organisation might be compromised from the start.

Our view therefore seemed the right one. It would oblige us to abide by the decision of the Council in disputes to which we were a party but, given the unanimity rule among the Great Powers, we were not likely to be faced with a decision against us in a matter of great importance. For example, if the question concerned Hong

---

(a) U8522/180/70. (b) APW (44) 117; U8381/180/70.

Kong, French interests would not be served by undermining our position, while in Middle Eastern questions the United States would be unlikely to combine with the U.S.S.R. in imposing a decision detrimental to us.

It was, however, clear that the Russians were most unlikely to give way, and that we might not even get American support in another attempt to persuade them. Before the Dumbarton Oaks Conference the United States Delegation had not reached a decision on the matter. Their memorandum included a paragraph to which Stalin and M. Molotov had drawn attention: 'Provisions will need to be worked out with respect to the voting procedure in the event of a dispute in which one or more of the members of the Council having continuing tenure are directly involved.'

At the Conference the United States Delegation came down on our side as a result of arguments put forward by us and a strong statement by Governor Dewey on behalf of the rights of small States. The Americans then stood firm even after the Soviet Delegation had refused our thesis, but there was likely to be a further conflict of views in the United States between those who suspected the State Department of trying to impose a non-democractic 'four-Power domination' on the world and those who regarded the Great Power veto as a safeguard against the possibility that the European and even the Latin American countries might line up against the United States. Furthermore the President and Mr. Hull had staked a great deal on securing a World Organisation, and the President in particular had set himself to secure Russia as a working partner.

We might therefore fail at the meeting of Heads of Governments to obtain agreement on our formula. If we did not accept the Russian thesis there seemed to be only three possible compromises. The first of these latter—put forward by us at the Conference—was that permanent Members of the Council should forgo the right of veto in the earlier stages of the pacific settlement of disputes. The Russians had rejected this plan; the United States Delegates did not think that the Administration would accept it, and our own Ministers had not approved of it. The proposal meant that a permanent Member party to a dispute could not prevent the Council from (*a*) investigating it, (*b*) calling upon the parties to settle it by various pacific means, (*c*) formulating recommendations with a view to a settlement. From this point, however, the Great Power concerned could block further action. This plan had considerable advantages. A Great Power could be brought to account and would lose the support of world opinion if it disregarded the recommendations made by the Council. Sanctions against a Great Power would probably be impracticable in any event, and the whole organisation would cease to function if the Great Powers were involved in war between themselves. The Russians, however, were unlikely to accept this compromise because it went so far in the direction of our original proposals. The smaller Powers would favour it in some respects but would dislike the idea that, in a dispute between a Great Power and a small Power, sanctions could be applied against the small Power but not against the Great Power.

A second possible compromise would be to draw up the procedure for voting on the Anglo-American plan but to add that this procedure would not necessarily apply when a permanent Member of the Council was a party to a dispute. The permanent Member could either accept the ordinary procedure or submit the case to the Council which would thereupon constitute itself a conciliation body, and try to find a solution in the presence not only of the Great Power concerned but also in that of the other Power or Powers concerned in the dispute. There would be no voting, and no question of sanctions.

The Russians might find this plan less objectionable, since there would be no question of putting the Great Power 'into the dock'. The plan would also secure the orderly discussion of the dispute in the presence of a number of small Powers, including the 'victim', and the Great Powers would be recognised as not altogether 'above the law'. On the other hand the smaller Powers would not like this plan because a small Power in dispute with a Great Power could not be assured even that the Security Council would go as far as making recommendations which might be in its favour. Furthermore the Security Council could still impose a settlement on a small Power if the Great Power concerned chose to abide by the ordinary procedure.

The third compromise proposal was on similar lines to the second, with the important difference that it would omit all provision for referring a dispute between a Great and a small power to the Security Council and would provide that, if a Great Power so demanded, the Council, as such, should not concern itself with such a dispute. On the other hand, provision would be made for a special meeting of the Permanent Members of the Council to consider disputes to which one of them was a party in the presence of the other party to the dispute. This meeting would try to conciliate the parties, but would otherwise take no action. If this proposal were adopted, the Dumbarton Oaks proposals would have to be modified in two respects. There would have to be changes in the provisions of Chapter V(B)1 which authorised the General Assembly to make recommendations for the settlement of any dispute not being dealt with by the Security Council. Otherwise the Great Power party to the dispute might be 'pilloried' even more effectively by the Assembly than by the Council. Chapter VIII(A)4 would also have to be changed. This Chapter laid down that if parties to a dispute likely to endanger the maintenance of international peace and security failed to settle it by peaceful means, they were bound to refer it to the Security Council. We should, in fact, have to lay down plainly that disputes to which Great Powers were a party were not necessarily the affair of the Organisation at all.

This plan would go a long way to meet the Soviet point of view. It might be supported as more in accordance with political realities; it would still be an improvement on the full Soviet thesis in that no State which was a permanent Member of the Council could refuse even to discuss with other Members a dispute between itself and a small Power. On the other hand the plan would put the Small Powers even more at the mercy of a Great Power; it would limit the scope of action—already very small—of the Assembly, and give the impression that a Great Power dictatorship was being established.

If we could not secure any of these compromises, could we accept, in the last resort, the Soviet proposals? Field Marshal Smuts and, later, the Australian Government, while maintaining their general objection to the requirement of unanimity among the Great Powers, considered that in the present circumstances we should accept the Russian view. The Canadian Government, while agreeing that Soviet participation in the Organisation was essential, thought it most important that public opinion throughout the United Nations should support the Organisation not only now but for many years to come. Mr. Mackenzie King considered that we should try for a compromise; his own suggestion was that we should accept the Soviet proposals as representing a necessary transitional stage in the organisation of World Security but not as part of a general and permanent system.

Sir A. Cadogan's view was that we should not accept the full Soviet proposals. Whatever the United States Administration might be prepared to do, there would be strong opposition from American public opinion to a completely 'Great Power' solution, and the Liberals and Isolationists in the Senate might combine to wreck American participation in the scheme. Canada and the smaller Western European States might agree to come into the Organisation, but they would almost certainly refuse to undertake the heavy obligations in the Dumbarton Oaks proposals. Sir A. Cadogan thought that if at the meeting of Heads of Governments we had to choose between accepting the Russian terms or failing to get their agreement to the scheme, we should try to get the matter postponed. The Russians appeared to want a World Organisation in which they would take a prominent part, but there would be no harm in a period of delay in which they could reflect on the consequences of refusing to accept a compromise.

Sir A. Cadogan therefore summed up as follows the course we should take at the meeting of Heads of Governments: (i) we should say that we were more impressed by the unanimity of view on essentials than by the division of opinion on the question of voting in the Security Council; hence we thought that a real effort at a compromise should be made. We should all admit that the Organisation must fail if the Permanent Members of the Security Council did not work in complete harmony, but on the British view the Soviet proposal whereby a Great Power could prevent the Security Council even from giving preliminary consideration to a dispute to which it was a party would make the formation of a World Organisation impossible.

(ii) If by this means we could persuade the Soviet Government to consider some compromise, we should put our three suggestions in the order listed above, and make it clear that, as we moved from one to the other, the process of reaching agreement, as far as we were concerned, was becoming increasingly difficult.

(iii) If we failed to get Soviet acceptance of any of these suggestions, we should say that, while we believed Anglo-Soviet co-operation to be the only real guarantee of future peace, and while we should do our best to maintain this co-operation, whatever happened, we could not agree to the circulation of any agreed proposals to the United Nations at any rate without further thought and consultation with the Dominions.

(a) On December 5, 1944, President Roosevelt telegraphed to the Prime Minister his views about the voting procedure. He said that he was also taking up the question with Stalin, in view of the fact that the prospects of an early meeting of the three Heads of Governments were uncertain, and because he was convinced that we should move forward as quickly as possible to convening a general conference of the United Nations on the subject of international organisation.

President Roosevelt's proposal was on the lines of the compromise suggested by Sir A. Cadogan at Dumbarton Oaks and repeated as the first solution in his paper of November 22. The President wanted to maintain the unanimity rule in all decisions of the Council relating to the determination of a threat to peace or to action for the removal of such a threat or for the suppression of aggression or other breaches of the peace. In these matters he accepted the Soviet view that the Permanent Members of the Council should always have a vote. At the same time he felt sure that the moral prestige of the Great Powers was an essential element in any successful scheme of international co-operation and that these Powers should not insist on exercising a veto

(a) T2265/4, No. 666; Premier 3/472; U8635/180/70; U8533/180/70.

in such judicial or quasi-judicial procedure as the international Organisation might employ in promoting the voluntary peaceful settlement of disputes. The willingness of the Permanent Members to abstain from the exercise of their voting rights on questions of this sort would immensely strengthen their own position as the principal guardians of the peace and would make the whole plan far more acceptable to all nations. The President therefore asked whether the Prime Minister would agree to a meeting of representatives of the three Powers to work out a plan on these lines and to discuss the arrangements necessary for a prompt convening of a general United Nations Conference.

The Prime Minister asked Mr. Eden on December 6 to give him a (a)
'short explanation' of what the President 'really meant'.[1] He also thought that the President should come to England to talk over the question. In a minute written on the same day—December 6—before (b)
the receipt of the President's telegram the Prime Minister had said that he differed fundamentally from the view taken by the Foreign Office, and that he was in entire agreement with the Russians. He thought that Mr. Eden was not well advised in 'marshalling opinion' on the subject before he knew the views of the War Cabinet and in taking a line which alienated us from the Russians. The Prime Minister could not understand why there was any hurry about a decision when there were so many urgent and vital matters to be decided. 'All these attempts to settle the world while we are struggling with the enemy seem to me most injurious.'

Mr. Eden replied on December 12 that the President was putting (c)
forward the solution suggested as 'Compromise A' in Sir A. Cadogan's memorandum of November 22. Sir A. Cadogan had suggested the compromise at Dumbarton Oaks. The Prime Minister and Mr. Eden had considered it at Quebec, but had thought that it went too far in the direction of the Russian proposals. The Prime Minister now said that he favoured the Russian proposals, but the Americans were clearly not prepared to accept them, and Sir A. Cadogan's memorandum had given strong reasons why we should not do so. There were also indications that the Russians themselves did not insist upon their full application. Mr. Eden repeated that he had not altogether made up his own mind, and that he did not want a Cabinet discussion before the question had been fully explored, but we were bound to examine the President's latest proposal urgently and to decide whether we could support it.

---

[1] The Foreign Office were, in fact, not altogether clear at this time about the meaning (d)
of the President's proposal.

(a) M1192/4, U8635/180/70. (b) M1191/4, U8635/180/70. (c) PM/44/762, U8635/180/70. (d) U8687/180/70.

(a) In a memorandum of December 18 Mr. Eden suggested that, if the Dominion Governments agreed, we should support the proposed compromise, but that we should not make any communication at the present stage to Stalin. Stalin was likely to reply with a suggestion for another meeting of experts to consider the President's proposal. In this case we might all agree on something nearer to the Russian point of view—i.e. the second or third of the compromises suggested by Sir A. Cadogan.

(b) The War Cabinet decided on December 20 to consult the Dominions and meanwhile to say nothing to the President or to Stalin.

(c) Lord Halifax reported on December 26 that, according to Mr. Stettinius, the Soviet Government appeared likely to accept the President's compromise proposal. Mr. Eden therefore suggested to the Prime Minister that the Armistice and Post-War Committee should discuss the question, and make a recommendation to the Cabinet.

(d) The Prime Minister agreed with this suggestion. On January 5, 1945, Mr. Attlee, as Chairman of the Armistice and Post-War Committee, circulated a report to the War Cabinet on the compromise solution suggested by President Roosevelt to Stalin. He explained that the Committee thought that the British Government should accept the compromise. In reply to the enquiries sent on the instructions of the War Cabinet, the Canadian Government had recognised that the compromise might be the best obtainable solution. The South African Government were willing to accept it; the Australian and New Zealand Governments had not yet replied.

The Committee thought that the President's proposal was similar in essentials to the first of Sir A. Cadogan's compromise suggestions. They considered that if a dispute involving one of the Great Powers came before the Security Council, and was not settled by agreement among the Great Powers, the World Organisation would have failed. Action involving the use of force against a Great Power would mean a major war, whatever the rules governing voting on the Security Council might be. The President's plan would ensure that a Great Power could not prevent a small Power from bringing a question before the World Organisation. During the discussion full publicity would be given to the matters in dispute and world opinion could make itself felt. Considerable pressure would thus be exerted on the parties to the dispute to seek a solution by negotiation or other peaceful means, and it would still be open to the Great Power concerned to submit the dispute to settlement by the Security Council, but there would not be in the background the prospect of the Great Power being placed against its will 'in the dock', and thus finding

---

(a) WP(44)747; U8709/180/70. (b) WM(44)172; U8709/180/70.
(c) U8815/180/70. (d) WP(45)12.

itself in a position from which it would be difficult to withdraw without humiliation.

The War Cabinet decided on January 11, 1945, to accept the recommendations of the Armistice and Post-War Committee and to (a) instruct Lord Halifax to tell Mr. Stettinius that we were prepared to accept the President's compromise proposals. Lord Halifax was instructed accordingly on January 13. He replied on January (b) 18 that Mr. Stettinius was most grateful for the decision, and that the President would like a message directly from the Prime Minister on the subject, since the original American proposal was made in a message from him (Mr. Roosevelt) to the Prime Minister.

On January 16, however, Mr. Harriman reported to Washington that the Soviet Government had replied unfavourably on December 27 to the President's proposal but that they were willing to discuss it at the forthcoming tripartite meeting. The Prime Minister, after hearing of the Russian attitude, sent a minute to Mr. Eden that, although he agreed about accepting Mr. Roosevelt's proposal, he did not wish to be committed to fighting against the Russians for it at this stage. He had not replied to the President's message of December 5 because he had thought that the matter lay with the Russians; if they would not agree, we should not take definite sides against them without hearing their views.

On January 20 Lord Halifax telegraphed that the President had (c) told him on January 17 that he was willing to go a long way towards meeting the Russian point of view about voting, and hoped to 'horse-trade' concessions on this question with Stalin against the withdrawal of the Russian claim for the separate representation of the sixteen Soviet Republics of the U.S.S.R.[1] The Foreign Office suggested that the Prime Minister's message to the President might state that we thought his compromise formula the best solution if there were general agreement to it. We noted the President's statement of January 17 to Lord Halifax. We still hoped that we should jointly succeed in persuading Stalin to accept, if not the proposed compromise, something which was at least a slight advance on the present position. Otherwise the Organisation might never come into existence owing to the unwillingness of the secondary Powers to agree to terms offering little advantage from membership, yet imposing heavy burdens upon them.

The Foreign Office believed that the President would press his proposal strongly on the Russians, and that it was essential that the Prime Minister should support him. Mr. Eden and Mr. Hopkins tried to put the arguments to him once again on January 24, but

---

[1] See section (iv).

(a) WM(45)4; U626/12/70. (b) U462/12/70. (c) U520/12/70.

(a) he remained convinced by Sir S. Cripps's views, and refused on January 25 even to send a telegram to the President in view of the fact that he was already on his way to Europe, and that there would soon be a chance of talking to him. The Prime Minister added:

> 'If the Russians agree about the American compromise I will accept it. I cannot undertake however to fight a stiff battle with them on the subject. I agree with the President that it is far more important to get the 16 Russian Republics argument out of the way. The only hope for the world is the agreement of the three Great Powers. If they quarrel, our children are undone.'

Mr. Eden's own comment on the President's 'horse-trading'
(b) proposal was made in a memorandum of January 25 to the Armistice and Post-War Committee. Mr. Eden said that the President was doubtless the best judge whether he would be able to persuade the American Senate and the rest of the world to accept a scheme for a World Organisation based on the Soviet thesis of the Great Power veto, and if he felt that he could safely accept the latter as part of the deal, we should not object. Mr. Eden's own view, however, was that the compromise was desirable in itself and that we and the President should do our best to try to persuade Stalin to accept it, and that, if necessary, we should fall back on one of the compromises suggested by Sir A. Cadogan. In any case, even if we were compelled to accept the Soviet thesis, we should do so only after we had tried our utmost to contest it, if only from the point of view of meeting the wishes of Canada and other States. It was indeed still open to doubt whether it would be possible to form a World Organisation on the basis of a Great Power veto. If we attempted to do so now, we might well be unable to get the agreement of other States without reducing heavily the obligations on member States, e.g. by the adoption of the Canadian proposal that no member State should be bound by a decision of the Security Council unless the latter had been endorsed by a two-thirds majority of the Assembly. Mr. Eden would not regard a World Organisation on this basis as worthless, but he would feel reassured if we also had a definite treaty guaranteeing American participation in action against a
(c) renewal of German or Japanese aggression.[1] The A.P.W. Committee considered Mr. Eden's memorandum on February 1, 1945. They decided that they would leave Mr. Eden to decide as he thought fit about the American proposals.

---

[1] See note (i) to section (iv).

(a) U626/12/70. (b) APW(45)12. (c) APW(45) 3rd Meeting.

(iv)

Soviet demands for the inclusion of the sixteen Soviet Socialist Republics as members of the World Organisation (August 29, 1944–January 5, 1945).

At a meeting of the Steering Committee of the Dumbarton Oaks Conference on August 29 the Russians proposed that all the sixteen Soviet Republics should be separately represented in the proposed Assembly of the United Nations. M. Sobolev, in putting this forward, said that these Republics were on the same footing as the British Dominions, having the constitutional right to remain neutral in time of war.[1] This proposal had greatly disturbed the President and the State Department and Mr. Stettinius asked M. Gromyko that it should not be made public or even recorded in the minutes of the Steering Committee. M. Gromyko promised not to raise the question at the Conference but to accept the principle that the United and Associated Nations[2] should be 'founder members'. Mr. Stettinius told Sir A. Cadogan on September 2 that the President had sent a message to Stalin on August 31 that it would be fatal to the chances of establishing a World Organisation if the Russian proposal were put forward. He added that he did not know whether the Prime Minister would care to endorse the President's message to Stalin. Stalin replied to the President on September 7. A week later Mr. Stettinius, Under-Secretary of State, told Mr. Hull how 'upset' he was that a message from Stalin had been received at the White House several days ago, but the State Department had not been told of it. Mr. Hull said that 'he was used to this kind of thing'. Mr. Stettinius could only comment that he was 'young and inexperienced'.[3] Later in the month he noted in his diary 'I told the President point-blank that I had heard a rumour that he and Churchill had sent a wire planning to send a joint cable to Stalin relating to world security and other matters, and that it would be most helpful to us in the Department to know if such a message had been sent.' The President replied that a general wire had been sent and that he would ask Admiral Leahy to send a copy of it to the Department. The copy was not sent.[4] (a)

The Foreign Office view was that for the time we should keep out of the discussion. The Soviet Government evidently feared that if

[1] The constitution of the Soviet Union had been amended on February 1, 1944, to allow each Republic of the Union the right to enter into direct relations with foreign States, conclude agreements with them, and exchange diplomatic and consular representatives. In fact, as was obvious, these constituent Republics had not the slightest opportunity of exercising any separate control of foreign policy.

[2] See above, p. 148–9, n. (2). [3] *F.R.U.S. 1944*. I, 811. [4] Ibid. I, 833.

(a) U7078, 7196/180/70; U7088, 7098/180/70.

they had only one seat in the Assembly the United Kingdom and the United States would have a preponderant influence owing to the number of votes which they would control. If the sixteen Soviet Republics were included as Members of the Assembly, and the Russians were also able to control the votes of their smaller neighbours, they might have at their disposal about one-third of the Assembly. They would not thereby control the Assembly because a two-thirds majority would probably be laid down for all important decisions, and the United Kingdom and the United States would each be likely to count upon a supporting bloc of fourteen or fifteen votes.

The real difficulty about the Soviet proposal was that the Americans could not accept it as long as the United States, with a population of 130 millions, had only one vote. The Soviet proposal would therefore probably lead to a demand for proportional representation in the Assembly, with absurd consequences, e.g. in the case of India and China, and the Assembly would cease to be based on the principle of the sovereign equality of States. The United States Administration would thus be wholly opposed to the Russian proposal. Sir A. Cadogan was instructed on September 6 that we had better leave the Americans to deal with the Russians.

The Soviet Government temporarily withdrew their proposal owing to American pressure, and, as a result (though it was uncertain whether the Soviet proposal had this end in view) prevented the Americans themselves from pressing their proposal to include the Associated Nations among the founder Members. The chapter on membership in the published proposals was therefore left unsettled, but the Soviet Government did not abandon their claim.
(a) Their delegation at Dumbarton Oaks stated that they would bring it forward at a later stage in the negotiations. They even suggested that the date of summoning a full Conference of the United Nations to discuss the recommendations could not be fixed until agreement was reached on the inclusion of the sixteen Republics as founder Members.

(b) In conversation with Mr. Jebb on November 24[1] M. Sobolev said that the Soviet Government attached the greatest importance to the admission of the sixteen Republics. They thought that the original membership of the World Organisation should be limited to those who had played a real part in the war. No one could deny that the Ukraine, for example, was more qualified in this respect than Guatemala or Nicaragua. M. Sobolev maintained that each of the Soviet Republics had an independent existence. He thought

[1] See also above, p. 164–5.

(a) U7665/180/70. (b) U8512/180/70; APW(44)122.

that, provided that the Great Powers were unanimous, no difficulty would arise even if the Security Council included representatives of the Soviet Union and of one Constituent Republic. Mr. Jebb had the impression that the Soviet Government would push their demand strongly, though they might not insist on it if they had their way over the Great Power veto.

On December 5, 1944, the Foreign Office drew up a memorandum (a) on the question. The memorandum pointed out that the status of the Republics had arisen in connexion with the Finnish armistice. The Russians had said that, if any of the Dominions were to sign the armistice, they would ask that the constituent Republics bordering on Finland should also sign. In 1943, during the negotiations for bringing the Russians into the War Crimes Commission in London, they had claimed the right of the constituent Republics to participate; their refusal to take part in the work of the Commission was partly due to the fact that this claim was not recognised. They did not put forward any such claims at the U.N.R.R.A., Bretton Woods, or Hot Springs Conferences. They had accepted a permanent seat for the U.S.S.R. on the Security Council. We could thus argue that they could not have dual representation, but we must expect the issue to be raised in connexion with any form of international organisation in which the Dominions and India took part. We might also have to face the question of recognising the constituent Republics and exchanging diplomatic representatives with them.

We did not know the views of the United States on the 'straight question' of recognition, but we had told the Dominions in June 1944 that we wished the issue to be postponed until the peace settlement because we might otherwise be represented as having recognised the claim of the Ukrainian and White Russian Republics to parts of eastern Poland, and the incorporation of the Baltic States into the U.S.S.R. It would, however, be difficult, if not impossible to withhold recognition indefinitely. The acceptance of the sixteen Republics as Members of the World Organisation would carry with it diplomatic recognition. Conversely, diplomatic recognition would imply the right—in the absence of express stipulation to the contrary—to independent representation on all forms of international organisation.

From the point of view of our interests, it would clearly be better that the U.S.S.R. should have one vote, and not sixteen (or seventeen) votes. On the other hand effective power in the Organisation would rest with the Council, and (as the Foreign Office had already pointed out) a two-thirds majority rule would prevent the U.S.S.R. from dictating policy, though it could block decisions in the Assembly of

(a) APW(44)123.

which it disaproved. The position of India made it awkward for us to argue against the Soviet case, since on paper the Soviet Republics had a greater measure of autonomy than India in foreign affairs. The United States Government, Senate and people, however, would certainly refuse to accept membership of a World Organisation in which they had only one vote, and the U.S.S.R. sixteen (or seventeen). Hence, if the U.S.S.R. would not withdraw its claim, an entirely new basis must be found for membership and voting as far as concerned the Assembly. It was extremely doubtful whether agreement could be reached on any workable plan. British policy aimed at making the World Organisation effective and at avoiding friction with the United States and the Soviet Union. Since no compromise on this particular issue ssemed possible, we had to choose between three courses of action: (i) We could agree to the Soviet proposals. This course would put us in an impossible position with the Americans, and probably wreck the Organisation. (ii) We could agree with the United States and oppose the Soviet proposals. Owing to the status of India we should be in some difficulty, and the Russians might think that we were opposing them on purely political grounds. (iii) We could leave the United States to deal with the U.S.S.R. and say that, as the United States would not join the Organisation unless their view prevailed, we felt bound to support them in the absence of positive evidence that the sixteen Republics had some measure of real independence; we were willing, however, to accept any compromise which did not exclude India. One of two possible compromises might be acceptable: (*a*) The sixteen Republics could send observers to the meetings of the Assembly with the right to speak but not to vote; (*b*) We would agree to the exclusion of the neutrals to whom the Russians objected (the Argentine, Portugal, Spain and Switzerland) if they withdrew their claim on behalf of the sixteen Republics. Meanwhile our first step would be to explain the situation to the Dominions and ask for their views.

(a) On January 5, 1945, the Armistice and Post-War Committee reported, after discussing the question, in favour of the third of the
(b) possible courses of action suggested by the Foreign Office. The War Cabinet agreed with their recommendation.

Note (1) to Section (iv). The proposals of Senator Vandenberg and Senator Connally regarding post-war organisation, January 1945.

(c) On January 25 Mr. Eden submitted to the Armistice and Post-War Committee a short memorandum referring to a proposal by Senator Vandenberg for the immediate conclusion of a 'hard and fast treaty to use an Allied force if necessary to keep Germany and Japan

(a) WP(45)12. (b) WM(45)4. (c) APW(45)12.

demilitarised' after the war. This treaty was, apparently, to be signed by the major Allies. Senator Vandenberg also favoured the immediate formulation of a United Nations Security Organisation on the lines of the Dumbarton Oaks proposals 'provided it sufficiently authorised the ultimate review of protested injustices in the eventual peace terms'.

President Roosevelt had told Lord Halifax on January 17 that he was 'neither enthusiastic about nor opposed to' Senator Vandenberg's proposal for a treaty. The Senator had described it to him as a 'temporary arrangement to be replaced by the Dumbarton Oaks plan'. The President added that he 'had no strong feelings against it, as a temporary substitute, if other people liked it'.

Mr. Eden thought that we should welcome the proposal, and might even go as far as suggesting to the President that we should be very glad if such a treaty could be concluded. There would be considerable advantage in a formal commitment by the United States Government and Senate to a treaty with ourselves, the U.S.S.R. and France whereby the United States would be pledged to join with their Allies in suppressing any renewed attempt at aggression by the Germans or the Japanese. Such a treaty would be similar to the ill-fated treaties of guarantee to France designed in 1919 to buttress the League of Nations, the treaty would be compatible with the World Organisation and parallel to the treaties concluded between ourselves and the Russians and the French. We should, however, have to insert a saving clause safeguarding the position of a World Organisation. If the Senate passed such a treaty we should have reinsured to a very large extent against any failure to establish a World Organisation.

Mr. Eden also mentioned another American proposal. Senator Connally was about to suggest to the State Department the formation of an 'Interim United Nations Council' when the United Nations met to agree on the terms of a World Security Organisation. Such a Council would be similar in constitution to the Security Council in the Dumbarton Oaks proposals. It would have no authority to use force, but, in Senator Connally's opinion, it might settle 'a great many vexing questions' and 'intervene in situations such as that which had arisen in Greece'.

Mr. Eden thought that the proposal was not quite clear. If it meant that the non-permanent members of the proposed Council would have to be co-opted by the permanent members, there might be a considerable advantage in that the first Security Council would have a 'comparatively respectable' membership. Mr. Eden suggested that we should tell the President at the forthcoming tripartite Conference that we had no objection to the scheme, but that it required some elaboration.

Note (ii) to Section (iv). Proposals by the Canadian Government.

(a) On January 11, 1945, the War Cabinet invited the Armistice and Post-War Committee to consider the comments received from the Dominion Governments on the Dumbarton Oaks proposals and to advise upon the terms of a reply. The questions of voting in the Security Council and membership of the Organisation by the constituent Republics of the U.S.S.R. were not included in the terms of reference to the Armistice and Post-War Committee since these questions were being given separate consideration.

The three most important points for consideration were raised by the Canadian Government. The latter had suggested (i) that, after the five Great Powers there should be a category of 'middle' or 'important secondary States' who should enjoy, in respect to election to the Council, a preferential position over other Members of the Organisation who were not Great Powers; (ii) that it would be difficult to secure acceptance by Members—especially by those not at the time on the Security Council—of permanent and indefinite obligations to take positive and possibly drastic action when prescribed by the Security Council; (iii) that limited arrangements might be made for a temporary period, by which the Great Powers would act together, and other Powers agree to act with them, to prevent renewed aggression by Germany or Japan. The Canadian Government considered that many countries would prefer to undertake obligations with this specific object rather than the indefinite obligations laid down in the Dumbarton Oaks proposals.

Lord Cranborne suggested on January 27 that the Foreign Office should summon an interdepartmental meeting to prepare the way for a full consideration of the issues on the A.P.W. Committee. He thought that this interdepartmental meeting might also take account of the views of foreign 'secondary' Powers. The next stage would be a Commonwealth meeting, a plan to which the War Cabinet had already given their approval.

(a) APW(45)11.

CHAPTER LXIV

The formulation of British policy with regard to a Western European bloc: proposals for the future of Germany and Austria, March–December 1944: Foreign Office opposition to the Morgenthau Plan: the work of the European Advisory Commission in 1944.

(i)

The problem of a Western European bloc: views of M. Spaak: Mr. Jebb's memoranda on Western Europe and a regional security system: consideration of Mr. Jebb's memoranda in the Foreign Office: provisional views of the Chiefs of Staff (March 23–July 27, 1944).

THE Foreign Office had also to consider from another angle the problems raised by the Prime Minister's proposals for a United States of Europe, or at all events a Council of Europe.[1] The smaller Western Powers were much interested in the matter, and anxious to know the views of the British Government on the future policy of Great Britain in Europe. Mr. Lie and Dr. Van Kleffens, the Norwegian and Dutch Foreign Ministers, and, in particular, M. Spaak, the Belgian Foreign Minister, wanted the British Government to take the initiative in proposals for collaboration between their countries and Great Britain. They had pointed out in conversations with Mr. Eden that their countries had learned a bitter lesson in 1940 and were determined in future to collaborate with Great Britain for the joint security of western Europe, and, in particular, to continue and expand the arrangements under which during the war we had trained and equipped their national forces. (a)

On March 23, 1944, M. Spaak again mentioned the matter to Mr. Eden. M. Spaak told Mr. Eden that the Belgian and Netherlands Governments had come to a financial agreement, and had determined to form a customs union which would include Luxembourg. M. Spaak asked what would be the attitude of the British Government if the arrangements were extended to include France. (b)

---

[1] See above, pp. 117–19, 122 for the Prime Minister's views.

(a) U6468/180/70. (b) WP(44)181; U4102/180/70; C4394/44/4.

The Belgian and Netherlands Governments wanted also to work out military agreements after the war with other countries of western Europe; they hoped that Great Britain would participate in these agreements.

M. Spaak was in favour of a western *bloc*, including Great Britain, from Norway to the Iberian peninsula. He thought that the British Government had not yet realised how much all the countries of western Europe looked to them though they sometimes wished the British would state more clearly their views. Mr. Eden answered that the question of 'speaking out more clearly' could not be separated from the need for preserving the maximum unity among the Allies in the conduct of the war. Mr. Eden said that he was not himself a supporter of the conception of spheres of influence in Europe and that he had to consider proposals for a western group in relation to the important problem of Allied unity during the war and European security after it. He promised, however, to consider M. Spaak's questions, and to give a reply to them. On March 24 M. Spaak sent Mr. Eden a memorandum summing up his views. He agreed upon the dangers of establishing two *blocs* in Europe, and, in particular, upon the risk that such a policy would result in each *bloc* trying to get Germany on its side, or, in other words, making Germany 'the arbiter of the situation'.

M. Spaak pointed out that in 1943 there appeared to have been general agreement about these dangers, but that the situation had now been affected by the conclusion of the Russo-Czechoslovak treaty,[1] and by M. Benes's comments that this treaty was open to the accession of Poland and eventually of other eastern European countries. Thus, without waiting for a solution of the European question as a whole, the Russians seemed to be engaged in organising eastern Europe.

M. Spaak thought that, while it would be a mistake to reply to the Russian action by adopting a similar policy for western Europe, and thus creating two *blocs*, it would be equally unsatisfactory to do nothing at all. He suggested that we should make it clear that we accepted 'certain geographical realities and their ensuing conclusions', but that nonetheless in our view peace could be assured only by the organisation of Europe as a whole. The first of these considerations would lead the British Government to associate themselves with the efforts towards a military and economic organisation which the Netherlands, Belgium, France and Luxembourg might attempt; the second consideration would suggest a statement that the Anglo-

[1] This treaty of mutual assistance and collaboration was signed on December 12, 1943. It included an undertaking by each of the Contracting Parties not to interfere in the internal affairs of the other. See also Volume II, Chapter XXXIV, note to section (v).

Soviet alliance would be a leading feature of a larger international organisation after the war.

M. Spaak's representations were made almost simultaneously with a message from Field-Marshal Smuts to the Prime Minister. In (a) this message of March 20 Field-Marshal Smuts suggested that the Foreign Office should prepare for the conference of the Dominion Prime Ministers a paper on the 'traditional trends of Russian policy', and, in relation to this policy, the advantages and disadvantages of a regional grouping of western Europe round Great Britain or otherwise.

In view of M. Spaak's question[1] Mr. Jebb had drawn up a memorandum on the question of a western *bloc*. This memorandum was circulated within the Foreign Office, and shown to other Departments concerned. The memorandum was then revised, or rather re-written, in the light of the comments made on it; the new version (b) was printed with the date of May 9, 1944, and the title 'Western Europe'. This printed version began by referring to the suggestion that we should work towards the creation of some regional system—in the first place, a security system—to cover western Europe and to include the United Kingdom. If, however, we were to regard the creation of such a system as an end in itself, we should be in danger of dividing Europe into British and Russian spheres of influence, with the result that each side would try to get the support of Germany. Since we were most anxious to avoid a situation of this kind, and since our policy was directed to the establishment of a world order, we could support a plan for western European system only if it were a part of some general European security scheme within the world order.

On this assumption, what form should a western regional system take? We might regard as significant the fact that, in a recent speech to a group of American editors, Mr. Walter Lippmann had said that 'the only way to prevent our [i.e. the United States] having again to fight our way across the Atlantic . . . is by measures which make France, the Netherlands, Belgium and Great Britain so united among themselves that, with the reinforcements we could bring them, they would never lose the military position on the Continent which this summer we are going to recover.'

Stalin himself, at all events early in 1942, had been in favour of Great Britain assuming certain defensive obligations in western Europe. Even so, the Russians might suspect special arrangements of

[1] In drawing up his memorandum Mr. Jebb had considered the question from the point of view of fitting a regional system into the framework of a World Organisation, based on the principle of Anglo-Soviet co-operation, whereas Field-Marshal Smuts had in mind a regional *bloc* to curb Soviet power. The later drafts of the memorandum took account of Field Marshal Smuts's suggestion.

(a) W4373/1534/68. (b) U4105/180/70.

this kind between ourselves and other European countries; their suspicions would be acute only if we made our plans without reference to schemes for a World Organisation and if our aims appeared to be not to keep Germany down but to build up a counterweight to Russian influence in Europe and a bulwark against Communist penetration. In any case we could take a much more effective part in a World Organisation if we were associated with our Western neighbours for purposes of defence, and especially for defence against Germany. In the United States and the U.S.S.R. and even in the Dominions there were doubts about our will and capacity to make an effective contribution as one of three World Powers to a security organisation. We could meet these doubts if we were generally thought to have improved our strategical position and increased our military potential by association with neighbouring States.

The first objective of a World Organisation would be to ensure against renewed aggression by Germany and other Axis States. In making preparations to this end we should work on the principle that, while we were prepared at first to carry a heavy burden, other States should share this burden as they recovered their strength. France might be unable for some time to carry her full responsibilities in the West, but her recovery might be more rapid than many people expected and her active co-operation was essential. We ought therefore to do everything possible to assist in the recovery of France and to bring her into any regional scheme. At the same time we should encourage the smaller Powers to take their part; we and they could no longer expect the taxpayers of the larger Powers to bear the whole burden of world defence.

We should have to arrange for the stationing of the forces of a regional association according to some plan, and for ensuring that the arms and equipment of the whole group were of uniform pattern, and produced within the area covered by the group (unless the French forces continued to be armed with American types of material). The location of the war industries of the group would be determined primarily by the relative immunity of the sites to air or other attack.

The purposes of the regional association would be limited to defence in Europe and would not extend to the overseas dependencies of any member of the group. This western association, and other regional associations, must not be allowed to develop into any exclusive spheres of influence; hence they must be integrated in the World Organisation; some members of one regional group would also be members of another group, and individual members of one group might have special ties with individual members of another group.

(a) Mr. Jebb also drew up early in May 1944 a paper on 'British

(a) U4366, 4367/180/70.

policy towards Europe'. He drafted this paper with the idea that it might be seen by the Prime Minister. He was, therefore, specially concerned to point out the dangers (i) that the Soviet Government might regard the Prime Minister's plan for a United States of Europe as an attempt to create a Continental *bloc* against Russia, (ii) that the *bloc* might ultimately be dominated by Germany. Mr. Jebb began by pointing out that the term 'United States of Europe' might mean a definite European State, excluding Great Britain, but extending from Cape St. Vincent to the Curzon Line, or a loose association of European States, including Great Britain and the U.S.S.R., with a common meeting place to discuss European problems and some central control of certain services such as transport. He then explained the danger to Great Britain from such a powerful unit as an 'integrated' Europe in the first sense of the term, and the likelihood that it would fall under German control. The Soviet Government would also regard the establishment of such a European State as contrary to their interests.

On the alternative explanation of the term we should have to face the danger that a weak and divided Europe would be a 'potential storm centre' and might be exploited by Soviet *Machtopolitik*. In a later version of his paper Mr. Jebb put these points slightly differently. (a) He assumed that we might work, as the Prime Minister had suggested, towards a 'United States of Europe'. He then politely set aside this proposal as a 'very long-term objective'; even the use of the phrase was dangerous since it would lose us Soviet support. In any case we ought to distinguish clearly between a 'Council of Europe' and a 'United States of Europe'.

Mr. Jebb's main thesis in each of his drafts was that if we were to set up a European Organisation, we could do so only through the establishment of a World Organisation of which the principal object must be to harmonise the policies of the three Great Powers. Otherwise there could be no stable conditions in Europe and no chance of securing even a minimum of European unity. Within the framework of the World Organisation we should try to further European unity in certain limited fields. Thus we might try to set up a 'United Nations Commission for Europe' in order to deal with the confusion resulting from the war. We had already made a proposal of this kind in an *aide-mémoire* of June 1943,[1] to the United States and Soviet Ambassadors. This proposal appeared to have made a strong appeal to the Russians at the Moscow Conference, though the Americans were a little afraid that we were attempting to establish a 'Council of Europe' before the creation of a World Council.

[1] The date of this *aide-mémoire* was July 1, 1943. See above, p. 50.

(a) U4366, 4922/180/70; U4635/180/70.

Our next step, after setting up a 'United Nations Commission for Europe' might be to organise a local scheme of western European defence designed to prevent a renewal of German aggression. This scheme would rest on mutual defence agreements between the United Kingdom and France in the first instance, and similar agreements with the Low Countries, Norway, and possibly Sweden. In the course of time Spain, Portugal and Italy might be brought into the scheme. This plan would not mean any great British commitment on the Continent, but would imply the standardisation of equipment, the elaboration of common plans for defence, and the maintenance in Great Britain and France of a very considerable volume of armaments. There were reasons for supposing that the Russians would favour an arrangement of this kind if they were satisfied that its object was to hold Germany down and not to form the basis of some *bloc* directed against themselves, and if they were allowed, under the direction of a United Nations Commission for Europe, to take the lead in organising the defence of eastern Europe against Germany.

It was also clear that if, in spite of our efforts, our relations with the U.S.S.R. deteriorated (with the consequence that there could be neither an effective World Council nor a European association in which the U.S.S.R. was represented) we should have at least some line of defence in western Europe against Russian or German domination.

Mr. Eden asked Mr. Law's Committee[1] to meet for a discussion of Mr. Jebb's two papers. The purpose of the discussion was to draw up a brief on the subject for the British Delegation to the forthcoming
(a) discussions at Dumbarton Oaks. The Committee therefore considered whether the association of the United Kingdom with a western European *bloc* would in fact be an accretion of strength by extending our defences in depth or whether it would weaken us by increasing our continental commitments and our reliance on the support of continental land armies.

The Committee agreed that the matter required expert examination on the hypothesis (*a*) of the existence, and (*b*) of the absence of a World Organisation or a three-Power Alliance. This examination would have to take account of the considerations that the U.S.S.R. might regard the proposed association not as a threat but as a contribution which it was incumbent on us to make towards the prevention of future German aggression, and that such an association would assist the political stabilisation of Europe after the war and also enable us to secure that other countries undertook part of the very

---

[1] See above, p. 89.

(a) U4922, 5051/180/70.

large financial burden which would otherwise be imposed on our national resources. The Committee also thought that the chances of the success of the proposed association would depend very largely on our reducing the economic power of Germany in key industries, e.g. steel and chemicals, in order to prevent her from retaining a dominant influence in the markets of the countries concerned and thus maintaining her industry in a state of relative preparedness for war.

On the other hand it could be argued from our experience between 1919 and 1925 that we could not easily reconcile the position of the Dominions with the assumption by the United Kingdom of obligations in western Europe unless these obligations were undertaken within the framework of a World Organisation. It might also be said that, from a military point of view, fixed regional defence schemes were not practicable, and also that, politically, it was unnecessary for us to demonstrate our importance as a partner in a World Organisation by the prior formation of a western European *bloc*. Our real strength, apart from our own resources, lay in the adherence of the Dominions and in our value as an ally.

The Committee agreed, however, that our representatives at Washington ought to have the proposed strategic appreciation, and that it was desirable for this purpose to put the two Foreign Office memoranda together and to submit them as a single memorandum to the Chiefs of Staff and subsequently to the Armistice and Post-War Committee.

On June 20, 1944, Mr. Jebb submitted the 'combined' memorandum, under the title 'Western Europe', to the Secretary of State. (a) With his approval the memorandum was sent to the Chiefs of Staff for their comments. The Chiefs of Staff were informed that it would then be sent to the Armistice and Post-War Committee, and given to the British Delegation for the World Organisation talks at Washington.

The memorandum pointed out that the question of regional security schemes might be discussed at Washington, and that, in any case, our action or inaction as regards western Europe might affect our relations with the United States and the Soviet Union. Our policy might well be—as the Prime Minister had suggested—to work for a 'Council of Europe'. Such a policy was dictated by the fundamental unity of European civilisation and by the urgent need to put an end to internecine conflicts between European States. Our political and strategic interests also required some drawing together of these States, since a weak and divided Europe would be a potential storm centre which might be exploited by Russia. It would be essential for

(a) U6139/180/70.

Great Britain to form part of any scheme for closer European co-operation; otherwise the plan might lead merely to another German attempt at European hegemony. Our participation must not be at the expense of our overseas commitments. We should need to maintain the traditional balance in our policy between Europe and the rest of the world, and also to keep in the closest association with the United States.

American opinion was still impatient of national feelings in Europe and suspicious of any tendency on the part of ourselves or other Continental countries towards closer mutual association in advance of the establishment of a World Organisation. American isolationists would be glad to say that, since Europe was organising itself, the United States should 'contract out'. On the other hand, we were now, in a sense, an advanced defence outpost of the United States; an increase in our security might be welcomed from this point of view.

We ought to avoid giving the Russians an impression that we were trying to create a continental *bloc* excluding the U.S.S.R. Apart from the danger that such a *bloc* might fall under German control, the Russians would certainly regard it as a threat. Hence we would be well advised not to use the term 'United States of Europe'.

The discussions with the Dominion Prime Ministers[1] had shown that there would be general Commonwealth agreement to the establishment, within a World Organisation, of some rather loose association of States to deal with European problems. The Dominions did not want us to engage ourselves too closely in Continental commitments or to increase the risk of involving them in another European war, but they recognised that two world wars had broken out in Europe; that it was desirable to take precautions against a third war; that British manpower and industry were essential to the strength of the Commonwealth, and that, for strategic reasons, new factors such as air power required a closer association between Great Britain and western Europe. Such an association should include the United Kingdom, the United States and, if possible, the U.S.S.R. It should have a common meeting place and some centrally controlled European services, e.g. transport.

The memorandum then referred to the *aide-mémoire* of July 1, 1943, proposing the establishment of a 'United Nations Commissions for Europe'. This *aide-mémoire* had later been embodied in the terms of reference of the European Advisory Commission. We hoped to advocate a 'United Nations Commission for Europe' in our proposals for a World Organisation. The question was whether we should try to work for some regional security system to cover western Europe and

[1] See Chapter LXII, section (iv).

include the United Kingdom. We could not yet say what shape such a system would take. We might have a multilateral treaty of mutual defence between the United Kingdom, France, the Netherlands, Belgium, Norway, Denmark and Iceland, with the possible inclusion of Sweden, Spain, Portugal and Italy. Or there might be a series of bilateral treaties of mutual defence, or merely arrangements for Staff defence talks and common defence plans. Any plan would have to be subordinated to the World Organisation. The memorandum then repeated the arguments in favour of a western European regional system; (i) We could take a more important part in the World Organisation if we were associated with our western neighbours for purposes of defence, especially against Germany. Such an association might refute American and Russian doubts of our will or capacity to act as a Great Power on the level of the two other World Powers. (ii) Stalin late in 1941 had spoken in favour of our assuming certain defence obligations in western Europe. Similar views had been put forward by influential persons in the United States. (iii) The Anglo-Soviet treaty was the basis of our European policy, and we should try to reinforce it. A western European security system would have this reinforcing effect especially if, with our approval, the Russians constructed a similar pact in eastern Europe. The Russians, in fact, were likely to do so, with or without our approval. (iv) We should have many calls on our manpower after the end of the war and of Lend-Lease. A western European security system might ease our manpower situation. (v) Such a system would also strengthen France. French co-operation would be essential for restraining Germany, and a strong and friendly France was essential to us. (vi) The association for security and political purposes could also be buttressed by an economic association which did not interfere with wider schemes of economic collaboration. (vii) From a military point of view, we should secure a good 'layout' of the western European forces, an arrangement of war industries with a view to protection against air attack, and greater flexibility and depth in our defence. The disadvantages would be an increased risk of getting involved in the defence of western Europe and the maintenance of land forces on a continental scale.

The Foreign Office were unable to make further proposals, or draw up definite instructions for the British Delegation to the Washington talks because the Chiefs of Staff did not give a full reply, or indeed any reply to this memorandum until July 27.[1] Their provisional reply then was that they could not at once give their (a)

[1] It should be remembered that these weeks covered a critical phase in the operations in northern France and in the Mediterranean area, and that the Chiefs of Staff were also occupied (from June 13) with the problem of dealing with flying bombs.

(a) U8652/180/70.

considered views on a matter of such importance for our security. In the immediate future this security would depend upon preventing the revival of Germany as an aggressive State, but in the long run the most important factor would be our relationship with Russia. It might be that we should obtain a World Organisation capable of resolving disputes between the major Powers. Otherwise we should be faced sooner or later with a clash of interests between ourselves and Russia in which the attitude and power of Germany would be of vital importance.

The Chiefs of Staff said that they were instituting an enquiry into our long-term military position which would have a considerable bearing upon the action to be taken towards Germany after her defeat. Meanwhile they saw great advantages from a military point of view in the Foreign Office proposals which would provide us with defence in depth, but it seemed unlikely that a western European association could be strong enough, or give sufficient depth, without the incorporation at a later stage of all or part of Germany. The Chiefs of Staff realised the importance of not antagonising Russia by giving the appearance of building up a western European *bloc* against her. For this reason the immediate object of a western European group must be to keep Germany down, but we should not forget the more remote but more dangerous possibility of the use of German resources by a hostile Russia and we should consider whether any measures we were prepared to take now would assist in preventing such a contingency.

Note to Section (i). Memorandum by Mr. Duff Cooper on some aspects of British post-war policy, May 30, 1944.

(a) On May 30, 1944, Mr. Duff Cooper, who was at this time British Representative with the French Committee of National Liberation, sent in a despatch to Mr. Eden his views on certain aspects of British post-war policy. Mr. Duff Cooper thought that we could not rely solely for our security on a World Organisation, and that we ought to reinsure ourselves by a system of alliances. In particular, we should take precautions against the domination of Europe by Russia. The surest method of preventing such domination would be an alliance of the western democratic Powers—Great Britain, France, Belgium, the Netherlands, Norway and Denmark, with the possible inclusion of Sweden, Portugal and Spain.

Mr. Duff Cooper's despatch was given full consideration in the
(b) Foreign Office, and was circulated on July 25, 1944, to the War Cabinet together with Mr. Eden's reply. The reply accepted Mr. Duff Cooper's view that we should not depend for our security solely on the

(a) U5407/180/70; U6543/180/70. (b) WP(44)409; U6594/180/70.

defence provided by a World Organisation. Mr. Eden, however, disagreed with Mr. Duff Cooper's view that the creation of a western European group should be undertaken explicitly as a precautionary measure against a Russian attempt at Continental domination. If the Russians came to regard this as our purpose, we should not only lose all chance of collaboration with them, but we should also drive them into working against us by all means in their power. There would be no possibility of a World Organisation, and no hope of European recovery. We should therefore base a western European system of alliances 'squarely' on the Anglo-Soviet alliance, on an expressed intention never again to permit the revival of a powerful Germany, and if possible, on a World Organisation which would itself rest upon an alliance, or close understanding, between Great Britain, the United States and the U.S.S.R.

Mr. Eden pointed out that we had also to take account of American suspicion of proposals tending to divide the world into *blocs*. We did not yet know whether the United States Senate would be persuaded to accept any European commitments, but they would clearly do so only in connexion with a World Organisation. For this reason the Foreign Office at this time considered it necessary to be extremely cautious in mentioning to other western European Governments plans for a closer western alliance.

(ii)

Further conversations between Mr. Eden and M. Spaak: the Prime Minister's doubts about a Western European defence bloc: Mr. Eden's reply to the Prime Minister (July–November, 1944).

In the middle of July 1944 Mr. Eden had further conversations (a) with M. Spaak, the Belgian Foreign Minister, and with the Dutch and Norwegian Foreign Ministers on the general question of present and future collaboration between their countries and the United Kingdom. Mr. Eden told the three Ministers that the reason why he had not replied to their approaches was not from lack of interest but because we had considered that in the present state of international relations we had felt it better not to enter into discussions about collaboration in any particular part of Europe. We had thought it especially undesirable to begin detailed conversations just before the conference at Washington on the structure of the World Organisation because we did not want to make it more difficult for Mr. Hull to deal with the isolationists in the United States. As soon as we knew the results of the Washington Conference, we should be willing to

(a) U6468/180/70.

open conversations with the Ministers, and we should probably make it plain in Washington that we felt free to do so.

(a) The three Ministers were fully satisfied with Mr. Eden's statement. Mr. Eden spoke in more detail to M. Viénot shortly before the latter's (b) death.[1] He also raised the matter with M. Massigli, the French Commissioner for Foreign Affairs, during his conversations in August[2] M. Massigli agreed with our proposed timetable, and put forward his own view that Western security should be based not only on the general idea of preventing German aggression but also on definite political and military arrangements to keep Germany down.

(c) On October 5, 1944, the Belgian Ambassador told Mr. Eden that M. Spaak proposed to come to England and wanted to begin conversations about the future relations of Great Britain, Belgium and the Netherlands. He said that Belgium would like to see her relations with the United Kingdom placed on a permanent footing by an alliance or any other method of which we approved. M. Spaak hoped that there would be no objection to discussing the matter now that the Dumbarton Oaks conversations were coming to an end. Mr. Eden answered that he would be glad to hear M. Spaak's views, but that the form in which Anglo-Belgian relations should be expressed was a matter to which considerable thought would have to be given.

(d) The Dumbarton Oaks Conference, in their final recommendations, stated (Chapter VIII (C) 1) that nothing in the Charter of the general International Organisation

> 'should preclude the existence of regional arrangements or agencies for peace dealing with such matters relating to the maintenance of international peace and security as are appropriate for regional action provided such arrangements or agencies and their activities are consistent with the purposes and principles of the Organisation.'

Sir A. Cadogan had also mentioned to the United States and Soviet Delegations at the Conference the ideas of the British Government with regard to closer association with the western European countries. Neither Delegation had objected to the proposal.

(e) Hence on October 20 a departmental meeting was held in the Foreign Office to carry the discussions a stage further. The meeting considered that France and the Low Countries should form the nucleus of an association and that Norway and Denmark should be included as soon as possible. The best method of procedure would be to begin with specific military and technical arrangements rather

---

[1] M. Viénot, French diplomatic representative in London, died suddenly on July 20.
[2] See below, pp. 239–41.

(a) U6381/44/70. (b) U7057/180/70. (c) U7917, 8652/180/70. (d) U7585/180/70; U8652/180/70. (e) U7956/180/70.

than to attempt the immediate conclusion of a formal and comprehensive agreement which might have to be modified in accordance with the Charter of the World Organisation. We should also make it clear that the security aimed at was security against Germany.

The meeting also decided to ask the Chiefs of Staff for their views. The Chiefs of Staff replied on November 8. They referred to their letter of July 27 as giving their agreement in principle, and accepted in general the Foreign Office suggestions. The Prime (a)
Minister was unwilling, however, that Mr. Eden should open discussions with the Western countries on the matter; though he agreed that we should not 'oppose any advance they made with a negative'. (b)
Mr. Eden therefore did not go beyond generalities in his discussions with M. Spaak during the latter's visit to London early in November. M. Spaak himself gave to the Foreign Office a memorandum on the 'Organisation of co-operation between Great Britain and Belgium within the framework of a West European Regional Entente'.

The Prime Minister's reasons for delay were based primarily on his view that the smaller States of western Europe would be liabilities rather than assets if we bound ourselves to them in a scheme of common regional defence. The Prime Minister put his argument (c)
shortly and firmly in a minute of November 25, 1944, to Mr. Eden. Two days earlier Mr. Eden had suggested certain changes in a message which the Prime Minister was sending to Stalin. The Prime Minister had proposed to say:

> 'There has been some talk in the Press about a western *bloc*. I have not given my agreement to any such plan. I trust first of all to our triple agreement embodied in a world organisation to ensure and compel peace upon the tortured world. It is only after and subordinate to any such world-structure that European arrangements for better comradeship should be set on foot, and in these matters we shall have no secrets from you, being assured that you will keep us equally informed of what you feel and need.'

Mr. Eden suggested that for the words 'I have not given my agreement . . . tortured world' the Prime Minister should substitute: 'I have not yet considered this. I trust first of all to our Treaty of Alliance, and close collaboration with the United States, to form the mainstays of a World Organisation to ensure and compel peace upon the tortured World.'

The Prime Minister replied on November 25 that he had accepted Mr. Eden's form of words. He then said that the Cabinet ought soon to discuss the question of a western *bloc*. Mr. Churchill himself thought that until a really strong French army was again in being,

---

(a) U8165/180/70. (b) U8146/180/70. (c) U8472, 8473/180/70.

that is to say, for another five or ten years, there was nothing in the smaller countries but

> 'hopeless weakness. The Belgians are extremely weak, and their behaviour before the war was shocking. The Dutch were entirely selfish and fought only when they were attacked, and then for a few hours. Denmark is helpless and defenceless, and Norway practically so. That England should undertake to defend these countries, together with any help they may afford, before the French have the second Army in Europe, seems to me contrary to all wisdom and even common prudence. It may well be that the Continent will be able to fire at us, and we at the Continent, and that our island position is damaged to that extent. But with a strong Air Force and adequate naval power the Channel is a tremendous obstacle to invasion by Armies and tanks.'

Mr. Churchill added:

> 'I cannot tell whether Parliament will be agreeable to the gigantic expense and burden of maintaining a large Army for Continental purposes. Even if they would, I should think it wiser to put the bulk of the money into the Air, which must be our chief defence with the Navy as an important assistant.
>
> The situation would change if the French became notably friendly to us and prepared to act as a barrier against the only other Power which after the extirpation of German military strength can threaten western Europe, namely Russia, and if at the same time they built up an Army comparable to that of 1914. But a second condition would also be necessary, as the French quite possibly may decide to work with Russia. This condition is the building up of the world organisation. I have accepted your expression "mainstay"[1] only for the moment, as I consider it must be an overall shield and canopy.'

Mr. Churchill said that he did not know

> 'how these ideas of what is called a "western *bloc*" got around in Foreign Office and other influential circles. They would certainly require the mature deliberation not only of the Cabinet but of Parliament before any effect could be given to them. The foreigners will also ask immediately: "How large an Army are you going to contribute?" I cannot imagine that even if we went on with taxes at the present rate, which I am sure would be ruinous for economic revival, we could maintain an Expeditionary Army of 50 or 60 divisions, which is the least required to play in the Continental war game. Perhaps you would enlighten me. I shall probably be writing a Paper for the Cabinet on this subject, and meanwhile there must be no committal.'

Mr. Eden replied on November 29 that he entirely agreed about the danger of entering into commitments for the defence of Norway, Denmark or the Low Countries except in conjunction with the

[1] i.e. in the message to Stalin.

French and as part of a general plan for containing Germany evolved under the aegis of a World Organisation. He agreed also that the western European countries had behaved very foolishly between the wars. Our own record, however, was not entirely praiseworthy. The lesson of the disasters of 1940 was that we needed to build up a common defence organisation in western Europe, which would prevent another Hitler 'whencesoever he may come, pursuing . . . the policy of "one by one"'. The best way of creating such an association would be to build up France, and we could hope that such a build-up would be possible during the period of the occupation of Germany. It would be, in fact, only after we had evacuated Germany that we should need a regional defence organisation for western Europe.

Nevertheless we ought to start thinking about it at once, since if our western Allies, and more especially the French, had the impression that we were not going to accept *any* Continental commitments, they might conclude that their only hope lay in making defence arrangements with the Russians. The development of long-range missiles had shown that, if we were to retain our independence, we must provide for our defence in depth. A properly organised Europe could provide this defence in depth and secure large resources in manpower which would greatly ease our burden and enable us to avoid maintaining a huge standing army. Hitler's strategy of 'one by one' not only gave him bases from which to bombard us and attack our sea communications, but also deprived us of a manpower pool of over sixty millions. Hence we had been compelled to strain ourselves to the utmost to raise a large army, and even so we could not have hoped for victory without the manpower of Russia and the United States. Meanwhile Hitler had been able to use the labour of millions of western Europeans, and thus to keep up the numbers of the German army. There was no reason to suppose that a common defence plan would compel us to maintain a huge standing army, though we should have to make a larger contribution than 'the famous two divisions which was all we had to offer last time'.

Mr. Eden then explained the origin of the idea of a western regional security plan, the present position of the discussions in the Foreign Office and the views of the Chiefs of Staff that there were great advantages in 'building up a strong association of nations in western Europe to provide us with the depth which is becoming increasingly necessary to our defence'. He said that the key to the matter was the attitude of the French. We had therefore to await the outcome of General de Gaulle's talks with Stalin.[1] In view of

[1] See Volume III, Chapter XXXVII, section (v).

Stalin's statement in December 1941, Mr. Eden did not expect him to oppose a special regional association in western Europe if it were part of the general system of world security under the control of the World Organisation and directed against a resurgence of Germany. During the discussions at Dumbarton Oaks neither the Soviet Union nor the United States Delegations had objected to the possible development of a western European association of this kind.

(a) After M. Spaak's visit in November 1944 the Foreign Office considered that it would be wise to say something to the Russians about the proposals for western regional security arrangements. We had not commented on M. Spaak's proposals outlining the first step to such arrangements, but we had received them from him, and had told M. Bidault of this fact. We had emphasised to the French Foreign Minister that we had made no commitments, and that any plans must be fitted into the framework of the World Organisation. General de Gaulle, who was about to visit Moscow, might well pass on this information in a more or less distorted form to Stalin. Russian broadcasts, and questions from members of the Russian Embassy in London, showed that the Soviet Government thought that some negotiations were taking place without their knowledge.

On November 26, therefore, Sir A. Clark Kerr was instructed to tell M. Molotov that there was a great deal of discussion in the British and foreign press about a so-called 'western European *bloc*'. Some press articles suggested that we were intending to organise a closely integrated western European system, and even that our object was to secure a counterpoise to the Soviet Union and the United States. Sir A. Clark Kerr was instructed to say that these rumours were largely fantasy. We should doubtless have to consider whether it would be desirable to devise a system for the organisation in west Europe of regional defence against Germany for the sole purpose of holding Germany down. During the Dumbarton Oaks Conference Sir A. Cadogan had said that we intended to make use of Chapter VIII(C) of the proposals in this sense; the Soviet and American representatives had raised no objection. Stalin himself had encouraged us in 1941 to think that such a system would be agreeable to him. If the arrangements were made subordinate to a World Organisation, we could not imagine that the Soviet Government would object to these either in the west or in the east of Europe. We had been approached at various times by the Norwegian, Dutch and Belgian Governments, and, recently, with more elaborate proposals from M. Spaak. We had not yet considered M. Spaak's memorandum,

---

(a) U8410/180/70.

though we had agreed to grant facilities for the training of Belgian troops in the United Kingdom and had undertaken to provide arms for a limited number of Belgian divisions to take part in the eventual occupation of Germany. We had not given any final indication of our views to any of the Governments concerned, and, in particular, we had not even taken up the question of regional defence with the French Government. We put the World Organisation first on our list of *desiderata*, and, in any case, we proposed to rely on the Anglo-Soviet alliance for the purpose of holding Germany down. There might well have to be similar arrangements between France and Great Britain and France and the U.S.S.R. but we might also find it desirable to have some regional defence arrangement in western Europe in order to work out a common defence policy against Germany, and to decide the role of each State. In accordance with our policy, we should discuss these matters in detail with the Soviet Government if and when they arose.[1]

Sir A. Clark Kerr saw M. Molotov on November 28. M. Molotov (a) said that the question of a western *bloc* could not but interest the Soviet Government. He thought that, from the newspapers, talk about the pact had been going on for some time; representatives of other Governments had also mentioned it. M. Molotov was grateful for the information given to him; he said that he would think about the matter, and that it would probably have to be discussed at the next meeting of Heads of Governments. Sir A. Clark Kerr commented in his telegram that our statement was timely; M. Molotov had clearly been watching the press closely and had probably attached undue importance to the reports about a western *bloc*.

During the visit of Mr. Churchill and Mr. Eden to France in November 1944[2] M. Bidault had asked Mr. Eden about M. Spaak's proposals. Mr. Eden told him that no definite agreement had been made with M. Spaak and that his written proposals had not yet been (b) considered. M. Spaak had suggested that the time was ready for an agreement, but Mr. Eden said that we needed discussions with the French and the Dutch.

No progress was made in the matter for the next eight weeks, mainly owing to the difficulties of negotiating an agreement with General de Gaulle, but in any case Mr. Churchill remained convinced that France, Belgium and the Netherlands were so weak that an agreement to defend them was not in British interests.

---

[1] The Foreign Office sent instructions that M. Bidault, who was on his way to Moscow, should be given a similar message. M. Bidault had left Cairo before the instructions (c) arrived. The message was therefore delivered to him by Sir A. Clark Kerr at Moscow. M. Bidault said that it corresponded with the views of the French Government.

[2] See Volume III, pp. 89–90.

(a) U8430/180/70. (b) E7627/217/89. (c) U8508/180/70.

The Foreign Office, however, still thought that the formation of a western regional defence group would be to our advantage. Mr. Bevin, the new Foreign Secretary, in a discussion at the Foreign Office on August 13, 1945, said that, in a long-term policy, he wanted to establish close relations between Great Britain and the countries on the Atlantic and Mediterranean fringes of Europe, but that he did not intend to take any immediate steps—starting with France—until he had had more time to consider possible Russian reactions.[1]

(iii)

Consideration of problems affecting the surrender and post-war treatment of Germany, January–October 1944: Sir W. Strang's memoranda of January 15 to the European Advisory Commission on the terms of a German surrender and the imposition of Allied military control: the question of a possible dismemberment of Germany.

The first formal statement to the United States and Russia of
(a) British views on the terms of surrender and post-war treatment of Germany was made in two memoranda[2] given by Sir W. Strang to the European Advisory Commission on January 15, 1944—a day after the first meeting of the Commission. In the first of these memoranda Sir W. Strang dealt with the terms of surrender. He pointed out that we could not forecast the circumstances in which hostilities would end, and the procedure most suitable for the German surrender, but it was 'possible to form some idea of the things the United Nations will desire to do in Germany' and even 'to evolve a general plan which will enable these things to be done whatever the procedure ultimately adopted'. The ideal conditions for the attainment of the United Nations' aims would be 'the existence of a German Government capable of assisting in the execution of the obligations which it will have undertaken' and the agreement of 'the United Nations primarily concerned' upon a 'single instrument terminating hostilities on behalf of all of them simultaneously'. Even if those conditions were not fulfilled, the material contained in a single full-length Instrument of Surrender would be useful. Hence the British Delegation to the Commission thought it desirable to put forward such a draft, though for the present the British Government did not wish to be committed to any of its terms. The draft was 'based on the principle of unconditional surrender and confers on the United Nations far-reaching

---

[1] See Volume III, Chapter XXXVII, p. 103, note 2.

[2] A third memorandum dealt with the actual machinery of control. The three memoranda are printed in *F.R.U.S. 1944*, Volume I, pp. 112–59.

(a) U407,408/104/70. EAC(44) 1 & 2.

powers which, under international law, they would not enjoy on a basis of ordinary military occupancy'. Certain general provisions 'entitle the United Nations to exercise all or any of the powers of the German Government, of the German Supreme Command, or of any local government or authority . . . In general, the draft armistice imposes on the German Government and people the obligation to assist in its execution and to carry on the national life, economy and administration under the direction of the United Nations'.

Conditions in Germany at the time of her surrender will almost certainly be chaotic, and the last thing the Allies will want to do is to saddle the High Command with all the vexations attendant on administering in detail a vast, hostile and bankrupt country. The draft terms were therefore based on the idea that the Germans should be enjoined to carry on all civilian activities until they are directed to do otherwise by the United Nations.

The second British memorandum dealt with the military occupation of Germany after the armistice. The memorandum began with a discussion of the arguments for and against a total occupation of Germany, i.e. the exercise of the right to move forces into any part of Germany, though this would not imply that there would be Allied troops in every part of the country at all times. The case was argued on the assumption that Austria would not form part of Germany after the war; that East Prussia and Danzig, and possibly other areas, would ultimately be given to Poland, and that elsewhere Germany would be confined within frontiers no wider than those of 1937. The objectives of the United Nations were described as the prevention or suppression of disorder in Germany, the rapid and total disarmament of Germany and break-up of the German military machine, and the complete destruction of the Nazi organisation. The Germans were also to be made to realise that they had suffered complete military defeat, but tolerable living conditions were to be ensured to them. For these purposes total military occupation was desirable though it need not be prolonged beyond the period necessary to achieve complete disarmament.

The chief argument against total occupation was the cost in manpower and material. Another argument was that it would be a political error unduly to prolong German humiliation with the risk of driving the whole German people into the nationalistic camp. The alternative of partial occupation, however, would mean that the non-occupied areas would become 'breeding grounds' for subversive activities, or even deliberately fomented disorders which would, as happened after 1918, lead to a German demand 'for permission to maintain military forces for the preservation of order'. Underground military activities were traditional in a defeated Germany, and total occupation was the only effective way of countering these activities.

If total occupation were adopted, it would be possible to reduce the strength of the occupying Army as soon as the process of disarmament was near to completion (probably within two years). During the next period, while the destruction of the German armament industry was being completed, air forces could be used increasingly to allow the reduction of land forces. The final period would last until a new German Government had been sufficiently established and the Allies were sufficiently convinced of its peaceful intentions entirely to withdraw their occupying force. During this last period it might be possible to use air forces alone or at all events to keep only a small land force in the country. The extent to which it would be possible to make these reductions of forces would largely depend on the progress made in the political re-education of Germany.

The memorandum also considered whether the occupation should be by zones in each of which one of the Allied Powers would provide the main occupying force, or carried out throughout Germany by a mixed force of soldiers of most of the United Nations. The mixed force plan would prevent the creation of spheres of interest by the occupying Powers and should ensure that a uniform policy was applied throughout the whole area, but there were insuperable administrative problems in maintaining troops of different nationalities differently armed and of using a mixed force and, above all, mixed staff if it became necessary to carry out operations against large-scale disturbances. Moreover the mixing of forces of different nationalities would increase the danger of trouble between the respective contingents; differences in rates of pay alone would cause discontent and envy. Most of the advantages which it was hoped to obtain from mixing could be got, under a policy of zones of occupation, from

> 'control by a United Nations High Commission at the top designed to bring the military policy, actions and behaviour of the contingents of the constituent armies into line'.

A further consideration in favour of zones of occupation was that, as after the last war, the defeat of Germany might be the signal for the re-emergence of separatist movements in that country.

> 'Whether the United Nations decide forcibly to split Germany up into smaller States, or whether spontaneous movements towards particularism or separatism are merely encouraged by the Allies, there must be advantage in dividing the country for purposes of occupation into areas whose boundaries approximate to the lines on which such tendencies towards division may be expected to develop'.[1]

[1] The memorandum went on to consider the best determination of the zones, with the Berlin area as a combined zone occupied by a mixed force and supporting the authority of an Allied Military Government, the Control Commission and other Allied bodies,

(*continued on page* 201)

These memoranda dealing with the more immediate issues of a German surrender and the imposition of Allied control had to take account of the fact that no British decisions had been reached on most of the complicated questions regarding the 'long-range' treatment of Germany. The British government had not even made up their minds about the amount of territory to be taken from Germany. Mr. Eden had asked for the authority of the Cabinet on September 27, 1943, to suggest at the Moscow Conference the cession to Poland of East Prussia, Danzig, and considerable areas of Silesia, including the Oppeln district, and consequent transfers of German populations. Some discussion had taken place on the subject at the Teheran Conference,[1] and on February 22, 1944, the Prime Minister had said in the House of Commons that he and Stalin had 'agreed upon the need for Poland to obtain compensation at the expense of Germany both in the north and in the west'. No decision had been reached on the amount of territory involved, but the Prime Minister had made it clear that we were not bound in the matter by any provisions of the Atlantic Charter. We had also not decided how far we would support the Polish and Czech desire to transfer German populations back to Germany.

We had not yet settled whether we wanted the dismemberment of Germany. Although the question had been raised at the Teheran Conference,[2] and referred to the European Advisory Commission, the latter body had been unable—owing to the Russian refusal—to discuss it. We had also not decided how far we wished to interfere with the existing constitutional arrangements of Germany. The Prime Minister had told the House of Commons on September 21, 1943, that 'Nazi tyranny and Prussian militarism must be exterminated'. We were preparing directives for the abolition of Nazi laws and institutions, and for a purge of the administration, but we had not reached any conclusion on such questions as the enforcement of a decentralised system upon Germany, the break-up of the Junker estates, and the removal of the control of the great industrialists over German industry.

Mr. Eden, in his paper of September 27, 1943, to the War Cabinet, had suggested, as matters for discussion in Moscow, the imposition of some form of international control of German industry and economic life. We had not decided about the form or precise objects of such control, though we were studying the matter, and, in particular, the problem of reconciling the demands of security with the need to use

---

(*continued*)
and ensuring the maintenance of order in the capital. For a short account of the prolonged discussions on the European Advisory Commission on the Instrument of Surrender and the mode of occupation and control of Germany, see below, section (viii) of this chapter.

[1] See Volume II, Chapter XXXV, section (v).

[2] See above, pp. 7–89.

German industry for the requirements of the United Nations and the question of German competition with our own industry, which was likely to be occupied for some time with the military needs of the war against Japan.

We had also to formulate our views on the whole question of reparation, and on what might be called the 'regeneration of Germany', though here our general view had been expressed in Mr. Eden's paper of September 27, 1943. Mr. Eden had said that 'the only policy holding out any real hope for the future is one which, while taking all necessary safeguards, aims ultimately at the re-admittance of a reformed Germany into the life of Europe'.

These questions were discussed between May and December 1944, at meetings of the Armistice and Post-War Committee. The Committee met twenty-one times between May 4 and December 31, 1944, and considered—in addition to matters affecting the proposed World Organisation—a large number of memoranda on subjects connected with the surrender and occupation of Germany and the treatment of Germany after the war. Owing to the number of subjects involved—most of them extremely complicated—as well as to the need for ascertaining the views of our Allies, the work of the Committee was, inevitably, somewhat piecemeal and tentative in character; the discussions were at times on detailed arrangements which in fact could not be settled before larger matters of policy had been decided. There was also, as in the case of the World Organisation, some trouble in getting the attention of the Prime Minister and of the War Cabinet—and the Chiefs of Staff—during a period when the military situation demanded incessant concentration and immediate decisions. Similar factors affected the formulation of American views, and, still more seriously, Russian views. In any case the Russians were extremely unwilling to commit themselves on post-war questions. Hence decisions were taken very slowly and many of the major problems left unsettled. Thus the terms of surrender for Germany were discussed at nine meetings between April 27 and September 21, while concurrently the Committee was considering subjects such as a proposed European Inland Transport Organisation, the re-education of Germans, and the problem of food and agriculture in Germany. Meanwhile no decisions had been reached on the larger questions of the future German frontiers or the extent to which administrative decentralisation should be carried—e.g. whether it should go as far as actual dismemberment. In view of this unavoidable delay and untidiness the British Delegation on the European Advisory Commission was concerned above all with securing that the Instrument of Surrender gave the Allies full and unlimited power to enforce, after the end of active hostilities, whatever terms they might think fit.

The discussions on the crucial question of dismemberment were indeed taken a stage further but reached something of a deadlock owing to differences of view between the Foreign Office and the Chiefs of Staff. The Foreign Office had asked the Chiefs of Staff on (a) June 7 for their views.[1] They stated in their letter that the matter had been referred at the Teheran Conference to a special committee of the three Powers, or a committee under the European Advisory Commission. The British representative had put the question on the agenda of the Commission in January 1944, but the Soviet representative had asked for discussion on it to be postponed for the time being; the reason which he gave was the insufficiency of his staff. No discussion had therefore taken place. The Foreign Office wanted, in particular, the views of the Chiefs of Staff on the possible effects of dismemberment on (i) the military occupation of Germany by the Allies, (ii) the machinery of inter-Allied control, (iii) the long-term prevention of rearmament, (iv) British strategic interests generally. The Chiefs of Staff could assume that a plan for dismemberment would follow, broadly, the three zones of occupation.

The Chiefs of Staff reported on September 9, 1944; a fortnight (b) earlier the Economic and Industrial Planning Staff (E.I.P.S.)[2] had completed their report on the economic aspects of dismemberment. The E.I.P.S. report was in general unfavourable to dismemberment. The Chiefs of Staff, on the other hand, regarded it, on balance, as to our strategic advantage in relation to the prevention of German rearmament and renewed aggression. They also considered the dismemberment of Germany as an insurance against the possibility of a hostile U.S.S.R. They pointed out that in the latter case we should require

> 'all the help we can get from any source open to us, including Germany. We must above all prevent Germany combining with the Soviet Union against us. It is open to argument whether a united Germany would be more likely to side with the U.S.S.R. than with ourselves. In any event, it is most unlikely that the U.S.S.R. would ever permit the rearmament of a united Germany unless she were satisfied that she could dominate a Germany so rearmed. Thus, we

[1] The Chiefs of Staff were informed that the Foreign Office were inviting the Economic and Industrial Planning Staff (see note 2 below) to study the problem in its economic aspect, and that they hoped eventually to prepare a single paper on the question for the guidance of the United Kingdom representative on the European Advisory Commission.

[2] The Economic and Industrial Planning Staff had been set up in February 1944 to consider the economic aspects of a German armistice. Their functions were, to arrange for consideration by the appropriate Departments of economic and industrial (not financial) questions connected with German armistice terms, to give advice to the Departments on these questions, and to collate the results for submission to the appropriate official or ministerial committees. On June 19 their terms of reference were extended to cover the European satellite States. See also section (iv) of this Chapter.

(a) C7021/146/18. (b) C13517/146/18.

are unlikely to secure help from the whole of Germany against the U.S.S.R. Our interests are therefore likely to be better served in this event by the acceptance of dismemberment, for we might hope eventually to bring north-western and possibly southern Germany also, within the orbit of a western European group. This would give increased depth to the defences of the United Kingdom and increase the war potential of that group.'

(a) On September 20 Mr. Eden submitted a Foreign Office memorandum on dismemberment to the Armistice and Post-War Committee[1] in the light of the two reports. In a covering note Mr. Eden wrote that he found it hard to resist the conclusion of the Foreign Office memorandum that dismemberment 'would fail to advance the main object we all have at heart, viz., security from the German menace. That it would have grave economic disadvantages is clear from the report of the E.I.P.S.' Mr. Eden would not, however, regard these advantages as conclusive if he were convinced that dismemberment would be in the interests of security.

Mr. Eden then said that, if we rejected dismemberment, we need not leave Germany in its present centralised state. There were other ways in which we might weaken the central Government. The French proposal for a special régime in Rheno-Westphalia[2] would remove from a central German authority the control over German basic industries. A return to the confederate or federal system based on the German States, or even a widespread system of decentralisation would also diminish the authority of the central Government. Either of these constitutional measures would have an appeal to German sentiment and historical tradition, and we had to face the fact that in the long run no constitutional settlement would be likely to last without the support of German opinion. In either case it should be possible to secure one vital change, i.e. the dissolution of Prussia into federal States or administrative areas.

Mr. Eden said that he proposed to circulate a paper on the merits and possibilities of confederation, federation, and decentralisation. Meanwhile he was strongly against consideration of the German problem from the point of view of reinsurance against possible Soviet aggression.

'If we prepare our post-war plans with the idea at the back of our minds that the Germans may serve as part of an anti-Soviet *bloc*, we shall quickly destroy any hope of preserving the Anglo-Soviet Alli-

---

[1] The Committee had agreed on August 31, see below, p. 218, that the 'dismemberment (b) of Germany was desirable, but that further consideration of this matter should be deferred until the reports which were being prepared on the subject, and the Foreign Secretary's paper on them, were available'.

[2] See below, section (VI).

(a) APW(44)90. (b) APW(44) 15th meeting.

ance and soon find ourselves advocating relaxations of the disarmament and other measures which we regard as essential guarantees against future German aggression.'[1]

The general conclusions of the Foreign Office memorandum were that the advantages claimed for dismemberment were illusory. There was little chance that the German people would regard it as acceptable or that the British or American people would be prepared to maintain it by force; British and American opinion was more likely to come to regard it as an injustice, and in such case the peace settlement as a whole would be prejudiced. Futhermore the Germans would have little difficulty in evading the necessary prohibitions and the continual need to prevent such evasions would endanger the unity of the Allies. We should require a great increase in Allied trained staff if we decided to enforce dismemberment; we might find that we had to govern Germany directly because German officials refused to co-operate in our policy. (a)

The memorandum dealt at some length with the possible effects of dismemberment on Anglo-Soviet relations, and with the arguments put forward by the Chiefs of Staff that dismemberment would be a form of insurance against the possibility of an eventually hostile U.S.S.R. The memorandum developed more fully the comments made by Mr. Eden in his covering note.

---

[1] The Foreign Office were already afraid that official references and 'careless talk' of the possibility of Anglo-Soviet hostility after the war might come to the notice of the Russians. On August 18, 1944, after reading the draft of the paper on dismemberment and another paper on the western *bloc* by the Post-Hostilities Planning Staff, Sir. O. Sargent thought it necessary to bring to Mr. Eden's notice the fact that the Chiefs of Staff were mentioning this possibility (and the corollary that we might need German assistance against Russia) in documents which had a fairly wide circulation. Sir O. Sargent considered it likely that both the Americans and the Russians would become aware of the attitude of the British military authorities. (b)

Mr. Eden spoke to General Ismay, Chief of Staff to the Minister of Defence, about the matter. General Ismay thought that the Chiefs of Staff had not given any directions to their subordinates on the lines of which Sir O. Sargent was complaining. Mr. Wilson, (c) Head of the Northern Dept. of the Foreign Office, however, on September 1, again raised the question of the general attitude of the Service Departments with regard to future Anglo-Soviet relations. Sir O. Sargent suggested that Mr. Eden might write to the Service Ministers on the danger of allowing the Russians to conclude that we were expecting them to be hostile to us after the war, and that our German policy was being framed partly at least with this consideration in mind. Later in September Mr. Wilson urged that some action should be taken. Sir O. Sargent thought that Mr. Eden might call the attention of the Prime Minister to the risks involved in anti-Russian talk. Sir O. Sargent had in mind not only that a warning should be given to the Service Departments but that—in view of the ill-mannered treatment which our Military Mission to Russia had received—the Prime Minister might send a message to Stalin or Mr. Eden himself might write to M. Molotov that we were taking special care to ensure that all our officials in contact with the Russians should do their best to establish frank and friendly co-operation, but that our instructions would be useless if the Russians were not given similar instructions, and if our representatives continued to be treated with suspicion.

After his meeting with the Chiefs of Staff on October 4, see below p. 209–10, Mr. Eden decided not to send this minute.

(a) C13517/146/18. (b) N5126/36/38. (c) N6214/36/38.

The argument [of the Chiefs of Staff] seems to be that dismemberment could be used to keep Germany prostrate just for so long as it might serve our purpose, and that at a given moment we could suddenly reverse our policy and find in Western Germany a reliable ally prepared to reinforce our war potential and to join us in battle against a combination of the strongest military Power in Europe and fellow-Germans in the East. Such a suggestion seems little less than fantastic. But it is worse than that. It is playing with fire. The policy of His Majesty's Government is to preserve the unity and collaboration of the United Nations. If we start preparing our post-war plans with the idea at the back of our minds that the Germans may serve as part of an anti-Soviet *bloc*, we shall quickly destroy any hope of preserving the Anglo-Soviet Alliance and soon find ourselves advocating relaxations of the disarmament and other measures which we regard as essential guarantees against future German aggression. This is not only a matter of strategy. It is a matter of high policy.

The question then arises whether dismemberment is likely to give rise to friction with the Soviet Government. This is not easy to answer because we do not know if they will advocate dismemberment or not. It is true that at Teheran Marshal Stalin advocated the division of Germany into smallish pieces and the use of force, if necessary, to prevent their reuniting. Against this we have M. Gusev's refusal to discuss the question in the E.A.C. and, still more significant, the Soviet proposals for control machinery for Germany to cover the first period of occupation. These proposals not only advocate the use of the German central Government and the German central organs for the purpose of carrying out the terms of surrender, but set out as one of the most important objectives of the Allied control agencies "the preparation of conditions for the creation in Germany of *central* and local organs based on democratic principles". It is difficult to believe that such realists as the Russians would wish to create central organs based on any principles if their purpose was to destroy the unity of Germany. At any rate, we cannot take it for granted that the Soviet Government are now in favour of dismemberment.

Should, however, we find them pressing for it, we shall be faced with a dilemma. If, on the basis of the arguments in this paper, we hold out against it, the Russians may suspect our motives and regard us either as appeasers or more probably as harbouring some deep-laid plot to bring Germany one day into an anti-Soviet *bloc*. This would be liable to vitiate all prospect of fruitful collaboration with the Soviet Union. The Russians' reaction would probably be to adopt whatever measures they considered necessary to achieve their own security, including all kinds of intrigue and intervention in every country of Europe and possibly an attempt to collaborate closely with Germany herself in order to counteract our supposed policy. If, on the other hand, we agree to dismemberment, acute differences are almost bound to arise in course of time over its policing. . . . It is not impossible too that dismemberment would lead to the division of former

Germany into Eastern and Western spheres of influence which it is our policy to avoid.

Either course, therefore, has its dangers. But the greater danger seems to lie in supporting a policy against our better judgment only to find when it had to be enforced that public support for the ruthless measures required was not forthcoming. If, therefore, we find the Russians bent on dismemberment, but decide that such a policy would be mistaken, it would seem best to make our views and our reasons abundantly clear to them, leaving no doubt in their minds that a soft peace is no part of our plan.

If we can convince the Russians that we harbour no designs of using the Germans against them—a point of particular current importance in the light of the Chiefs of Staff's Report—there is no reason to believe that the preservation of a united Germany would necessarily lead to a Russo-German combination. The more likely result of leaving Germany united would surely be to make the Russians more inclined to collaborate with us, always provided we remain strong and an Ally worth having. One can go further and suggest that the existence of a united Germany might prove a factor of the first importance in holding the Soviet Union and ourselves together.

Finally, in measuring the importance of Anglo-Soviet collaboration, we must not forget the equal importance of our relations with the United States. American opinion is in the long run unlikely to be favourable to dismemberment, at any rate, if it involves active policing measures on their part. Therefore, even if by supporting dismemberment we were to make Anglo-Soviet collaboration easier, we should run the risk of making Anglo-American collaboration more difficult.'

Before the Armistice and Post-War Committee discussed this (a) memorandum the Chiefs of Staff wrote to the Foreign Office on October 2, asking for a private meeting with Mr. Eden. They considered generally that the Foreign Office arguments were unconvincing, and in particular they questioned the view that a policy of dismemberment should be decided solely from the angle of security against Germany. They summed up their own case as follows:

'No one will dispute for a moment the value of friendship with Russia or of a successful world security organisation. No one would be better pleased than the Chiefs of Staff if a permanent solution to our military problems could be achieved by this means. We should be very foolish if we adopted measures which could hinder the perpetuation of the present close relations between the three great Powers. But it is the duty of the Chiefs of Staff to examine all serious eventualities. We cannot be debarred from taking into account the possibility that for some reason or other the world security organisation may break down, and that Russia may start forth on the path to world domination, as other continental nations have done before her.

(a) C13518/146/18.

When the Chiefs of Staff consider any important post-war problem, we start with the security of the British Empire as the cardinal objective, and try to examine the world situation with an open mind. In studying long-term strategical questions, we are bound to adopt two alternative hypotheses:

(*a*) That unanimity of view prevails among the three great Powers, and that a successful world security organisation results.

(*b*) That the world security organisation either fails to materialise, or later breaks down.

The first hypothesis presents no serious military problem. It is the second that cannot with safety be neglected. After the last war we made just that mistake; we assumed that the League of Nations would ensure the security of the British Empire, and we based all our post-war arrangements on that assumption. The results were disastrous. We found ourselves caught in a vicious circle. Our weakness led us to seek to appease our potential enemies. The more we appeased, the weaker we became.

If one looks at the situation which will exist in the world when Germany and Japan have been thoroughly beaten and demilitarised, one finds only two possible menaces to the security of the British Empire, namely the United States and Russia. We eliminate the United States, and are left with Russia, a country of enormous power and resources which had been cut off for 25 years from contact with the outside world and the trend of whose policy no one can foretell. Taking a long view, we cannot possibly afford to eliminate from our mind the conception of an expansionist and perhaps eventually aggressive Russia, and this applies whether we are considering the German problem or any other problem which affects our security.

The examination of an unpleasant situation which may perhaps arise is in no way incompatible with the pursuit of a policy designed to prevent that situation arising. Yet the Foreign Office seems to recoil from the precaution of considering how to insure against the failure of our policy. They seem in effect to presume that the policy we intend to pursue is bound to be successful provided no thought is taken to meet the possibility of failure. It is this attitude that we feel bound to challenge.

We ask that this fundamental question should be resolved before the Dismemberment Paper is taken by the A.P.W. Committee. We regard it as our duty as the military advisers of His Majesty's Government to examine quite freely those problems which affect the security of the British Empire, and we must be free to put forward the military view without being debarred from taking into account any consideration which we regard as relevant.'

(a) Sir O. Sargent re-stated the Foreign Office case in a note of October 4 for Mr. Eden's use in the discussion with the Chiefs of Staff.

(a) C13518/146/18.

'The Foreign Office do not deny the proposition that the Soviet Union is a possible enemy. But they think it unlikely that any cause of war between the Soviet Union and the British Empire will arise for, at the worst, a number of years.

In the meantime, H.M.G.'s policy is based on the Anglo-Soviet Alliance and every effort must be made in the interval, without sacrificing major British interests or jeopardizing the closest relations with the U.S.A., to get on good terms with the Soviet Government and accustom them, if possible, to the practice of frank and friendly relations and consultation. This may be facilitated by the establishment of a World Security Organisation. If it is not established, we must still pursue this policy.

It will be fatal to any chance of pursuing this policy successfully if the Soviet Government suspect H.M.G. of thinking in terms of a war with the Soviet Union, or of attempting to build up a *bloc* against the Soviet Union. Most fatal of all would be that the Soviet Government should suspect us of any intention in our policy towards Germany of combining with Germany or parts of Germany against the Soviet Union.

Not only would this make the establishment of good relations with the Soviet Government impossible, but the Soviet Government would immediately set themselves to making any western *bloc* ineffective, and to ensuring that Germany will be on the side of the Soviet Union and not on our side. There seems to the Foreign Office little doubt that the Soviet Union is in an excellent position to achieve both these aims.

It is therefore of vital importance that the Russians should not get to know that the Chiefs of Staff think in terms of a war against the Soviet Union, think of a western *bloc* as a potential safeguard against Russia, or, worst of all, dally with the idea of getting Germany or parts of Germany on our side against the Soviet Union.

It is therefore most undesirable that a considerable number of officers in the various Service Departments should be thinking in the above terms or that any thoughts of this kind should be committed to paper.'

At the meeting with the Chiefs of Staff on October 4, 1944, the (a) latter pointed out that the question of dismemberment had a most important bearing on the future security of the British Empire, and that they had felt bound

'to examinine it on various hypotheses, one of which was that in the course of time the World Security Organisation might break down on account of differences with Russia and that in the worst case we might find ourselves faced by a unitary Germany, dominated by or in collaboration with Russia.'

Mr. Eden said that, although we obviously could not exclude the possibility of differences with Russia, he had been worried by the

(a) N6177/183/38.

growing tendency in certain quarters for thought to swing too far in this direction. There were two dangers in this: firstly by focusing on the distant danger we might fail to guard against the more immediate one—the resurgence of Germany; secondly if study and talk about Russia as an enemy became widespread, the Russians would almost certainly come to hear of it, and would think that their suspicions of us were well-founded, and our talk of collaboration not sincere. After the first war, we had looked round for possible enemies, and had selected France, with the result that we had soon forgotten the real menace—namely Germany—and had awoken to the facts too late. As regards the second danger, Mr. Eden suggested that a general warning should be issued against indiscreet talk on the subject of Russia.

It was finally agreed at the meeting that Mr. Eden should withdraw the Foreign Office memorandum and his covering note, and that the Chiefs of Staff should also withdraw their paper, and prepare a fresh study. Mr. Eden would then submit a new memorandum after the Moscow Conference.[1] In view of the possibility that the question of dismemberment might be discussed at this conference, the Prime Minister should be informed of the existence of conflicting British views on the subject.[2]

It was also agreed that the assumptions to be made about Russia in strategical papers dealing with the post-war period raised a dilemma to which no solution had yet been found. Until such time as firm directions in the matter were given by the War Cabinet, the Chiefs of Staff should take steps to restrict to the narrowest possible limits discussions and circulation of papers in which the hypothesis of Russia as a possible enemy was mentioned.

(iv)

Consideration of further problems affecting the surrender and post-war treatment of Germany (July–October, 1944).

In spite of the lack of progress on the all-important question of dismemberment, a number of general discussions about Germany took place in the Armistice and Post-War Committee, though they consisted for the most part of expressions of opinion which could not be conclusive or definite until the three Powers had decided upon

[1] See below Section vi.

[2] General Ismay submitted a minute to the Prime Minister reporting that Mr. Eden was of opinion that 'it would not pay us to dismember Germany, whereas the Chiefs of Staff felt that the arguments for dismemberment were very strong'. The matter was therefore being given further study. The Prime Minister replied that he understood that both the President and Stalin were in favour of dismemberment, and that they went even further in the matter than he was inclined to go. The Prime Minister proposed to talk over the matter with Mr. Eden. On his return from Moscow Mr. Eden said that this proposed talk had not taken place.

their policy in regard to the larger issues. Thus one of the papers before the Committee early in July 1944 was a long report from an inter-departmental committee on the transfer of German populations. The committee had been set up to consider the following questions: (a)

'(i) having regard to the economic position in which Germany is likely to be placed as a result of defeat, and of the demands of the United Nations for disarmament, reparations, etc., how great will be Germany's capacity, to absorb emigrants from East Prussia (including Allenstein), Danzig, Upper Silesia, the Sudetenland, and from areas within the Polish frontiers of 1939 and the Czechoslovak frontiers of 1938? (ii) What conditions (both of time and administration) would be required to ensure that the transfer was carried out without undue suffering to the migrants and without serious economic dislocation both to Germany and to Poland and Czechoslovakia? (iii) What contributions in finance and personnel would be required from the United Nations to ensure these conditions? (iv) What possibility, if any, existed of settling the migrants in territories other than Germany?'

The Committee's answer to the fourth question was simple; no area outside Germany was likely to be available for a large-scale settlement of transferred populations. To the other questions they answered that the Czechoslovak Government would probably wish to expel some 1,500,000 Germans. If the Polish Government received Danzig, East Prussia, and the Upper Silesia, they might want to expel some 5,340,000 Germans. If they also received the Oder frontier north of Upper Silesia (including Stettin, Frankfurt-an-der-Oder, and Breslau, the figure might be increased by 3,300,000.[1] The Committee estimated that—allowing for German war casualties—the addition of these 10,140,000 migrants would increase the population of the 'rump Germany' by 15 per cent above the pre-war level.

The long-term economic problems of the transfer might not, in theory, be insoluble. The transfer might ultimately yield some advantages to all the countries concerned, but the short-term difficulties would be so great, especially for Germany, that—added to the general dislocation—they might cause a complete German economic collapse. The difficulties for Poland might also be insoluble without outside assistance.

The main problems for Poland and Czechoslovakia would be the resettlement of the vacated areas, retraining labour to take the place of the expelled personnel, and finding capital to restart industry and agriculture. The temporary fall in production, especially in agriculture, might have serious consequences. For Germany the main

[1] These figures took no account of possible transfers of Germans from other areas—e.g. Yugoslavia, Hungary, Roumania and Alsace-Lorraine.

(a) APW(44)34.

short-term problems could be summed up in the words 'homes, work, and food'. Housing would be the most serious problem; only about a third of the people transferred would have a reasonable chance of being absorbed in their former occupations. Most of the others, including those engaged in agriculture, would join the numbers of unemployed unskilled labourers. The problem of resettlement in Germany, however, might be eased if, at the same time, some millions of able-bodied Germans were employed as an organised labour force in devastated areas outside Germany, e.g. the U.S.S.R. The transfers would have an effect on the amount of reparation which could be secured from Germany, since some of the German resources which might have contributed to reparation would have to be employed in meeting the urgent subsistence needs of the migrants.

The Committee thought that the transfers could not begin in an organised way for about a year after the end of hostilities and that they would have to be spread over a period of at least five years. It would be necessary to set up a special transfer authority and not to leave the Poles and Czechs to eject the Germans as they might think fit. It would also be essential to adopt some criterion of selection, and not to allow any of the persons involved an option whether to go or stay. Half-measures—i.e. leaving large German minorities behind—would be useless. If, therefore, the transfers on the scale estimated by the Committee were regarded as impracticable, while it was still thought essential to remove all the Germans from areas ceded to Poland, the only solution appeared to be that the areas thus ceded should be smaller.

The Committee pointed out that the amount of human suffering involved would be very great; the migrants would be poor and embittered, and the mere transfer of persons of a particular nationality from territories long settled by them did not lessen the sentiment of the nation as a whole for the lost territory or the determination to regain it.

(a) Mr. Attlee submitted to the Armistice and Post-War Committee on July 11, 1944, a memorandum on policy towards Germany, with special reference to the conclusions of this report. He pointed out that the report raised a fundamental question which required discussion. It was generally agreed that our object in occupying Germany was to ensure that she should not re-emerge as a menace to peace. Ought we to act on the hypothesis that, subject to the disarmament and demilitarisation of Germany, the restoration of normal, orderly and organised life should be brought about as quickly as possible, and that Germany should be provided with food and facilities for economic, commercial and industrial revival? Or did we think that at all

(a) APW(44)43.

costs Nazi influence and the German war cult must be utterly rooted out, even if the result at first would be to make Germany feel the full impact of military defeat, including loss of territory, the influx of transferred populations, political and economic turmoil, etc.

Mr. Attlee considered that we were basing our plans on the first hypothesis. We wanted Germany to be able to provide reparation; we wanted to lighten as far as possible the tasks of our occupying forces, and we thought that the economic revival of Germany was essential to the general economic welfare of Europe. Mr. Attlee agreed that we should avoid creating a situation of chaos inside Germany which would be harmful to our own interests elsewhere or compel us to supply the Germans with food, etc., or provide large military forces for the maintenance of public order; the test of any policy, however, should be not so much how hardly it would bear upon Germany but how far it could be carried out without serious embarrassment or injury to ourselves.

Mr. Attlee thought that we should be wholly uncompromising, during the early stages of our occupation, in our measures for eradicating the whole German military machine and Nazi system. Such a policy might produce an internal crisis and subject the German people to great hardship. Even without taking an extreme view of their responsibility for the present situation, we could say that everything which brought home to them the completeness and irrevocability of their defeat was worth while. The only alternative to a policy of completely destroying German power would be an occupation lasting, perhaps for thirty years and a drastic 're-education'. It was impossible to suppose that we or the Americans would commit ourselves to a plan of this kind, or carry it through. We had therefore to take the line of drastic action at once, and to remember that in re-establishing Germany we must not restore the Prussian landowning class or the controllers of German heavy industry who looked to war, or the fear of war, to provide them with orders.

Mr. Eden commented upon Mr. Attlee's paper in a memorandum (a)
of July 19 to the Armistice and Post-War Committee. He agreed with Mr. Attlee that the test of our policy should be its effect on our own interests. Our main aims were to demilitarise Germany, to eradicate National Socialism, and to extract the maximum amount of goods and services from Germany for the general purposes of reconstruction. Would these purposes be promoted or would they be frustrated by economic chaos in Germany? Obviously Germany in economic chaos could supply neither goods nor services. We were also unlikely to obtain our desired political ends through economic chaos. The great depression had been one of the main factors in the growth of the Nazi party; we must not destroy the Nazis only to put something

(a) APW(44)47.

equally evil and dangerous in their place. Moreover our own troops would not carry out a policy which resulted in the starvation of Germany; public opinion in Great Britain—and even more quickly in the United States—would soon react too far in the other direction. Hence we could not remain indifferent to the results of political and economic confusion in Germany.

Mr. Eden thought that Mr. Attlee had not rightly interpreted the assumptions upon which the Foreign Office was basing its suggestions. We were not proposing to be over-tender to the Germans or—for reasons of efficient administration—to overlook the Nazi character of any German organisation. We proposed to abolish the Nazi party, its institutions, methods, and personnel, and to limit supplies to Germany to the minimum required for the avoidance of disease and unrest. In addition to our action against war criminals, the Foreign Office assumed that drastic measures would be taken against the German armed forces, the Gestapo, the party officials, the teachers, and the higher grades of the Civil Service. We were not hoping—as Mr. Attlee seemed to think—for a German Darlan or Badoglio; we regarded the Junkers and industrialists as our most dangerous enemies. Mr. Eden said that in fact we had to strike a balance and to act with determination, but also to avoid creating conditions likely to hamper the success of our policy.

(a) The Armistice and Post-War Committee discussed these two notes on July 20, 1944. Mr. Attlee considered that we ought to destroy what he called the 'central machine' of government in Germany. He said that it was an illusion to suppose that there was a 'normal Germany' to which one could return. There had been no normal Germany for fifty years or more, except one governed by a centralised and militaristic machine. Mr. Eden replied that we were in agreement about working for a maximum of separatism and decentralisation in Germany but we had not decided whether we should use force to stop a return to centralisation. Mr. Attlee said that military governments and control organisations always tended to work with what they considered to be the forces of law and order, since by so doing they felt they could create an efficient administration. He would be prepared to see a good deal of inefficiency in return for the destruction of the central machine and the substitution of local institutions.

Sir William Strang said that, if Ministers did not wish to work through a central German governmental organisation, they would have to change the policy hitherto put forward on the European Advisory Commission. The terms of surrender for Germany had been drawn up in the Commission on the assumption that a central German Government would exist. The papers which we had circulated to the

(a) APW(44) 10th meeting; U6568/180/70.

Commission on the machinery of control were also based on the assumption that the tripartite controlling authority would work through a central German Government. The Americans took much the same view; the Russians had not yet made any proposals in the matter but, if we judged by their ideas about the control of Berlin, they would assume a centralised Government. The argument in favour of operating the control through a central Government was that it offered the easiest and most effective way of disarming Germany and destroying the Nazi system. The occupation of Germany was to be in three zones demarcated in such a way as to suit a dismemberment of Germany into three parts, but it would not facilitate breaking up the country into its old States. In dealing with a central Government at the time of surrender we should not debar ourselves from working subsequently towards any end we desired. Sir William Strang had asked M. Gusev how he would deal with the surrender of Germany by an unsuitable Government. M. Gusev had said that he would accept the surrender and then get rid of the Government. Mr. Eden thought that it would certainly be necessary to accept the surrender of Germany by a central German Government, but that we should arrange our control machinery with a view to promoting the disruption of Germany as soon as possible after the surrender.

After the meeting Mr. Eden asked Mr. Attlee, as Chairman, whether he would arrange for a further discussion of the question. This discussion took place on July 27. Mr. Eden explained that there (a) were two points of fundamental importance: the dismemberment of Germany, and the dissolution of the central machinery of German Government. No one had as yet gone beyond saying that we wished to encourage dismemberment. The Chiefs of Staff, the Foreign Office, and the Economic and Industrial Planning Staff were studying the question; the Armistice and Post-War Committee could hardly come to a decision without seeing their reports. Mr. Eden's own view was that he would like to see dismemberment brought about from within; he was not sure that the right policy was to bring it about by force. On the second question, Mr. Eden's anxieties were 'short-term'. If we decided to break up the central government, what would be the effect on our arrangements for the indirect rule of Germany through the German administrative machine after the armistice? Should we have to make more heavy demands on our manpower? Could we possibly make Three Power control effective without a central Government at all events in the opening stages of the occupation? Mr. Eden thought that until these large questions had been further examined, the Armistice and Post-War Committee ought not to record conclusions as a result of their previous meeting. The Committee agreed with this view. Meanwhile they had already

(a) APW(44) 11th meeting.

(July 10) asked the Official Committee on Armistice Terms and Civil Administration[1] to prepare a report on the situation which might result from the absence of a formal surrender by a German central Government and of any central administration.

The report of the Economic and Industrial Planning Staff to (a) which Mr. Eden referred was completed on August 26, 1944. This report, which dealt with the issues affecting the economic obligations to be imposed on Germany, pointed out that some of our agreed objectives were conflicting. Thus, we wanted, whatever the economic cost to Germany or the United Nations, to eliminate, restrict or control German industries concerned with preparation for war. We also wanted to exact reparation from Germany and to secure from her goods and services required for the prosecution of the war against Japan or for meeting the needs of the United Nations after the war. It was, however, clear that the measures necessary to avoid any possible German aggression might impoverish Germany to the extent of rendering her incapable of providing reparation, or even to exist at a low standard of life without assistance; we had thus to strike a balance between the value of our restrictive economic measures from the point of view of security and the importance of the contribution which German industry could make to the rehabilitation of Europe and to world prosperity. There was also a further consideration. As long as the Allies were in occupation of Germany, our restrictive measures could be carried out, though for the period of occupation we should not need them as safeguards. Their value from the point of view of security must depend on their continuance after the occupation was over. The longer the period of occupation, the greater would be the permanent effects. Every year of direct control would have brought about a decline in the skilled labour force of Germany, encouraged the growth of a vested interest in a pacific German economy, and assisted Germany's former foreign customers to buy from elsewhere or develop their own manufactures. A ten-year occupation or direct control was the minimum period necessary to secure appreciable permanent effects of this kind.

The report therefore put three questions of principle: (i) were we to rely for security upon the will of the United Nations to keep Germany disarmed by effective sanctions or were we to reinsure against any weakening of that will by reducing German industrial capacity, and, if so, how far should we go? (ii) Should we limit our

[1] This body was a committee of officials under the chairmanship of Sir F. Bovenschen, Permanent Under-Secretary at the War Office. (It is referred to as A.C.A.O. as distinct from A.C.A., the former ministerial committee on Armistice Terms and Civil Administration, which had been renamed Armistice and Post-War Committee.)

(a) APW(44)66.

'reinsurance' measures to the period of occupation or should we impose continuing obligations even at the risk that a new generation might not regard their breach as justifying a recourse to sanctions? (iii) If we chose the former plan, could we count on a minimum ten-year period of occupation?

On August 29 Mr. Eden circulated a memorandum to the (a) Armistice and Post-War Committee on this report. He said that the United States Government had told us that they would like to hold conversations on an official level with the Russians and ourselves about reparation, restitution, and similar matters, including the means of re-starting German foreign trade after the war. Mr. Eden thought that these exploratory talks ought to cover the whole field of Allied policy towards Germany in the economic sphere. Reparation was only one of the ends to be served by this policy; it could not be isolated from economic security or from the commercial interests of the United Nations—particularly of Great Britain. The major Allies—including the French—should be in agreement on these matters before the German surrender. If there were to be preliminary talks—as the Americans now proposed—our own officials would require instructions. Mr. Eden suggested that they could take the Economic and Industrial Planning Staff report as a basis of discussion.

The Armistice and Post-War Committee considered on August 31, (b) 1944, the general issues involved in the E.I.P.S. report and Mr. Eden's comments. The broad issue of policy was whether we should aim at an efficient and highly industrialised Germany or a Germany industrially crippled. In favour of the first policy there were the arguments that the weakening of German industry would mean that we should get less reparation; that we should lose the contribution which Germany might otherwise make to world prosperity, and that the bitterness caused by our breaking up of the German industrial system would lead to another war. The arguments on the other side were no less obvious. The Committee thought that we should not try to destroy every aspect of German industrial development, but should eliminate entirely a relatively small number of industrial activities vital for war and also difficult to conceal; from this point of view, we should make a further careful examination of the industries likely to be of use in the development of the most modern instruments of war.

The Committee answered the three points of principle on which the report had invited their views. They thought that, in addition to the determination of the United Nations to keep Germany disarmed, we ought to take steps—for security reasons—to reduce the German industrial potential; that we should continue to occupy

(a) APW(44)72. (b) APW(44) 15th meeting.

Germany for at least ten years, and that the more we could do during this period to reduce her industrial potential, the stronger our ultimate position would be. We ought also to continue after the period of occupation arrangements for industrial inspection and supervision. The Committee also agreed with the American proposal for tripartite conversations; they suggested that these talks should be held under the direction of the European Advisory Commission.

(a) The Armistice and Post-War Committee also had before them on August 31 a copy of a telegram of August 23 from General Eisenhower, Supreme Commander, Allied Expeditionary Force, to the Combined Chiefs of Staff in which he raised the question of the possible collapse of Germany, the disappearance of all central authority, and a complete economic breakdown. Mr. Bevin, Minister of Labour, again expressed the view that we ought not to base our plans on the assumption that we should deal with a central German Government, but that from the outset we should organise our administration on a local basis. Mr. Eden repeated that the Committee agreed that the dismemberment of Germany was desirable. The Russians and Americans were of the same opinion. The original Allied plan to use a central Government had been adopted merely for convenience and was without prejudice to a subsequent decision about dismemberment. Mr. Eden admitted that the longer we used a central Government, the more difficult would be the task of dismemberment. He thought that the only differences of view were on the matter of timing and the question whether dismemberment should be effected by force if it could not be achieved by persuasion. Mr. Eden also mentioned M. Massigli's proposal for a permanent international control of Rheno-Wesphalia.[1]

The Committee recorded their opinion in favour of dismemberment, but agreed that a decision should be deferred until further reports were available. They were also interested in M. Massigli's proposals, and asked that they should be given careful examination.

In the autumn of 1944 a complete and rapid collapse in Germany (b) was a not unlikely hypothesis. The Joint Intelligence Committee had reported on August 10 to the War Cabinet that there might not even be a formal German surrender. The Committee reached this tentative conclusion after examining the possible ways in which the final collapse might take place. Another attempt at a military *coup d'état* was improbable. The failure of the first attempt by a group of senior military officers[2] had led to greater control of the army by the Nazi party. Himmler was now commander-in-chief of the German army inside Germany as well as in control of the internal adminis-

[1] See below, pp. 240–1. [2] i.e. the attempt to assassinate Hitler on July 20, 1944.

(a) SCAF 68, APW(44)71. (b) JIC(44)349; APW(44)60.

tration of the Reich. The German people wanted peace, but were unlikely to start a revolution or even to support an attempt to overthrow the régime at least until they were fairly sure that the attempt would succeed.

There were unconfirmed reports that Himmler wanted to open negotiations with the Russians on almost any terms but that Hitler refused to do so. These reports might well have been put out deliberately in order to cause discord among the Allies. There was no evidence that any influential person or group within the Nazi party was considering an approach to the British or Americans. As long, therefore, as we insisted on unconditional surrender the Nazi Government was unlikely to ask for an armistice.

The course of events was thus likely to be as follows. The army would continue to resist with diminishing effectiveness. Desertions and surrenders would increase, and the breakdown of resistance on one front might cause sudden disintegration elsewhere. As the army lost cohesion, supplies would run out and air force communications would break down. There would be a mass of refugees, especially in eastern Germany; an increasing number of the eight million foreign workers and working prisoners of war would be trying to get out of Germany, and deserters from the German army would be making their way home. These wandering masses of people would dislocate transportation, cause local famine and outbreaks of looting which the police would be unable to control. When at last—possibly not until after the Allied armies had crossed the frontiers of the Reich—the Germans realised their final defeat, Himmler's organisation would break down. Some of the Nazis might be assassinated; others might try to hide or to escape into neutral territory. There would be no effective authority to take their place, though individual service leaders might be found trying to prevent the country from getting into worse confusion.

The Chiefs of Staff thought that the conditions forecast in this report were not impossible, but that the Germans were so strongly disciplined that they would try to set up some authority to take the place of the Nazis, and that, even if a central government disappeared, local governing bodies such as town councils would continue to function. We ought, however, to take account of the possibility that there might be no central authority from whom we could accept an unconditional surrender.

In a revised estimate (September 6, 1944) of the conditions (a)
following a collapse the Joint Intelligence Committee repeated their view that no German military group would attempt to seize control from the Nazi party until it was clear either that Hitler was

---

(a) JIC(44)388; APW(44)80; C12207/1074/18.

dead or that Himmler's hold on the country was breaking. It would then probably be too late to get the situation under control before the Allies had occupied a substantial area of Germany. If, however, the military leaders were able to obtain control of Berlin, they might be able to set up an administration which would maintain some kind of authority over the greater part of Germany and form a body to which the Allies could address their demands.

(a) On September 21 the Armistice and Post-War Committee again considered the question of the machinery of control in Germany. Sir W. Strang, who had submitted a memorandum on the subject, said that he had drawn the attention of the European Advisory Commission to the possibility that there might be no central authority in Germany through which to exercise control, or that there might be an Allied decision to dismember the country. The American and Russian representatives on the Commission, however, thought that we must start with the assumption that a central government would exist and that a tripartite control could work through it. It was also pointed out to the Committee that Mr. Eden had discussed the matter with the Prime Minister at Quebec and that the Prime Minister had agreed that, if a central government or administration existed, we should use it, anyhow at the outset, as the vehicle of Allied control. Mr. Attlee repeated his view that we must have the intention of decentralisation, and, even if we began by using a central administration, base our plans on the building of provincial or local administrations. The Committee decided to recommend the acceptance of the proposal that the control should function at least in the first stages through a central German administrative machine, but that the arrangements should be sufficiently flexible to allow their adjustment to other conditions or policies.

The Armistice and Post-War Committee did not receive until October 20, 1944, the report (for which they had asked on July 10)[1] on the situation likely to arise if there were no formal German sur-
(b) render by a central Government. The general conclusion of the report was that some central administrative authority would have to be re-established, if only as an interim measure, whatever decision might be taken about decentralisation or dismemberment. The regional administrative machinery in Germany could not perform all the functions hitherto carried out by the central administration. Under the Nazi régime many powers previously exercised by the States had been transferred to the central Government. The Nazis had imposed their planned economy from the centre; we should have to continue the controls necessary to a planned economy if we were

---

[1] See above, pp. 215–16.

(a) APW(44) 17th meeting; APW(44)89. (b) APW(44)105.

not to allow Germany to fall into economic chaos, and if we wished to extract from her the maximum amount of goods for the benefit of the United Nations; these controls, e.g. over agricultural production, raw materials, foreign trade, prices and credit, tariffs, currency, banking, taxation, would have to be planned centrally. Moreover there were other matters such as transport, posts and telegraphs, and movements of population which could not be treated other than by a central administration.

The question therefore was not whether some central administrative machine would be necessary, but whether this machine should be a central Allied governing authority or a central German authority under Allied control. If the Allies were not themselves to provide a government of Germany, they would have to find an acceptable German authority; if no such authority existed, the Allies would probably appoint acceptable senior civil servants or other suitable persons to the Ministries concerned.

The arguments in favour of an Allied governing authority were that in any circumstances a certain amount of central Allied control would be necessary. If the Allies were to administer as well as control, they would merely have to expand their existing organisation; an Allied governing authority would be less of an obstacle to dismemberment and perhaps also to decentralisation, and 'spontaneous dismemberment' might occur in the absence of a central German administration. In any case, however, the Allied administration would be kept within certain limits. Certain functions, e.g. education, health and police could be left to local authorities, and as much use as possible made of the lower grades of the German civil service.

On the other hand, by taking over the direct government of Germany, the Allies would be committing themselves to an unlimited responsibility, whereas control implied only a limited responsibility. They would require a much larger staff. A tripartite governing authority of foreigners of different nationalities could not govern a country of 60–70 million people, and there would be much greater risk of divergencies of view among the Allies. Moreover the discussions on the European Advisory Commission had shown that both the Americans and the Russians—and especially the latter—wanted to control but not to administer Germany.

In a discussion of this report on November 2 Sir William Strang (a) told the Committee that the Foreign Office were revising the Instrument of Surrender to meet the possibility that there would be no German Government to sign it. The changes proposed were mostly verbal. The Committee agreed that a central administrative authority

(a) APW(44) 20th meeting.

in Germany would be necessary to deal with certain functions of Government which must be administered centrally. They thought, however, that a decision whether this body should be an Allied governing authority or a German authority under Allied control would have to be deferred until the question of dismemberment had been further discussed. The Committee considered generally that the establishment of an Allied governing authority would be a very formidable task, especially in relation to manpower, and that the use of a central German authority under Allied control would be more suitable.

(v)

Mr. Morgenthau's plan for the 'pastoralisation' of Germany: acceptance of the plan by the Prime Minister and the President at Quebec, September 15, 1944: Foreign Office opposition to the plan (September 1944–January 1945).

(a) Towards the end of August 1944 the Foreign Office received a certain amount of information[1] that Mr. Henry Morgenthau, United States Secretary of the Treasury, was talking a good deal about the necessity for a very severe treatment of Germany after the war, and was complaining of a tendency on the part of the Americans in London to make plans on the basis of building up Germany economically and to take little account of the President's policy for German (b) dismemberment. Lord Halifax confirmed these reports in a telegram of September 2. He said that there were signs that the Americans were giving urgent attention to the problems of policy towards Germany after the war. Mr. McCloy, Assistant Secretary of War, had told Lord Halifax that a committee at Cabinet level had been established to consider, among other questions, the partition of Germany into separate States; the trial and punishment of Hitler, Himmler, and other leading Nazis; the treatment of the Gestapo; the desirability—or otherwise—of an attempt to maintain the German economy; the possible internationalisation of the Ruhr.

Mr. Morgenthau was urging that the Allied Military Government should not go out of its way to maintain the German economy. He thought that a severe inflation, with the consequences of disruption and distress, might have a salutary effect upon the Germans. One of Hitler's difficulties had been to persuade the Germans to forget the economic consequences of the first World War. If another collapse of the mark occurred, the Germans might realise that war meant

[1] Later material (on the American side) about the origins of Mr. Morgenthau's plan for the treatment of Germany fall outside the scope of this *History*. I have limited myself, to the facts known about the matter at the time in the Foreign Office.

(a) U, 7039/4386/70. (b) C11631/146/18; C12121/1935/18.

economic ruin. Mr. McCloy did not agree with Mr. Morgenthau, but Lord Halifax thought that the question of policy would certainly be raised at the Quebec meeting. The Foreign Office considered that the Prime Minister should be warned that the President might raise the matter of the German economy, and might support Mr. Morgenthau's views. The Foreign Office hoped that the Prime Minister would try to persuade the President that these views were wrong, and that, while we should try to uproot and destroy the whole Nazi system, a starving and bankrupt Germany would not be in British or European interests.

Mr. Eden decided to raise the question with the War Cabinet. The (a) War Cabinet on September 11, 1944, agreed that he should submit to some of his colleagues and the Vice-Chiefs of Staff a draft message to the Prime Minister. Mr. Eden therefore consulted Mr. Attlee, the Chancellor of the Exchequer, Sir John Anderson, the Secretary of State for War, Sir James Grigg, and the Ministers of Labour and Production, Mr. Bevin and Mr. Lyttelton. He submitted to them a draft in which he said that there was some evidence that the Presi- (b) dent had been converted to a policy of letting Germany 'stew in her own juice after the surrender, imposing few controls in the sphere of civil admininistration, and letting chaos have its way'. The supporters of this policy regarded it as the true 'hard' policy, and thought it 'soft' to try to re-establish order.

This matter was of great importance, since our action in the first few weeks would influence the whole subsequent course of events. A failure to maintain economic controls would lead to inflation, with the result that the task of our occupying forces would be doubled, a few profiteers would gain, while the middle and working classes would suffer. We should be associated, not with just retribution, but with avoidable and purposeless suffering, and there would be no hope of getting an adequate contribution from Germany for the reconstruction of Europe. We might even have to send supplies into Germany, if only at the insistence of our own occupying forces who would be affected by the sight of starving children. A policy favouring chaos was not 'hard'; it was merely inefficient. We did not favour a 'soft' policy towards the Germans but we wanted the suffering which Germany must undergo to be the price of useful results for the United Nations. If, therefore, the President made any proposals supporting Mr. Morgenthau's ideas and therefore contrary to all previous Anglo-American plans, the Prime Minister might put our views to the President.

The Ministers—with the exception of Mr. Bevin—whom Mr. Eden (c) consulted agreed with his draft. Mr. Bevin wanted more information

(a) WM(44)122; C12208/1074/18. (b) C12121/1935/18. (c) C12560/547/18.

about the President's proposals, and the arguments on either side, (a) before he could express an opinion. The message was telegraphed to Mr. Eden, for transmission to the Prime Minister, on September 14.[1]

(b) Meanwhile on September 12 Lord Halifax had reported a conversation between Sir R. I. Campbell and Mr. Hopkins in which Mr. Hopkins had doubted the advisability of the internationalisation of the Ruhr. Mr. Hopkins thought that it would be better to deprive Germany of her steel industry by removing her steel plant, possibly to Belgium and the United Kingdom, and forbidding her to replace it.

The Prime Minister had heard from the President and Mr. Morgenthau their ideas on the treatment of Germany before the (c) arrival of the message sent to him through Mr. Eden. The Prime Minister telegraphed on September 15 to Mr. Attlee, the Chancellor of the Exchequer and the War Cabinet that he and Lord Cherwell, after discussing British munition and non-munition supplies, had been told by the President and Mr. Morgenthau that they had a plan for expanding the British export trade to meet the loss of foreign investments. They proposed that the steel industries of the Ruhr and Saar should be completely dismantled. The Russians would claim most of the machinery for the repair of their own plants. Some international trusteeship and form of control would be necessary to keep these potential centres of armament completely out of action for many years to come. The consequences would be to emphasise the pastoral character of German life; the goods supplied from these German centres—to the amount of £300–£400,000,000 a year—must be provided to a large extent by Great Britain.

The Prime Minister said in his telegram that he was at first taken aback by the proposal, but that he considered the disarmament argument to be decisive, and that the beneficial consequences to Great Britain followed naturally. The Prime Minister did not think it necessary to bring Mr. Eden into the discussions after his arrival in Quebec or to ask for the views of the Foreign Office on the proposals.[2]

---

[1] Mr. Eden had left for Quebec on the night of September 13–14 before the replies to his draft had been received. The Foreign Office had not regarded the matter as of immediate urgency, and had given the Ministers up to 1 p.m. on September 14 to send in their comments.

[2] No material, other than the telegrams quoted above has been found in the Foreign Office archives or the Churchill Papers, on the discussion of the 'Morgenthau plan' between the Prime Minister and the President or between the Prime Minister and Mr. Eden. *F.R.U.S. 1944. The Conference at Quebec*, 324–8, 342–6 and 360–3 respectively, prints accounts, compiled from various sources, of three conversations between Mr. Churchill and Mr. Roosevelt on September 13, 14 and 15, and also, pp. 328–30 and pp. 359–60 respectively, of conversations on September 14 and 15 between the Paymaster-General, Lord Cherwell, and Mr. Morgenthau. These indicate that Mr. Churchill, who initially opposed 'chaining himself to a dead German', was persuaded by Lord Cherwell to change his mind. Mr. Eden, however, did not like the plan.

(a) Cordite 251, C12560/547/18. (b) C12073/146/18.
(c) Gunfire 166, C12493/1935/18.

He and the President initialled on September 15, 1944, a document in the following terms: (a)

'At a Conference between the President and the Prime Minister upon the best measures to prevent renewed rearmament by Germany, it was felt that an essential feature was the future disposition of the Ruhr and the Saar.

The ease with which the metallurgical, chemical and electric industries in Germany can be converted from Peace to War has already been impressed upon us by bitter experience. It must also be remembered that the Germans have devastated a large portion of the industries of Russia and of other neighbouring allies, and it is only in accordance with justice that these injured countries should be entitled to remove the machinery they require in order to repair the losses they have suffered. The industries referred to in the Ruhr and in the Saar would therefore be necessarily put out of action and closed down. It was felt that the two districts should be put under some body under the world organisation which would supervise the dismantling of these industries and make sure that they were not started up again by some subterfuge.

This programme for eliminating the war-making industries in the Ruhr and in the Saar is looking forward to converting Germany into a country primarily agricultural and pastoral in its character.

The Prime Minister and the President were in agreement upon this programme.

(Initialled) O. K.
F. D. R.
(Initialled) W. S. C. September 15 1944.'

The Prime Minister telegraphed the text of this document to Mr. Attlee and the Chancellor of the Exchequer on September 15. They replied on September 16 with their warmest congratulations on (b) the arrangements made by the Prime Minister and Lord Cherwell. They had in mind mainly the arrangements to which the Americans had agreed for mutual Lend-Lease during the period between the surrender of Germany and the surrender of Japan;[1] they did not raise any question about the practicability of 'converting Germany into a country primarily agricultural and pastoral in its character'. On September 18, after Mr. Eden had returned from Quebec and (c) given the War Cabinet an account of the discussions, Mr. Attlee repeated his congratulations in another telegram to the Prime Minister. It seems probable that no reference was intended in these

[1] Mr. Hull has suggested (*Memoirs*, Volume II, p. 1613–15) that this offer of assistance which amounted to £3,500,000,000 in munitions and £3,000,000,000 in other assistance, was a return for the British acceptance of the Morgenthau plan. There is no evidence in the accounts of the Quebec Conference printed in *F.R.U.S.* that the two questions were so linked, or that the Prime Minister regarded the decisions in that light.

(a) Gunfire 169, Premier 3/192/2; C12405/547/18.
(b) Cordite 300, PM402/39A. (c) WM(44)123; Cordite 356; Premier 3/329/7.

telegrams to Mr. Morgenthau's plan, or to the document signed by the President and the Prime Minister. There was in fact no need for such reference. The earlier message delivered through Mr. Eden had already expressed the views of the War Cabinet on the larger question of policy. The Prime Minister was committed only to a general statement of principle; he also knew Mr. Eden's view.
(a) Mr. Attlee indeed raised the matter on September 21 at the Armistice and Post-War Committee. The Committee expressed doubts about the proposals, and decided to ask the Economic and Industrial Planning Staff to examine them, and to report as soon as possible.[1]

The Committee did not report until December 1944.[2] Meanwhile President Roosevelt himself seems to have regarded the acceptance of the plan as a mistake.[3] The President took no further action about the matter; on October 20 he told Mr. Hull that he regarded it as undesirable to decide upon 'detailed plans for a country which we do not yet occupy'.

Mr. Morgenthau, however, was not silenced by the defeat of his
(b) plan. On November 5 Lord Cherwell wrote a minute to the Prime Minister enclosing a memorandum which Mr. Morgenthau wished the Prime Minister to see.[4] This memorandum criticised very strongly what Mr. Morgenthau called the British 'draft of Policy Directive for Germany'. Lord Cherwell wrote that, in general, he thought that we should adopt an American draft expressing Mr. Morgenthau's views. The Prime Minister sent the memorandum to Mr. Eden and General Ismay (for the Chiefs of Staff Committee.)[5] The Prime Minister said that he had not seen the War Office draft, but that Mr. Morgenthau's criticism of it seemed 'very cogent'.

The Foreign Office—and the War Office—regarded the criticisms as ill-founded and impertinent. In a joint minute to the Prime Minister, Mr. Eden and Sir James Grigg pointed out in the first place that it was not the concern of the Secretary of the United States Treasury[6] but rather of the War or State Department to comment to the Prime Minister on British policy towards Germany. The docu-

[1] Mr. Attlee stated at the Committee that the Prime Minister had asked for the examination of the proposals.

[2] See below, pp. 237–9.

[3] The general facts about the plan reached the United States newspapers on September 21, and led to strong public criticism.

[4] In a minute to Mr. Stettinius Mr. Matthews (Deputy Director of the Office of European Affairs in the State Department) wrote that Mr. Morgenthau's memorandum 'could be most disturbing if there were any danger of its being taken seriously by the British, but I do not believe that this is likely'. Mr. Matthews said that Mr. McCloy had done his best to dissuade Mr. Morgenthau from giving the memorandum to Lord Cherwell. *F.R.U.S. 1944*, I. 381.

[5] General Ismay decided not to submit the memorandum to the Chiefs of Staff.

[6] The original draft included the words 'or of Lord Cherwell'. Sir A. Cadogan commented on these words: 'Toute verité n'est pas bonne à dire.'

(a) APW(44) 17th meeting. (b) C16256/1074/18.

ment to which Mr. Morgenthau referred was a handbook in which were printed together, for convenience, thirty-six separate directives on various aspects of the control of Germany. These drafts had been produced over a period of nine months. The more important drafts had been submitted to the A.P.W. Committee, where they had been approved by Ministers after detailed and often textual discussion. All the drafts had gone to the official Armistice and Civil Affairs Committee. They had been given, after approval, to Sir W. Strang for communication to the Americans and Russians on the European Advisory Commission.

Mr. Morgenthau's proposal that our drafts should be put aside, and that the document for immediate discussion should be an American draft directive ignored the fact that we had agreed to discuss on the European Advisory Commission questions affecting the treatment of Germany after the war. The Americans, however, had not sent their draft to the Commission; they had disregarded the important principle of tripartite discussions, and suggested that we should discuss their draft without reference to the Russians.[1] The joint minute then disposed briefly of Mr. Morgenthau's criticisms of detail.[2]

The minute was sent to the Prime Minister on November 21. The Prime Minister sent it to Lord Cherwell for his comments but did not reply to the minute until January 4, 1945. He then wrote that he (a) thought it too soon to try to decide such large questions as the treatment of Germany after the war. The first stage after German resistance would be severe military control lasting for many months, or even for a year or two if the German Underground Movement were active. We had yet to settle the practical questions of the partition of Germany, the treatment of the Ruhr and Saar industries, etc. These questions might be touched on at the forthcoming meeting in the Crimea; the Prime Minister doubted whether a final conclusion would be reached. No one could foresee at the present moment what the state of Europe or the relations of the Great Powers or the temper of their peoples would be after the war. The hatreds which Germany had caused in so many countries would find their counterpart in Great Britain. The Prime Minister wrote that he had been much struck by the depth of the feeling which would be aroused by a policy of 'putting poor Germany on her legs again'. He was also well aware

[1] The minute added that, as a result of our representations, the Americans had now agreed to table their document at the European Advisory Commission.

[2] No further references to Mr. Morgenthau's plan seem to have been received from Washington during the autumn of 1944. A note on a Foreign Office paper of November (b) 23 mentions that the plan had been strongly criticised in high quarters in the United States. A War Office paper of the same date (on the background of the United States draft directives) said that the Morgenthau policy was probably dead.

(a) Premier 3/195/2, M22/5. (b) C15888, 16546/1074/18.

of the arguments against having 'a poisoned community in the heart of Europe'. He thought that, with so much other immediate work on hand, we should not anticipate what might be very serious differences of view. We should have a new Parliament whose views we could not foresee, and we[1] should also have to consider very carefully our own election programme.

The Prime Minister himself preferred to concentrate upon the practical issues which would occupy the next two or three years rather than argue about the long-term relationship of Germany to Europe. He remembered the 'savage views' of the House of Commons and the constituencies after the 1914–18 war, and his own indignation at the French move into the Ruhr. Within a few years, however, the mood of Parliament and of the public entirely changed. The United States lent very large sums of money to Germany. The Prime Minister himself had supported the policy of tolerance towards Germany up till the Locarno Treaty and during the rest of Mr. Baldwin's Administration[2] on the grounds that Germany had no power to harm us. Then came a very rapid change with the emergence of Hitler. Thereafter the Prime Minister found himself again very much out of sympathy with the prevailing mood.

The Prime Minister thought it a mistake

> 'to try to write out on little pieces of paper what the vast emotions of an outraged and quivering world will be, either immediately after the struggle is over, or when the inevitable cold fit follows the hot. These awe-inspiring tides of feeling dominate most people's minds, and independent figures tend to become not only lonely but futile. Guidance in these mundane matters is granted to us only step by step, or at the utmost a step or two ahead. There is therefore wisdom in reserving one's decision as long as possible and until all the facts and forces that will be potent at the moment are revealed.'

The Prime Minister thought it possible that the approaching tripartite conversations might throw more light on the problem. (a) After writing this minute the Prime Minister received from the Chancellor of the Exchequer a letter from Lord Keynes, leader of a British financial mission to the United States[3]. Lord Keynes gave an account of a talk with the President. He thought that the President seemed in much the same state of mind as he had been at Quebec in regard to the post-war treatment of Germany. Representations from the State Department and others did not appear to have much effect on him, but he had not really made up his mind, and, in Lord

---

[1] The Prime Minister's reference here seems to have been to the Conservative Party.
[2] i.e. the Administration of 1924–9.
[3] This letter had been written to the Chancellor from Ottawa on November 30, 1944.

(a) Premier 3/195/2.

Keynes's judgment, did not intend to make up his mind for some time on the fundamental issues—he even spoke in this sense to Lord Keynes. At present he was only 'thinking aloud', and no premature importance ought to be attached to any statement reaching the Prime Minister about his plans.

On December 23 Mr. Law reported a conversation with the President in which the latter had said that it was most unwise as yet to attempt to reach any long-term decisions about Germany. We could not know in advance what the position would be at the time of the German surrender, and it would be folly to commit ourselves to plans which might turn out to be inappropriate or impracticable. (a)

(vi)

Discussions with regard to Germany during the visit of the Prime Minister and Mr. Eden to Moscow, October 1944: Foreign Office memoranda on the future of Germany, October–December 1944: French proposals for international control of the Rheno-Westphalian area, August 1944.

Meanwhile the future of Germany had been discussed during the Prime Minister's visit to Moscow in October 1944. At the first meeting with Stalin the Prime Minister said that both he and President Roosevelt were in favour of hard terms, though American opinion was divided. Stalin agreed that hard terms were necessary, and that, since these terms would certainly stir up a desire for revenge, our problem was to deny to the Germans the possibilities of revenge. Germany would have to be split up; her heavy industry and all industry producing war material would have to be destroyed and the country occupied for a long time. Stalin asked what the Prime Minister thought of Mr. Morgenthau's plan. Mr. Churchill gave no direct answer, but said that the President and Mr. Morgenthau were not very happy about the reception of the plan. Mr. Churchill suggested that M. Molotov, Mr. Eden and Mr. Harriman should talk over the German question and give a general picture of the various proposals to Stalin and himself. (b)

The records of the meeting do not contain an account of such a conversation, but at the final session on October 17 Stalin raised the question of the future of Germany. Mr. Eden explained that the British Government had not come to any conclusion. He mentioned three possible courses: dismemberment without reference to the old German States; the use of the States as a basis;[1] the imposition of a

[1] The record does not say what use was actually to be made of this 'basis'; i.e. whether the States were to form part of a federal State.

(a) C17873/1074/18. (b) Print 'Anglo-Soviet Political Conversations at Moscow, Obtober 9–October 17, 1944', Premier 3/434/4.

permanent international control on the chief industrial area (the Rhine, the Ruhr, the Saar and Westphalia) after the Soviet Union and the other Allies had taken all they needed in material. This area would be separated from Germany, and would be under the general control of the Allies.

Mr. Churchill thought that Prussia and the Prussian military caste were the root of the evil in Germany. He suggested the isolation of Prussia and, as Mr. Eden had explained, the control of the Ruhr and the Saar. The method of such control would have to be discussed. We should have first to take away all the machinery and machine tools needed by the U.S.S.R., Belgium, France and the Netherlands, and to ensure the repair of the damage to Russia in her western provinces and to the smaller Allies. This was the policy which Mr. Morgenthau had laid before the President, and which the President had liked. Mr. Churchill said that after the war Great Britain might make the things needed by Europe in fair competition with other countries. We would be the only great debtor nation and would have to increase our exports in order to buy food. The Russian intention to take away German machinery was thus in harmony with British interests in filling the gap which Germany would leave. Later in the discussion the Prime Minister suggested that Bavaria and Austria should form a State with Vienna as the capital, and that another State should be formed by Württemberg and Baden. The industrial areas on the Rhine would be under international control, and Saxony, when stripped of her industry, might go to Prussia. Germany would have no civil or military aviation; Mr. Morgenthau had also suggested that she should have no mercantile marine.

Stalin agreed with these views, and Mr. Eden suggested that the Russian representative on the European Advisory Commission might speed up its work. On this latter question[1] Mr. Eden had given M. Molotov a memorandum on the importance of completing as quickly as possible the joint plans of the three Great Powers for enforcing their terms of surrender on Germany and for the re-establishment of an independent Austria. If these plans were not settled before a German collapse, there was risk of confusion and misunderstanding. The European Advisory Commission had done useful work in preparing agreed drafts for the terms of surrender, but progress on the Commission was extremely slow. Urgent decisions were required especially with regard to the completion of the agreement (based on the Soviet draft) for the establishment of a Control Council and other three-Power machinery to co-ordinate the policy and actions of the forces of the three occupying Powers. The memorandum suggested that this agreement could be completed if the

[1] See also below, section (viii).

Soviet Government would accept the British proposal to allow the other United Nations to attach Military Missions to the Control Council, in order to represent their interests in German affairs but without weakening the principle of three-Power control.

After the Moscow discussions, and after the European Advisory Commission had agreed upon the machinery of control during the initial period of occupation, it was increasingly obvious that the War Cabinet could not postpone much longer a decision on the large question of policy with regard to the future of Germany. In particular, a decision was necessary on the question of dismemberment. On November 27, 1944, Mr. Eden circulated to the Armistice and Post- (a) War Committee a Foreign Office paper on 'Confederation, Federation and Decentralisation of the German State and the Dismemberment of Prussia'. Mr. Eden said that he would shortly submit another paper on the question of dismemberment but that he wanted the A.P.W. Committee also to consider—if dismemberment were regarded as impracticable—other possible ways of weakening Germany by constitutional readjustments.

The paper began by stating (i) that no political or constitutional arrangements would work unless they were broadly acceptable to the German people. We could disarm the Germans, destroy their industries, take away large areas of territory from them, but ultimately their constitutional and political arrangements must be of their own making.

(ii) The demand for political unity which had been a constant feature of German politics for a century would certainly reappear if Germany were broken up by foreign action or dictation.

(iii) An essential concomitant of a system of decentralisation must be the dismemberment of Prussia. The objections to the dismemberment of Germany as a whole did not apply in the case of Prussia. It would indeed be a paradox if by decentralising the German Government we were to revive the Prussian State as it existed before the Nazis had destroyed the powers of the Federal States. This revival would give those elements in Germany whom we wanted to suppress a platform for their authority over the rest of the country.

(iv) No constitutional system could be in itself a guarantee of security. We should have won security from Germany only by weakening her, and we should be safe only as long as Germany continued to be weak. If, through lack of will or a false sense of security or through quarrels with our present Allies, we relaxed our vigour or our vigilance, we should not save ourselves by the facts that Germany might be a democracy or a federal State or even that she had been

(a) C16291, 16550/146/18, APW(44)118.

dismembered. We should be aware of the danger that our public might be misled into thinking that political arrangements alone were an effective means of security and that we could abandon those parts of our security programme which involved enduring efforts and sacrifices on our part. 'We cannot afford to put our trust in political Maginot lines.'

The great objection to dismemberment was that it would be impossible to maintain it in the face of the German will to reunite, and that the obligation to maintain it would cause disagreement among the United Nations and in our own country. This main argument did not apply to various forms of decentralisation. First of all, there was the re-establishment of 'confederation'. This solution would be of little use. Either the Confederation would have to be so loose as to reproduce most of the features of dismemberment with all its disadvantages, but without the one advantage of obliterating the name of Germany, or the constituent States would come gradually to reinforce the central authority, until the latter was exercising the functions of a central government in a federal system.

A second solution would be a return to a federal constitution. The system of confederation had been discarded by the Germans themselves, but they had been proud of the achievement of national unity in the Bismarckian federal State. A return of federalism would not arouse bitter memories and might be welcomed as a relief from the excessive Nazi centralisation. It would be necessary, however, that the Germans should regard a return to federalism as a choice made by themselves, and not imposed upon them by their conquerors. We should also not wish to see a return to the Bismarckian régime, since this régime had two serious defects from our point of view. There was no 'responsible' Government at the centre and very little in the States, and the latter were very unequal. Prussian power was predominant before 1918, and remained too great under the Weimar Constitution, since its authors failed to carry out their original plans for dismembering Prussia.

Federation based on democratic government, and with the dismemberment of Prussia would have great advantages. The elimination of Prussia as created by the Hohenzollerns would remove one of the chief physical and spiritual foundations of German aggression. Economic planning for war would be more difficult under a federal system if sufficient economic control were vested in the States. Opposition to a war policy would be more effective if conducted by two or three federal States rather than by a national minority in the Reichstag.

The case for federalism rested even more strongly on the view that the chief political defect of the Germans was their submission to leadership; this submission was due to a feeling of impotence in face of the apparatus of government. Such a feeling, in relation to the Government of the Reich, was sustained by a carefully fostered nationalism which reckoned in terms of an undying race, and not in terms of the rights, quality, and dignity of individuals. The larger the community and the remoter the government, the greater was the strength of this German sentiment. One effect of federalism would be to re-educate the Germans to think of themselves more as Bavarians, Hanoverians, etc.—as their grandfathers thought—and not on Nazi lines, as *Reichsdeutsche*. Germans had also shown some capacity for local government but little for parliamentary democracy on a national scale. The small, autonomous State was the proper school for inculcating political responsibility in matters of larger import.

The two greatest difficulties in the way of re-establishing federalism were the unsuitability of many of the historic States as units, and the development in Germany, as elsewhere, of centralised political and economic authority. In order to arrive at a suitable balance between federal and State power we should have to get rid not only of the over-large Prussia but of the States which were too small. There would indeed be little difficulty in the south, where the existing States could be used. The present provinces of Prussia—excluding East Prussia—could provide nine federal States, and certain contiguous non-Prussian territories could be merged with them. Thus the State of Saxony and the Prussian province of Saxony, and Prussian and non-Prussian Hesse could be amalgamated.

A third possibility was regional decentralisation on the basis not of States but of provinces. The regions thus formed would take part in the execution of policy framed centrally, and would conduct their own local affairs through their regional machinery of government. This plan was preferable to the unitary system created by Hitler and might be less difficult to introduce than federation, since it would have less of the appearance of 'setting the clock back'. It might also train the Germans in self-government. In other respects, however, federation would suit us better, because it might weaken German nationalism by strengthening non-aggressive local patriotism and offer practical obstacles to the regimentation of German life by a central Government. Decentralisation would not have these effects. The provinces which derived their existence from the gift of the central Government would have no means and probably no will to obstruct any attempt by the central Government to withdraw the powers which it had granted to them.

Dismemberment would have to be imposed by force, but the only important measure which need be imposed by the Allies in the case of federation would be the dissolution of Prussia as an entity. The destruction of Prussian militarism was necessary in any case. The chief measure for getting rid of Prusso-German militarism would be the permanent abolition of the German armed forces and military establishments. The economic position of the Junkers was a subsidiary, though considerable problem, and was being given separate consideration. There remained the question of the Prussian State which comprised three-fifths of the total area and population of Germany proper and the mining and industrial area of the Ruhr. Measures of economic security with regard to the latter were again a separate problem.

The proposed Allied zones of occupation for Germany partitioned Prussia into four main areas: East Prussia under Soviet occupation pending an Allied decision about its future; the Prussian provinces of Upper and Lower Silesia, Pomerania, Mark Brandenburg and Saxony under Soviet occupation, with Berlin under tripartite occupation; the Prussian provinces of Schleswig-Holstein, Hanover, Westphalia and the Rhine under British occupation; the Prussian province of Hessen-Nassau under American occupation.

It could be said that for practical purposes this partition was adequate, and that we need do no more to destroy the State of Prussia. There was much to be gained by restricting Allied interference in German affairs to the essential minimum, and concentrating upon this minimum. The elimination of Prussia would be little more than a completion of the policy adopted by the Nazis. The State of Prussia was no longer an effective unit of administration and the Prussian provinces were administered on lines similar to the administration of the non-Prussian *Länder* and *Reichsgaue*. The connexion between Prussian militarism and National Socialism had been exaggerated, especially by German *émigrés* who were trying to sidetrack indignation against Germany as a whole. Munich was the capital of the Nazi movement; and in the Weimar period the Prussian Government which was suppressed in 1932 was democratic.

On the other hand Prussia had been the centre of German militarism since the days of Frederick the Great. The elimination of Prussia would thus appear as a strong and symbolic action, clear to all; it could be done without drastic measures or a large allocation of manpower. Furthermore this elimination of Prussia by dismemberment would be a good start for a general Allied plan of decentralisation for Germany. If we did not dismember Prussia now as a measure of security, the chances of a break-up in the future were unlikely. The cadre of the Prussian State would remain as a potential basis of a German militaristic revival. Such a revival would probably look to Prussian rather than to Nazi models. If Prussia were eliminated, the Germans might not find it easy to reconstruct it, and the Allies would regard an attempt to do so as a danger-signal. The

Germans themselves would probably not be wholly opposed to the plan. They had considered it after the first World War. The Rhinelanders and Hanoverians were not Prussian, and would probably emphasise the fact when the rest of Prussia was mainly under Soviet domination. In Bavaria *Schadenfreude* at the elimination of Prussia would probably be fairly widespread.

The arguments in favour of elimination thus greatly outweighed those against it. It would not be enough, however, to limit ourselves to the partition of Prussia during the Allied occupation. We ought to abolish the Prussian State and all surviving Prussian State offices and organs above the provincial level by a formal Act.

The two questions of the economic position of the Junkers—in other words, the future of the large estates in Germany and of the de-industrialisation of the Rhineland-Westphalia-Saar area were considered in two memoranda submitted to the Armistice and Post-War Committee in December 1944. The first of these questions had been raised by Mr. Bevin on July 20 when the Committee was dis- (a) cussing the subject of the transfer of German population. The Committee had asked the Foreign Office to report on the pre-war position of the great landed estates in Germany and on any plans for their distribution to the peasants.

The report—signed by Mr. Law—was submitted on December 15. (b) It pointed out that of the 27½ million hectares (68½ million acres) of agricultural land in Germany, 5 million hectares consisted of estates of 100 hectares (250 acres) or over. Of this area 3·8 million hectares were in private ownership and the rest was owned by public bodies—churches, schools, etc. Over 80 per cent of these 'large estates' were in the proposed Soviet zone of occupation (including East Prussia and Silesia). Farming methods on large and small estates differed widely; the large estates specialised in grain, potatoes and sugar beet, and the small farms more often in livestock products which had a greater food value. A given area devoted to small farms would support a larger agricultural population than a similar area given over to large farms; the small farmer employed a greater amount of capital and labour per hectare than a large estate. Hence there was an economic case for breaking up the large estates. This case was strengthened by the likelihood of a considerable surplus of labour in post-war Germany. If all the large estates in private and public ownership existing in Germany in 1937 were broken up, 150,000 peasant families could be settled on them.[1] If Germany lost East

[1] These figures assumed that the agricultural workers on the large estates would remain, and would work for the new settlers. An average peasant family was estimated at 4½ persons and 3 active workers.

(a) APW(44) 10th meeting. (b) APW(44)125.

Prussia and Upper Silesia, the number of large estates would be reduced by about a third, and only about 110,000 families would be settled. If Germany lost everything east of the Oder, this figure would fall to 82,000.

The long-run economic consequences would be advantageous, but the difficulties of the transitional period would be great. For some time the yield of grain, sugar beet and potatoes would decline without a corresponding increase in the yield of meat and milk. Building, livestock, roads and implements for resettlement would represent a large-scale capital programme which could be carried out only by reducing the amount of the German contribution to the rehabilitation of Europe. There might also be great difficulty in carrying out extensive agricultural reforms in an orderly manner. If the attempt to do so resulted merely in the labourers on the large estates seizing the land for themselves, the prospective economic advantages would be much delayed, and there would be little chance of settling peasants from elsewhere. It would be optimistic to hope that an orderly settlement would take less than five years; even this figure would mean multiplying fourfold the pre-war rate (when there was a fairly active process of peasant settlement).

The cost of creating 110,000 peasant holdings would be about RM.7,000 million. This sum—spread over five years—would probably represent annually a quarter of the German national savings; it would be required at a time when other forms of capital investment, e.g. house building and industrial re-equipment, and reparation, would make heavy demands on German resources. There would also be great difficulty in finding the livestock, building material and farm equipment. The report estimated that, ten years after the first settlement, the average holdings in the east could again be subdivided if sufficient capital were available for a costly irrigation scheme as well as for additional housing, roads, equipment, etc. This subdivision might allow the absorption in another five-year period of some 52,000 more families.

It was therefore clear that the break-up of the large estates, while creating very serious economic problems for ourselves and the Germans, would have little effect upon the problem of the transfer of population into Germany.[1] The estimated number of peasant families to be moved back into Germany on a 'transfer plan' from East Prussia and Silesia was 300,000; there were also some 400,000 other agricultural workers. If Germany lost all territory east of the Oder, more people would have to be moved, and the area for resettlement would be smaller. There would also be many non-agricultural

[1] On December 15, 1944, the day on which this report was submitted, the Prime Minister had said in a speech to the House of Commons that the Germans would be expelled from the territories ceded to Poland.

workers who would be unable to find employment in their former trades, and whom it would be desirable to absorb into agriculture.[1]

Although the report was concerned primarily with the economic aspect of the question, it pointed out that the existing concentration of so much landed property, with the economic and political power thus conferred, in the hands of so small a number of persons was undesirable in itself, but that we could not be sure that the break-up of the great estates would contribute much to our security. Other classes in Germany had supported Hitler as enthusiastically as the land-owning classes which dominated the old Prussian army and civil service, and indeed these other classes had been more faithful to him. The elimination of the Junkers as a decisive influence on German policy would be a gain to us only if their places were taken by less aggressively-minded Germans; there was nothing in the National Socialist experiment to suggest that this would necessarily be the case, or that the division of the land among a small proportion of the peasantry would have the effect of lessening the perennial German desire to acquire other people's farms and territory.

Finally, the greater part of the German large estates were in the zone of Germany which would come under Soviet occupation, and, if a land resettlement took place, the Soviet authorities would have to supervise it. The report suggested that we should take no initiative in the matter. If the Soviet Government were strongly in favour of the break-up of the large estates, we should support them. If they (the Soviet Government) took no steps in the matter, we should leave the Germans to do as they chose.

The Armistice and Post-War Committee, which had been asked on September 21 to consider the Morgenthau proposals for the de-industrialising of the Ruhr and the Saar, had referred these proposals to the E.I.P.S. The E.I.P..S did not produce a report on them until the latter part of December 1944. As the Committee must (a)
have expected, this report was unfavourable. The conclusions were that the direct and indirect effects on the Rhineland, Westphalia and the Saar would be to deprive about 2 million of the $6\frac{1}{2}$ million pre-war working population of their livelihood. Agriculture in the area was already on an intensive basis, and could not absorb an appreciable amount of additional labour. Even if new industries were established

[1] The report stated in a footnote (based, apparently, on the estimates made in the E.I.P.S. report on de-industrialisation referred to below,) that if, in addition to the great landed estates, medium estates were included in a general land resettlement, and if land used for aerodromes, defence works, etc., were brought back into cultivation, some 285,000 peasant families might be absorbed in fifteen years. This figure assumed the loss of East Prussia and Upper Silesia; it would be reduced to 220,000 if Germany lost all territory east of the Oder.

(a) APW(44)127; C22/22/18 (1945).

in the area, the people in it would be unable to maintain a standard of living comparable with that of the rest of Germany. It would be impossible to absorb the unemployed workers if at the same time employment had to be found for some 3–5 million workers from German territories ceded in the east.

The industries concerned provided before the war about 60 per cent of German exports, and the loss of production would far exceed the normal amount exported, with the probable result that Germany during the period of transition would require additional imports for which she would be unable to pay. Hence, except for certain 'once for all' deliveries, there might well be no means of getting reparation from Germany. If the elimination of the industries concerned were permanent, the Germans would be unable to build up a dangerous war potential, but they would almost certainly try to evade the prohibition, both locally and by the expansion of production in the industries concerned elsewhere in Germany. The United Nations would probably not be willing to use sanctions against such breaches of the prohibition since the Germans would begin them in a small way, and describe them as designed solely to give employment and to maintain a bare standard of living. Furthermore, we could obtain more easily such security as could be provided against the building up of a war potential by taking measures against certain selected industries over the whole of Germany.

The effects of 'de-industrialisation' on British commercial interests, though probably on the whole to our advantage would not be as favourable as was commonly supposed. The destruction of German productive power would impoverish the rest of the world with whom Germany traded. We might hope to obtain a share of the former German foreign markets larger than our pre-war share of imports into Germany, and larger also than the losses we might sustain in other exports owing to the increased competition from permitted German industries, and especially the coal industry. Any net advantage to us in our visible balance of trade would probably be nearer to £30 millions a year than the £300 or £400 millions which had been suggested. On invisible account, we should probably receive nothing in reparation (other than the plant transferred) or in respect of our large investments in Germany. The effects upon France, Belgium, and Luxembourg would be similar to those on the United Kingdom. Denmark and Norway would probably lose by the plan; the Dutch might gain in the long run through the expansion of their industry, but would lose the German market for agricultural produce, and also their valuable *entrepôt* trade. The report also suggested that the Morgenthau plan would be likely to be less effective from the point of view of 'economic security' than measures applied to a smaller range of selected industries over the whole of Germany.

In a covering note Mr. Eden accepted the conclusions in the report. He pointed out that, apart from the fact that we should gain on balance very little from the proposals, the area primarily affected was in the British zone of occupation, and that we should have to deal with the very serious additional problem of unemployment in the area which would result from de-industrialisation. Mr. Eden said that we need not take any action about the President's proposals unless the United States Government raised them again with us. Meanwhile he intended to circulate to the Armistice and Post-War Committee a report of M. Massigli's plan for leaving the industries of the Rheno-Westphalian area intact, but subjecting them to a permanent international control.

The French proposal to which Mr. Eden referred had been made by M. Massigli in August 1944. During the later stages of the negotiation of a civil affairs agreement with the French National Committee[1] Mr. Eden had invited M. Massigli to London to sign the agreement and also to hold a general discussion of matters of common Anglo-French interest. M. Massigli was in London during the last week of July for M. Viénot's funeral. Before leaving again for Algiers he submitted a list of subjects which he hoped Mr. Eden would be willing to discuss.

M. Massigli came to England again nearly a month later for these discussions.[2] At the first of them, which took place on August 22, (a)
1944, M. Massigli said that the French had given much consideration to the invitation from the European Advisory Commission to submit in writing their views on the terms of surrender to be enforced on Germany. They had thought at first of accepting this invitation, but had decided not to do so after the Prime Minister's speech of August 2 in which he had looked forward to France regaining her place as a Great Power and to the closest association of French representatives in the settlement of important European problems such as the problem of France and Germany along the Rhine. The French now felt that they could not accept the same procedure as the smaller States. They would ask to take part in the oral discussions of the terms of surrender. It was essential that Germany should not be able to say that she had surrendered only to the three Powers; the terms of surrender should efface once and for all the Franco-German armistice of 1940.

Mr. Eden said that he assumed that, in replying to the European Advisory Commission with a written statement, the French would ask for oral discussion. Sir W. Strang pointed out that the Soviet

[1] See Volume III, Chapter XXXVII, section (ii).
[2] See also Volume IV, Chapter LV, section (i).

(a) U7000/180/70.

Government held very strongly to the three-Power principle and that it had been difficult to get them to agree even to the invitation for a written statement. The United States attitude was also doubtful. M. Massigli said that the French were not asking at once for membership of the European Advisory Commission, but only for the right to discuss with the Commission the particular problem of the terms of surrender for Germany. Mr. Eden thought that this limited proposal had much more chance of success. He suggested that Sir W. Strang should see the French reply in draft in case he could give advice about the wording.

In answer to questions from M. Massigli Sir W. Strang explained that the main function of the European Advisory Commission was to prepare plans for the terms of surrender and control machinery for Germany. The work of the Commission covered similar preparation for the surrender of other enemy countries; it could deal with all aspects of the German problem. There was no question as yet of a German peace treaty. Sir W. Strang thought that the Advisory Commission might develop into an international forum for examining post-hostilities problems concerning enemy countries. M. Massigli then said that he must ask Mr. Eden for help in getting France a seat on the Commission, but Mr. Eden again advised him to concentrate for the moment on the terms of surrender for Germany and to leave the question of full membership until the French Government were re-established in France.

Mr. Eden told M. Massigli that the general plan was that Germany should be divided into three large zones of occupation but that it would be possible to bring in other Allied contingents. We were likely to propose that an area in our zone should be allotted to French troops. M. Massigli said that it was important to associate France with the occupation, to occupy a large area and to plan in terms of long-term policy. M. Massigli suggested permanent occupation or control of certain areas. He thought, for example, that the Rheno-Westphalian basin might be put under a special political régime, though it would remain German territory, and that this separation should take place immediately after the German surrender.

(a) At a second meeting with M. Massigli, on August 25, Mr. Eden said that—subject to the approval of the Prime Minister and the War Cabinet—he would support the French request for a seat on the European Advisory Commission as soon as the French Government were established in Paris. M. Massigli then spoke in more detail about the French plan for the Rheno-Westphalian area. He said that the French did not want to repeat the mistake of fixing the German

(a) U7057/180/70.

military frontier on the Rhine. They did not favour annexation, but thought that the Rheno-Westphalian area must be excluded from the western limits of the territory to be controlled by the future Germany. This special Rheno-Westphalian area should include the Ruhr, the regions around Frankfurt and Mannheim and the Black Forest. The area would be brought under permanent international control. It would remain German in administration, but should be linked economically with the West. It would be important to make the Germans realise from the outset that they would have to accept arrangements of this kind.

Sir W. Strang said that at present the European Advisory Commission had considered only the first stage of the occupation. This occupation would be on a 'total' basis, and would secure the complete military and economic disarmament of Germany. The Commission had not discussed a timetable for the reduction of the forces of occupation. We were at liberty to impose any conditions we thought desirable. There was no question of repeating the mistake of 1918 when the terms of the armistice had been fixed at the outset and made subject to renewal.

Mr. Eden said that we would certainly examine M. Massigli's proposals carefully. Mr. Eden mentioned the proposals to the Armistice (a)
and Post-War Committee on August 31. They agreed to ask for a report on the proposals from the Chiefs of Staff who had already been asked to advise on the military aspects of the dismemberment of Germany.[1] They also thought it desirable for the Foreign Office to report on the political aspects and to get the opinion of the Economic and Industrial Planning Staff on the economic aspects of the proposals. After full consideration, and the compilation of a number of drafts the Economic and Industrial Planning Staff produced a final report on January 8, 1945.[2]

The delay was due partly to uncertainty about the meaning of the French plan. It became clear that the French Government really had (b)
in mind the complete detachment of the Rheno-Westphalian area from Germany, and the establishment—in spite of the difficulties—of a state under permanent international control. The general con- (c)
clusions of the report were that the military occupation of the area defined as the Rhineland, Westphalia less the administrative area of Minden, and the Saar, without a separate economic régime, would make it easier to compel Germany to keep the terms of the Peace Treaty. If, however, the full objectives of the French were to be

[1] See above, p. 203.
[2] The Chiefs of Staff (who had in turn consulted the Post-Hostilities Planning Staff) informed the Foreign Office on January 12 that, on the information available to them, they were unable to commit themselves to any statement on the military implications of the proposals.

(a) APW(44) 15th meeting. (b) U8515/180/70. (c) C148/22/18.

realised, a separate economic régime would be necessary, but this régime could not be put into effect without separating the area from the rest of Germany. Complete separation would provide more economic security than any other measure hitherto considered, but if 'Rhenania' were also allowed—as the French proposed—a high degree of productivity, a dangerous source of war potential would remain in existence, and would be available to Germany if Allied occupation and control were removed. In other words, the success of the plan depended, as in the case of other plans for maintaining Allied security, on the will of the Allies to maintain their occupation and control and to refuse to allow a prosperous Rhenania to become reunited with Germany.

Meanwhile the Foreign Office and the Chiefs of Staff had not yet been able to put forward agreed recommendations on the question of (a) dismemberment. The Chiefs of Staff considered on December 5, 1944, a new report on the subject by the Post-Hostilities Planning Staff. This report concluded that, on balance, dismemberment would be to our military advantage as a means of weakening Germany and preventing German rearmament and a renewal of aggression. If dismemberment were accepted, however, the United Nations would have to regard its permanent maintenance as their settled policy. Public opinion would thus have to be educated to understand and approve the use of force as the ultimate sanction for keeping the new German State disarmed and separated. The education of public opinion in this matter would be easier because attempts at reunion would provide, at some stage, clearly recognisable danger signals justifying military action.

In accordance with their agreement with the Foreign Office,[1] the Chiefs of Staff had instructed the Post-Hostilities Planning Staff to deal in a separate appendix with the question of dismemberment in relation to the hypothesis of a hostile Russia. This appendix repeated the view that a hostile Russia might try to obtain German help against the western Powers, and that the reduction of the German military potential by dismemberment would be greatly to our advantage. Moreover the creation of a separate state in north-western Germany would make it more difficult for the U.S.S.R. to exert influence over the territory where the greater part of German industrial war potential was situated. We were unlikely, in any event, to secure the help of a united Germany against the U.S.S.R. since the latter would not permit us to do so. If we were to avoid provoking Russian hostility—'which we wish above all else to avert'—we must adhere firmly to the policy of eradicating German ability to

[1] See above, p. 210.

(a) COS(44)1012(o)(P.H.P.).

wage war. No change in this policy could be contemplated unless and until it was clear that a major clash between ourselves and the U.S.S.R. was inevitable. It might then be too late to achieve any full rearmament of Germany for our benefit. Nevertheless, if Germany were dismembered, our influence and that of our western Allies over the north-western and possibly the southern German States might be such that the Germans in these States would prefer to co-operate with us rather than the U.S.S.R. Such co-operation would be greatly to our strategic advantage since the territory of the north-western State in particular was of major strategic importance from the point of view of extending the defences of the United Kingdom. On the other hand, dismemberment might 'accelerate the inevitable tendency for eastern Germany to fall within the Soviet sphere of influence, thus bringing Soviet military power nearer the western nations'. On balance, the report concluded that the most important factor in dismemberment—in relation to the possibility of a hostile Russia—would be the reduction in the German help available to the Russians, and that for this reason dismemberment would be to our long-term strategic advantage.

The Chiefs of Staff did not commit themselves to any definite views on the paper submitted to them by the Post-Hostilities Planning Staff. They stated however that they regarded the paper as a 'most useful staff study'. Meanwhile the Foreign Office prepared a revised (a) draft of their original memorandum on dismemberment,[1] with a new covering note to the effect that, although the Secretary of State did not want as yet to express a definite opinion, he thought that dismemberment would raise 'grave political as well as practical issues to which an answer would have to be found before we could support such a policy'.

Mr. Eden was unwilling to circulate this memorandum. The Foreign Office view remained unchanged. Sir O. Sargent and Mr. Harvey minuted on the draft memorandum that public opinion in Great Britain and the United States would not be willing to maintain by force the dismemberment of Germany, and that the peace settlement generally would suffer from the collapse of one of its most important provisions. We should therefore concentrate upon weakening rather than destroying a central German Government by a restoration of a federal system based on the historic German States. These States would have to be more or less equal in strength in order to prevent the domination of the central Government by any one of

[1] See above, pp. 204–7. Mr. Eden made on December 31 a number of critical comments on the draft, though in most cases the text was unchanged from that in the memorandum which he had circulated previously to the Armistice and Post-War Committee. He commented that the paper showed 'little signs of any approach to this question with an open mind. It is merely the case against, which is, I admit, very strong.'

(a) C387/292/18.

them. Hence we should certainly have to break up Prussia into its component parts.

In view of Mr. Eden's unwillingness to circulate the revised memorandum, the Armistice and Post-War Committee did not discuss before the Yalta Conference the question of dismemberment.

(a) Although the Committee considered on January 4 the report on the break-up of large estates in Germany;[1] the discussion was somewhat inconclusive since Mr. Bevin, who was primarily interested in the subject, was not present at the meeting. Mr. Eden promised to submit further papers on the dismemberment of Germany, and German economic obligations; he also said that he would submit a paper dealing generally with all the various problems. The papers were not submitted before the Yalta Conference.

Since the European Advisory Commission continued to postpone their discussion of dismemberment, there was at the beginning of 1945 no agreed policy among the Allies whether or not to dismember Germany, and the British Government themselves had not made up their minds on this all-important matter.

(vii)

Consideration of post-war policy towards Austria: political and economic questions (October 1943–September 1944).

At the Moscow Conference of 1943 the Governments of the United Kingdom, the United States and the U.S.S.R. issued a declaration of their intention to establish a free and independent Austria. The three Governments at that time, however, took no steps either to define the boundaries of a free Austria or to consider the problems involved in re-establishing a viable Austrian State.

Early in 1944 the Foreign Office considered that we should agree as soon as possible with the United States and the U.S.S.R. on a territorial definition of Austria, since our policy was to detach Austria from the Reich immediately after the surrender of Germany and to give her preferential treatment in the application of the

(b) terms of surrender. The Foreign Office drew up a memorandum on the question in February 1944. Their general conclusion was that, while it might be convenient to restore initially the 1919 frontiers of Austria, these frontiers included certain debatable areas of which the most important was the South Tyrol. The Foreign Office pointed out that we could keep the Brenner frontier, or take the ethnic line run-

---

[1] See above, pp. 235–7.

(a) APW(45) 1st meeting. (b) APW(44)16; U2331/32/70.

ning roughly along the old Austrian districts of Upper Etsch and Trent, or we could adopt a compromise allowing Italy to retain the Salorno-Bolzano valley to a point north of the town of Bolzano, or we could hold a plebiscite in the province of Bolzano. The plebiscite plan was the least satisfactory, especially because it would raise the question whether the Germans, removed under Hitler's agreement of October 1939 with Mussolini, should be allowed to return and vote. The 'compromise' solution had much to be said for it, since it would meet Italy's economic requirements, satisfy to a large extent the local German population, strengthen Austria by showing confidence in her, and provide a fairly good strategic frontier. The Foreign Office also thought that a small area of Carinthia round the railway junction of Tarvis should be restored to Austria.

The Foreign Office memorandum was submitted to the Armistice and Post-War Committee on May 18, 1944. The Committee agreed (a) that, while for the immediate purpose of applying the terms of surrender, Austria should be defined as within the limits of her 1937 frontiers, we should not rule out the return to her, at a later date, of the South Tyrol and Tarvis, and that meanwhile Italian administration and jurisdiction should not be restored in those areas. The Committee thought it undesirable to decide upon further recommendations until they had received the report of the inter-departmental committee which had been studying the matter from an economic angle.

This Committee, which Mr. Eden had set up in October 1943, reported on September 22, 1944. Their report—a comprehensive and (b) well-planned document of 76 pages—showed the extreme difficulty of setting up an Austrian State which would not drift into economic bankruptcy and political subservience to Germany. A fundamental political obstacle was that, although Austria between 1918 and 1938 was ethnographically one of the most homogeneous nations on the European Continent, the Austrians, for historical reasons, had very little active national consciousness. There had been strong regional and local loyalties and, during the Habsburg régime, Austrian leadership of a multinational Empire had produced a broadly European type of outlook, but Austrians as a whole had shared the common German tendency to interpret their nationalism in terms of 'stock' rather than of State. At the time of the armistice in 1918 the Austrian Provisional Government had declared 'German-Austria' a 'constituent part of the German republic'.

The fact that Austria had become a separate and independent nation as the result of defeat reinforced this negative attitude towards

(a) APW(44) 4th meeting. (b) APW(44)93.

a national Austrian State. Unlike the new Slav succession States, 'Austria' was for the Austrians a come-down in the world, politically and economically insecure. The *Anschluss*, therefore, which was forbidden by the Allies, continued to attract many Austrians, especially at times of economic crisis. On the other hand this attraction had lessened even before the Nazis obtained power in Germany. After 1933 Austrian Pan-Germans and Nazis were active supporters of an *Anschluss*; the anti-Nazi elements were correspondingly hostile to it, and the bulk of the population more or less apathetic. The lack of resistance to the entry of the German army in March 1938 had shown almost a political vacuum. This vacuum was due largely to economic troubles, but it was partly the result of the internal political situation. About a third of the Austrian population of $6\frac{3}{4}$ millions was concentrated in Vienna. Vienna had become a distressed area, though the working class had gained from the active social policy of the Socialist municipal Government during the 1920s. Socialism was predominant in other Austrian towns, but the peasantry, as well as the Roman Catholic Church and big business, were opposed to it. The party division between the urban and rural populations had increased the tendency to substitute local and party loyalties for a loyalty to the Austrian nation State. Moreover as in Germany, violent party conflict led to the formation of private armies. After seven years of intermittent conflict between these armies of the Right and Left the Government of Dollfuss had suppressed the Viennese Socialists, and ruled as a dictatorship without nation-wide support, trying to hold down both the Socialists and the Nazis and looking to Italy to maintain Austrian political independence against Germany. In the last period before the German invasion there was a remarkable manifestation of Austrian patriotism, but it took the form of resistance to Nazi domination rather than pride and feeling for Austrian nationalism as such.

The Committee thought it imprudent to assume that after the war all pro-Nazi or pro-German sympathy in Austria would fade away. For many Austrian workers the Nazi régime had meant an end to a period of unemployment; a return to bad economic conditions might bring about a revulsion of feeling in favour of union with Germany. The memory of having fought in the German *Wehrmacht* might also exert, in the long run, an influence in favour of union with Germany. On the other hand the post-war situation would be very different from that of 1918. Since 1938 Germany had absorbed Austria, and then involved her in calamity. Austrian advocates of the *Anschluss* in 1918 had thought in terms of a federal union with Germany; total absorption had been widely resented, and feeling against the Nazi apparatus of terror, regimentation and propaganda would be reinforced by the traditional Austrian hostility to Prussia. Even so, the reaction would probably be negative rather than a positive affirmation of an Austrian national consciousness. There had been little evidence during the war that Austrians would make violent efforts in the cause of their national freedom or that they would give up their factional rivalries in the common interest of national reconstruction.

Hence we had to consider whether we could strengthen the basis of Austrian independence by some form of association between Austria and her neighbours. The report did not examine the possibility of a south German confederation based upon Austria and Bavaria, but it considered the possibility of a Danubian or central European confederation which, at its widest, might include Austria, Hungary, Czechoslovakia, Poland, Roumania, Bulgaria, and Yugoslavia. Some kind of grouping of this kind, possibly achieved in stages, possibly in a smaller form, would benefit all concerned in it, and was not wholly out of the question. The present Czechoslovak Government in exile had announced its desire for close collaboration with Austria. The difficulties were, however, very great. The war had probably increased nationalist sentiment generally in eastern and south-eastern Europe. Even the Czechoslovak Government regarded a political Czech-Austrian confederation as unlikely; Czechs in Czechoslovakia probably had stronger feelings on the subject. There was little chance of a Yugoslav-Austrian confederation. The existing Polish-Czech agreement was dropping into the background. The Slav States would suspect an attempt to restore Austrian hegemony over south-eastern Europe, and would be even more suspicious if there were a Habsburg restoration in Austria. Furthermore a Danubian grouping must include Hungary, but any Austro-Hungarian association would be disliked by all the Slav States; their distrust of Hungary indeed was greater than their distrust of Austria. Finally, the Russians had said at the Moscow Conference that some of the plans for federation were too much like the old policy of a *cordon sanitaire* against the Soviet Union and that it was premature to plan or encourage confederations of any kind. It seemed therefore that the prospects of an effective political Danubian Confederation were small and that we could not hope for more than some kind of economic association.

The report then surveyed the economic situation and prospects of Austria. The subordination of the Austrian economy to the German war machine would leave weaknesses in almost every important field of activity—e.g. transport, housing, industry, finance, agriculture, forestry, consumer goods, and foreign trade. There would also be the complicated but essential work of disentangling the Austrian from the German economy. On a longer view, Austrian productive capacity had been increased under German control; the development of hydro-electric power had meant a saving of about three-sevenths of the hard coal imports on a 1937 basis. We might assume that, if conditions of international trade were not worse than in the period before 1938, Austria could be economically viable even if she were not included in a Danubian grouping or in a wider international economic system. As far as Great Britain was concerned, our means of helping the Austrian economy were limited. We could not afford to provide a direct reconstruction loan; our main assistance must be in securing that Austria was given a good start.[1]

(a) Mr. Eden submitted a paper to the A.P.W. Committee on October 5, 1944, on some of the political aspects of this 'good start'. He pointed out that the British plan (not yet approved by the European Advisory Commission) for the occupation of Austria provided for a northern and a southern zone to be occupied respectively by Russian and British forces and a combined zone for the Reichsgau of Vienna. The absence of an American Zone was due to the decision of the United States Government to allocate only a token contingent to Austria; this United States contingent, however, would take part in the occupation of the combined zone.

Our proposals for the control machinery presupposed three stages. Supreme authority would reside at first with the Commander-in-Chief of each zone. Tripartite control would be established as soon as possible at Vienna, and authority would then rest with a tripartite Allied mission which would build up an Austrian administrative machine. The third stage would be the substitution of this Austrian administration for direct Allied control as soon as an Austrian Government were established. The creation of a fully representative Austrian Government would be a difficult matter, but it would be essential to hold elections to a constituent assembly as soon as practicable. These elections must be conducted by Austrians and not by the Allies. The Austrians must decide the method of election, e.g. whether they would use the system of proportional representation employed before 1938. For this task an administrative machine would be insufficient. Some kind of provisional government was required, possibly in the form of a Committee of Liberation. It would not, however, be easy to find a body of Austrians in whom sufficient confidence would be felt.

The method of appointing a Committee of Liberation must depend on the political situation in Austria. If political life revived quickly, we could ask all the political parties in Austria to nominate representatives to a National Committee. We could give provisional recognition to this Committee. On the other hand, if there were a

---

[1] The detailed proposals put forward to this end in the report are not discussed here.

(a) APW(44)99.

political vacuum in Austria, the Allied representatives would have to determine to a greater or less extent the constitution of the Committee from among seemingly qualified political leaders and party representatives or the heads of the civil service. We should have to ensure that the Committee was an adequate coalition body, and that we were not merely reviving the pre-1938 cleavage between the urban and rural populations. We should also have to be cautious about using returned Austrian *émigrés* who had done little more than perpetuate abroad the rivalries which had harmed the political life of republican Austria.

The A.P.W. Committee considered these two papers on October 5 and October 19, 1944. The Committee approved the first paper (post-war economic policy), with some minor modifications; they gave a general approval of the second paper on the understanding that an Austrian political machine should not be created until an efficient administrative machine had been set up. (a)

(viii)

The European Advisory Commission, March–December, 1944: delays in drawing up the Instrument of Surrender for Germany: British attempts to secure greater American and Russian co-operation and to speed up the work of the Commission.[1]

The memoranda and draft Instruments submitted by Sir W. Strang to the European Advisory Commission on January 15, 1944[2] had to be drawn up on the basis that the Allies had not come to a decision on the largest questions concerning the future of Germany. Nonetheless, as Sir W. Strang pointed out, it was possible, and indeed urgent, to settle the terms of a German armistice and the scope and form of an Allied control of Germany after this armistice had been concluded. The European Advisory Commission, which met in London, had taken some time in getting to work owing to the delay in the arrival of instructions—and staff—for the Soviet representative. There had also been important Anglo-American exchanges of opinion on what the tripartite Commission was expected to do and also what it ought not to attempt to do. The British Government hoped that the Commission would consider not only the treatment of Germany and other enemy countries but also questions connected with liberated territories. The Americans wanted to limit it to the consideration (b)

---

[1] It has not been possible, within the scope of this History, to deal at greater length with the work of the European Advisory Commission.

[2] See above, section (iii).

(a) APW(44) 18th and 19th meetings.

(b) U407,408/104/70, E.A.C. (44) 1 and 2; also *F.R.U.S., 1944*. I, 112–13.

of actual terms of surrender and machinery of control in enemy countries. One main reason for the wider British view was that if agreements on civil affairs with liberated countries, e.g. Norway, were brought before the Commission, they would thus become known to the Russians at an early stage, and in return we could ask the Russians to let us know their plans with regard to the treatment of civil affairs in eastern Europe. If we merely presented the Russians with *faits accomplis*, as in the case of Italy, they would treat us similarly.

President Roosevelt, Mr. Hull and the American Joint Chiefs of Staff, however, insisted on the Commission limiting itself to 'post hostilities' organisation to the exclusion of all matters concerned with military operations or the civil affairs of liberated territories before the end of hostilities. Mr. Hull told Mr. Winant on January 9, 1944, that the President had earlier said that he did not want the Commission 'to arrogate to itself the general field of post-war organisation'. Mr. Hull also wrote to Mr. Winant about 'the possible long-term repercussions on American public opinion should the impression be gained that this Commission sitting in London is secretly building the new world. The implications with regard to American participation in and co-operation with such an organisation are obvious'.[1]

For the time the Commission concentrated on the Instrument of Surrender for Germany. The Russian Delegation indeed refused to take up any other business until the German terms were settled. The Commission had before it three drafts, British, American and Russian. The British draft, a comprehensive document of some seventy articles including military, political and economic provisions, assumed that there would be a German Government competent to execute the terms. The draft was composed of a series of articles each of which imposed an obligation upon the Germans to submit to the exercise of a right conferred by the same article on the United Nations. The detailed application of these provisions would be effected by proclamations and orders issued by the Commanders-in-Chief on the basis of directives given to them by the three Governments. The draft assumed that the Commission would work out these directives on a uniform basis for the three Powers. The Russian draft, comprising twenty articles, also assumed the existence of a German Government which could sign terms of surrender. The view of the Russian Delegation was that the terms should be primarily military; that once Germany was occupied it would be easy to enforce additional terms agreed upon in the Control Commission. The important point, therefore, was to secure the military surrender as soon as possible.

The American draft of thirteen articles of a general military,

[1] *F.R.U.S., 1944*, I, 12–139.

political and economic character, seemed to assume that there would be no German Government capable of undertaking obligations and that the German High Command would have to carry out the terms of surrender. The draft gave the Allies unlimited powers in Germany, and spoke of the 'conquest' and 'governing' of the country; no details were given even in the military sphere. The British Delegation did not think the draft a technically good one; they considered that it had the double fault of making the German High Command responsible for obligations which it would not be competent to fulfil, and of omitting any mention of the military functions which the High Command would be able to carry out.

Sir W. Strang reported to Mr. Eden on February 22 that the (a) Commission was examining the principles upon which the drafts were based, and that he intended to put the case in favour of the British plan for a comprehensive Instrument of Surrender were a German Government capable of signing it. Five weeks later, on (b) March 29, 1944, Sir W. Strang again reported to the Secretary of State on the progress of the Commission. He explained that there was a deadlock between the Soviet and American Delegations on the question of the Instrument of Surrender for Germany; neither Delegation appeared to have authority to make concessions to the other or to consider a long and comprehensive draft on the British model. The Russians insisted on including in the signed Instrument a number of specific military provisions; the Americans declined to go beyond the most general terms. The Americans wanted a series of far-reaching general articles giving the Allies unlimited powers in Germany; the Russians thought that the necessary powers could be secured in one short article, and that the Germans would go on fighting rather than sign a document expressed in the far-reaching terms proposed by the Americans. The Russians wanted to concentrate on geting the earliest possible German signature to an Instrument securing the disarmament of the German forces; the Americans seemed more interested in taking the most complete and far-reaching powers in Germany.

On April 8 Sir W. Strang drew up another memorandum on the (c) work of the Commission. This memorandum was submitted to the Secretary of State for his use in discussions with Mr. Stettinius. Sir W. Strang wrote that the work of the Commission had not developed on the lines for which we had hoped when we had proposed its establishment, and that it had not made satisfactory progress even in dealing with the one question which it had seriously discussed, i.e. the terms of surrender for Germany. Sir W. Strang thought the Soviet and American Governments shared fairly equally the responsibility

(a) U1596/3/70. (b) U2770/3/70. (c) U3170/3/70.

for these disappointing results. We had hoped that the Commission would be a general clearing-house for three-Power discussions on the terms of surrender for the Axis Powers, the machinery of control, and the policy to be adopted in liberated countries—the Moscow Conference had referred all these questions to the Commission—and that it would also consider other European problems connected with the termination of hostilities. Even on the question of terms of surrender for Germany the United States War Department had insisted until the last few days upon the rigid adherence of the American Delegation to the terms of an Instrument of Surrender which was ill-conceived and ill-drafted. The Commission was unable to deal with the question of the occupation of Germany, which the British and Soviet Delegations had been ready to discuss for some weeks past, because the American Delegation was not ready.

The Soviet Government were also responsible for the delays. They had taken the line that the Commission should deal with the terms of surrender before discussing any other matters. Hence they had refused to begin the consideration of matters such as the dismemberment of Germany, the terms of surrender for the Axis satellites and the question of consulting the European Allies about terms of surrender for Germany. The refusal to discuss the terms of surrender for the satellites may well have been a retort to the American refusal to deal with the administration of liberated territory. Soviet delay in other matters might be due to the inadequacy (until lately) of M. Gusev's staff, difficulties of communication with Moscow, and the backward state of Soviet studies of some of the questions. The Soviet tactics in dealing with the Instruments of Surrender for Germany had not made for progress since they, like the Americans, had submitted a draft in regard to which they appeared to have little latitude. They had also taken the characteristic Soviet attitude of saying that detailed discussions were useless until all the broad principles were settled, whereas in fact much useful work could be done by subordinate advisers while leaving certain points of principle in suspense.

Sir W. Strang suggested a joint meeting with Mr. Stettinius, Mr. Winant and M. Gusev to review the position of the Commission. Mr. Eden agreed to this suggestion; such a joint meeting took place
(a) towards the end of April. Meanwhile Mr. Eden and Sir W. Strang had discussed the question of the Commission with Mr. Stettinius; Sir W. Strang later saw M. Gusev, and the latter also had a talk with Mr. Stettinius.

Mr. Stettinius was most sympathetic towards the British view that the American attitude towards the Commission was not in keeping
(b) with the original terms of reference. On April 24, 1944, however, he

(a) U3342, 3618, 4023, 4110/3/70. (b) U4110/3/70.

gave Mr. Eden a note from Mr. Hull in which the latter stated that it was inadvisable for the European Advisory Commission to assume additional duties for the present owing to the large amount of work still to be done on the Instrument of Surrender and the immense tasks before it with regard to the setting up of policies and controls for the post-hostilities period in Germany and the satellite States. The United States military authorities continued to oppose placing before the Commission matters involving military operations in the pre-surrender period, e.g. the Norwegian, Belgian and Dutch civil affairs agreements which the British Government had communicated to the Russians in Moscow.

Mr. Eden pointed out that Mr. Hull's note was not in accordance with the directives given to the Commission at the Moscow Conference, and that the Americans—as the Russians realised—were whittling down the activities of the Commission. Mr. Eden complained strongly of Mr. Hull's lack of support, and Mr. Stettinius agreed that the Russians were now regarding the Commission as less authoritative. Mr. Stettinius also agreed that the War Department in Washington was largely responsible for the American policy; he promised to send a 'strong telegram' to Washington on the general status and functions of the Commission.

After his return to the United States Mr. Stettinius had a conversation on May 23 with Lord Halifax. He said that the United States Administration had undoubtedly gone back on the arrangements in Moscow concerning the scope of the European Advisory Commission. He thought that the President might be afraid that, since the United States Government could be represented on the Commission only at an 'expert' level, the United Kingdom would take too much of a lead, 'get through solutions which the President might not particularly like, and generally organise Europe on lines of United Kingdom policy. The United Kingdom might thus figure in the eyes of European countries and the world as leaders in Europe of the Anglo-Saxon countries, something which he supposed the President might not wholly relish'. In his private report of May 30 to Mr. Eden, Lord Halifax commented that Mr. Stettinius's views were 'not without interest, perhaps, in connexion with the President's suggestion that he alone should issue a statement after D-day, instead of a tripartite statement'.[1] Mr. Stettinius also mentioned that the Combined Chiefs of Staff were hindering the efficient working of the (a)

[1] See below, p. 371. In his note of October 10, 1944, to Mr. Hull (see above p. 266) about avoiding detail on plans for Germany, President Roosevelt added that 'we must emphasise the fact that the European Advisory Commission is "advisory" and that you and I are not bound by that advice. This is something which is sometimes overlooked and if we do not remember that word "advisory" they may go ahead and execute some of the advice, which, when the time comes, we may not like at all.' *F.R.U.S.* 1944, I, 358.

(a) U5894/3/70.

European Advisory Commission 'in refusing to allow certain papers to come before it on the ground that they dealt with purely military matters'. Mr. Stettinius suggested that the British military authorities might be agreeing too much with the attitude taken by their American colleagues.

Mr. Eden decided on June 13 that Mr. Stettinius's estimate of the President's policy was of sufficient importance to be shown to the Prime Minister, Mr. Attlee and certain other members of the Cabinet. The Prime Minister made no comment. The Foreign Office considered, in general, that Mr. Stettinius's frank explanation was probably right, and that the President was inclined to see himself as a great Liberal leader and as a second and more realistic President Wilson. The President did not understand that British public opinion, remembering the consequences of accepting an American lead in 1919, would be very cautious about doing so again, and that his own policy, e.g. with regard to Admiral Darlan, had raised doubts whether he was qualified for the role of a liberal leader. Moreover American public opinion, though it would be gratified by the spectacle of America assuming the leadership, would feel uneasy if the President took too prominent a part in the affairs of Europe. At the same time the President and Mr. Hull might well think that, especially in an election year, they could not easily persuade their fellow-countrymen to take part in world affairs if the United Kingdom were too obviously settling the affairs of Europe, and particularly if the settlement seemed to consist of restoring dubious monarchies or retaining dictators.

Sir W. Strang pointed out that he was in fact taking the lead—on instructions—at the European Advisory Commission on the immediate question of consultation with the European Allies over the terms of surrender for Germany, and on the question of the participation of these Allies in the forces of occupation. Mr. Winant had been giving him steady and loyal support. Sir W. Strang thought that the Americans could not take an effective lead in Europe: 'Europe, still remembering 1919, and with the Darlan and other French episodes freshly in mind, is unlikely to follow.' At the same time Lord Halifax's report provided another argument against giving way to the President about the allocation of the British and American zones of occupation in Germany,[1] and against the perpetuation of the present arrangements for the Supreme Command after the cessation of hostilities in Europe.[2] We could not have a free foreign policy in Europe as long as there was an American

[1] See below, pp. 255–6.

[2] Sir A. Cadogan made a marginal note at this point: '? the Prime Minister's proposal in the Harvard speech.' In this speech on September 6, 1943, Mr. Churchill had expressed the view that it would be 'a most foolish and improvident act' to break up the system of military co-operation with the Combined Chiefs of Staff.

Supreme Commander responsible to the Combined Chiefs of Staff in Washington.

Meanwhile in March 1944 Sir W. Strang had been instructed to accept a shorter and less comprehensive document than the British draft on the understanding that the rest of the material in this British draft would be included in the proclamations and orders to be issued by the Commander-in-Chief. The Americans had then brought forward revised proposals (which they had discussed with the British representatives) for the Instrument of Surrender. These proposals went far to meet the Russian demands, and the Soviet Government seemed favourable to them. At last, after more discussion, a draft Instrument of Surrender, on the lines of the British compromise, was in fact submitted by the Commission to the three Governments on July 26, 1944, though the proposed detailed proclamations were not accepted in draft for another year. It was typical of the Russian attitude that for a long time they insisted on a proposal that all German forces surrendering at the final capitulation should be made prisoners of war. This proposal would have caused the greatest practical difficulty to the Western Powers, since it would have involved them in looking after large masses of Germans—feeding, clothing and housing them according to the standards laid down by the Geneva Convention—at a time when it was impossible to maintain such standards for the populations of liberated countries.

On September 12, 1944, the Commission accepted the plan for a division of Germany into three zones of occupation, with special arrangements for Berlin. The allocation of the British and United States zones was for some time a matter of Anglo-American controversy, partly, it would appear, owing to the President's exaggerated fear of disorders in France. The President wanted north-west Germany for their American zone. The Americans argued that 'it was not the natural task' of a distant country like the United States 'to bear the post-war burden of reconstituting France, Italy and the Balkans or to take part in internal problems in southern Europe'. The concern of the United States was that Germany should be eliminated 'as a possible and even probable cause of a third world war'. President (a)
Roosevelt had summed up the matter to Mr. Churchill as early as February in the words: 'I am absolutely unwilling to police France and possibly Italy and the Balkans as well. After all, France is your baby and will take a lot of nursing in order to bring it to the point of walking alone. It would be very difficult for me to keep in France my military force or management for any length of time'. Mr. (b)
Churchill replied that the American plan was extremely inconvenient from the point of view of communications; that the North-Western

(a) *F.R.U.S. 1944*, I, 184. (b) *F.R.U.S. 1944*, I, 166.

zone was far more suitable for British occupation in view of the need to secure naval disarmanemt, and that the question of 'policing' France did not arise since we were likely to recognise a French provisional Government which would exercise authority over the whole country. Mr. Churchill did not get an answer to this message, and therefore assumed that the President had accepted his view, but on May 27 Mr. Roosevelt telegraphed that he proposed to send in his and Mr. Churchill's name, instructions to General Eisenhower to prepare for American occupation of the North-Western zone. The matter was finally settled in principle at the Quebec Conference in September 1944, when the President accepted the British proposal.[1]

The plan of zonal occupation and division of Greater Berlin into three zones was considered by the Armistice and Post-War Committee, which accepted it on November 23, 1944. On July 27, 1944, Mr. Attlee had asked whether the working class area would fall within a single zone; he did not question the desirability of having three zones. On September 21 the Committee considered a memorandum on the allocation of zones at the Quebec Conference and the division of Berlin. The Committee was shown maps of the proposed zones. Mr. Attlee said that the agreement recorded at Quebec was very satisfactory to us. The Committee thought that there should be a recorded tripartite agreement on the common use of the aerodromes in the Greater Berlin area (Sir W. Strang informed them that the E.A.C. had intended such common use), but again the Committee did not raise any question about the viability of the arrangements either for Berlin or for the rest of Germany. The British and American military authorities do not appear to have expected any difficulties over the question of access to Berlin.

As the months passed the lack of progress on the Commission had become increasingly due to delays and obstruction from the Russian
(a) side. Sir W. Strang complained on August 18 to M. Gusev about these delays. He pointed out that military events were moving rapidly, and that Mr. Eden could not understand why the Commission had not even met for the last fortnight. Sir W. Strang had told Mr. Eden that M. Gusev was waiting for material from Moscow. M. Gusev said that he hoped that this material would soon arrive. Three weeks
(b) later—on September 7—Sir A. Clark Kerr, on instructions from the Foreign Office, wrote to M. Molotov pointing out that he had already sent a letter on August 8 explaining that the British Government wanted the Commission to begin at once their consideration of the machinery of control to be set up in Germany and the drafts of

---

[1] See also below, p. 320, note 1.

(a) U6970/3/70. (b) U7672/3/70.

the proclamations and orders to be issued by the Allied authorities. M. Molotov had not answered this letter, and the Commission had not met since August 4 except to discuss the Bulgarian armistice terms. M. Gusev had circulated on August 26 the Soviet plan for the machinery of control in Germany, but had not called a meeting[1] of the Commission although the British and American representatives had told him that they were ready to discuss the Soviet plan.

These representations had some effect. The Commission had several meetings in September, and made some progress. They were able to submit their plans for the occupation of Germany, though the allocation of the British and American zones had not yet been agreed. There was, however, little trouble about a general division into three zones. The actual lines of demarcation were indeed those suggested by the British Government after long interdepartmental discussion. In the light of later events these lines of demarcation turned out to be very favourable to the Russians,[2] but in the summer and early autumn of 1944 the Western Powers did not realise how deeply their forces would advance into Germany: they were not even sure whether the Russians would go beyond their own frontier.

The Foreign Office thought it desirable that during his visit to (a) Moscow in October Mr. Eden should talk to M. Molotov about accelerating the conduct of business. They suggested that he should ask the Soviet Government to appoint a full-time representative, since M. Gusev was much occupied with other affairs, and we had hoped not only that the Commission would hold frequent meetings, but that it would be assisted by expert committees, civilian and military, in making preparatory studies and doing the preliminary work of drafting. The Soviet representative, however, had insisted on dealing with one subject at a time, and finishing it off before starting on another subject; he had refused, except on one or two occasions, to remit any question to an expert committee. Thus the British and American representatives had been trying for months past to persuade him to agree to a meeting of the military advisers of the three delegations in order to work out arrangements for dealing with Allied prisoners of war in Germany after the surrender. In view of M. Gusev's attitude, the Commission had to deal with everything in full session, and a mass of business was accumulating which needed urgent treatment.

Mr. Eden gave M. Molotov on October 16 a memorandum on the (b)

---

[1] M. Gusev was at this time Chairman of the Commission.

[2] The Russian zone included 40 per cent. of the total area, 36 per cent. of the population, and 33 per cent. of the productive resources of Germany. One point of great importance was that the largest food-producing areas were in the Soviet zone.

(a) U7671/3/70. (b) U8042, 8043/3/70.

British views about speeding up the work of the Commission. The memorandum pointed out that other drafts had been before the Commission for several months (e.g. proclamations containing the necessary political administrative demands on the Germans, and directions to the Allied commanders-in-chief to ensure co-ordination of policy in their respective zones.) M. Gusev, had not been able to discuss these documents. The British representative on the Commission had also put forward draft schemes for a three-Power occupation and control of Austria. Developments in central Europe had made the matter an urgent one, and the British Government hoped that the Soviet Government would send immediate instructions to their representative to allow the discussion of Austrian affairs concurrently with those of Germany.

The British Government had also suggested that three-Power staffs forming a nucleus of control machinery in Germany and Austria should be set up in London. The British and American staffs had assembled or were in process of assembling. It would therefore be of the greatest advantage if the Soviet Government could send key representatives as soon as possible, and also supply M. Gusev with the additional subordinate assistance required for work on sub-committees. Hitherto, in the absence of sufficient assistance, M. Gusev had been unable to agree to the establishment of such committees, and all the work, including matters usually remitted to a drafting committee, had to be done in the full Commission.

M. Molotov told Mr. Eden that he would study this memorandum and reply to it in due course; there is no record that it was discussed at the meetings of the Conference. Mr. Eden also gave M. Molotov a separate note on the participation of France and other Allied Governments in the meetings. The note referred to the French application to discuss German matters with the Commission[1] and expressed the hope of the British Government that the Soviet Government would accept the French proposal without prejudice to a decision on any claims which the French might advance for a share in the occupation and control of Germany. The note also recommended that the Commission should be given discretion to invite the Governments of other Allied countries which had suffered from German aggression to send representatives to discuss matters of special interest to them in connexion with the German surrender, and to inform the other Allied Governments of the substance of the Instrument of Surrender, and, as soon as security considerations allowed, to show them the text. This recommendation was made in view of the importance of securing the agreement of the Governments concerned to the terms of surrender before these terms were presented to the Germans. The note did not

---

[1] See above, pp. 239–40.

mention the French request for permanent membership of the Commission.

Later Mr. Eden sent another note to M. Molotov entitled 'Representation of Interests of the other United Nations in the Control of Germany'. This note pointed out that, without impairing the basic principles of three-Power responsibility and authority for the control of Germany after surrender, arrangements would have to be made for the representation in Germany of the interests of other United Nations. Mr. Eden explained that the other Allied Governments had strong feelings in the matter.

The Soviet Government replied in two memoranda of October 25 (a)
and 26, 1944, from the Soviet Embassy in London. They met the British requests at every point, and even suggested the admission of France as a fourth permanent member of the Commission. M. Gusev was now more forthcoming and agreed to the reference of questions to sub-committees. On the other hand it was clear that, if the Russians were intending to be less obstructive in their methods, they were not less uncompromising in their demands. Thus, on November 30, M. (b)
Gusev rejected the British suggestion that the zones of occupation in Austria ought not to cut across the old provincial boundaries; the reason for this refusal was only too clearly that the Soviet Government wanted no intervening link between the central Government and the smaller units of local administration, and that they regarded even a provincial organisation as a possible challenge to the authoritarian rule of a 'Red Vienna'.

When it became clear in the early part of 1945 that a formal surrender by a German Government was unlikely, the Foreign Office suggested[1] that the four Allied Governments should announce, at the time of the German unconditional surrender, that, in the absence of any central German authority, they were assuming supreme authority over Germany. For this purpose it was necessary to redraft at least the preamble of the Instrument of Surrender. The draft was submitted by Sir W. Strang to the Commission on March 30, but was not formally discussed until May 1, or agreed, in the form of a Declaration, until May 12.

Meanwhile the Germans had surrendered, and the problem of the actual form of the Instrument of Surrender was settled by using a short military instrument. The Americans proposed that this instrument should be signed at General Eisenhower's headquarters at Rheims by a representative of the Supreme Allied Commander, General Eisenhower, and by a representative of the German High

---

[1] This suggestion was made on the initiative of Sir W. Strang, after consultation with Sir W. Malkin, Legal Adviser to the Foreign Office.

(a) U8103/3/70. (b) U8477/3/70.

Command. There would also be a Russian signature, but the Americans had not as yet suggested when and how this should be obtained. In fact this course was adopted, though the Russians caused difficulties.[1] The Instrument of Surrender contained an article authorising the Declaration which was made later at Berlin, on June 5, 1945.

[1] See Chapter LXVII, section (v). For a further account of the effect of Russian obstructiveness on the E.A.C., see below, pp. 338–9.

CHAPTER LXV

Discussions on the World Security Organisation and the treatment of Germany at the Yalta Conference,[1] February 4–11, 1945: the main issues at the San Francisco Conference

(i)

Proposals for a tripartite meeting: the Prime Minister's attempt to secure preliminary Anglo-American discussions: the Russo-American agreement about the Far East: the British attitude towards the American proposals for an Emergency High Commission for Europe and for a Declaration on Liberated Europe: discussion of the Declaration at the Conference.

At the time of the visit of the Prime Minister and Mr. Eden to Moscow, President Roosevelt appears to have suggested to the Russian Ambassador in Washington—through Mr. Hopkins—that a tripartite conference might be held somewhere in the Black Sea area towards the end of November;[2] Stalin agreed with the sugges- (a)
tion, and mentioned it to the Prime Minister. The Prime Minister, before leaving Cairo on his way back to London, told the President that he would come to any place chosen by him and Stalin. The President telegraphed to the Prime Minister on October 22 that the possibility (b)
of a meeting in the Black Sea region depended on 'our ability to get through the Dardanelles safely', since he (the President) wanted to come by sea. He asked Mr. Churchill whether Stalin would be

---

[1] For obvious reasons of convenience the discussions at the Conference on Poland, Yugoslavia, and the question of Turkey and the Montreux Convention have been dealt with separately. In order to get a complete view of the Conference, it is necessary to keep in mind these discussions—which took place at seven out of the eight plenary meetings—and, particularly, the compromise reached after long debate on the question of the Polish Government. For this subject, see Volume III, Chapter XL. For the discussions on Yugoslavia, see Volume III, Chapter XLII. For the discussion on the Montreux Convention, see Volume IV, Chapter LII.

[2] The Prime Minister, in a message of September 27, proposing a visit to Moscow, had said to Stalin that the President had in mind The Hague as a possible meeting place for (c)
a tripartite conference. The Prime Minister thought that the course of the war, 'even before Christmas' might 'alter the picture along the Baltic shore' to such an extent that a journey there by Stalin 'would not be tiring or difficult. However we shall have much hard fighting to do before any such plan can be made.' Stalin replied on September 30 (d)
that he too wanted a meeting but that his doctors had advised him not to take long journeys.

(a) T1946/4, No. 801, Premier 3/51/1. (b) T1950/4, No. 632, Premier 3/51/1. (c) T1828/4, Premier 3/434. (d) T1848A/4, Premier 3/434.

(a) likely to agree to Athens or Cyprus as a meeting place. The President
and the Prime Minister also suggested other places, including Salonika, Malta, and Jerusalem, but Stalin insisted on a Black Sea meeting
place and refused, for reasons of health, to travel anywhere by air.
No agreement about a meeting place had been reached at the
beginning of November. The Prime Minister then suggested that, if
(b) Stalin would not leave Russia, he (the Prime Minister) and the
President might hold a meeting in London and that M. Molotov
might be the chief Russian representative.

The President did not reply to this latter suggestion, but on
(c) November 14 proposed a postponement of a tripartite conference
until after his inauguration on January 20. He also wrote to Stalin to
(d) this effect, and mentioned an Adriatic port or Sicily as a meeting
place. Mr. Churchill telegraphed on November 19 his disappointment
(e) that the President would not agree to the London proposal. In view
of the number of important questions[1] awaiting a decision, he regretted the delay until the end of January. He also noted that the
President did not want any French representation at the meeting
with Stalin; Mr. Churchill's own view was that the French might
have come in 'towards the end in view of their vital interests in the
arrangements made for policing Germany as well as in all questions
affecting the Rhine frontier'.

In the end Stalin had his way once again over the meeting place.
He chose Yalta in the Crimea; the Prime Minister and the President
accepted the choice. The Prime Minister telegraphed to the President
(f) on January 5, 1945, his regret that the President would be unable to
visit Great Britain. He added: 'A very dismal impression would be
made if you were to visit France before you come to Britain. In fact,
it would be regarded as a slight on your closest ally. I gather however, that you will only go to the Mediterranean and Black Sea.' The
President was already proposing to spend one night at Malta on his
(g) way; Mr. Churchill suggested that the Chiefs of Staff might hold
(h) informal conversations there. He proposed on January 8 similar

[1] Mr. Churchill mentioned the treatment of Germany, the future World Organisation
the position in the Balkans, and the Polish question as matters which 'ought not to be left
(i) to moulder'. Mr. Roosevelt told Stalin on December 17 and again about ten days later
that he hoped that the Russians would not take any important decisions over Poland until
after the proposed tripartite meeting. The Russians, in fact, announced on December 31,
1944, their recognition of their own puppet 'Polish National Committee' as the Provisional
Government of Poland. See Volume III, pp. 241–5.

(a) T1957/4, Churchill to Roosevelt No. 804; T1964/4, Roosevelt to Churchill, No. 635; T2036/4, Roosevelt to Churchill No. 641, Premier 3/51/1.
(b) T2055–6/4, Nos. 814–15, Premier 3/51/1. (c) T2121/4, No. 648, Premier 3/51/1. (d) T2131–2, Roosevelt to Churchill Nos. 649–50, Premier 3/51/1. (e) T2137/4, No. 825, Premier 3/51/1. (f) T31/5, No. 874, Premier 3/51/1. (g) T35/5, No. 875, Premier 3/51/1; T59/5, No. 881, Premier 3/51/1. (h) T54/5, No. 880, Premier 3/51/1. (i) T2378/4, Roosevelt to Churchill No. 675, Premier 3/355; C17730/8/55; T2454/4, Roosevelt to Churchill No. 684, Premier 3/355; N309/6/55.

preparatory discussions—to which M. Molotov would be invited—between the Foreign Ministers. He asked the President how long he expected to stay at Yalta, and ended his message with the words: 'This may well be a fateful Conference, coming at a moment when the Great Allies are so divided and the shadow of the war lengthens out before us. At the present time I begin to think that the end of this war may well prove to be more disappointing than the last.'

The President did not want any of these preliminary meetings. He (a) explained that Mr. Stettinius could not reach Malta in time for a conference and that his own plans made it impossible for him to stay there. He also considered that the meeting at Yalta need not last longer than five or six days. The Prime Minister, however, argued once more in favour of some preliminary discussion. He told the (b) President on January 10 that Mr. Eden asked particularly that Mr. Stettinius might come to Malta for at least forty-eight hours in order to discuss the agenda for the conference, 'even though Molotov were not invited I am sure this would be found very useful. I do not see any other way of realising our hopes about World Organisation in five or six days'.[1] The President replied somewhat abruptly on January 12 that 'it is regretted that projected business here for the Secre- (c) tary of State will prevent Stettinius's arrival [at] Malta before January 31. It is my present intention to send Harry Hopkins to England some days in advance of the Malta date to talk with you and Eden'.[2]

The Prime Minister arrived at Malta on January 30, 1945, and the President on February 2. Mr. Eden and Mr. Stettinius and the Chiefs of Staff were able to hold short but important conversations[3] before the Delegations left by air for Yalta[4] where the Conference opened with a military discussion on February 4. The final meeting was on February 11, but the last important business meeting—at which all the final bargaining took place—was on February 10.

As the Prime Minister had foreseen, the time allocated for the Conference was too short, but it is unlikely that the decisions would

[1] The Prime Minister added: 'Even the Almighty took seven.'

[2] According to Mr. Hopkins, Mr. Churchill said to him that, from all the reports he had received about Yalta, 'If we had spent ten years on research, we could not have found a worse place in the world' (*F.R.U.S. 1945, Malta and Yalta*, p. 39). In fact, the conditions at Yalta, though far from satisfactory, turned out to be much better than the Prime Minister had anticipated. No record has been traced in the Foreign Office archives of Mr. Hopkins's conversations in London.

[3] The Prime Minister was unwell until the evening of January 30. The military discussions, at which there were sharp differences of opinion over the next step in the invasion of Germany, are not discussed here.

[4] At a luncheon on February 5, at which Mr. Eden, Mr. Stettinius, and M. Molotov were present, the latter suggested that the conference should be called 'The Crimea Conference'. This title was used during and after the conference, but later usage has adopted the title 'Yalta'.

(a) T65/5, No. 696, Premier 3/51/1.
(b) T69/5, No. 884. Premier 3/51/1. (c) T83/5, No. 699, Premier 3/51/1.

have been very different if they had not been taken in such haste, and if the President, partly because he was tired, had not tended to hurry the proceedings.[1] The fundamental problem for the British and Americans was to discover—if possible—how far the Russians intended to collaborate with the Western Powers after the war, or, to put the question in a slightly different form, what use the Russians intended to make of their military power. The Americans were not unaware of the uncertainties in this matter, but they were more easily satisfied with the Russian attitude. The President and his entourage continued to assume that, unlike Great Britain, Russia was not an 'imperialist' Power. This belief was important in relation to the two main questions which the President wanted to settle at the Conference: the conditions under which the Russians would fulfil their promise to enter the war against Japan, and the establishment of a World Security Organisation. A satisfactory settlement of the first of these questions would be evidence of Russian willingness to continue their wartime co-operation; the establishment with Russian co-operation of a World Security Organisation was, in the President's opinion, far more important than the immediate discussions over the future government or frontiers of Poland. With Russia inside the Security Organisation it would be possible to ensure the interests of the smaller European States.[2]

The settlement of the conditions of Russian entry into the Far Eastern war took place privately in discussions between the President and Stalin or Mr. Harriman and M. Molotov. The British representatives were not invited to these discussions or consulted about the
(a) terms, though earlier in the conversations between Mr. Eden and

[1] As at Teheran, the President seems to have been irritated by the length of the Prime Minister's speeches. At one point, when the Prime Minister began to speak, the President passed a note to Mr. Stettinius: 'Now we are in for half an hour of it.' The President had arranged to see King Ibn Saud, King Farouk and the Emperor Haile Selassie in his ship after the Conference, and was only persuaded with difficulty by the Prime Minister—with the support of Stalin—to prolong the Conference in order to finish the business. There is no evidence in the Foreign Office archives that the British Ministers were disquieted at the President's state of health, though Mr. Eden and Sir A. Cadogan, (who had last seen the President at Quebec in September 1944), expressed partly contradictory views on this point. Mr. Eden noted in his diary on February 2, 1945: 'I thought he looked considerably older since Quebec. He gives the impression of failing powers.' Later, however, he recorded his disbelief that the President's declining health altered his judgment, though his handling of the Conference was less sure than it might have been (Earl of Avon, *Memoirs*, II, pp. 512–13.) In his diary Sir A. Cadogan writes 'he looked rather better than when I last saw him. But I think he is woollier than ever' (*The Diaries of Sir Alexander Cadogan*, David Dilks, London, 1971, p. 704). But he told Mr. Stettinius, that he was shocked at the change in the President's appearance (E. R. Stettinius, *Roosevelt and the Russians*, London, 1950, p. 73.)

[2] Mr. Eden wrote at the time of the talks at Malta: 'they (the Americans) seemed to me to give rather too much weight to World Council and too little to Poland, in the sense that unless the Russians can be persuaded or compelled to treat Poland with some decency there will not be a World Council that is worth much. But this is more a matter of emphasis than anything else since they seem fully alive to "the seriousness of Polish issue".' (Earl of Avon, *op. cit.*, Volume II, p. 510.)

(a) WP(45)157, 1st F.S.M.

Mr. Stettinius at Malta Mr. Eden argued in favour of putting together all our requirements from Russia and considering what we had to give in return. Mr. Eden had said that, if the Russians decided to enter the war against Japan, they would do so because they thought it in their interests that the Japanese war should not be won by the United States and Great Britain alone. We had therefore no need to offer a high price for Russian participation and if we were prepared to agree to their territorial demands in the Far East, we ought to obtain a good return in the form of concessions to our requirements elsewhere.

The general impression of the British representatives at Malta was that the Russians would want southern Sakhalin and transit rights in southern Manchuria. In the event, the Russian terms were (*a*) the preservation of the *status quo* in Outer Mongolia; (*b*) the restoration to the Soviet Union of the rights lost by the Russian Imperial Government in 1905—that is to say, (i) the recovery of Southern Sakhalin and the islands adjacent to it, (ii) the internationalisation of the commercial port of Dairen, with safeguards for the pre-eminent interests of the U.S.S.R. and the restoration of Port Arthur as a Soviet naval base, (iii) the joint operation by a Soviet-Chinese company of the Chinese Eastern and South Manchuria railways, providing an outlet to Dairen, on the understanding that the pre-eminent interests of the U.S.S.R. would be safeguarded and that China would retain full sovereignty in Manchuria; (*c*) the acquisition by the Soviet Union of the Kurile Islands. On these terms Stalin promised that the Soviet Union would enter the war against Japan within two or three months after the defeat of Germany.

The President and Stalin reached agreement on the terms on February 10 but they were not shown to the British representatives until February 11, though the Prime Minister had learnt something of the Russian demands and the American reaction to them in a private talk on February 10. Mr. Churchill asked Stalin in a private conversation on February 10 what the Russians wanted in the Far East. Stalin said that they wanted a naval base such as Port Arthur, whereas the Americans would prefer the ports to be internationalised. The Prime Minister said that Great Britain would welcome the appearance of Russian ships in the Pacific, and that he was in favour of Russia making good her losses in the Russo-Japanese war.

The Prime Minister and Mr. Eden accepted the conditions of Russian entry into the Far Eastern war[1] on the understanding that the

---

[1] There is no evidence in the Foreign Office archives showing any difference of opinion between the Prime Minister and Mr. Eden on the question of approving the agreement. Mr. Eden, however, has written that his view, shared by Sir A. Cadogan, was, that the Prime Minister should not be a party to the agreement, and that he argued with Mr.

(*continued on page* 266)

matter was primarily an American affair and of concern to American military operations. The conditions were embodied in a personal agreement signed by the Prime Minister as well as by the President and Stalin; the agreement was not discussed at the meetings of the Conference. From the American point of view the document was remarkable. It not only accepted the claims of the Soviet Government to the rights obtained by the Tsarist régime at the height of Russian imperialism in the Far East;[1] it also agreed to the surrender of Chinese rights without previous consultation with General Chiang Kai-shek.[2] The document indeed recognised that Chinese consent was necessary, and the President undertook to obtain this consent, but the terms of the agreement guaranteed its fulfilment irrespective of any objections which the Chinese might make.[3]

The Foreign Office were much less ready to accept a favourable interpretation of Russian policy. The Russian conditions for entering the war against Japan were a reversion to Tsarist imperialism. Their action in Iran—the only country in which the three Great Powers were exercising a joint control—did not look well for the prospects of collaboration on a much larger scale in Germany. Even if their harsh and implacable policy towards the Poles were explained as a matter directly concerning their own security in relation to Germany, this explanation did not cover their lack of co-operation elsewhere. On the other hand, as earlier, the alternative to Anglo-Russian co-operation in Europe offered so dark a future, that the British Government were bound to continue the assumption that the Russians intended to honour their treaty with Great Britain and their other assurances of collaboration. Any open expression of doubt on the British side would have played into the hands of those members of the Russian governing oligarchy who, as the Foreign Office suspected, wanted to take full and cynical advantage of the change in the balance of power in Europe after the collapse of Germany.

As a matter of common prudence, however, the Foreign Office wanted to ensure that the Russians were committed to detailed declarations of common policy with the Allies which they could not easily elude and which might prevent them from pushing their own

---

(*continued*)
Churchill in the presence of Mr. Roosevelt and Stalin. Mr. Churchill felt that, 'whether we liked it [the agreement] or not, our authority in the East would suffer if we were not signatories, and therefore not parties to any later discussions'. (Earl of Avon, *op. cit.*, Volume II, p. 513).

[1] In fact the Russian occupation of Port Arthur had lasted only seven years.

[2] It should be remembered, however, (i) that the President knew that General Chiang Kai-shek wanted to obtain an agreement with the Russians which would preclude them from interfering in Chinese affairs on behalf of the Communists, and (ii) that General Chiang Kai-shek realised that he would have to pay a considerable price for such an agreement. Nevertheless, the President did not obtain from the Russians any promise that in return for the Chinese concessions they would agree not to support the Communists.

[3] The President at this time told Stalin that Hong Kong ought to be given back to China.

totalitarian measures to a point from which there could be no return.

The Americans agreed on the importance of committing the Russians to a common policy. In the discussions with the American (a) Delegation at Malta before the Yalta Conference Mr. Stettinius brought forward the two papers concerning a Declaration on Liberated Europe and an Emergency High Commission for Liberated Europe which they had communicated to the Foreign Office on January 24.[1] Mr. Hiss, of the United States Delegation, explained that the purpose of the American proposal was to secure unity of approach between the three Great Powers in relation to the difficulties which were certain to arise in liberated territories. The proposed High Commission would function only until the World Organisation had been set up, and it would not include Germany in its sphere of work. Mr. Stettinius then said that the Commission would be composed of four members (i.e. with the inclusion of the French) and possibly others. The Americans also pointed out that the presentation of the proposal to the Russians would require considerable care, since the question of Poland was involved.

Mr. Eden made it clear that the British Delegation were much attracted by the proposal. It would, however, be difficult—especially for the Russians—to find members of the Commission who would be ready to take responsibility for decisions of importance; in any case the responsibility to public opinion for such decisions must rest with the Foreign Secretaries of each country and these latter could not be permanently in session in a foreign country or go beyond a certain point in delegating their duties. Mr. Eden also raised the question of the connexion between the Emergency Commission and the quarterly meetings of Foreign Secretaries to which he attached importance.[2] The meeting then discussed the title to be given to the Commission. They felt that some title must be found which would not offend the smaller Allies or cut across the duties of the European Advisory Commission or of the Allied Control Commissions in certain countries. An American suggestion that the title should be 'Liberated Areas Emergency Council' was generally approved.

Mr. Stettinius pointed out that the whole proposal must be regarded as informal and unofficial; the President had not approved

---

[1] These proposals seem to have been under discussion for some time in the State Department. Mr. Jebb had put forward a similar plan in the spring and summer of 1943 and had mentioned it to the State Department when he was in America in March 1943 with Mr. Eden and Mr. Strang (see also Chapter LXI, pp. 36–8).

[2] The Prime Minister proposed later at the Conference the holding of such quarterly meetings. This proposal was accepted; it was decided that the meetings should be held at intervals of about three or four months, in rotation at the various capitals. The first meeting would take place in London.

(a) WP (45)157, 1st F.S.M.; U765/764/70.

it and was a little anxious lest it might prejudice the prospects of the more important World Organisation. The meeting therefore agreed that for the time the Prime Minister should be advised not to raise the matter with the President. The Foreign Office regarded these American proposals as of special importance in view of the information received about conditions in Soviet-controlled territory.[1] On (a) the night of January 31 Sir O. Sargent telegraphed to Mr. Eden a message from Mr. Law and himself about the proposals. Sir O. Sargent pointed out that, once a dictatorship approximating to the Russian model had been established, there was no possibility of getting a representative democratic régime according to English ideas. The Russians would enforce their system of representation according to which local Soviets sent 'representatives' chosen by the Communist Party to the next Soviet in the scale, and so on up to a National Assembly or Supreme Soviet, or, alternatively, general elections would be staged in the form of open voting for or against the party in power. In such conditions the proper application of the principle of voting by ballot became impossible, but the true situation could be disguised from the public in Great Britain and America by skilful propaganda and the rigging of the elections.

We had evidence that this process was well under way in Poland. There were increasing signs that a similar development was taking place in Bulgaria. The small Communist Party in Roumania was becoming more aggressive and self-confident. We could not yet judge what would happen in Yugoslavia, but Marshal Tito could establish a totalitarian system if he wished, in spite of his agreement with M. Subasić.[2] So also could M. Hoxha in Albania.[3] It was as yet impossible to make any forecasts about Hungary, Czechoslovakia, and Austria. We knew that our intervention alone had prevented the establishment of a totalitarian régime in Greece.

The American proposals—if enforced effectively at every stage—would go far to enable us to prevent developments of this kind. The American draft declaration, however, was vaguely worded on the crucial question of the interim régime to be set up pending the holding of elections. Sir O. Sargent thought that, whatever happened to the American proposals, we ought to try to get an undertaking or, at all events, an exchange of views on the best method of ensuring that the

---

[1] Mr. Jebb had in fact proposed a somewhat similar plan in a memorandum of January 23, 1945.

[2] Marshal Tito, President of the Yugoslav National Committee of Liberation, and Dr. Subasić, head of the Royal Government, had reached an agreement in October 1944 on the formation of a new Government. See Volume III, p. 351.

[3] M. Hoxha, a former schoolmaster, was the leader of a Communist-dominated Committee of National Liberation in Albania, which had set up a 'People's Republic' in the country after the withdrawal of the Germans in October 1944 and had suppressed rival political groups.

(a) Fleece 41, U815/764/70.

régimes about to be established in liberated countries were on lines of which we approved. We could suggest that on the liberation of a country the interim régime should be as representative as possible of all political parties, and should abstain from measures radically affecting the political or social structure of the country or from placing the power of 'making the elections' in the hands of a particular group or party. We might compel the Russians to declare themselves by asking them to agree to a formula of this kind either as part of the Declaration on Liberated Europe or independently. The formula would have to apply to all liberated countries in Europe with the exception of Germany. We could not limit it to eastern Europe. In view of the possibility of Russian interference in support of Communist groups and Communist-controlled Resistance movements in western Europe, and of the Russian tendency to accuse members of Right or Centre parties of being collaborationists, it was desirable to apply the formula to western as well as to eastern Europe, though for the present we could not agree that it should cover France and Belgium.

We should also try to ensure that representatives of the United Nations were completely free to reside and travel in the countries concerned and to report on political developments. The only foreign representative at present in Poland was a Frenchman; he was allowed to telegraph to Moscow only through the Russian authorities and his telegrams had not been arriving. In Bulgaria the Russians seemed to be hoping to make the position of our representatives so uncomfortable that we should withdraw them. If we had not been able to see what was going on in Greece, E.L.A.S.[1] would probably have been successful in imposing themselves on British and American opinion as the chosen spokesmen of all that was best in Greece.

In fact, the Americans dropped the plan for an Emergency Commission,[2] but maintained the proposal of a more general kind for a declaration on liberated Europe. This proposal was not considered by the Conference until the fifth plenary meeting on February 9. (a)
The American text brought before the Conference was as follows:

'The Premier of the Union of Soviet Socialist Republics, the Prime Minister of the United Kingdom and the President of the United States of America have consulted with each other in the

[1] i.e. the National Popular Liberation Army, a military resistance group under the control of the E.A.M., the left-wing Greek Liberation Front.

[2] According to Mr. Stettinius, the President, who had never much liked the European Advisory Commission, thought that there was no need for another organisation. Mr. Byrnes also thought that Congress might object to a United States Commissioner, with something like an independent authority, whose appointment was outside their control. The objection would be serious if the Commissioner agreed to decisions involving the retention of American troops in Europe. (Stettinius, *op. cit.*, pp. 87–8.)

(a) WP(45)157, 5th plenary.

common interests of the peoples of their countries and those of liberated Europe, They jointly declare their mutual agreement to concert during the temporary period of instability in liberated Europe the policies of their three Governments in assisting the peoples liberated from the domination of Nazi Germany and the peoples of the former Axis satellite States of Europe to solve by democratic means their pressing political and economic problems.

The establishment of order in Europe and the rebuilding of national economic life must be achieved by processes which will enable the liberated peoples to destroy the last vestiges of Nazism and Fascism and to create democratic institutions of their own choice. This is a principle of the Atlantic Charter—the right of all peoples to choose the form of government under which they will live—the restoration of sovereign rights and self-government to those peoples who have been forcibly deprived of them by the aggressor nations.

To foster the conditions in which the liberated peoples may exercise these rights, the three Governments will jointly assist the people in any European liberated State or former Axis satellite State in Europe where in their judgment conditions require (*a*) to establish conditions of internal peace; (*b*) to carry out emergency measures for the relief of distressed peoples; (*c*) to form interim governmental authorities broadly representative of all democratic elements in the population and pledged to the earliest possible establishment through free elections of governments responsive to the will of the people, and (*d*) to facilitate where necessary the holding of such elections.

The three Governments will consult the other United Nations and provisional authorities or other governments in Europe when matters of direct interest to them are under consideration.

When, in the opinion of the three Governments, conditions in any European liberated State or any former Axis satellite State in Europe make such action necessary, they will immediately establish appropriate machinery for the carrying out of the joint responsibilities set forth in this declaration.[1]

By this declaration we reaffirm our faith in the principles of the Atlantic Charter, our pledge in the Declaration by the United Nations, and our determination to build in co-operation with other peace-loving nations a world order under law, dedicated to peace, security, freedom and general well-being of all mankind.'

During the discussion the Prime Minister said that he did not disagree with the document, but would like to place on record the fact

[1] This clause, in fact, deprived the earlier clauses of most of their value. If action under these earlier clauses depended on the agreement of the three Governments, any one of them could exercise a veto merely by asserting the view that common action was unnecessary. Nevertheless, the earlier clauses remained mandatory, and any one of the signatory Governments failing to carry them out—as the Russians failed to do in Poland—could be held to have violated its obligations. This point was important in connection with the agreement about the zones of occupation in Germany (and to withdraw into these zones from the lines of military advance beyond them) until the Russians fulfilled their obligations under the Yalta declaration. (See also Volume III, Chapter XLVI, section (iii).)

that on his return from Newfoundland he had made a short statement interpreting the Atlantic Charter in which he had said that the British Government was already pursuing the principles of the Charter in the British Empire.

Mr. Eden pointed out that the earlier forms of the declaration had been drafted as a four-Power document. He did not want to propose any amendments, but suggested that the three Powers should be free to associate the French with the declaration if they thought fit to do so. Stalin considered that it would be better to leave the document as a three-Power declaration. M. Molotov then proposed, as an addition to the fourth paragraph, the words: 'and in this connection support will be given to the political figures of those countries who have taken an active part in the struggle against the German invaders.' The Conference agreed that the three Foreign Secretaries should consider this proposed addition.

At the next meeting of the Foreign Secretaries on the evening of (a)
February 9 M. Molotov put forward his amendment. Mr. Stettinius thought that it was not relevant, and Mr. Eden said that it would permit too much interference in the affairs of the liberated countries. M. Molotov said that the whole of the Declaration amounted to interference in the affairs of liberated Europe. He thought that there should be no doubt about our attitude towards those who had fought the Germans and those who had collaborated with them. He did not intend his amendment to have any bearing on the situation in Greece. He asked whether Mr. Eden objected to the amendment. Mr. Eden said that he did not see how it fitted in with the declaration. It was finally agreed to leave a decision on the amendment to the plenary meeting, and to consider at the meeting of the Foreign Secretaries on the following day a proposal by Mr. Eden for the addition of a final paragraph to the declaration inviting the Provisional Government of the French Republic to associate themselves with it.

Mr. Stettinius, at the meeting of the Foreign Secretaries on the (b)
morning of February 10, said that the United States delegation could not accept M. Molotov's amendment, since it would cause the greatest difficulty from the domestic standpoint in America. M. Molotov withdrew the amendment, and then suggested that the second part of paragraph 5 should be altered to read 'they will immediately consult together on the measures necessary to discharge the joint responsibilities set forth in this declaration'.

This amendment was accepted. M. Molotov would not yet agree to Mr. Eden's proposal to include an invitation to the French Government; later he accepted the proposal. The declaration was approved (c)
at the seventh plenary session in the afternoon of February 10, and

(a) WP(45)157, 8th F.S.M.
(b) WP(45)157, 9th F.S.M. (c) WP(45)157, 7th plenary.

published as part of the Communiqué of the proceedings of the Conference.

(ii)

Discussions at the Conference, February 4–9, 1945, the dismemberment of Germany: French participation in the occupation of Germany and representation on the Control Commission: the question of German reparation.

(a) At the meeting with the Americans at Malta on February 1 Mr. Eden and Mr. Stettinius agreed to propose that the French should be invited to occupy a zone in Germany and to join the Allied Control organisation. They discussed future policy towards Germany and agreed that both the political and economic aspects of this policy should be worked out by the European Advisory Commission, and that, with the Russians so close to Berlin, a tripartite agreement on common policy was urgently required.

(b) At a preliminary meeting between Mr. Eden and M. Molotov at Yalta at noon on February 4 M. Molotov at once said that the only fixed item on the Soviet agenda was the German question, and that the Russians wanted to begin with a discussion of the military situation.[1] In answer to a question from Mr. Eden, M. Molotov agreed that the political situation in Germany should also be discussed.

(c) On the following morning M. Molotov said that, at the plenary session to be held later in the day, the Soviet Delegation would discuss any question raised by the other Delegations, including matters relating to the dismemberment of Germany and other political and economic questions affecting Germany. Mr. Eden said that the British Government had not reached a decision in the matter; he suggested that the subject needed further investigation, and that the Prime Minister, the President and Stalin should discuss it in general terms, and then refer it back for further study to the three Foreign Ministers. M. Molotov agreed with this suggestion.

(d) On February 5, 1945, at the first plenary session Stalin said that he wanted to raise certain questions about Germany: They appeared to be agreed about the dismemberment of Germany, but no decision had been taken on the form which such dismemberment would take. Did they propose to set up a Government or Governments in Germany, or would they merely establish some form of administration,

---

[1] The military discussions were, in fact, of less importance than the political discussions.
(e) In a report of the night of February 7–8 to Mr. Attlee the Prime Minister said that 'all the Chiefs of Staff have taken a holiday today to see the battlefields of Balaclava. We are not stressing this in our contacts with our friends.'

(a) WP(45)157, 1st F.S.M. (b) WP(45)157, 2nd F.S.M.
(c) WP(45)157, 3rd F.S.M. (d) WP(45)157, 1st plenary. (e) Jason 220; Premier 3/51/10; U983/12/70.

either for Germany as a whole, or for the parts into which it was divided? They were agreed upon a policy of unconditional surrender. If Hitler surrendered unconditionally, would they preserve his Government? Did we propose at the Conference to work out definite terms (as in the case of Italy) for unconditional surrender?

Stalin reminded the Conference of the discussions at Teheran and at the recent conference in Moscow.[1] He thought that the time had now come to take a decision. The Prime Minister said that in principle they were all agreed about the dismemberment of Germany, but the actual method would need prolonged study of the historical, ethnographical and economic facts by a special committee and could not be settled in five or six days while they were at Yalta. The Prime Minister himself could not give an immediate answer upon the best way of dividing Germany in order to secure peace in the future; he would feel free, after detailed examination of the problem, to change the tentative views which he was now putting forward. He had in mind primarily the case of Prussia, the arch evil-doer. If Prussia were separated from the rest of Germany, her power to begin another war would be greatly limited. He also thought that the establishment of another considerable German State to the south, which might find its capital in Vienna, would provide a main line of division between Prussia and the rest of Germany, and would give approximately a fifty-fifty division in terms of population. Other questions which had been decided in principle needed consideration, e.g. the transfer of German territory to Poland, the future of the Ruhr and Saar industrial areas and the possibility of dividing Prussia after she had been isolated.

Stalin asked whether, if a group in Germany declared that they had overthrown Hitler, we should be prepared to negotiate with them. The Prime Minister said that, if Hitler or Himmler were to offer unconditional surrender, we should reply that we could not negotiate with the war criminals. If the Germans could not produce anyone else, we should have to go on with the war. It was, however, more likely that Hitler and his associates would be killed or disappear. We should then have to consider whether the people who offered unconditional surrender were worth dealing with. If we decided to deal with them, we should tell them the terms of surrender which we had already worked out. If they were not worth dealing with, we should continue the war, and occupy the whole country under strict military government.

Stalin asked when the question of dismemberment would be mentioned to the Germans, if it were not included, as he suggested, in the terms of surrender. The Prime Minister said that the Germans

---

[1] See above pp. 78–98 and 229–30. See also Volume II, p. 599 ff.

would surrender unconditionally: we therefore need not discuss the future of Germany with them. On the other hand the major Allies ought to begin the study of the question at once. Stalin suggested that, although we need not discuss it with the Germans, we ought to put forward our demand for dismemberment. The Prime Minister said there was no need to do so, and that before we made our demand, we must be sure what exactly we wanted. The President thought a decision should be taken on the principle at the Conference, and that the details should be worked out within thirty days; otherwise, if the question of dismemberment became a matter of public discussion a hundred different plans would be suggested. The President himself was in favour of decentralisation, and therefore of dismemberment, whether into five or seven, or more or fewer States.

Stalin accepted the President's proposal, but wished to add to the terms of surrender a general statement that Germany should be dismembered. The Prime Minister explained that for the present he could not go beyond saying that the British Government agreed in principle to dismemberment and were prepared to set up a body to discuss the best method of effecting it. He would agree to the three Foreign Secretaries considering article 12(a) of the terms of surrender[1] with a view to adding a reference to dismemberment, or words covering dismemberment.

(a) The Foreign Secretaries discussed the question on February 6. The discussion showed a difference between the Russian and British attitudes. M. Molotov wanted a form of words definitely showing that the Allies considered dismemberment necessary and proposed to carry it out. Mr. Eden said that a certain latitude was required; we could not say that dismemberment was 'necessary' until its practicability had been worked out. Mr. Eden added that the British were not responsible for the fact that the European Advisory Commission had not completed the study of dismemberment which had been agreed upon at Teheran. Mr. Eden would not go beyond the addition to
(b) article 12(a) of the terms of surrender of the words 'and the dismemberment'. At the second plenary session on February 6 M. Molotov accepted this proposal. At the next meeting of the Foreign Secre-
(c) taries on February 7 M. Molotov proposed the creation in London of a special committee, consisting of Mr. Eden and the United States and Soviet Ambassadors, to study the question of dismemberment. Mr. Eden thought that, in order to bring in the French, whose par-

---

[1] This article read: 'The United Kingdom, the United States of America, and the Union of Soviet Socialist Republics shall possess supreme authority with respect to Germany. In the exercise of such authority they will take such steps, including the complete disarmament and demilitarisation of Germany, as they deem requisite for future peace and security.'

(a) WP(45)157, 4th F.S.M. (b) WP(45)157, 2nd plenary. (c) WP(45)157, 5th F.S.M.

ticipation he regarded as most desirable, we should give the work to the European Advisory Commission. Mr. Stettinius thought that the presence of the French on the Advisory Commission was a reason for not referring the question to it. Mr. Eden said that we should be making a grave mistake if we kept the French out of the discussions. They were the neighbours of Germany, and had ideas about the future of the Rhineland. M. Molotov, with the agreement of Mr. Stettinius, suggested that the special body discussing the question could consider the participation of France.

Mr. Eden accepted the proposal for a special committee. He put forward—and his colleagues accepted—as terms of reference that the Committee should consider, 'on the assumption that Germany is to be split up, if necessary by force, into separate States (*a*) at what point of time the operation should be carried out; (*b*) what the boundaries of the States should be; (*c*) what measures would need to be taken by the occupying forces to ensure the more or less efficient functioning and survival of the States; and (*d*) what relationship should be allowed amongst the separate States and with other foreign Powers'. The Committee was instructed 'to submit a factual report indicating the advantages and disadvantages of this scheme from the point of view of general security'.

The Conference accepted the recommendations of the Foreign (a) Secretaries. The two other questions connected with Germany were more contentious. At the first plenary session the President raised (b) the question whether a zone of occupation in Germany should be allocated to the French. He said that he understood that the French did not claim to extend their sovereignty to the Rhine. Stalin said that General de Gaulle had told him in Moscow that France wanted to annex German territory up to the Rhine. The Prime Minister said that the Conference could not settle immediately the question of the French frontier. They were concerned only with the question of a zone of occupation. The Prime Minister was in favour of giving the French a zone, and would gladly let them have part of the British zone. All he wanted was the consent of the Soviet Government to an arrangement between the British and Americans and the French with regard to the areas which the latter would take over from the British and American zones. In answer to a question from Stalin the Prime Minister said that the British Government thought that the French should be admitted as a fourth Power to the Control Commission for Germany, and that, as the French army became stronger, the French could assume more responsibility. The French were unlikely to be lenient with the Germans. The British Government wanted France to be strong in order that Great Britain would not

(a) WP(45)157, 3rd plenary. (b) WP(45)157, 1st plenary.

have to bear the full weight of another German attack in the west. It was very uncertain whether the United States would share in the occupation of Germany for more than a few years. If the French army were not strengthened, the burden on the United Kingdom would be intolerable. We should not object if the Russians wished to make use of another Power, e.g. Poland, in their zone.

President Roosevelt said that the United States would take all reasonable steps to preserve peace, but not at the expense of keeping a large army indefinitely in Europe. For this reason the American occupation would be limited to two years. The President wanted, however, to keep the Control Commission small, and, although he was in favour of the French having a zone of their own, he did not think that they should become members of the Control Commission. Stalin said that the presence of France on the Control Commission might make it difficult to refuse other Powers. It was impossible to forget that the French had opened the gates to the enemy, and that otherwise the Great Powers would not have suffered so many losses. The Control Commission should consist only of those Powers who had stood firmly against Germany from the beginning. In any case the French had not been admitted so far to the meetings of the Great Powers.

The Prime Minister observed that we had all got into difficulties at the beginning of the war. France was the largest of Germany's immediate neighbours. Great Britain wanted a strong French army to contain Germany in the west, and British public opinion would fail to understand why the French were not brought into the discussion of questions relating to Germany. We could not deal with matters concerning north-west Germany and the frontiers of France without French participation. The Americans were free to go away from Europe, but the French would always remain next door to Germany. Moreover, unless the French were allowed to take their place on the central authority for Germany they would refuse to occupy a zone. Mr. Eden, and the Prime Minister, also pointed out that as a matter of practical administration the French zone could not be controlled if the French had no place in the central administration. Such a place would not imply French participation in the meetings of the Great Powers. The President maintained his opposition, and argued that the Dutch might also claim a seat on the Control Commission if—as might be necessary—they were given an area of farm land in Germany for five or six years while their own flooded lands were being rehabilitated. After further discussion, the Conference agreed to allocate to France a zone of occupation taken from the British and American zones and to ask the Foreign Secretaries to consider how control should be exercised over it.

The Foreign Secretaries did not deal with the matter at their meeting on the morning of February 6. At the plenary session later in the day the Prime Minister said that the position of France had become of great importance in view of the President's statement on the previous day about the withdrawal of American forces from Europe two years after the end of the war. Great Britain was not strong enough to do her part in the west against Germany unless there were a strong French army, and this fact must be considered in the light of the President's statement. The President said that what he wanted to make clear was that in present conditions public opinion in the United States was decisive. If it were possible to get agreement on something like the Dumbarton Oaks proposals, there was more chance of full American participation in the organisation of peace throughout the world. (a)

When the Foreign Secretaries discussed the matter on February 7 M. Molotov put forward a written proposal that the French authorities should exercise control in their zone under the general guidance of the Control Commission. Mr. Eden repeated the British view that, even if the French did not refuse a zone on these terms, we should find ourselves in great practical difficulties unless we agreed to French representation on the Control Commission. Mr. Eden suggested that they should report that France (and no other Power) should be accepted on the Control Commission, while the Americans and Russians were in favour of postponing a decision and referring the matter to the European Advisory Commission. (b)

At the plenary session later on February 7 the Prime Minister again argued in favour of the British proposal. He repeated that the admission of the French to the Control Commission would not give them a right to take part in three-Power Conferences, but that, unless they were represented on the Control Commission, they would certainly refuse—in the Prime Minister's view, rightly—to take over a zone of occupation. The President, with Stalin's support, suggested that the matter might be left to be settled by correspondence. The Prime Minister replied that this procedure would take months. The Conference agreed to discuss the matter again later. When this discussion took place on February 10 President Roosevelt said that he had come round to the Prime Minister's view that the French could not administer their zone adequately unless they were represented on the Control Commission. He said that they could do less harm as members than if they were not on the Commission, and that a concession on this point would make it easier to deal with the French in other matters. Stalin also withdrew his objection, and the Conference agreed with Mr. Eden's suggestion that the French Provisional Government should be sent at once an invitation to join the (c) (d)

(a) WP(45)157, 2nd plenary. (b) WP(45)157, 5th F.S.M. (c) WP(45)157, 3rd plenary. (d) WP(45)157, 7th plenary.

Control Commission. The French Government accepted this invitation and also the corresponding invitation in respect of Austria.

The third question affecting Germany was that of reparation. The (a) question was discussed at the first plenary meeting of the Conference. Stalin then asked M. Maisky[1] to explain the Russian plan for reparation in kind. M. Maisky said that two forms of reparation in kind would be demanded from Germany: the withdrawal of factories, plant, machine-tools, rolling-stock, etc., and yearly payments in kind for ten years after the war. It would also be necessary for the restoration of the Russian economy and the re-establishment of security in Europe that German heavy industries—iron, steel, heavy engineering, chemicals, electrical industry—should be reduced to about 20 per cent of their present figure. These industries could be used for making reparation payments. Furthermore all factories specialising in purely military products, aircraft factories and plants for making synthetic oil should be removed from Germany within two years. In order to maintain security after the ten-year period of payments an American-Russian-British International Control Commission should be set up to exercise strict control over the German economy for an indefinite period.

Reparation payments should cover only direct material losses, such as the destruction of public and private property, factories, cattle, corn, etc. Even so the payments would not cover the losses. We would therefore have to set up two criteria for establishing priorities among the countries claiming reparation: (i) proportionate contribution to winning the war, (ii) proportionate value of the direct material losses sustained by each country. The Russians proposed that a Reparation Commission composed of representatives of the three Great Powers should be established in Moscow to work out details. The Russians claimed as their share 10,000 million dollars over a period of ten years.

The Prime Minister's first comment was to refer to the disappointing experiences with regard to reparation after the first World War. He admitted that the sufferings of Russia had been greater than those of any other country, and that it would be reasonable, up to a point, to remove plant and factories from Germany, but he did not believe that it would be possible to get from Germany anything like the sum which the Russians claimed for themselves alone. He pointed out that Great Britain had also suffered greatly in the war. He referred to the seriousness of the British financial position and the problem of paying for British food imports. Great Britain had incurred in the common cause debts not far short of

[1] M. Maisky was at this time Deputy Commissar for Foreign Affairs. He and MM. Vyshinsky, Gusev and Gromyko attended the plenary conference.

(a) WP(45)157, 1st plenary.

£3,000 million. The Prime Minister also spoke of the damage done to other countries, e.g. France, Belgium, Holland and Norway, and asked what would happen if Germany were reduced to starvation? Should we do nothing, or, if we provided food to keep the Germans alive, who would pay for it? The Prime Minister favoured setting up a Reparation Commission, but insisted that it should explore the subject from the point of view of seeing what we could get in a sensible way.

The President also agreed with the proposal to appoint a Commission. He too thought it was impossible to get enough out of Germany to repair the material damage done to the U.S.S.R., Great Britain and France. The United States did not want manpower, tools or factories from Germany. They did not consider that the Germans should have a higher standard of living than the Russians; on the other hand they did not want them to starve, and could not feed or house them at American expense. The United States Government would be prepared to help the Soviet Government to get what they could out of Germany by the transfer of plant, etc. They would also help Great Britain to increase her exports, and would be glad to see these exports replacing German exports. In this way Great Britain would be helped to pay her debts. M. Maisky argued that the Russian figures were not too high. They did not involve transfer of currency. He agreed that the Germans must not be allowed to starve; they were not entitled, however, to live at a higher standard of living than the Central European standard. The Russian claim was equivalent only to a tenth of the United States budget for the present year, and to six months' British war expenditure.

The President and Stalin recommended a Commission limited to the three Great Powers. The Prime Minister thought that the Commission should begin in this way, but that it should also take account of the claims of other countries. Stalin said that the three Powers which had shared the main burden of the war were entitled to receive the maximum sum. He did not include France; the French had done nothing by way of sacrifice or action comparable to the achievements of the three Powers, and had indeed suffered less than Yugoslavia and Holland. France had only eight divisions and some naval forces at present in the war. Yugoslavia had twelve divisions, and the Lublin Poles thirteen divisions.

The Prime Minister suggested that during the Conference the Foreign Secretaries should draw up the heads of a draft directive for a Commission which would then take about a month to prepare a full report. He thought that it was for consideration whether exertion in the war should be the basis of claims or whether the sufferings endured at the hands of the enemy would not be a sufficiently all-embracing test for the allocation of all the sums likely to be received.

On either basis Russia would stand well, but the Great Powers must not allow it to be thought that they were merely looking after their own interests.

(a) The Foreign Secretaries began their discussion of a reparations directive on February 7. M. Molotov brought forward two documents. The first of these laid down certain basic principles for the exaction of reparation. (i) Reparation should be received in the first place by those countries which had borne the main burden of the war and had organised victory over the enemy. All other countries were to receive reparation in the second place. (ii) Apart from the question of the use of German labour for reparation, reparation in kind was to be exacted in two forms: removals in a single payment at the end of the war; and annual deliveries over ten years. (iii) The total sum under (ii) would be fixed at 20,000 million dollars, to be distributed as follows: U.S.S.R. 10,000 million, United Kingdom and United States 8,000 million, all other countries 2,000 million.

M. Maisky explained that these figures were based on a calculation of the national wealth of Germany before the war as 125,000 million dollars. As a result of the war and post-war difficulties, this figure could be reduced to 75,000 million dollars. The 'mobile' proportion of the industrial wealth of a highly industrialised country was about 30 per cent, i.e. in the case of Germany 22 to 23,000 million dollars. The Russians proposed to take 10,000 million dollars. This would leave Germany sufficient existence on 'a modest and decent Central European level'. The German national income before the war was 30,000 million dollars a year. After the war it would fall to 18–20,000 million. The Russians proposed to take 1,000 million dollars a year for ten years, i.e. 5 or 6 per cent. This would provide the second 10,000 million dollars.

Mr. Eden said that he could not give an opinion about M. Molotov's proposals without further study. He called attention to the Prime Minister's suggestion with regard to the basis of allocation. Mr. Eden would have preferred the inclusion of the Prime Minister's formula in order to avoid the impression that the Great Powers were taking everything. On the other hand, without committing himself to the Russian figures, he was inclined to agree in principle with M. Molotov's proposals under his second heading (i.e. (ii) above).

M. Molotov then brought forward his second document on the terms of reference of an Allied Reparation Committee.[1] He proposed that the Committee, which would meet at Moscow, should consist of a representative of each of the three Great Powers, and that the Soviet, American and British Governments should decide when repre-

[1] The record uses this term. The term 'Commission' was subsequently used.

(a) WP(45)157, 5th F.S.M.

sentatives of other Allied Powers should be invited to take part in its work. The functions of the Committee should be to work out a detailed plan of reparation in accordance with the principles adopted at the Conference. Mr. Eden accepted these proposals on the understanding that the term 'principle' did not mean acceptance of the details in the Russian plan.

The Prime Minister told the plenary conference on February 8 that he accepted the recommendations of the Foreign Secretaries. The next discussion took place at the Foreign Secretaries' meeting on February 9. Mr. Stettinius then submitted a memorandum on the basic principles of the exaction of reparation from Germany for study and recommendation by the Moscow Reparation Commission. This document followed generally the lines of M. Molotov's proposals (i) and (ii). It suggested that reparation should be received 'in the first instance' by those countries which had 'borne the main burden of the war and [had] suffered the heaviest losses and [had] organised victory over the enemy'. Mr. Stettinius included only one reference to an estimated sum. This reference, in his last sentence, ran: 'The Commission should consider in its initial studies the Soviet Government's suggested total of 20,000 million dollars for all forms of reparation'. (a) (b)

M. Molotov asked the meaning of this sentence. He thought that the Commission should consider the figure of 20,000 million dollars as a basis, and should reach their final figures by starting from this basis. Mr. Stettinius said that the figure should be 'taken into consideration and studied'. M. Molotov asked why the figure raised doubts. Was it too small or too large? Mr. Stettinius said that this could not be known until the Commission had studied the situation. The United States Government, however, were prepared to take 20,000 million dollars as a basis for discussion.

Mr. Eden said that an answer had not yet been received from the War Cabinet in London (whom he had consulted) but that the Prime Minister refused to insert any figures at the present stage. It was impossible to know what the figure should be. M. Molotov asked whether the Russian share (10,000 million dollars) could not be mentioned. Mr. Stettinius said that he was unable to go beyond agreeing that this share should be 50 per cent of the total. Mr. Eden also asked whether the policy of dismemberment might not reduce the total sum which could be obtained from Germany. M. Maisky thought this unlikely at all events as far as the lump sum, i.e. the single payment, was concerned. There might be variations in the annual payments during the first years owing to dismemberment, but these variations could be adjusted, and dismemberment would

(a) WP(45)157, 4th plenary. (b) WP(45)157, 7th F.S.M.

not make it impossible to take an annual sum amounting only to 5 or 6 per cent of the total income of Germany. Finally it was decided to report to the plenary conference later in the day (i) that the United States and Soviet Delegations had agreed to the figure of 20,000 million dollars as a basis of study and to the U.S.S.R. receiving 50 per cent of the total sum received, (ii) that Mr. Eden had reserved the British position. The Conference took note of the report and of the fact that Mr. Eden had said that he must await instructions from his Government.

(iii)

Discussions at the Conference, February 4–9, 1945: the World Organisation: voting on the Security Council: separate membership of the Ukraine and White Russian Soviet Republics: invitations to the Conference on World Organisation.

(a) At the meeting with the American Delegation in Malta Mr. Eden agreed to support the American compromise proposal for voting on the Council, i.e. a unanimous vote on the part of the Great Powers in cases involving the enforcement of a decision, but the exclusion from voting of parties to a dispute which was being dealt with by discussion on the Council.[1] The Americans explained that this proposal was not, from their point of view, a compromise but the solution which they preferred. During the discussion it was agreed that the Delegations should draw up two documents: a document setting out the proposals, to be given to the Russians and a brief and clear explanation of them for the President and the Prime Minister. If they accepted the plan, the President should present it formally to the Conference.

(b) At the second plenary meeting of the Conference (February 6) the President invited Mr. Stettinius to introduce the plan. Mr. Stettinius then repeated, with some changes in wording, the President's proposal of December 5, 1944, that the decisions of the Security Council on procedural matters should be made by an affirmative vote of seven members; decisions on all other matters should be made by an affirmative vote of seven members, including the concurring votes of the permanent members, provided that, in decisions affecting peaceful settlement, a party to a dispute should abstain from voting.

In a paper circulated to the Conference Mr. Stettinius listed five decisions relating to the peaceful settlement of disputes which would require the affirmative votes of seven members of the Security

[1] See above, pp. 170–1.

(a) WP(45)157, 1st F.S.M. (b) WP(45)157, 2nd plenary.

Council, including the votes of all the permanent members, but on which a member would not vote if the decision concerned a dispute to which it was a party.

These five decisions were as follows: (i) whether a dispute or a situation brought to the attention of the Council was of such a nature that its continuation was likely to threaten the peace; (ii) whether the Council should call on the parties to settle or adjust the dispute or situation by means of their own choice; (iii) whether the Council should recommend to the parties methods and procedures of settlement; (iv) whether the legal aspects of the matter before the Council should be referred by it for advice to the International Court of Justice; (v) whether, if a regional agency for the peaceful settlement of disputes existed, such an agency should be asked to concern itself with the controversy.

On the other hand, there would be no such restrictions on voting on six types of decision requiring the affirmative vote of seven members, including the permanent members. The most important of these six was that which related to the removal of threats to the peace and suppression of breaches of the peace, including the following questions: (*a*) whether failure by the parties to a dispute to settle it by means of their own choice or in accordance with the recommendations of the Security Council constituted a threat to the peace; (*b*) whether any other actions on the part of any country constituted a threat to the peace or a breach of the peace; (*c*) What measures should be taken by the Council to maintain or restore the peace, and how such measures should be carried out; (*d*) whether a regional agency should be allowed to take measures of enforcement.

The remaining five of these six types of decision requiring an affirmative vote of seven members, including the permanent members, related to: (i) recommendations to the Assembly on admission of new members, suspension or expulsion of a member and the election of the Secretary-General; (ii) restoration of the rights of a suspended member; (iii) approval of special agreements or agreements for the provision of armed forces and facilities; (iv) the formulation of plans for a general system of regulation of armaments, and the submission of such plans to the member States; (v) determination whether the nature and activities of a regional agency or arrangement for the maintenance of peace and security were consistent with the purposes and principles of the general organisation.

Mr. Stettinius said that these proposals recognised the need for unanimity among the permanent members of the Council in matters affecting the preservation of world peace, and at the same time made provision for a fair hearing for all members of the organisation. He explained that his proposals did not differ in substance from those of December 5. M. Molotov, however, asked for time to consider the proposals, and suggested that the discussion should be postponed until February 7.

The Prime Minister agreed about adjourning the discussion. He said that the British Government had given very serious attention to the President's proposals. He had not been altogether satisfied with the Dumbarton Oaks proposals, and had been anxious to make sure that the realities of the position of the three Great Powers had been fully faced. On studying the President's proposals his anxieties had been removed as far as concerned the British Empire and the self-governing Dominions. He thought that world peace depended, in the last resort, on the friendship and collaboration of the three Great Powers. It was, however, also necessary to provide for a full statement of grievances by the smaller nations of the world. Otherwise the Great Powers might appear to be seeking to rule the world, whereas their desire was to serve it, and to preserve it from the renewal of the horrors of war. The Prime Minister felt that, within the limits of the President's proposals, the three Great Powers should make a 'proud submission' to the general community of the world. He took an example from the British Empire to illustrate why he did not feel that this submission would be damaging to British interests. Thus, if China asked for the return of Hong Kong, the British Government would have the right to state their case fully against any case made by the Chinese, but they would not be allowed to vote on the five decisions mentioned by Mr. Stettinius. It would be open to China to state her full case, and to the Security Council to take a decision without the vote of the British Government.

Stalin asked whether Egypt would take part in the Assembly. The Prime Minister answered 'Yes', but that Egypt would not be a member of the Council unless she were elected to it. Stalin asked whether any member of the Assembly could express an opinion. The Prime Minister again answered 'Yes', but that if any of the five decisions were involved the British Government would not be allowed to vote. They accepted that position, agreeing to such procedural matters being decided without voting themselves. On the other hand the British Government could not agree that the six types of decision set out by Mr. Stettinius could be taken without their vote. The British Government would consider it too great an abrogation of sovereignty not to vote on such matters.

Because of their right to vote on the six types of decision, the British Government felt that they were sufficiently safeguarded and able to stop all further action against them by the Security Council. There could be no question of the Security Council compelling them to give back Hong Kong to China if they felt that this was not a right step to take. On the other hand they thought it right that China should have a chance of stating her case fully. Similarly, if

Egypt raised questions affecting the Suez Canal, the British Government would submit to the procedure laid down as to the five decisions on which the parties to the dispute would not vote, because British rights were reserved under the six types of decision; and Great Britain could prevent any action by the Council if she chose to do so. If Argentina raised a complaint against the United States, the United States Government would accept the procedure laid down in their proposals on the five decisions on which a party could not vote, but they would be free to oppose action under the six types of decision if, for example, they thought that the Monroe doctrine was being infringed.

Stalin asked for a copy of Mr. Stettinius's proposals. He said that the right merely to express an opinion was not of much value. A nation would raise a matter not in order to express an opinion about it but to get a decision. The question was therefore much more serious than securing the right to express an opinion. Stalin said that he would study the American document. At present he did not fully understand the proposals. What he feared was that, although the three Great Powers were Allies today, and would not commit acts of aggression, the three leaders would disappear in ten years or less, and a new generation would come into power which had not experienced the war. They wanted to secure peace for fifty years at least. The greatest danger was the possibility of conflict among themselves because if they remained united the German danger was not very important.

At the third plenary meeting in the afternoon of February 7, M. Molotov accepted Mr. Stettinius's proposal.[1] He then raised the question of the participation of the Soviet Republics as initial members of the World Organisation with votes in the Assembly. He asked that three, or at least two—he mentioned the Ukrainian, White Russian and Lithuanian Republics—should be given this position in view of their importance and their sacrifices in the war. The President suggested that the questions of invitations to a conference, and of the representation of different nations, should be referred to the Foreign Ministers. (a)

The Prime Minister agreed with this proposal. He pointed out that the four British self-governing Dominions had played a part in the organisation of peace before 1939. They had entered the war in 1939 of their own free will, and with full knowledge of our weakness. We could not agree to a system which excluded them from the position which they had held for a quarter of a century. The Prime Minister

[1] The Prime Minister telegraphed to Mr. Attlee that the Russians had said that their acceptance of the proposal was due largely to the British explanation of it. (b)

(a) WP(45)157, 3rd plenary. (b) Jason 220, Premier 3/51/10; U983/12/70.

therefore sympathised with the Russian proposals, though he could not give a final answer without consultation with Mr. Eden and possibly with the War Cabinet. He agreed, therefore, with the suggestion that the matter should be referred to the Foreign Secretaries.

(a) The Foreign Secretaries met at noon on February 8, 1945, to consider the two points referred to them, i.e. the membership of two or three Republics of the Soviet Union, and the time and place of the proposed conference. Mr. Stettinius proposed that the meeting should be held in the United States, not later than the end of April, and that invitations should be limited to those States which had declared war on the common enemy. After some discussion, the Foreign Secretaries agreed to recommend April 25 as the date and Washington as the place of meeting and to limit the invitation to States which had signed the United Nations Declaration before the last day of the Yalta Conference. The Conference on the World Organisation would itself determine the list of original members of the Organisation, and the British and American Delegations would support the proposal to admit two Soviet republics to original membership.

(b) These recommendations were considered at the plenary meeting of the conference on the afternoon of February 8. Mr. Eden explained that the proposal to invite only those States who had signed the United Nations Declaration was put forward because it was undesirable to allow other States to sign the Declaration merely in order to secure an invitation to the conference on World Organisation. Stalin said that ten of the States which had declared war on Germany, and would become members of the World Organisation, were not in diplomatic relations with the Soviet Union. It seemed strange that Russians should be partners in a World Organisation, the object of which was to attain international security, with these ten nations. The President said that there were probably special reasons why the States in question were not in diplomatic relations with Russia, e.g. in some States there was a strong Catholic influence. Representatives of these States, however, had been associated with Russia at a number of recent conferences, and Stalin's objective would be facilitated by inviting all of them to the Conference.

The President then said that he was in a difficulty because some time earlier Mr. Sumner Welles, who was then Acting Secretary of State, had told the South American Republics that, while they should break off diplomatic relations with Germany, they need not declare war. Five or six of the Republics had acted on this advice, and now felt themselves entitled to be invited to the Conference. Mr. Stettinius

---

(a) WP(45)157, 6th F.S.M. (b) WP(45)157, 4th plenary.

had brought these facts to the President's notice about a month ago. The President had then sent a letter to the Presidents of the six South American Republics explaining that, if they wished to be invited to the Conference they would have to declare war on Germany. One of them—Ecuador—had declared war, but had not yet signed the United Nations Declaration. Paraguay would declare war in a week or ten days' time. Declarations from Peru, Venezuela and Uruguay would shortly follow. The President would therefore find it embarrassing if, after declaring war, these States were not invited to the Conference. He regarded Mr. Welles's action as mistaken, but the States in question were among the Associated Nations, and had given help in the war, especially in the provision of raw material for munitions.

Stalin said that there would be some inconsistency in inviting to the Conference a number of States which had broken off relations with Germany but had not declared war, while other States in the same position, for example Turkey and Argentina,[1] were not invited. Furthermore, if invitations were to be sent to countries which declared war on Germany at this late hour, we should be inviting nations which had wavered, and looked to their own interests, and declared war only when they had seen who was going to win.

The President suggested that an invitation should be sent to those States who were willing to declare war against Germany at once. Stalin was willing to agree if the time limit were fixed at March 1. The Prime Minister supported the proposal that only those States which had declared war should be invited. He also agreed with Stalin that we should be inviting a certain number of nations which had not played a good part in the war. On the other hand we were recruiting nations to a World Organisation to oppose Germany, and declaration of war by another batch of nations would have a depressing effect on the Germans and on other hostile belligerents.

The President then proposed the inclusion of Iceland, and the Prime Minister mentioned the position of Egypt. Egypt had twice wanted to declare war on Germany and Italy, but we had advised her not to do so, partly because we wanted to spare Cairo and the rest of the country from heavy bombardment, partly because the nominal neutrality of Egypt had been more in our interest. We therefore felt that Egypt should be given the chance of declaring war now. The Prime Minister also supported the inclusion of Iceland in view of the fact that she had violated her neutrality by admitting British and American troops and had secured our 'lifeline' across the Atlantic. Stalin agreed, and added that we should not invite nations like Italy and Hungary, which had fought against us. The Prime Minister

---

[1] See also below, p. 309, note (1).

also said that we ought not to invite Eire. The President agreed. The Prime Minister then referred to Turkey. He said that Turkey had made an alliance with us at a dangerous time, and that her attitude had remained friendly and helpful in many ways although she had not taken the chance offered her a year ago. He thought that she should receive an invitation if she declared war now.

Stalin agreed with this suggestion. The President mentioned the case of Denmark, but the Prime Minister thought it better to wait until the country had been liberated. M. Molotov then asked whether the two Soviet Republics could not be allowed to sign the Declaration before March 1. The President said that the United States and Great Britain had agreed to support at the conference the claims of the two Republics to original membership, but that there would be some technical difficulty in including them among the States invited to the conference. Hitherto the question under discussion had been the issue of invitations to existing States which had not been admitted to the United Nations. In the case of the two Soviet Republics this question was whether the U.S.S.R. should in future have three votes. Stalin said that he would be content if the two Republics were mentioned by name in the report. The Conference therefore decided that 'The United Nations as they exist on the 8th February, 1945, and such of the Associated Nations as have declared war on the common enemy by March 1, 1945, would be the only States invited to the Conference on World Organisation. At that stage the delegates of the United Kingdom and the United States of America will support the proposal to admit to original membership two Soviet Socialist Republics, i.e. the Ukraine and White Russia.'

(iv)

Consideration by the War Cabinet of the Russian demands with regard to (a) separate membership of the United Nations for the Ukraine and White Russian republics, (b) the dismemberment of Germany, (c) German reparation: final resolutions of the Conference: the Prime Minister's report of February 19, 1945, to the War Cabinet.

(a) The War Cabinet met on February 8, 1945, to consider the questions raised by the Prime Minister in his telegrams from the Crimea. They began their discussions with the question of the acceptance of the Soviet claim to votes in the United Nations Assembly for the Ukraine and White Russia. This claim—which reduced the Soviet demand from sixteen votes to two votes—was based on the plea that the Ukraine and White Russia had suffered so greatly and had

(a) WM(45)16, C.A.; Jason 220, Premier 3/51/10; U983/12/70.

fought so well that they should be included as founder members of the Organisation. The President, who obviously saw difficulties from the American point of view, had not rejected the idea, but had proposed that it should be considered at a conference to be summoned in March. The Prime Minister felt that we had asked a great deal in claiming four or five members (six, if India were to be included), and that Russia was not demanding too much in asking for two votes in addition to that of the main Soviet vote. The Prime Minister also wished to make a friendly gesture to Russia in view of other important concessions on the Russian side which were achieved or impending. He asked that we should give an assurance to the Russians that we would support their request.

It was pointed out during the discussion that the President might not be able to maintain his support of the Russian claim if opposition developed in the United States. We also had no time to consult the Dominions. We might therefore find ourselves in the unfortunate position at the March conference of supporting the Russians against the Americans or the Dominions or both. There was also the difficulty that the Russians might claim later on that the other fourteen Soviet Republics should be given separate representation, since there was no difference in principle between the two selected Republics and the other fourteen. The test originally proposed had been that the States concerned should possess real independence in foreign affairs. The Ukraine and White Russia indeed had European and not merely internal frontiers, and might claim differential treatment on these grounds. In any case, Russia would have three seats, the British Empire five or six, and the United States (though she could influence the South American republics) only one. We should therefore find it very hard to resist the Russian demand. An alternative might be to agree to three places for Russia and allow her to choose whom she pleased.

The War Cabinet finally agreed that we should not go beyond the admission of the Ukraine and White Russia, and that the Prime Minister should be informed of their view of the importance of securing an understanding from the Russians which would protect us from subsequent claims for the admission of other Soviet Republics. The Prime Minister should also be told that some members of the War Cabinet, while accepting the decision, were not themselves in agreement with it.

The War Cabinet approved 'with great satisfaction' the agreement which the Prime Minister and Mr. Eden had secured over the question of voting on the Council of the World Organisation. They then discussed the proposal for a committee to study questions regarding the procedure for the dismemberment of Germany. The War Cabinet felt that the term 'dismemberment' needed a more precise definition.

It might mean (*a*) the severance from the pre-war Reich of areas such as Austria, East Prussia and parts of Silesia, (*b*) the break-up of unitary government in Germany, (*c*) the disintegration of Germany into a number of small States. The general issue of dismemberment raised a number of important economic and political questions. Neither the War Cabinet nor the A.P.W. Committee (except as far as East Prussia was concerned) had considered these questions.[1] It was therefore desirable to avoid any commitment until the War Cabinet could review the matter as a whole.

On the other hand the term 'dismemberment' might be intended to cover a wide range of possibilities which in any case would have to be examined by the proposed committee before a commitment was made. The War Cabinet therefore decided to ask Mr. Attlee to prepare a draft telegram to the Prime Minister and Mr. Eden stating that they did not want to commit themselves without further examination of the question. This telegram was considered at a later meeting of the War Cabinet on February 8 and sent to the Prime Minister on the following day.

The last subject considered by the War Cabinet was that of reparation. The War Cabinet regarded the Russian attitude on this question as in many respects fantastic. During the discussion the point was raised whether it was worthwhile to ask for any reparation. We were intending to impose very hard terms on Germany, and must carry our own public opinion with us. If we made extravagant demands for reparation we should lose the support of public opinion without getting the reparation; in this respect the history of reparation after the first World War was a warning to us.

The scale of the Russian demands for reparation was hardly compatible with their proposal for the dismemberment of Germany. A dismembered Germany deprived of 80 per cent of her machinery and equipment could not pay reparation on the scale proposed by the Russians; the only result of trying to secure such payment would be to destroy the German economy, reduce the Germans to the position of a slave nation, and make it necessary for the Allies, in the interests of Europe as a whole, to give them (as after the first World War) financial and economic assistance.

If we decided to demand reparation, we should be wise (apart from payments in kind, e.g. potash and timber) to limit the removal of machinery and equipment to those industries, such as synthetic oil, which had a potential war value. We should have the support of public opinion in breaking up these potential war industries, while we should leave Germany enough for the reconstruction of her economic life. We should remember, however, that by withdrawing obsolescent

---

[1] This statement was not entirely accurate. See Chapter LXIV, section (iv).

or heavily worn equipment and machinery from Germany we were making it necessary for her in due course to re-equip herself with modern machinery to our disadvantage.

Russia might have a strong case for drawing on German labour for a considerable time, but from our point of view the best plan was to get all we thought it wise to remove from Germany during the first two years after the war, and then give her a chance to do what she could with the remainder. We might, however, be unable to prevent the Russians from stripping their zone of occupation. The War Cabinet decided to reply in this general sense to the Prime Minister.

The reply, which was received at Yalta on February 9, stated that, (a) although the matter would require delicate handling with the Russians, we ought to make our position clear. We should emphasise, in particular, that reparation must be considered in relation to any policy of dismemberment and that the two Russian objectives of depleting German manufacturing capacity and preserving German ability to make large reparation payments were inconsistent. Our view on economic security was that we should eliminate certain selected fields of German war potential, but should leave the remaining industry more or less intact. We were more concerned than the Russians or Americans with the future of western Europe, and our public opinion would not tolerate for more than a short time the savage policy proposed by the Russians. Our greatest need for the delivery of reparation in kind (timber, potash, etc.) would arise during the first years after the war. We ought therefore to concentrate both on 'once for all' deliveries and on 'current' deliveries within a period of two years. The reparation problem after the last war, and the possibility of an early American withdrawal from the occupation of Germany, were strong arguments in favour of this policy. We should also insist that reparation demands must not be such as to put us in the position of having to finance Germany in order that she might fulfil obligations towards us or our Allies.

The War Cabinet also thought that France should be a member of the Allied Reparation Committee. The French had a great and legitimate interest in reparation; France was already a member of the European Advisory Commission which had the question on its agenda, and, unless the French were brought into the discussions on reparation, we could not count on their co-operation in settling the many questions which would arise. We should also have to secure, at some time, the consent of the other Allies; a statement to this effect in the terms of reference would make the Committee more acceptable to the Dominions. We could not agree to the Russian text which relegated to a second rank the claims of the smaller Allies. The

(a) Fleece 329–31, Premier 3/51/10; UE624/624/77.

claims, for example, of the Netherlands had high priority. The War Cabinet also thought it undesirable to specify the particular kinds of property which should be handed over. The Committee should be left to work out this question. It was important to secure possession of German assets abroad, but we might find difficulty in so doing in the case of neutral countries. There was more doubt about the question of shares in German enterprises. If German industry were depressed too far, standards of labour elsewhere might be affected, and capital might be attracted to Germany with a view to exploiting cheap German labour.

The use of German labour ought to be considered by the Committee as part of the general question of reparation. Thus, if the Russians took large numbers of Germans, this labour should be counted as a substantial contribution to reparation. Four million Germans at £40 a year over ten years would equal two-thirds of the Russians claims.

We could not possibly state, without further investigation, a figure for German deliveries. In any case the figure of 20,000 million dollars, or £500 million a year for ten years, was too high. This figure was, roughly, the equivalent of German pre-war gross annual exports (i.e. not allowing for imports). A Germany which had been defeated, bombed, and perhaps dismembered and was unable to pay for imports could not provide deliveries on this scale, even with the inclusion of some of her capital assets. Some account would have to be taken of payment for German imports; otherwise we should find ourselves paying for the imports necessary to keep Germany alive while others received the reparation. We had also to take our pre-war claims into account.

(a) Mr. Law and Sir O. Sargent also telegraphed to Mr. Eden on February 9 with regard to the omission of France from the membership of the proposed Dismemberment and Reparation Committees and from the Control Commission in Germany. The Foreign Office thought that the United States and Soviet Governments seemed unwilling to accept the policy of building up France under her present régime as one of the Great Powers. The American attitude might be due merely to prejudice and ignorance, but the Soviet attitude might well be part of a considered policy of weakening western Europe politically and militarily. The Soviet attempt to put France and other European Allies in a subordinate position with regard to reparation also suggested a policy of this kind.

If, after the admission of France to the European Advisory Commission, the Yalta Conference excluded her from participation in the settlement of German affairs, the effect upon General de Gaulle's

---

(a) Fleece 354, U1084/3/70.

position might be very serious. With all the General's shortcomings, his Government seemed to be the only alternative to civil disturbances and the emergence of a single-party Government with which we should find it difficult to work. Thus the policy of the Americans at Yalta might have a serious effect on our vital interests in Europe. Their declaration that United States troops would not stay longer than two years in Europe, and their veto on the participation of France in the settlement of German affairs meant upsetting the balance between eastern and western Europe to the advantage of Russia. Soviet forces of occupation would be established west of the Elbe, and possibly in Rheno-Westphalia; four Soviet satellites—Poland, Czechoslovakia, Yugoslavia and Bulgaria would be an advance guard pointing westwards and southwards. If France were weakened by civil disorder and estranged from Great Britain, and if the British army of occupation were cut down, and there were no American forces, the Russians would be in control of the situation. The future of Europe for some time to come might thus turn on the treatment of France at the Conference.

The main decisions of the Yalta Conference, as at most international meetings, were taken on the last full day of business. On this day, February 10, the three Heads of Government agreed to a formula to describe the 'reorganisation' of the so-called Polish Provisional Government. They accepted the Declaration on Liberated Europe, and an invitation, or exhortation, to Marshal Tito to fulfil the terms of his agreement with M. Subasić. They agreed to the admission of France to the Allied Control Commission for Germany, and set up arrangements for the discussion of German reparation. On this latter question Mr. Eden was able to give the views of the War Cabinet. He said at a meeting of the Foreign Secretaries that the British Delegation (a) held that reparation should be considered in relation to dismemberment and to the labour situation generally. We found it difficult to reconcile the two main Russian objects, namely the depletion of German industrial capacity and the payment by Germany of large annual sums. The British Government wished to avoid a situation in which they had to finance and feed Germany as a result of the reparations taken out of the country. Hence they could not agree to state a figure before the question had been examined by the Commission. They also thought that the French should be represented on the Commission from the start. Finally they wished to reserve their position with regard to pre-war claims.

M. Molotov said that without the mention of a figure the Commission would have no basis upon which to work. Mr. Eden said we would accept the principles laid down in the Soviet draft. He showed

(a) WP(45)157, 9th F.S.M.

M. Molotov a British redraft of the Russian proposals in the following terms:

'Basic Principles of Exaction of Reparation from Germany

1. The proportions in reparation allotted to the claimant countries shall be determined according to their respective contributions to the winning of the war and the degree of the material loss which they have suffered. Account shall be taken of deliveries made to the claimant countries by other enemy countries.

2. Reparation is to be exacted from Germany in the three following forms:

(*a*) Removals within two years from the surrender of Germany or the cessation of organised resistance from the national wealth of Germany located on the territory of Germany herself as well as outside her territory. These removals to be carried out chiefly for purposes of destroying the war potential of Germany. Subject to the fulfilment of these aims Germany's industrial capacity will not be reduced to a point which would endanger the economic existence of Germany and the execution of such obligations as may be imposed on her.

(*b*) Annual deliveries from current production for a period to be considered.

(*c*) Use of German labour and lorry service.

3. In fixing the amount of reparation to be exacted under paragraph 2 above account shall be taken of any arrangements made for the dismemberment of Germany, the requirements of the occupying forces and Germany's need to acquire from time to time sufficient foreign currency from her exports to pay for her current imports and the pre-war claims of the United Nations on Germany.

Regarding the Organisation of an Allied Reparation Committee

The Allied Reparation Committee shall be set up on the following basis:[1]

1. The Committee shall consist of three representatives: one each from the U.S.S.R., the United Kingdom and the United States. The French Provisional Government shall also be invited to nominate one representative. Each representative shall be entitled to call in to assist in the work of the Committee any number of experts.

2. The function of the Committee shall be to work out a detailed plan for exaction of reparations from Germany according to the principles adopted at the Crimea Conference of the Three Powers for acceptance by all Powers concerned, and to make recommendations to their respective Governments.

3. The Governments represented on the Committee shall deter-

[1] The wording of their proposals followed the text suggested by the War Cabinet.

mine the moment when the representatives of other Allied Powers will be invited to participate in the Allied Committee as well as define the forms of participation of these Powers in the Committee.

4. The activities of the Committee shall proceed in strict secrecy.

5. The Allied Reparation Committee shall be established in Moscow.'

M. Maisky said that the British reply was disappointing, and that we seemed to wish to take from Germany as little as possible. Mr. Eden answered that we had made no such reply, and that in our view the Russians were unlikely to get as much as they had hoped. M. Maisky agreed that the plan should be adjusted to meet dismemberment. He did not agree that there would be any difficulty in reconciling the two main Russian objects.

In the afternoon of February 10, 1945, the Prime Minister and Mr. (a) Eden had a conversation with Stalin and M. Molotov. Stalin asked why we could not take the Russian figure as a basis of work for the Reparation Commission and the Prime Minister explained that we thought it impossible to collect such a figure from Germany. He said that by removing factories and equipment from Germany the Russians would be doing us a service, since the removal would put an end to German exports which would then be replaced by British exports. The question was again discussed at the plenary session of (b) the Conference later in the afternoon. Stalin argued strongly for the inclusion of figures, and the Prime Minister refused. He quoted the telegram which he had received from the War Cabinet. Finally Stalin said that what he wanted to get settled was that Germany should pay reparations in kind and that the Moscow Commission should consider the amount to be paid. The Russians could put their figures before the Commission and the other parties could do the same.

It was therefore agreed to insert a clause relating to reparation in the communiqué on the Conference and to state that Germany would justly have to make the greatest possible compensation in kind for the damage which she had caused to the Allied Nations, and that a Commission on the subject of compensation for damage would be set up in Moscow. The Conference also accepted a secret protocol in the following terms:

'1. Germany must pay in kind for the losses caused by her to the Allied nations in the course of the war. Reparations are to be received in the first instance by those countries which have borne the main burden of the war, have suffered the heaviest losses and have organised victory over the enemy.

(a) WP(45)157, 6th plenary. (b) WP(45)157, 7th plenary.

2. Reparation in kind is to be exacted from Germany in the three following forms:

(*a*) Removals within two years from the surrender of Germany or the cessation of organised resistance from the national wealth of Germany located on the territory of Germany herself as well as outside her territory (equipment, machine-tools, ships, rolling-stock, German investments abroad, shares of industrial, transport and other enterprises in Germany, &c.), these removals to be carried out chiefly for the purpose of destroying the war potential of Germany.

(*b*) Annual deliveries of goods from current production for a period to be fixed.

(*c*) Use of German labour.

3. For the working out on the above principles of a detailed plan for exaction of reparation from Germany an Allied Reparation Commission will be set up in Moscow. It will consist of three representatives—one from the Union of Soviet Socialist Republics, one from the United Kingdom and one from the United States of America.

4. With regard to the fixing of the total sum of the reparation as well as the distribution of it among the countries which suffered from the German aggression the Soviet and American delegations agreed as follows:

"The Moscow Reparation Commission should take in its initial studies as a basis for discussion the suggestion of the Soviet Government that the total sum of the reparation in accordance with the points (*a*) and (*b*) of the paragraph 2 should be 20,000 million dollars and that 50 per cent of it should go to the Union of Soviet Socialist Republics."

The British delegation was of the opinion that pending consideration of the reparation question by the Moscow Reparation Commission no figures of reparation should be mentioned.

The above Soviet-American proposal has been passed to the Moscow Reparation Commission as one of the proposals to be considered by the Commission.'

(a) The Prime Minister telegraphed to Mr. Attlee—for the War Cabinet—on February 10 a general comment on the results of the Conference. He said that, in view of the fact that we had six representatives, he could not oppose the Russian request for separate representation of the Ukraine and White Russia on the United Nations; our six representatives might be in a safer position if Russia were also a 'multiple voter'. The question now was how the United States could place itself on terms of equality without raising further Russian demands. The actual voting in the Assembly was not of

(a) Jason 321. Premier 3/51/10.

much importance, but we could not say so without risk of affront to many smaller nations. All the Americans in the President's circle had told the Prime Minister that one of the principal reasons for the American withdrawal (*sic*) from the League of Nations was our having six votes to America's one. The Americans, however, were 'conscious of rejoinders about their South American tail' to which they were adding almost daily. Meanwhile they had agreed with us about recommending the inclusion of the Ukraine and White Russia as 'founder members'.

The Russians still held to the illusion of getting reparation on a great scale, and would certainly remove a great many plants and enforce other deliveries in kind. We must not commit ourselves to any figure. The Russians were as determined as the Americans to keep France, and especially General de Gaulle, out of the 'Big Three'. The Prime Minister had been surprised at the anti-French attitude of the Russians. The two other Great Powers were resisting our attempts to allow the French a seat on the Allied Control Commission for Germany, though obviously they must be on the Commission if they were to have a zone of occupation. The two Powers refused to agree to the French coming to a conference in the near future. All we could secure was French representation on the subordinate bodies.

The Prime Minister thought that we could put the position in the following way: 'The Powers on whom the brunt and burden of the war fell chiefly must preserve their right to meet together as and when the situation requires. Other meetings will no doubt be held at which representatives of other States will be present'. So far we alone had spoken a friendly word for France. Nevertheless the presence of General de Gaulle at the meeting 'would have wrecked all possible progress, already difficult enough'.

We had agreed in principle to the dismemberment of Germany, but all possibilities could be discussed, and, if no practical schemes were arranged, we should resume our liberty of decision. It was also clear that the French would have to be consulted on the question.

The Prime Minister explained that the British and American Combined Chiefs of Staff, with the approval of the President and himself, and after consultation with the Russians, had reached most satisfactory conclusions on all milltary questions. The Russians had been 'very open' with us. Shipping, stock-piling and oil questions had also been settled satisfactorily.

On February 12 the War Cabinet had before them the draft text of (a) the announcement to be issued at the end of the Conference. Mr.

(a) WM(45)18. 3, C.A.

Attlee said that the results achieved by the Prime Minister and Mr. Eden, in the face of great difficulties, were highly satisfactory.[1] There was agreement on the American proposals for the United Nations Organisation. We had had to concede membership to the Ukraine and White Russia, but the Americans had acted with us in the matter. The principle of the dismemberment of Germany had been accepted, but there remained ample room for discussion. France was to be invited to associate herself with the principles of the proposed declaration on liberated Europe, and would be given a zone in occupied Germany and a seat on the Allied Control Commission. A Reparation Commission in Moscow would consider the extent and methods of compensation for the damage caused by Germany to the Allied countries. The Tito-Subasić agreement was to be put into effect at once in Yugoslavia. At Mr. Attlee's suggestion the War Cabinet agreed to send the Prime Minister and Mr. Eden a telegram of congratulations on the skill and success with which they had conducted their discussions, and the results which they had achieved.

(a) On February 19 the Prime Minister gave the War Cabinet his impressions of the Conference.[2] After Mr. Attlee had repeated the hearty congratulations of the War Cabinet on the results obtained the Prime Minister spoke optimistically about the attitude of the Russians and his own confidence in the intentions of Stalin.[3]

The War Cabinet did not discuss any of the matters covered by the Prime Minister in his survey, but gave general approval to his statement.[4]

Meanwhile Mr. Eden had been in correspondence with the Foreign Office on the question of the invitations to the San Francisco Con-
(b) ference. He had telegraphed on the night of February 8–9, a summary of the discussion on February 8 about membership of the World Organisation, and had suggested that, in view of the 'hint' given to the South American 'clients' of the United States, we might give a similar hint to Egypt, Turkey, and possibly Iceland. Mr. Eden also asked whether the Foreign Office would approve of a hint to Portugal and King Ibn Saud (in view of the President's impending meeting with the latter).

(c) The Foreign Office replied to Mr. Eden on February 10 that in principle it would be desirable for as many of our 'clients' to be

---

[1] See also Volume III, p. 271.

[2] See Volume III, p. 272.

[3] See Volume III, pp. 271 and 437.

[4] On February 27 the Prime Minister made a statement on the Yalta Conference in the House of Commons. (Parl. Deb. Ser. V. 408; cols. 1275–1284.) Twenty-five members —most of them Conservatives—voted against the Government motion for approval of the British attitude at the Conference. Eleven others abstained. One junior Minister, Mr. H. G. Strauss, Parliamentary Secretary to the Ministry of Town and Country Planning, resigned a few days later.

(a) WM(45)22. 1, C.A. (b) Jason 257, U986/12/70. (c) Fleece 381, U986/12/70.

present as possible. Since Iraq and Iran had already qualified for membership, Egypt and Saudi Arabia ought to be given the opportunity of adhering to the United Nations Declaration—i.e. we ought to explain the position to King Ibn Saud and the Egyptian Government, but not to press them to join if they were reluctant to do so. In these circumstances it would be difficult not to give Turkey a similar hint, although we should find it somewhat humiliating to offer them this last-moment chance of obtaining a seat at the peace settlement; we had previously told them that unless they entered the war at the time we wished them to come in, they would forfeit the right to take part in the peace settlement. They had always denied this argument on the grounds that we should need them, and would have to invite them. We should in fact find it useful to have them with us in dealing with Balkan affairs. We could say, however, that action by them at this last moment would not constitute a claim to further military supplies or assistance.[1]

The United States Government were responsible for the military protection of Iceland, which was to some extent within their sphere of influence. They might have given a hint to the Icelandic Government, but Iceland had never had any armed forces and the Government had remained neutral in outlook. It was doubtful whether we should find it worth while even to mention to them that they might declare war.

The case of Portugal was more complicated. For political reasons we should wish not to leave her out if invitations were sent to Egypt, etc., but Dr. Salazar was most unlikely to give up his present policy of neutrality in the German war. He might be considering entry later on into the war against Japan, if the Japanese did not evacuate Timor; he was unlikely to declare war on Japan now owing to the effect which such a declaration would have on the position of the 200,000 refugees (in whose fate we also had an interest) at Macao. In the event of war between Portugal and Germany, no land or air threat from the Germans was to be expected, but the Germans might take naval action against Portuguese shipping, and thus add to Allied shipping difficulties. If we decided to give a hint to Dr. Salazar, we ought not to do more than explain the situation to him. We should not press him to declare war on Germany partly owing to the shipping question and also because he would resent pressure from us, and Russia might make difficulties over the adherence of Portugal to the United Nations Declaration.

There was also the case of Sweden. The Soviet Government had suggested more than once that we should bring Sweden into the war. Our own Chiefs of Staff were opposed to this suggestion because the

[1] See also Volume IV, Chapter LII, section (iii).

armed assistance which Sweden would require could be provided only by the Russians and there were obvious political objections against a course which would bring the Red Army into Scandinavia. The Foreign Office therefore were not in favour of saying anything to the Swedish Government.

These telegrams crossed a message from Mr. Eden on February 10
(a) to the Foreign Office stating that the Conference had agreed that the United Nations as they existed on February 9 should be invited to attend the Conference on the World Organisation, together with any of the Associated Nations (including Turkey) which might have declared war before March 1, 1945. This formula excluded an approach by us to Portugal or Saudi Arabia though, if they had declared war within the time-limit, we might hope that they might be invited. In any case, in order to diminish the preponderance of Latin America, we should give a hint to Egypt, Turkey and Iceland. The Americans agreed that we could suitably do so.

The Foreign Office replied on February 11 that they were doubtful
(b) about Turkey, and would wait until they had heard Mr. Eden's views on their telegrams of February 10. They thought, however, that Saudi Arabia should be regarded as an Associated Nation because she had broken off relations with Germany in 1940. The Foreign Office had therefore instructed the British representatives at Cairo, Jedda and Reykjavik to make the necessary communications. Mr. Eden replied on February 13 that he did not wish action to be taken
(c) as yet at Jedda, since he was discussing with M. Molotov the question of the inclusion of Saudi Arabia. He also wanted to consider further the inclusion of Iceland.[1]

(v)

Preparations for the San Francisco Conference: the question of postponement of the Conference: instructions for the British Delegation to the Conference.

The acceptance by the Soviet Government at the Yalta Conference of the compromise on the question of voting, and the Anglo-American agreement to allow separate representatives to the Ukrainian and White Russian Republics cleared the way for the founding conference of the United Nations. The United States Government, in particular, wished this Conference to take place as soon as possible. They sent out on March 1, 1945, invitations to a meeting in San Francisco.

---

[1] The States which in fact declared war on Germany before March 1 were Ecuador, Paraguay, Peru, Chile, Venezuela, Uruguay, Turkey, Egypt, Syria, Lebanon, Iran and Saudi Arabia.

(a) Jason 322, U987/12/70.
(b) Fleece 413, U987/12/70. (c) Jason 396, U1048/12/70.

There was an element of tragi-comedy in the fact that the question of invitations nearly wrecked the prospects of the Conference. The obvious difficulty was the position of Poland. Poland was undoubtedly qualified to receive an invitation since she was on the list of the United Nations. The difficulty was that until the agreement reached at Yalta on the creation of a new Polish Provisional Government of National Unity had been carried into effect, the British and United States Governments could not agree that the existing so-called Provisional Government should be taken to represent Poland; on the other hand the Russians had ceased to recognise the Polish Government in London. In order to get around this awkward situation the United States Government proposed a public statement expressing the hope that the Polish Provisional Government would have been established before the meeting of the San Francisco Conference on April 25, and would be in diplomatic relations with the major nations. In such case an invitation to the Conference could be sent to it.

This plan did not satisfy the Russians. In spite of a personal appeal from the President on March 24, Stalin refused to include M. Molotov in the Russian delegation, and the Soviet Government announced publicly their view that the existing Provisional Government should be invited to represent Poland. At the beginning of April the Foreign (a) Office considered the possibility of a postponement of the Conference. In favour of postponement there was the possibility that the Russians might refuse to attend until the deadlock over the Polish question had been settled. There was also a risk of Anglo-American disagreement over the question of territorial trusteeship. The Americans continued to insist on bringing forward proposals on this subject at the Conference, but, in spite of British enquiries, had not yet explained what they intended to propose. Finally, it was becoming clear that the conference, if it took place at the end of April, would coincide with the collapse and surrender of Germany; the Foreign Ministers of the European countries could not be as far away as San Francisco for a long period at such a critical time.

On the other hand the conference had been so much advertised by the United States Administration that any postponement would have a very serious effect on American public opinion and might even result in the rejection, later on, of the whole United Nations plan by the Senate. The risk of such a rejection would be greater if, in the interval, there were further disputes in Europe over a treaty of peace. It seemed therefore most undesirable to propose postponement, but the United States Government might suggest that, in view of the unexpectedly rapid collapse of Germany, the Foreign Ministers of the

(a) U2594/12/70.

leading European countries would be unable to attend a conference at the date proposed. In these circumstances the United States Government considered that the character of the conference should be changed, and that, instead of producing a charter agreed by Governments and capable of being submitted at once for ratification, it should rather be a preliminary meeting of experts from all the nations concerned. In other words, its object would be to secure agreement on a technical level to something like the Dumbarton Oaks proposals and to publish an expert report, probably in the form of a draft charter. After this document had been fully considered by Governments, the United States Government would summon the final conference at which the presence of Foreign Ministers would be essential. Sir A. Cadogan was away from the Foreign Office during the first discussion of this proposal, but his comment was that the proposal might be desirable. Mr. Eden, however, did not favour it, and nothing was said about it to the United States Government.

Meanwhile the Foreign Office had been considering the questions likely to arise at the Conference and the attitude which the British Delegation should take. In a memorandum of March 23, 1945, the
(a) Foreign Office drew up a list of questions on which the advice of the Armistice and Post-War Committee and the War Cabinet was necessary. The Foreign Office thought that, although the procedure to be adopted at the Conference was not yet known, the 'inviting States' (with whom France should be associated as far as possible), ought to agree upon their attitude towards proposals put forward by the 'invited States'. The four 'inviting States' had proposed that the Conference should consider the Dumbarton Oaks proposals 'as affording a basis for the Charter'. The United Kingdom Delegation, therefore, should not suggest or support major alterations without agreeing them at all events with the United States and Soviet Delegations, if the two latter were prepared to adopt a similar course.[1] On the other hand it would probably be necessary to make some changes in order to meet the wishes of the 'middle' and smaller States, to incorporate some improvements, and to deal with matters left out of the Dumbarton Oaks proposals by accident or design.

The first question raised by the Foreign Office was whether there should be a common centre for the World Organisation, and, if so, where this centre should be. The Foreign Office thought that, while some international organisations—e.g. the Monetary Fund and the Court—could be at different places, and the Security Council might vary its place of meeting, the Secretariat of the Organisation would

---

[1] The Chinese were obviously in a different position from that of the other 'inviting Powers'.

(a) APW(45)35.

have to be given a permanent centre, and that the Security Council and Assembly would tend to meet at this centre. The essential requirement of such a centre should be that it allowed freedom of communication and discussion. There would probably be general agreement upon the undesirability of locating the centre in the territory of a Great Power even if it were given special status, like the District of Columbia, as a kind of enclave, since there would be a risk that the Great Power concerned might be able to exercise undue influence upon the Secretariat. This objection would not hold in the case of an enclave in the territory of a smaller Power, but it was doubtful whether a small Power could provide the facilities. In any case long negotiations would probably be necessary, and these would have to be followed by a large building programme.

There would be no chance of getting agreement upon a place in Asia, Australasia, South America or Africa (with the possible exception of Tangier). Montreal, Toronto or Quebec would have advantages, but even if it were located in Canada, the Organisation would be too much overshadowed by the United States, while it would also be too far away from the political activities of Europe. From our point of view we should support a location in Europe; the choice of a place outside Europe would emphasise the declining position of the European Continent in world politics. Furthermore American opinion would be brought more into touch with political realities if the United States took part in an organisation situated outside the American Continent. The possible locations in Europe were Brussels, The Hague, Lisbon, Prague, Vienna, Copenhagen and Geneva. The first three could be ruled out, since the Russians would not come to western Europe. There were obvious disadvantages in choosing Vienna—a German-speaking city recently detached from the enemy. Prague might be regarded as too much in the Russian sphere of influence. There would be no objection to Copenhagen (except that its climate was not ideal). Geneva already had adequate facilities, and the whole area might perhaps be made into an international enclave. Unfortunately the Russians were most unlikely to agree to Geneva. Geneva might also be thought to be too much associated with the failure of the League of Nations. Nevertheless we might press for Geneva, though we were most unlikely to get this suggestion accepted. We might perhaps secure agreement upon Geneva as a temporary headquarters. Otherwise, unless the Russians agreed unexpectedly to one of the western capitals, we should support (i) Copenhagen, (ii) Prague, (iii) Vienna.[1]

[1] The Foreign Office regarded the name 'United Nations' (which had been suggested by the British Delegation at Dumbarton Oaks) as somewhat inconvenient, especially since it was not easily translated into Russian or Chinese. 'Union of Nations' might be a simpler term, but the United States Delegation had regarded it as seeming to denote too

(*continued on page* 304)

Certain important questions relating to membership were still unsettled. (i) At the Yalta Conference we had pledged ourselves to support the admission of White Russia and the Ukraine as 'founder members'. The Soviet Government were likely to insist on limiting initial membership, apart from the two Soviet republics, to the United Nations. Of the States to be represented at San Francisco only nine out of forty-five were European, while nineteen were Latin American. We ought therefore to try to secure early admission for such States as Sweden, Denmark, Switzerland, Spain (subject to a satisfactory change of Government) and our ally, Portugal. An attempt might be made to lay down criteria for determining whether (according to the Dumbarton Oaks proposals) a State was or was not 'peace-loving' and therefore eligible for membership. Such criteria as had been suggested—e.g. that the Government of the State should not be 'fascist' or that it should pay due regard to fundamental human rights, etc.—were open to the objections that they were difficult to interpret and presumed the right of the Organisation to concern itself with the internal affairs of a State. We ought therefore to define the term 'peace-loving' solely in an international sense—i.e. that a State would itself keep the peace and join in seeing that other States did so. (ii) The Conference would have to decide whether the non-permanent members of the first Security Council should be elected by the Assembly or nominated in the Charter. If they were to be elected by the Assembly, the Security Council could not meet until the Assembly had held a meeting. Furthermore the first two or three years would be critical for the success of the Organisation, and we might find it desirable to try to secure the nomination in the Charter of one of the Dominions or two of the smaller European Allies. (iii) A number of the smaller States would certainly ask for an increase in the powers of the Assembly over security questions. We ought to resist this demand, since it was counter to the arguments which we had put forward in our original proposals for the Dumbarton Oaks Conference, and which had been supported by the United States and the U.S.S.R. We might agree that the Assembly should have the right, in matters over which it had power of decision, to ask the Permanent Court for advisory opinions, but it should not be entitled to use this

---

(*continued*)
close an association of States. Hence there was no satisfactory alternative to 'United Nations'. This term at all events emphasised that responsibility for effective action lay with the nations themselves and not with a supra-national entity. Another point—the question of languages—was of some importance in relation to procedure. The Foreign Office considered that the French would make a considerable effort to try to re-establish French on an equal footing with English. The Spanish-speaking peoples might have similar ambitions, but would probably be content with French as representative of the Latin group. The Russians might make a stand for Russian, as they had done on the European Advisory Commission. The adoption of more than two official languages would be intolerably cumbrous. We should, however, have to agree at least to two languages, of which one would be English and the other—probably—French.

procedure in dealing with disputes, since it might thereby encroach on the sphere properly left to the Security Council. (iv) It had been suggested that the over-representation of Latin America in the voting in the Assembly might be countered by a system of weighted votes. This suggestion, however, was not practicable. The United States Government were considering whether they would ask for special representation to counterbalance the votes of the Soviet Republics, but they had not found a suitable formula, and all their public statements had emphasised the equality of States in the Assembly. A smaller point to be settled was the number of representatives of each State in the Assembly. The number three laid down in the Covenant of the League of Nations had been found too small; we should not object to a proposal to raise the number to six. (v) The question of 'disputes arising out of matters which by International Law were solely within the domestic jurisdiction of the State concerned' had not been properly discussed at Dumbarton Oaks. The Foreign Office, after taking legal opinion, proposed to support the continuance of the rule under the Covenant whereby States were under no obligation to submit such questions to methods of peaceful settlement, with a modification to the effect that the Security Council would be entitled to intervene to prevent or suppress a breach of the peace arising out of them. (vi) There was some criticism of the fact that the Security Council was not entitled to give an opinion—even if the parties desired it— on 'disputes the continuance of which does not threaten the maintenance of international peace and security'. This prohibition was intended to prevent a large number of small disputes coming before the Council, and would be in our interest, in view of our imperial responsibilities. The Foreign Office, however, saw no reason why the Council should not act in such a case if the parties—or even one of them—so desired. (vii) We had suggested in the Dumbarton Oaks proposals that regional agencies should be entitled to use force only with the approval of the Council. We did not see how the harmony of the Great Powers could be preserved without a rule of this kind, but the French Government was concerned with the bearing of this rule on the Franco-Soviet Treaty of Alliance of December 10, 1944. They were thinking of an amendment which would allow regional agencies to act merely after informing the Council, and without the obligation to obtain subsequent approval. The Belgian Government had also supported the right to act without prior approval, but wished to maintain the right of the Council to approve or disapprove. The French Government felt strongly on the matter. M. Bidault had mentioned it to Mr. Eden on February 25 as one of the reasons why the French Government could not sponsor the Dumbarton Oaks proposals. The French had always preferred action under special treaties of alliance to the slower and less certain method of decision by an international council. The Foreign Office considered that we could not give way on this point because it would deprive the United States and Great Britain of influence on decisions in Europe.

(a) The Foreign Office submitted three shorter memoranda, the first of which raised the question whether membership of the Organisation should be permanent. The question had been discussed shortly at Dumbarton Oaks; the American and Russian Delegations had agreed with the British view that there should be no right of withdrawal. The inclusion of such a right in the Covenant (at the wish of President Wilson in order to meet Republican criticism) had had a bad psychological effect in suggesting a lack of faith in the League. The Soviet Government had insisted upon giving the Organisation the right of expulsion, but they had admitted that such a right conflicted with the idea of permanence, and they might be persuaded to abandon it at San Francisco.

The second memorandum was concerned with the question of territorial trusteeship.[1] The third memorandum discussed four matters likely to arise at the Inter-Commonwealth meeting which was to take place immediately before the Conference. The first point concerned a possible guarantee of territorial integrity. In Article X of the Covenant the Members of the League of Nations had undertaken 'to respect and preserve as against external aggression the territorial integrity and existing political independence of all Members'. There was, however, no definite obligation upon Members to give effect to this provision, and the article in question had been counter-balanced to some extent by Article XIX whereby the Assembly was given powers to advise the reconsideration of treaties which had become inapplicable. Nevertheless the critics of the League had pointed out that it guaranteed the territorial *status quo* in perpetuity, since no frontiers could be altered without the consent of the country concerned.

Mr. Eden thought that the smaller Powers would criticise the absence of any such guarantee from the Dumbarton Oaks proposals; Australia and New Zealand in fact had already done so. We ought, however, to be firm about refusing such a guarantee since it would leave insufficient scope for future treaty revision. On the other hand we should argue that there was no question of the Council changing any frontier unless by the requisite majority it decided that a change was essential in the general interests of the preservation of international peace and security.

---

[1] See section (vii) of this Chapter.

(a) APW(45)46; WP(45)208–9.

The Dumbarton Oaks proposals also contained no guarantee of the political independence of member States. The reason for this omission was that it was very difficult to define exactly the meaning of 'political independence'. A State might control the actions of another State by indirect means, and it was impossible to lay down a line of division between the legitimate and illegitimate influence which one State might exercise upon the actions of another. A guarantee of political independence could thus extend only to external and legal forms, and could not take account of these indirect methods. The British view on this question was supported at Dumbarton Oaks by the United States and Soviet Delegations, but Australia and New Zealand were in favour of such a guarantee. Mr. Eden thought that we should give way if there were general support for a guarantee of political independence. The assumption that the independence of States would be 'respected' was implicit in the Dumbarton Oaks plan. If, however, a guarantee were given, we should have to give careful consideration to the drafting since, unless it were qualified in some way, it might commit us to recognising the full and immediate independence of India.

The third question was that of 'disputes arising out of matters within the domestic jurisdiction of the State concerned'. The Foreign Office had already stated their view[1] that the Charter should not do more than allow the Security Council to take action if such a dispute constituted a threat to the maintenance of peace or security. This would mean that we could not prevent the Security Council from considering a dispute, for example, with India, to which we were a party, if the Council had decided that the continuance of the dispute was likely to endanger the maintenance of international peace and security. It was, however, improbable that a dispute between two members of the Organisation, even if they were both members of the British Commonwealth, would be excluded from discussion by the Council on the ground that it was a matter of domestic jurisdiction; any such exclusion would be strongly resisted by a member of the Commonwealth wanting the dispute to be dealt with in this way. Under the Yalta voting formula we could indeed block any action against ourselves as the result of the consideration of such a dispute, but an inter-Commonwealth dispute was most unlikely to reach the stage where it constituted a threat to peace.

The fourth point concerned the control of enemy Powers. Mr. Eden thought that the World Organisation should be excluded from the control of enemy or ex-enemy States for the period of occupation, and that thereafter only the consent of the Security Council should be necessary for charging the Organisation with the general and ultimate

[1] See above, p. 305.

responsibility for preventing aggression on the part of ex-enemy States.

(a) At a meeting of the War Cabinet on April 3, 1945, it was thought that the best solution regarding non-permanent members of the Council would be that all members of the Organisation other than the five Great Powers should be eligible, but that the six non-permanent seats should be filled by electing one member for each of the six main territorial groups, Europe, Asia, Africa, Australasia, South America and North and Central America.

The War Cabinet accepted the Foreign Office view that we should maintain our objection to the inclusion in the Charter of a specific guarantee of the territorial integrity of member states, but it was suggested that if we did so it would be difficult also to oppose the demand of some Dominion Governments for a guarantee of political independence. It was pointed out, on the other hand, that in addition to the difficulty about India, we might find it embarrassing to press the suggestion that the political independence of territories such as the Ukraine should be guaranteed. In any event, could 'political independence' be defined for the purpose of such a guarantee? The War Cabinet therefore decided that we should try to persuade the Dominion Governments not to ask for a guarantee of political independence. The War Cabinet accepted the Foreign Office view on the questions of disputes arising out of matters within the domestic jurisdiction of the State concerned and of the position of the Organisation with regard to the control of enemy or ex-enemy States.

(vi)

The San Francisco Conference: crisis over the Russian interpretation of the Yalta formula with regard to voting on the Security Council.

The San Francisco Conference opened on April 25 and ended on June 26, 1945, with the signature of the United Nations Charter. The opening days were difficult because M. Molotov first objected to giving the chairmanship to Mr. Stettinius, and then after accepting a British compromise that each of the sponsoring Powers should take the chair in turn, tried to secure an invitation for the Polish Provisional Government—i.e. the Russian-sponsored Warsaw Government. The Conference refused to give this invitation until the agreed reorganisation of the Provisional Government had taken place. A third dispute broke out over Russian opposition to the admission of Argentina to the Conference. Here also the Russians were defeated.[1]

[1] The Americans were in a weak position on this question, since President Roosevelt had told Stalin at Yalta that Argentina would not be eligible for membership of the

(a) WM(45)38.

(*continued opposite*)

From this time until the dispute over the interpretation of the Yalta agreement on voting there was no serious and open division on a critical subject between the Russians and the British and Americans. The five Great Powers (i.e. the four sponsoring Powers and France) took care to settle matters before bringing them forward at the general sessions. The necessity for reaching agreement among the Five Powers delayed procedure, but since the basis of the Organisation was to be the unanimity of the Great Powers, it would have been incongruous and illogical not to have secured it in the acceptance of the original United Nations Charter.

In effect there were few important changes in the main features of the Dumbarton Oaks plan. A new chapter on trusteeship was added, but the change in American views on this question resulted in an arrangement much less dangerous to the interests of the European colonial Powers than had seemed probable in the first stages of the discussion of post-war arrangements. The Conference accepted the primary responsibility of the Security Council for the maintenance of peace and security, and, on the other hand, the limitation of the functions of the Council to those prescribed by the general purposes and principles of the United Nations Organisation. As a consequence the functions of the Assembly were those of discussion and recommendation on any question of international concern not being dealt with by the Security Council. The immense powers thus conferred on the Council were hardly even discussed at the Conference, partly because the attention of the smaller States was concentrated on a single matter—the so-called claim for a 'hidden veto' of the Great Powers.[1] The British Delegation was able to secure an amendment to the qualifications for election to the Security Council. This amendment provided that 'due regard' should be paid to the contribution of a State to security, and also to the need for an 'equitable geographical distribution' in the membership of the Council.[2] The provisions for the enforcement of decisions of the Council were altered only in two important respects:

(i) A new paragraph was inserted to the effect that in the case of a decision by the Council to employ the forces of a State not itself a member of the Council, the State concerned should be invited

United Nations unless she changed her policy. Mr. Stettinius, however, had agreed at an Inter-American Conference at Mexico City at the end of February to support the admission of Argentina. M. Molotov at San Francisco attempted to trade the admission of Argentina against that of the Polish Provisional Government.

[1] See below, pp. 311–12. In their summary of the results of the Conference the British Delegation described this concentration on a single question as probably 'a blessing in disguise'. The smaller States addressed a list of questions to the sponsoring Powers on the question of the application of the Great Power veto.

[2] This amendment was of particular importance to Canada, but it was likely to be of general value also to the European States.

to send a representative to discuss and vote on the employment of its forces. This clause was inserted largely at the request of the Canadian Delegation; their argument for it was that it would be difficult to justify to the Canadian Parliament the use of Canadian armed forces as a result of a decision by the Council on which Canada might not be represented.

(ii) The subordination of regional organisations and local security arrangements to the decisions of the Council was modified to meet Russian and American views. The Latin Americans—even more strongly than the United States—were afraid that the clause in the Dumbarton Oaks plan forbidding enforcement action under regional arrangements or by regional agencies without the authorisation of the Council might mean that the Russians could veto action, e.g. by the Pan-American Union. The Russians on the other hand considered that the operation of their bilateral pacts with Great Britain, France, Poland, Czechoslovakia and Yugoslavia might also be subject to veto. Hence a new article was inserted in the Charter asserting the inherent right of individual or collective self-defence in the event of an attack against a member State until the Council had taken the measures necessary to maintain international peace and security. The Russians were not satisfied with this clause; they pointed out that aggressive action by Germany short of armed attack might require immediate joint counter-action under their pacts. In order to cover this contingency the Charter excepted from the requirement of authorisation by the Council 'measures directed against any enemy State', i.e. a State which during the Second World War had been an enemy of a signatory of the Charter. This exception would lapse when the Council took over the responsibility for the prevention of aggression by the enemy States.

The most serious crisis over the interpretation of the Yalta voting formula arose over the Russian insistence that a Great Power should have the right to veto discussion by the Council of a dispute to which it was not itself a party. The Russian argument was that the decision
(a) to discuss a question was not a mere procedural matter but was of great political importance since it might lead to a chain of events ending in the imposition of sanctions.

On June 2 the Russian delegations insisted on their proposal, while the British and American delegations strongly opposed it; the Chinese and French supported the Anglo-American view. Mr. Stettinius said plainly that the United States Government could not sign a Charter which included the Russian proposal. There was thus a danger that at this late stage the whole of the work of the Conference would be

(a) U4292, 4348/12/70.

wrecked over this issue. The Foreign Office agreed with the view taken by Lord Halifax at San Francisco that the only way of inducing the Russians to give way was by personal appeals from President Truman and the Prime Minister to Stalin. The Prime Minister agreed to send a message to Stalin that it was unthinkable to allow the Conference to break down over a lesser restriction on the predominance of the Great Powers than that which all five had already accepted in the case of a dispute to which any one of them was a party. The Prime Minister, with the agreement of the Foreign Office, considered that the matter should be settled at once by correspondence with Stalin and that it should not be left to the forthcoming meeting of Heads of Governments since this delay would mean prolonging the Conference still further. It was impossible, without knowing Stalin's reply, to decide what to do in the event of failure to reach agreement with the Russians. The Foreign Office thought that the best course would be—as Lord Halifax had suggested—to let the Conference know the position and to take the line that other outstanding questions should be settled, and the Charter provisionally approved, and perhaps even signed, with the reservation that it would not come into force until this major question of interpretation had been settled to the general satisfaction. Other possible courses were to suspend the Conference altogether and temporarily to give up the idea of a World Organisation, or to go ahead without the Russians. The Foreign Office regarded the latter course as 'very dangerous indeed', since it would 'give full rein to the Russian obsession of a *cordon sanitaire*'.

The matter was, however, settled directly through the agency of Mr. Hopkins, who was already in Moscow.[1] Mr. Hopkins took the matter up with Stalin on June 6. Stalin swept aside M. Molotov's (a)
objections and (without apparently understanding the difficulty) said that the Soviet Government would accept the American thesis.

A further controversy arose over the question of voting procedure in the second stage of action by the Council.[2] The Yalta formula laid down that, while a party to a dispute should not vote, unanimity among the other four was required before action could be taken by the Council.[3] Hence there was a 'hidden veto'—as it was described by the smaller States. Thus if a dispute between Syria and France were brought before the Council, France would be debarred from voting on decisions designed to bring about a pacific settlement, but these decisions would have to be supported by the unanimous vote

[1] See Volume III, Chapter XLV, section (vii).

[2] i.e. efforts to bring about a pacific settlement. (The first stage was the hearing and discussion of the facts, and the third stage enforcement action.)

[3] See above, pp. 282–5.

(a) U4422, 4495/12/70.

of the other four permanent Members. It would thus be possible for, e.g. the United Kingdom, by withholding its vote, to prevent the Council from dealing with the dispute. In spite, however, of the efforts of the smaller Powers to get rid of this 'hidden veto', the Great Powers remained united in keeping it in the Charter.

(vii)

The question of trusteeship in relation to colonial territories: the change in American views: discussion at Yalta: the trusteeship chapter in the United Nations Charter.

One of the questions upon which the British Government felt considerable anxiety during the latter period of the war was the support given by American opinion to proposals for putting the colonial territories of the European Powers under what was somewhat vaguely termed 'international trusteeship'. President Roosevelt and Mr. Hull were known to favour plans of this kind, though they had given only superficial attention to them, and, in Mr. Hull's case, the main consideration was economic—the furtherance of free international trade—rather than political. Neither Mr. Roosevelt nor Mr. Hull knew much about recent developments in colonial government and administration in territories controlled by Great Britain and other European Powers. 'Imperialism' had still, in American opinion, a nineteenth-century, or even an eighteenth-century connotation. The President did not realise the practical difficulties in the way of international control. He was, as in other matters, curiously ready to override the legal rights and political interests of France, especially in relation to the French colonial empire in the Far East. He was also inclined to regard Mr. Churchill's vehement opposition to proposals for 'trusteeship' as due solely to the Prime Minister's wish to maintain an out-moded British Empire.

The President put his views to Mr. Eden during the latter's visit to Washington in March 1943. Later in the year at the Moscow Conference, Mr. Hull produced a memorandum in which he linked the question of international trusteeship with his favourite proposals for free international trade.[1] Mr. Eden definitely rejected these proposals, and the matter was left for further study. No progress was made in this study at the Teheran Conference, though the President—against the protests of the Prime Minister—did not disagree with a suggestion by Stalin that the French should lose all their Empire.

Somewhat to the surprise of the British Delegation, no decision was

---

[1] See above, p. 73, note 3.

taken at Dumbarton Oaks on the inclusion of a statement about territorial trusteeship in the recommendations of the Conference. The Americans themselves discreetly dropped the matter for the time. Military and naval opinion—and especially naval opinion—in the United States, with considerable support in Congress, had begun to think of the future of the Pacific islands, which were formerly under Japanese control, as of great strategic importance. The Americans wanted to hold and to fortify bases in these islands. They wanted to occupy the islands without appearing to possess theoretical sovereignty over them, and thereby incurring the charge of 'imperialism'. On the other hand, a plan for trusteeship involving, as its purpose, the ultimate independence of the islands would place them in an awkward position. Hence, although certain members of the State Department did not give up their advocacy of the original plans for transforming all the colonial possessions of the European Powers into trusteeships, the policy accepted by the President became much less drastic and much closer to the British and French views.

The British Government, on the other hand, wanted to go as far as possible in meeting the criticisms of non-colonial Powers. They had in fact a very strong case in that they could demonstrate both the liberal character of their own colonial policy and the dangers of granting full independence too rapidly to peoples as yet incapable of self-government. In December 1944 the Colonial Secretary submitted to the (a) War Cabinet a paper setting out the principles of a system of international co-operation in colonial development which would satisfy American and other opinion and at the same time safeguard the sovereignty and administrative authority of the responsible Metropolitan Powers. The War Cabinet agreed on December 20 to send (b) this memorandum to the Dominions and, possibly, after their replies had been obtained, to communicate it to the State Department as the basis of an exchange of views before the Yalta Conference. The Prime Minister, however, was still extremely nervous—and irritated —over the long-standing American pressure which seemed to take no account of British interests and to threaten the whole fabric of the British Empire. On December 30 Lord Halifax telegraphed that the (c) State Department had again raised the question of trusteeship, and had pointed out that, although the question need not be settled at the forthcoming United Nations Security Conference, some discussion would be inevitable in relation to the former Italian colonies and the Japanese-mandated islands. The State Department suggested that a preliminary Anglo-American discussion was desirable and that Mr. Stanley, who was in the West Indies, might talk informally about it on his return through Washington.

(a) WP(44)738. (b) WM(44)172. (c) U8861/910/70.

(a) The Prime Minister sent Mr. Eden on December 31 a very strong minute on the subject:

> 'How does this matter stand? There must be no question of our being hustled or seduced into declarations affecting British sovereignty in any of the Dominions or Colonies. Pray remember my declaration against liquidating the British Empire. If the Americans want to take Japanese islands which they have conquered, let them do so with our blessing and any form of words that may be agreeable to them. But "Hands off the British Empire" is our maxim, and it must not be weakened or smirched to please sob-stuff merchants at home or foreigners of any hue.'

(b) The Foreign Office thought that the Prime Minister had not given adequate consideration to Mr. Stanley's memorandum. Mr. Eden replied to the Prime Minister on January 8, 1945, that there was

> 'not the slightest question of liquidating the British Empire. On the contrary, we are anxious to persuade the Americans not to go in for half-baked international régimes in any ex-enemy colonies they may take over, nor to advocate them for others, but to accept colonial responsibilities on the same terms as ourselves.'

The Prime Minister replied on January 18 after considering Mr. Stanley's proposals. He said that he understood these proposals to be the best possible scheme

> '(i) to secure international agreement to the termination of the Mandate System and avoid its extension to enemy territories conquered in the present war, and (ii) to allow foreign Powers a means of expressing their reasonable and legitimate interest in Colonial territories *without* affecting our sovereignty and executive authority, or entitling them to meddle in constitutional questions, or establishing international bodies possessing powers of interference devoid of responsibility.'

If Mr. Eden were satisfied that this was so, and that the proposals involved no danger to our Colonial Empire, the Prime Minister had no objection to communicating them to the United States Government.

After discussion with Mr. Stanley, Mr. Eden replied on January 24 that the proposals, if generally adopted, would be favourable to us, and that there was great advantage in taking the initiative and preventing the Americans from circulating schemes of their own which might be dangerous to our interests. Mr. Stanley had already put our views unofficially to members of the United States Administration, and our proposals had been sent for comment to the Dominion Governments. If the President should raise the question at the forth-

(a) U235/191/70(1945). (b) U681/191/70.

coming meeting in the Crimea, the Prime Minister might say that we would shortly present to his Government a well-considered plan for international collaboration in colonial matters and that we hoped that the Americans would not circulate proposals until they had studied our plan.

During the Yalta Conference Mr. Jebb, at Mr. Harry Hopkins's (a) suggestion, had an informal discussion on February 4 with Mr. Byrnes and Mr. Hiss about various outstanding points. Mr. Hiss argued that the British view on territorial trusteeship did not go far enough. Mr. Hiss wanted a declaration on colonial policy to be signed by all the Colonial Powers. He also thought that in any case we and the Americans and Russians should agree, and record our agreement in an unpublished protocol, that the subject of trusteeship and dependent areas should be discussed at the United Nations Conference and that provision should be made in the Charter 'covering these points'. Mr. Hopkins, however, advised Mr. Eden to wait until the President raised the matter, and hinted that Mr. Roosevelt might not go as far as some of his subordinates wanted to go.

Mr. Eden, at Sir A. Cadogan's suggestion, after hearing of Mr. Hiss's proposal, warned the Prime Minister that the question might be raised. Mr. Eden did not want to make any commitment on the subject, but thought that if we had to accept the proposal for a discussion at the United Nations Conference we should try to get the reference in Mr. Hiss's formula to 'the subject of territorial trusteeships and dependent areas' amended to read simply 'the subject of territorial trusteeship'. We should then avoid committing ourselves in advance to an extension of the system of mandates.

The Americans, in fact, brought up the question at the Yalta Conference, but in a guarded way. Mr. Stettinius, however, used (b) Mr. Hiss's formula in proposing at a meeting of the Foreign Secretaries that, before the United Nations Conference, the five Governments with permanent seats on the Council should consult one another on the subjects of territorial trusteeship and dependent areas and that these subjects should also be discussed at the United Nations Conference. Mr. Eden and M. Molotov agreed with this proposal, but, at the plenary Session on February 9, the Prime Minister said that he (c) could not agree, at all events without consulting the Dominions, to making any British territory the subject of a system under which other Powers could criticise the work we had done in our colonies or call upon us to justify our administration. Mr. Stettinius explained that this proposal merely enabled the World Organisation to set up a Territorial Trusteeship if it so desired. We might have to do so in order to deal with territories taken from the Japanese. There was also

(a) U1047/191/70. (b) WP(45)157, 7th F.S.M. (c) WP(45) 157, 5th plenary.

the question of the future of the Mandated Territories under the League when the latter had been wound up.

The Prime Minister said that his objection would be met if it were made clear that the proposed system of territorial trusteeship would not in any way affect the integrity of the British Commonwealth and Empire. The Conference accepted Mr. Stettinius's proposal subject to an amendment making it clear that territorial trusteeship would apply only to existing mandates of the League of Nations, territory detached from the enemy as the result of the present war or any other territory which might be placed voluntarily under trusteeship. The Conference also agreed to state[1] that it would be a matter for subsequent agreement which territories within these three categories would be placed under trusteeship; that no discussion of actual territories was contemplated at the forthcoming United Nations Conference, and that only principles and machinery of trusteeship would be formulated by the Conference for inclusion in the Charter.

The wording of the secret protocol of the conference was thus in accordance with the British view. Mr. Stettinius's phrase about 'trusteeship and dependent areas' was altered to read only 'the question of territorial trusteeship', and the protocol did not state definitely that the subjects would be discussed at the United Nations
(a) Conference.[2] In a minute of February 22 to the Prime Minister Mr. Eden said that we had committed ourselves only to discussion of the general nature of the future international machinery which would be responsible for carrying out the functions now exercised by the League of Nations in respect of mandates, and any similar functions which the new Organisation might exercise in regard to territories detached from the enemy.

(b) Mr. Eden raised the question of the British attitude in a memorandum to the War Cabinet on the policy to be adopted at San Francisco. Mr. Stanley, with the agreement of the Armistice and Post-War Committee, thought that we ought to agree to the continuance of a mandatory system in respect of existing Mandated territories, and territories taken from the enemy but that we should not agree to an extension of the system 'to any territory which might voluntarily be placed under trusteeship'. Mr. Eden pointed out that, in view of the Yalta agreement, we were committed to agreeing that, if any system of trusteeship were set up, it should apply 'to any other

---

[1] i.e. in the Protocol of the Conference.

[2] i.e. Mr. Stettinius's original wording to this effect was taken out of the resolution. On the other hand the phrase 'no discussion of actual territories is contemplated at the forthcoming United Nations Conference, or in the preliminary consultations', implied that a discussion of principle was likely to take place.

(a) U1521/191/70. (b) WP(45)200 and 208; WM(45)38; U2432/191/70.

territory which might voluntarily be placed under trusteeship'. We were not therefore free to oppose such a plan on principle. There was a slight risk in our agreement to an extension since, if the United States voluntarily put her existing colonial dependencies under a system of trusteeship agreed at San Francisco, the other colonial Powers would thereby be placed in an invidious position. The Foreign Office, however, did not expect this to happen: in any case we and the other colonial Powers could refuse to follow the American lead.

The War Cabinet considered the question on April 3 in their review of British policy in regard to the Conference. They agreed that the intention of the Yalta form of words was limiting and that we were not committed to the acceptance of any particular view. We could argue at San Francisco that, since it would clearly be within the powers of the World Organisation to arrange for a mandatory trusteeship, there was no reason to make specific provision to this effect in the Charter. If such provision were made, we should have to make an immediate declaration that we did not intend to use it in respect of any territories under our control. We should also make it clear beyond doubt that the term 'voluntarily placed under trusteeship' meant that a request for trusteeship must come from the Power exercising sovereignty over the territory concerned. At a meeting of Commonwealth representatives, however, on April 4–5, 1945, in London the representatives of Australia and New Zealand argued strongly in favour of making specific provision in the Charter; they also urged the United Kingdom Government to take the lead in placing all British colonies under some measure of trusteeship.

In a memorandum submitted by Lord Cranborne, and considered (a)
by the War Cabinet on April 12, it was suggested that we should tell the Dominion representatives that we could not place under any form of trusteeship any of our colonial territories other than those at present administered under mandate, but Lord Cranborne thought that, having regard to the views expressed by the Dominion representatives, we should consider whether we should refrain from arguing at San Francisco against the inclusion of any specific enabling provision in the Charter.

The War Cabinet agreed with Lord Cranborne's first recommendation. On the question of our attitude at San Francisco the Prime Minister thought that the French and Dutch would certainly object to arrangements for placing their colonies under voluntary trusteeship and that, as a matter of tactics, we might let them take the lead and then support their arguments. We need not assume the initiative in opposing the inclusion of provision for territories to be placed

(a) WP(45)228; WM(45)43; U2842, 2959/191/70.

voluntarily under trusteeship provided we made it clear that we had no intention of applying the provision to any of our Colonial territories not at present administered under mandate. The War Cabinet agreed with this view.

The five-Power 'consultations' envisaged at Yalta did not take
(a) place. British representatives who went to Washington to discuss the matter in April before the meeting of the Conference were unable to make any progress owing to President Roosevelt's death. They were told that the President had not given a ruling on the difference of view between the State Department and the Service Departments, and that there was now no possibility of holding five-Power talks before the Conference. The United States Delegation therefore
(b) submitted proposals to the representatives of the Five Powers at San Francisco on April 30, 1945.

These proposals were based on the American requirements in the Pacific Islands. They put forward two categories of mandated territory. The first category consisted of territories designated as strategic areas; in these areas the functions of the Organisation, including the approval or amendment of the trusteeship arrangements, would be exercised by the Security Council. All other areas were placed in the second category; the functions of the Organisation with regard to them were to be exercised by the Assembly working through a Trusteeship Council. All the territories in which the United States Government were interested would fall into the first category. On the other hand the British Government would find it difficult in many important cases to establish their claim for inclusion of territory in this category without clearly indicating a potential enemy. The Chiefs of Staff and the Foreign Office argued that the British Delegation could not use this argument at San Francisco, but they could point out that it was extremely difficult to draw a line between territories of which the defences were or were not sufficient to justify their inclusion in the category of strategic areas and that the strategic importance of territories was liable to change; a proposal to transfer an area from the second to the first category, however, might well provoke international suspicion. Furthermore, whereas the territories which the Americans wished to acquire were small islands, the territories under British control included large and populous countries which could not easily be divided administratively into 'strategic' and 'non-strategic' areas. It was also thought that the large powers of interference allowed in the American proposals to the Assembly and the Trusteeship Council in the case of territories in the second category would put the British Government in a very difficult position especially with regard to Palestine.

(a) U2771/191/70. (b) U3304/191/70.

The British Delegation circulated a draft based on the policy agreed by the War Cabinet, and without the undesirable features of the American draft. The final arrangements made were not unsatisfactory from the British point of view. (a) The United States Delegation insisted on maintaining the category of 'strategic areas' which would be subject to the Security Council and not to the General Assembly and Trusteeship Council. On the other hand British defence interests were safeguarded by a clause allowing the State administering a 'trust territory' to ensure that the territory played its part in the maintenance of international peace and security. It would therefore be possible to take all necessary defence measures without designating all or part of a territory as a strategic area; such measures also were not included among those upon which the General Assembly, acting through the Trusteeship Council, would be entitled to ask for reports.

The British Delegation also secured a satisfactory compromise on two other points:

(i) The Russians and Chinese wished to insert a statement that the ultimate objective for Trust territories and colonies generally was independence. With the support of the American and French Delegations the British Delegation secured a more limited statement that the objective was 'to develop self-government in forms appropriate to the varying circumstances of each territory'.

(ii) The Russian delegation wished to include among the powers and functions of the Trusteeship Council a clause authorising the latter to control the fulfilment of its instructions and recommendations by sending their representatives and inspectors to the Trust territories. The British Delegation secured the rejection of this clause which would have allowed unlimited and irresponsible interference in administration. They tried to secure that visits by the Trusteeship Council should be at the invitation of the administering State. The actual wording adopted in the Chapter was 'periodic visits . . . at times agreed upon with the administering State'. The Chapter included the limitations agreed at Yalta that the system of trusteeship should apply only to territories at present held under mandate, or detached from enemy States as a result of the war, or voluntarily placed under the system by States responsible for their administration. The position of the British Government was also safeguarded by the over-riding provisions elsewhere in the Charter relating to domestic jurisdiction.

(a) U4829/12/70.

CHAPTER LXVI

The formulation of British policy with regard to Germany from the Yalta Conference to the Potsdam Conference: British proposals on procedure for the conclusions of treaties with the European enemy states

(i)

Foreign Office memorandum of March 19 on the dismemberment of Germany: Sir J. Anderson's memorandum of March 7 on reparation and dismemberment: discussion in the War Cabinet on March 22, 1945.

THE three Powers had settled before the opening of the discussions at Yalta on February 6, 1945, the delimitation of their respective zones of occupation in Germany.[1] The European Advisory Commission had drawn up an Instrument for the Unconditional Surrender of Germany, and a Protocol dealing with the administrative machinery of occupation. The Conference accepted these documents and mainly on the insistence of the British representatives, allowed France a zone of occupation and admitted her to the Allied Control Council. A number of important administrative questions, however, remained unsettled, and the Conference had postponed for further study the most important problems of German reparation and of possible dismemberment of the country. Special committees had been appointed to discuss these two questions.

(a) The Committee dealing with the question of the dismemberment of Germany held its first meeting on March 7, 1945. At this meeting it

[1] President Roosevelt had accepted in principle, at the Quebec Conference in 1944, the British argument in favour of allocating north-west Germany as the British zone, and south-west Germany as the American zone of occupation on condition that the Americans were guaranteed the use of the ports of Bremen and Bremerhaven. The American military authorities for a long time disputed over the communication arrangements through Bremen, and the ratification of the agreement was thus delayed. The Americans finally gave way since, in the military situation as it was towards the end of the year, there was some probability that the Russians might advance far into Germany before the Anglo-American forces had crossed the Rhine, and—if no previous agreement had been reached—might then make difficulties about withdrawing from any of the areas into which their armies had moved. The Anglo-American Agreement was approved by the E.A.C. and recommended to the Governments concerned on November 18, 1944. The British Government approved the Agreement on December 5, 1944, the U.S. Government on February 2, 1945, and the Soviet Government on February 6, 1945.

(a) APW(45)40; C1113/292/18.

became clear that the Governments of the three Powers were already engaged in studying the problem; the Committee therefore agreed that as soon as any member had material ready he would communicate it to his colleagues. Meanwhile the Committee could not get far owing to differences of opinion about its terms of reference. The British Government, after much hesitation in the matter, had to decide their policy.

Mr. Eden submitted to the Armistice and Post-War Committee on March 19, 1945, a memorandum stating from a British angle the main issues involved in the question of dismemberment. He suggested that, if the A.P.W. Committee approved generally of the statement, they should send it to the Chiefs of Staff and the E.I.P.S. for urgent comment with particular regard to the commitments which dismemberment would involve in respect of troops and administrative staff, to the capacity of each of the new States of a dismembered Germany to pay reparation, and the scale of 'economic security measures which could be borne by the new States'.

The memorandum began by noting the decisions already reached, or proposals made, about the future of Germany, including the territorial claims against Germany, the agreement reached at Yalta on reparation, and the announcement at Yalta that the three Powers intended to eliminate or control all German industry which could be used for war purposes. These decisions must affect plans for dismemberment, since, if Germany lost a large part of old Prussia, and the whole of the Rhine-Ruhr industrial area, any further partitioning might be found unnecessary.

Dismemberment implied that the States into which Germany was divided would be completely independent of one another and have no common political or economic institutions. If dismemberment were a reality, it could not be achieved by any single measure, since its effects would enter into the political, economic, and social life of the German people. The Allies would therefore have to maintain control for a considerable time over the new States and to impose permanent restrictions upon their dealings with one another. Hence the Allied manpower commitments would be increased both as regards numbers and as regards the time for which they would be required. Any plan for dismemberment would thus have to give the new States, or at least some of them, a reasonable chance of reaching political and economic equilibrium; if they remained in a state of political unrest and economic distress, our commitments would be heavy especially if, as stated by the President, American troops were withdrawn after two years, and Europe would not enjoy the full benefits of peace.

A plan for dismemberment must take into account, wherever possible, German historic traditions and associations, but several of the old States had shown themselves unsatisfactory units of self-government, and too much attention need not be paid to old boundaries. It was more important to secure a suitable distribution of economic resources and to avoid separating industries from the areas supplying their needs. We should also have to keep in mind that a dismembered Germany would probably not be able to make the same reparation deliveries as a united Germany. The work of the Dismemberment Committee in London must therefore be co-ordinated with that of the Moscow Commission on Compensation for Damage. The surest way to ensure the permanence of the new States would be to make them look outward towards their non-German neighbours rather than inwards towards one another; at the same time we must avoid the risk that they might draw their neighbours too closely into their own orbit. Thus close ties between a South German State and Austria might lead to the absorption of the latter. In any case the Germans for some time to come would certainly do their utmost to keep alive and to extend a movement towards reunion. We should therefore have to impose restrictions on the dealings of the States with one another. (i) We should have to prevent them from setting up machinery—on the lines of the old Germanic Confederation—for concerting a common foreign policy, though even without this machinery a common foreign policy would be possible. (ii) We should also have to prevent any German State from interfering in the internal politics of another German State. (iii) We should have to forbid the formation of a *Zollverein*. It would not, however, be easy to stop evasion of a veto on preferential trade arrangements or financial relations. (iv) We should have to consider how we could deal with the various official and semi-official organisations which Germans had used in the past for political ends, though here again the Germans might find ways of evading our veto. We could ensure that no German could be simultaneously a citizen of two or more German States, but we could not prevent each State from granting many of the advantages enjoyed by its citizens to visitors or settlers from other German States, e.g. the right to practise a trade or profession, or to enjoy the benefits of social or educational services. We could not easily forbid educational interchange or rule that legal or medical qualifications acquired in one State must not be recognised as entitling the holder to practise in another German State.

The trade unions and the Churches were also a problem. We should have to forbid trade unions on a national German basis, but if the unions formed in the various German States were members of a World Federation of Trade Unions, their representatives would probably act together as a German delegation. Similarly with the Churches, some of which had acted as agents for the encouragement of German nationalist feeling outside the frontiers of Germany. It would be awkward to have dioceses straddling the frontier between two German States, yet a move to reshape the dioceses would meet with opposition, especially from the Catholics.

One of the great difficulties in effecting dismemberment would be that the Control Commission would have to carry out at first a number of measures requiring central planning and direction and, as had been foreseen, the existence of some central German administration. The Commission would have to deal with disarmament, reparation in kind, the suppression of Nazi organisations and underground movements, the control of transport and the repatriation of displaced persons. The settlement of the uprooted population in Germany would also be a serious problem. Migration had taken place on a very large scale. This migration had begun with the transfer of labour to new centres of war industry, and had continued owing to the bombing of cities and the further dispersal of factories, and latterly, with the movement of thousands of refugees from the advancing armies in east and west. If drastic restrictions were put on German industry, in addition to the Allied demands for reparation, the economic structure of Germany would be changed and a redistribution of labour would be needed. The housing problem would be most serious, and emergency measures would have to be taken to feed the population and prevent the spread of epidemics.

Obviously these enormous problems could be dealt with only by a central administration; until they were settled, the new States would lack the essential foundations of a political and economic system, i.e. a definite body of citizens resident within their frontiers. If the transfer of populations from the ceded territories were made at once, dismemberment would take longer to complete. A central authority would also be necessary for 'unscrambling' finance and property, e.g. the issue of new currencies, the division of Reich and State debts, and the redistribution of insurance, banking and property to ensure that no citizen of one State owned large amounts of property in another State.

Nevertheless certain steps towards the establishment of new States could be taken at once; regional administrative centres could be built up for matters of local government, public health, education, etc. The zones of occupation need not coincide at first with the boundaries of the new States, but in the final stages of setting up German Governments in these States it would be necessary for each State to fall within only one of the zones of occupation. The Central Control Commission would have to remain for some time after the central German administration had ceased to exist and there were only the German authorities in the various States; otherwise the Germans would try at once to evade the restrictions placed on them. There was, however, no reason why the Control Commission—which would then merely be co-ordinating the policy of the occupying Powers—should be situated in Germany.

The memorandum dealt finally with possible plans of dismemberment. It did not recommend the creation of a considerable number —twelve to twenty—of small German States since such States, having in most cases only German neighbours, would lean on one another and try to form a confederation which would soon become a first step towards reunion. The simplest plan of partition would be along two lines, north–south and east–west. The north–south line would run through Prussia which we could not safely leave intact. The western boundary of the Russian zone would be a good dividing line. This line was more satisfactory from a political than from an economic point of view, since it would separate the provinces of Hanover and Saxony, but these two provinces could not be united in a single State unless the Russians withdrew from a large part—and the richest and most populous part—of their zone of occupation. An area in the province of Saxony north of Magdeburg and west of the Elbe might be attached more satisfactorily to Hanover than to central or eastern Germany.

The east–west line would cut off Bavaria, Württemberg and Baden from the north, and create a non-Prussian south German State with a fair amount of homogeneity. On general grounds of political affinity, the Saar and the Palatinate, and the southern half of Hessen should go with it, but if a 'Rhenania' under international supervision were set up, it would be desirable to include in it all the area west of the Rhine in order to bring the Saar mines and the Rhine frontier under control.

These three States would be large; the eastern State and western States would each contain about 27 million people, and the southern State about 14 million. Each would have a common frontier with the other two. A further subdivision might therefore be necessary. The southern area could easily be divided into the three States of Bavaria, Württemberg and Baden, but little would be gained by enforcing complete severance between the three; the three former State Governments might be revived and a federal constitution imposed upon them.

The main argument for subdividing the western region would be to use the links binding the Rhineland with western Europe in such a way as to detach it from its German hinterland. This process would be much more difficult if the Rhineland were joined to Hanover. If the French proposals for a western region under international supervision were accepted, a sub-division would be essential since this region could not include all north-western Germany.

The purpose of sub-dividing the eastern region would be to separate old Prussia—the seat of German militarism—from the rich industrial area of the province and State of Saxony. Furthermore, if a Rhineland State were brought closely under the influence of the Western Powers, the Soviet Government might claim that the eastern German State should be under their influence. In such case it might be an advantage to limit the size of the eastern State and to have a central area as a kind of buffer composed of two States, one of which—the eastern sub-division of the western State—would be based on Hanover, and the other—the western sub-division of the eastern State—based on the province and State of Saxony. We could not, however, propose a definite plan for eastern Germany until a decision had been taken on the amount of Prussian territory to be ceded to Poland. If the Polish frontier were advanced to the Oder-Neisse line, an eastern State composed of Mecklenburg and the remains of Pomerania, Brandenburg and Silesia would have a poor chance of achieving political or economic stability.

The memorandum, for obvious reasons, did not pronounce a judgment on the merits of the policy of dismemberment as such, though in its listing of the difficulties it showed fairly clearly that the Foreign Office, at the least, felt no enthusiasm for the plan. In putting forward for the consideration of the United States and (a) Russian representatives draft terms of reference for the tripartite Committee on Dismemberment, Mr. Eden was careful to avoid a definite commitment.

The directive to the Committee was agreed at the beginning of April in the following terms:

'In studying the procedure for the dismemberment of Germany, the Committee on Dismemberment set up by the Crimea Conference will approach its work in the light of the following considerations:

(*a*) The primary objective of the Allies in their dealings with Germany after the surrender or the cessation of German resistance is to prevent future German aggression.

(*b*) In considering how best to achieve this objective, the question arises whether, as a complement to disarmament and demilitarisation, it can be achieved by such measures as the elimination or control of all German industry that could be used for military production, or whether, in addition, it will be necessary to divide Germany.

(*c*) If it should be found necessary, for the achievement of this objective, to divide Germany, it is necessary to enquire: (i) in what manner Germany should be divided, into what parts, with what boundaries, and with what inter-relationship among the parts; (ii) at what point of time the division should be effected; (iii) what measures would be required on the part of the Allies in order to effect and maintain such division.'

On the day of the first meeting of the Dismemberment Commission, (b) March 7, 1945, Sir John Anderson, the Chancellor of the Exchequer,

(a) APW(45)56; C1854/45/18. (b) WP(45)146; UE1159/624/77.

submitted to the War Cabinet a memorandum dealing with reparation and the dismemberment of Germany. He pointed out certain conditions which were essential to our interests.

(i) We ought not to incur expense arising out of the supply of permitted imports into Germany while at the same time Germany was making reparation deliveries either of a 'once for all' or of a current and continuing character. Otherwise we would be paying for German reparation. We must therefore insist that any relief and other supplies necessary to put Germany into a condition to pay reparation should be a first charge on deliveries taken from her, and must be paid for by those receiving the deliveries as long as the supplies required exceeded the value of German overseas earnings apart from reparation.

(ii) The permitted imports into Germany should be sufficient, but not more than sufficient, to give effect to the Prime Minister's statement that the Allies did not intend to leave the German people without means of subsistence.

(iii) No 'once for all' deliveries should be taken from any zone of occupation unless the Allied Control Commission had decided, in agreement with the occupying Power, that they could be taken without risk of creating conditions contrary to the administrative interests of the occupying Power.

(iv) An occupying Power should not be responsible for securing reparation deliveries beyond the limit judged by this Power to be within the capacity of its zone of occupation.

(v) Except with the consent of all the interested Powers no equipment or stocks should be taken from parts of Germany to be detached from German sovereignty, whether for inclusion in Poland or to form a zone (in the west) under international control.

Germany would be unlikely, after meeting her necessary imports, to be able to provide current reparation deliveries on a substantial scale during the first five years after the war. In the following five years much larger deliveries should be possible but there was at present no basis for an estimate of the amount. During the first five years the net reparation would consist mainly or entirely of 'once for all' deliveries (though their equivalent value might be needed in large part to cover necessary imports) and the services of German labourers. These labour services should be included in the reparation account.

Dismemberment would greatly impair German capacity to make reparation and should therefore be considered mainly as an alternative to reparation; a sound scheme of reparation on an important scale required a unitary German Government which would be responsible for delivery. The dismemberment of Germany under the occupation of four several Powers who could not themselves take the responsibility of procuring reparation deliveries from their zones was incompatible with the practical working of a sound scheme.

After stating these general considerations the Chancellor turned to a detailed analysis of the economic issues arising out of the surrender of Germany. He dealt with these issues under three main headings:

(*a*) The responsibilities of the British zone of occupation.
(*b*) Reparation.
(*c*) Dismemberment.

(*a*) The British zone was not self-supporting, but would normally draw additional food supplies from Brandenburg, Pomerania, East Prussia and overseas. For some time we should obtain little from the eastern zone or the American south-western zone. The British zone also depended on an industrial economy and would probably have a large number of refugees from eastern Germany. The zone—and western Germany as a whole—would need relief imports. We could not have a British army of occupation surrounded by semi-starved and partially homeless women and children. On the other hand, we could not support the zone from our own resources or buy requirements for it from abroad. Our policy must therefore be to make our relief imports—as had already been stated—a first charge on German deliveries.

(*b*) Our short experience in a part of Italy had shown the enormous cost in which we should be involved if we had to maintain at our expense even a minimum standard of living in the British zone of Germany. If the zone had been unduly stripped of its capital resources for reparation, large sums would also be needed for working capital. Hence the importance of the third and fourth conditions stated above that no Power should be required to secure reparation deliveries beyond its estimate of the capacity of its zone. If Russia could claim that any deficiency of deliveries in the Russian zone should be made up to the agreed Russian share of reparation by deliveries from the other zones, our liabilities might be seriously increased. Similarly, if we were to allow a situation to develop in which each occupying Power had sole responsibility for its own zone, the situation might be equally serious. For this reason we must ensure the maintenance of the collective responsibility of the occupying Powers.

The Chancellor suggested that we ought to consider whether it would not be wise for us to refrain from giving an undertaking to occupy Germany for a longer period than that for which the four occupying Powers would each and all be prepared to make themselves responsible. We had also to keep in mind the effect of reparation payments on Europe as a whole. The Russian proposals envisaged a large 'once for all' delivery of all kinds of materials, machinery, transport, and other forms of 'German national wealth' within two years and further deliveries annually over ten years. This policy would provide some immediate compensation for the destruction carried out by the Germans in Russia, and would reduce German industrial strength so that for a number of years the Germans would be able to do little more than rebuild their immediate physical necessities. The policy would give some economic security against Germany. The German standard of living would be reduced. The Russians regarded this reduction as just, but we had to remember that standards of living elsewhere in Europe would be affected.

The Chancellor agreed that security was the first consideration in our policy towards the industrial and economic structure of Germany; the Germans must adapt themselves to our requirements, and we and other countries affected must adjust our own economies accordingly, but we had to keep in mind that Germany was a source of supply and a market to much of Europe as well as to ourselves. The European standard of living might be lowered by these changes in the centre of its economy; if, however, we obtained security, the standard would rise again before long. On the other hand, the more we stripped Germany of her industrial equipment and the more changes we enforced upon her economy, the slower would be the return to higher general standards in Europe, and the greater the risk of social disturbances in Germany. These disturbances would endanger the stability of western European political institutions, especially since Europe, at the best, would be in a very weak economic condition. Moreover, as the occupying Power in the most industrialised areas we should have to deal with the social disturbances, and our action would be open to misrepresentation in our own country and elsewhere.

(*c*) The Chancellor feared even graver consequences from the dismemberment of Germany urged by the Russians if this plan meant not only the transfer of part of eastern Germany to Poland and the creation of some special 'international system' in the industrial area of western Germany (a scheme which could not lightly be assumed as practicable), but also the break-up of the unitary German State into three or four separate and self-supporting States. The Chancellor thought that such an attempt to break up Germany would meet with serious political difficulties because (i) public opinion in Great Britain and the Commonwealth and in the United States did not yet understand its implications, (ii) the Germans would resist it, and the more dangerous German elements use it as a rallying cry for their own purposes. The Chancellor asked whether consideration had been given to the means whereby political stability could be established in the separate States or their separation maintained and enforced. From the economic point of view we should have to meet opposition for some time, and find ourselves involved thereby in heavy commitments. Had we examined economic questions such as a prohibition of a common currency or a Customs Union between the separate States, or the development of a free trade union movement, or the position of unitary services such as transport and communications?

Apart from these questions requiring detailed study, the Chancellor considered that we could not have both reparation and dismemberment. He repeated that a practicable reparations policy must be one which left to the Germans some prospects of a minimum subsistence and, to the extent to which reparation deliveries were to be continued for a period of time, some prospects of an export trade which could pay for the necessary imports. A policy of substantial reparations was thus possible only by bringing the whole of the German economy within the reparation field.

The Chancellor pointed out that the whole matter was affected by the American decision to withdraw their occupying troops from their zone within two years. Two years was the period within which the military authorities expected to achieve the disarmament of Germany, but we could not hope within this time to have taken more than the first steps towards clearing up the economic and political confusion in the country, and possibly to have made some progress towards the 'once for all' reparation deliveries. If the United States zone were to be developed into a new south-west German State, American interest during and after their occupation was likely to be limited to that area. They might put financial help at its disposal as some justification for the removal of their troops, but it was essential to us that American help should be extended consistently to the economic problem of Germany as a whole, or at least to western Germany. Thus, unless we maintained the principle of a unitary German State, both for reparation and necessary relief imports, we should have to meet a financial and economic liability which we could discharge only by making our own people pay not merely for the defeat of Germany but for its revival. Many of these heavy charges would fall on us in the early period. We should have to maintain an army of occupation, wage war against Japan, strengthen our garrisons, finance relief and help to restore our damaged colonies and dependencies in the East. Even if some of this money came back to us later, the costs would have to be financed meanwhile, at a time when our reserves were dangerously inadequate, and we were borrowing largely from poor countries to whose development repayment of our debt would be essential. The Chancellor believed that at present we could carry this debt and by our own energies repay it over a number of years. We might perhaps hope for some American help, but we could not risk becoming financially dependent upon the United States.

If we had to assume that the Russian zone of occupation would gradually include the area of Berlin and develop into a governmental or administrative system amenable to Russian policy, we should at least consider whether there should not be a unified western Germany which could be fitted into the general economy of the western European countries.

Finally the Chancellor wrote that, in the grave issues which we had to face, we must be sure above all that our policy rested solidly upon the considered judgment of our own people and of the Commonwealth, and that it was a policy within our means, physically and financially. If certain trends in the Yalta discussions became firm conclusions without substantial modification, the result might well prove beyond the financial strength of the United Kingdom and the Commonwealth—which looked to us for help—and might impair our capacity for proper leadership in Europe.

(a) The War Cabinet considered the Chancellor's memorandum on March 22, 1945. In introducing his memorandum Sir J. Anderson said that he was disturbed over the implications of Russian policy which apparently aimed at combining the maximum reparation with the maximum dismemberment. He regarded these aims as incompatible and, in their application to the most productive area of Germany under Allied control, likely to make Germany incapable of an independent existence. Great Britain, in particular, would thereby be left in charge of a deficit area in the north-west requiring imports which we could not afford.

Mr. Eden agreed that the policies of reparation and dismemberment could not be considered in isolation, but these policies did not seem to him to be mutually exclusive. Some of the problems raised by the Chancellor would arise irrespective of dismemberment. Mr. Eden suggested that the War Cabinet ought to consider the Chancellor's memorandum in conjunction with his own memorandum of March 19.[1] The Prime Minister thought that the two problems of reparation and dismemberment were not linked to the extent that they could not profitably be examined by separate bodies. He saw no reason to change the arrangements agreed at Yalta whereby a Commission in Moscow considered reparation and a Committee in London considered dismemberment.

The Prime Minister said that we had been faced with three main problems of which the first was that of the military zones. We had

---

[1] See above, pp. 321–5.

(a) WM(45)35. 3, C.A.; UE1299/624/77.

settled this problem in principle, though we ought to press the Russians to agree to a measure of uniformity of treatment in each of the three zones. The second problem was that of dismemberment. The Russians attached the greatest importance to it, and the term now appeared in the Instrument of Surrender. It raised matters of great difficulty with a vast historical background, and required the most careful and prolonged study by experts. We might find that no conclusions would be reached on it for a year or more after the collapse of Germany. The Prime Minister himself had always favoured the isolation of Prussia and the establishment of a south German State, including Austria and the south German Kingdoms,[1] which could be treated more leniently than Prussia. With regard to the third problem—reparation—we must recognise that the Russians were determined to get everything possible out of Germany. They had not shared our own disillusionary experience of reparation, and their economy could probably absorb more reparation than we could absorb. In any case, they would certainly want to remove machinery and plant from all parts of Germany, including Silesia and the Ruhr, in order to re-establish their own industry to which the Germans had done so much damage. The Prime Minister thought that, in view of the sufferings and losses of the Russians, there was justice in their claim and that it would be very hard for us to resist it. In general the Prime Minister thought that there was a serious risk of confusing the issues if we tried to link the problems of reparation too closely with those of dismemberment. He repeated his view that we ought not to disturb the arrangements already made for their examination respectively in Moscow and in London.

In the course of discussion the War Cabinet agreed that we should have to accept the Russian claim to remove machinery and plant from Germany for industrial re-equipment, but we should try to secure two points: (i) there should be some special protection to territories to be assigned to one or other of the Allies under the peace settlement, i.e. Russia should not be free to move a substantial portion of the industrial equipment from Silesia before it was handed over to Poland, and (ii) arrangements should be made to protect the interests of the other occupying Powers during the period of military occupation. If the Russians moved machinery from the British zone they should be required to supply food to the zone from surplus areas in Eastern Germany.

The War Cabinet felt anxious over the Russian plan to exact reparation not only in 'once for all' deliveries but also in annual instalments over a period of years. Such annual deliveries of manufactured or consumer goods would help to maintain the existing

---

[1] In spite of this term, the Prime Minister evidently meant to include the Grand Duchy of Baden.

German industrial structure and thus assist the Germans to reconstruct their war potential. They might lead to demands for supplying Germany with machine tools and money to enable her to discharge her industrial obligations. We might thus have a repetition of the disastrous loans to Germany after the first World War. From our point of view, there would be great advantages in restricting deliveries from Germany to capital goods and raw materials such as timber, potash, etc. Furthermore, although one main object of our reparation policy should be to secure for ourselves the export markets for manufactured goods which Germany held before the war, we did not want to destroy the German economy without hope of recovery, and could not therefore allow the heavily industrialised areas to be stripped of machinery.

The War Cabinet agreed that, while we had to accept the procedure laid down at the Yalta Conference, the instructions to our representatives on the Moscow Commission and the London Committee might well be considered together, and that the A.P.W. Committee might be invited to examine the question of reparation on the hypothesis (*a*) of a unified Germany (*b*) of dismemberment. The Prime Minister said that he would consider the whole question in the light of the discussion and arrange to bring it again before the War Cabinet.

On March 26, 1945, a sudden change in the Russian attitude towards dismemberment[1] put the relations between this question and the problem of reparation in a different light. Mr. Eden wrote
(a) a minute to the Prime Minister on March 31 that the complications of the dismemberment question were such that no acceptable scheme was likely to be suggested in time to be of help in the discussion of reparation. The Russians were asking us to make an early start with the latter discussion. Mr. Eden therefore thought that we should consider at once the instructions to our delegates in Moscow and that these discussions should be confined to the determination of Germany's capacity to make reparation and the form in which it should be made. In present circumstances the calculations would have to be made on the basis of a unitary German State; they would be subject to modification in the light of any subsequent decisions about dismemberment (including the Rhenania proposals).

(b) The Prime Minister agreed with this plan. He also noted that, in his view the separation of Prussia from southern Germany, and the favourable treatment of southern Germany compared with Prussia, would not necessarily affect the total obtainable amount of reparation.

Another report dealt with the question of reparation, and the

---

[1] See below, p. 335.

(a) PM/45/143, UE1159/624/9. (b) M288/5. UE1542/624/77.

economic treatment of Germany from a different angle. At their consideration on August 31, 1944, of the E.I.P.S. report on the economic obligations to be imposed upon Germany the A.P.W. Committee had decided that British policy towards Germany in the field of economic security should be to apply severe measures within a selected field and to leave the rest of German industry more or less undisturbed.[1] The E.I.P.S. were therefore asked to prepare another report putting forward specific proposals regarding the industries to be restricted and the types of restriction to be applied. They were also asked to consider what measures could be taken to prevent the development of weapons of the V1 and V2 types.

This second report was circulated to the A.P.W. Committee on (a) April 19, 1945. In a covering note Mr. Law pointed out that the matter was of particular importance in view of the appointment at the Yalta Conference of a special Commission to consider questions of reparation. Reparation and economic security could not be dealt with in isolation because the types and quantities of goods which could be made available for reparation either as 'once for all' or as continuing deliveries depended on the measure of restrictions enforced from the point of view of economic security. Furthermore the protocol of the Yalta Conference dealing with reparation provided that the removals to be made from the national wealth of Germany within two years from her surrender were to be carried out chiefly for the purpose of destroying German war potential. The British delegation to the Reparation Commission would therefore have to be aware of the 'economic security' policy which we should wish to apply to a unitary Germany. In this regard Mr. Law also pointed out that the report would need reconsideration if a policy of dismemberment were finally accepted. This was no reason for delaying the report. On the contrary the terms of reference of the Dismemberment Committee in London suggested that dismemberment would be considered from the point of view of its necessity as an addition to other measures; hence there was greater reason for deciding as soon as possible what measures, including measures of economic security, should be imposed upon a unitary Germany.

The report assumed, therefore, a unitary Germany, with the subtraction of East Prussia and certain parts of Pomerania and Upper Silesia, a period of occupation lasting not less than ten years,[2] the permanent prohibition on the maintenance by Germany of armed forces and on the possession or manufacture of arms and

---

[1] See above, pp. 217–18.

[2] This period had been suggested in the first E.I.P.S. report and was agreed by the A.P.W. Committee on August 31, 1944.

(a) APW(45)57; UE1734/86/77.

munitions and of plant required for their manufacture. The E.I.P.S. concluded that no measures of industrial restriction or control could be devised to prevent Germany from developing weapons of the V1 and V2 types. In the view of the Scientific Adviser to the Army Council the only practicable form of restriction would be to prohibit the Germans from arranging, carrying out, or attending any trials or experiments involving the projection or propulsion of missiles by any means over ranges greater than one kilometre, and from possessing or manufacturing rocket or jet propulsion units. We should have to maintain efficient intelligence services to give us early warning of any German attempt to evade these prohibitions.[1]

The E.I.P.S. had borne in mind that, beyond a certain point, the benefit to economic security of additional restrictions, considered in relation to their effect on the German economy, was subject to diminishing returns. The effect upon the German economy of all the restrictions which they were proposing would not—taken by themselves—be very great, but they could not be assessed in isolation from other adverse factors likely to be present, and the total effect might not only make reparation from current German production impossible but also necessitate the provision of outside help to Germany during the first five to ten years after the war. The report then gave a list of those industries upon which a decision in principle should be taken at once, and a second list upon which a decision should be deferred until after further investigation. In the first category, the report proposed an indefinite prohibition upon the manufacture of civil aircraft, and upon the production of synthetic oil and certain chemicals. It also proposed a prohibition for the period of occupation (i.e. not less than ten years) on merchant ship-building, on the acquisition of a merchant shipping fleet, and on the manufacture of ball and roller-bearings and steel and machine tools beyond the needs of 'peaceful domestic requirements'. The second category included other chemicals (including synthetic rubber), locomotives, motor vehicles, agricultural tractors, aluminium and magnesium.

The E.I.P.S. pointed out that these measures of restriction would limit the number of industries available to absorb the unemployment created partly by the restrictions themselves but principally by transfer of population and the general post-war dislocation. In order to prevent a drift back into war industries after the period of occupation, we must not merely avoid discouraging, but even facilitate the development of 'peaceful' industries. We should thereby

---

[1] The E.I.P.S. stated that they had also been advised that no industrial restrictions would suffice to limit German ability to develop bacteriological warfare, but that the danger of such development would be greatly lessened if Germany could be prevented from developing and using aircraft and long-range weapons.

increase competition with our own exports, but on balance we stood to gain from the proposed restrictions. In any case, the risk would be the price which we should have to pay for economic security.[1]

The Armistice and Post-War Committee on May 10 accepted in general the recommendations of the E.I.P.S. report. The Committee agreed that they should be taken as the basis of instructions to Field-Marshal Montgomery, Commander-in-Chief, British Forces of Occupation in Germany, regarding the initial measures to be taken in the British zone of occupation for the destruction of Germany's war potential, and that they should also be communicated to the British representative on the Reparation Commission in Moscow. (a)

In fact the question of dismemberment faded out of practical consideration before the Potsdam Conference. The Soviet Government in giving its views over the terms of reference of the Committee, informed the Foreign Office on March 26, 1945, that they understood the decision of the Yalta Conference 'regarding the dismemberment of Germany not as an obligatory plan . . . but as a possibility for exerting pressure on Germany with the object of rendering her harmless in the event of other means proving inadequate'. The British and United States Governments were only too glad to accept this Russian change of view. At their second formal meeting on April 11, the tripartite committee merely decided that, as soon as any of the three representatives had proposals or suggestions to make, he should communicate them to his colleagues. (b) (c)

No such proposals were brought forward, and the committee did not hold a third meeting.[2] The term 'dismemberment' was not introduced into the Allied Declaration regarding the unconditional surrender of Germany, though the possibility was covered by the words that the four Governments 'will hereafter determine the boundaries of Germany or any part thereof, and the status of Germany or of any area at present being part of German territory'. The Russian view was made clear by Stalin in a proclamation of May 9 to the Soviet people that the Soviet Union was celebrating (d)

---

[1] These views were not in accord with those of Lord Cherwell, who had concluded in a paper of April 7: 'It is far more important to this country to re-establish British exports than to obtain German manufactured goods as reparations. For this reason alone, we should discourage the restoration of German industry. But quite apart from this, such a policy would give far more military security than any other scheme likely to be devised. The instructions to our representatives on the Reparations Commission should therefore be to try to confine reparations to existing equipment, raw materials and, if the Russians insist, indentured labour.' (e)

[2] The French proposals for a 'Rhenania' also faded out. The Foreign Office received on April 12 a copy of a French memorandum on the question, but the memorandum had not been approved by the French Government, and the latter did not submit any detailed proposals. (f)

(a) APW(45) 11th meeting. (b) C1354/292/18. (c) C1490/292/18, (d) C2158/292/18. (e) WP(45)244 (f) C1644, 3268/22/18.

victory, although it did not intend either to dismember or to destroy Germany.

The Commission set up at the Yalta Conference to study the question of reparation did not meet until more than four months (a) after its establishment. On March 14, 1945, Mr. Eden instructed Lord Halifax and Sir A. Clark Kerr to reopen with the United States and Soviet Governments the question of French membership of the Reparation Commission.

The British arguments in favour of such membership were very strong. Mr. Eden pointed out that the French were being given a zone of occupation in Germany and would be represented on the Control Commission. They would thus be in a position to influence the execution of reparation policy and ought therefore to take part in its formulation. They also had a vital interest in Allied policy towards Germany and would have a sense of grievance if they were excluded from the consideration of reparation questions.

(b) The Soviet Government replied on April 2 agreeing with the proposal, but suggesting at the same time that Poland and Yugoslavia should be represented on the Commission. The United States Government agreed to the inclusion of France but not of Yugoslavia or Poland (at least until the establishment of a new Government in Poland). On April 9 the British Government answered that, in their (c) view, the Netherlands or Norway had stronger claims than Yugoslavia, and that the question of finding a generally acceptable Polish representative remained to be solved. In any case there were overwhelming advantages in getting the talks started by the four Powers who would be controlling the German economy and upon whom the execution of any reparation policy would primarily rest.

(d) The Soviet Government, however, maintained until May 21 their demand for the inclusion of Yugoslav and Polish representatives. (e) They then suggested that, in view of the failure to reach agreement on this point, and of the need for urgent action, the Commission should begin its work as a tripartite body according to the decisions (f) of the Yalta Conference. The Foreign Office wished to insist on French participation, but the United States Government were unwilling to do so. In these circumstances the British Government gave way on June 9, though they hoped to bring in the French as soon as possible.

The Commission thus met for the first time in the last week of June. Its main work before the assembling of the Potsdam Conference was to fix the percentages of reparation payment. The figures

(a) UE1083/624/77. (b) UE1353, 1429/624/77. (c) UE1458/624/77.
(d) UE1896, 2104/624/77. (e) UE2259, 2349, 2420/624/77.
(f) UE2104, 2139, 2421/624/77.

agreed after much discussion were 56 per cent for the U.S.S.R., 22 per cent for the United Kingdom and 22 per cent for the United States. In order to satisfy the claims of other nations, each of the three Powers would agree to 'give up from their share in the ratio that each share bore to the total'. In view of the heavier British losses, the British Delegation had tried—unsuccessfully—to get the United States Delegation to agree to a larger figure for the United Kingdom than for the United States. The American representative Mr. Pauley, refused to 'go home with the lowest figure of the three'. Mr. Harriman supported Mr. Pauley's view. The British Government decided, reluctantly, to accept it, in the general interest of Anglo-American relations, and especially since they had reason to assume that the Americans would in fact release the bulk of their claim for the benefit of other countries. On the other hand, in order to allow for the reduction of their share to meet the claims of other nations and at the same time to maintain their claim to a total of 50 per cent, the Russian percentage was raised first to 55 and then to 56.[1]

(ii)

Foreign Office briefs on the economic treatment of Germany for the British Delegation to the Potsdam Conference.

The British Delegation went to the Potsdam Conference with a number of briefs on questions affecting Germany. These briefs, taken together, show that the Foreign Office had a fairly comprehensive general policy on the economic treatment of Germany, although, in the absence of an agreement between the three Great Powers, it was impossible to put forward any definite long-term political plans. The question of dismemberment was now out of the way, but the (a)

[1] A good deal of consideration was given during the latter part of 1944 and early in 1945 to the possibility of recovering from the Nazis what was loosely described as 'ill-gotten gains'. On August 2, 1944, the Committee on Armistice Terms and Civil Administration asked the Treasury, the Foreign Office and the Trading with the Enemy Department to consider the question. A number of interdepartmental meetings were held, but no agreement could be reached. A general examination of the problem showed that the only practical method of dealing with the question of restitution would be on an arbitrary basis and outside ordinary processes of law. Some of the Nazis had enriched themselves by means which could not be technically described as illegal. We could not deal with all Germans who had made money through their support of the régime, any selection of persons would be a matter of great difficulty. The Foreign Office held strongly that we should be compromising our own efforts to re-establish the rule of law in Germany if we had resort to action outside the ordinary legal methods of procedure. On the other hand there was no reason why the property of war criminals and Nazi criminals generally should not be confiscated by order of the court pronouncing sentence upon them. Furthermore, if Nazis could be proved to be in possession of stolen goods, such goods could be taken from them by ordinary process of law. The Foreign Office view was accepted by the British Government. (b)

(a) F.O.934/6/5. (b) ACAO/P(45)65; ACAO/M(45)25 and 26; UE2645/152/77.

Foreign Office thought that, since Mr. Eden was chairman of the committee appointed to study the matter, and therefore accountable for its work, we might ask the Russians and Americans whether they intended to encourage separatist tendencies in their zones—a policy which we had always favoured—and whether they wished the committee to take any action.

The Foreign Office were more concerned with the immediate problems of the administration of Germany. Russian obstructiveness on the European Advisory Commission had hampered the settlement of a number of these problems, and of other matters concerned with the treatment of Germany. The Foreign Office pointed out that the promises of a change in the Russian attitude made to
(a) Mr. Eden by M. Molotov at the Moscow Conference in 1944 had not been fulfilled.[1] In spite of repeated undertakings, the Russians had not sent their representatives on the Control Council to London. We had therefore not been able to discuss or make any preliminary plans for the establishment and operation of control machinery. M. Gusev had refused to discuss any of the British and American directives dealing with the policy to be pursued in different fields in Germany and Austria. Hence there was no agreement on Allied policy in any of these matters. Even on questions which the Soviet Government had declared to be, in their view, of primary importance the Commission had made no progress. Committees had been set up to deal with two of these questions—the repatriation of prisoners of war and internees, and the detailed measures for the disarmament and demilitarisation of Germany. The Russians either failed to nominate a representative on these committees or refused to come to meetings. Hence in both cases it was necessary to take unilateral action when the emergency arose. The European Advisory Commission had never discussed the two other subjects suggested by the Russians—i.e. (i) the abolition of the Hitlerite régime and the surrender of war criminals, and (ii) the control of the German economy. These subjects were being dealt with through other channels.

The European Advisory Commission had recently concluded agreements on the control machinery in Germany and the control and occupation of Austria, but again the Russians had been dilatory and obstructive. We had tabled in August 1944 the General Order (or Additional Requirements) designed to supplement the Declaration on the Defeat of Germany which was signed in Berlin on June 5, 1945.[2] The Order was not discussed until May 1945. Several months

[1] Mr. Eden's complaints to M. Molotov had only a temporary effect. See above, p. 259.
[2] See above, p. 260.

(a) F.O.934/6/46.

passed before M. Gusev had been willing to discuss our papers on Austria. The French amendments to the 'basic' European Advisory Commission documents, which in the case of the Instrument of Surrender and the Control Agreement were purely formal, were tabled in January, but not agreed until May. The Agreement about the French Zone was still held up by M. Gusev owing to difficulties about the French sector in Berlin. Our proposals for a Restitution Commission were tabled in November 1944; they were not discussed until the summer of 1945 and were then rejected by the Russians. We had tabled papers on the Disposal of Enemy War Material in August 1944, and, later, on Foreign Representation in Berlin. Neither paper had been discussed.

The Foreign Office hoped that the Allied Control Council in Berlin would succeed in co-ordinating Allied policy and that it would meet as soon as possible to draw up a Four-Power agreement over a wide field. The British and American Commanders-in-Chief had already received a large number of directives from their Governments. The directives had been circulated in the European Advisory Commission; the Soviet and French Governments therefore knew about them, though they had not approved them or tabled any directives of their own. On certain important matters the Heads of the three Governments might therefore give direct guidance to the Control Council. The most urgent question was that of building up a central German administration in order to give effect to the Allied policy that the burden of administering Germany should fall on the Germans themselves, subject to an over-riding Allied control.

The question of treating Germany as a single economic unit was of equal, and perhaps of greater importance. In their brief on this (a)
subject for the British Delegation the Foreign Office suggested that, although the four Controlling Powers might not treat Germany for all purposes as a single political unit, they should agree upon a common economic policy for the country as a whole in regard to the free inter-zonal exchange of foodstuffs and other goods and services (e.g. public utilities and transport) essential to the economic existence of the German people. Such exchange should enable local deficiencies to be met from German national sources and not from imports. The standard of living implied by the term 'economic existence' would not exceed during the period of reparation payments the average of the standard of living in all European countries other than the United Kingdom and the U.S.S.R. The agreed policy of the four Powers should also prevent 'artificially stimulated disparities in wages, rationing, price levels, and standards of living', ensure a unified currency and banking system, uniform taxation, and a

(a) F.O.934/6/58.

central budget, and secure a 'uniform visitation upon the German people of the economic penalties' resulting from their war of aggression. On the other hand the treatment of Germany as an economic unit should not imply the preservation in an undesirable form of German economic strength. The uniform application of agreed measures of industrial disarmament would indeed have an opposite effect.

The brief pointed out that the alternative policy was to regard each zone of occupation as autonomous. This plan would be unnecessarily expensive in goods and manpower for each of the Occupying Powers; it would delay 'once for all' deliveries and economic disarmament, since some installations would have to be kept in existence merely in order to maintain the economic life of a particular zone. One zone might have to import grain for cattle-feeding merely because the surplus fodder in an adjoining zone was not available. Furthermore anarchy could be prevented in Germany only by the maintenance of certain economic controls of a national kind. Some German industries, e.g. textiles and chemicals, were closely integrated on a national basis. It was undesirable that the textile industry, which was necessary for German minimum requirements and also for assisting the rehabilitation of Europe, should break down owing to the establishment of artificial zonal barriers between its component parts. On the other hand we should probably wish to reduce the chemical industry, but measures to this end would fail if they were applied in one zone and not in another.

The British Government had a special interest in treating Germany as an economic whole because the area included in the Soviet zone of occupation normally had a surplus of foodstuffs whereas our zone and, to a somewhat lesser extent the American zone, had a deficiency. If we could not secure supplies from eastern Germany for the heavily populated and devastated Ruhr area, we should be compelled to use shipping to import food—and in the present shipping situation we could do so only at the expense of the liberated countries—or we should have to meet widespread disorder and the disorganisation of essential industries such as coal-mining.

The Foreign Office called attention to the administrative difficulties which would follow from a failure to reach agreement on a common policy in the matter. On July 7, 1945, Marshal Zhukov, Commander-in-Chief of the Soviet Zone, had made it clear that the Russians expected each of the Occupying Powers to be responsible for food and fuel in its own sector of Berlin. In the case of coal, the Russians had assumed that two-thirds of the estimated requirement for public utilities would come from the Ruhr, whereas in 1936–7 as much as 50 or 60 per cent of the hard coal used in Greater Berlin was drawn from German Upper and Lower Silesia. If we had accepted the Russian assumption, some 900,000 Germans in the British sector might have been without food, and largely without public utilities while the Berlin Conference was meeting.

There were two ways of securing the adoption of a common policy by the other Controlling Powers. We could convince them of the merits of this policy, or we could threaten to withhold the resources of our zone from the other zones. The French and Americans would probably accept our view of the merits of a common economic policy. The Russians were likely to agree only if the policy were based on a substantial reduction of the German standard of living and a consequent increase in the available loot.

The second course would lead us to consider the value of our bargaining assets. Our position would be fairly strong in relation to the French and American zones since we controlled the Ruhr coal. We also had a strong short-term bargaining position in relation to the Russians owing to the fact that they wanted to obtain from our zone very considerable 'once for all' reparation deliveries of capital goods.

Obviously we should try the first course, since we might otherwise be obliged to barter our short-term assets against long-term promises which the Russians might not observe. We knew how little value we could put on formulae agreed with the Soviet Government when the latter did not intend to cary them out. The Foreign Office therefore recommended that the British Delegation should try to secure the agreement of President Truman and Stalin to a statement of policy which could be sent to the four Commanders-in-Chief. These latter would draw up an administrative agreement on the lines suggested to them. If there were not time at the Conference to secure such a statement, the Control Council should be asked to prepare one as soon as possible.

The Foreign Office also drew up a brief on the industrial dis- (a)
armament of Germany. They defined 'industrial disarmament' (or 'economic security') as, the elimination, restriction, or control, in the interests of security, of the industrial and economic basis of Germany's war potential'. The measures thus envisaged did not imply the de-industrialisation of Germany; as a complement to industrial disarmament, other forms of German economic activity might require to be stimulated.

The policy suggested by the Foreign Office had not yet received final assent from the Cabinet; the principles upon which it was based were as follows:

(i) Germany must be disarmed for an indefinite period, and her war potential reduced. The proposals for economic disarmament

(a) F.O.934/6/57; UE3034/624/77.

were limited to civilian industries because there would be a permanent prohibition of the possession of arms and munitions and the plant required to manufacture them.

(ii) Industrial disarmament should be completed as far as possible during the period of occupation, though we ought to impose upon Germany economic obligations extending beyond the period of occupation. In order to ensure the observance of such continuing obligations, German industrial development after the period of occupation must be subject to Allied observation and inspection.

(iii) Plans for industrial disarmament must be made and applied on a national basis.

(iv) Since the value in terms of security of measures of industrial disarmament depended on their continuing effect after the end of the occupation, a period of ten years was the minimum requirement for this occupation or at least for the direct control of German industry. Every year of direct control would bring about a decline in the skilled labour forces of the industries chosen for 'disarmament' and would increase the growth of a vested interest in a pacific German economy. This natural development would be a surer safeguard than any obligations laid on Germany in a peace treaty.

(v) The problem for us was to strike a balance between the value of economic measures as a means of maintaining world peace and their cost in relation to other economic policies affecting Germany, e.g. reparation. The Foreign Office agreed with the proposal to concentrate upon the complete elimination of a relatively small number of industries which were of the greatest military importance and also difficult to conceal. Any action outside these limits would tend to defeat its purpose by creating conditions of unrest and resentment.

(vi) Within the limits stated under (v) industrial disarmament should come before other objectives such as reparation. In some respects, e.g. 'once for all' deliveries of capital equipment, there would be no conflict.

(vii) The will to achieve industrial disarmament would be strongest in the early period of occupation. We should therefore apply our measures as soon as possible on a four-Power basis, and in regard to such industries as civil aircraft, merchant shipbuilding, steel, machine tools, ball and roller bearings, synthetic oil and the production of ammonia and methanol by high-pressure hydrogenation.

(iii)

British list of questions for discussion at the Potsdam Conference: American proposals for discussion.

The Foreign Office regarded the Conference as an attempt to ascertain whether it was possible to regulate the affairs of Europe on a basis of co-operation between the three Great Powers. Hence, in addition to preparing briefs for the British Delegation, they wished to co-ordinate British policy, as far as was possible, with that of the Americans. With this purpose in mind, they drew up a list of questions for discussion at the Conference, and sent it on May 29, 1945 (a) (when they expected a date of meeting earlier than July 15), to the United States Government. The list did not include all the questions requiring settlement, but rather those which had created, or were likely to create, friction with the Soviet Government.

The State Department had not replied to this telegram at the end of June. Meanwhile the Foreign Office had been revising their list in the light of developments. On June 30 the revised list was sent to Lord Halifax. The list was as follows: (b)

1. *GENERAL*

(*a*) Question of procedure for a general European settlement.
(*b*) Application of Yalta Declaration on Liberated Europe.
(*c*) Permission for representatives of the press to function freely in countries of Eastern Europe.
(*d*) War crimes.

2. *POLAND*

3. *GERMANY*

(*a*) Polish Western Frontier. Status of Polish administration in former German territory.
(*b*) Transfer of German populations from Poland and Czechoslovakia.
(*c*) Exchange of views about setting up a central German administration in Berlin to co-ordinate transport etc.; future German Government.
(*d*) Attitude towards political parties and activities.
(*e*) Treatment of Germany as an economic whole.
(*f*) Co-ordination of propaganda and information services to Germany.

(a) U4204/3628/70. *F.R.U.S., 1945. The Conference of Berlin, I,* pp. 158–9.
(b) Tels. 6972–3 to Washington, F.O.934/6.

4. *ITALY*

Conclusions of a peace treaty.

5. *BALKANS*

(*a*) Internal situation in ex-satellite countries with particular reference to the form of governments which have been set up.
(*b*) The question of eventual peace treaties with these countries.
(*c*) The status of the British and American representatives on the Control Commissions pending the conclusion of peace treaties.
(*d*) The removal of industrial equipment, especially in Roumania, under the guise of booty.
(*e*) The situation in Yugoslavia and the implementation of the Tito-Subasić Agreement.
(*f*) The assurance of free elections in all the Balkan countries.

6. *TURKEY*

(*a*) Russo-Turkish relations.
(*b*) Modification of the Montreux Convention.

7. *IRAN*

Question of mutual withdrawal of troops.

Lord Halifax was informed that Poland had been retained in the list in case any matters arose or were left outstanding in the negotiations which were being carried on in Moscow. Under item (1)(*a*) it would be possible to discuss such questions as the holding of a Peace Conference, the future of the European Advisory Commission, and permanent machinery for dealing with problems of countries in Allied occupation. We did not propose to discuss at the meeting details of the actual European settlement—frontiers, etc. Item (*b*) might be covered largely by the discussions under Items 5 (*a*) and (*f*); in any case we thought that the Americans might take the initiative in raising it. Item 1(*d*) was new,[1] and might prove unnecessary in view of the discussions taking place in London. Items 3(*a*) and (*b*) ought certainly to be discussed, and, again, we suggested that the Americans might take the initiative under 3(*b*), since they had already raised the matter with us, and under 5(*a*), (*c*) and (*f*).

We did not propose ourselves to raise other German topics such as the disposal of German merchant ships, the future of German industry, reparations, or the disposal of Russian and German displaced persons in Germany. We thought of telling the Russians in general terms of our intention to conclude a treaty of peace with Italy and to express the hope that they would agree. We did not think it necessary to discuss with them at present the redefinition of

[1] i.e. not in the first list. For this question see below, Chapter LXIX, section (iii).

our policy and interests in Italy, though we would be glad to discuss it in London if a meeting could be arranged there with members of the United States Delegation after the conference. We considered it inevitable that, in view of the recent Russo-Turkish exchanges,[1] the question of the Straits would be discussed.

On July 2 the Foreign Office consulted the Prime Minister (in Mr. Eden's absence) on a number of points requiring decision with regard to our list of questions. (a)

(i) Should we give the list to the Russians, and try to get an agreed agenda? The Foreign Office considered that an agreed agenda would make for the efficient conduct of business, but that we were unlikely to get it.

(ii) Could we arrange a preliminary meeting with the Americans? The Prime Minister and the President, and Mr. Eden and Mr. Stettinius had met at Malta before the Crimea Conference, but Mr. Truman was unlikely to agree to a preliminary meeting of this kind, and circumstances might make it impracticable. On the other hand a meeting at some level would be extremely useful. The Foreign Office proposed suggesting that a member or members of the State Department should pass through London for an exchange of views before the conference.

(iii) No final decisions on Germany could be taken without French agreement, since they could block action on the Control Commission. The Foreign Office realised the difficulty of arranging for French representation at any stage of the conference, but considered that the disadvantages arising from the absence of such representation should be understood.

(iv) Tactics at the Conference. The Foreign Office were preparing a list of the few bargaining points on the Anglo-American side. The most important of these would be American credits. We ought not to give away any of these assets early in the Conference. Even if the Russian requests were reasonable, we should not grant them except in return for their agreement to reasonable requests on our part.

The Prime Minister commented only on the proposal for a meeting with the Americans. He said that no meetings could be arranged before reaching Berlin. We could then have appropriate contacts at several levels with the Americans, but 'let the Americans come to us, if they want preliminary arrangements, and not we to them'. (b)

On July 4, however, a Reuter report (subsequently confirmed by a (c)

[1] See Volume IV, Chapter LII, section (iv).

(a) PM/45/309, Premier 3/430/3.
(b) M675/5, Premier 3/430/3. (c) Washington tel. 4641, F.O.800/416/63/14.

telegram from Lord Halifax) announced that Mr. Joseph E. Davies, former American Ambassador to Moscow, was coming at once to London on a new mission. The Foreign Office did not regard him as the most suitable person with whom to discuss the agenda of the Conference, but considered that we might suggest that he should be accompanied by a representative of the State Department. Mr. Eden supported this suggestion, and the Prime Minister agreed to it. It turned out to be too late to make any arrangement of this kind, but Mr. Dunn of the State Department said that he expected to reach
(a) Berlin on July 13 and would be free to discuss questions with the British Delegation on July 14. The State Department, however, did not want the Russians to think that there was a joint Anglo-American agenda or that we or the Americans wished to agree with the Russians on a tripartite agenda.

(b) On July 7 the State Department gave to the British Embassy their own list.[1] Their proposals for discussion were:

1. Procedure and machinery for peace negotiations and territorial settlements.
2. Policy towards Germany:
   (*a*) Establishment of a Control Council;
   (*b*) Agreement on treatment of Germany in initial control period;
   (*c*) Establishment of German local administration;
   (*d*) Treatment of Germany as an economic unit.
3. Implementation of the Yalta Declaration on Liberated Europe.
4. Policy towards Italy.
5. Co-operation in solving European economic problems.
6. Freedom of communication and information in Europe.

The State Department also expected a discussion of policy with regard to the Far East.

Mr. Matthews, in commenting on various items in this list, explained that the United States proposed the establishment of a Council of the five Foreign Ministers—i.e. the 'Big Three', France and China, to deal with the urgent problems of peace negotiations and territorial settlements. This Council would draw up, for submission to the United Nations, treaties of peace with Italy, Roumania, Bulgaria, and, at a later date, if the five Governments so wished, with Germany when it was 'mutually agreed that a German Government adequate to the purpose is functioning'. Mr. Matthews said that the limitation of the Council to the 'Big Five' had been put

[1] The State Department had given this list to the Russians.

(a) Washington tels. 4758, 4712, F.O.800/416/63/23 and 22.
(b) Washington tels. 4708–09, F.O.800/416/63/40–41.

forward as the most convenient way of avoiding a multiplication of claims for other parties—e.g. Byelo-Russia—to take a hand in drafting the treaties.

Mr. Dunn said[1] that the State Department were also much concerned with the problem of France. They wanted to help France to take her place again, as quickly as possible, as a free, democratic, and strong country, as an effective 'outpost' of western influence. One of the principal advantages in the proposal for a Council of Five was that it would associate France at once with Great Britain, the United States, and the U.S.S.R. in the discussion of the most difficult problems. The United States Government had been afraid that, if they suggested bringing in France alone, the Soviet Government might object, but that the latter might agree more readily if the matter were on the basis of the five major Powers. China was unlikely to make any difficulties for the United States and Great Britain and would probably be helpful. (a)

(iv)

British attitude towards the United States proposal for a Council of Foreign Ministers: Foreign Office brief on procedure for the conclusion of treaties with the European enemy States.

Mr. Winant on July 7, 1945, sent a letter to Mr. Eden giving a list (b) of the topics which the President might wish to raise at the Conference. On the following day he communicated formally the American (c) proposal for a Council of Five. The American argument was stated as follows: 'With the termination of hostilities in Europe the United Nations are faced with the urgent problem of peace negotiations and territorial settlements without which the existing confusion, political uncertainty and economic stagnation will continue to the serious detriment of Europe and the world. The experience at Versailles following the last war does not encourage the belief that a full, formal peace conference is the procedure best suited to obtain the best results or to arrive at a solution conducive to those conditions of permanent peace which the United Nations Organisation is dedicated to uphold. Such a formal peace conference would necessarily be slow and unwieldy, its sessions would be conducted in an atmosphere of rival claims and counter-claims and ratification of the resulting documents might be long delayed. On the other hand, a formal peace conference limited to the three or four principal nations

[1] It is not clear from this telegram whether Mr. Dunn's comments were made to Lord Halifax or to one of his staff.

(a) Washington tel. 4759, U5559/5559/70.
(b) U5466/3628/70. (c) U5559/5559/70.

would almost certainly encounter much opposition on the part of other members of the United Nations not invited to participate. They would feel that problems of direct concern to them were decided in their absence.' Hence the proposal for a Council of Five Foreign Ministers to draw up treaties for submission to the United Nations.

The Council would not be limited, however, to this function, but might consider such other common European problems of an emergency character as it could properly take up. Whenever it was considering a question of 'direct interest to a State not represented' on it, such a State should be

> 'invited to send representatives to participate in the discussion and study of that question. It is not intended, however, to fix hard and fast rules, but rather to permit the Council to adapt its procedure to the particular problem under consideration. In some cases it might desire to hold its own preliminary discussions prior to the participation of other interested States. In other cases the Council might desire to convoke a formal conference of the States chiefly interested in seeking a solution of the particular problem.'

The Foreign Office gave full consideration to the American proposal. They also wanted a definite settlement to be made as early as possible, since a continuance of uncertainty would make it impossible for Europe to settle down, and, in particular, if territorial disputes were left open, there would be a constant risk of local fighting and direct action by minor States as had happened after the first World War. Delay would be greatly to the disadvantage of ourselves and the Americans, who had to demobilise while still faced with the Japanese war. The 'unfortunate experience' of the Versailles Conference was also a warning against holding a general Conference before the ground had been fully prepared. While we were drawing up the terms of surrender for the enemy countries, we had observed the advantages of the major Allies taking the lead, and securing the concurrence of the interested lesser Allies at a comparatively late stage in the proceedings. We ought to aim at dealing with each enemy country separately and at establishing some body representing the four principal European Allies to do the preparatory work, and draft the terms for subsequent ratification by the other Allied States concerned at a general Conference or by whatever means might be found expedient.

The American proposal showed that the United States Government had been thinking on the same lines as ourselves. Their proposal had the following important advantages:

(i) It would secure the principle that the Great Powers should do the essential preliminary work;

(ii) A Council of Foreign Ministers would have the necessary status and prestige to handle the great problems involved. The importance of this point had been shown by the difficulties and delays of the European Advisory Commission, i.e. a body set up on an 'official' level;

(iii) If, as the Americans suggested, the Foreign Ministers also had deputies to represent them, their work could go on continuously; the deputies would deal with complicated details—i.e. with the kind of business for which the European Advisory Commission was set up—with the authority and backing of the Foreign Ministers.

(iv) We and the Americans would have a better chance of obtaining an effective share in drawing up the treaties with the 'satellite' States.

(v) The Council would be available to deal, if necessary at short notice, with any dangerous territorial or other disputes arising between the Allies as a legacy of the war. Here again the Foreign Ministers could do with greater authority work which we had hoped might be done by the European Advisory Commission.

(vi) Although the Council would have to have a regular seat at some convenient place, there would be an advantage in leaving it free to meet elsewhere; the Russians would no doubt be reconciled to the plan if the meetings concerned with the satellite States were held in Moscow or somewhere in eastern Europe.[1] The plan had three main disadvantages.

(i) The introduction of China into the detailed European settlement. China was not a party to the four-Power assumption of complete authority over Germany and was not at war with any of the satellites. The Soviet Government were unlikely to agree to her inclusion as a principal party on the Council for all purposes.

(ii) If—as appeared to be the case—the Americans wished us to await the emergence of a German Government capable of signing a treaty before we settled German problems, the delay would be dangerous and would certainly cause many difficulties.

(iii) The U.S.S.R. and China would be brought from the outset into the preparatory work of the Italian treaty, whereas our policy had been to agree to the draft settlement first with the Americans, and only at the second stage with the French and Russians.

These three drawbacks could be overcome. China might be, nominally, a member of the Council, without taking part in treaty-making in the case of the satellites with whom she was not at war. She would have the right to participate in discussions about Germany, but any action with regard to Germany in advance of the final settlement would continue to be taken by the four Powers in virtue

---

[1] The Foreign Office noted that M. Maisky had suggested to Mr. Roberts, Minister in H.M. Embassy at Moscow that the 'Peace Conference' should be held in Prague.

of their supreme authority over the country. We need not await the emergence of a German Government before we settled urgent questions affecting Germany by further declarations of the four Powers, e.g. on the German-Polish and German-Czechoslovak frontiers. The Council could draw up the terms of these Declarations as they would draw up the Treaties with the other enemy States, and leave the assent of the other interested United Nations to be obtained by a conference or other suitable means in the light of circumstances. Finally the advantages we should gain from putting the Council in charge of treaty-making with the satellites would offset the disadvantages of closer Soviet intervention in the arrangements for Italy.

The Foreign Office pointed out that the establishment of the Council would make the European Advisory Commission superfluous. The European Advisory Commission had practically completed the main plans for Germany and Austria; subsidiary matters could now be best discussed by the Four-Power Commissions in Berlin and Vienna and other current questions with which the European Advisory Commission might have dealt could obviously be handled best by the Council.

The Foreign Office therefore recommended that we should welcome the American proposal, while pointing out the difficulties about China and suggesting that she should be admitted as a kind of 'sleeping partner'. We should emphasise the importance of giving the new body a permanent seat, especially for its secretariat, though it might meet elsewhere. We might recommend London as the permanent seat—provided this did not mean M. Gusev—but could agree to Prague if the Russians insisted.[1] We should also agree to the dissolution of the European Advisory Commission on the understanding that the Council would meet regularly, and deal not only with matters of policy, but with the detailed preparatory work on frontiers, etc. We should urge strongly the need for the deputies to be specially appointed, since they would have full time work which could not be performed adequately by local Ambassadors—least of all by M. Gusev. The Council ought also to deal with the peace treaty for Finland;[2] the United States representative would become, like his Chinese colleague, a 'sleeping partner' on this occasion.

(a) The Foreign Office, before hearing of the American proposal, had drawn up a brief for the British Delegation on the procedure for reaching a settlement with (i) Germany, (ii) Austria, (iii) Italy,

[1] Mr. Eden, who agreed with the rest of the statement of Foreign Office views, noted that he saw no reason for going to Prague.

[2] The American proposal had excluded this treaty from the consideration of the Council, since the United States was not at war with Finland.

(a) U5559/5559/70.

(iv) the Axis satellites, (v) territorial and connected disputes between the lesser European Allies or quasi-Allies.

(i) Germany. Here the position was very different from that of 1918, when an armistice was concluded with the German Government. There was now no German Government or central administration; the whole country was under Allied occupation, and the four Allies had assumed supreme authority over it by the Four-Power declaration signed at Berlin on June 5, 1945. It was impossible to put through a treaty of the Versailles type at any foreseeable time, even if it were desirable to do so. We did not even know whether Germany would be dismembered into several States with separate Governments.

If we were unwilling to wait indefinitely for a suitable German Government—or Governments—with whom we could sign a formal treaty, we should have to impose our peace terms by Allied declarations based upon the powers conferred by the Declaration of June 5. This method would be without precedent, but the condition of Germany and the character of the occupation were also without precedent. By the method of declaration we could choose our own moment for ending the war and making a final settlement without depending upon the development of German internal politics.

If the settlement were imposed by successive declarations, we could deal first with the most urgent problems—e.g. frontiers—without waiting for the result of discussions over contentious matters such as reparations, property rights, debts, etc. We ought not to bring the state of war formally to an end before we had reached a final decision on the major problems, and on the machinery required to ensure the observance of our terms by Germany. We should have to obtain at some stage the assent of the other Allies at war with Germany. We could do so by means of a general conference at which the various declarations might be brought together in a single document.

As soon as a German Government or Governments emerged, they should be required to notify their formal acceptance of the terms laid down in our declarations. We should make Allied recognition conditional on such acceptance. If we recognised a German Government or Governments before we had issued any of our declarations, we should probably have to give up the method of peace-making by declaration, and sign a peace treaty in the normal way. This was an argument in favour of proceeding by declaration without great delay. The signature of humiliating terms would—as in 1919—damn any German Government in the eyes of the German people. Since a German Government would be likely to be composed of persons whom we would wish to hold power in Germany, we should not want to weaken their internal position. The formal acceptance of an accomplished fact would be less damaging than the signature of a new treaty.

(ii) Austria. We wanted to encourage in Austria a sense of independence. To this end we hoped that it might be possible to re-establish an Austrian administration and recognise a representative Austrian Government without much delay. Questions regarding nationality, property, etc. between Germany and Austria would raise complicated issues which might take years to settle; the establishment of peace with Austria should not therefore be delayed until these details had been settled. We could not decide whether it would be better to proceed by declaration or treaty until we knew when an Austrian Government would be recognised and the terms we should wish to impose upon it. In either case the four major Allies ought to be in broad agreement over the terms before bringing them before the other Allies, though two of the latter—Czechoslovakia and Yugoslavia—were closely concerned.

(iii) The Foreign Office memorandum here referred to the proposals about an Italian peace treaty already before the War Cabinet.[1] On these proposals territorial questions would be left over for later settlement, and Italy would cede the disputed territories, including the Italian colonies, to the four Powers. The Foreign Office had proposed that, after we had reached agreement, first with the Dominions, then with the United States Government, and lastly with the French and Soviet Governments, we should consult the other Allies at war with Italy, who had a direct interest in the settlement. After the four Allies were in agreement, we could draft the actual treaty, and possibly hold a small inter-Allied conference. The Italians would be admitted to the later stages of the negotiations, and given opportunities for comment, but would be required to sign the treaty without any major change in the terms.

(iv) The Satellites. We had recently suggested to the United States the desirability of concluding early treaties of peace with the four satellites,[2] partly because we had no other way of securing the withdrawal at least of the greater part of the Russian troops in the countries, and also because we could not expect the Russians to agree to broadening the satellite governments or to operate the Control Commissions on a genuinely tripartite basis. The Americans were not in favour of our plan. We had therefore agreed to let them make one more attempt to persuade the Russians to allow the broadening of the governments and to operate the armistice régimes on a

---

[1] See Volume III, Chapter XLIV, section (iv).

[2] The Foreign Office and the State Department regarded Finland, and to a lesser extent Hungary, as in a different category from Roumania and Bulgaria.

genuinely tripartite basis. If, as we expected, this attempt failed, we should bring forward our proposals.

On the other hand we had conceded during the armistice proceedings that the Soviet Government had a primary interest in the four satellites. We had therefore to accept the facts that the Soviet Government would wish to play a leading part in the arrangements for those peace treaties and that our suggestions would have to be marked into the Russian drafts.[1]

(v) If general tranquillity were to be restored in Europe, we should have to reach and, if necessary, impose a settlement of territorial and other outstanding questions between Allied countries. The three major Allies had reached agreement at the Yalta conference over the Soviet-Polish frontier; their decisions had now been recognised by the new Polish Government in Warsaw. The Soviet Government were settling their own problems with Poland and Czechoslovakia bilaterally under the general cover of the Treaties of Alliance which they had concluded with these States. The Soviet Government considered that the Polish-Czechoslovak dispute over Teschen was a matter to be settled between the Slav peoples concerned, and not by a general peace conference.

There would remain, however, certain potentially dangerous questions in south-east Europe which we could not allow the Soviet Government to decide without our participation. These questions included the future of Albania (with Yugoslav and Greek territorial claims to Albanian territory) and the Greek-Yugoslav frontier. In general—if the time-factor allowed—it would be desirable to bring such questions before the World Organisation which might be established by the spring of 1946.

In a note of July 10, 1945, to the Prime Minister, Mr. Eden summed up the Foreign Office view on the question 'what cards we hold for a general negotiation with the Russians, in the shape of things which the Russians want from us and which it is in our power to give or to withhold'. (a)

The list was as follows:

(i) *Credits*. The Russians would not be interested in credits from us of a size we could afford to give, but they had approached the

[1] After submitting this brief the Foreign Office heard from Lord Halifax that the State Department was opposed to any negotiation with the existing governments of Roumania, or (though their opposition here was less strong) with the Governments of Bulgaria and Hungary. Mr. Eden minuted this telegram: 'They [the Americans] are right.' On July 21 the Foreign Office noted that opinion in the British Delegation was hardening against peace proposals and unlikely to bring them forward. The Foreign Office thought that we might make the proposals again in a month or six weeks after the Conference, especially if any Russian concessions had proved valueless. See also Volume III. (b)

(a) PM/45/322, F.O.800/416/63/27. (b) R11596, 11658, 11694 and 11909/81/67

Americans for very large credits and the Americans had told them that such a proposal would require special legislation which was at the moment out of the question.

(ii) *Germany.* Here we held a certain number of assets which the Russians required, e.g. the merchant navy, a substantial part of German industry and industrial resources, including, in the British Zone, 75 per cent of the German steel-making capacity. Physical control of these assets gave us a bargaining advantage in securing acceptable reparation and other settlements. We and the Americans also held the greater part, and possibly the whole, of the German diplomatic archives. The Russian were pressing for access to them. Our intention had been to grant access on a basis of reciprocity, though this would be largely a formality, since we doubted whether the Russians held anything of importance for us. In view, however, of the recent Russian behaviour to us, we ought not to give them access to these archives until they met us on other issues. The Russians might also ask for information about German secret devices, but we should not wish to use this matter for bargaining. Finally, we had most of the German fleet and indeed all the ships which were seaworthy. The Russians wanted their share of the ships; here again we ought not to meet their demands without getting our requirements on other issues.

(iii) *The Italian fleet.* The Russians had claimed one battleship, one cruiser, eight destroyers, four submarines, and 40,000 tons of merchant shipping.[1] Many of our claims on the Russians were at least as well-founded as their claims to the Italian ships; we should therefore refuse to agree without a *quid pro quo*.

(iv) *The Straits.* We had promised to consider sympathetically Russian proposals for a modification of the Straits régime, but we were not committed to accepting them, and our consent was necessary if they were to be accepted. Furthermore, any new régime which the Russians might wish to establish would probably require reference to the World Organisation, where again our consent would be necessary. Similar considerations applied to any Russian proposals about access to the Baltic and control of the Kiel Canal, though here we were even less committed.

(v) *The Baltic States.* If the Russians requested our recognition of their annexation of these small States, we had numerous demands to make in return, and especially with regard to our interests in the countries.

(vi) *Tangier.* The Russians had asked to participate in discussions on Tangier and, presumably, in any future international régime. We should certainly not agree to this with a *quid pro quo*.

---

[1] See Volume II, Chapter XXXIV, section (vii).

Mr. Eden, in submitting to the Prime Minister on July 12 the various Foreign Office briefs for the Conference, wrote that on returning to the Foreign Office (after his illness) he found 'the world outlook gloomy, and signs of Russian penetration everywhere'. (a)

Mr. Eden pointed out that, although the United States Government agreed generally with our list of topics for discussion, and although we and the Americans had communicated our lists to the Soviet Government, there was no agreed agenda for the meeting. We did not know the views of the new American Secretary of State,[1] Mr. Dunn and Mr. Matthews had each given a somewhat different emphasis to the order of importance of the subjects to be discussed. It was impossible to arrange any preliminary discussion with Mr. Byrnes since he and the President seemed to be arriving at Berlin on the opening day of the Conference.[2] We could not therefore decide the order in which we should raise the subjects on our list.[3]

---

[1] Mr. James Byrnes had succeeded Mr. Stettinius as Secretary of State on June 30, 1945.

[2] Sir A. Cadogan was able to hold a meeting with members of the United States Delegation, at which Mr. Byrnes was not present, on the afternoon of July 14. The meeting showed that the two delegations were in general agreement on policy to be adopted at the conference, except that the United States Delegation did not agree with the British view that early peace treaties with the Soviet-controlled Balkan countries offered the best line of approach. (b)

[3] In conversation with Mr. Eden on the evening of July 16, M. Molotov said that the Soviet Delegation wanted to add to the subjects already listed for discussion: (*a*) The disposal of the German Navy and Merchant Marine. (*b*) Reparation. (*c*) Territorial Trusteeship and the role of the U.S.S.R. (*d*) Poland. (*e*) Diplomatic relations with the satellite States. (*f*) Spain, (*g*) Tangier. (*h*) Syria and the Lebanon. M. Molotov agreed that a discussion under (*c*) would be a continuation of the conversations at San Francisco. On (*d*) he complained that 'the government of M. Arciszewski' still existed. Mr. Eden said that it was gradually being liquidated. He also told M. Molotov that the British Delegation wished to discuss the fulfilment of the Yalta Declaration on Poland. (c)

(a) PM/45/324, U6125/3628/70. (b) U5679/3628/70. (c) F.O.934/2/8(3).

CHAPTER LXVII

German peace-feelers in 1942, 1943 and 1944: Allied discussions with regard to the maintenance of the demand for German unconditional surrender: the unconditional surrender of Germany and the end of hostilities

(i)

German peace-feelers in 1942–3: the question of unconditional surrender at the Moscow and Teheran Conferences: further German peace-feelers.

(a) DURING the last three years of the war the British Government had no reason to change their attitude towards German peace overtures.[1] The Foreign Office continued to take the view that many—perhaps the majority—of these offers were set going by the German secret service, which appeared to have made a special study of the strategy and tactics of peace-feelers. The German purpose was obviously to cause dissension among the Allies and to slow down their war effort.[2] Neutral countries were favourable ground for these manoeuvres in view of the general anxiety of the neutrals to see the end of the war before they were forced—for one reason or another—to take part in it. Turkey, for example, was particularly open to such intrigues; von Papen as German Ambassador played with skill on Turkish suspicions of Russia, fears of becoming involved in the war, and the desire of the Turkish Government to act as an intermediary between the combatants.

The dissident generals and the civilian groups of moderates in Germany wanted to replace Hitler and his associates by a govern-

[1] See Volume II, Chapter XXV, for peace-feelers in 1939–41.

[2] One typical attempt to divide the Allies was made in an approach to the United States Government in March 1943 through the usual devious channels. The Argentine Minister in Madrid reported to the American Minister a conversation with the Roumanian Minister who had been instructed by the Roumanian dictator Antonescu to let it be known to the Americans that he (Antonescu) had seen Hitler. Hitler, who no longer thought it possible for Germany to win the war, wanted an understanding with the United States and Great Britain on the basis that Germany was a bulwark against communism which would otherwise engulf Europe. Hitler would agree to restore all conquered territories, including Poland, but would want part of the Ukraine (as a protectorate). Peace would be guaranteed by the united forces of the Germans and Anglo-Saxons. Hitler himself would stay in power; the German people had confidence in him and were solidly behind him. The American Minister said that he would transmit the message, but was sure that the answer would be 'no'. The Minister, in fact, was instructed not to give any answer. *F.R.U.S., 1943*, I, 485–6.

(a) C7180/416/18.

ment which would make a compromise peace; they were still unable to devise a successful plan for getting rid of Hitler, and the peace terms which they regarded as essential if their 'moderate government' were to secure popular support were, as earlier, wholly unacceptable from an Allied point of view. An overture purporting to come from von Papen in December 1943 is an odd example of the kind of terms suggested. These particular terms were that Germany should keep the *Anschluss* with Austria and should 'rent' Danzig and the Corridor from Poland. The approaches, therefore, were met either with complete silence, or—in the case of neutral governments—with the statement that there could be no talk of peace terms until the Nazi régime had been broken.

The public statements of Ministers continued on similar lines. (a)
Thus on May 8, 1942, in a statement subsequently described in a Foreign Office minute of August 20, 1945, as representing the policy (b)
of His Majesty's Government towards approaches on the part of German 'opposition movements', Mr. Eden said that the longer the (c)
Germans supported and tolerated the Hitler régime, the heavier their responsibility. 'If,' continued Mr. Eden, 'any section of the German people really wants to see a return to a German State which is based on respect for law and respect for the rights of the individual, they must understand that no one will believe them until they have taken active steps to rid themselves of their present régime.'

About a fortnight later Lord Cranborne, while reaffirming that a negotiated peace with the Nazi leaders would be 'an unpardonable betrayal' of Great Britain and the world, mentioned that Germany (d)
would be disarmed but that the Allies had no intention of imposing permanent measures of economic discrimination against her. At the Casablanca meeting of 1943 President Roosevelt, with the Prime Minister's endorsement, used the term 'unconditional surrender.'[1] The acceptance of this term made all German peace-feelers useless, at least in the sense of feelers after a bargain in which the Allies would commit themselves to definite promises about the future of Germany. The Germans themselves in the early months of 1943 were not inclined to lower their minimum terms and to acquiesce in a 'dictated' peace. They could no longer hope for complete victory, but did not expect complete defeat. They felt strong enough to hold out in the areas of Europe—outside Russia—under their occupation until Allied opinion became war-weary and ready to accept a compromise peace—not indeed on the terms for which the Germans had hoped, but at all events on terms short of unconditional surrender.

---

[1] See Chapter LXI, section (ii).

(a) C1410/1410/18 (1942). (b) C4832/45/18 (1945). (c) Speech at Edinburgh, *The Times* May 9, 1942. (d) H.C.5s. Vol. 122: 1177–9.

This view was less easily held in Germany after the surrender of Italy and the Russian advances in the latter part of 1943. It was untenable after the Allied invasion of France in 1944 except by those who shared Hitler's delusions about secret weapons or about the chances of dividing the Allies. There were in 1944, as earlier, two different kinds of peace-feelers—those put forward through secret channels by Germans who now realised the utter ruin into which Hitler was leading the country, and those suggested by the German authorities themselves as a means of causing suspicion among the Allies.[1]

The British Government had no reason to pay attention to either type of approach. The Germans hostile to the régime never gave the impression that they had the capacity to overthrow it; their most important attempt to get rid of Hitler in July 1944 was a failure for which they themselves paid a terrible price. After this failure a spontaneous movement to break the régime was even more unlikely. Except for a few outstanding individuals, most of the 'moderates' continued to live in a world of opinion totally different from that of the Allies. The younger generation had been brought up in an atmosphere of absolute moral condemnation of the terms of the Treaty of Versailles as a violation of promises under which an allegedly undefeated German Army had surrendered in 1918. This view of a 'wronged' Germany made it impossible for them to realise the strength of Allied feeling about German aggression and the Allied determination not merely to avert the results of this aggression, but to make sure it could not be repeated. In any case it was very difficult, if not impossible, for the British authorities to know whether this or that secret overture was at all genuine, and not part of the German attempt to cause distrust between the Western Allies and Russia. The Foreign Office continued to be aware of this latter possibility—indeed the Russians left them in no doubt about their suspicions. All German approaches were therefore mentioned at once to the Soviet Government, though even this policy did not
(a) quieten Russian fears.[2]

(b) Meanwhile Mr. Eden had decided to raise the question of peace-feelers at the Moscow Conference in October 1943, and to point out that we had made a practice of communicating to the United States and Soviet Governments particulars of all the more serious attempts of enemy nationals to establish contact with us but that we had received very little information in return. At the Conference Mr.

---

[1] See also below pp. 360–3.

[2] For a report in *Pravda* on January 17, 1944, of an alleged secret meeting between Ribbentrop and, on the Allied side, 'two leading English figures' about conditions for a secret peace, see Volume II, pp. 542–5.

(a) C15307/155/18. (b) C11894/155/18.

Eden brought forward a resolution providing for the exchange of information between the three Governments and mutual consultation in regard to any peace approaches. The draft text of this resolution was accepted. The Russians, however, proposed the addition of a third paragraph bringing in the demand for unconditional surrender. The Russian wording was clumsy, and, in view of the four-Power Declaration,[1] Mr. Eden regarded the reference as unnecessary, but was prepared to agree to it. The Americans then raised difficulties about Finland, and the Russian proposal was dropped. (a)

The Foreign Office telegraphed to Mr. Eden on November 26, 1943, while he was on his way to the Teheran Conference, that the three Allied leaders might find it suitable to issue an appeal to the German people. There was evidence that the Germans were now deeply concerned about the casualties and material damage resulting from air raids. In these circumstances it might be worth while warning the German people of the uselessness of further resistance. We should say that our terms were unconditional surrender, to be followed by the military occupation of Germany by forces of the United Nations. It would be of great importance to make it clear that the military occupation would be carried out by Anglo-American as well as by Russian forces, since one of the main factors sustaining German resistance was a fear that the armies of occupation would be mainly Russian. (b)

No decision was reached on this proposal at the Teheran Conference. Mr. Eden telegraphed to the Foreign Office on December 1 that Stalin had spoken to the President on November 29 about unconditional surrender and had said that it was 'bad tactics' and that we should work out terms together and make them generally known to the German people.[2] Mr. Eden said that the Prime Minister considered this a better suggestion than the Foreign Office proposal. He (Mr. Eden) thought that the terms would have to be worked out as soon as might be possible through the European Advisory Commission. Mr. Hopkins took a similar view. On December 17, therefore, the Foreign Office asked the United States and Soviet Governments whether they would be willing to send instructions to this effect to their representatives on the Commission. (c)

---

[1] See Volume II, pp. 587–8.

[2] At a dinner meeting with the British and Russian military representatives on November 28, Stalin questioned the advisability of the principle of unconditional surrender without defining the exact terms which would be imposed upon Germany. He felt that to leave the principle of unconditional surrender unclarified merely served to unite the German people, whereas to draw up specific terms, no matter how hard, and tell the German people that this was what they would have to accept, would, in his opinion, hasten the day of German capitulation. *F.R.U.S., 1943, Cairo and Teheran Conferences*, 513.

(a) C13324, 13432/155/18. (b) C14543/155/18. (c) C14544/155/18.

(a) Lord Halifax, however, telegraphed on December 24 that Mr. Hull had taken up the matter with the President, but that the latter had said that he had no recollection of any discussion about it in his presence at Teheran. He was asking Mr. Winant to talk over the question with the Prime Minister on his return to London. Mr. Eden telegraphed to the Prime Minister on December 31 that he thought Stalin had raised the matter with the President at dinner, but that in any case we should try to begin the preliminary consultations as soon as possible.

The Foreign Office had considered in August 1943 the question of (b) modifying to some extent the insistence upon unconditional surrender. The context was a minute from the Prime Minister on a report of August 10 from Sir H. Knatchbull-Hugessen of a conversation with the Turkish Minister for Foreign Affairs. The Minister said that he had received clear hints from von Papen that the latter expected to be summoned to replace Ribbentrop (who was 'discredited') and that he was considering the possibility of an approach to the Allies. Sir H. Knatchbull-Hugessen asked 'What about Hitler?' The Minister then said that 'Hitler's fate would follow after Papen's appointment'. Sir H. Knatchbull-Hugessen replied that, in view of Papen's past record, we would not listen to advances either through or from him, and that our terms were unconditional surrender.

The Foreign Office approved of Sir H. Knatchbull-Hugessen's reply, but the Prime Minister minuted to Mr. Eden from Quebec on the telegram: 'All this is quite true, but it might better have been left unsaid. The displacement of Ribbentrop would be a milestone of importance, and would probably lead to further disintegration in the Nazi machine. There is no need for us to discourage this process by continually uttering the slogan "Unconditional Surrender". As long as we do not have to commit ourselves to dealing with any particular new figure or new Government our advantage is clear. We certainly do not want, if we can help it, to get them all fused together in a solid desperate block for whom there is no hope. I am sure you will agree with me that a gradual break-up in Germany must mean a weakening of their resistance, and consequently the saving of hundreds of thousands of British and American lives.'

The Foreign Office decided, with Mr. Eden's approval, that the Prime Minister's minute did not propose any general change of policy, and that it would be sufficient to tell Sir H. Knatchbull-Hugessen that, while unconditional surrender remained, and was known to be, our basic policy, we thought it expedient not to stress this fact too often, since we did not want to defeat our object by producing a desperate and united *bloc* of resistance in Germany.

(c) In the third week of December 1943 an approach to the British

(a) C15131/155/18. (b) C9134, 9706, 10041/155/18. (c) C14851/155/18.

Government was made indirectly through a Swedish business man at Stockholm. This man, who had maintained relations with high Nazi officials, returned from Berlin to Stockholm on December 16 with a message alleged to come from Himmler. According to this message Himmler, after consulting Göring and Generals Milch and Rommel (but not Ribbentrop), had been authorised by Hitler to try to secure secret contact between British and German representatives. Himmler's proposal was that the Germans should send two representatives—one from the party and one from the army—in order to clarify the meaning of the term 'unconditional surrender'. Himmler told the emissary that, although he and Hitler realised that the political system must be changed, the change could not be brought about before the terms of surrender had been considered, since otherwise the whole country would fall into anarchy and no responsible representatives would be available for the negotiations.

The Foreign Office did not regard the approach as likely to be genuine. Mr. Eden wrote that his instinct was to 'turn this down flat'. One motive for it might be to threaten Great Britain with the German 'secret weapon', if we refused to accept a compromise peace. In any case as Mr. Eden also noted, the Germans, after hearing our terms, might use them for propaganda to convince the German people that we intended their total destruction. Mr. Eden therefore recommended that we should inform the United States and Soviet Governments of the approach and should ask whether they agreed that our reply should be that we had nothing to say to Hitler, Himmler, and those associated with him except that our terms were unconditional surrender and that 'unconditional surrender' needed no definition.

The Prime Minister, who was on a visit to Tunisia, agreed with (a) this decision, but in his reply on December 23 to a telegram from Mr. Eden explaining what we proposed to do, he added that he had been greatly interested in Stalin's statement at Teheran that the term 'unconditional surrender' needed some definition. The Prime Minister said that he would shortly ask Stalin whether he would elaborate this suggestion, since an agreed public announcement might undermine the position of the Nazi leaders. The United States and Soviet Governments agreed with the terms of the proposed reply to the German approach. On January 1, 1944, Mr. Mallet, the Minister at Stockholm, was instructed to pass on the reply through the Swedish intermediary.[1]

---

[1] On November 13, 1943, Sir A. Clark Kerr had telegraphed information from M. Molotov about an approach to the Soviet Mission in Stockholm by representatives of a (*continued on page* 362)

(a) WM(43)172.2, C.A.; Grand 734, C14851/155/18, Frozen 805, Premier 3/197/7; C14851/155/18.

There appear to have been no German peace-feelers to the British Government of any importance in the early months of 1944. Reports continued to be received about opposition movements in Germany, but there were no grounds for acting on them, or for a change in the policy described in Mr. Eden's speech of May 8, 1942, that any German opposition must itself take steps to get rid of the régime before the Allies could accept it as genuine.

On June 1, 1944, an interdepartmental meeting was held in the Foreign Office to consider whether these opposition movements were in any way organised or co-ordinated, and, if so, whether they were strong enough to carry out a *coup* against the régime. The meeting examined the information available about the two main opposition groups: those who, like the Christian Socialists, were concerned mainly with the future of Germany after the war, and the high military officers who might help us during our military operations if they had some inducement or offer better than unconditional surrender. The first of these groups would be of no immediate help. A careful scrutiny of the evidence available during the past three or four years about the second group suggested that some at least of it was reliable enough to show that some German generals were now genuinely anti-Nazi and that the stories of opposition movements were not merely planted by the secret service in order to cause confusion and dissension among the Allies. There seemed, however, to be no evidence at all of any co-ordination between these generals;[1] isolated action was unlikely and could not succeed. In any case, though we might make an attempt to do so, it was not certain that we could get into contact with the generals concerned. The War Cabinet was also unlikely to agree to any offers or promises which would have to be made to the generals before they would take action. Hence the committee came to the conclusion that, on the evidence, it was not practicable to obtain any help in our forthcoming operations from this military opposition. Here the matter remained for the rest of the year. No steps were taken to qualify or mitigate the 'unconditional surrender' as far as concerned Germany.

(a) Early in November 1944 the British Government received information that von Kessel, Counsellor at the German Embassy to the Vatican, wanted to desert to the British authorities in Rome, and that von Weizsäcker, formerly State Secretary for Foreign Affairs

---

(*continued*)
number of German industrialists (said to be in touch with Ribbentrop) who wanted a Russo-German peace. The Soviet Government had refused all contact or conversations with these German representatives.

[1] There were also differences of view among the opposition groups, civilian and military, whether to look to the Western Powers for defence against Russian communism or to try to get from the Russians an offer of better terms than the unconditional surrender laid down by the Allies.

(a) C15074, 15253, 16142, 16143/180/18.

and at this time German Ambassador to the Vatican, knew of, and sympathised with, Kessel's intentions. Kessel asked that he might see a British officer in order to give oral explanations which he claimed might be connected with a new *coup* against the régime. The Foreign Office suspected this approach, but allowed an interview in order to discover whether Kessel had anything useful to say.

The interview was of no value. Neither Kessel nor Weizsäcker was willing to renounce publicly his German allegiance; both seemed to be acting mainly to reinsure themselves. Weizsäcker, in a message, alleged that he had the means to bring about the downfall of Hitler, but that for his own safety he would tell his plan only to a responsible British official personally known to him. Kessel offered to go to Switzerland to establish contact with Guderian or von Rundstedt, who, in his view, might be willing to negotiate peace. In informing the United States and Soviet Governments on December 13, 1944, of this approach, the Foreign Office explained that they thought it purely a manoeuvre and did not propose to continue contact with Kessel.

On this same day M. Dahlerus, a Swedish business man, who had (a) carried messages from Göring to the British Government in 1939, visited a member of the staff of the British Legation at Stockholm to give information which he had received from a German friend about the position in Germany. This German said that Hitler had undergone an operation on his ears after the attempt on his life; that he had lost his capacity for work, though otherwise he appeared quite normal, and that he was no longer important for purposes of practical leadership. Himmler, who had come to an agreement with the military authorities, was now in fact the dictator of Germany, probably with the support of Goebbels. Ribbentrop, Ley and other extremists were opposed to Himmler; so also was Göring, but the latter was of no importance except for the fact that he still had some popularity in Germany. Himmler hoped to be able to produce a force of 5,000,000 (*sic*) men with which to hold the Russian and western fronts long enough to convince the Western Powers that they must make terms with him. M. Dahlerus said that he thought of going to Germany and arranging to see Himmler in order to find out his intentions. He wanted, however, an assurance that the Foreign Office would believe the report which he brought back. M. Dahlerus was told at once that no such assurance could be given to him; that there was no chance whatever that the British Government would negotiate with Himmler, and any information brought from Germany by M. Dahlerus would be of interest only from an Intelligence point of view.

The Foreign Office took the view that this move might well be

(a) C17717, 17735/180/18.

merely a German attempt—at the time of their counter-offensive in the Ardennes—to cause dissension and suspicion among the Allies, with the purpose of securing compromise terms from one or the
(a) other of them. The Prime Minister thought that we should keep entirely clear of contacts involving 'people going to and fro from Germany'. The Foreign Office therefore instructed Sir V. Mallet that no discussions should take place with M. Dahlerus or with anyone else. The United States and Soviet Governments were again given full information of M. Dahlerus's approach. The Foreign
(b) Office also sent out a general telegram on January 4, 1945, to His Majesty's Representatives in neutral capitals warning them that the Germans might accompany or follow their military counter-offensive by peace offers designed to cause dissension among the Allies. Any approaches, including those from neutrals, should therefore be reported at once, and no encouragement should be given to them.

(c) Sir V. Mallet dealt according to these instructions with an approach in March 1945 by Dr. Hesse, a high official in Ribbentrop's entourage, who came to Stockholm in an attempt to get into touch with western Allied officials. Hesse argued that, if the Western Powers wanted to prevent Germany from fighting to the end and capitulating finally to Russia they must make peace with Hitler on terms which would give adequate guarantees. Otherwise the Germans would ally themselves with Russia and drive the Western Powers out of the European Continent. The intermediary through whom Hesse made his approach was told that the British Government were not in the least interested in anything he had to say.

(ii)

British discussions on the question of unconditional surrender; Foreign Office proposal for a tripartite declaration to the German people: exchanges with the United States and Soviet Governments: the Prime Minister's doubts about the effect of a declaration: further American proposals for a statement to the German people (January–December 1944).

(d) On January 15, 1944, the Prime Minister wrote a short note for the War Cabinet on the question of unconditional surrender.[1] He said that President Roosevelt had used this term without previously consulting him, but that he had thought it right to endorse the President's statement and that the statement might well have been appropriate to the circumstances of the time at which it was made. The Prime Minister understood by 'unconditional surrender' that

---

[1] On the question of unconditional surrender in relation to Japan see below Chapter LXX.

(a) C18029/180/18. (b) C17791/103/18. (1944). (c) C900/45/18.
(d) WP(44)33; C1859/1236/62.

after it the Germans had no rights to any particular form of treatment, e.g. the Atlantic Charter would not apply to them as a matter of right. On the other hand the victorious nations owed it to themselves to observe the obligations of humanity and civilisation. The President, in a statement[1] of December 24, 1943, had given a 'very good popular rendering of this conception'. The Prime Minister thought that his own speech at the Guildhall in November 1943 was relevant.[2] We ought to consider what was going to happen to the Germans before deciding whether more precise statements would induce them to surrender. They were to be completely disarmed and deprived of all power to rearm. They were to be forbidden all aviation, civil or military, and all training in flying. Large numbers of persons alleged to be guilty of atrocities were to be handed over for judgment to the countries where their crimes were committed. Stalin had said at Teheran that he would require at least four million Germans to work for many years in building up the ruin they had caused in Russia. The Russians would doubtless take away from Germany vast quantities of machinery to make up in a generous fashion for their losses at the hands of the Germans. Other Powers might make similar claims; such retribution would not seem to be devoid of justice in view of the great severity practised upon immense numbers of French, Italian and Russian prisoners of war and internees.

The Prime Minister added:

> 'The British, United States and Russian Governments are I understand agreed that Germany is to be decisively broken up into a number of separate States. East Prussia and Germany east of the River Oder are to be alienated forever and the population shifted. Prussia itself is to be divided and curtailed. The Ruhr and other great centres of coal and steel must be put outside the power of Prussia.'

Finally, the entire core of the German army comprised in the General Staff was to be broken up, and the Russians might put forward a demand that very large numbers of the General Staff should be put to death or interned for many years. The Prime Minister himself had wished to publish a list of some 50 to 100 outlaws of first notoriety with a view to dissociating the mass of the people from those who would suffer capital punishment at the hands

---

1 'The United Nations have no intention to enslave the German people. We wish them to have a normal chance to develop in peace, as useful and respectable members of the European family. But we most certainly emphasise the word "respectable", for we intend to rid them once for all of Nazism and Prussian militarism and the fantastic and disastrous notion that they constitute the "Master Race".'

2 This speech, which was delivered at the Mansion House (the Guildhall had been bombed) did not in fact contain any explanation of the term 'unconditional surrender'. The Prime Minister merely repeated his conviction that 'not only Germany, but Japan, with whom the British Commonwealth and Empire have an inexpiable quarrel, will be forced into unconditional surrender'.

of the Allies and of avoiding anything in the nature of mass executions. This would tend to reassure the ordinary people. But these proposals were scouted at Teheran as being far too lenient, though the Prime Minister was not sure how far Marshal Stalin was serious in this part of the conversation.

The Prime Minister's conclusion was that a frank statement of what was going to happen to Germany might not necessarily have a reassuring effect upon the German people and that they might prefer the vague terms of 'unconditional surrender', with the mitigations put forward in statements such as that made by the President.

(a) The Chiefs of Staff drew up on January 26 and submitted to the War Cabinet on February 5, 1944, a memorandum of their views on the effect of the formula of unconditional surrender on German military and civilian morale. They pointed out that Nazi propaganda was using the term to convince the Germans that the loss of the war would be infinitely worse than their present sufferings. Germany could expect no mercy. The German nation would be blotted out and the German people held collectively responsible with their leaders for all the crime and misery of the war. There was ample evidence that this talk was having an effect, mainly upon the uneducated masses, but to some extent upon all civilians; they felt that they would be involved with their country in complete social and economic collapse. Although fear of the Gestapo remained the most important factor in inducing the German civilian population to continue the war, the use of the formula of unconditional surrender appeared to be a contributory influence.

The mainspring of the German armed forces, especially of the professional officer class, continued to be discipline; this discipline would be broken only by defeats in the field. Nevertheless German soldiers, sailors, and airmen who were personally aware of the atrocities committed by their countrymen and of the ferocious retaliation by the Russians had better reason still for believing the propaganda which warned them against the retribution and revenge of their enemies.

Since Nazi propaganda had succeeded in converting the formula of unconditional surrender into one of the props supporting the German will to resist, could we do anything to remove this prop? The Chiefs of Staff were convinced that it would be a mistake to abandon the formula. It had stimulated Allied morale; it left the Governments of the United Nations a free hand to take such action as might be necessary to bring home to the German people that their defeat was complete and that they had acknowledged it. Nevertheless, without giving up the demand for unconditional surrender we might weaken the will to resist and separate the German people

(a) WP(44)83; C1861, 1864/1236/62.

from their leaders if the three Heads of Government made a public statement on the kind of future which they proposed to secure for the German people. The draft statement suggested by the Chiefs of Staff was to the effect that (i) Germany would be deprived of the fruits of her greed and aggression and held responsible for all the loss and damage caused by the war. (ii) German war criminals would be 'handed over to punishment', but there would be no mass reprisals against the German people. (iii) Steps would be taken to ensure that German aggression could not be renewed and that the Nazi party system and Prussian domination and militarism were extirpated. (iv) We should assist in building up a new Germany based on the rule of law and truth and it would be our desire to maintain the livelihood of the German people whom we wished to have a normal chance to develop in peace as useful and respectable members of the European family.

The Foreign Office considered on February 2, 1944, what recom- (a) mendations they should make in regard to the Prime Minister's minute of January 15. They drew up a memorandum and a draft declaration for submission to the War Cabinet. They pointed out that there had been no answer from the Soviet Government to their suggestion of December 17, 1943,[1] that the question of a draft declaration might be examined urgently by the European Advisory Commission, and that President Roosevelt thought that his statement of December 24, was sufficient. They agreed with the Chiefs of Staff that it was neither possible nor desirable to abandon the demand for unconditional surrender, though there were advantages in not overstressing it in our propaganda. In spite of the difficulties mentioned by the Prime Minister, a pronouncement by the three Heads of Government would be helpful if it were made at a suitable psychological moment and if the contents did not expose us later to a charge of bad faith. The Nazi use of the alleged repudiation of Mr. Wilson's Fourteen Points was a warning of the long-term dangers involved in any statement. The Foreign Office draft declaration therefore attempted to cover, broadly, all the points made by the Prime Minister, and to avoid any commitment likely to prove embarrassing in the future. At the same time the declaration might encourage the Germans to feel that even in defeat there was some hope for their future.

The draft declaration (after certain amendments had been made) was in the following terms:

'... Germany shall be punished for her aggression. Those responsible for that aggression and for the crimes accompanying it must be handed

[1] See also above p. 359–60.

(a) C1860/1236/62, 3029/1211/55; WP(44)125.

over for punishment. Justice will govern the actions of the United Nations. There will be no mass reprisals against the people of Germany.

Germany shall be deprived of the fruits of her aggression and will be held responsible for all that she has robbed from the countries occupied by her armies and for the loss and damage which she has caused to the United Nations during the war.

German aggression shall not be renewed. The most complete material guarantees will be exacted from Germany to destroy her power of aggression.

Germany will be purged of the National Socialist party and system. Prussian domination and militarism will be extirpated. The military forces of the United Nations will jointly occupy Germany and German civil administration will be controlled and supervised as may be necessary.

It is in the interests of our own peoples and of the world

(1) that there shall be established in Germany the rule of law and not of arbitrary violence, and a system of education based on truth, not on perverted history. Only thus will the nations of the world be secured from the rise of a new German tyranny, which would again disturb the peace:

(2) that Germany shall not be a centre of economic collapse and consequent chaos, which might infect the world:

(3) that when the German people have been purged and regenerated and have shown themselves capable of becoming law-abiding members of the world community, they shall eventually find their place in the world family of democratic nations and in the world system of security.'

(a) Mr. Eden sent the draft to the Prime Minister. The Prime Minister replied that the draft might be circulated to the War Cabinet, but that he did not at all like it or think that it would attract the Germans.

'The time would be better chosen if we had won a few victories against their Armies. If we are going to take all this territory away from them and shift 6 or 7 million people out of their homes, and if several millions of them are to go and work in Russia, I doubt very much whether we are in a position to give these assurances, bleak though they be.'

Mr. Eden answered that he had not proposed issuing the declaration until a favourable moment, but that, after we had ourselves come to a decision, lengthy consultations would be necessary before the principle and a draft text could be agreed by President Roosevelt and Stalin.

The memorandum and draft declaration were circulated to the
(b) War Cabinet on February 15 and discussed on March 13 in conjunc-

(a) M86/4, C1865/1236/62. (b) WM(44)34; C3517/1236/62.

tion with the memoranda by the Prime Minister and the Chiefs of Staff. The Prime Minister said that there was some criticism in the House of Commons that we were not adhering strictly to the terms of the Atlantic Charter. This criticism was based on some remarks of his own about the transfer of territory,[1] but we had never bound ourselves to apply the terms of the Charter to ex-enemy countries, e.g. the United Nations had a right to make territorial changes in the Reich. This was a strong argument for holding to the term 'unconditional surrender' which gave a free hand to the United Nations. On the other hand there was force in the argument that the Germans might surrender more easily if they were assured that in doing so they would not lose everything. The Prime Minister, however, doubted whether we could gain any real advantage at the present time by such attempts at reassurance. The War Cabinet accepted the Prime Minister's view and thought that the matter should be reconsidered later. Mr. Eden suggested that this reconsideration should take place after the European Advisory Commission had examined the armistice terms for Germany.

The Foreign Office, however, with Mr. Eden's approval, did not give up the idea of raising once again their general proposal for a declaration to the German people. They had unexpected support from General Eisenhower's headquarters. Mr. Stettinius, who was visiting General Eisenhower, telegraphed on April 13, 1944, to Mr. (a) Hull and the Chief of Staff of the American Army, General Marshall, that General Eisenhower and his Chief of Staff, General Bedell Smith thought that the term 'unconditional surrender' should be 'clarified by announcing the principles upon which the treatment of a defeated Germany would be based'. Sir A. Cadogan therefore (in Mr. Eden's absence) submitted a memorandum to the Prime Minister on April 15 pointing out that this proposal would have to be discussed with the Americans and that the Foreign Office needed guidance on the matter from the War Cabinet. Sir A. Cadogan noted that the Foreign Office continued to favour a declaration, and

---

[1] The reference appears to be to a statement by the Prime Minister in the House of Commons on February 22, 1944, that 'the term "unconditional surrender" does not mean that the German people will be enslaved or destroyed. It means, however, that the Allies will not be bound to them at the moment of surrender by any pact or obligation. There will be, for example, no question of the Atlantic Charter applying to Germany as a matter of right and barring territorial transferences or adjustments to enemy countries. No such arguments will be admitted by us as were used by Germany after the last war, saying that they surrendered in consequence of President Wilson's Fourteen Points. Unconditional surrender means that the victors have a free hand. It does not mean that they are entitled to behave in a barbarous manner or that they wish to blot out Germany from among the nations of Europe. If we are bound, we are bound by our own consciences to civilisation. We are not to be bound to the Germans as the result of a bargain struck. That is the meaning of unconditional surrender.' Parl. Deb. H. of C. 5th S. vol. 397: 698–9.

(a) C3022/1077/55.

that the evidence suggested that a statement of the Allies' intentions towards Germany, 'however grim it might appear to us, would appear necessary to German soldiers and civilians, and so put before them an acceptable alternative to the continuation of the war'. It would be undesirable, however, to accept Mr. Stettinius's suggestion that in addition to a tripartite declaration defining unconditional surrender there should also be a joint Anglo-American statement of the principles upon which the military government of Germany would be conducted. We could not dissociate ourselves and the Americans in this way from the Russians.

(a) The Prime Minister, however, disliked the whole of Mr. Stettinius's plan. He replied to Sir A. Cadogan on April 19 as follows:

> 'This matter is on the President. He announced it at Casablanca without any consultation. I backed him up in general terms. Subsequent correspondence with the President has shown him very much disinclined to remodel his statements now. He has given us several examples.
>
> I have pointed out to the Cabinet that the actual terms contemplated for Germany are not of a character to reassure them at all, if stated in detail. Both President Roosevelt and Marshal Stalin at Teheran wished to cut Germany into smaller pieces than I had in mind. Stalin spoke of very large mass executions of over 50,000 of the Staffs and military experts. Whether he was joking or not could not be ascertained. The atmosphere was jovial but also grim. He certainly said that he would require 4,000,000 German males to work for an indefinite period to rebuild Russia. We have promised the Poles that they shall have compensation both in East Prussia and, if they like, up to the line of the Oder. There are a lot of other terms implying the German ruin and indefinite prevention of their rising again as an Armed Power.
>
> On the other hand, they know that Unconditional Surrender was interpreted in a very favourable manner in the case of the Italians, and we see now what the Roumanians are offered if they will turn their coats, as they have so often done.
>
> By all means make a historical summary of events and circulate it to the Cabinet. Personally I am not going to address the President on the subject. For good or ill, the Americans took the lead, and it is for them to make the first move.
>
> I may say I think it all wrong for the Generals to start shivering before the battle. This battle has been forced upon us by the Russians and by the United States military authorities. We have gone in wholeheartedly, and I would not raise a timorous cry before a decision in the field has been taken.
>
> The Cabinet should certainly consider the matter but we should wait until Mr. Eden's return. It is primarily a United States affair.'

(a) C5183/1236/62.

The Foreign Office thought that, in view of the Prime Minister's attitude, there was no use in putting their case again to the War Cabinet. Mr. Eden, on his return, minuted that he was 'not enthusiastic' about the proposal. No further steps were therefore taken in the matter.

On May 20, 1944 the President telegraphed to the Prime Minister (a) a new proposal that he (the President) should issue a statement to the German people after D-Day.[1] The Foreign Office did not object to this proposal. The Prime Minister replied on May 22 to the President (b) that he would bring the matter before the War Cabinet, and that he thought it would be best for the President to speak 'for all three of us', but that the 'main principle of the note we should strike towards Germany' required considerable thought, and that the timing of the statement would have to be related to 'the success or otherwise of our operation'. The Prime Minister was, in fact, suggesting tactfully that the President should not issue his proposed statement. In a (c) minute of May 23 asking for Mr. Eden's views on the President's proposed declaration, Mr. Churchill said that he did not much like the President's tone towards Germany. It seemed more suitable after a victorious battle than before the hazards were encountered. Mr. Eden inclined to agree with the Prime Minister.

The War Cabinet discussed the matter on May 24, and (with the (d) support of Field-Marshal Smuts and Mr. Curtin, the Australian Prime Minister, who were present at the meeting) asked the Prime Minister to telegraph to the President in favour of postponement. Mr. Churchill therefore telegraphed on May 25 that the War Cabinet (e) were afraid that, if the message were sent before the battle was won, the Germans might distort it 'into a sort of peace appeal'. The Prime Minister added:

> 'If there were nothing between us except that the Germans have an evil philosophy, there would be little ground for the War going on. I think myself that the message might conceivably be taken as a peace feeler, and that the Germans might reply that they accepted your note as a basis for further discussion.
>
> In truth there is much more between them and us than a philosophy. Nearly all Europe cries for vengeance against brutal tyranny. At Teheran my suggestion for the isolation of Prussia was considered far too modest by you and U.J. Everybody expects complete forcible

[1] The statement called upon the Germans to realise that they would be totally defeated, and that a continuance of the war would be 'unintelligent' on their part. The Allies had already made it clear that they did not intend the total destruction of the German people, but merely that of 'the philosophy of those Germans who have announced that they could subjugate the world'.

(a) T1099/4, No. 541, Premier 3/472; C6776/1236/62. (b) T1109/4, No. 679, Premier 3/472; C7294/1236/62. (c) C7504/1236/62. (d) WM(44)68.2, C.A. (e) T1123/4, No. 680, Premier 3/472; C7294/1236/62.

disarmament of Germany, possibly extending to civil aviation, to be made and maintained. There are other very grave questions open. For instance, how are the Poles going to be compensated if they do not get East Prussia and certain territories up to the line of the Oder in return for the Curzon Line which the Russians will certainly demand?'

The Prime Minister said that the War Cabinet also thought that 'a document so grave addressed to the enemy should emanate from the (a) three Allies'. The President replied on May 27 agreeing not to make any statement.

(b) The President proposed again to the Prime Minister on November 22 the issue of a joint declaration to the German people that the Allies did not wish to devastate Germany or destroy the German people, but only to eliminate Nazi Control. The President told the Prime Minister that General Eisenhower thought that such a declaration would help to break down German morale. General Eisenhower had in fact reported to the Combined Chiefs of Staff on (c) November 20 that one of the factors prolonging German resistance was the success of Nazi propaganda in convincing every German that unconditional surrender meant the complete devastation of Germany and her elimination as a nation.

(d) The Prime Minister, after consulting the War Cabinet and the Chiefs of Staff, replied on November 24 that

'we all gravely doubt whether any such statement should be made. I do not think that the Germans are very much afraid of the treatment they will get from the British and American Armies or Governments. What they are afraid of is a Russian occupation, and a large proportion of their people being taken off to toil to death in Russia, or as they say, Siberia. Nothing that we can say will eradicate this deep-seated fear.

2. Moreover U.J. certainly contemplates demanding 2 or 3 million Nazi youth, Gestapo men, etc., doing prolonged reparation work, and it is hard to say that he is wrong. We could not therefore give the Germans any assurances on this subject without consultations with U.J.

3. It seems to me that if I were a German soldier or general, I should regard any such statement at this juncture, when the battle for Cologne is at its height, as a confession of weakness on our part and as proof positive of the advantages of further desperate resistance. The Chiefs of Staff and the Ministry of Information both independently agree with me that this might well be the consequence of any such announcement now. I do not see any alternative to the General Grant attitude; "to fight it out on this line, if it takes all summer". We

---

(a) T1141/4, No. 543, Premier 3/472; C7295/1236/7. (b) T2155/4, No. 655, Premier 3/193/2; C16361/103/18. (c) SCAF 134, Premier 3/193/2.
(d) WM(44)155; T2171/4, No. 828, Premier 3/193/2.

therefore are opposed to any reassurance being volunteered by us at this juncture.

4. The brilliant French success in the south, your capture of Metz and the break-through of the Seventh American Army upon Strassbourg (*sic*) now taken are substantial facts which must be added to the intense pressure of the American First and Ninth Armies and our own British efforts towards Venlo. Even if we do not conquer at the strongest point towards Cologne enough has already been gained to make the battle a notable step towards our goal. Words, I am sure, would play no part now, and we can, it seems to me, speak no words to which the Russians, who are still holding on their front double the number of divisions opposite us, are not parties.

5. I therefore earnestly hope that we shall fight the battle out till winter comes about the middle of December and throw extra weight into the points of penetration. I am sure it would be hurtful to our prestige and even to our initiative if we seemed to try high-level appeals to the Germans now. All kinds of propaganda can be thrown across the battlefronts locally as they do to us, and the Staffs are working at a plan, on which separate telegrams will be sent, which is designed to meet Eisenhower's desire to get at German morale by underground methods. But to make the great Governments responsible for anything which would look like appeasement now would worsen our chances, confess our errors and stiffen the enemy resistance. Please however do not hesitate to correct me if you think I am wrong. Meanwhile I remain set where you put me on unconditional surrender.'

The President again accepted the British view, and did not issue (a) any statement.[1]

At the beginning of March 1945, however, the Prime Minister thought that the time had come for a warning to the Germans of the situation they would be bringing upon themselves if they went on fighting. The Prime Minister told the War Cabinet on March 6 that (b) he was considering the possibility of issuing a warning to the German people (possibly in conjunction with President Roosevelt and Stalin) about the effects of continued resistance. This warning would state clearly that if the Germans prolonged their resistance, especially beyond the time of the spring sowing, they would increase the risk of famine in Germany after the final surrender. In these circumstances the Germans could not rely on the Allies to provide food for them, since they would have brought famine on themselves.

[1] The Prime Minister telegraphed to General Eisenhower on November 25 that it (c) would be a mistake to show the Germans that 'we were anxious for them to ease off their desperate opposition. Goebbels would certainly be able to point to the alteration of our tone as an encouragement for further resistance, and the morale of the German fighting troops would be proportionately raised.' General Eisenhower replied on November 26 (d) agreeing with the Prime Minister's view.

(a) T2171/4, No. 657, Premier 3/193/2. (b) WM(45)26; C867/47/18.
(c) T2180/4, Premier 3/193/2. (d) T2194/4, Premier 3/193/2.

(a) The Prime Minister read the draft of his proposed telegram to President Roosevelt to the War Cabinet on March 14. He said that Mr. Eden had pointed out that the declaration might increase the risk of the Germans conserving their own food supply by reducing the rations of prisoners of war and other Allied nationals now in Germany. There was also some danger that the Germans might take the declaration to mean that, if they surrendered, the United Nations would see that there was no acute food shortage in the country. This point could be met by wording the declaration in such a manner that the Germans would realise that anyhow they must suffer from a very grave food shortage, and that if they delayed their surrender this shortage would develop into a famine.

The Prime Minister said that he would mention to the President the disadvantages as well as the advantages of his proposal. The
(b) President replied on March 21 that the time did not seem appropriate for such a proclamation; he suggested that the point should be made in our propaganda. The Foreign Office pointed out that this was
(c) already being done. On March 22 the Prime Minister withdrew his suggestion for a declaration.

(iii)

German approach with regard to the surrender of the German forces in Italy: Russian misunderstanding of the situation: British and American exchanges with Stalin (March 8–April 14, 1945).

The approach made by Dr. Hesse,[1] and rejected out of hand by the British Minister in Stockholm, was typical of the last phase in the attempt of the Germans to escape from the consequences of their acts. Their only chance of alleviating their fate was to try to divide the Allies, and, when this attempt was shown to be useless, to surrender to the Western Powers while holding off—as far as was possible—the Russian advance from the East. A first large-scale offer, or rather approach, on the question of a military surrender in Italy did in fact cause serious trouble between the Western Allies and the Soviet Government, but this trouble was not lasting, and was due mainly to the extreme suspicion on the Russian side, together with a certain failure on the side of the British and, more seriously, the American military authorities in handling the situation with the Russians.

The German approach was made in the first instance to the

[1] See above, p. 364.

(a) WM(45)30; C1013/47/18; T300/5, No. 915, Premier 3/193/6A; C1085/47/18. (b) T316/5, No. 721, Premier 3/193/6A; C1128/47/18. (c) T319/5, No. 919, Premier 3/193/6A C1128/47/18.

United States Intelligence Service through Italian intermediaries. The Germans making this approach, which Field-Marshal Alexander, Supreme Allied Commander in the Mediterranean Theatre, regarded with some suspicion, included General Wolff, senior S.S. officer in north Italy, and a representative of Marshal Kesselring. In fact, the approach at this time had no military result. Kesselring, whom General Wolff hoped to win over to his plan, was transferred to another command, and the plan—if indeed there was anything more in it than an attempt to cause confusion—petered out.

In the first stage, on receiving the information from American sources that General Wolff had arrived in Switzerland on March 8, 1945, Field-Marshal Alexander proposed to instruct the Germans in question to produce signed authority from Marshal Kesselring that they had authority to treat with the Allies. Field-Marshal Alexander would send representatives to examine their credentials in Switzerland, and, if this examination proved satisfactory, inform them that they must come to his headquarters for military discussions. These discussions would deal only with the method of surrender on a purely military and not on a governmental or political basis.

Field-Marshal Alexander's report of the approach and of his (a)
proposed reply was telegraphed to London on March 11. The Foreign Office instructed Sir A. Clark Kerr during the night of March 11–12 (b)
to inform the Soviet Government at once, on behalf of the Prime Minister and Mr. Eden, of the approach and to say that Field- (c)
Marshal Alexander was being instructed to send officers to Switzerland to meet the German emissaries and to deal with them as he had suggested, but that he had been told not to make any contact with them until the view of the Soviet Government had been received.

The Soviet Government replied on the night of March 12–13 that (d)
they considered the talks of the highest importance, and agreed that they should be held. They proposed to send three Soviet officers to take part in them. In the evening of March 13 the Foreign Office instructed Sir A. Clark Kerr to inform the Soviet Government that (e)
we agreed that Soviet officers should take part in the proposed talks. Sir A. Clark Kerr was also told, for his own information, that we did not know how the British and American officers were being brought into Switzerland, i.e. secretly or with the knowledge of the Swiss Government, and that the absence of diplomatic relations between the U.S.S.R. and Switzerland might raise difficulties with regard to the Soviet officers.

Later on March 13, however, a telegram was received from the (f)
British Joint Staff Mission in Washington reporting that, on the

---

(a) NAF878, C1575/45/18. (b) Tels. 1213–4 to Moscow, C1575/45/18.
(c) FAN506, C1575/45/18. (d) Moscow tel. 769, C1575/45/18.
(e) Tel. 1234 to Moscow, C1575/45/18. (f) JSM597–8, C1575/45/18.

advice of Mr. Harriman, the United States Ambassador in Moscow, the United States Chiefs of Staff were unwilling to agree to Soviet participation in the preliminary talks in Switzerland. They pointed out that Field-Marshal Alexander's proposal was for a military surrender which would not involve political matters; the negotiations would be conducted at his headquarters, and the meeting in Switzerland was merely to arrange for accredited representatives of the German Commander to go to Allied Force Headquarters. Mr. Harriman thought that the Soviet claim to take part in the discussions in Switzerland was unjustified, since the German proposal was for the surrender of a military force on a United States–British front. This surrender was 'not a parallel to the capitulation of a Government'; Mr. Harriman felt that in similar circumstances the Soviet Government would not allow the participation of American officers. He also considered that if we gave way to their request, the Soviet Government would take it as a sign of weakness and put forward other untenable demands.

With the agreement of the State Department, the United States Chiefs of Staff therefore proposed that the State Department and the Foreign Office should reply to the Soviet Government that the Russian representatives were 'welcome', and that Field-Marshal Alexander was being instructed to arrange for them to be present at his headquarters where all matters concerning a German surrender would be discussed. The meeting in Switzerland was merely for the purpose of establishing contact in order to get the German representatives to Allied headquarters.[1]

(a) The Prime Minister, to whom this telegram was sent, minuted on March 14 that the American argument seemed 'good and logical' and also 'extremely important', but that their proposed reply expressed their views 'in a very weak and reserved form'. Did they mean that the Soviet representatives would take no part in the discussions and be present only as observers? 'This is what I think it means, but it is expressed so politely that there may be subsequent recrimination. "Welcome" to what? They have nothing to do with a purely military surrender of the German army in Italy.'

The Chiefs of Staff agreed with the Prime Minister's view of the American reply and with the assumption that the Russians should attend merely as observers. The Foreign Office, however, pointed out that it was undesirable to use the word 'observer', since it would

---

[1] Sir. A. Clark Kerr telegraphed on the morning of March 14 a summary of Mr.
(b) Harriman's views and said that he had agreed with his (Mr. Harriman's) request to take no action on his instructions until Mr. Harriman had heard from the United States Government. The Prime Minister minuted this telegram on March 15 with the words: 'These are tremendous arguments. I feel we were too complaisant—I especially.'

(a) D73/5; C1575/45/18. (b) Moscow tel. 797, C1575/45/18.

certainly give offence to the Soviet Government; in any case we had to keep in mind that we might be creating a precedent for ourselves in the event of a similar situation arising on the Eastern front. The Foreign Office therefore suggested to the Chiefs of Staff a revised (a) wording in which, after an explanation that the meeting in Switzerland was merely to establish contact, the relevant sentences were as follows:

'Field-Marshal Alexander is being instructed to make all necessary arrangements for the presence of Soviet representatives at any discussions which may take place at A.F.H.Q.: but, as the German proposal is for the surrender of a military force on a United States–British front, Field-Marshal Alexander, as Supreme Commander in this theatre, would alone be responsible for conducting negotiations and reaching decisions.'

The United States Government accepted these suggestions. The (b) British and United States Ambassadors in Moscow were instructed (c) on the evening of March 15 to inform the Soviet Government of them. Sir A. Clark Kerr telegraphed during the night of March 16 that he had received an angry reply from M. Molotov that, after the Soviet Government had agreed to the contacts in Switzerland provided that Soviet representatives took part in the talks, and after they had appointed their representatives, we were denying them the right to participate in the talks. This denial seemed to them 'utterly unexpected and incomprehensible' as between two Allies. Hence the Soviet Government considered it impossible to give their consent to the talks and insisted that they should be broken off, and that in future there should be no question of conducting separate talks between one or two of the Allied Powers and German representatives without the participation of the third Allied Power.

In a second telegram on March 17 Sir A. Clark Kerr pointed out that we could easily retort that the Soviet Government had consulted us only in a very perfunctory way over their declaration of war on Bulgaria and the end of hostilities in Bulgaria and the other satellites. There was, however, nothing to be gained by an argument on these lines, and we need not agree to the interruption of the talks in Switzerland. We might reply that we also held that all three major Allies should be represented at future conversations with the Germans, and that we intended to include Soviet representatives if the present contacts for establishing the credentials of the German emissaries were followed by discussions at Field-Marshal Alexander's headquarters.

The Foreign Office considered it desirable to concert at once with

(a) COS(W)681 2, C1575/45/18. (b) JSM604, FAN508, C1575/45/18.
(c) Tels. 1267–8, 1285 to Moscow, C1575/45/18.

the United States Government a reply to M. Molotov's complaints. Lord Halifax was therefore instructed on March 18 to tell the State Department (i) that it should be clearly understood by all concerned that we had been willing to let the Russians come to Switzerland as well as to Field-Marshal Alexander's headquarters so that they would be fully aware of what was taking place. We had not intended and did not intend that they should take an active part in negotiations of a purely military kind for the surrender of Kesselring's army. These negotiations should obviously be conducted by Field-Marshal Alexander. It was probably now too late to bring the Russians to Switzerland. In any case the contacts there were merely for establishing the credentials of the German emissaries, and ought not to be delayed. (ii) the Prime Minister and the President might repeat the facts in a personal message to Stalin, and say that, in the light of this explanation, they hoped that the Soviet Government would not press their request for the contacts in Switzerland to be broken off and would maintain their readiness to be represented at any negotiations which might take place at Field-Marshal Alexander's headquarters. These negotiations would deal only with the military surrender of the German armies; any political questions would be referred at once to the three Governments.

The United States Government agreed with the terms of this message, but suggested that it should be sent to M. Molotov and not to Stalin, and that the reference to the Soviet Government not pressing their request should be omitted. The Foreign Office accepted these suggestions (though, on balance, they would have preferred a direct approach to Stalin) and sent instructions to Sir A. Clark Kerr to deliver the message. Mr. Harriman received similar instructions. M. Molotov, however, refused to be satisfied with the explanation.
(a) He replied in a letter to Sir A. Clark Kerr on March 22[1] that the Soviet Government saw in the matter 'not a misunderstanding but something worse'. He complained that, for a fortnight, 'behind the back of the Soviet Union, which is bearing the brunt of the war against Germany, negotiations have been going on' between representatives of the German and Anglo-American commands.

Meanwhile Marshal Kesselring had been transferred to the western front, and the approaches in Switzerland were for the time halted. The Prime Minister in explaining the situation to the War Cabinet on March 19, 1945, said that this development would solve the immediate difficulties which had arisen with the Russians, but that we ought to reach a clear understanding with them about the treatment of any future approaches. Any German proposal for the

---

[1] The letter was dated March 22, and appears to have been received early on March 23.

(a) Moscow tel. 921, C1577/45/18.

surrender of a military force must be made to the Allied Commander on the front concerned; this Commander alone would be responsible for conducting the negotiations and reaching decisions. Since, however, political questions might emerge in the discussions, the three main Allied Powers should be informed, and should be entitled to send representatives to be present throughout the negotiations.

The War Cabinet thought that the Foreign Secretary should try to reach agreement with the Soviet and United States Governments on these lines. The Foreign Office had begun to draft the necessary procedure (which, as they pointed out, would have to cover the preliminary stage for the establishment of the credentials of German emissaries) when the text of M. Molotov's letter of March 22 was received. The Prime Minister's first comment—on March 24—was (a) that for the moment the negotiations had been dropped. They might be reopened in an area far more vital than Italy,[1] and would then include political as well as military considerations. The Russians might have a legitimate fear of our doing a deal in the west to hold them well back in the east. The Prime Minister therefore thought it would be a good thing not to send an answer to M. Molotov until we had discussed the matter with the United States Government.

Sir A. Clark Kerr also agreed that M. Molotov's letters should be (b) ignored. He suggested, however, that since the letters showed a real suspicion which we could not safely ignore, we should be most careful to carry out our part of the plan, i.e. we should keep the Soviet Government fully informed of developments and give them an opportunity to take part in any meetings at Allied Headquarters. Sir A. Clark Kerr's recommendation was handed to the Chiefs of Staff. They telegraphed on March 29 to the British Joint Staff (c) Mission at Washington, for the information of the Combined Chiefs of Staff, that Field-Marshal Alexander did not appear to be giving effect to his instructions to keep the Russians informed of the results of any contacts, and that he should be instructed to do so.

Lord Halifax telegraphed on the night of March 26–7 that the (d) United States military authorities had also decided to ignore M. Molotov's letter. The Prime Minister had shown a copy of the letter to General Eisenhower.[2] In a minute to Mr. Eden on March 25 the Prime Minister reported that General Eisenhower was 'deeply (e) stirred with anger at what he considers most unjust and unfounded charges about our good faith'. He would himself, 'as military commander, accept the unconditional surrender of any body of enemy

---

[1] i.e. owing to Marshal Kesselring's transfer to the western front there was now a possibility that he might offer to negotiate the capitulation of the armies on this front.

[2] The Prime Minister went to General Eisenhower's headquarters on March 25.

(a) M254/5, C1577/45/18. (b) Moscow tel. 959, C1577/45/18. (c) COS(W)717, C1577/45/18. (d) Washington tel. 1984, C1577/45/18. (e) M262/5, C1577/45/18.

troops on his front from a Company to the entire Army . . . he had full authority to accept such a surrender without asking anybody's opinion', but would 'consult the Governments' if any political question arose. He was afraid that, if the Russians were brought into a question of the surrender of Kesselring's forces, a matter which could have been settled by himself in an hour might be prolonged for three or four weeks with heavy losses to our troops. General Eisenhower said that he would insist upon all the enemy forces laying down their arms, and remaining where they were until further orders. so that there could be no possibility of transferring them across Germany to the eastern front. He would also advance as rapidly as possible eastwards through the surrendered troops.

The Prime Minister thought that these matters should be left to General Eisenhower's discretion, and that the Governments should come in only if political issues were raised. There was no reason 'why we should break our hearts if, owing to mass surrenders in the West, we get to the Elbe or even further before Stalin'. The Prime Minister, on further reflection, considered that we should send no answer to the 'insulting letter' from M. Molotov. He assumed that the Foreign Office had sent a copy to Washington pointing out 'in no spirit of complaint that it was they who particularly wished that the Russians should not come to Switzerland'. The Prime Minister was sure that we ought 'to get absolutely in line with the United States, which should be easy, and meanwhile let Molotov and his master wait'.[1]

(a) The Foreign Office drew up on March 29, 1945, a minute for the Prime Minister with special reference to the question whether an offer of surrender—whether arising out of military operations or otherwise—from the German Commander-in-Chief on the western or Italian fronts should be regarded as a purely military matter. In itself such a surrender, as General Eisenhower had claimed, would be a purely military affair, but the consequences of a surrender on this scale would go far beyond the military sphere. It was also clear that, unless we were willing to go some way to meet the Russians on the question of the presence of Russian observers at any negotiations which might take place, the political consequences might be very serious over the whole field of allied relations.

The Foreign Office explained that, in accordance with the War Cabinet decision on March 19, they had been in touch with the Chiefs of Staff on procedure in the event of any cases analogous to

[1] This message, which also dealt with the critical position at the San Francisco Conference, included a characteristic sentence: 'We have had a jolly day, having crossed the Rhine.'

(a) PM/45/141, C1577/45/18.

the present German approach.[1] They submitted to the Prime Minister a draft telegram on the subject. They added that we might assume that the war in the West was moving so fast that a general capitulation was no longer likely and that we could safely let matters rest as they were. On the other hand from a political point of view we ought to agree with the United States Government to communicate to the Soviet Government the formula set out in the draft telegram. This telegram was sent to Washington on April 4, (a) but at the same time a new development from the Russian side aggravated the position.

Although the Americans had suggested that the Anglo-American reply to the Russian complaints should be made to M. Molotov and not to Stalin, the President had addressed two messages to Stalin on the subject. The second of these messages, which was sent on April (b) 1, included the words 'No negotiations for surrender have been entered into, and if there should be any negotiations, they will be conducted at Caserta with your representatives present throughout.'

Stalin replied as follows on April 3: (c)

> 'I have received your message on the question of negotiations in Berne. You are absolutely right that in connection with the affair regarding negotiations of the Anglo-American command with the German command somewhere in Berne or some other place "has developed an atmosphere of fear and distrust deserving regrets".
>
> You insist that there have been no negotiations yet.
>
> It may be assumed that you have not yet been fully informed. As regards my military colleagues, they, on the basis of data which they have on hand, do not have any doubts that the negotiations have taken place and that they have ended in an agreement with the Germans, on the basis of which the German Commander on the western front—Marshal Kesselring—has agreed to open the front and permit the Anglo-American troops to advance to the East, and the Anglo-Americans have promised in return to ease for the Germans the peace terms.
>
> I think that my colleagues are close to the truth. Otherwise one could not have understood the fact that the Anglo-Americans have

[1] These discussions with the Chiefs of Staff had shown a difference of opinion with the Foreign Office on the procedure to be followed on the preliminary establishment of the *bona fides* of a German approach. The Chiefs of Staff wanted to give the Allied Commanders discretion to act as Field-Marshal Alexander had acted. The Foreign Office pointed out that, if we were to conceal from the Russians the fact that the military representative of an Allied Commander was in touch with enemy emissaries on neutral territory, we should again have trouble with the Russians. The Foreign Office view appears to have been that secret organisations such as S.O.E. and the American O.S.S. ought to be able to establish the *bona fides* of an approach and that investigation through such channels (unknown to the Russians) differed in kind from direct action by the Allied commander. The Foreign Office held up their minute to the Prime Minister until—on March 30—the Chiefs of Staff accepted in principle the Foreign Office view.

(a) Tel. 3212 to Washington, C1578/45/18. (b) MX23589, C1578/45/18.
(c) T402/5, Roosevelt to Churchill No. 734, Premier 3/198; C1578/45/18.

refused to admit to Berne representatives of the Soviet command for participation in the negotiations with the Germans.

I also cannot understand the silence of the British who have allowed you to correspond with me on this unpleasant matter, and they themselves remain silent, although it is known that the initiative in this whole affair with the negotiations in Berne belongs to the British.

I understand that there are certain advantages for the Anglo-American troops as a result of these separate negotiations in Berne or some other place since the Anglo-American troops get the possibility to advance into the heart of Germany almost without resistance on the part of the Germans, but why was it necessary to conceal this from the Russians, and why your Allies—the Russians—were not notified?

As a result of this at the present moment the Germans on the western front in fact have ceased the war against England and the United States. At the same time the Germans continue the war with Russia, the Ally of England and the United States. It is understandable that such a situation can in no way serve the cause of preservation of the (*sic*) strengthening of trust between our countries.

I have already written to you in my previous message and consider it necessary to repeat it here that I personally and my colleagues would have never made such a risky step, being aware that a momentary advantage, no matter what it would be, is fading before the principal advantage of the preservation and strengthening of the trust among the Allies.'

The President answered on April 5 in very strong terms.

'I have received with astonishment your message of April 3 containing an allegation that arrangements which were made between Field-Marshal Alexander and Kesselring at Berne, "permitted the Anglo-American troops to advance to the east and the Anglo-Americans promised in return to ease for the Germans the peace terms".

In my previous messages to you in regard to the attempts made in Berne to arrange a conference to discuss a surrender of the German Army in Italy, I have told you that (1) no negotiations were held in Berne; (2) that the meeting had no political implications whatever; (3) that in any surrender of the enemy army in Italy there could be no violation of our agreed principle of unconditional surrender; (4) that Soviet officers would be welcomed at any meeting that might be arranged to discuss surrender.

For the advantage of our common war effort against Germany, which to-day gives excellent promise of an early success in a disintegration of the German Armies, I must continue to assume that you have the same high confidence in my truthfulness and reliability that I have always had in yours.

I have also a full appreciation of the effect your gallant army has had in making possible a crossing of the Rhine by the forces under General Eisenhower and the effect that your forces will have hereafter on the eventual collapse of the German resistance to our combined attacks.

I have complete confidence in General Eisenhower and know that he certainly would inform me before entering into any agreement with the Germans. He is instructed to demand and will demand unconditional surrender of enemy troops that may be defeated on his front. Our advances on the western front are due to military action. Their speed has been attributable mainly to the terrific impact of our Air Power resulting in destruction of German communications, and to the fact that Eisenhower was able to cripple the bulk of the German forces on the western front while they were still west of the Rhine.

I am certain that there were no negotiations in Berne at any time, and I feel that your information to that effect must have come from German sources which have made persistent efforts to create dissension between us in order to escape in some measure for responsibility for their war crimes. If that was Wolff's purpose in Berne, your message proves that he has had some success.

With a confidence in your belief in my personal reliability and in my determination to bring about together with you an unconditional surrender of the Nazis, it is astonishing that a belief seems to have reached the Soviet Government that I have entered into an agreement with the enemy without first obtaining your full agreement.

Finally I would say this, it would be one of the great tragedies of history if at the very moment of the victory, now within our grasp, such distrust, such lack of faith should prejudice the entire undertaking after the colossal losses of life, material and treasure involved.

Frankly I cannot avoid a feeling of bitter resentment towards your informers, whoever they are, for such vile misrepresentations of my actions or those of my trusted subordinates.'

On receiving copies of these two messages Mr. Churchill himself (a)
sent a message to Stalin on April 6.

'The President has sent me his correspondence with you about the contacts made in Switzerland between a British and an American officer on Field-Marshal Alexander's Staff and a German General named Wolff relating to possible surrender of Kesselring's Army in northern Italy. I therefore deem it right to send you a precise summary of the action of His Majesty's Government. As soon as we heard of these contacts we immediately informed the Soviet Government on March 12, and we and the United States Government have faithfully reported to you everything that has taken place. The sole and only business mentioned or referred to in any way in Switzerland was to test the credentials of the German emissary and try to arrange a meeting between a nominee of Kesselring's and Field-Marshal Alexander at his Headquarters or some convenient point in northern Italy. There were no negotiations in Switzerland even for a military surrender of Kesselring's Army. Still less did any political-military

(a) T404/5, Premier 3/198; C1578/45/18.

plot, as alleged in your telegram to the President, enter into our thoughts, which are not as suggested of so dishonourable a character.

Your representatives were immediately invited to the meeting we attempted to arrange in Italy. Had it taken place and had your representatives come, they would have heard every word that passed.

We consider that Field-Marshal Alexander has full right to accept the surrender of the German Army of 25 divisions on his front in Italy and to discuss such matters with German envoys who have the power to settle the terms of capitulation. Nevertheless we took especial care to invite your representatives to this purely military discussion at his Headquarters should it take place. In fact however nothing resulted from any contacts in Switzerland. Our officers returned from Switzerland without having succeeded in fixing a rendezvous in Italy for Kesselring's emissaries to come to. Of all this the Soviet Government have been fully informed step by step by Field-Marshal Alexander or by Sir Archibald Clark Kerr, as well as through United States channels. I repeat that no negotiations of any kind were entered into or even touched upon, formally or informally, in Switzerland.

There is however a possibility that the whole of this request to parley by German General Wolff was one of those attempts which are made by the enemy with the object of sowing distrust between Allies. Field-Marshal Alexander made this point in a telegram sent on March 11 in which he remarks "Please note that two of the leading figures are S.S. and Himmler men, which makes me very suspicious." This telegram was repeated to the British Ambassador in Moscow on the March 12 for communication to the Soviet Government. If to sow distrust between us was the German intention, it has certainly for the moment been successful.

Sir Archibald Clark Kerr was instructed by Mr. Eden to explain the whole position to M. Molotov in his letter of the March 21. The reply of the March 22 handed to him from M. Molotov contained the following expression: "In this instance the Soviet Government sees not a misunderstanding but something worse."

It also complains that "in Berne for two weeks behind the backs of the Soviet Union, which is bearing the brunt of the war against Germany, negotiations have been going on between representatives of the German Military Command on the one hand and representatives of English and American Commands on the other". In the interests of Anglo-Russian relations, His Majesty's Government decided not to make any reply to this most wounding and unfounded charge but to ignore it. This is the reason for what you call in your message to the President "The silence of the British". We thought it better to keep silent than to respond to such a message as was sent by M. Molotov, but you may be sure that we were astonished by it and affronted that M. Molotov should impute such conduct to us. This however in no way affected our instructions to Field-Marshal Alexander to keep you fully informed.

Neither is it true that the initiative in this matter came, as you state to the President, wholly from the British. In fact the information given to Field-Marshal Alexander that the German General Wolff wished to make a contact in Switzerland was brought to him by an American Agency.

There is no connection whatever between any contacts at Berne or elsewhere with the total defeat of the German Armies on the western front. They have in fact fought with great obstinacy and inflicted upon us and the American Armies since the opening of our February offensive up to March 28 upwards of 87,000 casualties. However being outnumbered on the ground and literally overwhelmed in the Air by the vastly superior Anglo-American Air Forces, which in the month of March alone dropped over 200,000 tons of bombs on Germany, the German Armies in the west have been decisively broken. The fact that they were outnumbered on the ground in the west is due to the magnificent attacks and weight of the Soviet Armies.

With regard to the charges which you have made in your message to the President of April 3, which also asperse His Majesty's Government, I associate myself and my colleagues with the last sentence of the President's reply.'

Stalin replied on April 7:

'Your message of April 5 received. In my message of April 7 to the President, which I am sending to you also, I have already replied to all the fundamental points raised in your message regarding the negotiations in Switzerland. On the other questions raised in your message I consider it necessary to make the following remarks. (a)

1. Neither I nor Molotov had any intention of "blackening" anyone. It is not a matter of wanting to "blacken" [anyone] but of our having developed differing points of view as regards the rights and obligations of an ally. You will see from my message to the President that the Russian point of view on this question is the correct one, as it guarantees each ally's rights and deprives the enemy of any possibility of sowing discord between us.

2. My messages are personal and strictly confidential. This makes it possible to speak one's mind clearly and frankly. This is the advantage of confidential communications. If, however, you are going to regard every frank statement of mine as offensive, it will make this kind of communication very difficult. I can assure you that I had and have no intention of offending anyone.'

Stalin replied to the President at greater length; he repeated the Russian argument, though in much less offensive terms, and claimed that the lack of resistance by the Germans on the western front was not due solely to the fact that they had been defeated. He also maintained that his informants were 'honest and modest people who discharge their duties conscientiously'.

(a) T419A/5, Premier 3/198/2; C2465/45/18.

(a) The Prime Minister sent to the President a copy of Stalin's message to him with the comment that 'this is about the best we are going to get out of them, and certainly it is as near as they can get to an apology'. He did not want to send a reply until he knew how (b) the President thought the matter should be handled. Before the Prime Minister sent his reply President Roosevelt was dead. On the (c) night of April 14–15 the Prime Minister repeated the reply to Mr. Truman. He had thanked Stalin for the 'reassuring tone' of his last message, and hoped that the misunderstanding might now be considered at an end. He explained why he thought the Russians had imagined that we 'were trying to get a walkover' on the western front at their expense; he also referred to the British proposal that the contacts in Switzerland should be broken off at once, since there was now no chance that they would procure the surrender of the German forces in Italy.

The Foreign Office had strongly urged this break-off. Field-Marshal Alexander had withdrawn his officers from Switzerland on (d) April 4. Lord Halifax was instructed on the night of April 13–14 to suggest with emphasis to the State Department that, since the German Commander-in-Chief in Italy clearly had no intention, at all events at the present stage, of surrendering his forces on terms acceptable to the Allies, the American Intelligence Service should break off contact with the German emissaries. We regarded it as essential, in view of the Russian attitude, to put a stop at once to the (e) whole business. The State Department accepted this view, and for the time the matter was at an end.

The Foreign Office, however, thought that some further step was necessary both to reassure the Russians and to make explicit our own position with regard to united Allied action in dealing with Ger- (f) many. Sir A. Cadogan sent a minute to the Prime Minister on April 16, 1945, pointing out that for the past fortnight the Soviet press had been repeating the allegations made by Stalin that the Germans were attempting no serious resistance in the west, and that this fact might have some deep and possibly sinister significance. Sir A. Cadogan thought that the handling of Germany might be the crucial factor in our own and American relations with Russia, and that it was desirable to note some of the reasons why the Russians had developed their suspicions, and to consider how we could deal with them: (i) the contacts in Switzerland were a 'prime irritant'; (ii) it was now fairly certain that the Germans had been giving the Russians tendencious reports about these and other contacts; (iii)

(a) T433/5, No. 940, Premier 3/198/2; C2466/45/18. (b) T460A/5, Premier 3/198/2; C2466/45/18. (c) T475/5, No. 4, Premier 3/198/2; C2466/45/18.
(d) Tel. 3640 to Washington, C1578/45/18. (e) FAN527, C1578/45/18.
(f) C1579/45/18.

the Russians knew that most Germans preferred us and the Americans to themselves; (iv) they (the Russians) were afraid that we and the Americans would be too 'soft' with the Germans. The anti-Soviet tone of the Catholic press and of 'reactionaries' here and in the United States had given rise to suspicions that we might yet be tempted to set up 'some kind of pseudo-democratic western German buffer State between ourselves and Russia'; (v) professional military jealousy doubtless played some part, especially as the Russian people had been constantly assured that they, practically alone, had defeated the Germans. The further east we met the Russians, the less plausibly could this argument be maintained. These facts had implications as regards Russian prestige in the world generally and also on the plans which the Russians had intended to put into effect if they had been the first to occupy the greater part of Germany.

Sir A. Cadogan thought that the Prime Minister and President Roosevelt had done everything possible to dispel these Russian suspicions, but that it would be of great value and importance if the Prime Minister at an early date could make a public reference to the Russian press allegations and at the same time reaffirm our intention to keep to the principles laid down in the section of the Yalta communiqué dealing with Germany. Sir A. Cadogan suggested a statement rebutting the allegations that there had been no German resistance in the west. We had always given generous acknowledgment to the part played by the Red Army, but we and the Americans now had on the Continent armies of vast dimensions and unparalleled equipment. These armies, together with an overwhelming air power, had shattered German resistance in the west. We should also reaffirm our intention to exact unconditional surrender, and give a warning against German attempts to create dissension between the Allies. We might repeat the phrases in the Yalta communiqué about Germany, with special emphasis on our intentions to be 'tough but just to the Germans', and refer to the agreements reached in the European Advisory Commission on the control of Germany and to our firm intention to work in unison with our Russian, American and French allies in our dealings with the Germans.

A copy of this minute was also sent to Mr. Eden in case he might have a chance of speaking on similar lines to M. Molotov.[1] Owing to pressure of business the Prime Minister had not been able to read this minute before May 1. The Prime Minister's secretariat then suggested that, in the circumstances, the minute might be withdrawn. The Foreign Office agreed to its withdrawal.

[1] Mr. Eden had no opportunity to do so at San Francisco.

(iv)

Approach to the British and United States Governments from Himmler: rejection of the approach (April 25–7, 1945).

(a) On April 25, 1945, Sir V. Mallet reported from Stockholm that the Swedish Minister for Foreign Affairs had asked him, and the American Minister to call at 11 p.m. on the evening of April 24. The Swedish Minister had with him Count Bernadotte, head of the Swedish Red Cross, who had just come back from Germany via Denmark. He had seen Himmler, with whom he had had previous conversations, at the latter's request at 10 a.m. on April 24 in Lübeck. Himmler said that Hitler was desperately ill, and might be dead already. In any case he would not live for more than two days. Himmler was therefore now in a position of full authority to act. He asked Count Bernadotte to inform the Swedish Government of his desire that they should arrange a meeting between him (Himmler) and General Eisenhower in order to capitulate on the whole western front. Count Bernadotte said that such a meeting was unnecessary since Himmler could order the German forces to surrender. He therefore refused to forward Himmler's request unless Norway and Denmark were included in the capitulation. In this case there might be some point in a meeting since special arrangements might be necessary for accepting the German surrender. Himmler answered that he was ready to order the troops in Denmark and Norway to surrender to British, American or Swedish troops. He hoped to continue resistance at least for a time on the eastern front. Count Bernadotte told him that it would be scarcely practicable for him to do so, and that in any case the Allies would not allow it. Himmler said that he hoped the Western Allies and not the Russians would be the first to enter Mecklenburg in order to save the civilian population.

Count Bernadotte explained that General Schellenberg, a member of Himmler's staff, was waiting near the Danish border and could ensure the immediate delivery of any message to Himmler. The Swedish Minister added that he thought the information of such importance that he should communicate it at once to Sir V. Mallet and the United States Minister. They replied that Himmler's refusal to order a surrender on the eastern front looked like a last attempt to create discord between Russia and the Western Allies; obviously the Nazis would have to surrender to all the Allies at the same time. The Swedish Minister admitted this possible explanation of Himmler's motive, but said that the capitulation of all the German troops on the western front and in Norway and Denmark would be

---

(a) C1706/45/18.

of great advantage to all the Allies, including Russia, and would lead rapidly to a total surrender. The British and United States Governments were free to pass on Count Bernadotte's information to the Soviet Government; the only reason why the Swedish Government could not inform the Soviet Government directly was that Himmler had stipulated that his message was for the Western Allies only.

The War Cabinet met at 4.30 p.m. on April 25 to consider Sir V. (a)
Mallet's telegram. The Prime Minister said that the facts must be told to Stalin at once, and that we should say also that, as far as we were concerned, there could be no question of anything less than a simultaneous and unconditional surrender to the three major Powers. The reply to Himmler should be that German troops should give themselves up as individuals or units to the Allied troops or representatives on the spot. Until this happened, the Allies would continue their attacks with the utmost vigour in all theatres of war. The Prime Minister thought we could safely send this message to Stalin without first consulting the United States Government; he proposed, however, without delaying the message to Stalin, to let President Truman know by telephone what he had done and to invite him to telegraph to Stalin on similar lines.

The Prime Minister said that Himmler was claiming to act on behalf of the German Government. The surrender which he offered was therefore a matter for discussion between Governments and did not require a meeting with General Eisenhower. It would indeed be unsuitable for a proposal for a general surrender to be discussed with the military commander in the field. General Eisenhower, however, should be told of the approach and informed that the matter was being dealt with between Governments.

The War Cabinet agreed with the Prime Minister's suggestions. Later in the meeting the Prime Minister telephoned accordingly to General Eisenhower. The War Cabinet then considered the question of the surrender of German forces in territories where there were no Allied troops. They decided that representatives of the Norwegian Government and British military officers should be flown to Norway in order to be ready to accept the surrender of the German troops in Norway and that a similar procedure should be adopted for Denmark. The Prime Minister sent his message through the Foreign (b)
Office in the agreed terms to Stalin after the War Cabinet meeting, and at 8.10 p.m. telephoned to President Truman. The President agreed at every point with his action.

Stalin's reply was transmitted through the Soviet Embassy in (c)

(a) WM(45)52, C.A.; WP(45)270; C1767/45/18.
(b) T629–30/5, Premier 3/197/6; C1767/45/18.
(c) T646/5, Premier 3/197/6; C1769/45/18.

London on April 26. Stalin considered the Prime Minister's proposal 'to present to Himmler a demand for unconditional surrender on all fronts, including the Soviet front, the only correct one'. He added: 'Knowing you, I had no doubt that you would act just in this way. I beg you to act in the sense of your proposal, and the Red Army will maintain its pressure on Berlin in the interests of our common cause.'

(a) The Prime Minister, in telegraphing the text of this message to Mr. Eden at San Francisco and to Lord Halifax in Washington thought that the sentence beginning 'knowing you' was so personal and friendly that it would be better not to repeat it to the United States Government, since we did not know whether Stalin had used
(b) a similar wording to President Truman. The Prime Minister replied to Stalin on April 27 that he was most pleased to know that he (Stalin) was in no doubt how he would act, and 'always will act'
(c) towards him. Meanwhile on the night of April 26–7 Sir V. Mallet was instructed to tell the Swedish Minister for Foreign Affairs that, as far as the British Government were concerned, there could be no question whatever of anything less than unconditional surrender by the Germans simultaneously to the three major Powers. German forces, either as individuals or in units, should everywhere surrender themselves to the Allied troops or representatives on the spot. Until this happened, the attacks of the Allies upon them on all sides and in all theatres where resistance continued would be prosecuted with the utmost vigour. The United States Government gave a similar reply to Himmler's overture.

(d) Sir V. Mallet telegraphed in the afternoon of April 27 that the British and American replies would be passed on by Count Bernadotte, who was leaving at once by air for Denmark. The Swedish Government would not add any official comments, but Count Bernadotte intended to emphasise unofficially that 'surrender now' was the only possible course.[1]

(v)

The unconditional surrender of Germany: exchanges with the Soviet Government regarding the announcement of the surrender (April 16–May 8, 1945).

(e) On April 16, 1945, the United States Chiefs of Staff, after considering the views telegraphed by the Foreign Office that some step

[1] In order to make it clear that the Germans would not be able to cause a split in the allied front, an official communiqué was issued from No. 10 Downing Street on the night of April 28–9 with regard to Himmler's approach and the British reply.

(a) T651/5, Premier 3/197/6; C1769/45/18.
(b) T650/5, Premier 3/197/6; C1769/45/18. (c) C1769/45/18.
(d) C1760/45/18. (e) C1964/45/18.

was necessary to avoid more misunderstandings, recommended a message to the Russians on the question of a German surrender.[1] They expected the unconditional surrender of German forces on a large scale on all fronts in the immediate future. They thought it desirable that each of the Allies should be able to observe the negotiations for any such surrender, but that no German offer should be refused because one of the Allies was not present. They suggested that the Russians should nominate representatives to be available immediately at Allied Forces Headquarters in Italy and on the western front in the event of any negotiations. The United States Chiefs of Staff considered it no longer necessary to envisage merely local surrenders. Hence the appointment of accredited military representatives at each Allied headquarters would meet the situation. The Commanders-in-Chief would report any German approaches to them, and if these approaches developed into widespread surrenders with obvious political implications, the three Governments would be able to deal with them.

The Foreign Office agreed with this proposal with an additional paragraph suggesting that the appointment of representatives should be reciprocal. The proposal did not deal explicitly with the case of negotiations on neutral territory, but the likelihood of such negotiations had now decreased, and, if a case arose, the Commanders-in-Chief would not open discussions without previously seeking authority from their Governments. The proposal was put to the Soviet Government and accepted by them. (a) (b)

The final stages of the German surrender came very rapidly. The capitulation on the Italian front took place between April 26 and 29, 1945. The German envoys, with whom contact had been broken off, returned to Switzerland claiming to have full powers to surrender the German forces in Italy. Field-Marshal Alexander on April 24 (c) reported their arrival and asked for instructions for dealing with them. He was informed on April 26 that he could instruct them to come at (d) once to his headquarters in Italy, but that there must be no bargaining or negotiating in Switzerland. If the German envoys would not go at once to Field-Marshal Alexander's headquarters, all contact with them must be discontinued. Field-Marshal Alexander was instructed to tell the Soviet General Staff at once, through the Military Missions in Moscow, of this renewed approach and to say

[1] For an account of messages exchanged between British, American and Russian authorities about the final objectives for their armies and about arrangements for their junction, see John Ehrman, *Grand Strategy*, Volume VI (H.M.S.O., 1956), pp. 131–61. The Americans did not accept the Prime Minister's view that 'we should join hands with Russian Armies as far to the East as possible, and, if circumstances allow, enter Berlin' (cited *ibid.* p. 138).

(a) C1965/45/18. (b) C1969/45/18. (c) NAF931, C2236/45/18.
(d) FAN532, C2236/45/18.

that it had been made on German initiative. He was to give our reply, and to ask that a Russian representative should be nominated to attend the negotiations at his headquarters.

(a) Meanwhile on the night of April 25–6 the Prime Minister sent a personal message to Stalin explaining the situation, and saying that Field-Marshal Alexander was free to accept the unconditional surrender of the considerable army on his front, but that all political issues were reserved to the three Governments. The Prime Minister pointed out that the surrender in Italy was not mentioned in the telegram which he had sent about Himmler's proposed surrender.[1] 'We have spent a lot of blood in Italy, and the capture of the German armies south of the Alps is a prize dear to the hearts of the British Nation with whom in this matter the United States have shared the costs and perils.'

(b) Stalin replied on April 26 thanking the Prime Minister for his message, and notifying him of the appointment of a Soviet representative to take part in the conversations at Field-Marshal Alexander's headquarters.[2] These conversations took place at Caserta on
(c) April 28 and 29. The Instrument of Surrender of the German Forces in Italy,[3] and in the Vorarlberg, Tyrol and Salzburg provinces of Austria and in part of Carinthia, was signed on April 29, and took effect at noon on May 2.[4]

(d) The Prime Minister kept Stalin informed of the proceedings at Field-Marshal Alexander's headquarters. In the early hours of April 30 he telegraphed the news of the signature of the Instrument of Surrender in the presence of the Russian representatives. The Prime Minister said that no publicity should be given to the news until the terms became effective. President Truman had sug-
(e) gested that the announcement of the surrender should be made first by Field-Marshal Alexander. The Prime Minister told Stalin: 'As your officers were present, I have given instructions to Field-Marshal

---

[1] See above p. 389.

[2] In a message to President Truman on May 1 the Prime Minister described the tone
(f) of Stalin's reply as 'greatly improved'.

[3] Except the portion of Venezia Giulia east of the Isonzo river.

[4] The French Ambassador asked the Foreign Office on the evening of April 30 that the French Government should be informed in advance of the publication of any events, such
(g) as the surrender offer of Himmler, or any other surrender, and that they should not be left to read of such offers in the newspapers. The Foreign Office suggested to the Prime Minister on May 1 that it would be desirable to inform the French Government of the impending German surrender in Italy. Sir O. Sargent therefore proposed to tell the French Ambassador the facts in strict confidence on the night of May 1 or early on May 2. There is no record of the Prime Minister's reply, but the Foreign Office seem to have given the information to M. Massigli.

(a) T638/5, Tel. 2176 to Moscow, Premier 3/198/2; C2236/45/18.
(b) T660/5, Premier 3/198/2; C2236/45/18. (c) COS(45)115; C2266/45/18.
(d) T680/5, Tel. 2265 to Moscow; T689/5, Tel. 2269 to Moscow, Premier 3/198/2; C2237/45/18. (e) T683/5, No. 16, Premier 3/1982; C2237/45/18.
(f) T709/5, No. 27, Premier 3/198/2; C2237/45/18). (g) C2000, 2237/45/18.

Alexander accordingly'. Stalin agreed with this proposal. Field Marshal Alexander made the announcement at 18.30 on May 2. (a)

The complete unconditional surrender of all the German forces soon followed. This surrender was by definition a military affair, but the Foreign Office were concerned to see that the Instrument of Surrender was duly carried out, and that the process by which the surrender took place did not lead to friction or misunderstanding between the Allies. Sir O. Sargent, on May 4, sent a minute to the (b) Prime Minister to the effect that within the next forty-eight hours Admiral Dönitz who had been nominated in Hitler's will as his successor would have to decide whether to surrender Germany unconditionally to all the Great Powers or whether to continue to resist in Norway, Bohemia, and an Austrian redoubt. In the former case we should have to designate a British signatory who could go at short notice to the place where the document would be signed. There would be some advantage if the British signatory were also the British Commander-in-Chief designate in Germany. In any case it would be necessary to appoint a British Commander-in-Chief immediately on the signature of the document in order to enable the Control Commission to be set up at once. Sir O. Sargent thought that the Instrument of Surrender should be signed inside Germany. There was something to be said for signing it in Berlin, but the disadvantage was that at the moment Berlin was occupied by Soviet troops alone. Sir O. Sargent therefore suggested a place like Torgau, where American and Soviet forces had met on April 25. He thought that we could accept Dönitz's signature. Dönitz claimed that Hitler had appointed him as Head of the State and Supreme Commander of the German Armed Forces; he was as likely as any other German to secure the obedience of the Wehrmacht.

The Instrument of Surrender prescribed two German signatures: (i) a representative of the Government, and (ii) a representative of the Wehrmacht. Dönitz might be said to represent both these elements, but Sir O. Sargent considered that it would be useful to have another signature—that of Himmler, for example, if he were available—definitely committing the Nazi party. Another possible signatory was Keitel who had been for a long time Chief of the High Command of the Armed Forces. The possible combinations might be (i) Dönitz as Head of the Government and Keitel for the Wehrmacht, or (ii) Dönitz for the Wehrmacht and Himmler (as Minister of the Interior) for the Government. What we wanted to avoid was that the surrender should be signed by unrepresentative nonenties as was the case with the Treaty of Versailles.

These suggestions were overtaken by the events of the German

(a) NAF941, C2237/45/18. (b) PM.OS/45/67, C2005/45/18.

surrender. On May 3 Dönitz's Emissary, Admiral von Friedeburg, the new Commander-in-Chief of the German Navy, with a German staff officer, had come to Field-Marshal Montgomery's headquarters with an offer to surrender those German armies which had been fighting the Russians. They also asked to be allowed to send refugees through the British lines. Since they obviously wanted to avoid surrendering to the Russians, Field-Marshal Montgomery refused to discuss a surrender with them. On the following day Admiral von Friedeburg returned with an offer to surrender all the German forces in north-west Germany, and also those in the Netherlands and Denmark. Field-Marshal Montgomery already had authority from General Eisenhower to accept the military surrender of any or all the German forces within his zone of operations. He therefore
(a) accepted the capitulation. On May 5, about 5 p.m., Admiral von Friedeburg came to General Eisenhower's headquarters with an offer to surrender all the remaining German forces on the western front. He was told that General Eisenhower would not discuss a surrender on this basis. He then said that he wished to make a full and complete surrender of all German forces everywhere, but had
(b) no authority to do so. He sent a message to Admiral Dönitz asking
(c) for this authority. On the night of May 6 General Jodl, Chief of the German Armed Forces Staff, arrived at General Eisenhower's headquarters, and, with Admiral von Friedeburg, continued the negotiations. General Eisenhower reported that it was clear from the outset that the Germans were stalling for time in order that they might evacuate the largest possible number of soldiers and civilians from the Russian front to within the British and American lines. They continued their attempt at a separate surrender on the western front, and even said that, whatever General Eisenhower's answer might be, they intended to order all German forces on the western front to cease fire. They asked for a meeting on May 8 for the signature of the surrender terms, and a forty-eight hours' interval thereafter in order to get the instructions to their outlying units. Their actual purpose was to gain time. General Eisenhower finally said to the emissaries that unless they accepted his terms, he would break off negotiations, and seal the western front, i.e. prevent by force any further westward movement by German soldiers or civilians.

The Germans then telegraphed to Admiral Dönitz for authority to make a full and complete surrender, but again wished to stipulate that actual fighting would cease forty-eight hours after the signature of the terms. General Eisenhower refused this proposal, and stated that all fighting would have to cease on both fronts forty-eight hours

(a) SCAF345, C3117/45/18. (b) SCAF347, C3117/45/18.
(c) SCAF354, C3117/45/18.

from midnight on May 6; otherwise he would carry out his threat of sealing the front. In reporting his action General Eisenhower repeated that the Germans were trying to continue to make a front against the Russians as long as possible in order to evacuate the maximum number into our lines. In any event fighting would cease almost at once on the western front since, with minor exceptions, General Eisenhower's troops were on the line which they had been ordered to occupy. General Eisenhower therefore suggested that, if matters went as he had proposed, a proclamation should be made by the Governments announcing Wednesday, May 9, as VE Day, with a statement that fighting had already largely ceased throughout the front, and that, by the terms of the German surrender, hostilities would come to an end formally at 12.1 a.m. on May 9.

Early on May 7 General Eisenhower reported that General Jodl (a) had signed the Act of Military Surrender[1] at midnight (the actual time was 2.41 a.m.) and that the official termination of hostilities would be, as previously stated, at 12.1 a.m. on May 9. General Eisenhower suggested that, if it were thought necessary that the official announcement should be close to the termination of hostilities, the announcement should be made at 3 p.m. on May 8. Since, however, in most cases the orders to troops in enemy commands would go out *en clair*, and since it would be impossible to keep millions of individuals in France and neutral countries from knowing the facts, General Eisenhower suggested that the Governments might announce, as soon as they had agreed upon a time, that Germany had surrendered unconditionally, and that the cessation of hostilities on land, at sea, and in the air would be effected as soon as possible. If this announcement were made on May 7 VE Day might be May 8. In a second telegram General Eisenhower reported that, in addition to the (b) act of military surrender, General Jodl had signed an undertaking that the Chief of the German High Command and the Commanders-in-Chief of the army, navy and air forces would arrive at a place and time designated by himself (General Eisenhower) and the Soviet High Command with plenary powers to execute a formal ratification of the act of unconditional surrender of the German armed forces.

General Eisenhower had notified the Russian High Command on (c) the night of May 5–6 of the presentation to Admiral von Friedeburg of the terms of surrender. He said that Admiral von Friedeburg had

[1] The Instrument which had been prepared by the European Advisory Commission was overlooked in the press of business, and the document signed was one drawn up at General Eisenhower's headquarters. See Robert Murphy, *Diplomat Among Warriors* (New York 1964), pp. 240–1.

(a) SCAF 357–8, C3117/45/18. (b) SCAF359, C3117/45/18.
(c) SCAF348, C3117/45/18.

transmitted the terms to Admiral Dönitz and that a reply was expected on May 6. If Admiral von Friedeburg received authority to sign the act of military surrender, General Eisenhower would accept it, and the Russian representative—General Susloparov—would sign it on behalf of the Russian High Command. General Eisenhower asked whether the Russian High Command (i) wanted to make any addition to or modification of the terms; (ii) wished the formality of signing to be repeated before any other Russian representatives at any other place or (iii) desired to take part in the more formal meeting of ratification which would follow the signature at his headquarters. He asked for an answer as soon as possible in order that he might know the wishes of the Russian High Command before the signature which would probably take place on the morning of May 6.

(a) On May 6 the Russians gave the Allied military representatives in Moscow a note to General Eisenhower in answer to his message of May 5. The note, which was not received in Washington until 1.0 a.m. on May 7, reversed the approval which the Russians had given to the signing of a document of military surrender at General Eisenhower's headquarters. They suggested certain changes in the text, and also wished the formal act of military surrender to be signed in Berlin, with Marshal Zhukov as the Soviet signatory. They also complained that Admiral Dönitz was continuing resistance in the east, and that public opinion would conclude that he had made a separate truce with the western allies and was continuing the war in the east. The Russian note pointed out that such a truce would be
(b) contrary to the agreement made with them. General Eisenhower replied on the morning of May 7 that the Act of Military Surrender had been signed at 2.41 a.m. before the receipt of the Russian message, and that it provided for a more formal signature. He said that he would be glad to come to Berlin for this signature at any time on May 8 convenient to Marshal Zhukov, but that he would like the hour to be as near to noon as possible. He pointed out that the Western Allies had scrupulously adhered to the engagement of no separate truce on their front. When large-scale surrenders of enemy troops began to take place on the flanks of his armies, General Eisenhower had offered to keep pushing on in the right centre until he met the Red Army. He had not continued this movement owing to information from the Russian High Command that the commitment of large forces to the area involved would certainly result in confusion and entanglement. He repeated that the Western Allies had 'consistently refused to discuss a separate truce with anyone', and had 'proceeded exactly in accordance with our understanding

(a) MX24200, C3117/45/18. (b) SCAF361, C3117/45/18.

of Russian desires'. In reporting the Russian note to the United States and British Governments General Eisenhower stated that he must now withdraw his recommendation about a public announcement, since obviously it would be unwise to make any such announcement until the Russians were satisfied. (a)

On May 8 the Russians sent another letter to General Eisenhower for delivery to the United States and British Governments. They stated that they were not convinced that the order of the German High Command on unconditional surrender would be carried out by the German forces on the eastern front. Hence they feared that an announcement 'today' by the Soviet Government on the surrender of Germany would put them in an embarrassing position and mislead public opinion in the Soviet Union. The Soviet High Command therefore wished to wait until the moment when the German surrender went into effect, and thus to postpone the announcement until 7 p.m., Moscow time, on May 9. (b)

The formal Act of Surrender was signed in Berlin between 11.15 and 11.45 p.m. on May 8. General Eisenhower himself did not go to Berlin for the signature.[1] On the Allied side the act was signed by his Deputy Air Chief Marshal Tedder and Marshal Zhukov, with General Spaatz, Commander of the U.S. Strategic Air Forces in Europe, and General de Lattre de Tassigny, representing General de Gaulle as witnesses. The German signatories were Field-Marshal Keitel, Admiral von Friedeburg and General Stumpff. (c)

The Russian demands for delay led to an exchange of messages between the Prime Minister and Stalin over the timing of the announcement of the German unconditional surrender. The Prime Minister sent a message to Stalin on the evening of May 5. He said (d) that President Truman had told him of a message which he (the President) had sent to Stalin asking that the three heads of Governments should announce VE day at the same time. Mr. Churchill said that the best time for this would be noon (British double summer time), but that since this time would be 6 p.m. in Washington, he proposed 3 p.m., which would be 4 p.m. in Moscow and 9 a.m. in (e) Washington. Stalin agreed with the proposed times. At 12.47 a.m. on May 7 the Prime Minister sent another message to Stalin that (f) the President agreed to this hour. The Prime Minister said that Tuesday, May 8, was the 'target day' but he would telegraph on May 7 whether a postponement to May 9 was necessary. After hearing

---

[1] General Eisenhower mentions in his book *Crusade in Europe* (London 1948), p. 467 that he later saw in Moscow a film portraying the Berlin ceremony. No reference was made in the film to the prior surrender at General Eisenhower's headquarters.

(a) FWD20809, C3117/45/18. (b) MX24218, C3117/45/18. (c) C3118/45/18. (d) T779/5, Premier 3/197/7; W6234/341/49. (e) T812/5, Premier 3/197/7; W6348/341. (f) T804/5, Premier 3/197/7; W6233/341/49.

(a) from General Eisenhower of the signature of the Instrument of Surrender President Truman confirmed the hour—9 a.m. Washington time—and day—May 8.

(b) At 1.30 p.m. on May 7, the Prime Minister sent a telegram to Mr. Roberts at Moscow containing a message for Stalin. Mr. Roberts was instructed not to deliver this message until the Prime Minister had heard from the President. The message was to the effect that Stalin would have seen General Eisenhower's telegram on May 7, that it would be impossible to keep the news of the German surrender secret until May 8, and that the announcement should therefore be made at the earliest possible moment. The Prime Minister thought this change of time inevitable. He proposed making the announcement 'today, Monday', at 6 p.m. London time, and hoped that Stalin would find this time (7 p.m. in Moscow) convenient. He added: 'I understand from General Eisenhower that he is arranging with you for the formal signature of the agreement . . . to take place in Berlin on Tuesday.'

(c) The President agreed with this change and so informed the United States Embassy in Moscow, but Mr. Roberts telegraphed from Moscow at 4 p.m. that the Soviet Government had informed the United States Embassy orally that as they had received no information through their own channels about the surrender, they were unable to comment on the Prime Minister's proposal[1] before 7 p.m.

(d) At 4.26 p.m.—before Mr. Roberts's telegram had been received—the Prime Minister sent instructions to him to substitute another message. In this message the Prime Minister said that the German radio had just broadcast an address to the German people by Admiral Dönitz's Foreign Minister, Count Schwerin von Krosigk, that Admiral Dönitz had declared the unconditional surrender of all the German fighting forces. Since the whole world had now been informed of the surrender the Prime Minister proposed to make an announcement at 6 p.m. 'this evening'. He hoped that Stalin would agree that the announcements were necessary, since otherwise it would appear that only the Governments did not know about it. Mr. Roberts was instructed to do everything possible to get an immediate answer before 6 p.m.

(e) At 9.10 p.m. the Prime Minister sent another message through Mr. Roberts to Stalin that in view of the difficulty of concerting an

[1] Mr. Roberts had not as yet communicated the Prime Minister's proposal to Stalin, but it is evident that the latter had heard of it through the message from the President to the United States Embassy.

(a) T808/5, No. 29, Premier 3/197/7; W6348/341/49.
(b) T809/5, Tel. 2468 to Moscow, Premier 3/197/7; W6348/ 341/49.
(c) W6348/341/49. (d) T813A/5, Tel. 2473 to Moscow, Premier 3/197/7; W6348/341/49. (e) T815/5, Tel. 2483 to Moscow, Premier 3/197/7; W6348/341/49.

earlier announcement he had decided with much regret to postpone his broadcast announcement until the time earlier arranged, i.e. May 8, 3 p.m. Meanwhile a statement had been issued to the British press giving the time of the announcement on May 8 and saying that the day would be treated as VE day in Europe, and regarded as a holiday. This statement was necessary on account of the large numbers of work people who had to be considered. The Prime Minister added that he had informed President Truman accordingly.

A telegram from Mr. Roberts was received at 12.20 a.m. on May 8. (a)
He said that the Prime Minister's second message had not reached him until 8 p.m. British time (i.e. 9 p.m. Moscow time). He had then already sent the first message to Stalin. The Soviet Government, however, must have known of the German broadcasts. The Soviet General Staff had now informed the head of the American military mission that they did not consider the fighting on their front to be over, and that they wanted the announcement to be made on May (b)
9. A message from Stalin to this effect was received through the Soviet Embassy on the morning of May 8.[1]

The Prime Minister replied to Stalin that he could not wait until (c)
May 9 before making his announcement. He would also have to inform Parliament of the signature of the Instrument at Rheims and the formal ratification which was taking place in Berlin. He had telephoned to General Eisenhower and had been assured by him of his intention to use all his forces against any fanatical enemy groups who might disobey the orders which they had received from their own Government and High Command. General Eisenhower's instructions would apply to all British troops under his command. The Prime Minister intended to say in his announcement that the Germans were still resisting in some places. In view of the immense length of the front and the disorganised condition of the German Government (*sic*) this fact was not surprising. The Prime Minister believed that the President was making his announcement 'today' at 9 a.m. Washington time. He hoped that Stalin would also be able to make an announcement 'under the necessary reserves'.

The Prime Minister informed the War Cabinet on May 7 of the (d)
signature of the Instrument of Surrender and of the developments, up to the time of the Cabinet meeting, regarding the public announcement. He mentioned General Eisenhower's proposal for an immediate announcement in view of the fact that the German surrender would be generally known. He then referred to Stalin's refusal to change the time and the President's unwillingness to make a

[1] The text was similar to that of the message sent to General Eisenhower. See above, p. 397.

(a) W6348/341/49. (b) T820/5, Premier 3/197/7; W6348/341/49. (c) T823/5, Tel. 2489 to Moscow, Premier 3/197/7; W6348/341/49. (d) WM(45)59; W6347/341/49.

change even though the Germans had announced full details of the surrender and the Columbia Broadcasting Company was sending news of it throughout the world. The Prime Minister had therefore thought it inexpedient to carry out his plan for announcing the news at 6 p.m. He thought it unfortunate that the official announcement should be delayed, and a matter for special regret that the British public should be deprived of the chance of a spontaneous celebration of the victory, but on balance it seemed preferable to avoid the risk of a reproach from Stalin for changing the arrangements previously agreed between the three Powers.

The War Cabinet agreed with this decision, but considered that, since the news had become so widely known on an unofficial basis, some guidance should be given to the public. They agreed therefore to a statement by the Minister of Information that an official announcement would be broadcast by the Prime Minister at 3 p.m. on May 8, and that this day would be treated as 'Victory in Europe Day' and regarded—with May 9—as a holiday. The War Cabinet were also informed that General de Gaulle intended to announce the German surrender in a broadcast at 8 p.m. on May 7. They decided to tell General de Gaulle of the plans for synchronising the official announcement, and to advise him to postpone his broadcast. If he were unwilling to do so, no further pressure could be brought to bear on him.

The Prime Minister then said that, after making his broadcast on May 8 he would go to the House of Commons and ask leave to interrupt the business for the purpose of repeating the announcement in the House. He would thereafter propose an adjournment of the House to St. Margaret's Westminster, for a service of thanksgiving.

CHAPTER LXVIII

The Potsdam Conference (I): the general background: Mr. Byrnes's compromise proposals on the main questions at issue: the Polish problem at the Conference

(i)

Procedure at the Conference:[1] *acceptance of the American proposal for a Council of Foreign Ministers: the deadlock on the main issues at the Conference: changes in the British representation: Mr. Byrnes's compromise proposals.*

THE formal procedure at the Potsdam Conference followed that adopted at Yalta. At the first plenary meeting on July 17, 1945, after President Truman had been invited to take the chair at these meetings,[2] the delegations submitted lists of subjects which they desired to bring forward for discussion. They agreed that the Foreign Secretaries should meet to discuss the lists and to select three or four items for discussion at the next plenary meeting. The Foreign Secretaries were also asked to indicate those items in the lists which called for discussion in the first instance at a plenary meeting, and those which might be remitted at once for examination at their own meetings.

This procedure was continued throughout the Conference; that is to say, the main subjects listed for discussion and the memoranda submitted by the Delegations were examined by the Foreign Secretaries either before or after a preliminary discussion at the plenary sessions, and the Foreign Secretaries prepared the agenda for these

---

[1] For American records of the Potsdam Conference, see *F.R.U.S., 1945, The Conference of Berlin*, 2 vols. 1960. Russian records of the plenary meetings of the Conference are published in *The Teheran, Yalta & Potsdam Conferences* (Eng. trans. Moscow, 1969), 147–316. For Mr. Churchill's attempts to secure a tripartite meeting at an earlier date, and his correspondence on the subject with President Truman, see above, Volume III, pp. 571f.

[2] President Truman appears to have come to the Conference with the hope that he would be able to mediate between the 'special' interests of Great Britain and Russia. He wrote later that he did not underrate the difficulties confronting him as Chairman of the Conference. He would be faced with many problems, and knew that Stalin and Mr. Churchill would have these 'special' interests which might lead to conflict. On meeting Stalin, however, Mr. Truman was impressed by his direct manner and speech, and felt hopeful of reaching an agreement with him which would be satisfactory to the world and to the Western Powers. (See H. S. Truman, *Years of Trial & Hope* (Eng. ed., 1956), 265 & 267.

sessions. There were in all eleven formal meetings of the Foreign Secretaries and thirteen plenary meetings.[1]

Perhaps the most significant question of the period was, however, excluded from this procedure. The atomic bomb was not discussed at a formal meeting of the Potsdam Conference, even though the knowledge that a new dimension in warfare now existed was an unexpressed factor affecting the balance of power at the Conference. Mr. Churchill was informed by Mr. Stimson on July 17 of the successful detonation in New Mexico. The new situation was discussed by Mr. Churchill with Mr. Truman when he lunched with him on July 18[2]. In a brief note for the Cabinet he recorded that they agreed that Stalin should be informed that the Americans had a new form of bomb which was likely to have decisive effects upon Japan.[3] The President accordingly spoke to Stalin after the plenary meeting on July 24 and formed the impression, probably erroneously, that Stalin did not seem to have any conception of what he was talking about.[4]

In the case of the American proposal for a council of Foreign Ministers the procedure worked smoothly. President Truman intro-
(a) duced the proposal at the first plenary session of the conference. The British delegation had agreed to support it, and the Russians had no reason to oppose it since it was for the most part an adaptation of existing machinery and its acceptance did not commit any of the Powers to decisions on policy.

Stalin asked why China was included in a body which was to deal primarily with European questions. He also asked whether the Council would take the place of the European Advisory Commission and of the permanent machinery for regular consultation between the three Great Powers set up at Yalta. President Truman said that he had suggested the inclusion of China because China was a member

[1] Mr. Byrnes called an informal meeting of Foreign Secretaries to discuss German reparation on July 23. After Mr. Eden had left the Conference, and before the arrival of Mr. Bevin, Sir A. Cadogan acted as deputy for the British Foreign Secretary at two meetings of the Foreign Secretaries.

[2] The conversation at this luncheon appears to have been mainly concerned with the
(b) British financial position, Imperial preference, the American tariff, and the question of American bases in British territory, especially in Africa. Churchill, *Second World War*, Volume VI, pp. 546–8.

[3] *Ibid.* pp. 551–4. Mr. Churchill noted that British consent to the use of the atomic bomb had been given on July 4 (see below, p. 524 n.2) and that he never doubted that President Truman was right in deciding to use it. For British official accounts in this connexion see John Ehrman, *Grand Strategy*, Volume VI, pp. 275–313, and Margaret, Gowing, *Britain and Atomic Energy, 1939–45* (London 1964), pp. 370–86.

[4] *F.R.U.S., 1945, The Conference of Berlin*, II 378–9.

(a) F(Terminal) 1st Meeting; P(Terminal)2. Records of Plenary Meetings and Meetings of Foreign Secretaries at the Berlin Conference were classified as P(Terminal) and F(Terminal) respectively, and related memoranda as P(Terminal) Nos. 1–81. These records are contained in the Print '"Terminal", Record of the Proceedings of the Berlin Conference, 17th July to 1st August, 1945' filed as U6197/3628/70. Also included in this Print as an appendix were records of conversations between British and Polish representatives. (b) Premier 3/430.

of the Security Council of the World Organisation. Mr. Churchill also thought it unnecessary to bring China into discussions on the detailed settlements in Europe. He considered that the new Council need not interfere with the work of the European Advisory Commission or with the regular meetings of the Foreign Secretaries. Stalin asked whether any indication could be given of the date of the Peace Conference for which the Council was to make preparations. President Truman said that the Peace Conference should be held 'as soon as it could be held successfully, but not before'.

The proposal was remitted to the Foreign Secretaries for consideration. At their first meeting (July 18) M. Molotov said that there (a) would be no objection to the inclusion of China if the functions of the Council were not limited to European questions. Mr. Byrnes suggested that the Chinese representative might take an active part in the Council's work only when it was discussing 'matters of Asiatic interest or matters of world-wide concern'. The United States Government had proposed the inclusion of China because China was a permanent member of the Security Council of the World Organisation; and because the Council would be available to deal with Far Eastern problems if the war against Japan were to end 'soon'. Mr. Byrnes explained further, in answer to questions, that the United States Government wanted to avoid delay in the preparation of peace treaties and therefore proposed that the Council should be limited to this work and should not be burdened with current problems. Mr. Eden hoped that the Council might take over the tasks assigned at Yalta to the three Foreign Secretaries. Mr. Byrnes said that his proposal did not affect the Yalta decision and that the three Foreign Secretaries would continue to meet for the discussion of problems of common concern. M. Molotov agreed with Mr. Byrnes. Mr. Eden said that he had hoped that the meetings of the three Foreign Secretaries might have become, with the inclusion of France, meetings of four, but that he must accept the views of his two colleagues on this point.

M. Molotov pointed out that the primary tasks of the Council included the preparation of peace treaties with countries with which France had not signed any armistice and that France ought not to participate in the preparation of the treaties. Mr. Byrnes said that the United States Government had not been at war with Finland, but would wish to express views on the Finnish Peace Treaty. There was a case for giving similar weight to French views in the preparation of peace treaties with Roumania, Bulgaria, Hungary and Finland. It was then agreed to draw up a formula ensuring that the peace treaties should be prepared only by representatives of the

(a) F(Terminal) 1st meeting.

States which had signed armistice terms with the countries concerned This formula was subsequently modified to include the participation of France in the preparation of the peace treaty with Italy.

The Foreign Secretaries also agreed that, after the establishment of the Council, the Control Councils for Germany and Austria could take over the remaining tasks of the European Advisory Commission, though Mr. Eden pointed out that a decision to abolish the European Advisory Commission required the consent of the French.

At the consideration of the final draft of the proposal, the Prime (a) Minister suggested that London should be the permanent home of the Secretariat and the place at which the first meeting should be held, though meetings might take place in other capitals from time to time. He said that 'London had been the capital most under fire, and longest in the war. It had claims to be the largest city in the world and one of the oldest, and, moreover, it was more nearly half-way between the United States and Russia than any other place in Europe.' Stalin said that 'this counted more than any other factor'. Mr. Churchill continued that 'it was also London's turn'. Mr. Attlee supported Mr. Churchill's view. Stalin and President Truman accepted the proposals and the Conference agreed that the first meeting of the Council should be held in London on September 1, 1945.

The discussions on the more contentious business of the Conference were much less satisfactory. They ranged from subject to subject because the main issues were so closely connected. The British and Americans refused to consider the question of reparation apart from the immediate problem of finding the Germans in the western zones of occupation sufficient means to live without external (that is to say, British and American) assistance. The settlement of the German–Polish frontier was relevant to these two questions, since the food supplies of the industrial areas were drawn largely from the territory claimed by Poland which the Russians had already handed over to Polish administration. German reparation, again, was an immediate issue to the Russians because they wanted—in their interest—the enforcement in western Germany of the policy of 'stripping bare' which they were applying to the German capital assets in the Soviet zone of occupation. The discussion of an Italian peace treaty and the admission of Italy to the United Nations was widened by the Russians into a general proposal for giving similar treatment to the former satellite States of south-eastern Europe. This proposal in turn had a direct bearing on the American and British demands for a loyal fulfilment by the Russians of the Yalta Declaration on Liberated Europe. The conclusion of treaties with these satellite States would have implied recognition of their Governments, but the Western

(a) P(Terminal) 4th meeting.

Powers, and in particular the Americans, refused such recognition until they were satisfied that the Governments were freely chosen and genuinely independent. The Russians—since it was obvious that they would not allow free elections or genuine independence in the countries concerned—attempted a political counter-attack by complaining of the state of affairs in Greece and by making charges that the Western Allies themselves—and particularly the British—were not fulfilling their engagements.

A meeting between Mr. Churchill and Stalin on the second evening of the Conference showed the general 'offensive-defensive' line which the Russians intended to take. Mr. Churchill dined with Stalin. He has recorded that they 'conversed agreeably from half-past eight in the evening to half-past one next morning without reaching any crucial topic'. The Prime Minister mentioned the (a) Russo-Turkish negotiations. Stalin said that Russia wanted the return of Kars and Ardahan; he gave no details about the Russian requirements in the Straits. Stalin asked for a share in the German fleet. He then spoke of Greek aggression. The Prime Minister replied that the Greeks were greatly alarmed about Yugoslav and Bulgarian intentions, but there had been no serious fighting. He suggested that the Conference should warn the small Powers that frontier changes could be made only at the Peace Conference. The Prime Minister also proposed that the Great Powers should send observers to Athens. Stalin thought that this would show a lack of confidence in the honesty of the Greek people, and that reports from the Ambassadors in Greece would be sufficient.

Stalin said that Russian policy in the countries liberated by the Red Army was directed towards the establishment of strong, independent, sovereign States. He did not want to 'sovietise' the countries. They should have free elections in which all except Fascist parties would take part. He protested against Mr. Churchill's complaints that, instead of the agreed '50-50' arrangement,[1] the Russians had a 99 per cent control of Yugoslavia. He said that he had been 'hurt' by the American demand for a change of Government in Roumania and Bulgaria 'where everything was peaceful'. He denied any intention of advancing westwards, and claimed that Russia was withdrawing troops from the west and demobilising them as rapidly as railway transport allowed.

The Russians were in fact deeply suspicious of British and American action, and ready to misinterpret it at almost every point. Thus during the Conference they complained that 10,000 alleged Soviet (b)

---

[1] See Volume III, pp. 349–51 for the percentage agreements at Moscow in 1944.

(a) Premier 3/430/8. (b) P(Terminal) 6th and 8th meetings; F.O.934/5/42(1), tels. Target 157 and 161, F.O.934/5/42(6), Onward 171 and 205.

citizens who were prisoners of war under British control in Italy were being organised in a division under officers who had served in the German army. In answering this complaint the Prime Minister pointed out that we had just taken about a million prisoners of war in Italy; that there were in fact some 10,000 men in the camp of which the Russians were complaining. Most of these men were non-Soviet Ukrainians; a number were Poles not domiciled within the 1939 Russian frontiers. The Russian Mission in Rome had been given full access to the camp, and were in process of 'sifting' the men. 665 of them wanted to go back to Russia, and their wish would be immediately fulfilled. We would also hand over at once any others who would go without the use of force. The Prime Minister also said that the Russian general upon whose report M. Molotov had based his complaint might well have made enquiries at Field-Marshal Alexander's headquarters.

(a) After this complaint had been disposed of the Russians made another ill-founded assertion that we had not disarmed 400,000 German troops in Norway. The facts were that the 365,000 Germans in Norway had been collected into reservations after VE-day, and disarmed except for the officers and 2 per cent of other ranks who were allowed to retain respectively pistols and rifles with a small quantity of ammunition in order to maintain order and discipline in the camps. 25,000 Germans had already been sent back to the British and American zones of occupation: 150,000 would have gone back by the end of August. 108,000 of the Germans in Norway came from the Russian zone of occupation; these 'Russian-owned' Germans were the most difficult problem. We wanted the Russians to take as many of them as possible without delay directly into their zone.[1]

Meanwhile the Russians themselves had given the Western Powers

---

[1] Other Russian complaints submitted in the form of memoranda were (i) that 'White'
(b) *émigrés* and other Russians or persons hostile to the U.S.S.R. were trying to hinder the
(c) return of Soviet citizens to Russia from Germany and Austria; (ii) that, on instructions from the British Government, the British military authorities in Norway were refusing to hand over to the Soviet repatriation authorities Soviet citizens from the Baltic Republics, the western Ukraine and Byelo-Russia. Similar complaints were made about the detention of Soviet citizens in Great Britain.

(d) The Soviet Delegation also drew up a long memorandum alleging in detail the removal of industrial equipment, etc. and of rolling stock from the Soviet zone by the British and United States armies. The memorandum was largely a counter-charge to the Allied charges that the Soviet authorities were moving very large quantities of machinery etc.
(e) from their zone, and that they had taken equipment from British oil companies in Roumania. Stalin first tried to deny these latter charges and then suggested that the matter might be dealt with through ordinary diplomatic channels, but President Truman pointed out that the United States had an interest in the matter. At the Prime Minister's proposal the question was referred to the Foreign Secretaries. After further discussion agreement (*continued on page* 407)

(a) P(Terminal) 9th meeting; F(Terminal) 10th meeting; P(Terminal) 43 and 64; F.O. 934/5/51(2), tels. Target 238–9, Onward 264. (b) P(Terminal) 44. (c) P(Terminal) 60. (d) P(Terminal) 47 and 60. (e) P(Terminal) 3rd meeting; F(Terminal) 5th and 11th meetings; P(Terminal) 40 and 46.

grounds of complaint over the attitude of the Soviet military commander in Austria. The Foreign Office transmitted to Berlin on July 19 a message of the previous day from General McCreery, (a) Commanding the British Eighth Army, on two meetings between British, American and French representatives and the Russians at Vienna. These meetings were held on July 16. The Russians claimed that the agreements made in the European Advisory Commission for the zones of occupation and machinery of Allied control in Austria had not yet been ratified by the four Governments, and that they had no authority from Moscow to implement them.[1] They could not therefore discuss the occupation of Styria by the Eighth Army or the move of an advance party of the three Allies into Vienna. Although Marshal Koniev had written to General McCreery agreeing to the meeting, and stating his belief that many questions could be settled at it, the Russians also declined to discuss matters such as signal communications, roads, railways, and civilian supplies. On the insistence of the Allied representatives, the Russians referred again to Marshal Koniev. The Marshal agreed to an immediate discussion of the points raised, and good progress was then made.

The Allied representatives left Vienna on July 17. General McCreery reported that the Russians could continue to stall the Allies with regard to a move into Styria and Vienna unless steps were (b) taken at the highest level to ensure the despatch of the necessary instructions to Marshal Koniev from Moscow. The Foreign Office thought that the reason for the deliberate stalling was that the Russians wanted to complete the stripping of Styria before the entry of the Allies. There was circumstantial and reliable evidence of large-scale removals of machinery and industrial equipment from Vienna and Styria, and also of large-scale requisitioning by the Red Army of food stocks, cattle, farm implements, etc. in Styria. In April 1944 we had sent an official letter to M. Vyshinsky to the effect that we were sure of Soviet agreement to our view that 'our common purpose might be prejudiced by unilateral action on the part of any one of the Occupying Powers in regard to the removal of industrial plant and equipment' etc. The Foreign Office thought that attention might be drawn at the Conference to this unilateral action on the part of the Russians, and to the difficulties which it would cause to

---

(*continued*)
was reached that the three Governments should appoint representatives on a commission of investigation. This commission would begin work not later than August 10, and would be given all the necessary facilities for carrying out a full examination in the places concerned.

[1] These arrangements had been delayed by the dispute with the Russians over their action in setting up unilaterally an Austrian Provisional Government (see Volume III, p. 585). The agreements, however, had been completed in the European Advisory Commission on July 4, 1945.

(a) F.O.934/4/25(1), Onward 72. (b) F.O.934/4/25(4), Onward 86.

the Allied Council and in particular to the British Commander-in-Chief. The Prime Minister raised the question in emphatic terms at the plenary session on July 20. Stalin made some complaints—(a) which the Prime Minister at once questioned—about the attitude of Field-Marshal Alexander but said that he had now approved the recommendations of the European Advisory Commission and that the British and American armies could move at once into Vienna and their allotted zones in Austria.

On July 20 the Foreign Office telegraphed that General Mc-(b) Creery foresaw that the Russians would try to place on us—as in the case of Berlin—the responsibility for feeding our sector in Vienna. We could not supply food or fuel, however, except for a short period, without American help. The Foreign Office thought that, in spite of the political importance of maintaining our position in Austria, we might have to consider whether we should give up the occupation of our zone in Vienna, or indeed Styria, unless the Russians would agree that deficiencies of supplies in Austria were to be met from the normal sources. In the case of food supplies for Vienna, these sources were mainly in Lower Austria and the countries of the Danube basin now under Russian control, while the supplies of coal came mainly from Silesia and Poland.

The Prime Minister raised the question at the plenary session on (c) July 23. He pointed out that there were some 500,000 civilians in the British zone of Vienna, and that their supplies of food had always come from the Soviet zone. He therefore proposed that the Soviet army should continue to provide supplies for this population until other arrangements could be worked out. Stalin promised to discuss the matter with Marshal Koniev. On the following day Stalin agreed that the Russians would undertake to provide food for the whole of Vienna from the eastern area until other arrangements had been made.

Against the background of suspicion and bickering over particular questions, and of deep divergence of policy on the largest issues, little progress had been made by July 25 at the plenary sessions, and the reference of the main interlocked questions to the Foreign Ministers resulted merely in a tiresome repetition of the same arguments and the same disagreements. After July 25 the plenary sessions and the meetings of Foreign Ministers were suspended in order to allow Mr. Churchill and Mr. Eden to return for the declaration of the result of the British elections.

Mr. Attlee and his Foreign Secretary, Mr. Ernest Bevin, did not reach Potsdam until the evening of July 28. The change in the

---

(a) P(Terminal) 4th meeting. (b) F.O.934/4/25(5), Onward 112.
(c) P(Terminal) 7th and 8th meetings.

British representation did not mean a break in the continuity of British policy. At the Prime Minister's invitation, Mr. Attlee had attended the earlier meetings of the Conference; he and Mr. Bevin had been members not only of the War Cabinet but of the Armistice and Post-War Committee. They knew the background of the questions in dispute at the Conference and had approved of the general instructions and briefs given to the British Delegation. Sir A. Cadogan was at Potsdam throughout the Conference and was in touch with Mr. Byrnes during the absence of the political chiefs of the British Delegation. He recommended the British acceptance of Mr. Byrnes's proposals for a compromise.

These proposals, which broke the deadlock between the Western Powers and the Russians, were made after Mr. Churchill and Mr. Eden had left Potsdam. They ultimately involved an acceptance in full of the Polish claims to the line of the Oder and the western Neisse. A final settlement was deferred, nominally, until the Peace Conference, but if the Western Powers were willing to give a provisional consent to the claims, they were unlikely to dispute them later. In any case there was evidence during the Conference that M. Mikolajczyk, the former leader of the Polish Government in London, who was now Deputy Prime Minister and Minister of Agriculture in the Polish Provisional Government of National Unity,[1] was already losing the battle with M. Bierut[2] over the freedom of political parties and the holding of free elections in Poland; the Soviet Government, even if their armies and secret police withdrew from the country, would continue to exercise an indirect control, and to prevent the alignment of Poland as a parliamentary democracy with the Western Powers.

On the question of reparation, the Western Powers were in a stronger position, since the Russians wanted to receive large quantities of machinery and plant from the British and American zones, and especially from the Ruhr. The Russians themselves were indifferent to the problem of keeping the Germans in the British and American zones from starvation, although this problem had been greatly aggravated by the mass expulsion—and flight—of Germans from the territory which the Russians had already handed over to the Poles. The Americans, however, remembering the dismal history of reparation after the First World War, were unwilling to put themselves into the position of supplying the Germans (or, for that matter, the Austrians and Italians) with the means of paying reparation to Russia. Even so, the Americans conceded to the Soviet Government

[1] For the formation, on June 21, 1945, of this Government, which was based upon the Soviet-supported Polish Provisional Government which had been set up at Lublin, upon democratic leaders who had remained in Poland and upon representatives of the Polish Government in London, see Volume III, Chapter XLV.

[2] President of the Polish National Council since June 21, 1945.

a larger share of reparation from western Germany than seemed reasonable to the British Government.

Mr. Byrnes included in his compromise proposals a formula to meet the Soviet demands with regard to the satellite States, while reserving the rights of the Western Powers to judge for themselves whether the Governments of these States were satisfactorily constituted. The formula was largely face-saving, or, at best, a means of postponing the real issue between the Russians and the British and Americans, but, as in the case of Poland, the Russians were in possession and, short of the use of force, could not be turned out.

Mr. Byrnes insisted that the terms of his proposed compromise were indivisible. He also said that, if the Russians did not accept them, the United States Delegation would leave the Conference on August 1. The British Ministers were disquieted and uneasy, especially over the concessions to the Poles, but, even if they had thought it possible by resisting longer, to get better terms, and to do more to safeguard the supporters of democracy, in the western sense of the term, in Poland and in the satellite States, they could not hold out against Mr. Byrnes's tactics and against President Truman's wish to close down the conference. Hence a general agreement was reached on July 31, the final details agreed on August 1, and the communiqué on the Conference signed in the early hours of August 2.

(ii)

The Polish western frontier: Foreign Office memorandum of July 12, 1945: Sir A. Clark Kerr's conversations with M. Bierut and M. Mikolajczyk in Warsaw (July 12–14, 1945).

With the conclusion of an agreement between the Communist and non-Communist Poles, and the recognition of the reorganised Polish Government a few days before the assembling of the Potsdam Conference,[1] the three Great Powers had settled, at least formally, the most serious immediate difficulty in the way of their co-operation. They had also removed from the field of their discussions at Potsdam the question of the eastern frontier of Poland. There, is, however, especially from the Polish point of view, an element of tragic irony in the fact that, having given way to one of the partitioning Powers—Russia—in regard to the eastern frontier, the British Government were now concerned with the effect on the other partitioning Power—Germany—of an extension of the Polish frontier in the west.

The Foreign Office had been troubled since the Yalta Conference over the extent of the Polish claims to territorial compensation at

[1] See Volume III, Chapter XLV, section (vii).

German expense and over the Russian action in allowing their puppet Provisional Government to extend Polish administration up to the line of the Oder and the western Neisse. As the Russian armies advanced westwards from the Vistula to the Oder many Germans in the area had left it; the Foreign Office had no means of estimating the numbers either of refugees or of those who had remained. The introduction of a Polish administration obviously affected any later decision by the Peace Conference, since it would be almost impossible to push the Poles back from the western Neisse. The Russians, who had an interest of their own in intensifying Polish-German hatreds, would certainly support the extreme Polish claims to former German territory. Meanwhile the matter gravely affected the problem of supplying the rest of Germany. The area handed over by the Russians to the Poles had been one of the main sources of German grain supplies. The Poles were likely to withhold these supplies, and also to refuse to send coal from Silesia. The Western Allies would thus have to meet the needs of a starving population greatly increased by the number of refugees. The problem would be especially serious in the devastated industrial areas of the Ruhr which were in the zone of British occupation.

On March 23, 1945, Sir A. Clark Kerr had been instructed to (a)
raise the question with the Soviet Government. M. Molotov, in a (b)
letter of April 2, replied that in entrusting to Polish administration the civil administration of former German territory conquered by the Red Army the Soviet Government were not contravening their agreement with the British and United States Governments on the occupation of Germany, and on the control machinery in Germany, and that the organisation of Polish administration in Silesia could not be connected or identified with the question of the future frontiers of Poland.

On May 14, again on instructions from the Foreign Office, Mr. (c)
Roberts sent a letter to M. Vyshinsky taking note of M. Molotov's assurances but drawing attention (i) to the agreement reached in the European Advisory Commission on the occupation of Germany; this agreement created zones in a 'Germany within her frontiers as they were on the 31st December, 1937': (ii) to a further agreement that members of the Control Council would jointly exercise supreme authority on matters affecting Germany as a whole. In view of these agreements the British Government assumed that the Soviet authorities were entrusting the local administration in the areas concerned to Polish officials merely on grounds of convenience; that such officials were the agents of the Soviet Government as the occupying Power and were not responsible to Polish authority; that the

(a) N2620/6/55. (b) N3588, 4098, 4305/6/55; N4700/6/55. (c) N5123, 6122/6/55.

authority of the Control Council would extend to the areas in question within the 1937 frontiers of Germany. Mr. Roberts also asked whether the Soviet Government accepted responsibility for measures enacted by the Polish officials, and whether they agreed that, in view of the Yalta Declaration, none of these measures could be understood as establishing the incorporation of such territory in the Polish State. Finally Mr. Roberts asked what was the position in Danzig and what was the area within the 1937 frontiers in which Polish officials had been entrusted with administrative responsibility.

(a) M. Vyshinsky replied on June 1 that in the Soviet view the supreme authority of the Allies in Germany—i.e. the Control Council—extended over the separate zones of occupation only in respect of questions common to the whole of Germany; the Polish administration in former German territories was operating under the direction of the Polish Provisional Government and was not responsible to the Soviet Government; the activities of the Polish authorities could not be taken as prejudging the question of the frontier. This question
(b) remained for settlement at the Peace Conference. The British Embassy in Moscow, however, reported on July 11 the receipt of a note from the Polish Ambassador setting out in detail the Polish claim to all territories up to the line of the Oder and the western Neisse, including the port of Stettin.

The British Delegation had, therefore, to raise the matter at the Potsdam Conference. The Foreign Office drew up a memorandum
(c) on July 12, as a brief for the Delegation, summing up the arguments for and against reaching an agreement on the frontier question at the Conference. The main conclusions were as follows:

(1) The Poles and Russians had now committed themselves to the Oder-western Neisse line. If we postponed a settlement, we should only be aggravating the difficulties; meanwhile, we should have allowed the Soviet Government to disregard the authority of the Control Council and thereby set a precedent for trouble in other matters.

(2) If we accepted the Polish claims now, such a precipitate concession of the maximum Russian demands would be regarded as a sign of weakness and provoke other demands.

(3) British public opinion was unlikely to give lasting support to a settlement which deprived Germany of about one-fifth of her territory, and over 10,000,000 persons of indisputably German stock. Such a settlement might lead to another war.

(4) The immediate transfer of the territories to Poland would withdraw them from the authority of the Control Council, and from the area of German reparation and supply, including the food supplies of western Germany. Marshal Zhukov had already said at a tripartite

(a) N6328/6/55. (b) N8448/6/55; F.O.934/2/10(32). (c) N8810/6/55.

military meeting in Berlin on July 7, when the question of food and fuel supplies was under discussion, that the territory east of the Oder and Neisse was under Polish control and that Silesia was not available to him for fuel supplies since the eastern frontier of his zone was the Oder and Neisse 'as agreed at the Crimea Conference.'

(5) M. Vyshinsky's assurances were thus of little practical value. In any case he had stated that the Soviet Government had no authority over, or responsibility for the territory under Polish administration. We could not accept the right of the Soviet Government to place a part of their zone outside the authority not only of the Control Council but also of the Soviet Commander-in-Chief. The Soviet Government would certainly object if we or the Americans handed over the Ruhr or the Rhineland to the French on similar conditions.

(6) We should therefore state at the Conference, if the United States Government agreed, that we could not accept the Soviet view of the situation. We ought also to make some positive proposals. We should say that we were willing to reach an understanding with the Soviet Government on a reasonable western frontier for Poland. This frontier would be short of the Polish claims, and should not go beyond Danzig, East Prussia south and west of Königsberg, Oppeln Silesia and the most eastern portion of Pomerania. We would also agree, subject to French concurrence, to the transfer of the territories east of such a frontier to permanent Polish administration subject to ratification at the Peace Conference.

(7) If we failed to persuade the Soviet Government to accept a compromise of this kind we should state that we would consent to the transfer to Polish administration only of such German territories as the four controlling Powers were prepared to allow Poland to acquire permanently. If the Soviet Government nonetheless insisted on handing over parts of Germany to Poland without our consent, and thereby reduced the capacity of Germany as a whole to pay reparation, we should have to insist upon the proportionate reduction of the Russian share of German reparation. If necessary, we should have to tell the Soviet Government that we should not allow them any reparation deliveries from the British and American zones unless these issues were settled to our satisfaction.[1]

The Russian action was so clearly a breach of the Yalta Agreement that the Foreign Office could not feel much confidence—even if there had been no other reason for doubt—in the general intention of the Russians to observe their later promises with regard to Poland. It was impossible to judge whether the moderates—represented generally by M. Mikolajczyk—would be able to hold their own against the Communists, or whether the Russians would loosen

[1] A statement on the lines of this memorandum was also telegraphed to Washington on the night of July 12–13 for the information of the State Department. (a)

(a) N6767/6/55.

their control on the Provisional Government and allow free elections. The Russian behaviour elsewhere did not give much ground for confidence. The Polish situation, however, differed from that of the Balkan countries. There was a stronger body of left-wing but anti-Communist opinion in Poland; the Russians in their own interest might find it desirable to give way—at least to some extent—to this opinion and to the strong pressure of the Western Powers.

A first impression of the new régime came to the Foreign Office (a) from Sir A. Clark Kerr. On July 12 Sir A. Clark Kerr reached Warsaw on his way to the Potsdam Conference. He stayed in Warsaw until July 14, and saw most of the Polish Ministers. Mr. R. M. A. Hankey, His Majesty's Chargé d'Affaires with the Provisional Government, arrived in Warsaw on July 14. Sir A. Clark Kerr was well received by M. Bierut. M. Bierut spoke of the wish of the Polish Government to establish good relations with Great Britain and to maintain the former contacts of Poland with the west. He seemed inclined to accept the suggestion put by Sir A. Clark Kerr (on the confidential advice of M. Romer, Minister for Foreign Affairs in the former Polish Government in London) that leading members of the Polish Government should go to London to try to win over the waverers. M. Osubka Morawski, the Prime Minister, told Sir A. Clark Kerr on the following day that the Provisional Government had considered this suggestion and were proposing to send a representative group of junior Ministers. Sir A. Clark Kerr said he thought that the mission should carry full authority, and that for this purpose, it should include the two Deputy Prime Ministers, MM. Mikolajczyk and Gomulka.

(b) M. Mikolajczyk—who had been much pleased with his own reception in the country—told Sir A. Clark Kerr that Poland was 'in a state of chaos so complete that he was inclined to believe that there had been a brain at work behind it'. The type of official who had formerly administered the country had been drawn mainly from the upper and middle classes—the latter were largely Jews. These classes had practically disappeared, but their disappearance was not enough to account for the chaos. M. Mikolajczyk suspected that the Lublin Government had been trying to 'sovietise' the country. He thought that, although much time had been lost, this danger had now been averted. Thus, the agricultural policy of the Lublin Government had been a complete failure. The new peasant landowners had been unable to hold their own with the established peasants and the Ministry of Agriculture was daily receiving communications such as: 'The acres we have been given are no good to us. Take them back and give us work.'

(a) N8746/211/55; F.O.934/2/10(10), Target 45–6. (b) N8746/211/55; F.O. 934/2/10(10), Target 47.

M. Mikolajczyk said that assurances given to Sir A. Clark Kerr in Moscow by M. Bierut about the widespread release of political prisoners were not being carried out, and that arrests were still being made. He discussed his own position, especially in relation to the Polish secret police working under Russian control. He said that he felt no real uneasiness in the matter but that a settlement would take time. Poland was approaching two uncomfortable and even critical months during which most of the Red Army was to be withdrawn, and after which certain points only would remain in Russian occupation. He expected the N.K.V.D.[1] to go with the army, and once the N.K.V.D. had gone he and the people of Poland would know how to deal with the local secret police.

M. Mikolajczyk was counting on the support of the younger peasants, many of whom were still in hiding. The Peasant Party would probably issue their programme early in the following week; the reaction of the Government to it would be a test whether the expression of party opinion was to be free. After the issue of the programme the party would start its own newspaper. This would be a further test, since at present the Polish press was—with two exceptions—not free. The Communist Party wanted to put off the elections in the hope of gaining strength during the period of delay. M. Mikolajczyk himself thought that the best time for the elections would be at Christmas or early in the New Year. He was anxious to see the return in time for them of large numbers of Poles from the west, and especially from Great Britain. Although the Government professed also to hold this view, they were in fact in no hurry to facilitate their return. M. Mikolajczyk said that the harvest promised well, but might be lost owing to the pillaging of the countryside by the troops of the Red Army who were taking away every machine and every animal within their reach. On the high roads over which the Russians were withdrawing the peasants were escaping to the woods and leaving their villages to be pillaged. These facts were causing great anxiety, but there was some hope of improvement after the arrival of Marshal Rokossovsky.[2]

M. Mikolajczyk said that the most useful contribution from Great Britain would be an immediate suggestion for a Trade Agreement and the provision of technical advisers. If possible, some British firms should offer help, on a commercial basis, in the rebuilding of Warsaw, and thus give a start to the recovery of Polish private enterprise. The Government had been planning to restrict reconstruction work to State enterprises, but were now giving way to popular demand, though, obviously, some kind of general control would be necessary.

[1] i.e. the Russian Secret Police.
[2] Poland was included in the area of Marshal Rokossovsky's command.

(a) Sir A. Clark Kerr asked M. Morawski about the intentions of the Government with regard to political prisoners. After saying at first that the matter was a domestic question, M. Morawski explained that many prisoners had already been released and that towards the end of August the Government proposed to introduce a bill providing for an amnesty; this bill would exclude only collaborators, that is to say, Poles who had registered themselves during the occupation as *Volksdeutsche.*

(iii)

Refusal of Mr. Churchill and Mr. Eden to agree to the extension of Polish administration to the Oder and western Neisse (July 17–22, 1945).

(b) Mr. Churchill introduced the subject of Poland at the first plenary meeting of the Potsdam Conference on July 17. He said that there had recently been a substantial improvement in the Polish situation, but that various aspects of the problem ought to be discussed—e.g. the holding of free elections at an early date, the winding up of the former Polish Government in London, and the future treatment of the Poles who had fought with the United Nations under the protection of the British Government and from a base in the United Kingdom.

(c) On the following day the Conference began a discussion of the problems connected with the liquidation of the Polish Government in London. Stalin handed in a draft statement to the effect that the British and American Governments, and the Governments of the other United Nations should sever all relations with 'the Government of Arzishevsky'; that all the property and assets of this Government should be transferred at once to the Provisional Polish Government of National Unity, and that all the Polish armed forces and merchant navy should be subordinated to the latter Government. The Prime Minister pointed out that the burden of the matter lay on Great Britain since we had sheltered the Poles since their homeland had been overrun and they had been driven from France. The Polish Government in exile had very little property. The Central Bank of Poland had frozen assets in London and Canada of some £20,000,000 but this sum was not in the possession of the Polish Government in London. We had provided the Polish Government with some £120,000,000. Since the recognition of the new Provisional Government we had arranged to pay three months' salary to the employees of the former Government; after the expiry of this period they would be dismissed.

(a) N8746/211/55; F.O.934/2/10(10), Target 49.
(b) P(Terminal) 1st meeting. (c) P(Terminal) 2nd meeting.

We had also to consider the liquidation or transfer to Poland of the Polish forces which had fought with us. These forces—amounting to 180–200,000 men—had fought with great bravery and good discipline. They were now in a state of grave mental and moral distress. Their proper treatment was a matter affecting the honour of the British Government. These men had taken an oath of loyalty to President Raczkiewicz whom we had now ceased to recognise. Our policy was to persuade as many as possible of the soldiers and of the civilian employees of the Government to go back to Poland. We had been disturbed by the allegations of General Anders, the Polish former Supreme Commander, that if they went back they would be sent to Siberia. We had taken disciplinary action against General Anders and would not allow him to make such prejudicial statements to his troops, but the Prime Minister himself had said in the House of Commons that if there were any Polish soldiers who did not want to return to Poland, we would keep them in Great Britain. He hoped that, with the continued improvements in Poland, the majority would wish to return.

The Prime Minister suggested that the meeting should discuss this aspect of the question but Stalin—without commenting on the Prime Minister's statement—asked whether he had read the Soviet draft statement. Mr. Churchill proposed that the draft should be submitted for discussion by the three Foreign Secretaries. It was also agreed to submit to the Foreign Ministers the question of elections in Poland.

At the meeting of the Foreign Secretaries on July 19 Mr. Eden (a)
proposed a revised draft of the statement on Poland in the following terms:

'(1) We have taken note with pleasure of the agreement reached amongst representative Poles from Poland and abroad which has made possible the formation, in accordance with the decisions reached at the Crimea Conference, of a Polish Provisional Government of National Unity recognised by the Three Powers. The establishment by the British and United States Governments of diplomatic relations with the Polish Provisional Government has resulted in the withdrawal of their recognition from the former Polish Government in London, which no longer exists.

(2) The British and United States Governments express their willingness to discuss with properly accredited representatives of the Polish Provisional Government the orderly transfer to it of Polish State property, including the Polish Embassies in London and Washington, in regard to which measures of conservation have been taken by the two Governments. They assume that such discussions would embrace also the questions of the acknowledgement by the

(a) F(Terminal) 2nd meeting.

Polish Provisional Government of liability for the credits advanced to the late Polish Government and other outstanding debts, and the relation of such advances to any assets of the Polish State available abroad.

(3) The Three Powers are anxious to assist the Polish Provisional Government in facilitating the return to Poland as soon as practicable of all Poles abroad who wish to go, including members of the Polish Armed Forces and Merchant Marine. It is their desire that as many of these Poles as possible should return home, and they consider that the Polish Provisional Government could itself greatly assist in this regard by giving specific undertakings that those Poles who return will do so with full assurance of their personal security, freedom and livelihood.

(4) The Three Powers note that the Polish Provisional Government is pledged to the holding of free and unfettered elections as soon as possible on the basis of universal suffrage and secret ballot, in which all democratic and anti-Nazi parties shall have the right to take part and to put forward candidates. It is the confident hope of the Three Powers that the elections will be so organised as to enable all sections of Polish opinion to express their views freely, and thus play their full part in the restoration of the country's political life. The Three Powers will further expect that representatives of the Allied Press shall enjoy full freedom to report to the world upon developments in Poland before and during the elections.'

There was sufficient agreement upon this draft to allow it to be referred to a drafting committee, but M. Molotov objected to the suggestion that the Polish Provisional Government should 'acknowledge' liability for credits advanced to the former Polish Government. Mr. Eden explained that we did not ask that the new Government should accept liability before any discussion; he agreed to a change of wording. M. Molotov also said that the Polish Government could not guarantee a 'livelihood' to all Poles returning to Poland. Mr. Eden agreed to withdraw this term, and suggested the addition of words to show that there should be no discrimination between Poles returning to Poland and their fellow-citizens already in the country.

(a) The drafting committee reported to a meeting of the Foreign Secretaries on July 21. In the discussions the Russians again defended the interests of the Polish Provisional Government on all points and tried to cut out of the draft, or to qualify, any references to the conduct of elections or the freedom of the press in Poland. They wanted to omit from the draft all reference to the liability of the Polish Provisional Government for the credits advanced to the late Government and the relation of such advances to the assets of the Polish State abroad. Mr. Byrnes and Mr. Eden pointed out that it was

(a) P(Terminal) 17; F(Terminal) 4th meeting.

impossible to refer only to the assets of the Polish Government and not to its liabilities. M. Molotov would not give way; the matter was therefore referred to a plenary session.

The Russians then objected to a statement in the draft that the Polish Government might assist in the return of Poles abroad by giving suitable assurances and to the use of the word 'pledge' with regard to the holding of elections. The Russian view was that the Polish Government had already accepted the decisions of the Crimea Conference that a pledge should be given, and that the three Powers had only to note this acceptance. The Russians also objected to a phrase that all sections of Polish opinion should be enabled to express their views freely and that representatives of the Allied Press should enjoy full freedom to report upon developments in Poland before and during the elections. The Soviet Government could not allow freedom to Fascist or Nazi organisations; they also considered that the freedom of the press in Poland was already covered by a general agreement of the Conference that wide facilities for press representatives should be provided in all countries of eastern Europe.

The draft was submitted to the fifth plenary meeting of the Con- (a)
ference on July 21. The Russians then accepted an American redraft of the clause regarding the assets and liabilities of the Polish Government. Mr. Eden had already agreed to modify the sentence about the assurances which the Polish Government might give to facilitate the return of as many Poles as possible to Poland. After some discussion in which the Russians tried to maintain that the references to the freedom of the press were an unnecessary slur on the Polish Government and that there was complete freedom of the press in the country, a compromise sentence was accepted. The statement in its final form was embodied in the Protocol of the (b)
Conference.[1]

The questions of the western frontier of Poland and of the Russian action in admitting the Poles to the western Neisse were also discussed at this meeting of the Conference. The Soviet Government had submitted on July 20 a memorandum stating that they recog- (c)
nised it as necessary and equitable to fix the frontier along the line of the western Neisse and the Oder to the sea west of Swinemünde and including Stettin in Poland. The Polish Government themselves had put forward a claim to this frontier, and M. Molotov had written a letter to Mr. Eden on July 20 enclosing a message from MM. Bierut and Morawski to the effect that only this boundary line could be considered a just frontier guaranteeing 'successful development

---

[1] See below, pp. 438–9.

(a) P(Terminal) 5th meeting. (b) P(Terminal) 23.
(c) P(Terminal) 12; N9026/6/55; F.O.934/2/10(38), Target 154.

to the Polish nation, security to Europe, and a lasting peace to the world'.

(a) When the discussion opened on July 21 President Truman said that according to the agreement reached at Yalta the final delimitation of the western frontier of Poland would await the Peace Conference. It had also been agreed at the present Conference that the 1937 frontiers of Germany should be taken as a starting point. The three Powers had agreed upon the boundaries of their respective zones of occupation in Germany. The United States and British Government had moved their troops back in an orderly fashion to their own zones, but the Soviet Government, without consulting the other two Governments, appeared to have given a zone to the Poles. The President thought that this action should have been agreed beforehand between the three Governments. The question of reparation, and other matters affecting Germany, could not be settled until it was made clear that the part of the Soviet zone occupied by Poland was a part of Germany.

Stalin said that at the Yalta Conference the three Heads of Government had decided that Poland should receive accessions of territory in the north and west, that at the appropriate time the opinion of the Polish Provisional Government should be obtained on the size of the accessions, but that the final settlement should be put off until the Peace Conference. The Polish Government had now expressed their view and the Soviet Government proposed that the Conference should state an opinion in sympathy with the Polish proposals, though the final settlement would not take place until the Peace Conference. Stalin argued that the Soviet Government had not given Poland a zone of occupation without agreeing it with the other two Governments. The Soviet Government had not been able to accept the British and American proposals that Polish administration should not be admitted into 'western Poland' until the frontier problem had been settled. The German population in these areas had retreated with the German armies, and the Polish population alone had remained. The Soviet armies needed a local administration in their rear areas; they were readier to admit the Polish Government and administration since they felt sure that Poland would secure an accession of territory to the west of her former frontier.

The President repeated his statement that the frontier question could not be settled until the Peace Conference, and that if Germany were not occupied in accordance with the agreed zones there would be difficulties over reparations. Meanwhile he would not object to the use by the Soviet Government of a Polish administration in the

(a) P(Terminal) 5th meeting; U5639/3628/70; F.O.934/3/18(b), Target 156.

Soviet zone of occupation. The Prime Minister, however, doubted whether the boundary line could in fact remain unsettled, since the matter seriously affected the question of food supplies. If the Polish demands, which the Soviet Government were supporting, were accepted in full, one quarter of the arable land within the 1937 frontiers of Germany would be alienated, and some 8¼–9 million Germans would have to be moved into the territory remaining to Germany. Mr. Churchill disputed Stalin's assertion that all the Germans in the area had left it.

Stalin again said that there were no Germans in the territory between the Oder and the Vistula and that it would be unlikely that the Poles working the land would have them back. The Prime Minister replied that he was deeply concerned to support compensation for Poland, at the expense of Germany, for the territory she was losing to the east of the Curzon line but the Poles were now claiming far more than they were giving up. The transfer of some 3–4 million Germans to make room for the Poles who were to be moved from the east of the Curzon line would cause a great shock to the British people; the movement of 8¼ million would be more than he could defend. If the Germans had run away from the territory in question, they should be allowed to go back. Furthermore the Poles had no right to follow a policy which might well involve a catastrophe in the feeding of Germany. The British Government, which had the responsibility for feeding the vast population of the Ruhr, could not agree that this population should be deprived of the sources of supply upon which they had previously depended; hence we could not allow territory in the east of Germany which had been overrun by the war to be regarded as having become Polish territory. We stood on the general principle that the supplies of food and fuel available from the Germany of the 1937 frontiers should be available to the whole of the German people within these frontiers, irrespective of the particular zone in which they lived.

The Prime Minister reminded Stalin of his statement at the previous meeting[1] that we should not allow our policy to be governed by memories or by feelings of retribution. Stalin said that his statement did not apply to war criminals. The Prime Minister answered that not all of the 8¼ million Germans who had fled from eastern Germany were war criminals. After further inconclusive discussion in which Mr. Churchill supported Mr. Attlee's view, Stalin said that it was impossible to compel the Poles to produce bread and give it to the Germans and the position could not be changed, since it was a result not of deliberate policy but of the course of events, for which the Germans themselves were to blame. After President Truman

---

[1] See below, p. 472.

had refused to agree that parts of eastern Germany should be detached from the rest of the country in matters concerned with reparation and supplies, the discussion was adjourned.

(a) The discussion was resumed at the plenary meeting on July 22. Stalin again proposed that the Polish demand should be accepted. Mr. Churchill repeated the reasons which he had already given to explain why the British Government could not accept the demand: (i) the final decision on all boundary questions could be reached only at the Peace Conference; (ii) it would not be advantageous for the Polish nation to take over so large an area as they were asking for; (iii) acceptance of the Polish demands would break the economic unity of Germany and put too heavy a burden on the Powers occupying the Western Zones, particularly in the supply of food and fuel; (iv) we had grave moral scruples about vast movements of population, and could not accept a transfer of 8–9 million Germans; the British and Soviet Governments did not agree upon the numbers of Germans still remaining in the territory.

During the discussion Stalin suggested that representatives of the Polish Provisional Government might come to the Conference to state their views or that the Council of Foreign Ministers to be set up in London should invite the attendance of Polish representatives. President Truman accepted the latter proposal, and argued that there was no reason for haste. The Prime Minister, on the other hand, repeated his view that the matter was urgent. There was no point in the Poles going to London if the Conference had been unable to agree. Meanwhile the food and fuel problems would remain, and the burden would fall particularly on the British. The Prime Minister put forward a possible compromise that the Polish authorities might extend their occupation, as Poles, up to a certain line, and that west of this line they would act as agents of the Soviet Government in accordance with the agreement already reached on the occupation of Germany. The Conference, after further discussion in which no new arguments were brought forward, finally agreed to invite the attendance of Polish representatives.

(iv)

The Polish Delegation at the Conference: Mr. Churchill's and Mr. Eden's conversations with the Polish delegates: Mr. Hankey's report of July 23 from Warsaw (July 23–5, 1945).

The Polish Delegation—which was larger than the British representatives had expected—included M. Bierut and M. Mikolajczyk.

(a) P(Terminal) 6th meeting.

On July 24, M. Mikolajczyk gave Mr. D. Allen, on the British Delegation, a note summing up his reasons why the Polish frontier question should be settled at once. These reasons were as follows: (a)

(i) The Polish population east of the Curzon Line must be encouraged to return to Poland and move into the western territory.

(ii) The Polish population of this western territory must be repatriated at once. The date of the election was contingent on their return.

(iii) If these movements of population were delayed until a later fixing of the frontiers, the Soviet Armies would remain in control and Poland would have no chance of directing her national economy within the area of the entire State. Partial elections would cover only a small portion of the State.

(iv) This state of affairs would not only overthrow 'the State system of economy', but would 'render impossible any normalisation of conditions in the country, which might prejudice the question of the State's independence or of its system'.

(v) The lack of opportunity for transfer to the west from the overcrowded districts of central Poland was leading to the parcellation of farm holdings and large estates, and preventing an agricultural recovery.

(vi) If Poland did not take over these territories soon there would be no point in a later occupation of these derelict areas.

The Polish delegation was invited to state its case at the meeting of Foreign Ministers on the morning of July 24. They were strongly supported by M. Molotov (although the matter was not being argued before the meeting) who claimed that the Soviet Government had a special responsibility in the matter. Mr. Eden pointed out that the British Commonwealth had declared war on Germany in 1939 on behalf of Poland. Mr. Eden, however, did not restate the British views on the Polish demands but—correctly—left discussion to the plenary session later in the day. (b)

At the plenary meeting in the afternoon of July 24 Mr. Byrnes, who had taken the chair at the meeting of Foreign Secretaries, summed up the Polish arguments as follows: (i) Poland would lose 180,000 square kilometres of territory in the east, and should receive some compensation in the west. (ii) The territory under consideration was a single economic unit. (iii) Poland would receive less territory than she was giving up; the total area of the Polish State would be reduced from 388,000 to 309,000 square kilometres and the population from 34 to 26 million, though it would be more homogeneous. (iv) The 1–1½ million Germans left in the area would (c)

(a) N9609/6/55; F.O.934/2/10(60). (b) F(Terminal) 7th meeting.
(c) P(Terminal) 8th meeting.

probably be willing to leave it. The acquisition of the territory would enable Poland not only to support her own population, but also to employ those Poles who had formerly been in the habit of going every year to work in Germany. (v) From the point of view of security the proposed frontier provided the shortest and most defensible line. (vi) Germany had tried to destroy the Polish nation and to ruin Polish culture. It would be an expression of justice to compensate Poland in this way. (vii) Poland had ceded territory in the east for the sake of preserving peace. It would be right for Germany to cede territory in the east which had been a fortress of German aggression. (viii) The transfer of territory would reduce German capacity for war production, and leave Poland without any national minorities. (ix) Before the war Poland had an excess of rural population. The new territory would provide employment for this population in Poland and thus allow the return of Poles who had been forced to emigrate. (x) The area had been one of the bases of the German armament industry. It contained an important coal basin and large supplies of zinc, and had been one of the centres of German imperialism. (xi) German transit trade before the war had been very large; great quantities of goods had been transported across Germany from Czechoslovakia, Hungary, Roumania and Yugoslavia. The natural route for these goods was through Stettin, but the Germans had sent them through Hamburg. With Stettin in Polish control, the natural route would be used. (xii) The whole Oder basin—i.e. including the western Neisse—was necessary to Poland in order to enable her to control its water resources, since the river was not naturally navigable. (xiii) Even with the transfer of territory Poland would still lose 20 per cent of her pre-war territory while Germany would lose only 18 per cent. Finally, the Polish representatives asked for a speedy decision in order to promote the return from abroad of the Poles whose work was necessary for the rebuilding of Poland.

The Conference decided to adjourn until a later meeting the discussion of the Polish claim. The Prime Minister also said that he
(a) intended to see M. Bierut. Mr. Churchill and Mr. Eden had in fact received the Polish Delegation before the Plenary Session. They had explained the British doubts whether Poland could absorb such large territories, and had also pointed out our difficulties in relation to the supply of food to Germany. They warned the Poles not to repeat in the west the mistake which they had made after the last war in pressing too far to the east. M. Bierut in reply merely brought forward the arguments which he had mentioned already at the meeting with the Foreign Ministers. Mr. Churchill also appealed to the Poles

(a) Terminal, Appendix; N9389, 9536/6/55.

to allow full freedom for Polish political parties and for the Allied press in Poland before and after the elections. Later on July 24 Mr. Eden had a long talk with M. Bierut, M. Mikolajczyk and two other members of the Polish Delegation. M. Bierut again summarised the Polish case on the frontier question, and showed no sign of modifying his claims. On the question of freedom for the political parties M. Bierut argued unconvincingly that everything would be well. He said that all parties—of which there were twenty-three—would be able to take part in the elections if they had not supported the Fascists and Hitlerites; the Government were merely trying to consolidate this large number of parties into a few large groups. He also said that if the great Allies carried their interest in Polish affairs to the extent of bringing pressure to bear on the Poles, they would be encroaching on Polish sovereignty. He claimed that British press correspondents who had visited Poland were satisfied with the conditions in which they worked, and that foreign correspondents in Poland had the same privileges as Polish correspondents in other countries. Mr. Eden then mentioned a report in *The Times* of July 24 that 300 trials were taking place in Poland, and that 6,000 more were pending. M. Bierut doubted whether this number was greater in proportion to the population than in other liberated countries. He said that traitors must be punished. At a session of the Polish National Council on July 22 a resolution had been passed to introduce a bill for a general amnesty; many people had been released earlier. Other resolutions provided for the cancellation of wartime restrictions, such as the existing state of emergency.

On the morning of July 25 the Prime Minister saw M. Bierut alone. He said again that our only wish was to see Poland strong and prosperous, and that for this reason we were greatly interested in the holding of free elections, the restoration of normal civil liberties, the independence of the law courts, as opposed to the tendency towards police government developing in the Balkans. The Poles abroad would be encouraged to return. M. Bierut said that the policy of the Polish Provisional Government inclined not towards a Communist or sovietised Poland, but towards the forms of democratic political life current in western Europe. The Poles were not in favour of police régimes; 99 per cent of them were Catholic. M. Bierut repeated that all Polish parties other than those of active collaborationists would be free to take part in the elections; he suggested that the elections would probably be even more 'democratic' than those in England. Mr. Churchill said that M. Bierut had asked that the Great Powers should not stand in the way of Poland's development, and that this question was closely linked with the frontier problem. We were not standing in the way, but the frontier question was tangled up with the problems of reparation and supply. We had been ready to support Polish claims up to the Oder at some points but not along its whole length. The Poles were now asking for too much. 'In consequence there might be failure to reach agreement. We and the Americans might pursue one policy on our side and the Russians another. That would have serious consequences.'

(a) At the plenary meeting of July 25 the Prime Minister mentioned his own and Mr. Eden's discussions with the Poles. He said that the question of the Polish western frontier could not be settled without taking into account the large number—about 1½ million—of Germans whom M. Bierut admitted to be still in the area, and without reference to the question of reparations, occupation zones, etc. which were still undecided.

President Truman agreed with the Prime Minister. He said that he and Mr. Byrnes had also seen the Poles and that Mr. Byrnes was to have further conversations with them. The best course therefore was to postpone a discussion until the next plenary meeting. Meanwhile, if Poland were to become a fifth occupying Power, the position must be regularised, and the Polish Government made properly responsible for the area under their occupation, while the final delimitation of frontiers must be left for settlement at the Peace Conference. The President stated that a Peace Treaty with the United States could be ratified only with the consent and advice of the Senate: that the Polish question was of particular interest to American public opinion, and that any decision on this question must be one which he could honestly recommend to the Senate and which the Senate would be likely to accept.

The Prime Minister then spoke of the importance of a settlement of the Polish question, and of other matters bound up with it (such as reparation and the feeding of Germany) from the point of view of the success of the Conference. The Conference would have failed if Poland were allowed to assume the position of a fifth occupying Power without any arrangements for sharing the food produced in Germany equally over the whole German population, and without agreement on a reparation plan or a definition of war booty. The Prime Minister hoped that a broad agreement might be reached on 'this network of problems lying at the very heart of their work'. So far, however, they had made no progress towards such an agreement.

Stalin said that the question of obtaining for the rest of Germany supplies of coal and metals from the Ruhr was even more important than the question of food supplies. The Prime Minister replied that supplies from the Ruhr for the Russian zone of Germany or for Poland would have to be bartered against food from these areas. He could not accept a position whereby the Soviet Government had the

---

(a) P(Terminal) 9th meeting.

right to dispose unconditionally of all supplies in the Russian zone, and to the east of it, and at the same time to share in the products from other zones. After more discussion on the usual lines the Conference again adjourned a decision.

Meanwhile on the night of July 24–5 the Foreign Office forwarded (a) to Mr. Eden a telegram of July 23 from Mr. Hankey at Warsaw.[1] Mr. Hankey had attended meetings of the Polish National Home Council on July 21 and 22 and a public demonstration on July 22. The proceedings did not strike him favourably. The names of the new members of the Council,—and especially those of MM. Mikolajczyk, Grabski, Witos, and Zulawski who had not been members of the Lublin Government, were greeted with acclamation, but M. Witos was not present and everyone knew that he had not yet accepted office. M. Mikolajczyk did not take the oath and did not speak because M. Bierut had refused to accept any of his nominations from the Peasant Party to the National Home Council. The Prime Minister received a vote of confidence by a perfunctory show of hands before anyone had been allowed to comment on his speech. The Council was 'not a people's democratic assembly but a voting machine carefully parked on them'. The public demonstration consisted almost entirely of Communists 'with a carefully arranged *claque* of speaking choruses'. Mr. Hankey's general conclusion was that at present things were 'moving in the wrong direction'.

Mr. Eden's comment—'This is bad'—in sending the telegram to the Prime Minister was the last of his notes on the Polish question. He went back to England with the Prime Minister in the afternoon of July 25. On the following day the Government resigned as a result of the General Election.

M. Mikolajczyk, accompanied by Sir A. Clark Kerr, also saw Mr. (b) Eden alone on the morning of July 25. He described as 'all nonsense' M. Bierut's talk about the twenty-three political parties in Poland and much of his comment on the freedom to be allowed to the expression of opinion at the elections. M. Mikolajczyk said that the position had changed markedly for the worse during the last ten days; M. Bierut had gone back on many of his undertakings, and was clearly aiming at the establishment of a one-party system. M. Mikolajczyk thought that the Communists would not get more than one per cent of the vote in a free election, owing to the popular hatred of the Government and the N.K.V.D.

After Mr. Eden had left for a meeting M. Mikolajczyk continued the conversation with Sir A. Clark Kerr. The latter summed up

[1] It is uncertain whether Mr. Eden read this telegram from the Foreign Office before the plenary meeting on July 25. The Prime Minister does not seem to have read it before he saw M. Bierut.

(a) N9107/6/55. (b) N9720/6/55.

M. Mikolajczyk's views as follows: Poland would be able to establish her independence only if the elections were held without delay; the holding of elections depended upon the fixing of the frontiers and the withdrawal of the Red Army from Polish territory. M. Mikolajczyk argued in favour of the full Polish claim to the western Neisse frontier. He said that Poland could fill the areas for which she asked. Two out of the eight million inhabitants were already Polish; one million could be made up of the migrant agricultural labourers from Poland; four million would consist of the population of the area taken over in the east by Russia. There was also a surplus population in central Poland.

(v)

Conversations between Mr. Attlee and Mr. Bevin and the Polish delegates: M. Bierut's assurances to Mr. Bevin: acceptance by Mr. Attlee and Mr. Bevin of the American proposal that the Conference should agree to the extension of Polish administration to the Oder and the western Neisse: Protocol of the Conference (July 28–August 1, 1945).

Mr. Attlee and Mr. Bevin reached Berlin in time to visit first the American and then the Russian leaders[1] before a plenary session of the Conference was held in the late evening of July 28. The Polish question was not discussed at this meeting. A plenary session arranged for July 29 had to be postponed until July 31 owing to the illness of Stalin.[2] No meeting of the Foreign Secretaries was held on July 29.

(a) Mr. Attlee and Mr. Bevin were given on their arrival a note by Sir A. Cadogan on the outstanding problems of the Conference.[3] This note mentioned the compromise proposals which Mr. Byrnes was intending to put forward, and which included the acceptance

[1] No record of these meetings has been traced in the British archives. For American accounts of the former, see *F.R.U.S., 1945, The Conference of Berlin, II*, pp. 458–9. According to the account by Mr. Byrnes there cited, when President Truman explained the proposed new boundaries of Poland 'Mr. Bevin immediately and forcefully presented his strong opposition'. Sir A. Cadogan recorded in his diary that Stalin 'was interested to know how to account for the election result. He asked whether it meant that the British were tired of the Japanese war?' (*The Diaries of Sir Alexander Cadogan*, p. 776). M. Mikolajczyk in a memorandum recounting a party given by Stalin for the Polish ministers on July 27, says that Stalin said to him (apropos of the change of government in Great Britain) that 'Churchill did not trust us, and, in consequence, we did not fully trust him'. *F.R.U.S., 1945 The Conference of Berlin* II, 531.

[2] There is no evidence in the British archives to show whether Stalin's illness (a cold) was genuine or whether it was a diplomatic move to gain time in the hope either that the Poles would convince Mr. Attlee and Mr. Bevin or that the Americans—in view of President Truman's desire to bring the Conference to an end and to return to the United States—would be persuaded to suggest a compromise which would give M. Bierut and the Russians what they wanted. Stalin invited M. Bierut to see him on the evening of July 29.

[3] See below, pp. 449–50.

(a) F.O.934/2/8(19).

of the Polish administration of the areas claimed by them pending a final arrangement of the frontier at the Peace Conference. Sir A. Cadogan considered that the British Delegation would be wise to accept the compromise proposals as a whole.

Mr. Attlee and Mr. Bevin discussed Mr. Byrnes's proposals at a meeting with the staff of the British Delegation on the morning of Sunday, July 29. Mr. Bevin thought that a concession on the frontier question might be used as an opportunity for a general settlement of problems raised at the Conference. We might try to get a provisional agreement on the western frontier which would enable us to secure the withdrawal of Soviet troops and the holding of elections and also the provision of supplies for Germany and Western Europe from the enlarged territory of Poland during the next three years or so. As part of the general understanding, we would ourselves promise to try to get early elections in Greece and Italy. We could then press for similar elections in the satellite states. Mr. Bevin said that, if such a general agreement could be reached, he would be prepared to make some concession on reparation—e.g. an offer, possibly up to 20 per cent, of 'once for all' deliveries from the Ruhr to Russia. (a)

Mr. Bevin said that he would have preferred the western frontier of Poland to follow a line running to the east of the Oder and along the eastern Neisse. Sir A. Cadogan said that the Americans were thinking in terms of a line along the Oder which would leave Stettin to the Poles, and would then follow the eastern Neisse. The Americans would resist Polish claims to territory west of the eastern Neisse and, if their proposed line were accepted, they would favour the immediate holding of elections in the territory ceded to Poland.

Sir A. Clark Kerr said that the Russians and the Poles would press strongly for the western Neisse. He thought that there was much to be said for accepting this claim now as part of a general settlement, since we should otherwise be forced into acquiescing in it as a *fait accompli* after it had been brought about by unilateral Soviet action. Mr. Attlee pointed out that there was a difference between accepting a *fait accompli* and becoming accessories before the fact. The general view, however, was that we should do better to make the concession as part of a general settlement. We might avoid taking a definite decision between the eastern and western Neisse by asking for a report by experts, or we might decide provisionally in favour of the western Neisse on the understanding that the matter remained open to review in the light of a report by experts. The suggestion of a special enquiry would also allow time for public opinion in Great Britain to become accustomed to the idea of allowing Poland so large an addition of territory in the west.

Mr. Bevin said that, while he would still prefer to be left free to

(a) F.O.934/2/8(15).

choose between the eastern and western Neisse, he would like to know what the Soviet Government would concede in return for a full recognition of the Polish claim. He proposed that he and Mr. Attlee should see Stalin and M. Molotov before putting forward any proposals at a plenary meeting. If the Russians understood that we were prepared to make a general settlement, they might be more accommodating on some of the points to which we attached importance. Sir A. Cadogan thought that it might be better first to approach President Truman. Mr. Attlee said that he and Mr. Bevin would see the President and Mr. Byrnes during the course of the day and would explain to them what the British Delegation had in mind; subject to this interview they would then make a separate approach to Stalin.

(a) In the afternoon of July 29 Mr. Attlee and Mr. Bevin met the Polish Delegation. The Poles repeated their case for the proposed frontier, with M. Mikolajczyk explaining in particular that homes had to be found for the four million Poles from east of the Curzon Line, and that if Poland was to make her proper contribution to the needs of Europe, agriculture and industry in the new territories must be brought into production as soon as possible. Only the Poles could undertake these tasks.

Mr. Bevin asked that British representatives should be able to investigate the situation on the spot, and pointed out that the British Government was being asked in fact to settle Poland's territorial status now. Both he and Mr. Attlee expressed concern about the movements of population and Mr. Bevin made plain the British preference for a boundary on the eastern Neisse. In this context Mr. Bevin put to the Poles questions about the date of, and the participants in, the elections in Poland, about the withdrawal of Soviet troops, and about the willingness of Poland to assist in supplying the rest of Europe and Germany in particular.

Mr. Bierut replied that elections could be held within a few months of the definition of the frontiers, and that all groups of Poles with a programme could participate. Soviet troops, he said, were already withdrawing. M. Mikolajczyk said that the Poles would have no export surplus from the next harvest, but that in their own interest they would want to do all they could in the matter of coal and industrial products.[1]

(b) At a second meeting on the morning of July 30 Mr. Attlee and

[1] Following this meeting Mr. Attlee and Mr. Bevin held a meeting with Mr. Truman and Mr. Byrnes. No official records of this meeting have been traced but Mr. Truman has stated that the British leaders were informed of the suggestion previously made to him by M. Molotov that the U.S.S.R. should be formally requested by her Allies to enter the war against Japan (cited *F.R.U.S., 1945, The Conference of Berlin,* II, 476–7). No records of any British interview on July 29 with Stalin and M. Molotov have been traced in British archives.

(a) Terminal, Appendix; N9539/6/55. (b) Terminal, Appendix; N9608/6/55.

Mr. Bevin closely questioned M. Bierut on the position of the political parties in Poland, the freedom which they would enjoy during the elections and the procedure and date of the elections. M. Bierut gave assurances on the points raised though he admitted that the National Council would have power to exclude from the elections parties of which it did not approve. He explained that the date of the elections was related to the problem of repatriating the several million Poles still abroad. Mr. Bevin asked whether the Provisional Government could not give an assurance that the elections would be held, at the latest, by February 1946. M. Bierut said that the date could be fixed only by the competent Polish authorities, and that the Polish Government could not accept commitments in the matter, particularly when it might be felt that these commitments were being forced upon the Polish nation from outside. The Polish nation was conscious of having reached political maturity and would not accept any foreign guarantee of its political rights.

Mr. Attlee asked M. Bierut what provision would be made for the Polish troops returning to Poland. M. Bierut answered that 'both the men and the officers would be welcomed back' and that no distinction would be made between those who had served Poland at home and those who had fought abroad. All Polish troops and workers abroad would be given protection and facilities for finding work and land on equal terms with all other Polish citizens. M. Bierut also repeated the assurance which he had given to Mr. Eden that British press correspondents in Poland would in general be granted the same treatment as Polish correspondents in British territory. In answer to a question he confirmed that freedom of religion existed and would be maintained in Poland. (a)

On the morning of July 30, 1945, Mr. Bevin also had a conversation with M. Mikolajczyk in which the latter explained his fears about the situation in Poland.[1] The only British record of this conversation is in a note to Mr. Bevin from Sir A. Clark Kerr evidently recording a further conversation that afternoon with M. Mikolajczyk, who recapitulated that, in the hurry of the morning conversation he had been trying to tell Mr. Bevin that his chief preoccupation was to secure the independence of Poland, which he felt to be in doubt, but even so still within reach if something like the following conditions were secured: (i) The Soviet army would have to be withdrawn. This withdrawal was in progress, and was to be completed within

[1] The time of this conversation is uncertain. There is no record stating whether it took place before or after the meeting between Mr. Attlee and Mr. Bevin and the Polish representatives at 11.30 a.m. on July 30, but it would appear (from M. Mikolajczyk's later reference to Sir A. Clark Kerr to the conversations of 11.30 a.m.) to have taken place before 11.30 a.m. Otherwise M. Mikolajczyk would probably have warned Mr. Bevin against accepting M. Bierut's statements about free elections.

(a) N9659/6/55. 'Terminal', Appendix.

the next two months except at certain points designed to safeguard the Russian lines of communication. (ii) The N.K.V.D. must also leave Poland. M. Mikolajczyk hoped that they would go with the army. The Polish people would know how to deal with the Polish version of the N.K.V.D. which the Russians had set up in Poland. (iii) There must be 'free and unfettered elections'. This freedom could be achieved only by the unrestricted expression of opinion by all political parties—i.e. political manifestos and party newspapers and by Allied supervision of the elections. (Sir A. Clark Kerr thought that we should not be able to secure supervision because M. Molotov would reject it as wounding to Polish pride.) (iv) We must agree to the Polish territorial claim. M. Mikolajczyk said that he must have land to offer the four million Poles now east of the Curzon line in order to tempt them to come into Poland. An arrangement had been reached with the Russians whereby Poles wishing to opt for Poland had to do so by January 1, 1946. These people were still doubtful whether it was worth their while to move into Poland. A second reason for granting the full territorial claim was that, unless the region between the eastern and western Neisse were in Polish hands, the Germans would retain control of the waters of the Oder, and would be able to make the river unnavigable. M. Mikolajczyk suggested that in time these regions would be able to contribute to the supply of food and coal to Germany, but that meanwhile the stripping of factories must stop. He also emphasised that the Communists would use our hesitation over meeting the Polish territorial claims as evidence that all good things in Poland came from Russia while we and the Americans were unsympathetic and niggardly. This propaganda would help M. Bierut and his associates to bring back into the arms of Russia a Poland which he (M. Mikolajczyk) was trying to turn to the West. But whatever we did, the Russians would see to it that the Poles got the western Neisse, and the credit would go to them.

In his minute on this conversation Sir A. Clark Kerr repeated his view that we ought to maintain the impression that M. Mikolajczyk had our confidence. Such strength as he had—and it was still by no means negligible—rested in the belief of his Communist colleagues that the British Government was wholly behind him. During the afternoon conversation M. Mikolajczyk told Sir A. Clark Kerr that M. Bierut's remarks on the institutional position and freedom of elections during the conversation of the morning of July 30 with Mr. Attlee and Mr. Bevin was largely nonsense, and a deliberate attempt to deceive them. M. Mikolajczyk therefore hoped that Mr. Attlee and Mr. Bevin would take another opportunity to put to M. Bierut some of the searching questions which he had had to answer in the conversation. M. Bierut, on his way home, had complained bitterly of our 'intolerable interference in the internal affairs of Poland', and had rejected the argument that the interest of the British Government was justified by the pledges undertaken as a result of the Yalta Conference.

On the evening of July 30 Sir O. Sargent telegraphed to Sir A. Cadogan that it appeared from M. Mikolajczyk's statements to Mr. Eden and Sir A. Clark Kerr on July 25 that the struggle between him (M. Mikolajczyk) and the Communists had already reached a crucial stage. Our friends in Poland were likely to be defeated unless we could secure proper opportunities for M. Mikolajczyk and M. Popiel[1] to organise their parties, secure that the National Council accepted M. Mikolajczyk's candidates, and prevent the Praesidium from becoming a super-Government. From what M. Mikolajczyk had said to Mr. Eden, M. Bierut's promises and talk about twenty-three political parties and freedom of expression at the elections seemed to be worth nothing. (a)

We ought therefore to get at Potsdam, if there were still time, formal assurances of a satisfactory kind from the Poles in full conference, and undertakings from the Russians about the withdrawal of the Red Army and N.K.V.D. from Poland. Furthermore, we and the Americans should have some sanction to apply if those assurances were not fulfilled. The Foreign Office did not know how it was proposed to leave the question of the western frontier of Poland at the end of the conference. They suggested that, if we were prepared to do anything for the Poles in the matter, we should use our concession as a sanction, i.e. we should withhold the fulfilment of anything we were prepared to do pending the carrying out to our satisfaction of the assurances we required. As an alternative we might link with the carrying out of these assurances our attitude on the questions of the Polish armed forces and merchant marine, the return of refugees, reparation, and indeed everything which we should have to discuss, sooner or later, with the Warsaw Government.

The Foreign Office had not enough knowledge of the state of the negotiations to say whether these suggestions were practicable; they did not even know whether the Poles were still at Potsdam. Sir O. Sargent, however, was sending the telegram because he had read the report of the interview between Mr. Attlee and Mr. Bevin, and the Poles on the afternoon of July 29. On the question of political freedom in Poland, M. Bierut seemed 'only to have repeated the same sort of stuff as he had said to Mr. Churchill and Mr. Eden'.

Mr. Byrnes put forward his proposals at a meeting of the Foreign (b)

---

[1] Leader of the Christian Democrat Party in Poland.

(a) N9539/6/55. (b) F (Terminal) 10th meeting; U5870/3628/70; F.O.934/2/10(9), Target 305.F.O.934/4/22(16), Target 308.

Secretaries in the afternoon of July 30 before the British Delegation had formally agreed to them, and apparently without telling the Delegation in advance that he was intending to state them at this meeting. He proposed that agreement should be reached concurrently on the three main outstanding questions relating to German reparations, admissions to the United Nations and the western frontier of Poland. On this latter question the United States Delegation was prepared to admit administration by the Poles of the area claimed by them pending a final delimitation of the frontier at the Peace Conference. This involved a 'sacrifice of the views of the United States Delegation' but he was willing to agree if all three questions were settled at once. Mr. Bevin pointed out that the British Delegation had not yet agreed to the American proposals regarding the Polish western frontier or to those regarding reparation.

(a) Mr. Bevin saw M. Mikolajczyk again on the morning of July 31.[1] Mr. Bevin said that he understood his difficulties, and wished him to understand the difficulties with which he (Mr. Bevin) was faced. The Labour Party had always held that the Polish frontier should not go beyond the eastern Neisse. If he (Mr. Bevin) and the Prime Minister were to agree to anything more than this, they must have in return satisfactory assurances about internal conditions in Poland. Mr. Bevin gave M. Mikolajczyk a paper containing five points, and asked him to urge the Polish Delegation to return helpful replies. The paper ran as follows:

'Before they express a final opinion in regard to the claim of the Polish Provisional Government to a frontier on the western Neisse and the Oder including Stettin, the British Delegation desire to receive satisfactory assurances from the Polish Delegation on the following points:

1. What measures do the Polish Provisional Government propose to take to carry out the decision of the Crimea Conference, which has been accepted by the Polish Provisional Government, in regard to the holding of free and unfettered elections as soon as possible on a basis of universal suffrage and secret ballot, in which all democratic and anti-Nazi parties shall have the right to take part and to put forward candidates?

2. Will there be freedom of the press in Poland and will foreign correspondents be permitted to enter and to move freely in whatever territories may be transferred to Polish administration and to send

---

[1] The Polish question was not discussed at a meeting of the British Delegation on July
(b) 30. At a meeting of the Delegation in the morning of July 31, Mr. Bevin said that, although the United States Delegation had announced that they would accept the whole Polish claim, the British Delegation had not yet assented to it. Mr. Bevin hoped that we might still secure further assurances from the Poles, especially with regard to the holding of elections. We had made it clear that our assent to the Polish claims would be easier if we had satisfactory assurances on the matter.

(a) Terminal, Appendix. (b) F.O.934/2/8(18).

out uncensored news concerning developments in Poland before and during the elections?

3. Will there be freedom of religion throughout all territories under Polish administration?

4. Amongst the Poles in the West there is an absence of confidence in the new Government. It is important that confidence should be established. Will the Polish Provisional Government issue a public declaration in such terms as to reassure these Poles and to encourage them to return? Such a declaration should make it clear that members of the Polish armed forces under British command who wish to do so will return to Poland with the same rights as those enjoyed by the Polish forces now serving in Poland. Similarly, it should be made clear that all Poles who return to the new western territories transferred to Polish administration will be given the same opportunities for finding homes and work as Poles in pre-war Polish territory.

5. Will the Polish Provisional Government do all in their power to facilitate the early establishment of a British military air service between London and Warsaw via Berlin to enable His Majesty's Government to maintain regular official communication with His Majesty's Embassy at Warsaw?

The attitude of the British Delegation towards the proposal of the Polish Provisional Government that the present Conference should endorse the transfer to Polish administration of all German territory up to the line of the Oder and the western Neisse will be influenced by the nature of the replies received to the above questions.'

At 2.45 p.m. on July 31 Mr. Bevin again saw the Polish Delegation. (a)
He said that the Polish claims raised new problems upon which the British Delegation had had no opportunity of consulting the recently formed British Government. Hence they must satisfy themselves that they could justify their action to British public opinion and that they had taken all precautions to make sure of the conditions in the new Poland that they were helping to create. He had therefore submitted certain questions to M. Mikolajczyk not with any idea of interfering with Polish sovereignty, but in order to ascertain how the Polish Provisional Government intended to carry out the Yalta decisions if the British Government supported their claims. Mr. Bevin wanted to be able to give Parliament a satisfactory indication of the attitude of the Polish Government on the points which he had raised. He therefore hoped that the Polish Delegation would give short and direct answers to his questions.

M. Bierut said that he had already given broad and exhaustive answers to these questions at previous meetings. In reply to a comment from Mr. Bevin that the answers had been evasive and

(a) Terminal, Appendix; N9922/6/55.

indefinite, M. Bierut said that he would reply in writing if Mr. Bevin wished him to do so, but that all the members of the Polish Delegation agreed with the positive answers which he had already given. The policy of the Polish Government was to hold elections as soon as possible, but their attitude on this question could not be considered as a concession to the point of view of another Government.

Mr. Bevin asked M. Bierut to be frank. He was not himself in the habit of evading the issue. The position was that, if the Polish Delegation wanted the vote of the British Delegation in support of their proposals, they must give a definite answer to our question 'what will happen to the people who live in the territories transferred to Polish administration?' British opinion would ask this question. The British Government were not making any demands; they were giving something away, and were entitled to have an answer. Could not the Polish Delegation, in reply to Point 1, give an assurance that, subject to the withdrawal of Soviet troops, and the speeding up of the repatriation of Poles abroad, the Polish Provisional Government would make every effort to hold free elections early in 1946?

M. Bierut said that elections in accordance with the Yalta declaration would be held after a provisional settlement of the frontier question had been reached and as soon as repatriation had been completed. The Polish Government would try to make a declaration to this effect. Mr. Bevin said that he had not consulted the American or Soviet Delegations on the matter because he regarded Poland as a Sovereign State. He wished, however, to be able to tell Parliament that the Polish Delegation had given him an assurance that they would hold elections under the 1921 Constitution, and would, if it lay within their power, aim at carrying through these elections in the early part of 1946. Meanwhile the Polish Provisional Government, in conjunction with their Allies, would do all they could to secure the fullest repatriation of Poles abroad. The precise date of the election would be affected by the date of the withdrawal of Soviet troops from territory under Polish administration.

M. Bierut repeated that the whole Polish Delegation, which represented the three most important parties in the Government Coalition and spoke for the Polish Government and nation, were agreed in their intention to see elections held within the shortest possible time. Mr. Bevin replied that he must be able to give some indication of the date. Otherwise the British Government and Parliament would feel that the matter was being put off indefinitely. M. Bierut said that in any case the elections would take place early in 1946, and possibly sooner. He agreed that a statement might be made to the effect that the elections would be held as early as possible, and not later than the early part of 1946.

On Point 2 M. Bierut complained at first that it would be difficult for him to give an assurance which might enable foreign countries to send unlimited numbers of press correspondents to Poland. Mr. Bevin said that he was asking only for the normal facilities. M. Bierut finally agreed that this question might be answered in the affirmative.

Point 3 was also answered in the affirmative. M. Bierut said that freedom of religion already existed in Poland.

On Point 4 M. Bierut pointed out that a declaration on the lines desired had already been made by the Polish Prime Minister in a recent statement before the Polish National Council. He undertook to see that a further statement was made in order that the intentions of the Polish Provisional Government might be placed beyond doubt. Mr. Bevin said that he would like to ask—as a suggestion and not as a condition—whether the Polish Government, after a provisional frontier settlement had been reached, would not send representatives to make personal contact with the Poles abroad and seek to remove their fears about conditions in Poland. M. Bierut agreed to this suggestion.

On Point 5 M. Bierut said that he had spoken to the Soviet Delegation about the proposed British air service to Warsaw; they had stated that the matter must be taken up with them by the British Delegation.

Mr. Bevin said in conclusion that, on the strength of the assurances received from the Polish Delegation and in the belief that the Polish Government would give effect to them, and in the spirit of friendship which he hoped would animate future Anglo-Polish relations, he was ready, if the American and Soviet Delegations also agreed, to support the claim of the Polish Provisional Government to a provisional frontier on the Oder and the western Neisse. He proposed, in informing the Conference of his agreement, to refer to the assurances which he had received from the Polish Delegation. M. Bierut agreed to this.

At the plenary meeting of the Conference, at 4 p.m. on July 31, (a)
after agreement had been reached on Soviet reparation claims to assets in the Western Zones of Germany,[1] Mr. Bevin asked three questions about the American proposal that, pending the final (b)
delimitation of Poland's western frontiers at the Peace Conference, Poland should administer the territories east of the Oder and the western Neisse, which should not be considered as part of the Soviet zone of occupation in Germany. He wished to know whether the administration of this territory,[2] which was within the Soviet Zone,

---

[1] See below, pp. 454–5.

[2] Mr. Bevin also said that his instructions were to stand out for the eastern Neisse: *F.R.U.S. 1945, The Conference of Berlin*, II, 518.

(a) P(Terminal) 11th meeting. (b) P(Terminal) 70.

could be handed over entirely to the Polish Provisional Government, whether all Soviet troops would be withdrawn from this area, and what assurances would be given that the Polish Government would carry out their undertakings. He then recapitulated the assurances he had received from M. Bierut. Mr. Bevin did not press the point that the Soviet transfer to Poland of part of its zone of occupation in effect removed this area from the jurisdiction of the Control Council, and accepted Stalin's reply that this transfer was a special case because Poland's western boundary could not be settled in advance of the Peace Treaty. Stalin further replied that all Russian troops would be withdrawn from the area except those required to protect the lines of communication to Germany. The Conference then accepted the American proposal.

The Protocol of the Conference contained the following summary of the agreed policy of the three Powers with regard to Poland:

'A. Declaration

We have taken note with pleasure of the agreement reached among representative Poles from Poland and abroad which has made possible the formation, in accordance with the decisions reached at the Crimea Conference, of a Polish Provisional Government of National Unity recognised by the Three Powers. The establishment by the British and United States Governments of diplomatic relations with the Polish Provisional Government of National Unity has resulted in the withdrawal of their recognition from the former Polish Government in London, which no longer exists.

The British and United States Governments have taken measures to protect the interests of the Polish Provisional Government of National Unity, as the recognised Government of the Polish State, in the property belonging to the Polish State located in their territories and under their control, whatever the form of this property may be. They have further taken measures to prevent alienation to third parties of such property. All proper facilities will be given to the Polish Provisional Government of National Unity for the exercise of the ordinary legal remedies for the recovery of any property belonging to the Polish State which may have been wrongfully alienated.

The Three Powers are anxious to assist the Polish Provisional Government of National Unity in facilitating the return to Poland as soon as practicable of all Poles abroad who wish to go, including members of the Polish armed forces and the merchant marine. They expect that those Poles who return home shall be accorded personal and property rights on the same basis as all Polish citizens.

The Three Powers note that the Polish Provisional Government of National Unity in accordance with the decisions of the Crimea Conference has agreed to the holding of free and unfettered elections as soon as possible on the basis of universal suffrage and secret ballot in which all democratic and anti-Nazi parties shall have the right to take part and to put forward candidates; and that representatives of the Allied Press shall enjoy full freedom to report to the world upon developments in Poland before and during the elections.

B. Western Frontier of Poland

In conformity with the agreement on Poland reached at the Crimea Conference the three Heads of Government have sought the opinion of the Polish Provisional Government of National Unity in regard to the accession of territory in the north and west which Poland should receive. The President of the National Council of Poland and members of the Polish Provisional Government of National Unity have been received at the Conference and have fully presented their views. The three Heads of Government reaffirm their opinion that the final delimitation of the western frontier of Poland should await the peace settlement.

The three Heads of Government agree that, pending the final determination of Poland's western frontier, the former German territories east of a line running from the Baltic Sea immediately west of Swinemünde, and thence along the Oder River to the confluence of the western Neisse River and along the western Neisse to the Czechoslovak frontier, including that portion of East Prussia not placed under the administration of the Union of Soviet Socialist Republics in accordance with the understanding reached at this conference and including the area of the former free city of Danzig, shall be under the administration of the Polish State and for such purposes should not be considered as part of the Soviet zone of occupation in Germany.'

On August 1 Sir A. Clark Kerr gave M. Bierut a message of good-will from Mr. Bevin and explained that he (Mr. Bevin) counted confidently on the faithful fulfilment of the assurances given to him on July 31. M. Bierut expressed his own joy and the gratitude the Poles felt for all that Great Britain had done for Poland. He said that the new Polish Government would make every effort to maintain the closest and friendliest relations—diplomatic, cultural, and economic—with Great Britain. He knew that some mistrust was felt of his Government, but hoped that it would soon pass. Sir A. Clark Kerr reminded him that there were ways in which the Polish Government could help in dispelling the mistrust. (a)

M. Bierut then said that President Truman had told him of the decision taken by the Conference on July 31 about the western frontiers of Poland. He expressed the warm thanks of the Polish Government for this 'happy solution' of Poland's difficulties.

(a) Terminal, Appendix.

CHAPTER LXIX

The Potsdam Conference (II): the treatment of Germany: acceptance of Mr. Byrnes's compromise over reparation: the status of Italy: the question of the recognition of the governments of the satellite states: Anglo-American complaints about the non-fulfilment of the Yalta declaration on liberated Europe: Russian counter-charges: Russian demands with regard to Turkey

(i)

Discussion of political and economic principles governing the initial period of control: German reparation: British and American opposition to the Russian claims.

APART from the question of the Polish western frontier, the main issues at the Potsdam Conference concerned the treatment of Germany. At an early stage in the Conference the United States Delegation took the initiative in bringing forward comprehensive proposals on the subject. The Delegation circulated a
(a) memorandum containing a draft of a proposed agreement on the political and economic principles which should govern Allied action in the initial control period and proposals for German reparation.
(b) The Conference accepted on July 19, 1945, the main political principles set out in the American draft. In the text as approved the purposes of the Allied occupation were described as, primarily, the complete disarmament and demilitarisation of Germany and the elimination or control of all German industry which could be used for military production. The Allies also wished to convince the German people that they had suffered a total military defeat and could not escape responsibility for the destruction which they had brought upon themselves owing to 'their own ruthless warfare and the fanatical Nazi resistance', to destroy the National Socialist Party and to ensure that the Party and its organisation and activities were not revived in any form, and to prepare for the eventual reconstruction of German political life on a democratic basis and for the

(a) P(Terminal) 3 and 6. (b) P(Terminal) 3rd meeting; P(Terminal) 7.

eventual peaceful co-operation of Germany 'in international life'. All Nazi laws which provided the basis of the Hitler régime or established discrimination on grounds of race, creed or political opinion were to be abolished. War criminals should be brought to judgment. All members of the Nazi Party who had been more than nominal participants in its activities, and all persons hostile to Allied purposes should be removed from public or semi-public office and from positions of responsibility in important private undertakings, and should be 'replaced by persons who, by their political and moral qualities, are deemed capable of assisting in developing genuinely democratic institutions in Germany'. German education should be 'so controlled as completely to eliminate Nazi and militarist doctrines and to make possible the successful development of democratic ideas'. The judicial system should also be reorganised in accordance with the principles of democracy.

The administration of affairs in Germany should be 'directed development of local responsibility'. To this end

> (i) local government should be restored on 'democratic principles and in particular through elective councils as rapidly as is consistent with military security and the purposes of military occupation: (ii) all democratic political parties with right of assembly and of public discussion shall be allowed and encouraged throughout Germany: (iii) representative and elective principles shall be introduced into regional, provincial, and state (*Land*) administration as rapidly as may be justified by the successful application of these principles in local self-government; (iv) for the time being no central German Government shall be established.'

Subject, again, to military security, freedom of speech, press, and religion would be permitted, religious institutions would be respected, and the formation of free trade unions permitted.

At a later stage in the Conference—on July 24—the British Delegation with American support, suggested two additions to this (a) statement on political principles. They proposed that so far as was practicable there should be uniformity of treatment of the civilian population throughout Germany, and that, subject to normal regulations, there should be free circulation of the nationals of the Powers represented on the Control Council in all zones by land and air. Representatives of the two Delegations had made these proposals on the Economic Committee, but the Soviet representative had regarded them as political matters.

When the Foreign Ministers discussed the proposals on July 30, M. Molotov put forward a third addition, that assistance would be (b)

(a) P(Terminal) 39. (b) F(Terminal) 10th meeting.

given 'to the establishment of a central German administration composed of secretaries for respective branches of administration—in the first instance of central administrative institutions for foreign trade, industry, finance, transport and communications'. The central German administration should act under the direction of the Control Council and it would be their task to co-ordinate the activities of the Provincial Governments in order to ensure the fulfilment of the decisions of the Control Council and 'the exercise of functions connected with the solving of problems of an all-German character'.

The Conference accepted the first British proposal, and agreed to invite the Control Council to consider the second proposal and report upon it to the Council of Foreign Ministers in September. The British Delegation thought that the Russian proposal was too
(a) detailed. At the Plenary meeting on July 31 Mr. Bevin suggested that the relevant paragraph in the statement of principles should read: 'For the time being no central German Government shall be established. Notwithstanding this, however, certain essential central German administrative departments, headed by State Secretaries, shall be established, particularly in the fields of finance, transport, communications, foreign trade and industry. Such departments will act under the direction of the Control Council.' The Conference accepted this wording. The statement on political principles was agreed without much difficulty since it dealt only with the immediate and initial period of control and did not touch the more contentious question of the German frontiers or the ultimate constitution of the German State or States. The consideration of economic problems was much more difficult.

(b) At the first meeting of Foreign Ministers (July 18) Mr. Byrnes suggested the appointment of a committee to survey the economic problems of Germany and—significantly—'to define the issues on which agreement could not be reached among members of the
(c) Delegation staffs'. The Economic Committee produced a first report on July 20. Here also they were agreed on most of the general economic principles suggested in the American memorandum. These suggestions were that the Controlling Powers should (i) prohibit the manufacture of armaments, munitions, all types of aircraft and sea-going ships, and control all production directly necessary to a war economy; (ii) decentralise the German economy for the purpose of eliminating the existing excessive concentration of economic power in cartels, syndicates, trusts, etc. (iii) emphasise primarily the development of agriculture and peaceful domestic industries; (iv) treat Germany as a single economic unit; (v) impose Allied control to the extent necessary to (*a*) carry out programmes of

(a) P(Terminal) 11th meeting. (b) F(Terminal) 1st meeting. (c) P(Terminal) 15.

industrial disarmament and demilitarisation, reparation, and approved exports and imports; (*b*) assure production adequate to the needs of the occupying forces and displaced persons in Germany and to maintain average living standards not exceeding the average of the standards of living of European countries (excluding the United Kingdom and the U.S.S.R.); (*c*) secure the equitable distribution of essential commodities between the several zones in Germany in order to produce a balanced economy and reduce the need for imports; (*d*) prevent Germany from developing a war potential; (*e*) control all German research institutions connected with economic activities.

The British and American representatives also proposed, under heading (v) (c) that, in the absence of special reasons to the contrary, each of the zones of occupation, including the Greater Berlin area, should draw its supplies from the areas in Germany on which it had drawn before the war. The Conference had already discussed—at the second plenary meeting—what was meant by the term 'Germany'. The British and American view was that the Germany of 1937 should be taken as the basis of discussion. Stalin had agreed, after suggesting that the territory lost by Germany in 1945 should be deducted from the 'Germany of 1937'.

The Soviet representative on the Committee, however, refused to accept the British and American proposal with regard to supplies until the Conference had taken a decision on the future boundaries of Germany. In other words, the Soviet Government wished to exclude the area which they had already handed over to Polish administration,[1] whereas the British and American proposal would have included all territory which had been German in 1937 whether or not it was administered by or ceded to another State in 1945. This question was linked with the larger question of priority for reparation payments or for payment—by German exports—for necessary imports. The American memorandum on reparation had included a reference to the failure of the Moscow Commission on Reparations to reach agreement on the final words[2] of a 'principle' to the effect that 'after payment of reparations, enough resources must be left to enable the German people to subsist without external assistance. In working out the economic balance of Germany, the necessary means must be provided for payment of imports approved by the Governments concerned *before reparation deliveries are made from current production or from stocks of goods.*

The memorandum stated that the United States Delegation fully concurred in this principle, and must insist that the necessary approved imports into Germany should be a first charge against

---

[1] See above, pp. 410–13 ff.

[2] i.e. the words italicised in the text.

exports from Germany of current production and stocks of goods. Otherwise the Allies would either be repeating their mistakes at the end of the first World War or be unable to bring about the desired industrial disarmament of Germany.

The Economic Committee considered that this question related both to the general economic principles and to reparation. They were unable to agree upon it. The British and United States representatives recommended the adoption of the following text as an economic principle:

> 'The Control Council shall formulate as soon as possible a programme of minimum required imports for Germany as a whole. Such a programme shall include provision for equitable inter-zonal distribution of supplies available within Germany, so as to minimise the net deficit for, and imports into, Germany as a whole. Responsibility for the procurement and financing of approved imports for Germany as a whole shall be shared on a basis to be negotiated in the Control Council. Reimbursement for all the net advances made for approved imports into Germany shall be a first charge against the proceeds of both exports of capital equipment, and of current production and stocks from Germany.'

The Soviet representatives on the committee would not accept this clause. They held—as before—that reparation deliveries should have priority and that imports into Germany should, if necessary, be confined to the amount which could be paid for by exports from Germany after reparation schedules had been met.

Apart from these more fundamental differences the Committee submitted the formula for allocation of reparations between the three Great Powers and for meeting the claims of other Powers agreed by the Moscow Commission on Reparations, namely 56 per cent for the U.S.S.R. and 22 per cent each for the United Kingdom and the United States with proportional relinquishment to meet the other Powers' claims.[1] The Committee also agreed on certain principles of reparation which had been proposed by the Allied Commission and repeated in the American memorandum: (i) removals of property would be directed primarily to the elimination of the 'war-making power of Germany'. (ii) reparation should be such as would 'speed recovery and reconstruction' in countries devastated by Germans; (iii) for the purposes of making a reparation plan Germany would be treated as a single economic unit; (iv) reparation payments should not involve external financial assistance or prejudice 'the successful execution of the task entrusted to the Armies of Occupation'. (v) Reparation should be taken, as far as possible, from the existing wealth of Germany. Claims might be stated, for

---

[1] See above pp. 336–7.

convenience, in money, but—in contrast to reparation after World War I—reparation would be 'assessed and exacted in kind in the form of things such as plants, machines, equipment, stocks, foreign investments, etc.' (vi) 'In order to avoid building up German industrial capacity and disturbing the long-term stability of the economies of the United Nations, long-run payment of reparations in the form of manufactured products shall be restricted to a minimum.' (vii) 'In justice to those countries occupied by the enemy, reparations shall be calculated upon the basis that the average living standards in Germany during the reparation period shall not exceed the average standards of living of European countries.'[1]

At a preliminary discussion of this report by the Foreign Ministers (a)
on July 22 M. Molotov again raised objections to the proposal that Germany should be treated as a single economic unit; he thought it necessary to allow the Control Council to issue detailed instructions from time to time on the extent to which such treatment was possible. M. Molotov also objected to the provision that the various zones of occupation should continue to draw their supplies from the areas upon which they had drawn before the war. At the meeting of Foreign Ministers on July 23, M. Molotov referred to the discussions on the western frontier of Poland.[2] He offered to withdraw his (b)
proposal to qualify the statement that Germany should be treated as a single economic unit, but at the same time asked for the deletion of the clause regarding the drawing of supplies. Mr. Eden and Mr. Byrnes could not agree to this latter proposal. The matter was then referred to a plenary meeting. M. Molotov also proposed a new formula as a substitute for the clause on priorities recommended by the British and American representatives on the Economic Committee. His wording was as follows: 'After payment of reparations, (c)
enough resources must be left to enable the German people to subsist without external assistance. In working out the economic balance of Germany, the necessary means must be provided to pay for imports in so far as they are approved by the Control Council; in case the means are insufficient to pay simultaneously on reparations account and for approved imports, all kinds of deliveries (internal consumption, exports, reparations) have to be proportionately reduced.' (d)

M. Molotov explained that under his formula any 'short-fall' on estimated production would be divided in such a way as to fall equally on exports and reparation deliveries. Mr. Eden and Mr. Byrnes pointed out that this plan would merely put on one or more

---

[1] As in the general statement of economic principles, European countries were defined as excluding the United Kingdom and the U.S.S.R.

[2] See Chapter LXVIII, section (iv).

(a) F(Terminal) 5th meeting. (b) F(Terminal) 6th meeting. (c) P(Terminal) 15.
(d) *F.R.U.S., 1945, The Conference of Berlin*, II, 810.

of the Powers the burden of supplying a part of the 'necessary imports' without payment. As an alternative M. Molotov then suggested that exports should have the first priority to the extent previously agreed by the Control Council. Since the Ministers could not reach a decision, the matter was referred to a plenary meeting.

The Soviet Delegation also submitted to the Conference on July 23 two memoranda on reparation from Germany. The first of these (a) memoranda repeated the Russian proposals at Yalta that out of the total sum of 20,000 million dollars accepted as the figure for reparation, about one half would be taken in the form of 'once for all' removals, within two years, from the national wealth of Germany, and the other half would come from annual deliveries in kind over a period of ten years.[1] The second memorandum proposed that, (b) pending the establishment of a permanent Allied reparation agency, removals should be based upon the urgency of need among the nations which had suffered from German action.

(c) In the afternoon of July 23, at Mr. Byrnes's suggestion, the Foreign Ministers held an informal meeting to discuss their differences over the questions of reparations and supply. Mr. Byrnes asked M. Molotov about the removals which were already taking place in the Russian Zone. M. Molotov said that perhaps 300 million dollars' worth had already been removed, and that the Russians might reduce their claims by that amount. They had asked for 10,000 million dollars of reparation payments and would be ready to take nine. Mr. Byrnes then pointed out that the coal mines in Silesia were now in Polish possession; he asked about the position of other resources in the area. M. Molotov argued that the territory now being administered by Poland contained only 16 per cent of the national wealth of German territory in 1937; Mr. Pauley, of the United States Delegation, put the figure as 20 per cent. Mr. Byrnes said that the Russians were now proposing to give to Poland 20 per cent of the amount which at Yalta had been considered available for general reparation purposes. Mr. Eden agreed, and pointed out that we had never contemplated that this area of German territory should not be available for reparation. Mr. Byrnes said that the figure of 9,000 million dollars mentioned by the Russians was meaningless. When M. Molotov said that at Yalta the United States Delegation had not objected to the total estimate of 20,000 million dollars Mr. Byrnes replied that this figure had been agreed only as a basis of discussion, and that since Yalta all our armies had

[1] The memorandum also laid down lists of industries from which 'once-for-all' and 'current' deliveries should be made, and gave the approximate value of removals from each industry. The memorandum specified Germany within her 1937 frontiers as the area from which removals would take place.

(a) P(Terminal) 29. (b) P(Terminal) 30. (c) P(Terminal) 38, UE3238/86/9.

moved into Germany and we had also destroyed thousands of millions of dollars' worth of property by air bombardment.

M. Molotov then reduced his figure to a possible 8,000 million dollars. Mr. Byrnes said that the principal concern of the United States was the amount in food and coal which 'would have to be taken from their people[1] to pay reparation for someone else'. Owing to the expulsion of the Germans from Silesia there were now some 4 million more people in the American Zone and about 800,000 more in their sector of Berlin. According to American estimates the Russian Zone (including the territories now administered by Poland) included about 50 per cent of German resources. Mr. Byrnes then made a new suggestion. He said that if the Russians collected their reparation from their own zone, and if the British, French and Americans did likewise from their respective zones, and also undertook to pay out of the amount collected the claims of Belgium, the Netherlands, and other United Nations, we should at least avoid the questions which were now being raised and would cause great irritation in the future.

M. Molotov asked what would happen to the resources of the Ruhr. He said that the Russians wanted to receive supplies from other zones as reparation, and that they could not agree to Mr. Byrnes's plan unless they were given 2 or 3 thousand million dollars' worth of machinery from the Ruhr; they might then take the rest of their reparation from their own zone. At all events they would be willing to discuss proposals on these lines. M. Molotov also argued that the Russian Zone contained less than 40 per cent of the total resources of Germany.

'Mr. Eden said that from his point of view the difficulty was that owing to the allocation of large areas to Poland, the Russian Zone would contribute no food or fuel to the other areas of Germany which were formerly supplied from this zone. How were these supplies to be made good? If we had to supply coal to Berlin to make up for the Silesian supply, it would be at the expense of France, the Netherlands and Belgium, to whom we could send no coal after August 1. What could Russia supply in the way of food and coal? M. Molotov said that this question must be discussed.[2]

On July 26 the Economic Committee, which had been asked also to consider the reparation problems of Italy and Austria, issued a second report. They stated that no agreement had been reached on (a)

---

[1] It is not wholly clear whether Mr. Byrnes meant the people of the United States or the people in the American zone of occupation in Germany.

[2] Mr. Eden, in a note to the Prime Minister on this meeting, wrote: 'It remains to be seen if a bargain acceptable to both sides can be struck.' (b)

(a) P(Terminal) 41. (b) PM/45/12T, F.O.934/1/4(17).

the method of obtaining substantial reparation from Germany. The British and American representatives were prepared to consider certain 'once for all' removals from the war industries of Austria and Italy, but were opposed to any levies on the current production of these countries, since in fact they would be paid for by the United Kingdom and the United States.

(a) M. Molotov said at the meeting of Foreign Secretaries on July 27 that the United States Government seemed to have gone back on their assumption that the total figure of German reparation should be 20,000 million dollars. Mr. Byrnes repeated his previous statement that this figure had been taken only as a basis of discussion and that in the changed circumstances it did not apply. In addition to the destruction of property by military action, and the exclusion of large parts of Germany from the area over which reparation could be exacted, the Russians had given an interpretation of their own to 'war booty', and had already seized and removed a large proportion of the plant and equipment in Germany from which reparation might have been payable. Thus in the American sector of Berlin they had stripped almost all the machinery from the International Telegraph and Telephone Company and from four other plants. Mr. Byrnes added that the United States sought nothing for themselves by way of reparations, but that they asserted their claim because they would have to look after the interests of other Allied countries.

M. Molotov said that neither Great Britain nor the United States had been occupied by the German armies. The Soviet Union and Poland had been invaded, and had suffered great losses of life and property. They therefore had an indisputable right to claim reparation. He admitted that the Soviet authorities might have removed some machinery, but they had taken only a fraction of the amount destroyed in the Soviet Union during the German occupation. M. Molotov also disagreed with the conclusions of the Committee on the question of reparation from Austria and Italy.[1]

(ii)

Mr. Byrnes's compromise proposal on reparation: disposal of the German navy and merchant fleet.

The Conference had thus failed to reach agreement on the most important issues at the time when Mr. Churchill and Mr. Eden left for England. At this point Mr. Byrnes took the lead in proposing a

---

[1] For the question of Italian and Austrian reparation see below, pp. 481–2.

(a) F(Terminal) 9th meeting.

bargain on the two major questions of reparation and the Polish western frontier.[1] He suggested to Sir A. Cadogan on the evening of July 27 that on the reparation question we might accept an arrangement whereby the Russians would take what they required from their own zone of occupation and should also be allowed 1,500 million dollars[2] worth of equipment from the Western Zones on the condition that they supplied an equivalent value, over a period of five or six years, in coal and foodstuffs from German territory under their control. On the other hand we should have to agree to the immediate transfer to Polish administration of all the territory up to the eastern Neisse. These two solutions were interdependent, and the transfer of the territory to Polish administration would depend on the firm agreement of the Soviet Government to provide the requisite quantities of coal and foodstuffs. (a)

In a note of July 28 for the use of Mr. Attlee and Mr. Bevin on their arrival at Potsdam, Sir A. Cadogan therefore explained that Mr. Byrnes was intending to put forward a 'comprehensive' solution of these three main outstanding problems of reparation, the 'economic treatment of Germany as a whole', and the Polish western frontier.[3] Sir A. Cadogan thought that we ought to accept this comprehensive solution. He explained, with special reference to the proposals on reparation, that until recently we and the Americans had been strongly in favour of treating Germany as a single economic unit. General Eisenhower and Field-Marshal Montgomery thought that we should make a genuine effort to get agreement on this principle, but some members of the American Delegation had been greatly impressed by seeing how thoroughly the Russians had stripped Berlin, and had come to the conclusion that it would be unrealistic to suppose that all four zones could in fact be treated as a single economic unit. (b)

Sir A. Cadogan said that it had been agreed that Russia should receive 50 per cent of German reparation. One half of the national wealth of Germany was in the Russian Zone. The Russians were already taking material from their zone, and would strip it far more

---

[1] Mr. Byrnes subsequently added to his compromise proposals a new formula on the recognition of the Government of the satellite States with a view to the admission of the latter to the United Nations. See below, pp. 478–87.

[2] The British documents do not explain why Mr. Byrnes here used a figure, and not a percentage.

[3] Sir. A. Cadogan had telegraphed earlier on July 27 to the Foreign Office, in answer to a telegram of that day asking for information for Mr. Bevin, that the British Delegation thought that agreement ought to be reached on reparation and the outstanding economic principles with regard to the treatment of Germany, on the western frontier of Poland, the question of admissions to the United Nations, Austrian and Italian reparations, and the transfer of populations from Poland and Czechoslovakia. He mentioned other matters which might, however, be left to the Council of Foreign Ministers. (c)

(a) F.O.934/2/8(20). (b) F.O.934/2/8(19). (c) F.O.934/2/8(15), Target 259.

completely than the Western Powers would strip their zones. We could therefore say that by this process the Russians were in practice satisfying their claim. They were, however, in great need of machinery from the Ruhr, and we could require, in return for allowing them a fixed proportion of the machinery which we decided to take from this area, that they should supply coal and food to Berlin and other parts of Germany normally dependent on the Russian (and Polish) areas of administration. We should have to make a detailed agreement about the amount of coal and food to be supplied, and the period during which deliveries would take place. Sir A. Cadogan drew up a draft statement for use by the Prime Minister, if he should approve of Mr. Byrnes's proposal and decide to support it at the Conference. The draft did not mention any definite frontier for Poland, but referred only to the transfer to Polish administration of certain areas of Germany within the agreed Russian zone of occupation.

(a) The British Delegation discussed Mr. Byrnes's offer on reparation at their staff conference on the morning of July 30. Mr. Attlee asked whether the proposed deliveries to the Russians from the Western Zone should not be expressed as in exchange for deliveries of food and other supplies from the Russian Zone. Sir D. Waley of H.M. Treasury, explained that the British representatives on the Control Council were anxious that the agreement should not be expressed in these terms, i.e. so much machinery in exchange for so much food, since there would be continual disputes over each particular consignment in either direction. The point of principle was, however, covered by the opening words of the statement which made it clear that the offer was made 'as part of a settlement covering this and other matters'.

Mr. Bevin suggested that we should make it clear that the reparation plan would have to provide for eliminating the German war potential and for leaving Germany sufficient industrial equipment to enable her to maintain an approved standard of living.

(b) At the meeting of the Foreign Ministers on July 30 Mr. Byrnes submitted a paper in which he developed in more detail his proposal of July 23, and tried to combine it with the Russian claim to a share in the German assets in the Ruhr. He suggested that the reparation claims of the U.S.S.R. and Poland should be met from the Russian Zone plus (*a*) 25 per cent of the industrial capital equipment removed from the Ruhr as unnecessary to a peace economy, on condition that the Russians would make available an equivalent value in food, coal, potash, zinc, timber, and clay and oil products and (*b*) an additional 15 per cent of such industrial capital equipment

(a) F.O.934/2/8(16). (b) F(Terminal) 10th meeting; P(Terminal) 63.

from the Ruhr. This additional percentage would be transferred to the Soviet Union without payment or exchange of any kind.[1]

Mr. Byrnes, as he had explained to Sir A. Cadogan, made this proposal conditional upon agreement on his two other compromise proposals. Mr. Bevin then read out a paper which the British Delegation was submitting for circulation. This paper, which had been drawn up after consultation with the Treasury, stated that the British Government, as part of a general settlement, would agree that the U.S.S.R., in addition to obtaining reparation removals and deliveries from their own zone of occupation, should also receive 'from the Western Zones and particularly from the Ruhr 10 per cent of such equipment, particularly from the heavy metal industries, as it is decided to remove under an agreed Reparation Plan' which would have to provide for eliminating German war potential while leaving sufficient industrial equipment to maintain approved living standards. These removals would be on a very considerable scale, but the precise amount could not be estimated until a comprehensive plan had been worked out. This plan would 'have to be such as to enable the Powers (other than the Soviet Union and Poland) entitled to reparation to obtain from the Russian Zone adequate amounts of annual deliveries of timber and potash'. (a)

M. Molotov commented that this plan would give the Russians only 10 per cent of the equipment from the American and British Zones, whereas under the American proposal they would get 25 per cent with payment and 15 per cent without payment. Mr. Bevin explained that the question was whether the Russians would choose 10 per cent from the British and American Zones or a higher percentage from the Ruhr alone. The British Delegation had taken account of the economic principles which they wished to apply to the treatment of Germany. They preferred to deal with the supply of goods rather separately from reparations. Mr. Bevin was concerned lest the supply of goods between zones might lead to disputes—e.g. he foresaw difficulty in finding an agreed basis in exchanging machinery for potatoes. He hoped therefore that the Conference would agree upon the sources of supplies for all the zones of Germany as a separate matter from the question of reparation.

Mr. Bevin then read out a second paper—which was subsequently circulated to the British Delegation—on the sources of supply for the zones of occupation, including the greater Berlin area. This (b)

---

[1] Mr. Byrnes explained that he had put forward a percentage of machinery and equipment from the Ruhr because the Soviet Government were specially concerned with the Ruhr. The United States Government would compensate the British Government with machinery from the American zone in respect of any excess of machinery drawn from the British Zone.

(a) P(Terminal) 65. (b) P(Terminal) 65.

memorandum repeated the British proposal that, as a general principle, each of the zones of occupation—including the Greater Berlin area—would draw its supplies as far as was practicable from the area of Germany on which it had drawn before the war. Until the 1946 harvest the zone for which the Soviet Government were responsible might have little or no surplus foodstuffs, but during this period the zone in question should supply enough food for its own needs and those of the Greater Berlin area. After the 1946 harvest the Soviet Zone would provide for supplies to the Greater Berlin area and Western Germany approximately to the extent usual in the past. This result would follow from the general principle of treating Germany as a single economic unit. Arrangements on similar lines were suggested for coal.

(a) Mr. Bevin also read a third British paper which suggested for inclusion in the economic principles governing the treatment of Germany, a statement that 'payment for approved imports into Germany shall be a first charge against the proceeds of exports out of current production and out of stocks of goods'.

M. Molotov then restated the Soviet view. The Soviet Government wanted to receive German equipment to restart their own factories. Mr. Byrnes's proposals were therefore nearer than Mr. Bevin's to the Soviet wishes, but each was obscure in speaking of percentages of an unknown figure. Would the 25 per cent quoted by Mr. Byrnes be not less than 800 million dollars or 2 million tons of equipment? If so, the question could be settled at once. Mr. Byrnes said that it was impossible to give an estimate in dollars or tons. They did not know how much German equipment could be taken for reparation or how much was required to maintain the essential economy of Germany. Was each piece of equipment to be assessed at the cost price or the present value? The Soviet Government would have to trust the good faith of their Allies.

M. Molotov asked whether Mr. Bevin's proposal meant 10 per cent of all equipment in the Western Zones or 10 per cent of the equipment which could be removed from these zones. Mr. Bevin said that he was referring to the equipment which could be removed, and pointed out that the position of the other Allies had to be taken into account. He also supported Mr. Byrnes's argument that it was impossible to state any figures. Mr. Bevin supposed that Great Britain would not obtain much in the way of reparation, and pointed out that he would find it difficult to explain to the British public why under Mr. Byrnes's plan the greater part of the Soviet demands were to be met from the British Zone. M. Molotov suggested that the plan might apply to the British and American Zones. Mr. Byrnes

---

(a) P(Terminal) 65.

agreed, but said that in this case the percentages allocated to the Soviet Government would have to be halved.

M. Molotov then proposed that the percentages should be 25 per cent from the two Western Zones by way of exchange, and 25 per cent without payment. Mr. Bevin said that he would be saved much political difficulty if the United States proposal could be expressed at $12\frac{1}{2}$ per cent on the basis of exchange and $7\frac{1}{2}$ per cent without payment from both zones. M. Molotov suggested 20 per cent from both zones by exchange, and 20 per cent without payment, mainly from the Ruhr.

Mr. Byrnes said that he had linked his proposal about reparation with the concessions on the Polish western frontier suggested by the United States Delegation and with the declaration about admission to the United Nations[1] which involved a concession by the British Delegation. He hoped that the Soviet Delegation would make the concession he had suggested about percentages.

Mr. Bevin said that the British Delegation had not agreed to the American proposal about the Polish western frontier or to the proposal about reparation, but that he thought the figures of $12\frac{1}{2}$ and $7\frac{1}{2}$ per cent very favourable to Russia. After further discussion the matter was referred to a plenary meeting.

M. Molotov next proposed, as an addition to Mr. Bevin's formula on the 'first charge' the words: 'As regards the rest, priority should be given to reparations, as compared with the satisfaction of other economic needs.' Mr. Byrnes explained that, on his proposals, the Soviet Government need not concern themselves with German imports or exports because they would get the agreed percentage from the Western Zones. M. Molotov said that he thought agreement could be reached provided that a definite figure were settled for the total of reparation due to the Soviet Union. Mr. Byrnes reminded the meeting that his three points had to be taken together. The meeting accordingly agreed that all three must be submitted to the Plenary Meeting.

The British Delegation discussed the position on the morning of (a)
July 31. Mr. Bevin thought that since Mr. Byrnes had made his offer of a general settlement, the Russians would try, first, to get an absolute figure of deliveries from the Western Zones. After this demand had been refused they would probably attempt to get agreement on 10 per cent of deliveries from the two zones without exchange, and 10 per cent with exchange.

Sir D. Waley said that the most disturbing feature of the new American plan was its implication that the United States Govern-

---

[1] See below, section (iv) of this chapter.

(a) F.O.934/2/8(18).

ment had given up hope of co-operation with the Russians in the administration of Germany as a single economic unit. They seemed to take the defeatist view that the Russian Zone would be administered as a separate unit, with lower standards of living and few facilities for the interchange of goods with the rest of Germany. Even at this stage there was something to be said for making a last attempt to get the reparation problem handled on a different basis.

Mr. Bevin saw no practical advantage in further discussion with the United States Delegation on the basis of their plan. They clearly wanted to make the best bargain they could and to end the discussion as soon as possible. We should therefore agree to their plan, and pursue the question of treating Germany as an economic unit in separate discussions on the exchange of supplies between the various areas of the country. The Russians were willing to consider proposals for treating Germany as an economic whole—e.g. their suggestion for a central German administration.

Sir D. Waley accepted Mr. Bevin's view and the meeting agreed that we should state our readiness to accept a basis of deliveries of equipment to Russia from the two Western Zones up to 10 per cent against exchanges and 10 per cent without exchanges.

(a) Mr. Byrnes summed up his proposals at the plenary meeting of the Conference on July 31.[1] The Soviet Delegation put forward a demand for 15 per cent by exchange and 10 per cent without payment; in addition they claimed 500 million dollars' worth of shares in industrial and transport undertakings in the Western Zones, 30 per cent of German foreign investments and 30 per cent of German gold now at the disposal of the Allies.

After some discussion during which it had been accepted that the Control Council should, subject to the final approval of the zone commander concerned, determine what equipment was not necessary to Germany's peace economy. Mr. Byrnes refused to accept these additional Soviet claims. Stalin then said that it might be necessary for the Soviet Delegation to raise their percentage claims. President Truman offered to agree to the Russian figures of 15 and 10 per cent if the Soviet Delegation would withdraw their additional claim. Mr. Bevin said we should find it difficult to meet the claims of other Allies, e.g. France, Belgium or the Netherlands, if the Russian figures were accepted. He suggested, as a compromise, 12½ and 10 per cent. Stalin asked why the British Delegation was un-

(b) [1] Before the plenary meeting, Sir D. Waley had shown to the Delegation a copy of Mr. Byrnes's proposals which (with some minor changes) were those put forward by Mr. Byrnes on July 30, though the figures were now 12½ and 7½ per cent from the two zones. Sir D. Waley had told the Americans that this latter change was essential, but he understood that nonetheless the Americans might propose, as an alternative, 25 per cent and 15 per cent from the Ruhr.

(a) P(Terminal) 11th meeting. (b) P(Terminal) 67.

willing to accept the Russian proposals although the United States Delegation had accepted them. Mr. Bevin said that most of the equipment would be taken from the British Zone; that we wanted little for ourselves, but that we would have to satisfy the claims of our Allies. Stalin said that France did not deserve to obtain much in reparation. She had signed an armistice with Germany, and had broken the common Allied front. Stalin estimated that 150 enemy divisions had been provided or supplied from France and that these facts should be set against any French claim for reparations. Finally, after he had tried to get the figures to 17½ per cent against exchanges and 7½ per cent in direct reparation, Mr. Bevin accepted the Russian figures of 15 and 10 per cent.

After this agreement had been reached, and the two other proposals dealt with in Mr. Byrnes's compromise proposals had been accepted,[1] the Conference returned to the consideration of the draft statement on economic principles governing the treatment of Germany which they had agreed to postpone. They decided that, in view of the agreement reached on the reparation problem, it was no longer necessary to include the paragraph—to which the Russians had objected—that each zone should draw its supplies from the area of Germany upon which it had been accustomed to draw them before the war. Stalin referred to the new paragraph which M. Molotov had suggested on July 22 with regard to priorities.[2] Mr. Byrnes thought that this paragraph was now unnecessary since it had been agreed that the Russians would receive a specific percentage of the plant and equipment scheduled for delivery as reparation from the Western Zones. Mr. Bevin, however, said that he was still concerned to secure that payments for approved imports into Germany should be a first charge against the proceeds of exports. It would be most unfortunate if the decision reached on reparation payments had the effect of dividing Germany into separate zones for economic purposes. Mr. Bevin was therefore more anxious to secure agreement that Germany should be treated as an economic unit for purposes of the normal exchange of goods. Stalin thought that Mr. Bevin's point would be met by the establishment of a central German administration for economic purposes. It was agreed therefore to hold over a decision until the Conference had discussed the question of a central administration.[3]

At the first of two plenary meetings on August 1 Mr. Byrnes reported that the Committee appointed to draft a statement of (a)
plan on the agreement on German reparation had been unable to

---

[1] See above, pp. 437–8, and below, p. 479.
[2] See above, pp. 445–6. [3] See above, p. 442.

(a) P(Terminal) 12th Meeting.

agree on the reference to German external assets. Mr. Byrnes had thought that the Russians had withdrawn any claim in the matter in return for the agreement of the United States Delegation to the high percentages of deliveries of capital equipment from the Western Zones, but the Soviet representative on the drafting committee would not accept this interpretation.

Stalin said that he had intended to withdraw only the claim to a share in German undertakings in the Western Zones, and a share in the gold found in these zones, and in German external assets. All assets in countries west of the demarcation line between the Russian and the Western Zones should be at the disposal of Great Britain and the United States and all assets east of the line should be at the disposal of the Soviet Union. Mr. Bevin asked whether Stalin's proposal meant that all German external assets in the areas occupied by the Russian armies would go to the Russians while all such assets located elsewhere would go to Great Britain and the United States. Thus German assets in Yugoslavia and Czechoslovakia would be at the disposal of Great Britain and the United States while those in Austria would be divided between the three Powers. Stalin agreed with this interpretation, and the proposal was then accepted by the Conference.

Finally the Conference agreed—after further discussion—to settle the question of priorities by including in the statement of economic principles two new paragraphs. The first paragraph ran as follows: 'Payment of reparations should leave enough resources to enable the German people to subsist without external assistance. In working out the economic balance of Germany the necessary means must be provided to pay for imports approved by the Control Council in Germany. The proceeds of exports from current production and stocks shall be available in the first place for payment for such imports.' The second paragraph laid down that this clause would not apply to the equipment and products included in the percentages allocated to the U.S.S.R. from the Western Zones.

The agreement on German reparation, as embodied in the protocol and communiqué of the Conference, was therefore in the following terms:

'1. Reparation claims of the U.S.S.R. shall be met by removals from the zone of Germany occupied by the U.S.S.R., and from appropriate German external assets.

2. The U.S.S.R. undertakes to settle the reparation claims of Poland from its own share of reparations.

3. The reparations claims of the United States, the United Kingdom and other countries entitled to reparations shall be met from the Western Zones and from appropriate German external assets.

4. In addition to the reparations to be taken by the U.S.S.R. from

its own zone of occupation, the U.S.S.R. shall receive additionally from the Western Zones:

(*a*) 15 per cent. of such usable and complete industrial capital equipment, in the first place from the metallurgical, chemical and machine manufacturing industries, as is unnecessary for the German peace economy and should be removed from the Western Zones of Germany, in exchange for an equivalent value of food, coal, potash, zinc, timber, clay products, petroleum products, and such other commodities as may be agreed upon.

(*b*) 10 per cent of such industrial capital equipment as is unnecessary for the German peace economy and should be removed from the Western Zones, to be transferred to the Soviet Government on reparations account without payment or exchange of any kind in return.

Removals of equipment as provided in (*a*) and (*b*) above shall be made simultaneously.

5. The amount of equipment to be removed from the Western Zones on account of reparations must be determined within six months from now at the latest.

6. Removals of industrial capital equipment shall begin as soon as possible and shall be completed within two years from the determination specified in paragraph 5. The delivery of products covered by 4(*a*) above shall begin as soon as possible and shall be made by the U.S.S.R. in agreed instalments within five years of the date hereof. The determination of the amount and character of the industrial capital equipment unnecessary for the German peace economy and therefore available for reparations shall be made by the Control Council under policies fixed by the Allied Commission on Reparations, with the participation of France, subject to the final approval of the Zone Commander in the Zone from which the equipment is to be removed.

7. Prior to the fixing of the total amount of equipment subject to removal, advance deliveries shall be made in respect of such equipment as will be determined to be eligible for delivery in accordance with the procedure set forth in the last sentence of paragraph 6.

8. The Soviet Government renounces all claims in respect of reparations to shares of German enterprises which are located in the Western Zones of occupation in Germany as well as to German foreign assets in all countries except those specified in paragraph 9 below.

9. The Governments of the United Kingdom and United States renounce all claims in respect of reparations to shares of German enterprises which are located in the Eastern Zone of occupation in Germany, as well as to German foreign assets in Bulgaria, Finland, Hungary, Roumania and Eastern Austria.

10. The Soviet Government makes no claims to gold captured by the Allied troops in Germany.'

The document published in the communiqué also has as a preamble a sentence as follows: 'In accordance with the Crimea decision that Germany be compelled to compensate to the greatest possible extent for the loss and suffering that she has caused to the United Nations and for which the German people cannot escape responsibility, the following agreement on reparation was reached . . .'

(a) In addition to the reparation demand the Soviet Government also put forward claims to a third share in the German navy and mer-
(b) chant marine. At the discussion of this claim on July 19[1] President Truman said that the first step was to decide what was booty and what was reparation. Material defined as booty belonged to the nation whose forces captured it. Material defined as reparations should be divided in agreed proportions. The President thought that the German merchant fleet should fall under the latter heading. He was interested primarily in the merchant fleet since he wished it to remain under the present control until the end of the Japanese war.

Stalin's view was that the German battle fleet was booty, and belonged to those who accepted the German surrender. The merchant fleet could be regarded either as booty or as reparations. Mr. Churchill said that he did not want to approach the matter from a juridical standpoint, but rather to reach a fair and friendly settlement between Allies. Most of the fleet was in British hands. If the three Powers came to a fair and friendly general settlement of the affairs before the Conference, he would not oppose a fair division of the fleet. The question of losses, however, was very relevant; Great Britain had lost some ten capital ships, some twenty cruisers, and hundreds of small craft. Mr. Churchill thought that the German U-boats were in a different category from other warships, and that they should be sunk or destroyed, with the exception of a few of the latest types which had devices of interest to the three Powers. These few should be shared.

Mr. Churchill proposed that the German merchant navy should be used for the war against Japan for which shipping was greatly needed. He also asked whether the Russians had not obtained control of 400,000 tons of Finnish shipping and of a number of Roumanian ships. Stalin said that the Russians had not taken a single Finnish ship, and that they were using only one Roumanian ship.

Mr. Churchill then mentioned the claims of other Allied nations—e.g. Norway. He suggested that the German merchant navy might

---

(c) [1] Stalin had already asked at the first plenary meeting why Mr. Churchill did not agree that Russia should have a third of the German fleet. Mr. Churchill said that this was not the position. He thought, however, that the Conference should consider whether the fleet should be divided up or sunk. Stalin answered that he did not intend to sink the ships allotted to Russia.

(a) P(Terminal) 9. (b) P(Terminal) 3rd meeting. (c) P(Terminal) 1st meeting.

be divided into four parts, one of which would be allocated to meet the needs of nations not represented at the Conference. After considerable discussion Stalin accepted the proposal that the matter should be left over to the end of the Conference with a view to a settlement on the basis of a three-fold division of the warships. He agreed that a large proportion of the U-boats should be sunk, and that the merchant ships should be used for the war against Japan, and then divided equally among the three Powers.

The subject was not discussed again at the Conference until August 1. Meanwhile on July 30 the British and Soviet Delegations submitted memoranda on the question to the Conference. The Soviet memorandum merely repeated the claim to a third of the war and (a) merchant fleets, with the suggestion that the transfer should begin on August 1, 1945, and be completed by November 1, 1945. No reference was made to the use of the merchant fleet in the war against Japan, but the Soviet Government agreed that most of the U-boats should be destroyed.

The British memorandum suggested that a share in the German (b) war fleet should be given to France, and repeated the view that, in allocating the Soviet share, account should be taken of the Roumanian and Bulgarian warships available to the Soviet navy. On the question of merchant shipping the memorandum again proposed that account should be taken of the satellite (Roumanian and Finnish) merchant shipping which had passed under Soviet control. Subject to these conditions, and to the provision of ships for local German purposes, the British Delegation renewed the suggestion that a fourth part should be made available for division between the other Allied States whose merchant marine had suffered losses at the hands of Germany. The British Delegation proposed that the transfer should not take place until the end of the Japanese war.

The Conference appointed a special committee of three admirals to consider the British and Soviet memoranda. The Committee reported on August 1. The American and Russian representatives (c) did not support the British recommendation that a portion of the German War Fleet should be given to France. On the other hand the British and American representatives suggested that only thirty submarines should be preserved, and divided equally among the three Powers. The Soviet representative claimed 'about 30' submarines for the U.S.S.R.

There was a similar division of opinion over the allocation of the German merchant marine. The American and Soviet representatives did not support the British proposal for allocating a quarter of the merchant fleet to other Allied States, and the Soviet representative

(a) P(Terminal) 55. (b) P(Terminal) 52. (c) P(Terminal) 75.

opposed the British and American proposal to allow for the inland and coastal ships necessary to maintain a 'basic German peace economy'. The Soviet representative also disagreed with the British view that the shares of the Allied States could count as reparation receipts. The United States representative expressed no view on this matter.

(a) In the discussion of this report at the meeting of Foreign Secretaries on August 1 Mr. Bevin said that he was prepared to agree to a three-fold division of the war fleet (i.e. excluding France). He was unwilling to make any concession on the number of submarines. M. Molotov accepted ten as the number to be retained by each of the three Powers. Mr. Bevin then said that the British Delegation wanted to ensure that Germany should retain a reasonable amount of shipping for the purpose of carrying on the economic life of the country. The balance should then be divided into thirds on the understanding that the Soviet Government would allocate a fair proportion of their share to Poland, and the British and United States Governments a proportion of their respective shares to France and other Allied countries. M. Molotov was unwilling to assume any special responsibility for Poland. M. Molotov then said that Yugoslavia would be offended if she were left out, and that Great Britain and the United States should make an allocation to her as well as to the other Allies. Mr. Bevin replied that, in view of the very heavy British losses, he must leave this matter to the Soviet Union.[1] Mr. Byrnes thought that it would be unwise to mention recognition of any claimants, since we should be inviting claims, e.g. from some South American countries which had lost ships. Finally, after Mr. Bevin had offered to be responsible for Yugoslav claims if the Soviet Union would deal with Poland, M. Molotov said that he must reserve the position
(b) of the Soviet Government. At the plenary meeting on the afternoon of August 1, however, Stalin agreed that the Soviet Government should be responsible for meeting Polish claims.

---

[1] Mr. Bevin pointed out that of the total shipping losses of the Allies, Great Britain had suffered 48 per cent, the United States 15 per cent, Norway 10½ per cent, France 7 per cent, Poland 5½ per cent, and the U.S.S.R. 1 per cent ('Poland' is evidently an error for 'Holland' in the British record of the discussions: cf. the American record in *F.R.U.S.* 1945, *The Conference of Berlin*, II, 560.) M. Molotov disputed these figures and asked what was the figure for Poland. Mr. Bevin replied that the losses of Poland were 'about the same as those of Holland'.

(a) F(Terminal) 11th meeting. (b) P(Terminal) 12th meeting.

(iii)

The trial of war criminals: earlier British objections to the establishment of a tribunal for the trial of major criminals: American and Russian insistence upon an international tribunal: agreement at the Potsdam Conference to an Allied statement.

The three Heads of Governments at the Teheran Conference had issued a declaration on German atrocities stating that the Allied Governments would track down individuals responsible for massacres, executions and other crimes, and send them for trial and punishment to the countries where they had committed their crimes. Major criminals, such as the leading members of the German Government, whose acts had no geographical location, would be punished by joint action on the part of the Allied Governments. Nothing further was said in the declaration about the form which this joint action would take. At this time the British Government inclined to a legal form of trial, while the Russians and Americans appeared to favour the summary execution of Hitler and his principal associates.

No agreement had been reached on this question before the Yalta Conference. The Conference itself referred the matter to later meetings of the Foreign Ministers. No such meetings had taken place before the assembling of the San Francisco Conference. The United States Government, however, sent Judge Rosenman to London to discuss the question with the Lord Chancellor (Lord Simon). Lord Simon submitted to the War Cabinet a memorandum (a) on the discussions. The War Cabinet considered this memorandum on April 12, 1945. They agreed with the American view that a pro- (b) posal for a treaty creating an inter-Allied Criminal Court for the trial of war criminals was unsuitable, and that the appropriate tribunal should be a military tribunal. They had changed their view about the treatment of major criminals. They now proposed summary execution for them, whereas the Americans were in favour of a formal trial or judicial enquiry. The War Cabinet asked Lord Simon to communicate their conclusions to Judge Rosenman and to prepare for transmission to the United States Government a statement of their objections to a formal trial for the major criminals.

While this statement was in preparation the Foreign Office were informed that M. Molotov was going to San Francisco. They thought that he might raise the question of war criminals (which was now becoming urgent in view of the rapid German collapse). Lord Simon and the Attorney-General therefore gave Sir A. Cadogan, who (c)

(a) WP(45)225. (b) WM(45)43. (c) WP(45)281.

was about to leave for San Francisco, a short paper on the British view.

In this paper Lord Simon assumed that the major criminals would be executed. The question whether they should or should not be tried by a tribunal depended on the nature of the charge which the Allied peoples and the world in general made against Hitler. 'It is the totality of his offences against the international standard which civilised countries try to observe which makes him the guilty man that he is.' If he were indicted formally in a court, the trial would be long and elaborate. He would have to be given all the rights properly conceded to an accused person. He must be defended, if he so wished, by counsel, and must be allowed to call relevant evidence. According to British methods, his defence could not be forcibly shut down or limited because it involved a great expenditure of time.

If the method of public trial were adopted, there would certainly be comment that the whole affair was a 'put-up job' designed by the Allies to justify a punishment upon which they were already resolved. Hitler and his associates would be very much alive to the opportunities which a long trial would offer them. It was difficult to suppose that anyone would look on Hitler as an injured man, but a long trial might result in a change of feeling with regard to the justification of trying him at all, rather than shooting him out of hand. Furthermore, if 'in the complicated and novel procedure which such a trial is bound to adopt—for Russian, American, and British ideas must in some way be amalgamated—the defence secured some unexpected point, is there not a danger of the trial being denounced as a farce?'

Among Hitler's crimes were his conduct leading up to the war and his unprovoked attacks, during the war, on various countries. These acts, however, were not war crimes in the ordinary sense; it was not at all clear that they could properly be described as crimes under international law. They would have to be part of the charge, and, if the tribunal—as was presumably the case—had to proceed according to international law, the accused might argue that this part of the indictment should be struck out. It might well be thought that these acts ought to be regarded as crimes under international law, but this would be a matter for the tribunal, and the accused could argue from 'what has happened in the past and what has been done by various countries in declaring war which resulted in acquiring new territory, which certainly were not regarded at the time as crimes against international law'.

Lord Simon suggested that a document should be drawn up at once giving the reasoned basis for the punishment of the persons concerned. He added that such a document might be served upon each of the principal criminals on an agreed list. Each should be told that, if he wished to make an answer he must do so in writing within, say, fourteen days, and that his answer would be submitted to the Government in whose charge he was, and that the Allies would thereafter promulgate their decision upon his case. This procedure would not be in the nature of a trial and would not involve the attempt to set up a judicial tribunal, but it would 'give the accused the opportunity of putting forward what he wished to say, and might conceivably, in some cases, influence the decision'.

Sir A. Cadogan telegraphed from Washington on April 22 that he had shown Lord Simon's paper (excluding his personal suggestion about procedure) to Judge Rosenman, but that the latter had said that he had discussed the matter with President Truman, and had found him strongly of opinion that we could not dispose of the major criminals by political decision and without some form of judicial process. Judge Rosenman thought that the United States Government might accept an 'arraignment' procedure if it were sufficiently 'dressed up'. (Sir A. Cadogan took this to mean that there would have to be proper provision for verification of documents, etc.) Judge Rosenman suggested that each of the Allies should nominate representatives to draft an 'arraignment'. On May 2 Sir A. Cadogan telegraphed from San Francisco that Mr. Stettinius proposed to hold a meeting of the three Foreign Ministers in the afternoon of May 3 (United States Pacific Time) to consider a short report from Judge Rosenman. Mr. Eden therefore wanted to know the views of the War Cabinet.

The War Cabinet considered the matter forthwith. At their (a) discussion Mr. Law summed up the problem as follows: There were three types of war criminal: (*a*) the 'ordinary' type charged with an offence committed in the territory of an Allied Government. These men could be handed over to be dealt with by the Government concerned, (*b*) an 'intermediate' category such as Kramer, the Commandant at Belsen, and the local heads of the Gestapo throughout Germany. Judge Rosenman had suggested that these cases might be dealt with by first establishing in a single conspiracy trial that the Gestapo was a criminal conspiracy, and arranging that thereafter individual members could be punished on proof of membership of the conspiracy. We could accept such a plan if the handling of individual cases did not put an intolerable burden on the occupying authority. (*c*) the major criminals whose offences had no geographical location. The Americans and Russians wanted to have these cases tried by judicial procedure. The Foreign Office now thought that, with the death of Hitler, Mussolini, and other leaders, circumstances

(a) WM(45)57.

had changed. It would be inexpedient to have State trials of the lesser leaders; we should therefore try to bring all the offenders under the first or second category. Most of the leaders could be dealt with under the Moscow declaration[1] of October 1943, as having been responsible for specific war crimes against specified Allied nationals, and most of the remainder could be treated as having been parties to a general conspiracy.

The War Cabinet agreed about the difficulties of procedure in a State trial of the major criminals, but thought that we ought not to continue to oppose the combined wishes of the United States and Soviet Governments or give an impression that we were trying to deny to the individuals charged an opportunity of answering the charges against them. We should therefore accept the American and Russian view in principle, but leave them to draw up a workable procedure before finally committing ourselves.

The War Cabinet accepted the Prime Minister's summary that (i) war criminals whose offences were committed on Allied territory should be handed over for trial to the Government concerned: (ii) war criminals whose offences were committed on enemy territory should be dealt with by military courts under a manual of guidance agreed by the Allies: (iii) we should support Judge Rosenman's proposal for establishing that the leaders and active members of the Gestapo were members of a common enterprise engaged in a criminal conspiracy, though we should ask for a statement of the procedure proposed for the main trial and for the punishment of persons subsequently found to have been members of the conspiracy: (iv) we should not oppose the joint view of the Russians and Americans but should invite them to draw up a workable procedure with regard to the trial of major criminals before we agreed to put such criminals on trial: (v) we should point out that the situation had changed with the death of Hitler, Mussolini, and other prominent leaders, and that others would probably be killed before the fighting was over. A telegram was sent to this effect to Mr. Eden in time for the meeting at San Francisco.

The discussions at the War Crimes Commission in London for the establishment of an international tribunal for the trial of major criminals were not concluded before the Potsdam Conference, though general agreement had been reached. The British Delegation at the Conference had included the subject among the questions which they wished to raise. The matter was not discussed, however, until a meeting of the Foreign Secretaries on July 30. The discussion then

---

[1] This declaration laid down that Germans accused of war crimes would be tried in the countries where the crimes had been committed, except for the major war criminals whose offences had no particular geographical location and who would be punished by the joint decision of the allied governments.

took place on two memoranda—British and Russian. The British memorandum stated that it was 'most desirable, in view of the great public interest throughout the world in the major criminals being brought to just and speedy punishment that an agreement should be reached between the Three Governments' to insert a paragraph on the matter in the protocol and communiqué of the Conference. (a)

The wording suggested by the British Delegation was as follows:

> 'The Three Governments have taken note of the discussions which have been proceeding in recent weeks in London between British, United States, Soviet and French representatives with a view to reaching agreement on the methods of trial of those major war criminals whose crimes under the Moscow Declaration of October 1943 have no particular geographical localisation. The Three Governments re-affirm their intention to bring these criminals to swift and sure justice. They hope that the negotiations in London will result in speedy agreement being reached for this purpose, and they regard it as a matter of great importance that the trial of these major criminals should begin at the earliest possible date.'

The Russian memorandum also proposed a paragraph for insertion in the protocol or communiqué of the Conference in the following terms: (b)

> '1. The Conference recognised it as necessary that an International Tribunal should be set up in the near future to try the principal war criminals whose crimes, as is stated in the Moscow Declaration of the 1st November, 1943, have no geographic location.
>
> 2. The Conference decided that in the first place the following chiefs of the Hitler clique should be tried by the International Tribunal: Göring, Hess,[1] Ribbentrop, Ley, Keitel, Doenitz, Kaltenbrunner, Frick, Streicher, Krupp.[2]
>
> 3. The leaders of the three Allied Governments declare that, in accordance with the Moscow Declaration of the 1st November, 1943, they will take all measures in their power to secure the surrender for trial of war criminals who have taken shelter in neutral countries. Should any of these countries refuse to surrender the war criminals who have taken shelter in its territory the three Allied Governments will consult each other as to the steps which it will be necessary to take to ensure the implementation of their firm decision.'

At the meeting on July 30 M. Molotov accepted the British and American view that the trials should be held at Nuremberg. Mr. Byrnes thought it undesirable to mention any war criminals by name. (c)

---

[1] Rudolf Hess had been a prisoner in England since May 10, 1941. The Russians continued to suspect the British Government of protecting him from being brought to trial. See Volume II, pp. 277, 278, 280.

[2] The British list during the London discussion had not included Dönitz or Krupp but had included Rosenberg and Hans Frank.

(a) P(Terminal) 53. (b) P(Terminal) 57. (c) F(Terminal) 10th meeting.

The representatives of the three Governments on the War Crimes Commission would be in a better position to know which cases should be tried first; the publication of a selected list could also give rise to difficulties, since there would be differences of opinion about the composition of the list.

(a) On July 31 the British Delegation put forward a revised draft of (b) their proposed paragraph, but the Russians, at a plenary meeting of the Conference, again asked the for insertion of the names of some of the 'major criminals'. Mr. Attlee and Mr. Byrnes repeated the argument against publishing a list; Stalin said that, if no names were mentioned, some people might think that the three Powers had the intention of saving some of the criminals.

In view of the fact that the War Crimes Commission was about to report the Conference agreed to defer their discussion until the (c) following day. Meanwhile, since the British representatives on the Commission thought that the Americans were inclining to the idea of trials by individual nations rather than trials on a quadripartite basis, Mr. Attlee mentioned the question to President Truman. The President agreed that the latter basis should be adopted, and that the trials should begin soon.

(d) At the meeting of the Foreign Secretaries on August 1, M. Molotov continued to ask for the inclusion of names. Mr. Bevin said that the British Delegation opposed this proposal, and thought the most effective way of meeting the Russian demand was to get the trials started at the earliest possible moment. Mr. Byrnes said that the determination of the criminals to be tried had been left to the selected prosecutors, and that this responsibility should not be taken from them. Since M. Molotov refused to give way, the question was again referred to a plenary meeting.

(e) Stalin said at this meeting on August 1 that a list of names was necessary in order to satisfy public opinion in the Allied countries. A list would also make it clear that some German industrialists were to be tried. Finally it would remove any uncertainty about Hess. Mr. Bevin said that he could give a clear undertaking that Hess would be handed over for trial without delay, but Stalin thought it desirable to dispel any doubts on the matter in the minds of the general public in Allied countries. President Truman informed the Conference on August 1 that Mr. Justice Jackson, the United States representative on the Commission, had told him that the publication of names would handicap the work of the Commission, and that the Commission hoped to begin the trials within thirty days. Stalin then agreed to accept the British draft statement if a sentence were added to it that

(a) P(Terminal) 71. (b) P(Terminal) 11th meeting. (c) F.O.934/1/5(15), Onward 317 & Target 283, U5882/29/73, Target 332. (d) P(Terminal) 11th meeting. (e) P(Terminal) 12th meeting.

the first list of war criminals to be tried would be published within thirty days. The Conference agreed to this addition.

(iv)

American proposal for the admission of Italy to the United Nations: British attitude to the proposal: the question of an Italian peace treaty: Russian proposals for breaking off relations with General Franco and for the recognition of the Governments of the Satellite States: Mr. Byrnes's compromise proposal.

Although the two Western Powers had decided to raise at the Conference the question of a peace treaty with Italy, their ideas on procedure, and indeed on the general status of Italy, were affected, as earlier, by a difference in background.[1] The Americans continued to think that the British Government, in their own imperialist interests, wanted to 'keep Italy down', while the British view was that the State Department took too little account of the fact that Italy had been the Fascist ally of Germany; that she had attacked Great Britain at a most critical time, and had changed sides only in the hope of avoiding the consequences of military defeat.

The Foreign Office also felt a certain irritation that, in spite of the prior British concern in Italian affairs, the State Department was too much inclined to take unilateral decisions and announce them without giving the British Government a chance of stating the case on the other side. The Foreign Office had reason to complain of action of this kind immediately before the opening of the Conference. They were told on July 15, 1945, by the United States Embassy that the (a) Italian Ambassador at Washington had recently informed the State Department of Italy's intention to declare war on Japan. The declaration of war would be published on July 15. The State Department would accordingly announce on July 17 the intention of the United States Government to support the admission of Italy to the World Security Organisation. They hoped that the British Government would support this announcement.

The Foreign Office pointed out to the United States Embassy that the Italian decision to declare war against Japan had been known for several weeks. Hence there was no reason why the State Department should not have let us know earlier of their intention. 'To expect us to give a snap decision on an important question' in the absence of the Prime Minister and Foreign Secretary was 'bad enough. It was even worse when a matter concerning Italy was at stake.' We had

[1] For the Foreign Office brief on Italy for the British Delegation to the Conference, see Volume III, Chapter XLIV, section (iv).

(a) ZM3829/1/22.

already tried to co-operate most closely with the United States on questions of principle concerning Italy, and, 'in view of all we had had to put up with from Italy during the war', we were entitled to more consideration from the United States authorities. Moreover the admission of Italy to the World Security Organisation was closely connected with the question of an Italian peace treaty. We had consistently argued that it would be a mistake to make a preliminary treaty 'merely giving Italy all the jam and none of the powder'. We thought it undesirable to make concessions or promises to Italy about her future status until we were agreed upon the complete peace treaty. We agreed on the conclusion of a peace treaty as soon as possible, but we regarded it as important that any statement to this effect should be tripartite. We therefore hoped that the United States Government would take no action until the matter had been discussed at the Potsdam Conference.

(a) In view of the British representations Mr. Byrnes agreed to telegraph to Washington to get the announcement postponed, but at
(b) the first plenary meeting of the Conference on July 17, President Truman asked whether the Conference would accept the admission of Italy to association with the United Nations in view of the fact that she had now declared war on Japan. Mr. Churchill said that the matter would require careful consideration. The British people could not easily forget the conduct of Italy in declaring war on the British Commonwealth at the hour of its greatest danger when French resistance was on the point of collapse. They could also not forget the long struggle against Italy in North Africa before the entry of the United States into the war, and the severe British naval losses in the Mediterranean. Nevertheless we had shown the greatest goodwill to Italy, and had provided fourteen out of the fifteen ships lent to Russia to meet the Russian claim to an immediate share of the Italian fleet.

(c) The United States Delegation circulated a memorandum to the Conference summarising their view that the anomalous status of Italy as a 'co-belligerent and unconditionally surrendered enemy' was hampering every effort by the Allies and by the Italians themselves to improve the economic and political situation of the country. This anomaly could be solved only through the negotiation of a definitive peace treaty. Such a negotiation would take at least several months, and might be one of the first tasks of the proposed Council of Foreign Ministers. Meanwhile an improvement in the internal situation of Italy would be greatly facilitated by an interim arrangement providing tangible recognition of the Italian contribution to the defeat of Germany.

(a) ZM3861/122; F.O.934/2/6(1), Target 54. (b) P(Terminal) 1st meeting.
(c) P(Terminal) 5.

The United States Delegation therefore recommended that the short terms of surrender, and the numerous obsolete clauses of the long terms of surrender[1] should be replaced by certain undertakings on the part of the Italian Government to meet the requirements of the existing situation. These undertakings should provide that the Italian Government (i) would refrain from any hostile action against any of the United Nations pending the conclusion of the treaty of peace; (ii) would maintain no military, naval or air force or equipment except as authorised by the Allies, and (iii) would comply with all instructions from the Allies with regard to such forces and equipment. Under this interim arrangement control of Italy would be retained only as far as was necessary to cover Allied military requirements while Allied forces remained in Italy or were operating therefrom, and to safeguard the equitable settlement of territorial disputes.

At a meeting of the Foreign Secretaries on July 18 Mr. Byrnes proposed that the Plenary Meeting should discuss at once the question of the admission of Italy to membership of the United Nations. (a) M. Molotov asked for delay. Mr. Byrnes therefore did not raise the matter again until July 20. The discussion was then linked with a proposal about Spain. As the Foreign Office expected, the Soviet (b) Delegation had presented to the Conference a memorandum suggesting that the three Powers should recommend to the United Nations that they should break off all relations with the Government of General Franco and give support to the 'democratic forces' in Spain and thus enable the Spanish people 'to establish such a régime as will respond to their will'. The reasons put forward for this proposal were that the Franco régime originated not as a development of internal forces in Spain but as a result of outside interference by the principal Axis countries; that the régime was a grave danger to freedom-loving nations in Europe and South America, and that in the face of the brutal terror instituted by General Franco the Spanish people had repeatedly expressed themselves against the régime and in favour of the restoration of democratic government in Spain.

This memorandum was discussed at a plenary meeting of the (c) Conference on July 19. Mr. Churchill said that the present and previous British Governments had a strong dislike of General Franco and his régime, and that he regarded the cruelties perpetrated by it as wholly distasteful and undemocratic. On the other hand he was afraid that the Russian proposal—given the nature of the Spanish people—might have the effect of rallying round General Franco those elements which were now deserting him. Moreover, though the

[1] See Volume III, Chapter XLIV, Section (iv).

(a) P(Terminal) 1st meeting. (b) P(Terminal)8; Z8637, 8853, 9049/537/41.
(c) P(Terminal) 3rd meeting.

rupture of relations might give some satisfaction, in practice Ambassadors were needed.

The Prime Minister thought that we should not interfere in the internal affairs of another country, though we had a right not to allow a system of government repugnant to us in a country which had fought against us or which we had liberated. Spain had not been liberated by us and had not fought against us. It was to be hoped that the Franco régime would soon pass away, and all proper diplomatic action should be taken, but we did not want to countenance action which might lead to a renewal of the horrors of the civil war. In any case the World Organisation now set up made provision against interference by one country in the affairs of another. We could not without inconsistency take action contrary to the Charter at the time we were preparing to ratify it.

Stalin argued that the Franco régime was gaining strength, and that it was dangerous to leave matters as they were. He was, however, willing to take a milder and more flexible method of showing that the three Powers had no sympathy with the Franco régime, and that the aspirations of the Spanish people towards democracy were just. He proposed that the matter should be submitted to the Foreign Secretaries for consideration. President Truman was willing to accept this proposal, but the Prime Minister thought that the question was one of principle—non-intervention in the affairs of another country—and should be decided by the plenary Conference. He would do nothing to support the Franco régime, and would be glad if a change took place in Spain resulting in a constitutional monarchy on democratic lines, and an amnesty for political prisoners. If, however, the Conference announced its views in the matter we should merely turn Spanish opinion against us. President Truman again gave his support to the proposal for referring the matter to the Foreign Secretaries, but, after
(a) the continued opposition of the Prime Minister, suggested that the discussion should be left open for the time.

In a note of July 19 to Sir A. Cadogan on this discussion Mr. Hoyer Millar, Head of the Western Department of the Foreign Office, suggested that, while it was impossible to accept the Russian proposal as originally drafted (since it implied direct intervention in Spanish internal affairs), we might well agree to some form of resolution definitely disapproving of General Franco and his régime. If we continued to resist the Russians altogether on this matter, they would become more obstinate on matters to which we attached greater importance. We might also give the Americans the impression that we were favourable to General Franco, whereas in fact we should welcome his disappearance. Mr. Hoyer Millar suggested a resolution on the following lines:

(a) Z9237/537/41.

> 'The three Governments, while recognising that it rests with the Spanish people themselves to choose the type of government under which they wish to live, feel bound to make it clear that, in so far as they themselves are concerned, they will find it difficult to place their relations with Spain on a better footing so long as General Franco and the Falange régime remain in power. In particular, as long as the present régime in Spain remains unaltered, the three Governments will feel unable to support any application from the Spanish Government for membership of the World Organisation.' (a)

Mr. Byrnes, at the meeting of Foreign Secretaries on July 20, suggested that the statement which President Truman had proposed with regard to the admission of Italy to the United Nations might include a reference to Spain: i.e. the Great Powers might state that they would not favour the admission of Spain as long as she remained under the control of the existing régime. Mr. Eden said he was attracted by the suggestion, but thought that the statement would be strengthened if it included references to other neutral countries. It would be simpler to contrast the position of Spain with other neutrals rather than with the position of States which had waged war against the United Nations, since in the case of the latter a peace settlement must precede admission.

From this point the question of Spain became overshadowed by the Soviet demand that any declaration should include a reference to the four 'satellites'—Finland, Roumania, Bulgaria and Hungary. Mr. Byrnes's suggestion was, however, carried over to the final draft of a declaration with regard to the conclusion of peace treaties and admission to the United Nations Organisation. Meanwhile the Foreign Secretaries on July 20 appointed a Committee to draft such a (b) declaration.

The American proposals with regard to an Italian peace treaty were considered at a plenary meeting of the Conference on July 20. Stalin then proposed that the position of Roumania, Finland, Hungary and Bulgaria should also be considered. Bulgaria had provided eight or ten divisions, and Roumania ten or twelve in the last stages of the war against Germany. President Truman explained that he had singled out Italy because she had been the first country to surrender, and the armistice terms imposed on her were harder and more binding than those imposed on the other States. He agreed, however, that the Foreign Secretaries might consider the position of these States.

The Prime Minister recapitulated the special position of Great Britain as the country which had suffered most from Italian aggression. Nonetheless we did not oppose the suggestion for preparing a peace treaty with Italy. The work of preparation would take several months, and might not be completed very long before the meeting

(a) F(Terminal) 3rd meeting; Z8854/537/41. (b) P(Terminal) 4th meeting.

of a general Peace Conference. Mr. Churchill pointed out that the existing Italian Government had no democratic foundations, since it was not based on free, fair, and unfettered elections. The Ministers were simply politicians who called themselves leaders of political parties. He understood that they were proposing to hold elections before the winter. It was therefore undesirable—although we might start work on a treaty—to come to final conclusions with the Italians before their Government stood on a recognisable democratic foundation.

Mr. Churchill did not agree with the American proposal for the replacement of the Terms of Surrender by undertakings on the part of the Italian Government. The electorate might repudiate the present Italian Government which was dependent on the political parties of twenty years ago. If we gave up our rights under the Terms of Surrender, and if there were a long interval before the Peace Settlement, we should have lost our power to secure our requirements from Italy other than by the exercise of force which we wished to avoid. The undertakings listed in the United States memorandum did not cover vital questions such as the future of the Italian fleet and colonies and the payment of reparation. Thus we should lose our rights under the Terms of Surrender without having made satisfactory arrangements to replace them. Moreover these terms were signed on behalf of many other nations—including the Dominions—who had suffered great losses at the hands of the Italians. We ought not to go further than to assent in principle to the preparation of a peace treaty with Italy and to ask the Council of Foreign Ministers to give priority to the matter. Mr. Churchill also referred to the other countries mentioned in the discussion. He said that Bulgaria had no claim on Great Britain. In the first World War Bulgaria had inflicted great suffering on Russia, and in the second war she had greatly injured Yugoslavia and Greece and had been a constant threat to Turkey. Bulgaria was still armed, and no arrangements had been made for the payment of reparation by her. Mr. Churchill was much less favourably inclined to start preparations for a peace treaty with her than with Italy.

Stalin said that we wanted to separate the satellite States from Germany in order to reduce her power. We could not achieve this by the use of force alone, but must alleviate the position of these States. In comparison with these considerations of high policy all other questions of complaint or revenge must lapse. The spirit of revenge or redress from injuries was a very bad adviser in politics. It was not for him to teach his colleagues in this matter, but 'in politics one should be guided by the calculation of forces'.[1] The practical question

[1] Mr. Truman agreed with these remarks that peace could not be made on the basis of revenge. The Prime Minister said that he also agreed with them, and that it gave him great pleasure to hear 'these sentiments expressed with such solemnity and authority'.

was whether we wanted Italy or the other satellites on the side of the United Nations. He supported President Truman's proposals on Italy and thought that diplomatic relations should be resumed with the satellites.

The Conference agreed to submit to the Foreign Ministers the question of interim arrangements pending the conclusion of peace treaties with Italy and the other satellite States.

On July 21 the United States Delegation presented to the meeting (a) of Foreign Secretaries two memoranda; the first dealt with policy towards Roumania, Bulgaria, Hungary, and Finland, and the second with policy towards Italy. The first memorandum stated that the objectives of the three Great Powers were the early achievement of the political independence and economic recovery of the countries in question, and the exercise of the right of the respective peoples ultimately to choose their own forms of government. The Council of Foreign Ministers should therefore undertake as soon as possible the preparation of peace treaties with the four countries, and the three Governments should make 'such public declarations on matters of joint concern to those countries as may be appropriate'. Meanwhile they would take steps through the Control Commissions for the progressive transfer of responsibility to the Governments concerned.

In the memorandum on Italy the objectives of the three Governments were described as in the other memorandum, with an additional sentence that 'the three Governments agree to certain steps which would afford some further acknowledgement of Italian contribution towards the defeat of Germany'. Then followed three clauses: (i) the three Governments would announce their intention to conclude an early peace treaty with Italy and to provide her with such economic assistance as was practicable. They would also repeat their view on the desirability of early elections in Italy; (ii) the Allied Commission in Italy would 'accelerate the steps already taken' (*sic*) to transfer increasing responsibilities to the Italian Government; (iii) the three Governments would ask their Ambassadors in Italy, in consultation with the Supreme Allied Commander, to report before September 1, 1945, on those provisions of the Terms of Surrender which might be considered as inoperative.[1]

M. Molotov tried to get the two memoranda combined into a single (b)

[1] The British Delegation—in private conversation with the Americans—had pointed (c) out once again their doubts about an interim arrangement with Italy which would terminate the armistice and therefore make it impossible to enforce upon Italy certain provisions, particularly those relating to territorial questions, which we wished to include in the treaty. The British Delegation suggested as an alternative method the termination of such parts of the armistice terms as were no longer applicable. This would mean in fact terminating the larger part of the terms. The United States Delegation accepted this suggestion.

(a) P(Terminal) 19–20. (b) F(Terminal) 4th meeting. (c) F.O.934/2/6(4).

declaration, but Mr. Byrnes did not agree that there was sufficient similarity between the case of Italy and that of the four other countries. The question whether there should be a single declaration covering both Italy and the satellites was referred back to a plenary meeting. M. Molotov stated that he must place on record the Soviet view that the time had come for the British and United States Government to extend diplomatic recognition to the existing Governments of Roumania, Bulgaria and Hungary. When the question was (a) brought before the plenary meeting on July 21 Stalin repeated the Soviet view that the three Governments should agree to resume diplomatic relations with the four countries. The Prime Minister and President Truman refused this suggestion. Stalin then said that he was not prepared in the circumstances to discuss policy either towards Italy or towards the satellites.

Meanwhile the Soviet delegation had brought forward the (b) question of the future of the Italian colonies. They had suggested in a memorandum of July 20 that the Conference should authorise the Council of Foreign Ministers to consider proposals for bringing into effect the system of trusteeship in accordance with the provisions of the United Nations Charter. The memorandum referred to

> 'the necessity of solution in the nearest future of the problem relating to the terms of trusteeship on [*sic* ?of] the former colonial possessions of Italy in Africa and in the Mediterranean, having in view herewith the possibility of establishing the trusteeship system exercised by individual States or by U.S.S.R., U.S.A. and Great Britain jointly on the above-mentioned former colonial possessions of Italy.'

There was a further reference to proposals regarding the régime of territories at present held under mandate of the League of Nations.

(c) M. Molotov explained this memorandum to the plenary meeting of the Conference on July 22, and added that the question of Korea should be discussed. Mr. Churchill pointed out that, since the matter had been discussed at San Francisco and was already in the hands of the World Organisation, there was not much point in considering it at the Conference. President Truman, however, supported the Russian demand for a discussion on trusteeship.[1] Stalin then asked what had happened to the Italian colonies? Mr. Churchill replied at once that the British army 'through heavy losses and indisputable victories had conquered them'.[2] We had come out of the war as the

[1] President Truman said that he thought it just as appropriate to discuss the Italian colonies as to discuss Poland.

[2] Stalin here interjected that the Red Army had taken Berlin.

(a) P(Terminal) 5th meeting.
(b) P(Terminal) 13. (c) P(Terminal) 6th meeting; U5677/3628/70.

world's greatest debtor, and would never regain naval equality with the United States. Nevertheless we had made no territorial claims. 'For us there was no Königsberg, no Baltic States, nothing.' We would therefore approach the question raised by Stalin with complete disinterestedness. Italy had lost her colonies, and had no claim of right to regain them, but these facts did not preclude the return of some of them to her on certain conditions at the Peace Settlement. Mr. Churchill did not say that he favoured their return but he did not preclude it. At present we held the colonies. Mr. Churchill 'wondered who wanted them; if there were claimants at the table they should come forward'.

President Truman said that the United States did not want them, or want to undertake trusteeship for them; they already had enough poor Italians in the United States. Mr. Churchill said that we had considered whether any of the colonies would be suitable for Jewish settlement, but the Jews had not favoured the suggestion. We had great interests in the Mediterranean and any change in the *status quo* would require long consideration on our part. Mr. Churchill asked whether the Russians wished to put forward claims for some of the colonies or for trusteeship of them? M. Molotov replied that the Soviet Government would like to know whether we thought it advisable for Italy to lose her colonies, and, if so, to what State should they be given or what State should have trusteeship over them? Mr. Churchill said that we had reached no conclusion in the matter, but he had not thought of the possibility that the Soviet Government might want large tracts of the North African shore. If this were the case, the matter would have to be considered in relation to many other factors. Stalin replied that the Soviet Delegation at San Francisco had said that the Soviet Government wished to secure the mandates for certain territories.

Mr. Churchill pointed out once more that the question could be decided only at the Peace Conference. Stalin, however, with Mr. Truman's support, again proposed that the matter should be referred to the Foreign Secretaries. The latter discussed the subject on July 23. Mr. Eden then said that our view was only that Italy had no (a) right to recover any of her colonies. The Peace Conference would decide whether in fact any of these colonies should be restored to her. After this decision, consideration could be given to the form of trusteeship appropriate to any colonies which were not to be restored to Italy. The World Organisation would probably be the proper body to consider the matter. Mr. Byrnes supported this view. M. Molotov then withdrew his request for an immediate discussion and the three Foreign Secretaries agreed to note that the Soviet Government would

(a) F(Terminal) 6th meeting.

raise the matter at the first meeting of the Council of Foreign Ministers in September 1945.[1]

The Committee appointed to draft a statement about the admission of neutrals to the United Nations failed to reach agreement. The Foreign Secretaries therefore considered the question again on
(a) the morning of July 24. Mr. Byrnes proposed a draft which the British Delegation were in general prepared to support. M. Molotov, however, refused to consider the draft unless it included a reference to the position of the four satellite countries which, in his opinion, had done more than Italy to help in bringing about the ultimate defeat of Germany. Mr. Eden and Mr. Byrnes repeated the unwillingness of their respective Governments to recognise the Governments of the satellite States—and especially those of Roumania and Bulgaria on the ground that these governments were not sufficiently representative. After further discussion—including some plain speaking by Mr Eden about the Roumanian Government—Mr. Byrnes proposed an additional paragraph to the draft statement to the effect that 'the three Governments also hope that the Council of Foreign Ministers may, without undue delay, prepare peace treaties for Bulgaria, Roumania, Hungary and Finland. It is also their desire, on the conclusion of peace treaties with responsible democratic Governments in these countries, to support their application for membership of the United Nations Organisation.' M. Molotov was willing to take this draft as a basis for discussion, but he insisted that the satellite countries must not be put in a worse position than Italy. Mr. Byrnes repeated that the United States would not recognise the existing Governments in the satellite States.

Mr. Eden—in reply to M. Molotov—said that it was a mistake 'to use words to paper over cracks'. There was, in fact, a difference between Italy and some at least of the four satellite countries in which the Soviet Government were specially interested. The British Government would be ready to make a peace treaty and renew diplomatic relations with the present government in Italy, but not, on their present information, with the existing Governments of

---

[1] The Secretary of State for the Dominions, on hearing of the Russian proposal, tele-
(b) graphed on July 24 to Mr. Eden that at San Francisco the Soviet Delegation had tried repeatedly to cut out from the Trusteeship chapter of the United Nations Charter all safeguards with regard to existing Mandates. If they had had their way, there would have been no security for existing mandatories pending the negotiation of new Trusteeship arrangements. We did not know the Russian motive, but it was significant that they should have raised the matter again. The question concerned the Dominions as well as ourselves; we could not enter into any new arrangements with the United States and Russia unless we had full consultation with the Dominion Governments. Mr. Eden replied on July 25 that he was in entire agreement. He added: 'We had a bit of a dust-up with the Russians, but have yielded nothing. They will no doubt return to the charge on the next international occasion.'

(a) F(Terminal) 7th meeting.
(b) F.O.934/3/18(7), Target 173, F.O.934/4/30(7), Onward 194 and Target 220.

Bulgaria and Roumania. In view of the failure of the Foreign Secretaries to reach agreement, the matter was referred to a plenary meeting.

(a) At the plenary meeting on July 24 Mr. Churchill used even stronger language than Mr. Eden about the Governments of Roumania and Bulgaria. He complained about the treatment of British representatives in Roumania, and contrasted the position in the satellite States unfavourably with that of Italy.[1] The Soviet Government, however, maintained their refusal to agree to any declaration which did not include a reference to the possibility of diplomatic recognition of the four satellite Governments. Stalin said that the 'artificial distinction' between Italy and the four satellites compelled him to think that these four were 'being treated as lepers'. In this he saw 'an intention to discredit the Soviet Union and the Soviet army'. Italy had been the first to surrender, but in all other respects she had done far more harm than the four countries to the Allied cause. Stalin doubted whether the Italian Government were really more democratic or responsible than the other Governments.[2] President Truman, after repeating that the United States would not recognise the satellite governments until they had been reorganised on a democratic basis, finally said that he would accept a compromise formula proposed by M. Molotov (as an addition to Mr. Byrnes's formula) that the three Governments agreed 'to consider, each separately, in the immediate future, the question of the establishing of diplomatic relations with Finland, Roumania, Bulgaria, and Hungary'. Mr. Churchill said that in accepting this formula, there would be a risk that the Conference was covering up with words a real difference of view, and that the formula would give the impression that we intended a speedy recognition of the four Governments. Mr. Churchill asked Mr. Truman whether he had not previously said that he was not prepared to recognise these Governments. He asked the President whether he would recognise the representatives of Roumania and Bulgaria and invite them to the Council of Foreign Ministers in September to discuss the preparation of Peace Treaties. Mr. Truman replied, enigmatically, that the only Governments so invited would be those which the United States would recognise; he then suggested that the Foreign Ministers might reconsider the draft in the light of the discussion.

(b) Mr. Eden had left Berlin, and Mr. Bevin had not arrived when on July 27 the Foreign Ministers again discussed the matter. Sir A. Cadogan, on behalf of the British Delegation, proposed, as an alternative to the Russian wording, a form of words to the effect

[1] In speaking of the restriction put on the British Missions in Roumania and Bulgaria Mr. Churchill said that 'an iron curtain had been rung down'.

[2] Stalin said later that the satellite governments were 'more democratic and nearer to the people than was the Italian Government'.

(a) P(Terminal) 8th meeting. (b) F(Terminal) 9th meeting.

that 'the conclusion of peace treaties with responsible[1] democratic Governments in these States (i.e. the satellites) will enable the three Governments to establish normal diplomatic relations with them and to support their application for admission to the United Nations'. Sir A. Cadogan repeated the statement which the British Delegation had already made that Great Britain could not constitutionally resume normal diplomatic relations with States with which she was technically at war.

Mr. Byrnes then said that when President Truman had put forward his original suggestion that the Conference should give public support to the Italian application for admission to the United Nations, he had not expected serious objection. It had appeared, however, that this proposal would not be accepted unless the statement included a reference to the other ex-enemy satellite States. It had also been impossible to reach agreement on the terms of this reference. Mr. Byrnes therefore thought it better to withdraw the original American proposal.

M. Molotov, however, wanted to continue the attempt to get an (a) agreed statement and was unwilling to allow the proposal to be withdrawn. At the plenary meeting on July 28, Mr. Attlee and Mr. Bevin maintained the attitude taken by Mr. Churchill and Mr. Eden on the question of recognition of the satellite Governments. Stalin again put forward his view that there was no reason for making any difference between Italy and the other satellites. Italy had already been given full diplomatic recognition by the United States and Soviet Governments, and 90 per cent recognition by the British Government. Mr. Bevin said the difference was that we had known a great deal about the Italian Government before we recognised it and we knew nothing about the governments in the other countries. Stalin suggested that the Russian formula might be amended to read: 'The three Governments agree to consider, each separately, the question of establishing complete or partial diplomatic relations.' Mr. Attlee would not accept this formula. Mr. Bevin added that he wanted to be 'absolutely straight with the British people', and that we did not want to cover up with words the real effect of a decision. It we were going to recognise the satellite States, we should be ready to say so, but we could not recognise them at the present time. Mr. Bevin then supported Mr. Byrnes's proposal that the project for a declaration about the admission of neutral and ex-enemy States to the United Nations should be withdrawn. Stalin consented to the withdrawal.

Mr. Byrnes, however, reconsidered the matter, and decided to suggest a new formula as part of his general compromise proposals. (b) He told Sir A. Cadogan of his intention; the British Delegation at

[1] At the wish of the Soviet representatives, this word was later changed to 'recognised'.

(a) P(Terminal) 10th meeting. (b) F.O.934/2/8(15).

their staff meeting on the morning of July 29 decided to accept the formula, though they thought that it would at first seem discouraging to the genuinely democratic parties in the countries concerned. On the other hand the formula would not commit us to recognition unless we were satisfied that responsible democractic governments had been established. We might also link acceptance of the formula with the request which we had already made for better facilities for the press and for the expression of public opinion. We should make it clear that we felt free to announce that we had agreed to the declaration in the expectation that these facilities would be granted.

Mr. Byrnes introduced his new formula, as part of his compromise, (a)
at the Foreign Secretaries' meeting on July 30. At the plenary meeting on July 31 he said that on further reflection the United States Dele- (b)
gation had decided to put forward this new draft as part of their attempt to secure agreement on the three outstanding problems of reparation, the western frontier of Poland and the attitude of the Great Powers towards the admission of certain States to association with the United Nations. They now suggested two new sentences to the draft in order to cover the satellite States: (i) 'The three Governments agree to examine, each separately, in the near future, in the light of the conditions then prevailing, the establishment of diplomatic relations with Bulgaria, Finland, Hungary and Roumania, to the extent possible prior to the ratification of peace treaties with those countries.' (ii) 'The three Governments express the desire that, in view of the changed conditions resulting from the termination of the war in Europe, representatives of the Allied Press shall enjoy full freedom to report to the world on developments in Bulgaria, Finland, Hungary and Roumania.'

Mr. Byrnes said that the first of these sentences was designed to meet the Soviet views as well as those of the British and United States Delegations, and the second used substantially the same language as that already approved in the proposed statement on Poland. Stalin accepted the sentences with the substitution in (i) of the words 'conclusion of peace treaties' for 'ratification of peace treaties', and in (ii) of the words 'have no doubt that . . . representatives of the Allied Press will enjoy' for 'express the desire . . . shall enjoy'. President Truman and Mr. Attlee accepted these amendments. The draft was then agreed without further discussion. The terms of the Allied statement as recorded in the Protocol and published report of the Conference were as follows:

'The three Governments consider it desirable that the present anomalous position of Italy, Bulgaria, Finland, Hungary and

(a) F(Terminal) 10th meeting; P(Terminal) 58. (b) P(Terminal) 11th meeting.

Roumania should be terminated by the conclusion of Peace Treaties. They trust that the other interested Allied Governments will share these views.

For their part the Three Governments have included the preparation of a Peace Treaty for Italy as the first among the immediate important tasks to be undertaken by the new Council of Foreign Ministers. Italy was the first of the Axis Powers to break with Germany, to whose defeat she has made a material contribution, and has now joined with the Allies in the struggle against Japan. Italy has freed herself from the Fascist régime and is making good progress towards re-establishment of a democratic government and institutions. The conclusion of such a Peace Treaty with a recognised and democratic Italian Government will make it possible for the Three Governments to fulfil their desire to support an application from Italy for membership of the United Nations.

The Three Governments have also charged the Council of Foreign Ministers with the task of preparing Peace Treaties for Bulgaria, Finland, Hungary and Roumania. The conclusion of Peace Treaties with recognised democratic Governments in these States will also enable the Three Governments to support applications from them for membership of the United Nations. The Three Governments agree to examine, each separately in the near future, in the light of the conditions then prevailing, the establishment of diplomatic relations with Finland, Roumania, Bulgaria and Hungary, to the extent possible prior to the conclusion of Peace Treaties with those countries.

The Three Governments have no doubt that in view of the changed conditions resulting from the termination of the war in Europe, representatives of the Allied press will enjoy full freedom to report to the world upon developments in Roumania, Bulgaria, Hungary and Finland.

As regards the admission of other States into the United Nations Organisation, Article 4 of the Charter of the United Nations declares that:

1. Membership in the United Nations is open to all other peace-loving States who accept the obligations contained in the present Charter, and, in the judgment of the organisation, are able and willing to carry out these obligations;
2. The admission of any such State to membership in the United Nations will be effected by a decision of the General Assembly upon the recommendation of the Security Council.

The Three Governments, so far as they are concerned, will support applications for membership from those States which have remained neutral during the war and which fulfil the qualifications set out above.

The Three Governments feel bound, however, to make it clear that they for their part would not favour any application for membership put forward by the present Spanish Government, which, having been founded with the support of the Axis powers, does not, in view of its origins, its nature, its record and its close association with the aggressor States, possess the qualifications necessary to justify such membership.'

At the meeting of the Foreign Ministers on July 20 M. Molotov had raised the question whether Italy was to pay reparation. The Foreign Ministers gave separate consideration to this question after they had decided to appoint a sub-committee to draft a statement about Italy. Mr. Byrnes said that he doubted whether in fact Italy could pay anything. The United States Government had already advanced some 200 million dollars to Italy and would probably have to advance another 400 or 500 million dollars. They were not prepared to advance money to Italy, or any other country, for the purpose of enabling her to pay reparation. (a)

M. Molotov pointed out that, if Finland could pay reparation, a large country like Italy ought not to go free. Mr. Eden inclined to agree with Mr. Byrnes's view. Italy was liable in principle to pay reparation, but the extent to which this liability could be enforced would be a matter for consideration when the Italian Peace Treaty was being drafted. The Foreign Ministers agreed to refer the question of Italian and of Austrian reparation to the committee of the Conference which was considering German economic problems.

On July 24 the Soviet Delegation circulated a memorandum to the Conference suggesting that Italian reparation payment should be fixed at 600 million dollars payable over six years by means of goods produced by Italian industry and agriculture. This reparation would serve as compensation for damage inflicted upon the U.S.S.R., Great Britain, the United States, Yugoslavia, Greece and Albania as a result of Italian participation in the war. (b)

The Economic Committee was unable to produce an agreed report. The Soviet representatives maintained their figure of 600 million dollars for Italy. The British and American representatives argued that Italy would continue to require aid from abroad for some time to come; the United Kingdom, the United States and Canada had already supplied more than 500 million dollars' worth of goods to Italy to prevent disease and unrest, and any reparation payments from Italy would in fact be financed by the nations supplying such goods. The British and American representatives therefore could not agree to the imposition of reparation levies on the current production of Italy.[1] They were, however, prepared to consider the possibility of certain 'once for all' removals of machinery and equipment from direct war industries having no peace-time utility. (c)

---

[1] Similar arguments applied to Austria.

(a) F(Terminal) 3rd meeting. (b) P(Terminal) 37. (c) P(Terminal) 41.

(a) The Foreign Secretaries discussed this report at a meeting on July 27, but again reached no agreement. They therefore referred (b) the question to a plenary meeting on July 28. Stalin then said that while the Soviet Union would agree not to ask reparation from Austria, they felt bound to secure it from Italy. President Truman said that he was concerned that the first charge on Italian exports must be the repayment of the advances already made to Italy. Mr. Attlee agreed with this view. Mr. Bevin suggested that the matter was one of priorities; the first priority must be the repayment of the advances, and the second, reparation. They must therefore find out how much would be left over after allowance had been made for the (c) first priority. At the meeting of the Foreign Secretaries on July 30 Mr. Bevin circulated a British draft recommendation that the Council of Foreign Ministers should deal with the problem on this basis. M. Molotov wanted a discussion at the meeting. Mr. Byrnes pointed out that it had been discussed at length. There seemed to be no prospect of agreement, but M. Molotov could raise the matter at the plenary meeting. M. Molotov did not raise the question, and nothing further was said about it at the Conference.

(v)

The question of the fulfilment of the Yalta Declaration on Liberated Europe: Russian attitude towards Anglo-American complaints: Russian proposals with regard to Greece: President Truman's refusal to continue the discussion of Yugoslav affairs: Russian demands with regard to Turkey: President Truman's proposal for the unrestricted navigation of inland waterways.

Stalin and M. Molotov had deliberately widened the discussions on Italy in the hope of obtaining British and American recognition of the Russian-controlled Governments of Roumania, Bulgaria and Hungary. If they had granted this recognition, the western Allies would not only have committed themselves to an admission that the Governments concerned had been appointed and were acting in accordance with the Yalta Declaration on Liberated Europe; they would also have ruled out, in practice, any chance of securing free elections and the establishment of democratic liberties generally in these countries.

In accordance with the policy upon which they had decided before the Conference, the United States Delegation submitted a memoran- (d) dum on July 17 1945, pointing out that the obligations assumed under the Declaration had not been carried out, and that the continued failure of the three Powers to secure that these obligations were

(a) F(Terminal) 9th meeting. (b) P(Terminal) 10th meeting. (c) F(Terminal) 10th meeting. (d) P(Terminal) 4.

honoured would be regarded throughout the world as evidence of their lack of unity and would undermine confidence in the sincerity of their declared aims. The United States Government proposed that the three Governments should take the following steps to carry out their obligations under the Declaration:

(i) They should agree on the immediate reorganisation of the Governments in Roumania and Bulgaria, in accordance with paragraph 3 clause (c)[1] of the Declaration.

(ii) They should work out procedures for such reorganisation to include the representation of all significant democratic elements. Diplomatic recognition should be accorded, and peace treaties concluded with the countries in question as soon as the reorganisation had taken place.

(iii) They should consider how best to assist (in accordance with paragraph 3, clause (d) of the Declaration) any interim Governments in the holding of free and unfettered elections. Such assistance was required in the case of Greece and would be required in Roumania and Bulgaria and probably in other countries.

On July 20 the Soviet Delegation replied to this memorandum (a) stating that they disagreed with the statements regarding Roumania and Bulgaria. They maintained that due order and legal power existed in these countries and in Hungary and Finland as well; that the Governments of Roumania and Bulgaria had authority, were trusted by the population, and were faithfully carrying out their obligations. There was no reason for interfering in their domestic affairs. In Greece on the other hand no due order existed, law was not respected, and terrorism raged against the 'democratic elements which had borne the principal burden of the fight against German invaders for the liberation of Greece'. The Greek Government were also threatening Albania and Bulgaria with military action. Urgent measures were therefore necessary to 'eliminate such a situation in Greece'. The Soviet Government therefore proposed the restoration 'in the nearest days' of diplomatic relations with Roumania, Bulgaria, Finland, and Hungary, and a recommendation to the Regent of Greece to take immediate measures towards the re-establishment of a democratic Government according to the Varkiza agreement of February 12, 1945.[2]

The Foreign Office considered this Russian document as 'astonishing'. (b) We could not possibly accept the statement that 'due order' existed in Roumania and Bulgaria and that the Governments of

[1] See above, p. 270.

[2] For this agreement between the Greek Government and representatives of E.A.M (National Liberation Front) and E.L.A.S. (National People's Liberation Army) see Volume III, pp. 436–8.

(a) P(Terminal) 11. (b) R12360/5063/67.

these countries were 'trusted by the population'. Our briefs for the Conference had already drawn attention to the terrorist activities of the Communist-controlled secret police and militia in the two countries, and especially in Bulgaria. We could add that, according to reports which we believed to be approximately accurate, some 40–50,000 persons had been murdered by the militia in the past six months, excluding the 2,000 executed after trials as 'war criminals'. The 'offence' of most of these people was not collaboration with the Germans, but opposition to the present Government.

The Russian assertion that the two Governments were carrying out their agreements under the armistice was equally unacceptable. The failure of the Bulgarian Government to make reparation deliveries to Greece was a serious example. The Bulgarians also, instead of demobilising their army, as they were required to do under the armistice terms, appeared to have been allowed by the Russians to increase it. Many of the fascist organisations, e.g. the Roumanian Iron Guard, had been only nominally suppressed, and had transferred their allegiance to the Communists who had welcomed them. The Russians would, of course, deny our evidence, but we could point out the contrast between the severe censorship imposed on Soviet-controlled Balkan countries and the complete freedom of speech and the press permitted in Greece. If the situation in the Soviet-controlled countries was as satisfactory as the Russians pretended, why should they continue to prevent newspaper correspondents from entering them?

(a) At the Foreign Secretaries' meeting on July 20 Mr. Eden objected very strongly to the statements in the Soviet memorandum, and particularly to the allegations with regard to Greece. He referred to
(b) the Prime Minister's statement at the plenary meeting on July 19 that there was no truth in a report—mentioned by Stalin on the previous day—of trouble on the Greek frontier. Mr. Churchill had said that there were no Greek field divisions in northern Greece, but only 7000 National Guards armed and deployed for security purposes. On the other side of the frontier, however, there were said to be 30,000 Albanian, 30,000 Yugoslav and 24,000 Bulgarian troops.

Mr. Eden said that the Soviet memorandum—which had been submitted after the Prime Minister's denial of the report mentioned by Stalin—was a complete travesty of the facts. The Soviet Government did not know the situation in Greece; the British Government were fully informed of it, and the press of the world were free to see for themselves and report on conditions in Greece. This could not be said of Roumania and Bulgaria. Furthermore the Greek Government had invited the Powers to supervise the elections in Greece; here again there was no comparable situation in Roumania or Bulgaria.

(a) F(Terminal) 3rd meeting. (b) P(Terminal) 3rd meeting.

Mr. Byrnes supported Mr. Eden. He said that American hopes with regard to the fulfilment of the Yalta Declaration had been disappointed in Roumania and Bulgaria. The Governments of these countries had restricted the movements of United States representatives; members of the Control Commission had been refused entry into Bulgaria for a month or six weeks. The press too had been denied entry. There were also no signs that elections would be held at the earliest possible moment. Mr. Byrnes said that American opinion was irritated by these facts, and that one of the Great Powers had no right to deal with the situation alone. In view of the attitude of the Roumanian and Bulgarian Governments it was impossible for the United States to recognise them.

M. Molotov continued to argue that the situation was satisfactory in Roumania and Bulgaria, but not in Greece; that free elections would be held in the first two of these countries—in Bulgaria on August 26[1]—and that there was no need for Allied supervision of the elections. He did not comment when Mr. Byrnes and Mr. Eden said they had sent invitations to the Soviet Government to join in supervision of elections.

Mr. Byrnes said that Allied supervision of elections was necessary. Mr. Eden pointed out that the Bulgarian electors were being asked to vote for a list, and that this method was not what we understood by democracy or free elections. After M. Molotov had complained again about the situation in Greece, Mr. Eden said that he must take the gravest exception to his (M. Molotov's) statements and to the Soviet memorandum, and that they were a serious reflection on the British Government.

Mr. Eden suggested that the British and American Delegations should submit memoranda setting out their requirements with regard to the rights of the Control Commission, free elections, and the freedom of the press in Roumania and Bulgaria. M. Molotov accepted this suggestion. He admitted that more freedom should be given to the press, but repeated his view that supervision of the elections was unnecessary.

The United States Delegation submitted another memorandum on (a)

[1] After hearing that the Bulgarian elections had been fixed for August 26, the Foreign Office telegraphed to Mr. Eden that all the available evidence showed that these elections would be wholly unrepresentative. The Foreign Office suggested that we might warn the Bulgarian Government that we should be unable to accept as representative any Government elected in the manner now proposed. Even if the Russians agreed to Allied observation of the elections, the electoral machinery would render the polling a complete farce. As an alternative to a communication to the Bulgarian Government, Mr. Eden and the Americans might make a statement at the Conference in answer to the Soviet memorandum of July 20. If we said nothing, the Soviet Government would claim that, apart from Great Britain, Bulgaria was the first and only European country to hold free and democratic elections. (b)

(a) P(Terminal) 21. (b) R12490/81/67.

July 21 putting forward three 'steps of immediate urgency in the implementation of the Yalta Declaration':

(i) The three Governments should 'adopt adequate measures to enable them to become informed of proposed electoral procedures, and to provide for the observation[1] of elections, in Italy, Greece, Bulgaria, Roumania and Hungary for the choice of Governments responsive to the will of the people'.

(ii) The three Governments should agree to adopt measures for facilitating the entry of representatives of the press into liberated or former Axis satellite States; these representatives should be allowed freedom of movement, and facilities for the despatch of their reports without restriction by political censorship. Any restrictions on the freedom of the press within the countries concerned should also be removed.

(iii) The three Governments should agree that the Control Commissions in Roumania, Bulgaria, and Hungary should henceforward operate on a tripartite basis, with revised procedures 'taking into account the interests and responsibilities of the three Governments which together presented the terms of armistice to the respective countries'.

Mr. Eden associated the British Delegation with the terms of this memorandum. The Foreign Secretaries discussed the memorandum
(a) at a meeting on July 22. M. Molotov—while complaining of the position of the Soviet representative on the Allied Council in Italy—agreed to put forward a memorandum on changes which the Soviet Government were proposing to introduce into the Control Commissions. He had no doubt that—in the new situation since the war had ended—everything practicable would be done to give increased facilities to press representatives. He suggested that a public declaration in the matter was unnecessary. Mr. Eden said that the question was not only one of freedom of movement for press representatives but of freedom to despatch reports without political censorship. Mr. Byrnes and Mr. Eden repeated that, although their respective Governments would have preferred not to assume the responsibility of supervising the elections, they were convinced that it was necessary to do so in order to fulfil the spirit of the Yalta Declaration and remove the suspicions of world opinion.

M. Molotov objected again to the proposals for the supervision of elections, though he would be more ready to discuss the points raised in the memorandum if the other Delegates would discuss at the

---

[1] Mr. Churchill had suggested the use of this word rather than 'supervision' (which might seem to imply some kind of control).

(a) F(Terminal) 5th meeting.

same time the restoration of diplomatic relations with ex-enemy satellite States. Mr. Eden said that it would be easier to consider recognition in some form of the Governments established as a result of elections held under the conditions recommended by the United States Delegate, though we could not resume normal diplomatic relations with countries with which we were still at war. Mr. Byrnes said that the United States Government would recognise any Government established as a result of elections held under the conditions which the Delegation had proposed, but could not recognise the existing Governments. M. Molotov, however, persisted in refusing, even in principle, the supervision of elections in the ex-enemy satellite countries by observers nominated by the Great Powers.

In view of this Soviet refusal no further discussion took place on the question of elections or of the freedom of the press. Mr. Byrnes, however, at the plenary meeting of July 31, suggested that consideration should be given to the third proposal in the United States memorandum, i.e. the operation of the Control Commissions in Roumania, Bulgaria, and Hungary on a tripartite basis. This proposal was accepted, and a statement introduced into the protocol and communiqué of the Conference giving details of the changes. The other proposals, on Mr. Bevin's suggestion, were dropped. The British and United States Governments thus gave up any hope of securing that the elections in these countries were held on a basis which the western democratic Powers would regard as satisfactory. (a)

The attitude of the Soviet Government increased the difficulties of the position in Greece. Mr. Churchill had thought it desirable to refute in a written statement the Soviet allegations about the state of Greece. Mr. Eden gave copies of this memorandum to Mr. Byrnes and M. Molotov on July 23. The memorandum consisted of a covering note by Mr. Churchill, a report by Field-Marshal Alexander, and an earlier report of a visit to Greece by a delegation of the British Trades Union Congress in January 1945. (b)

The most alarming feature of the situation, however, was not the obstinacy with which the Russians attacked Greece at the Conference but the increasing evidence that they were conducting a campaign of propaganda inciting the Bulgarians, Yugoslavs and Albanians to enforce their territorial claims by direct action. The Prime Minister had denied Stalin's charge that the Greeks were stirring up trouble on the frontier; the real cause of the unrest lay with the Russians themselves. The British Delegation indeed were fully aware of what the Russians were doing, and the Foreign Office

(a) P(Terminal) 11th meeting. (b) F(Terminal) 6th meeting. P(Terminal) 25.

were greatly concerned over the question whether we could do any-
(a) thing to counter it. The Foreign Office telegraphed on July 27 to the British Delegation that a concerted campaign of a dangerous kind was being launched against Greece by all her neighbours, and that it was difficult to believe that this campaign was not being directed by the Russians. It was bad enough that the Allies of Greece should attack her in this way, but much worse that the defeated Roumanians and Bulgarians should be encouraged to slander her. We had protested, with little or no result, in Moscow, and we had told Marshal Tito that, if he had complaints to make against the Greek Government he should do so through ordinary diplomatic channels and not through public speeches. If, however—as seemed likely—the Russians had ordered a continuance of the press campaign, our representations would have no effect.

The Foreign Office considered that if Marshal Tito, counting on Russian support, actually invaded the Greek frontier, we should have to intervene. The military position was serious, in view of the numbers of Yugoslav, Bulgarian and Albanian forces on the Greek frontier, and also of the fact that, in spite of Stalin's statement that there were only 30,000 Russian troops in Bulgaria, our estimate of the number was 100,000 or perhaps even 200,000, whereas we had—as the Russians knew—only 40,000 troops, without any armoured division in Greece.

The Foreign Office thought that the Soviet Government were trying to challenge our policy of building up a strong, independent Greece and Turkey friendly to Great Britain; they were also attempting to strengthen their own client, Bulgaria. As long as Yugoslavia, Greece and Turkey were in good relations, Bulgaria would be isolated. Hence the Russians wanted to set Greece and Yugoslavia against each other in the hope that they would hereby compel Yugoslavia to co-operate with Bulgaria. If we countered this challenge in its early stages, the Soviet Government would probably abandon it, but if any part of Greek territory were invaded without counter action on our part the Yugoslavs and Bulgarians might well attempt a large-scale military invasion to secure their objective—i.e. Salonika and Thrace. The Soviet Government would be able to overthrow the Greek Government, revive E.A.M., bring Turkey into the Russian orbit and secure bases in the Straits.

(b) On July 30 the British Delegation suggested in a memorandum that the Conference might issue at its conclusion a statement to the following effect:

'The three Heads of Government noted with regret that charges of aggressive action were being made by Governments in South-

(a) R12717/11875/19. (b) P(Terminal) 51.

East Europe against their neighbours, and that fears were entertained of attempts to anticipate the peace settlement by violent and unilateral action. The three Heads of Government would be strongly opposed to any such attempts, which would be contrary to the principles for which the war has been fought and which are embodied in the Charter of the United Nations. They are confident that the Governments of the countries concerned, which have so recently suffered in common the trials of war and of Fascist occupation, will find peaceful means of solving their differences, and that their people will now be enabled to enter a period of prosperous and democratic development, on the lines laid down in such documents as the Varkiza Agreement and the Tito-Subasić Agreement.'[1]

The Soviet Delegation replied, indirectly, by a memorandum on (a)
conditions in the Trieste-Istria area. The discussion of these two
memoranda was deferred on July 30, and in fact did not take place.[2] (b)
M. Molotov, at Mr. Bevin's suggestion, agreed on July 31 that the (c)
Soviet memorandum on Trieste-Istria should be withdrawn from consideration. No reference was made to the British memorandum, and no statement on the lines suggested by it appeared in the protocol or communiqué of the Conference. Later developments of the matter therefore remain outside the scope of this *History*.

The Soviet Delegation also agreed on July 31 that no further discussion should take place on their earlier memorandum about
conditions in Greece. Nevertheless on August 1 they circulated (d)
another memorandum repeating in the following terms their demand for a change of government in Greece:

'In view of the fact that at the present time in Greece order has been disturbed, law is not being observed, and, moreover, the Varkiza agreement between the Greek Government and democratic elements is obviously not being carried out, it should be recommended to the British Government to cause the Regent of Greece to modify the composition of the Greek Government in the spirit of the agreement concluded in Varkiza on the 12th February, 1945, between representatives of the then existing Greek Government and representatives of Greek democracy.'

The Conference neither discussed this memorandum, nor referred to it in the protocol and communiqué. The demand for a change of

---

[1] This agreement of November 1, 1944, between Marshal Tito and Dr. Subasić, Prime Minister of the Royal Yugoslav Government, provided for the appointment of a Regency Council and for the formation of an interim government. A further agreement of December 7 provided for elections for a constituent assembly. See Volume III, pp. 351–7.

[2] See further below, pp. 492–3.

(a) P(Terminal) 61. (b) F(Terminal) 10th meeting.
(c) P(Terminal) 11th meeting. (d) P(Terminal) 76.

government, however, was already part of the Soviet-directed propaganda against Greece, and the Foreign Office felt that some positive statement of the British attitude was necessary, and ought not to be delayed. They sent telegrams on the question to the British Dele-
(a) gation on July 27 and 30. They were opposed to any change in the government, and suggested that we might put forward as our reasons, that such a change would interrupt the measures being taken to restore the economy and finances of Greece at a time when these measures were producing results; that the last all-party government under M. Papandreou had failed, and that there was now even less chance of success after the civil war; that an all-party government would not be able to organise and hold elections on a fairer basis than the present 'service' government. On the contrary, party rivalries would be brought into the government, and the chances of free elections would be 'very remote'. In any case, even if we wished to establish an all-party government we could not do so since the Popular Party, which represented about half of Greece, would refuse to co-operate with the Republicans and Communists. The Foreign Office thought, however, that, if the campaign for an all-party Government continued, the Communist and Republican parties might make it impossible for the elections to be held in 1945, or might boycott them.

The Foreign Office considered that we should make our views known at once. The simplest method of stating our policy would be an answer to a parliamentary question, but it might be dangerous—in view of the continued Russian-directed agitation—to delay until the meeting of Parliament. The best plan would therefore be a message from the Prime Minister to the Regent of Greece. We need not state explicitly that we were against a change of government, but it should be clear that this was our view. We might emphasise our continued interest in Greek affairs and our desire to assist the Greek people in restoring their country and in choosing their future régime and Government in conditions of freedom and tranquillity. We might refer to our desire to see the full implementation of the Varkiza agreement and our concern at reports of right-wing excesses in contravention of the agreement. We could emphasise our view of the importance of the Greek Government carrying out, without fear or favour, the measures adopted to prevent violation of the agreement by the Right or the Left, and we could say that law and order must be established throughout Greece on a fair and impartial basis in order that the Greek people might be enabled to express their will as soon as possible.

Mr. Attlee agreed to this suggestion from the Foreign Office. He

(a) F.O.934/1/1(21) and (26), Onward 248, 289.

sent a message to the Regent of Greece on August 1 in the following terms: (a)

> 'Your Beatitude must be aware that it is the desire of His Majesty's Government to assist the Greek people both in restoring their country and in choosing their future régime and Government in conditions of freedom and tranquillity. We hope to see the Varkiza Agreement fully carried out, and we are concerned at reports of right-wing excesses in contravention of this Agreement. We attach importance to the execution by Admiral Voulgaris's Government of the measures they have adopted to prevent all violations of the Agreement by extremists either of the right wing or of the left. It is our earnest hope that law and order may be established throughout Greece on a fair and impartial basis, in order that the Greek people may be enabled to express their will as soon as possible.'

While the Russians were trying to upset the Government in Greece, and, for this purpose, making use of the Varkiza agreement, they had taken a very different line in regard to the Tito-Subasić agreement over Yugoslavia. Here the Russians followed the defensive policy which they had adopted over Poland, Bulgaria and Roumania, i.e. they assumed that the Governments under their control were acting independently, and were fulfilling the terms of the Yalta Declaration on Liberated Europe.

The British Delegation submitted a memorandum to the Conference calling attention to the fact that the Heads of the three Governments, at the Yalta Conference, had endorsed the Tito-Subasić agreement of November 1944, with its guarantees of the basic principles of democratic liberties, and with the promise of a general election within three months of the liberation of Yugoslavia. The principles of this agreement, however, had not been fully carried out, doubtless owing to war conditions. The British Delegation therefore thought it desirable that the three Heads of Governments should issue a statement recalling the fact that they had recognised the Yugoslav Government on the basis of the Yalta and Tito-Subasić agreements, and that they expected these agreements to be carried out in the near future.[1] (b)

The discussion of this memorandum at the plenary meeting on July 19 was something of an anticlimax, since it came at an un- (c)

[1] In conversation with M. Molotov on the evening of July 16 (see also above, p. 355, note 3), Mr. Eden had raised the subject of Yugoslavia. He said that the Tito-Subasić agreement had hardly begun to work. M. Molotov explained that, except for the U.S.S.R., Yugoslavia was the most devastated country in Europe. Mr. Eden replied that there had not been much fighting there. M. Molotov pointed out that the fighting had been of a partisan nature. Mr. Eden went on to say that the Yugoslav parliament had not been called. M. Molotov's answer was that most of its members had been pro-German, and that all the anti-German members had left it. He (M. Molotov) had read in the press that a meeting of some kind had been called for July 23. (d)

(a) Target 311, R13007/4/19. (b) P(Terminal) 22. (c) P(Terminal) 3rd meeting. (d) F.O.934/2/8(3).

fortunate moment after an acrimonious debate on Spain.[1] Stalin made the first comment on the memorandum. He said that no result could be achieved without inviting Yugoslav representatives to the Conference. Mr. Eden pointed out that the original declaration at Yalta had been made without hearing Yugoslav representatives. Stalin answered that there was now a legitimate Government in Yugoslavia, and that accusations against it could not be settled in the absence of its representatives. He also denied that there was any difference between Marshal Tito and Dr. Subasić.[2] President Truman asked whether the state of affairs in Yugoslavia was sufficiently serious to make it necessary to call Yugoslav representatives. Mr. Churchill repeated that, while great allowance had to be made for Marshal Tito owing to the disturbed state of his country, the Tito-Subasić agreement had not been carried out; that Marshal Tito's administration had imposed a strictly controlled party organisation backed by political police and that the control of the press was almost as strict as in Fascist countries.

Mr. Churchill was not unwilling to invite Yugoslav representatives to the Conference but President Truman did not think the matter worth pursuing. He said that he had come to Berlin for a discussion of world affairs with Stalin and Mr. Churchill. He did not want to sit on a court hearing complaints about the affairs of small States. His purpose was to discuss matters as between Heads of Government on which they could come to an agreement; otherwise he would be wasting his time. Stalin agreed, and, in view of this American refusal, Mr. Churchill said he would not press the matter for the moment, but that the question of Yugoslavia could not be dropped; he had thought that the United States were interested in the matter, since they had submitted a paper about the Yalta Declaration on Liberated Europe.[3]

The British Delegation was later told privately that the President's attitude was as much a shock to the State Department as to themselves, since the State Department had drawn up an even stronger brief on the subject than that prepared for the Foreign Office. It was, however, now impossible to go back to the original proposals. The
(a) British Delegation therefore brought forward its memorandum calling in a general way on the governments of the south-east European States not to anticipate the peace settlement by violent and unilateral action.[4] The Soviet Government also circulated a memo-

---

[1] See above, pp. 469–70.

[2] In fact the British proposal that the Yugoslav Government should be reminded of their unfulfilled obligations was in part the result of suggestions from Dr. Subasić himself. Dr. Subasić thought that a three-Power declaration might help him in maintaining his position in Belgrade. See Volume III, p. 381.

[3] See also Volume III, Chapter XLII, section (vi).

[4] See above, pp. 488–9.

(a) P(Terminal) 51.

randum on 'Conditions in the Trieste-Istria district' merely restating the Yugoslav claim with regard to the civil administration in the area of Military Government. (a)

These two papers were brought up for discussion at a meeting of the Foreign Secretaries on July 30. Mr. Bevin introduced the British memorandum, but M. Molotov at once replied by referring to the Soviet memorandum. It was obvious that this latter memorandum had been drawn up in order to counter our proposals, and that the Soviet Delegation would insist on bringing it into the discussion. We could not agree to a tripartite discussion of civil administration in Venezia Giulia on the basis of the Soviet arguments. The whole question of Yugoslavia was therefore dropped, and discussions on it were not resumed at the Conference. (b)

The Conference also reached a deadlock on the question of the Russian claims with regard to the Straits.[1] This subject was among those proposed by the British Delegation in view of the known fact that the Soviet Government wanted a drastic revision of the Montreux Convention. In opening the discussion at the plenary meeting on July 22 Mr. Churchill said that he had told Stalin at Teheran that we would support the revision of the Convention, but that the consent of all the signatories except Japan would be necessary. We should welcome the free movement of Russian warships or merchant ships in and out of the Black Sea, but we regarded it as important not to alarm Turkey. (c)

Turkey had been much alarmed by the strong concentration of Bulgarian and Russian troops in Bulgaria, the continuous attacks on her in the Soviet press and radio and the turn of the conversations between M. Molotov and the Turkish Ambassador in Moscow, at which the former had mentioned modification of the Turkish eastern frontier, including Kars and Ardahan, and a Russian military base on the Straits. The Prime Minister understood that these were not demands made by Russia, but that Turkey had asked for an alliance, and M. Molotov had stated the conditions on which such a proposal would be considered. The Prime Minister enquired what had happened since these conversations.

M. Molotov said that he would give the Prime Minister and the President a written statement of the Russian point of view. The Turkish Government had first raised the question of an alliance. M. Molotov had held two conversations with the Turkish Ambassador in Moscow, and had laid down as conditions: the return of Kars and Ardahan, which Russia had lost in 1921, and a modification of the régime in the Straits.

[1] See also Volume IV, Chapter LII, section (iv).

(a) P(Terminal) 61. (b) P(Terminal) 10th meeting. (c) P(Terminal) 6th meeting; P(Terminal) 26.

M. Molotov argued that the conclusion of a treaty meant that Russia and Turkey jointly undertook to defend all their frontiers, but that Russia could not give this undertaking in regard to certain sections of the Turkish frontier which she thought unjust. Russia therefore asked for the return of Kars and Ardahan. As for the Straits, both the President and the Prime Minister as Allies had admitted the necessity for a change. M. Molotov had told the Turkish Ambassador that if Turkey was not prepared to settle the two points raised by Russia, the Soviet Government was still ready to make an agreement regarding the Straits.

M. Molotov then produced his written statement of the proposals which he had given to the Ambassador. The proposals were: (i) that the Montreux Convention should be abrogated; (ii) that the régime of the Straits should be determined by Turkey and Russia as the States chiefly concerned and capable of ensuring freedom of commercial navigation and security in the Straits; (iii) that in the interests of their own security and the maintenance of peace in the Black Sea area, Turkey and Russia, by their common facilities in the Straits, should prevent their use by other countries for purposes inimical to the Black Sea Powers. This third proposal referred to the establishment of Russian military bases in the Straits.

Mr. Churchill pointed out that these proposals went far beyond anything discussed between Stalin and himself. M. Molotov answered that at the time of the discussions there was no question of a treaty with Turkey. Mr. Churchill said that M. Molotov's paper raised the new issue of a Russian military base in the Straits, and also proposed that no one except Russia and Turkey was to have anything to do with the passage of vessels through the Straits. He felt certain that Turkey would never agree to such conditions, and he would not be prepared to press her to accept them. He had already made it clear that he could neither support nor ask the Turks to agree to the fortification of the Straits by a Russian base. M. Molotov argued that the Russo-Turkish treaties of 1805 and 1833 gave Russia military bases.[1] The Prime Minister said that he must 'ask for the opportunity to look up these ancient treaties'. He would stand by his agreement with Stalin to support the revision of the Convention, but he felt quite free on these new proposals. Stalin agreed that Mr. Churchill was quite free in the matter. President Truman asked for time to consider the proposals before further discussion.

(a) At the seventh plenary meeting of the Conference on July 23, President Truman suggested that the discussion on Turkey should be

[1] This argument was without historical foundation. Russia obtained a privileged position by the treaties, but not a right to construct or maintain military bases in the Straits.

(a) P(Terminal) 7th meeting: R12516/44/61.

resumed. Mr. Churchill said that he had already made clear that he could neither support nor ask the Turks to agree to the fortification of the Straits by a Russian base. Stalin said that Mr. Churchill had spoken of Russia frightening Turkey and that a main reason was the concentration of too many Russian troops in Bulgaria. He claimed that there were only 30,000 as against the 40,000 British troops Mr. Churchill stated were in Greece. Stalin further reminded the meeting that Mr. Churchill thought Russia was frightening Turkey by proposing a rectification of her frontiers. Kars, however, was part of Armenia and Ardahan part of Georgia. These questions of frontier restoration would not have arisen if Turkey had not asked for an alliance. An alliance meant that Russia undertook to defend the Turkish frontiers and Turkey undertook to defend the Russian frontiers. Russia considered the existing frontier in the region of Kars and Ardahan to be incorrect and had told Turkey that it must be rectified. If Turkey did not agree, the question of an alliance would be dropped.

Stalin then spoke of the Straits. He said that the point of issue was to give Russia the right to pass freely to and from the Black Sea. As Turkey herself was too weak to guarantee the passage of the Straits, Russia would like to see it guaranteed by force. Mr. Churchill asked whether Stalin suggested that it should be guaranteed by force or by law. Stalin said that right must be guaranteed by force as it was in the Panama Canal by the United States Navy and the Suez Canal by the British Navy. He asked whether Mr. Churchill thought that a naval base in the Straits would be acceptable to Turkey. Mr. Churchill said that he thought it would be unacceptable. Stalin said that in that case Russia should be given a base elsewhere for the repair and refuelling of the Russian fleet so that, together with its Allies, it could keep order in the area.

President Truman then said that in the view of the United States the Convention should be revised. The Straits should be a free waterway for all and guaranteed by the Great Powers. The President said that after much study he had come to the conclusion that all the wars[1] in the last 200 years had originated in the area bounded by the Baltic Sea and the Mediterranean and by the eastern border of France and the western border of Russia. In the last two wars the peace of the world had been overturned first by Austria and then by Germany. The present Conference and the coming Peace Conference should see that this did not happen again. To a great extent such a purpose could be accomplished by securing 'freedom for the passage of goods and intercourse' in the area concerned as in the United States.

---

[1] It must be assumed that the President was referring to European wars, but even so the generalisation is, obviously, erroneous.

President Truman then read out a paper entitled 'Free and Unrestricted Navigation of International Inland Waterways'. The President said that his proposals for international control of these waterways should apply to the Kiel Canal and to the Straits. He did not want to see another war in twenty-five years starting perhaps on the Danube. The United States Government wanted Europe to be self-supporting, and the United Kingdom, Russia and France to be prosperous and satisfied. The proposals which he had read out were a step in this direction.

The Prime Minister said that he was in general agreement with the President's proposals and that he supported freedom of navigation through the Straits under the guarantee of the Powers. He hoped that Stalin would accept this proposal rather than press for a Russian base near Istanbul.[1]

(a) The discussion on Turkey was resumed at the eighth plenary meeting of the Conference on July 24. President Truman asked for the views of his colleagues on his paper on international inland waterways. Stalin observed that the President's paper did not deal specifically with Turkey and the Straits, but rather with the Danube and the Rhine. The Soviet delegation wanted to discuss the question of the Straits and bases in the Straits for Russia. President Truman said that he wished to see both these questions considered together. Stalin thereupon suggested that consideration of the question should be postponed; he feared that the meeting would not reach agreement since their views differed too widely.

Mr. Churchill then said that, on the previous day, the President had favoured the view that the freedom of the Straits should be guaranteed by an international authority including the three Great Powers. The President agreed that he had made this suggestion. Stalin said that the Soviet Government were in favour of freedom of passage, but they thought that it would also be necessary to have bases in the Straits. Mr. Churchill said that we had hoped that an international guarantee would be more than a substitute for fortifications. His Majesty's Government would be prepared to join with other nations in guaranteeing freedom of passage and would be prepared to press Turkey to accept this arrangement. Freedom of passage could be obtained without either trouble with Turkey or expense. The proposed guarantee gave every security to Russia.

President Truman said again that he was prepared to support an

---

[1] During a dinner given by the Soviet Delegation to the Prime Minister and the President on July 23 Stalin asked the Prime Minister whether he would not agree to allow the Russians a base at Dedeagach if he refused to let them have a fortified position in the Sea of Marmora. Mr. Churchill answered: 'I will always support Russia in her claim to the freedom of the seas all the year round.' Churchill, *Second World War*, VI, 578.

(a) P(Terminal) 8th meeting.

international guarantee of the freedom of the Straits for all nations without reservation. He contemplated no fortifications at all. Mr. Churchill said that he fully agreed. Stalin said that it had become evident that the opinions at the table differed. He again proposed a postponement of the discussion. He said that the Soviet Government had interrupted their talks with the Turks but only for the time. They could resume these talks and Great Britain could do the same. He was not certain whether Turkey would be prepared to agree to an international guarantee. Mr. Churchill replied that they were more likely to agree to such a guarantee than to a large fort being erected near Istanbul. Stalin thought that this was very likely, but he was not sure. President Truman said that the United States Government would try to make the Turkish Government see the advantages of international control. The discussion upon Turkey was thereupon adjourned. The question of Kars and Ardahan was not mentioned on July 24.

Although it was now clear that no agreement would be reached about the Straits the President insisted on further notice being taken of his proposal about internationalising inland waterways. On July 31 he repeated his view that, if these lines of communi- (a) cation were internationalised and properly controlled, the result would be an important factor in preventing future wars. If the Conference had no time to agree upon the details of the scheme, the matter should be considered before the final Peace Treaties were made.

M. Molotov pointed out that the Conference had agreed to postpone the question of the Straits, on which the President's proposal had first been made. It would be impossible to consider the proposal without the advice of a number of experts familiar with the details of the Central European waterways. President Truman then suggested that the question might be considered at the meeting of Foreign Ministers in September 1945. The Conference agreed with this proposal.

The British and Soviet Delegations accepted a short reference to the proposal in the Protocol of the Conference. This reference, how- (b) ever, did not satisfy the President. At the afternoon meeting on August 1 he asked that there should also be a reference in the communiqué. He was anxious to be able to say, on his return to the United States, that he had not entered into any secret agreements and that all the effective decisions of the Conference were recorded in the communiqué.

Stalin refused, rather abruptly, to agree,[1] but then explained that

[1] For President Truman's anger at Stalin's attitude, see Margaret Truman, *Harry S. Truman* (London, 1973) pp. 278–9.

(a) P(Terminal) 11th meeting. (b) P(Terminal) 12th meeting.

at earlier Conferences the Protocol had recorded all agreed decisions, and that the communiqué had contained only those decisions on matters of political principle which were of general interest. Formal decisions—such as the reference of the proposals on Inland Waterways to the Foreign Ministers Council—should not be included in the communiqué; such decisions, however, were not 'secret agreements'.

President Truman accepted this decision on the understanding that he would be free to disclose the fact that his proposals had been referred to the Council of Foreign Ministers. On August 9, in a broadcast on the Potsdam Conference, President Truman said that one of the persistent causes of war in Europe during the past two centuries had been selfish control of inland waterways and that the United States had proposed free navigation of those waterways with agencies to secure equal treatment for all nations. Membership of the agencies would include the United States, Great Britain, Russia, France and the States bordering on the waterways. The President said that his proposal had been referred to the Council of Foreign Ministers, where the United States intended to press for its adoption.

(a) At the end of the Conference Mr. Attlee sent a personal message to the Dominion Prime Ministers. He explained that he had had the advantage of attending the Plenary Meetings from the beginning, and had thus been 'able to maintain the continuity of the British side in spite of the change of Government. The atmosphere has been one of good will and cordiality combined with the utmost freedom and frankness of discussion. It has been evident that all three Delegations have felt deeply their responsibility for the future of the world; and in our approach to all major questions we have throughout had it in mind that the unity and continued co-operation of the three Governments is the first and greatest essential for the preservation of world peace.'

Mr. Attlee then dealt with the four most important items in the report of the Conference:

(i) *Poland*

The conclusion on the Polish boundary was only reached after long and searching discussions with the Polish representatives. In this matter as in some others we found decisions already being shaped for us by events. We made it our prime concern to see that the new Poland would be independent, democratic and in free communication with the world at large. We have obtained assurances from the Polish representatives of their firm intention to put into full effect the political settlement in Poland which the Conference had already agreed.

(a) F.O.934/2/8(22), Target 318.

(ii) *Treatment of Germany*

The political principles and some of the economic principles were settled without much difficulty. The rest of the latter turned mainly on the decision about German reparations which proved one of the most difficult questions to settle, provoking long and arduous discussion. Our object throughout was to avoid any plan which would stultify the principle of the economic unity of Germany or produce a situation in which Germany could pay reparations only at the indirect expense of the U.S. and ourselves. The plan finally agreed on is in substance the American plan.

(iii) *Italy and South-East Europe*

We were under pressure from the American side to take some further step towards admitting Italy to the United Nations and from the Soviet side to recognise the Governments of the satellite states. The statement (on 'Admission to the United Nations') secures both these without prejudicing any points which we regard as essential. We found greater willingness than hitherto to admit the Press to South-East Europe though whether we shall see free elections is more open to doubt. The statement has the advantage of administering a public rebuke to Franco.

(iv) *The Council of Foreign Ministers*

In the new Council of Foreign Ministers we hope we have a machine for continuing co-operation between the Great Powers. While the immediate task is to formulate Peace Treaties and prepare for the eventual Peace Settlement in Europe we hope to use the Council as an instrument for the settlement of other outstanding questions some of which, as you will have seen, have already been referred to it.

In general I feel that we have made considerable progress towards a better understanding between the three Governments and that the decisions reached will provide a firm basis for a further advance.

Mr. Bevin, speaking in the House of Commons on August 20, 1945, was more guarded in his survey of the achievements of the Conference and in his general estimate of the situation. He said frankly that in Hungary, Bulgaria and Roumania, 'the impression we get from recent developments is that one kind of totalitarianism is being replaced by another'. During this same debate Mr. Churchill gave a sombre description of what was happening in the areas under Russian control, and a warning against the delusion that 'the most serious questions' at the Conference 'were brought to good solutions'.

CHAPTER LXX

The surrender of Japan: British and American planning for the treatment of Japan after the war

(i)

Japanese peace-feelers in 1944: approach through the Swedish Minister at Tokyo, September 1944: Japanese approaches through Swedish channels in 1945: approaches to the Soviet Government.

THE Japanese had lost the initiative before the Allies landed on the coasts of Normandy. In November 1943, the Americans had begun the new tactics of using carrier-borne aircraft to protect a whole landing-force. They were thus able to approach the centre of Japanese power far more quickly; they could threaten Japanese sea communications, and, possibly, compel a general surrender without a large scale invasion of the mainland. The Americans first attacked the Gilbert Islands; in January and February 1944, they gained bases in the Marshall Islands, and in June and July captured Saipan and Guam in the Marianas. Another line of attack in the south-west Pacific was equally successful, and in July 1944, American and Australian forces were in key positions along the northern coast of New Guinea. In October the Japanese lost a great part of their remaining naval strength in an attempt to prevent the Americans from taking the island of Leyte in the Philippines. In Burma the Japanese forces had begun to retreat in June 1944. The Japanese, in August and September, destroyed the airfields in China constructed for eventual American use but this success was now of less strategic importance, since the Americans expected to be able to use Russian airfields, and, in any case, were no longer hoping for much military help from the Chinese.

At the second Quebec Conference in August 1944 the Combined Chiefs of Staff estimated that the complete defeat of Japan would follow within eighteen months of the end of the war with Germany. The Japanese leaders themselves were, obviously, aware of their position. Although they might still hope to resist the invasion of their country, they were faced with the collapse of their plans for a New Order under their control in East Asia. They had risked the whole economy of Japan in the attempt to carry out this plan. They had been aggressors for too long and on too large a scale to escape severe retribution. The Western Allies (or, for that matter, the

U.S.S.R.)[1] were unlikely to give the slightest attention to Japanese approaches for a compromise peace. A few indirect approaches were made, but the Japanese Government themselves seem to have recognised their futility.

The attitude of the Foreign Office towards these manœuvres was that they would not receive any approach from individual intermediaries. If the Japanese Government wanted to make peace proposals, they must do so themselves; in such an event, their normal and obvious course would be action through a neutral Government. One view in the Foreign Office was that the attitude of British (a) Missions should be even more stringent towards Japanese approaches than towards those made by German nationals, in view of American suspicions that the Japanese would appeal to Great Britain on the basis of past friendship and business connexions. On October 11, (b) 1944, therefore, the Foreign Office instructed the British Embassy at Lisbon—in reply to an enquiry from them about possible Japanese overtures—that, if the Japanese had a serious proposal to make, they must put it forward through a third Government.

An unofficial Japanese overture for peace had been made to the British Government before these instructions were sent to Lisbon. On September 20, 1944, the Swedish Minister for Foreign Affairs told (c) Sir V. Mallet of a telegram just received from the Swedish Minister at Tokyo, whom he described as a 'man of calm and good judgment'. The latter had reported that important civilian circles in Japan were discussing the peace problem with increasing anxiety. They expected a speedy German collapse, and doubted whether Japan could then continue the war. They thought it necessary to get peace as soon as possible before Japanese towns were destroyed. They considered that Japan would have to surrender all territories taken from Great Britain during the war, and recognise all former British investments and interests in east Asia. They realised that all other territories occupied during the war would have to be restored to their former owners and that Japan would probably lose Manchuria. They were ready for preliminary talks through Swedish channels. The Swedish Minister at Tokyo reported: 'Behind the man who gave me this message there stands one of the best-known statesmen in Japan and there is no doubt that this attempt must be considered as a serious

---

[1] In September 1943, and again in April 1944, the Japanese Government had suggested to the Soviet Government the despatch of a mission to Moscow to discuss Soviet-Japanese (d) relations. The Soviet Government refused these suggestions, and, in informing the British Government of them, said that they knew the purpose of the mission was to explore the chances of a separate Russo-German peace. For the Japanese peace-feelers and the course of events in Japan before the Japanese surrender, see R. J. C. Burton, *Japan's Decision to Surrender* (Stamford, U.S.A., 1954).

(a) C9145/155/18 (1943). (b) F4410/208/23. (c) F4370/208/23.
(d) F4370/208/23.

one.' The Foreign Office regarded this approach as a serious peace-feeler, of which they should inform the United States Government at once. They recommended that (if the United States Government agreed) we should tell the Swedish Minister for Foreign Affairs that we were not prepared to reply to indirect Japanese approaches. The Swedish Ministers could reply if he wished that he knew it would be useless to deliver the Japanese message to us. On September 24 the Foreign Office instructed Lord Halifax to inform Mr. Hull of the peace-feeler and to obtain his approval of the proposed British attitude.[1]

(a) Mr. Hull agreed with the proposed action. He hoped that we would tell the Russians of it 'promptly', though he agreed that they need not be consulted about our answer. On September 29, therefore, the Foreign Office informed Sir V. Mallet of the answer to be given to the Swedish Minister for Foreign Affairs. Sir A. Clark Kerr was instructed to inform the Soviet Government of the Swedish communication and our reply. He was also told that the protocol of the Moscow Conference of October 1943[2] might be held to commit us to consult Russia before replying to such an approach. In our reference to peace-feelers we had had in mind at the Conference the Axis satellites and not Japan, with whom Russia was not at war. We thought it unlikely that Russia would expect to be consulted about a peace-feeler from Japan; she might even prefer not to be consulted. The Foreign Office, however, thought it expedient—and Mr. Hull had agreed—to inform Russia of the Japanese approach.

(b) Sir V. Mallet carried out his instructions on September 30, 1944. The Secretary-General of the Swedish Ministry of Foreign Affairs said that he would telegraph to Tokyo that his Government knew by experience that the British Government would not answer indirect approaches. They had therefore thought it useless to pass on the message. The Secretary-General said that the Swedish Minister at Tokyo had recently telegraphed that the new Japanese Minister for Foreign Affairs was preparing to approach us.[3]

The Japanese Cabinet resigned in April, 1945. Admiral K. Suzuki (reluctantly) became Prime Minister and Mr. S. Togo (with equal reluctance) Foreign Minister.[4] The civilians who secured these appointments for Admiral Suzuki and Mr. Togo realised that Japan had lost the war and should try to find a way to make peace. Their hopes of getting terms easier than the 'unconditional surrender' upon

[1] The Foreign Office gave Mr. Eden a statement for the War Cabinet, but the matter does not appear to have been discussed there.

[2] See above, pp. 358–9.

[3] On November 1 the Foreign Office repeated to the Missions concerned their previous instructions with regard to Japanese peace-feelers.

[4] For Mr. Togo, who was Foreign Minister in 1941–3, see Volume II, p. 151.

(a) F4465, 4679, 4813/208/23. (b) F4497/208/23.

which the United States and Great Britain were insisting lay in possible Russian mediation. The Japanese did not share the British or American hopes of Russian willingness to co-operate with the western democracies: they expected that Stalin, who had shown himself to be concerned solely with Russian interests in Europe, would also think solely in terms of Russian interests in the Far East. The Japanese also knew of the agreement made by Mr. Roosevelt which gave Stalin everything he wanted for Russia in the Far East.[1]

There were no more peace overtures from Japan until May 1945, (a) but the Swedish Minister at Tokyo reported to Stockholm in April that the new Japanese Prime Minister was in favour of making peace. The nature of this peace was not explained. The Swedish Minister was instructed that, if the Japanese Government put forward peace proposals to him, Sweden would not act as mediator but would only forward them to Great Britain and the United States.

On May 23, 1945, the State Department spoke to Sir G. Sansom[2] (b) about rumours in the United States press of peace-feelers by Japan. The State Department was embarrassed by these rumours, since they reinforced a trend of public opinion in favour of a negotiated peace with Japan. Although this trend was not important, it had been stimulated by the heavy losses in the operations at Okinawa.[3] The State Department had sent to the Foreign Office from time to time reports in which Japanese diplomats and others had spoken about the terms which Japan should or might accept. So far there had been no peace-feeler arising from an initiative by the Japanese Government. A report had, however, just been received from the United States Minister at Stockholm; if it were well-founded, it might show that responsible Japanese circles wanted to arrange mediation by a neutral power.[4] The United States Legation at Stockholm had been approached by an unnamed person, who claimed that he had been acting as an intermediary in negotiations between General Onodera, Japanese Military Attaché at Stockholm, and Prince Carl, brother of the King,[5] with a view to mediation by the Swedish Royal Family.

---

[1] See above, pp. 264–6.

[2] Sir G. Sansom, who had served for many years in Japan, was adviser on Japanese affairs to the British Ambassador in Washington from 1942 to 1947.

[3] The British Government were also embarrassed by these rumours. There was no movement in Great Britain in favour of a negotiated peace, but the Japanese might think otherwise and infer that, if only they held out long enough, they had a chance of escaping with less than unconditional surrender.

[4] On May 5 the Swedish Minister at Tokyo reported that the two last raids on Tokyo (c) had done more damage than that done by all the previous raids. The industrial area between Tokyo and Yokohama had been devastated. Great fires were raging in the centre of Tokyo. According to official statements, 500,000 homes had been destroyed in Tokyo and two million people were homeless. Reliable information put the dead at over 100,000.

[5] Prince Carl of Sweden was President of the Swedish Red Cross till November 1945. His nephew, Count Folke Bernadotte, was Vice-President, but succeeded him as President as from January 1, 1946.

(a) F2391/630/23 (1945). (b) F3121/630/23. (c) F2780/630/23.

According to this unnamed person, General Onodera said that American propaganda in Japan had been more effective than was generally realised. The Russians were moving troops to the Manchurian border and intended to declare war on Japan; the Japanese realised that they had lost the war and so could try only to avoid further destruction. The intermediary stated that he had been authorised—he did not say by whom—to arrange for a member of the Swedish Royal Family to act as mediator between Japan and the Allies; and that, as he was representing the Emperor, the mediator must be a member of the Royal Family. He suggested Prince Carl. The only definite point which he mentioned was that there could not be unconditional surrender because Japan must 'save face' *vis-à-vis* China.

The intermediary said that at first Prince Carl had been unwilling to consider the matter because, as Chairman of the Swedish Red Cross, he felt that he should avoid entanglement in international politics. He agreed, however, to consult the Swedish Government and Count Bernadotte. Later the intermediary was told that the King of Sweden was taking an interest in the matter, and that various unspecified contacts had been made, and something could be arranged. The Foreign Office commented that the United States and Great Britain were committed to the unconditional surrender of Japan, to which the Japanese were opposed; hence there was no basis for negotiation.

(a) Early in June 1945 the Soviet Political Representative at Budapest, M. Pushkin, asked the United States Representative whether he had any information about a recent Japanese peace-feeler. The United States representative said that he had no information, whereupon M. Pushkin said: 'The Soviet Union had a bone to pick with Japan.'

(b) The Swedish Government informed the British Legation at Stockholm on July 17 of a report that Stalin was bringing Japanese peace proposals to the Potsdam meeting, and that his late arrival was due to the last-minute discussions with the Japanese.

(c) Two days later the Foreign Office heard that Mr. Hirota, a former Japanese Prime Minister and Ambassador to Russia, had held conversations in June with M. Malik, Russian Ambassador to Japan. Mr. Hirota had tried to find out the Russian views on the Far East and to come to some understanding for future Soviet-Japanese relations. M. Malik had been instructed to reply that any proposal for closer relations after the expiry in 1946 of the Soviet-Japanese Neutrality Pact of April 1941 which the U.S.S.R. had denounced on April 5, 1945, must come from the Japanese side. On June 29 Mr. Hirota had put

(a) F4007/630/23. (b) F4320/630/23. F.O.934/3/14(3).
(c) F.O.934/3/14(6), (16).

proposals to M. Malik for an agreement on mutual assistance and non-aggression. He suggested that the two countries should recognise the 'neutrality' of Manchuria; and they should agree upon equal fishing rights in northern waters in exchange for supplies of oil from Russia, and discuss any other questions which the Soviet Government might wish to raise. Mr. Sato, the Japanese Ambassador in Moscow, had been instructed to ask M. Molotov, before the latter left for Berlin, to support Mr. Hirota's proposals and to expedite a Russian reply.

On July 10, 1945, the State Department released to the press a statement by Mr. Grew[1] commenting on reports that peace offers had been received from the Japanese Government. Mr. Grew said that conversations about peace had been reported to the Department from various parts of the world, but that no approach had been made to the United States Government, directly or indirectly, by anyone who could establish his authority to speak for the Japanese Government, and that there had been no offer of surrender. After referring to President Truman's statements of May 8[2] and June 1, in which the President said that unconditional surrender did not mean the destruction or enslavement of the Japanese people, Mr. Grew said: 'The policy of this Government has been, is and will continue to be unconditional surrender as defined by the President in these statements, that is the best comment I can make upon peace feelers and rumours of peace feelers of whatever origin.' (a)

(ii)

The demand for the unconditional surrender of Japan: the Cairo declaration of December 1, 1943: the meaning of 'unconditional surrender': the Potsdam Declaration of July 26, 1945.

Even if they had received official peace overtures from Japan in 1944 or in the early part of 1945, the British Government would have found it difficult to give an answer except in general terms of unconditional surrender. They had not decided upon their own policy on the treatment of Japan—except in regard to the dissolution of the Japanese overseas empire—and did not know in any detail the views of the United States Government. Apart from the fact that American views would probably be decisive in a sphere which United States opinion regarded as primarily an American concern, the Foreign Office could not make plans without a general directive from the War

[1] Special Assistant to the Secretary of State and formerly United States Ambassador to Japan.

[2] See below, pp. 507–8.

(a) F4181/584/61; F4216/584/61; F.O. 934/3/14(4).

Cabinet. In 1944 the end of the war with Japan seemed a long way off; the time and attention of Ministers—and especially of the Prime Minister—were concentrated first on the hazards of the cross-Channel invasion, and then on the exploitation of the Allied victories, and on the immediate problems likely to follow the German defeat and surrender. A number of questions of strategic planning for the ultimate defeat of Japan could not be postponed, since, unless they were decided, the direction and area of current operations could not be determined. In view of American suspicions of British 'imperialism' and of local friction in the Far Eastern theatres of war over spheres of command, these strategic questions were often controversial, but there was no urgent reason for deciding what was to be done to the Japanese after their defeat. The formula of unconditional surrender announced at the end of the Casablanca Conference[1] applied to Japan as to Germany and Italy. The Declaration issued on December 1, 1943, after the first Cairo Conference, on the post-war treatment of Japan, announced that the 'three Great Allies'—Great Britain, the United States, and China—intended to punish as well as restrain the aggression of Japan. They had 'no thought of territorial expansion' for themselves, but their purpose was that Japan should be 'stripped of all the islands in the Pacific which she has seized or occupied since the beginning of the First World War in 1914', and that she should be compelled to restore to China all the territories such as Manchuria, Formosa, and the Pescadores, stolen from the Chinese. 'Japan will also be expelled from all other territories which she has taken by violence and greed', and 'in due course Korea shall become free and independent'.

The Declaration envisaged that 'serious and prolonged operations' would be necessary to procure the unconditional surrender of Japan. Later in December 1943, Mr. Grew spoke in Chicago about the need to go on fighting, 'regardless of time or losses', until the Japanese army, navy, and air force were out of action. An inconclusive peace would mean that the 'militaristic cancer would dig in underground as it did in Germany'; the Japanese would not give up their attempt to control East Asia until they had been reduced to military impotence.

In the course of 1944, however, the Foreign Office—and the British military authorities in south-east Asia—came to the view that the Allied pronouncements on Japan were likely to prolong a suicidal resistance, and that it was desirable to qualify, though not to get rid of the demand for unconditional surrender. On the other hand the publication of details of the savage treatment of prisoners of war by the Japanese strengthened the demand in Great Britain and

---

[1] See above, Chapter LXI, section (ii).

the United States for harsh terms.[1] The Foreign Office thought, however, that the Allies might assure the Japanese that they would take measures to relieve distress in Japan after the war; that they wanted to secure a reasonable standard of living and adequate economic opportunities for the Japanese people. The greatest fear of the Japanese seemed to be that the Allies would humiliate them by requiring the deposition of the Emperor. This fear persisted in 1945 and was indeed manifest in the latter stages of the Japanese surrender.

In May 1945 the Swedish Minister at Tokyo, on his return to Stockholm, reported that a Japanese surrender was unlikely as long as the Emperor remained on the American list of war criminals. The Foreign Office had not seen any American list of war criminals; their only information related to an American list of military offences committed in the field against United States troops and prisoners of war. The Emperor was not on the United Nations War Crimes Commission's list of war criminals, but the United States had not submitted a list to this Commission. The Foreign Office thought that the Japanese might have mistaken the unofficial opinions of the Institute of Pacific Relations for the policy of the United States Government, and have deduced therefrom that the Emperor was to be regarded as a war criminal.[2] They asked the British Embassy at Washington to find out the position. By July the Embassy had discovered only the opinion of the United States representative on the United Nations War Crimes Commission, though his views were believed to be those of the State Department. He thought that the Commission should do nothing about Japanese war criminals which might lengthen the war or give cause for reprisals against United States prisoners of war. (a) (b) (c)

On May 8, 1945, President Truman took the opportunity of the German surrender in Europe to explain to the Japanese what the United States Government meant by the formula of 'unconditional surrender'. The President began by saying that Nazi Germany had been defeated, but that the blows against Japan would increase in power and intensity as long as their leaders and armed forces continued the war, and would totally destroy Japan's industrial war production, its shipping and everything that supported its military activity. The blows would not cease until the Japanese military and naval forces surrendered unconditionally. Mr. Truman said that (d)

---

1 The Prime Minister was reported to have summed up the matter at the second Quebec Conference by saying that the Japanese must be put into a position in which neither their vices nor their virtues could be inflicted on their fellow men. (e)

2 The United States delegates to a meeting of the Institute of Pacific Relations in January 1945 had suggested that the Emperor and his family should be excluded from the throne.

(a) F2874, 3018/630/23. (b) F3018, 4050/630/23. (c) U4362/211/73.
(d) F3620/364/23. (e) F4785/94/23 (1944).

unconditional surrender of the armed forces meant for the Japanese people the end of the war and of the influence of the military leaders; it meant also provision for the return of soldiers and sailors to their families, farms and jobs. It did not mean 'the extermination or enslavement of the Japanese people'.

(a) On May 27, 1945, Mr. Grew told Sir G. Sansom that he had been considering whether this last assurance should not now be repeated again, indicating—at least to responsible civilian leaders in Japan—not only that 'unconditional surrender' did not mean the extermination of the Japanese people, but also that we did not intend to impose any form of government on the Japanese people against their will i.e. we should not interfere with the constitution or the position of the Emperor, nor did we intend to destroy permanently the basis of their economic life, but wanted them to be able to develop a peacetime economy which would promote the welfare of the Japanese people as a whole without permitting aggressive policies. Mr. Grew proposed to speak to the President on these lines.

Sir G. Sansom said that it was a 'very nicely balanced question' for the Administration whether, in view of United States public opinion, they could afford to sponsor such an announcement. The Foreign Office and Sir G. Sansom agreed that unqualified insistence on unconditional surrender was helping to prolong Japanese resistance.

Mr. Grew approached the President on May 28, 1945, with his suggestion. After the heavy bombing of Tokyo he thought the occasion favourable for a definite statement that unconditional surrender would not mean the elimination of the Emperor, if the Japanese people wanted to keep him and the dynasty. Mr. Grew's proposal had considerable support in the State Department and from Mr. Stimson and some other members of the Administration, but President Truman accepted the contrary view that the Japanese might regard a statement on Mr. Grew's lines as a sign of weakness.[1]

At the beginning of July the Japanese situation was such that an Anglo-American warning combined with some reassurances about Allied intentions might have an effect on Japanese opinion. Between February and June 1945 the Americans had occupied the islands of Iwo Jima and Okinawa, though at heavy cost owing to the tenacity of the garrisons and to the 'suicide' attacks of Japanese pilots on American warships. In Burma Admiral Mountbatten's forces[2] had captured Rangoon on May 3: scattered Japanese forces remained in the country, but their expulsion was only a matter of time. On July 7

---

[1] J. C. Grew, *Turbulent Era* (Eng. Edition, Hammond and Hammond, 1953) pp. 1421–40. See also *F.R.U.S., 1945 The Conference of Berlin* I, 834–903.

[2] Admiral Mountbatten was Supreme Commander, South East Asia 1943–6.

(a) F3620/364/23.

General MacArthur, Allied Supreme Commander in the south-west Pacific, announced that—except for isolated bodies of troops—the American re-occupation of the Philippines was complete. Furthermore, the Soviet denunciation in April of the Soviet-Japanese Neutrality Pact of April 1941 could be taken by the Japanese as a sign that the Russians intended to enter the Pacific war.[1]

Meanwhile although the President had rejected Mr. Grew's suggestion, the United States Government were considering the issue of a warning to the Japanese people of the consequences of prolonging a hopeless resistance. Lord Halifax, on July 4, 1945, re- (a) ported a remark by Mr. Harry Hopkins that Stalin was likely to raise at the Potsdam Conference the question of an interpretation of 'unconditional surrender' for the Japanese.[2] Admiral King, U.S. Commander-in-Chief of Naval Operations, who told Lord Halifax of Mr. Hopkins's remark, had said that the United States would favour a discussion of the matter, though they realised the need for caution. The Foreign Office thought that their views on the meaning of unconditional surrender agreed with those of the United States Government, but that, in view of future Anglo-American relations, an initiative for modifying the phrase should come from the American or Russian, and not from the British Delegation. They also thought that, as China had been a principal in the war against Japan for eight years, the Chinese reaction to a statement about unconditional surrender should be taken into account. Although China was not to be represented at Potsdam, there would be less danger of friction with her if a public statement were not made without Chinese agreement.[3]

Mr. Grew continued to have Mr. Stimson's support for a more explicit statement about the possibilities of a constitutional monarchy under the Emperor as the future government of Japan. Mr. Stimson drew up a draft declaration on July 2 and brought it forward again

---

[1] According to the terms of the Pact the denunciation would not take effect until a year after notice had been given. The Russians, when they declared war, evaded this revision by claiming that they were acting under their obligation to co-operate with other members of the United Nations in the maintenance of peace and security. It is a matter of interest that, in negotiating with Stalin the terms of Russian entry into the war against Japan, neither President Roosevelt nor Mr. Churchill (as a co-signatory of the agreement) regarded this provision in the Russo-Japanese treaty as an obstacle.

[2] Stalin had told Mr. Hopkins that he favoured getting rid of 'the institution' of the Emperor. *F.R.U.S., 1945 The Conference of Berlin*, I, 46.

[3] These fears were not without foundation. When the draft of the proposed Potsdam declaration was shown by the U.S. Ambassador at Chungking to General Chiang Kai-shek, the General said that it would be helpful to his position in China if his name and title—President of the Republic of China—followed those of the President of the United States and preceded Mr. Churchill. The General said that he and Mr. Truman were supreme heads of State, whereas Mr. Churchill was only a secondary official. He also asked that China should be invited to take part in all future U.N. conferences on Asia. *F.R.U.S., 1945 The Conference of Berlin*, II, 1283.

(a) F4058/584/61.

on July 16—the day of the successful experimental detonation of an atomic bomb. The United States authorities also knew at this time from intercepted telegrams that the Emperor of Japan wanted to negotiate a surrender, and that the Japanese Supreme War Council had suggested to him that he should send Prince Konoye on a secret mission to Moscow.[1] The Emperor agreed, and on July 12 told Prince Konoye to accept whatever terms he could get. Mr. Togo, the Japanese Foreign Minister, telegraphed the same day to Mr. Sato, the Japanese Ambassador in Moscow, asking him to get a reply as soon as possible to the request to the Soviet Government to receive Prince Konoye. Mr. Togo told Mr. Sato that if Great Britain and the United States would recognise Japanese 'honour and existence, we would terminate the war . . . but if the enemy insists on unconditional surrender, we and His Majesty the Emperor would fight to the end'.[2] The instructions reached Mr. Sato too late for him to present them to M. Molotov (who might anyhow have refused to see him because the Russian Delegation was about to leave for Potsdam. On July 18 Mr. Sato reported that M. Lozovsky, Deputy Commissar for Foreign Affairs, had told him that the terms of the Japanese message were not clear, and that the Soviet Government could give no reply to the Emperor's message or to the proposal for a visit by Prince Konoye.

Meanwhile at Potsdam on July 17 Stalin (not knowing that the United States Government already had this information) had asked Mr. Churchill to tell President Truman of the Japanese *démarche*.[3] Mr. Churchill saw the President on July 18 and said during the conversation that we might avoid using the term 'unconditional surrender' to the Japanese by expressing our demand in some other way. The Japanese were ready to face certain death in large numbers on a question which to them was one of military honour, but which might not appear so important to us.[4] Mr. Truman, however, was receiving other advice not to make any change in his present declaration. Mr. Hull had sent a message to Mr. Byrnes at Potsdam that he was uncertain how a declaration about the maintenance of the Emperor and the dynasty would work out, and that it would be

---

[1] The Foreign Office also had information about the Japanese decision to send Prince Konoye on a mission to Moscow. On July 26 the Foreign Office received a report that Admiral Nomura and other Japanese representatives were in Moscow to ask for Soviet mediation to end the war with Japan. The Japanese were reported to be uneasy about the Potsdam talks, and to be preparing for an early Russian entry into the Far Eastern war. The Foreign Office thought the report about Admiral Numura was improbable, and probably came from a leakage about the proposal to send Prince Konoye to Moscow.

[2] Telegrams exchanged between Mr. Togo and Mr. Sato, and some of the memoranda etc. on the subject of the proposed proclamation to Japan, are printed in *F.R.U.S., 1945, The Conference of Berlin* I, 873–903.

[3] Stalin said that he did not want himself to mention the Japanese approach to Mr. Truman because he wished to avoid giving the impression that the Soviet Union had any desire to mediate between the U.S.A. and Japan. He does, however, seem to have spoken directly on July 18 to Mr. Truman of the approach. *Op. cit.*, II, 87–8, and 1587–8.

[4] Churchill, *op. cit.*, Volume VI, p. 555.

better to wait before making it. The American Joint Chiefs of Staff telegraphed to the President that, while they did not want anything in the declaration to make it difficult or impossible to use the authority of the Emperor to order a surrender of the Japanese forces outside as well as inside Japan, they thought it best to exclude a statement about constitutional monarchy under the existing dynasty and to make no commitment to support any particular form of Japanese government. They pointed out that the second statement might be misconstrued, on the one hand, by those who would take it to mean, either that the United Nations would depose the Emperor and substitute some other member of his family, or, on the other hand, that the United Nations would be prepared to continue the institution of the Emperor and Emperor-worship.

Mr. Byrnes gave Mr. Churchill the draft of the declaration on July 24.[1] He said that the United States Government wished to put it forward in the names of the three Governments (United States, Great Britain and China) at war with Japan.[2] The British Delegation thought that it was unrealistic in that it seemed to address the Japanese people over the head of their Government. There was no organised civilian group in Japan who could overthrow the Government; the mass of the people were loyal to the Emperor and therefore obedient to a lawfully constituted administration. The proclamation would have a better chance of achieving its object it if were framed in recognition of these facts. (a) (b)

Mr. Eden advised the Prime Minister to accept the draft, but suggested some amendments to convert the document from a proclamation to the Japanese people to a communication to the Japanese Government. The President accepted all the British amendments. On July 25 the Prime Minister told the President that he would agree to the amended draft. He hoped that the President would issue it as soon as possible. The declaration was issued on July 26 in the following terms: (c)

(1) We, the President of the United States, the President of the National Government of the Republic of China and the Prime Minister of Great Britain, representing the hundreds of millions of our countrymen, have conferred and agree that Japan shall be given an opportunity to end this war.

(2) The prodigious land, sea and air forces of the United States,

---

[1] This date is inferred from a footnote in *F.R.U.S., 1945, The Conference of Berlin*, II, 1275, n. (1) which quotes Mr. Truman as saying he '. . . gave him (Churchill) a copy of the draft proclamation on July 24.'

[2] Mr. Byrnes said that the President did not think it necessary to consult General Chiang Kai-shek, but the final text was telegraphed to, and approved by, him before it was issued.

(a) C.P.(45)89. F4606/364/23. (b) F.O.934/3/14(9). (c) PM45/8T; F4789/364/23.

the British Empire and of China, many times reinforced by their armies and air fleets from the west, are poised to strike the final blows upon Japan. This military power is sustained and inspired by the determination of the Allied nations to prosecute the war against Japan until she ceases to resist.

(3) The result of the futile and senseless German resistance to the might of the aroused free peoples of the world stands forth in awful clarity as an example to the people of Japan. The might that now converges on Japan is immeasurably greater than that which, when applied to the resisting Nazis, necessarily laid waste to the lands, the industry and the method of life of the whole German people. The full application of our military power, backed by our resolve, will mean the inevitable and complete destruction of the Japanese armed forces and, just as inevitably, the utter devastation of the Japanese homeland.

(4) The time has come for Japan to decide whether she will continue to be controlled by those self-willed militaristic advisers whose unintelligent calculations have brought the Empire of Japan to the threshold of annihilation or whether she will follow the path of reason.

(5) The following are our terms. We will not deviate from them. There are no alternatives. We shall brook no delay.

(6) There must be eliminated for all time the authority and influence of those who have deceived and misled the people of Japan into embarking on world conquest, for we insist that a new order of peace, security and justice will be impossible until irresponsible militarism is driven from the world.

(7) Until such a new order is established and until there is convincing proof that Japan's war-making power is destroyed, points in Japanese territory to be designated by the Allies shall be occupied to secure the achievement of the basic objectives we are here setting forth.

(8) The terms of the Cairo Declaration shall be carried out and Japanese sovereignty shall be limited to the islands of Honshu, Hokkaido, Kyushu, Shikoku and such minor islands as we determine.

(9) The Japanese military forces, after being completely disarmed, shall be permitted to return to their homes with the opportunity to lead peaceful and productive lives.

(10) We do not intend that the Japanese shall be enslaved as a race or destroyed as a nation, but stern justice shall be meted out to all war criminals, including those who have visited cruelties upon our prisoners. The Japanese Government shall remove all obstacles to the revival and strengthening of democratic tendencies among the Japanese people. Freedom of speech, of religion and of thought, as well as respect for the fundamental human rights, shall be established.

(11) Japan shall be permitted to maintain such industries as will sustain her economy and permit the exaction of just reparations in kind, but not those industries which would enable her to rearm for war. To this end, access to, as distinguished from control of, raw materials shall be permitted.

(12) The occupying forces of the Allies shall be withdrawn from Japan as soon as these objectives have been accomplished and there has been established, in accordance with the freely expressed will of the Japanese people, a peacefully inclined and responsible Government.

(13) We call upon the Government of Japan to proclaim now the unconditional surrender of all the Japanese armed forces, and to provide proper and adequate assurances of their good faith in such action. The alternative for Japan is prompt and utter destruction.

Stalin told the other delegates at the tenth plenary meeting of the Potsdam Conference on July 28 that the Japanese Government had (a) proposed that the Soviet Government should act as mediator in an approach to the British and United States Governments. Although he had not been informed in advance of what he called the Anglo-American ultimatum to Japan, he thought it his duty to tell the British and Americans of this latest development.[1] He had received a letter from the Japanese Ambassador at Moscow. In this letter Mr. Sato had said that, when he had last wanted to state the policy of his Government about Japanese-Soviet relations and the war, the Soviet Government had replied that they could not answer since the message from the Japanese Emperor—which Prince Konoye was to convey—had not contained a sufficiently definite proposal. Mr. Sato had therefore been instructed to explain that Prince Konoye's proposed mission was to ask the Soviet Government to mediate between the Japanese Government and the British and United States Governments in order to end the war and negotiate about Soviet-Japanese interests. The Emperor had authorised the mission, and the only object of it was to avoid more bloodshed on both sides. Stalin said this was simply another attempt to obtain Russian collaboration in forthcoming Japanese policy, and that the Soviet Government had given 'an unhesitating negative'. In view of the Japanese Prime Minister's press statement of July 28,[2] no action was taken on Stalin's statement.

(iii)

Preliminary British and American planning for the treatment of Japan after the war: Foreign Office memorandum of May 1945: Sir G. Sansom's memorandum of June 20, 1945.

Meanwhile, the Foreign Office had been examining the problems which would follow the surrender of Japan. In September 1944 the

[1] Mr. Togo (as the Americans already knew from their intercepts) had instructed Mr. Sato to say to M. Lozovsky that Prince Konoye's mission would be to ask for Russian help in ending the war and to negotiate on matters of Soviet-Japanese interests. Mr. Togo repeated that Japan could not accept 'unconditional surrender'. He seems to have sent this message on the night of July 21, but it does not appear to have reached Mr. Sato until July 24. See *F.R.U.S. The Conference of Berlin*, II, 1257–9.

[2] See below, p. 524.

(a) P(Terminal) 10th meeting. F.O./934/3/14(15).

War Office informed the Foreign Office that they were considering the question of civil affairs for Japan and the possible extent of the British commitment. They had as yet no official knowledge of American intentions, but had heard unofficially that the Americans had at first envisaged a thirty per cent British participation but had decided later in favour of an all-American civil affairs plan; they had now made much progress in training their personnel. The War Office thought that we should enquire about these plans, in order to be ready if we were suddenly asked to take part in them. The War
(a) Office sent a cable to the Joint Staff Mission in Washington to find out the position. No reply had been received to this cable at the end of February 1945.

(b) Before this date the War Office heard unofficially that the United States War Department had in view plans for the civil administration of Japan, which would be undertaken by the nation whose land forces had been engaged in operations against the mainland of Japan.[1] The preliminary view of the Foreign Office on the matter was that Russia was the 'great question mark', since it was not known whether she would join in the fighting or simply demand a voice in the peace settlement. China might want to participate for reasons of prestige. The Dominions Office had pointed out that Australia expected to be consulted, and New Zealand and Canada might have similar views. The Foreign Office thought that we should come to an agreement with the Dominions before we approached the United States.

The Foreign Office proposed preliminary talks with the Dominions Office. If they agreed, a committee with Dominion participation might decide on the extent of Japanese territory to be occupied and the personnel to administer it. British participation in the control of Japan would not be satisfactory if it were only regional and did not extend to participation in control of the central Government and the central organs of finance, communications and industry. It might be difficult to dispute the American argument that, if they supplied the land troops, they must have sole responsibility for civil affairs administration during the pre-surrender period in Japan. If, however, we shared in the post-surrender administrative period, we should probably inherit an American legacy in policy, administrative methods and Japanese personnel which might give rise to difficulties.

A Foreign Office minute of December 21, 1944, pointed out the relevance of the manpower problem in the post-surrender period. We might not be able or willing to allocate powerful British forces for a

[1] i.e. if (as the War Department appeared to assume) the land forces of the United States alone were to be engaged on the mainland of Japan the control of civil affairs would be wholly in American hands.

(a) NOD350, F4230/4230/23 (1944). (b) F5877/4230/23.

long-term occupation of Japan if Great Britain were to take one of the islands or have a zone on the German model. The question of troops was vital since, if we did not share in the occupation, we could not provide more than a token number towards the higher control staffs.

In the early part of 1945 the Australian Department of External (a) Affairs suggested to the Foreign Office the establishment of a committee similar to the European Advisory Commission to deal with Far Eastern affairs. The Foreign Office gave full consideration to this proposal, but their general view was that there were so many difficulties in the way of the successful establishment and functioning of a formal inter-Allied body that it would be better to drop the idea of a Far Eastern Commission for the time being and concentrate on an attempt to get problems discussed on an informal Anglo-American or Empire-American basis. The Foreign Office thought Lord Halifax should be asked to discuss the matter with the Head of the British Joint Staff Mission in Washington, Field-Marshal Sir H. Wilson, and advise whether an approach through Washington was the best initial course.[1] On May 10, 1945, the Chiefs of Staff discussed a proposal that these problems might best be considered through (b) military channels in Washington, but agreed that they should be dealt with through political channels and not through the Joint Staff Mission.[2]

Before the Foreign Office sent any instructions to Lord Halifax, they received a letter of May 3 from Sir G. Sansom, who had just been (c) told unofficially that the State Department for a long time had been examining the problems which would arise with the end of the war in the Far East. They had reached agreement with the Service Departments at the highest level and had almost come to the stage where they could submit a short paper to the President; if approved, this would become a statement of United States policy. Plans seemed to

[1] The Foreign Office prepared a brief for the San Francisco delegation in which they discussed a report that the United States had in mind a Pacific Security Council under the (d) auspices of the United Nations. It seemed doubtful whether this problem would come up at the San Francisco conference, since the conference was to be limited to working out the charter for the world organisation. A special body deriving its powers from the world organisation might be needed eventually to discuss and co-ordinate post-war questions in the Far East and Pacific; but these were long-term matters, and it was not clear how such a body would fill the immediate need for a committee to plan on behalf of the main belligerents the arrangements for the surrender, occupation and control of Japan, i.e. the counterpart for the Far East of the European Advisory Commission.

[2] A Foreign Office minute of May 17 read: 'I think both our own and the U.S. Chiefs of Staff are becoming less "military" and more inclined to leave "armistice and civil (e) affairs" matters to Foreign Offices. Hard experience has knocked holes in the original 1942 military thesis that "civil affairs" were merely the handmaid of operations. Our own C.O.S. have long since been inclined to leave the F.O. to take the lead, e.g. F.O. leadership in civil affairs (Allied), the "diplomatic" character of the E.A.C. and F.O. responsibility for planning the Control Commission in Germany.'

(a) F584/584/61. (b) COS(45)122, F2847/584/61. (c) F2774/364/23.
(d) F2574/584/61. (e) F2847/584/61.

have been laid for a period of military government in Japan, followed by an interim period of administration by the Japanese under a control commission, and a subsequent period of 'normal' government under agreed conditions.

Sir G. Sansom thought that the United States Government meant to take the lead where Japan was concerned. He regarded the information which he had received as advice to the British Government to decide their policy quickly. The State Department had found that the greatest obstacle to their plans for military government and subsequent dealings with Japan was lack of adequate personnel in both numbers and quality. China had apparently no well-considered plans for dealing with Japan, although the State Department thought that they wanted to dominate Korea and Thailand. Sir G. Sansom reported that the United States Government planned to delay the restoration of Japanese industry and accelerate the growth of Chinese industry, until the difference of potential between Japan and China was reduced to a point where Japan would not be a danger.

(a) On May 12 the Foreign Office telegraphed to Lord Halifax that any proposal to set up a Far Eastern counterpart of the European Advisory Commission would probably break down on the question of membership. They thought it unlikely that the United States Government would agree to the establishment of an inter-Allied body of wide membership to discuss problems arising after the defeat of Japan. They doubted indeed whether the United States service authorities would accept an inter-Allied body for this purpose. The problems, however, could not be held indefinitely in suspense or left to the Americans alone. Without prejudice to the ultimate establishment of an inter-Allied body, discussions should begin at once on an Anglo-American or Empire-American basis. The Foreign Office informed Lord Halifax that they had intended to suggest to Mr. Eden that he should sound Mr. Stettinius on the subject at San Francisco. Meanwhile—at the suggestion of the Chiefs of Staff—they asked Lord Halifax for his views and those of Field-Marshal Wilson on the best mode of approach to the United States Government.

(b) Lord Halifax replied on May 26. Field-Marshal Wilson had told him that the question of the occupation of Japan had been under discussion by the United States Joint Civil Affairs committee for some months, and was now being considered by the United States Chiefs of Staff and State Department. He understood that surrender terms and proclamations had been drawn up, and that machinery for co-ordinating these with other Powers had been sketched out. United States plans seemed to envisage an allied occupation of

(a) F2847/584/61. (b) F3178/584/61.

Japan by Americans, British, Chinese and possibly Russians with some form of co-ordinating Allied control. These plans would probably be complete in about a fortnight, when the United States Government would approach the British Government and perhaps China to suggest the establishment of an advisory commission to consider the United States drafts.

Until this time the Foreign Office had not known that American planning was so far advanced and that there was so much agreement between the State and War Departments. The Foreign Office now drew up a memorandum[1] to initiate discussion of the problems in- (a) volved in the Committee on Armistice Terms and Civil Administration. This memorandum pointed out that, although the idea of a large-scale and perhaps lengthy occupation of Germany was generally accepted, very little thought had been given to the corresponding problem in Japan or the obligations which it might entail on Great Britain and the Dominions. The Foreign Office thought that the occupation and control of Japan to ensure the elimination of militarism might raise more difficult questions than the suppression of Nazism in the west, owing to the limitations of manpower and the remoteness of Japan, the nature of the Japanese people and the comparative scarcity of Allied personnel with knowledge of the country and the language. The problem and the role of the British Commonwealth in its solution ought to be considered at once.

Hitherto the United States had taken the major part in the war against Japan, and expected to continue to do so in dealing with her after defeat. The defeat and disarmament of Japan were, however, very important politically to the United Kingdom and to Canada, Australia and New Zealand, who had been harmed by Japanese aggression and had a vital interest in future peace and security in the Pacific. Australia and New Zealand had contributed to the limit of their strength and with notable results to the defeat of the Japanese in the south-west Pacific area; Canada had shared in the defence of Hong Kong, and intended to take part in the war until the end. The

---

[1] The history of this memorandum shows the delays in the consideration of Far Eastern post-war questions. On December 21, 1944, after receiving the 'unofficial' information about American plans (see above, p. 514), the Foreign Office suggested that a paper on the subject might be prepared for the official Committee on Armistice Terms and Civil Administration. The Far Eastern Committee of the War Cabinet agreed to this suggestion on January 17, 1945. On March 2 the Foreign Office sent to the War Office a draft (which had not yet been seen by the Secretary of State or the Permanent Under-Secretary) with the idea that it should be made into a joint Foreign Office and War Office paper. The War Office replied on March 21 that they thought it better for the paper to come from the Foreign Office only, since if it were a joint paper the Admiralty and Air Ministry might feel that they ought to be consulted, and this consultation would mean more delay. The Foreign Office then revised their paper. The revised paper was sent by Sir O. Sargent on May 9 to the Chiefs of Staff with the proposal that, if they agreed, it might go directly to the Prime Minister. The Chiefs of Staff agreed on May 17.

(a) COS(45)324(o); F3220/364/23, F1834/364/23.

United Kingdom and India had committed forces to the south-east Asia campaigns, and a powerful British fleet had been deployed in the Pacific. After the defeat of Germany, it was intended to send more British troops to the Far East. The Foreign Office thought that the British Commonwealth must share in the control of Japan after her defeat. It was most important for the future peace of the Pacific area that the Japanese people should be impressed with the conception of the United Nations marshalled to vindicate the principles of civilisation violated by Japan. There was no reason yet to think that American policy was opposed to allowing us a part in the occupation and control of Japan.

The Foreign Office foresaw three phases of the problem: (i) the pre-surrender period, with Allied forces established in Japanese territory, (ii) the post-surrender period, when Japan was under Allied military control, and (iii) the High Commission period, with either civil or military control until Japan was considered fit to control her own affairs. Planning for the pre-surrender period was difficult until we knew what land forces would conquer the Japanese mainland, since the American attitude was understood to be that the nationality of these forces would decide responsibility for civil affairs. Even if British troops could not take part in the landing and establishment of Allied forces on Japanese home territory, the British Commonwealth should have a share in formulating Allied policy for the control of Japan.

The Foreign Office memorandum then discussed whether the occupation of Japan was to be short or long, and whether it was to cover the whole country or only a minimum number of key points. The nature of the central control over the Japanese administration would have to be decided, and also whether regional control was to be integrated, or whether zones or key points were to be allotted to the several Allies. It seemed too early for proposals about the final High Commission period, but full British Commonwealth participation in the control of Japan during this period was important. The Foreign Office did not know American or Chinese intentions or Russia's future attitude towards Japan. The fanatical nature of the Japanese and their numbers might make a large occupation force necessary. The British manpower problem would be more difficult than that of the United States; this fact might make it necessary to limit occupation to a minimum, and rely on economic controls, which could be used with great effect in view of Japan's geographical position and lack of raw materials. On the other hand, economic controls might give rise to inter-Allied suspicion and jealousy, especially if they conflicted with the post-war trading policies of the controlling Powers. If military occupation were decided on, the Foreign Office thought it politically desirable that British Commonwealth forces should take part. For the same reason, the British Commonwealth should be adequately represented at all levels in central control over the Japanese Government. A Commonwealth policy should be formulated in consultation with the Dominion Governments for discussion with the United States and other Allied Governments concerned.[1]

Sir O. Sargent, on reading this memorandum, pointed out that much time would be lost if discussion began in the Committee on Armistice Terms and Civil Administration and worked up gradually through various stages to the War Cabinet, without any previous indication of the Government's intentions about sharing in the occupation and control of Japan, and that it would be better to begin with a directive from the Prime Minister.

On May 26 Mr. Eden therefore raised the matter with the Prime (a)
Minister. He said that American planning had reached an advanced stage. He thought that we should take part in the military occupation of Japan, if there were an Allied occupation, and that we should share in political and economic control and in the planning of that control as we had done in Europe. Hence the study of the problems involved should start at once; unless we opened discussions with Washington in the near future, American views might crystallise before we had had time to influence them. The Chiefs of Staff also had this view. The Prime Minister agreed that the Foreign Office and Chiefs of Staff should report jointly to the War Cabinet.

On May 28 the State Department showed Sir G. Sansom inform- (b)
ally a draft document on United States policy to Japan. The preamble stated that United States objectives were (*a*) unconditional surrender or the total defeat of Japan; (*b*) execution of the territorial provisions of the Cairo Declaration; (*c*) prevention of future aggression; (*d*) development of a Japanese Government which could be trusted in international relations; (*e*) eventual participation of Japan in a world economic system on terms consistent with (*c*) and (*d*).

The United States planned to realise these objectives, firstly, by securing for the Supreme Allied Commander complete authority

---

[1] A suggestion seems to have been made in the War Office for something like a 'Morgenthau plan' for Japan. The War Office informed the Foreign Office in May 1945 of (c)
details of this plan. It was based on the argument that, since the Japanese had contributed so little to world economy that could not be replaced from elsewhere—notably China and India—the best policy would be to drive them back to the islands of Japan, destroy their industry and merchant fleets and reduce them to their position of seventy years before. They should be left alone as cultivators, fishermen and craftsmen until the United Nations were satisfied that a change of heart made it safe to admit them to the comity of nations. By the exercise of limited central control, the United Nations would see that they were adequately fed and clothed. The War Office thought that in view of the speed of events and the British position regarding planning for Japan, such a policy might have much to commend it. The Foreign Office did not even comment on the plan, and no further attention appears to have been given to it.

(a) PM/45/205, F3220/364/23. (b) F5400/364/23 (c) F2821/364/23.

over all domestic and foreign affairs. The constitutional powers of the Emperor and all organs, e.g. the Diet, for considering and formulating policy would therefore be suspended, and the military government would assume their functions. Secondly, military government, which would be stern but just, would repeal obnoxious laws, dissolve all political parties and societies, proclaim freedom of worship, institute a new system of public information in place of the existing systems, and control education.[1] Thirdly, civil courts of justice would continue to function under the control of the military government.

The State Department had in mind three periods: one of severe military government, one of close surveillance during which some restrictions might be relaxed and the Japanese allowed to carry out some civil functions, and one looking forward to the re-entry of Japan into the family of nations. The duration of each period would depend on the behaviour of the Japanese. The general political aims of the United States were the abolition of militarism, the emergence and encouragement of liberal political elements, and the development of a political system consistent with United Nations principles.

The State Department envisaged reparation, but not until productive machinery was partly restored. They had in mind the destruction of industries related to war and an emphasis on light industries in the process of restoring a normal economy. The programme of industrial rehabilitation should not aim at a standard of living out of line with standards in other parts of Asia. The programme would encourage local self-government and provide for a more extended ownership of means of production, financial organs and so on.

(a) A State Department official told Sir G. Sansom that the United States Government did not intend as yet to inform other Governments of their views and invite participation. They felt that the main responsibility for the defeat of Japan and carrying out the surrender terms lay with them. If the other Allies did not want to share in carrying out the surrender terms, they would not object, but would welcome any participation or opinions offered. The Foreign Office accepted the general statement of American objectives, but thought that the Americans might not have counted the cost to themselves of a protracted total occupation of Japan and the assumption of

[1] In a minute of June 9 on these proposals, Sir G. Sansom wrote: 'With regard to in-
(b) doctrination, it is extremely doubtful whether, even if the Allies had at their disposal a host of erudite arch-angels, the Japanese people would respond to their teaching. Many Japanese, I feel sure, would prefer the horrors of war to the ministrations of a kind of U.N.R.R.A. [United Nations Relief and Rehabilitation Administration] operating in the cultural field.'

(a) F3238/364/23. (b) F4052/584/61.

all the functions of government. The Japanese were a proud and stubborn race who had never known foreign control, and a foreign military government could function only if it were backed by an army of occupation much larger in proportion to the population than in the case of Germany. Political assassinations during the period of foreign rule were likely. Although the Allies might have to decide to accept the burden of total occupation if it were the only way to render Japan permanently harmless, less drastic and burdensome arrangements might be more effective. Without her overseas territories, Japan was so poor in natural resources that it should not be difficult to exercise economic controls. The fact of defeat had to be impressed upon the masses; this could be done by a triumphal march through Tokyo, by the long-term occupation of four or five easily-held key points, by keeping Allied war vessels at the ports and by occasional demonstration flights of massed aircraft. Instead of suspending the constitutional powers of the Emperor, the Allies ought to work through these powers, and to secure compliance with their demands by the use of economic sanctions. The Foreign Office suggested that they should now bring the problem to the notice of the Dominion Governments in order to formulate a Commonwealth policy on the control of Japan.

Sir G. Sansom came to England early in June to take part in the discussions on British policy. On June 20 he summed up the position (a) in a memorandum which was later approved by the Far Eastern Department and the Chiefs of Staff. He wrote that no exception could be taken to the American objectives, but that a number of American officials were known to have doubts about the feasibility of their own plans. He suggested therefore that the Foreign Office should formulate their views and put them to the Americans.

Sir G. Sansom pointed out that after defeat Japan would be militarily impotent and financially weak, with much of her industrial equipment destroyed. She would be unable to borrow capital, and had only scanty capital resources of her own. It should be possible to influence the course of events after defeat without protracted occupation and a costly machinery of internal controls since the control of Japanese imports and exports and the deferment of new commercial treaties offered a more effective means of compulsion than Allied prescription of specific political and social institutions. The employment of these economic sanctions should enable the Allies to induce Japan to reform her institutions.

On the other hand Sir G. Sansom pointed out that, if it were decided that even partial restoration of Japan's industries was of the lowest priority, much of the urban population of Japan (more than

(a) F3768, 5400/364/23.

half the total of 76 million) would be unemployed and inadequately fed, if not starving. This would not favour the evolution of a democratic type of government in Japan, since the limited internal resources would have to be husbanded by strict controls imposed by autocratic methods. It would be useless for a military government of the kind contemplated by the Americans to embark on ambitious projects for the political re-education of a starving and miserable people. The prospects of Japanese political liberalisation might be improved if Japan could engage in some foreign trade as soon as possible, and then turn to developing an internal market. There were objections to such concessions, but the hard alternative seemed to be the creation of a political vacuum, which would have to be filled either by costly total Allied control of a pauperised Japanese population or by violent revolution with its dangerous implications for the future. These considerations affected the scale and length of occupation. Sir G. Sansom thought that the Foreign Office should make up their minds about the advantages and disadvantages of participation in the political and economic control of Japan as the Americans seemed to envisage it. 'There is a danger that we might be dragged along behind the American chariot and become implicated in policies in which we had little faith.'

Sir G. Sansom considered that, instead of suspending the constitutional powers of the Emperor, the Allies ought to work through them or whatever State administration they found in being in Japan. He repeated his view that they should use economic sanctions to secure compliance with such requirements as the repeal of obnoxious laws, dissolution of political societies, reform of education, and freedom of speech and worship.

He suggested that the State Department should be told informally of the British views, and that detailed studies of some of the problems should be undertaken in London. He stated four of the problems. Firstly, would the loss of her colonies and strategic bases, her navy, air force and merchant marine, her weapons and arsenals and much of her industrial equipment, with the strain of reparations, make Japan so weak that she would not be able to support her population without outside help? Secondly, was it necessary, in addition to these disabilities, to impose on Japan terms as to her political and social structure in the hope that a democratic and peace-loving state would emerge? Or were there other means more likely to produce the desired result at less expense and effort to the Allies? Thirdly, to what extent was long-range economic control physically and politically feasible? Lastly, if the Americans insisted on total occupation and military government of Japan, would British abstention from anything but token participation injure her interests and prestige in the United States, and in Asia?

On July 18 the Foreign Office sent Lord Halifax their views tentatively and without commitment in a telegram based on Sir G. Sansom's memorandum.[1] They asked Lord Halifax to make an oral communication to the State Department on the lines of their telegram, and to say that it represented only their preliminary reactions and was without prejudice to the views of the Dominions, which must be expressly reserved, and to the final views of the British Government. (a)

The telegram to Lord Halifax was however altered on the instructions of Mr. Eden, who had not seen it before despatch.[2] He did not agree with the view of the Far Eastern Department and Sir G. Sansom that the Allies should work through whatever administration they found in being in Japan, probably the Emperor. Mr. Eden minuted: 'I do not want us to recommend to Americans that Emperor should be preserved. They would no doubt like to get such advice and then say they had reluctantly concurred with us.' (b)

On July 29 therefore the telegram to Lord Halifax was amended by deleting the reference to the Emperor. The amendment ran: 'Might it not be preferable also for the Allies, instead of assuming all the functions of government in Japan, to work through a Japanese administration, using economic sanctions to secure compliance with such requirements as the repeal of obnoxious laws, the dissolution of political societies, and the reform of education, freedom of speech and worship, etc.?'[3] (c)

---

[1] This telegram to Washington, and the substance of the telegram from Washington containing the proposals mentioned to Sir G. Sansom, were sent to the Dominion Governments. The Foreign Office did not think that there was anything in the memorandum which needed Cabinet approval at the time; on the other hand they wanted to get their views to Washington as soon as possible in view of the likelihood that the question would be discussed at least informally between the Delegations at Potsdam. Sir G. Sansom's memorandum which was taken to Potsdam by the British delegation, and the Foreign Office comments on it were shown informally to the State Department (*F.R.U.S., 1945, The Conference of Berlin*, I, 581–4.)

[2] Mr. Eden had been away from the Foreign Office for most of June and early July owing to illness, although during part of the time papers were sent to him. On July 15 he went with the Prime Minister and Mr. Attlee to Potsdam.

[3] When Mr. Grew received the preliminary British views, he made little comment beyond pointing out that the Potsdam surrender formula represented a modification in American ideas somewhat in the direction of the British paper, particularly in its reference to the establishment of a responsible Japanese Government. (d)

(a) F4310, 5400/364/23; Onward 51/2, F.O.934/3/14(2). (b) Target 95, Onward 51, F.O.934/3/14(1); F4396/364/23.
(c) Target 95: F4396, 5400/364/23. (d) F5032/364/23.

(iv)

The Japanese attitude towards the Potsdam Declaration: atomic bombs dropped on Hiroshima and Nagasaki: the Japanese offer to surrender, August 10, 1945: Allied acceptance of the surrender of Japan, August 14: President Truman's appointment of General MacArthur to receive the Japanese surrender: signature of the Instrument of Surrender, September 2, 1945.

The Japanese Government neither accepted nor directly rejected the opportunity given to them by the Potsdam declaration. They decided to take no positive action, but to ignore the declaration pending further developments and especially the outcome of their *démarche* with the Soviet Government. They considered that the declaration had not been addressed to them (the Japanese Government) officially by the three signatory Powers: they had heard it only as a radio broadcast, and did not think they need answer it. Unfortunately, from their point of view, they did not keep a complete silence about it. Mr. Suzuki, the Japanese Prime Minister, made a press statement on July 28 that the declaration was nothing but a rehash of the Cairo declaration, and that the Japanese Government set no value upon it, and had no recourse other than to ignore it entirely, and resolutely to fight for the successful conclusion of the war.[1]

The United States Government, not unnaturally, took the statement as a refusal to surrender even on the terms that the Japanese people would ultimately be free to choose their own form of responsible Government. The President then decided that the atomic bomb should be used after August 3 if Japan had not surrendered.[2] A bomb was dropped on Hiroshima on August 6, and another on Nagasaki two days later. On August 9 the U.S.S.R. declared war on
(a) Japan. On August 10 the Japanese News Agency announced that

[1] *See F.R.U.S., 1945, The Conference of Berlin*, II, 1293. The Japanese word translated as 'ignore' could also have meant 'make no immediate comment' (i.e. until more information had been received). The 'anti-peace' party in the Japanese army asked for a more definite statement and obtained it from the Prime Minister on July 30. See Butow, *op. cit.*, pp. 145–7. On August 2 Mr. Togo again instructed Mr. Sato to make further efforts with the Russians. Mr. Togo said in his message: 'It is our intention to make the Potsdam three-Power Declaration the basis of our study regarding the terms (of the Japanese capitulation)'.

[2] Under the terms of the Quebec Agreement of August 19, 1943, British concurrence was required for the use of the bomb. Field-Marshal Wilson told the United States authorities on July 4, 1945, that H.M.G. agreed to the use of the bomb against Japan. He added that the Prime Minister might wish to discuss the matter with President Truman at the Potsdam Conference. Mr. Churchill has stated (*Second World War*, VI, p. 639) that 'there was never a moment's discussion at the Conference whether the bomb should be used or not'. Mr. Churchill's view—which was obviously also that of the Americans—was that the use of the bomb in bringing the war rapidly to an end would in fact mean a smaller expenditure of lives—Japanese as well as British and American and Russian—than would have been likely with the weapons already in use. No record has been found in the Cabinet or Foreign Office archives of any discussion of the matter.

(a) F4974, 4975/630/23.

the Japanese Government had addressed on that day the following communication to the Swiss and Swedish Governments respectively for transmission to the United States, Great Britain, the Soviet Union and China:

> 'In obedience to the gracious command of His Majesty the Emperor who, ever anxious to enhance the cause of world peace, desires earnestly to bring about an early termination of hostilities with a view to saving mankind from the calamities to be imposed upon them by further continuation of the war, the Japanese Government asked several weeks ago the Soviet Government with which neutral relations then prevailed, to render its good offices in restoring peace *vis-à-vis* the enemy powers.
>
> These efforts in the interest of peace unfortunately having failed the Japanese Government in conformity with the august wish of His Majesty to restore the general peace, and desiring to put an end to the untold sufferings entailed by war as quickly as possible have decided upon the following.
>
> The Japanese Government are ready to accept the terms enumerated in that joint declaration which was issued at Potsdam on July 26, 1945, by the heads of the Governments of the United States, Great Britain and China and later subscribed to by the Soviet Government, with the understanding that the said declaration does not comprise any demand which prejudices the prerogatives of His Majesty as a sovereign ruler. The Japanese Government hope sincerely that this understanding is warranted and desire keenly that an explicit indication to that effect will be speedily forthcoming.'

Since the Foreign Office had not received official confirmation of the offer they asked the United States, Chinese and Soviet Governments at 5.25 p.m. on August 10 urgently for their views on the statement, and in particular on the condition about the Emperor in the penultimate sentence. In view of the difficulties in administering Japan, they were inclined, provided the United States Government agreed, to allow the Emperor to remain as a symbol, but they could not accept the term 'prerogatives' until it was more closely defined. If the Allies insisted on the disappearance of the Emperor, the Japanese might continue a suicidal resistance. The Potsdam Declaration had not mentioned the Emperor, though it had implied elimination of the military clique.[1] The Foreign Secretary told the American Ambassador on the afternoon of August 10 that he would not discuss the matter with other Governments until he was certain that Great Britain and the United States were in accord. Mr. Winant replied that the State Department were working out a formula for putting Japan under Allied control, and using the Emperor as the instrument of control. He expected to receive the formula about 9.30 p.m.

---

[1] Mr. Bevin had put these views to a meeting of the Cabinet at 3 p.m.

(a) On the evening of August 10 Mr. Winant sent to the Prime Minister the following message from Mr. Byrnes about the reply which the United States Government proposed to send: 'With regard to the Japanese Government's message accepting the terms of the Potsdam proclamation but containing the statement "with the understanding that the said declaration does not comprise any demand which prejudices the prerogatives of His Majesty as a sovereign ruler" our position is as follows: "From the moment of surrender the authority of the Emperor and the Japanese Government to rule the State shall be subject to the Supreme Commander of the Allied Powers who will take such steps as he deems proper to effectuate the surrender terms. The Emperor and the Japanese High Command will be required to sign the surrender terms necessary to carry out the provisions of the Potsdam declaration, to issue orders to all the armed forces of Japan to cease hostilities and to surrender their arms and to issue such other orders as the Supreme Commander may require to give effect to the surrender terms. Immediately upon the surrender the Japanese Government shall transport prisoners of war and civilian internees to places of safety, as directed, where they can quickly be placed aboard Allied transports. The ultimate form of government of Japan shall, in accordance with the Potsdam declaration, be established by the freely expressed will of the Japanese people. The armed forces of the Allied Powers will remain in Japan until the purposes set forth in the Potsdam declaration are achieved." '

The message to the Prime Minister expressed the hope that the British Government would join in this reply in order to end the war and prevent further loss of life. Mr. Attlee and Mr. Bevin told Mr. Winant at midnight on August 10–11 that they agreed in principle with the American proposals but doubted whether it was wise to ask the Emperor to sign the surrender terms. They suggested the formula:

> 'The Emperor shall authorise and ensure the signature by the Government of Japan and the Japanese General Headquarters of the Surrender Terms necessary to carry out the provisions of the Potsdam Declaration, and shall issue his commands to all the Japanese Military, Naval and Air authorities and to all the Forces under their control wherever located to cease active operations and to surrender their arms etc. (as in the United States draft).'

Mr. Attlee and Mr. Bevin believed that this suggestion was in keeping with the Potsdam Declaration, and that it would secure the immediate surrender of the Japanese in all outlying areas and thereby save Allied lives.

(a) F4975/630/23.

Meanwhile, on the morning of August 10, the Japanese Government had also made a communication to the Soviet Ambassador in Tokyo on the lines of their News Agency announcement. At midnight M. Molotov showed the communication to the United States and British Ambassadors. Sir A. Clark Kerr asked him for his views, in particular on the stipulation about the Emperor. M. Molotov said that he was 'sceptical' about the Japanese offer, which fell short of unconditional surrender, and that he did not propose to pay any attention to it. The offensive in Manchuria would continue. Sir A. Clark Kerr asked him whether or not the Emperor was to play a part in future Japanese politics. M. Molotov said that this point was not clear. While M. Molotov was enquiring about the views of the British and United States Governments, a member of Mr. Harriman's staff arrived with a telegram from Washington. This telegram conveyed the hope of the United States Government that the Soviet Government would join in replying that, from the moment of surrender, the Emperor should be subject to the Supreme Allied Commander; that the ultimate form of Government in Japan, in accordance with the Potsdam declaration, would be determined by the freely expressed will of the Japanese people; and that Allied Forces would remain until the purposes of the Potsdam declaration had been achieved. M. Molotov seemed inclined to agree, but said that he would have to consult his Government. At 1.45 a.m. on August 11 he summoned Sir A. Clark Kerr and Mr. Harriman again, and began by accepting the draft American reply to the Japanese Government. He said that the Soviet Government considered that this reply should be delivered in the name of the principal Powers at war with Japan, and that, in the event of an affirmative answer from the Japanese Government, the Allied Powers should agree on a candidate or candidates for a representative of the Allied High Command to which the Emperor and the Japanese Government would be subject. Mr. Harriman asked M. Molotov the meaning of the last sentence. M. Molotov replied that, as there was no United Command in the Far East, it would be necessary to decide on one or two persons as representatives of the Allied High Command. Mr. Harriman suggested that the Russian reply imposed a veto on American freedom of action. M. Molotov said that this was not so, but Mr. Harriman insisted that the Soviet Government's reply meant the imposition of a veto. Sir A. Clark Kerr suggested that by force of circumstances the Supreme Command would fall to the Americans; he was sure that the British Government would accept their choice. Mr. Harriman thereupon made it clear that the United States meant to appoint the Supreme Commander. M. Molotov observed sharply that he assumed that the

(a) F4974, 4976/630/23. (b) F4977/630/23.

Soviet Government would learn of this appointment from the press; Mr. Harriman rejoined that they would learn it from the President. Sir A. Clark Kerr later reported: '. . . and so it went on ding-dong, tempers ever rising'. Mr. Harriman suggested that the Soviet Government should confine their demands to consultation, rather than insist on agreement. M. Molotov refused, and asked why the surrender should not be accepted in any case by [more than][1] one person. Why not, for example, Marshal Vassilevsky[2] as well as General MacArthur? Mr. Harriman said that this was inconceivable. After an angry rejoinder by M. Molotov, Mr. Harriman reminded him of America's four-year effort in the Far East in contrast with Russia's two-day excursion into Manchuria. M. Molotov spoke of the part which Russia had played in liberating Europe. The two Ambassadors then withdrew. At 3 a.m. M. Molotov's secretary telephoned to say that Stalin had consented to substitute 'consult' for 'agree' in the third sentence of M. Molotov's reply, and to drop the words 'or candidates'.

(a) Early on the morning of August 11, the United States Ambassador at Chungking informed General Chiang Kai-shek of the American draft reply to the Japanese statement. General Chiang Kai-shek agreed with the draft, and was particularly pleased with the inclusion of the stipulation that the Emperor himself should sign the surrender terms.[3]

(b) The United States Government sent the following message on behalf of the Four Powers on August 11 to the Swiss Government for the Japanese Government:

> 'With regard to the Japanese Government's message accepting the terms of the Potsdam Proclamation but containing the statement "with the understanding that the said declaration does not comprise any demand which prejudices the prerogatives of His Majesty as a Sovereign Ruler", our position is as follows:
>
> From the moment of surrender the authority of the Emperor and the Japanese Government to rule the State shall be subject to the Supreme Commander of the Allied Powers who will take such steps as he deems proper to effectuate the surrender terms.
>
> The Emperor will be required to authorise and ensure the signature by the Government of Japan and Japanese Imperial General Headquarters of the surrender terms necessary to carry out the provisions of the Potsdam Declaration, and shall issue his commands to all the Japanese Military, Naval and Air Authorities and to all the Forces

[1] These words are not in the text as received in London, but seem to be required by the sense of M. Molotov's question.

[2] The Soviet Chief of General Staff.

[3] The Chinese Government later accepted the amendments which the British Government had proposed to Washington.

(a) F5018, 5024, 5039/630/23; F5034/630/23. (b) F4974/630/23.

under their control, wherever located, to cease active operations, surrender their arms, and to issue such other orders as the Supreme Commander may require to give effect to the surrender terms.

Immediately upon the surrender the Japanese Government shall transport prisoners of war and civilian internees to places of safety, as directed, where they can quickly be placed aboard Allied transports.

The ultimate form of Government of Japan shall, in accordance with the Potsdam Declaration, be established by the freely expressed will of the Japanese people.

The armed forces of the Allied Powers will remain in Japan until the purposes set forth in the Potsdam Declaration are achieved.'

President Truman telegraphed to Mr. Attlee on August 12 that he (a) proposed General MacArthur 'as Supreme Commander for the Allied Powers to accept, co-ordinate and carry into effect the surrender of the Japanese armed forces'. He would make arrangements for a British representative to be present at the surrender. Japanese forces in south-east Asia and parts of Malaysia were to surrender unconditionally to Admiral Mountbatten or his subordinate commanders. Mr. Attlee replied that he agreed, and designated Admiral Sir Bruce Fraser to accompany General MacArthur. By the morning of August 13, General Chiang Kai-shek had agreed to nominate a representative to be associated with General MacArthur in the surrender negotiations. Fleet Admiral Nimitz was to be present as the United States representative.[1]

---

[1] The Dominion Governments were informed of the procedure agreed between the President and the Prime Minister for acceptance of the Japanese surrender by General MacArthur, and for the presence of Admiral Sir Bruce Fraser as the British representative. The Dominion Governments were invited to arrange for a senior Service representative of each to be attached to Admiral Fraser. The Australian Government nominated General Blamey, Commander-in-Chief, Australian Military Forces and Commander of Allied Land Forces in the South-West Pacific Area, but asked that he should attend as the direct representative of the Australian Government. On August 14 the Foreign Office pointed out to Lord Halifax that if the Australian representative had separate status, it would be (b) necessary to make the same arrangement for the other Dominion representatives. They wanted nevertheless to meet Australian wishes on the point if the United States authorities saw no objection. Lord Halifax was asked to take the matter up with them urgently.

On August 15 Mr. Dunn told Mr. Balfour, Minister in H.M. Embassy at Washington, (c) that the United States Government were willing that Admiral Fraser should be accompanied by Dominion representatives, but could not agree to granting them independent status. He explained that the act of surrender would be signed by General MacArthur, and that his signature would be endorsed below by Admiral Fraser, Admiral Nimitz, a Chinese and a Soviet General. The Australian Government were informed of the American decision, and subsequently made direct representations to the United States Government in favour not only of independent Australian representation, but also of signature by the Australian representative. On August 23 the Foreign Office were embarrassed to learn from the press that the United States Government had invited the Australian, New Zealand, Canadian, and the French and Dutch Governments to be represented and to sign. The Foreign Office instructed Lord Halifax to point out to the State Department the difficult position with regard to the Australian Government in which the United States action had placed them.

(*continued on page* 530)

(a) F4974, 5071, 5213/630/23. (b) F4974/630/23. (c) F5157/630/23.

(a) The Foreign Office prepared a draft act of surrender for Japan and sent it to the British Embassy at Washington on the morning of August 12, although they realised that an American draft might be used. This preliminary draft was still subject to the views of the Chiefs of Staff and the Dominions; it was modelled on the German Act of Military Surrender, but was intended for signature on behalf of the Japanese Government as well as the High Command.

Mr. Balfour was instructed to inform the State Department that the Foreign Office had followed the United States lead in the reply to the Japanese Government, and had acquiesced in their procedure of acting in the name of the British Government without prior consultation. The details of the formal act of surrender were, however, so important that both the text and the procedure must be settled by agreement, and there must be an opportunity for the concurrence of the Dominions before action or publication by the United States Government.

(b) Mr. Balfour carried out these instructions on August 12. On the afternoon of August 13 Mr. Dunn telephoned to Mr. Balfour to say that the United States Government had completed the draft act of surrender, and that in its preparation they had benefited from the 'timely delivery' of the British draft. He said that the United States Government were not in a position to consult their Allies about the act. Mr. Balfour reminded him that, when he had delivered the British draft, he had spoken of the importance of giving the British Government an opportunity of obtaining the concurrence of the Dominions. Mr. Dunn thereupon showed Mr. Balfour the United States draft and explained that the United States Government were unwilling to consult us formally because they did not intend to invite Soviet or Chinese comments on the text. Mr. Dunn made it clear that he was not authorised to discuss the terms of the United States Act, or even to let Mr. Balfour have a copy of it, but he undertook to pass on certain amendments suggested by the British Chiefs of Staff and any later British suggestions. He implied, however, that it was too late for any more amendment of the United States act.

(c) On August 14 (at 6 p.m. Washington time) the Japanese Government replied through the Swiss Chargé d'Affaires in Washington to the communication which the United States Government had made

---

(*continued*)

(d) Mr. Balfour spoke to Mr. Dunn on August 25. Mr. Dunn said that the State Department had 'thrown the matter into the lap of the military'. Exchanges of telegrams had taken place between General MacArthur and the War Department, and it had been decided to allow the officers concerned to sign the Act of Surrender. He implied that the State Department had not been kept informed of this development.

(a) F5048/630/23. (b) F5110/630/23. (c) CM(45)22; F4974/630/23.
(d) F5754/630/23.

on August 11 on behalf of the Four Powers. Their reply was as follows:[1]

'With reference to the announcement of August 10 regarding the acceptance of the provisions of the Potsdam Declaration and the reply of the Governments of the United States, Great Britain, the Soviet Union and China sent by Secretary of State Byrnes on the date of August 11, the Japanese Government has the honour to communicate to the Governments of the four Powers as follows:

(1) His Majesty the Emperor has issued an Imperial rescript regarding Japan's acceptance of the provisions of the Potsdam Declaration.

(2) His Majesty the Emperor is prepared to authorise and ensure the signature by his Government and the Imperial General Headquarters of the necessary terms for carrying out the provisions of the Potsdam Declaration.

(3) His Majesty is also prepared to issue his commands to all the Military, Naval and Air Authorities of Japan, and all the Forces under their control, wherever located, to cease active operations, to surrender arms and to issue such other orders as may be required by the Supreme Commander of the Allied Forces for the execution of the above-mentioned terms.

(Signed) TOGO'

Mr. Byrnes telephoned to Mr. Bevin to inform him of the Japanese reply. He said that the United States Government considered the reply a satisfactory acceptance of the terms of the Potsdam declaration. They proposed that the Allied Governments should accept the Japanese surrender and announce it at once. Mr. Byrnes sent a further message that the Soviet and Chinese Governments had accepted his proposal for an announcement at 7 p.m. Washington time.

The Cabinet met at once to consider the Japanese reply. They (a) discussed the interpretation of the third paragraph of this reply. It was suggested that the Allied demand had been that the Emperor should comply with the directions of the Allied Commander, and that the proper construction of the reply was that the Emperor would command his military, naval and air authorities to comply with those directions. The Cabinet agreed that the Japanese reply was a satisfactory acceptance of the Allied conditions, and that the Prime Minister should announce at midnight the news of Japan's surrender.

Early in the morning of August 15, President Truman telegraphed (b)

[1] The Japanese acceptance of the terms was again brought about by the direct personal intervention of the Emperor. Unsuccessful attempts were made in Tokyo by the military extremists to carry out a *coup* against the 'evil advisers' who had persuaded the Emperor to agree to the terms of surrender.

(a) CM(45)22; F4974/630/23. (b) COS(45) 199th meeting; F6041/630/23.

to Mr. Attlee that instructions had been sent to United States commanders in the Pacific and western Pacific areas to suspend offensive operations against the Japanese as far as was consistent with the safety of Allied forces. Admiral Mountbatten received similar in-
(a) structions. On the same day President Truman sent Mr. Attlee the General Order which he had approved for issue to General MacArthur, covering details of the surrender of Japanese armed forces.[1]

The signature of the formal Instrument of Surrender, which contained the detailed terms, took place in the American warship *Missouri* in Tokyo Bay on September 2, 1945.[2] On this day an American force, with a small number of British marines, landed on Japanese territory, and established themselves in the outskirts of Tokyo as the first contingent of the Allied occupying force.

---

[1] The terms of the Instrument of Surrender for Japan laid down that the Japanese forces in each area of fighting should surrender to the Commander-in-Chief, or an officer designated by him, in the area concerned. General Chiang-Kai-shek claimed that Hong Kong was a part of China and therefore within his area of command. The British authorities notified Chiang Kai-shek that a British force was on its way to Hong Kong to receive the surrender and restore the British administration. Mr. Attlee asked President Truman to instruct General MacArthur so ensure that the Japanese High Command ordered the Japanese forces in Hong Kong to surrender to the British naval commander on his arrival. President Truman (while remembering, (as he points out in his *Memoirs*, I, 379), President Roosevelt's wish that Hong Kong should be returned to Chinese sovereignty) considered that, although the status of Hong Kong might be discussed later, the United States should respect established rights. He therefore instructed General MacArthur in accordance with Mr. Attlee's request. General Chiang Kai-shek protested strongly to President Truman that the Japanese surrender should be made to China. (Among other reasons for maintaining General MacArthur's instructions was the obvious fact that it was impossible for any Chinese force to get to Hong Kong unless the Americans brought them there.)

General Chiang Kai-shek then said he would delegate his authority to a British commander. The British Government refused to accept General Chiang Kai-shek's claim, and took no notice of his 'delegation of authority'. The Japanese surrender was made to the British naval commander. No mention was made of the General at the ceremony of surrender in Hong Kong, but he continued to list it as one of the several surrenders to be made to him.

[2] Although the United States Embassy communicated to the Foreign Office on August
(b) 16 the text of the instrument of surrender which the Japanese were to be required to sign, the Foreign Office had not received by October 9 a copy of the document actually signed. The delay in the signature of the Instrument of Surrender was due partly to the time taken in assembling and transporting a force of occupation. A typhoon also caused further postponement.

(a) F5348/630/23. (b) F5213/630/23.

INDEX